PRAISE FOR

SAXOPHONE COLOSSUS

Longlisted for the PEN/Jacqueline Bograd Weld Award (2023)

****Winner, Biography/Autobiography of the Year, 2023
Jazz Journalists Association Jazz Awards****

Boston Globe, "Best Books of 2022"

WBGO, "Jazz Lovers' Gift Guide"

———————◆◦▸———————

"A revealing, comprehensive biography... [and] a brimming and organized compendium, something to keep returning to like Rollins's records..." —*New York Times*

"Levy paints a vivid picture... Throughout *Saxophone Colossus* he weds his extensive research to a feel for detail and narrative; the book is certainly long, but it has too much great reporting to be dry." —*Los Angeles Times*

"[Author Aidan Levy] distills essential truths... and ties strands of Mr. Rollins's history together in poignant ways." —*Wall Street Journal*

"Aidan Levy's indefatigable research and interviewing process has allowed him to fill *Saxophone Colossus* with a vast chorus of voices." —*The Wire*

"An incredibly deep, well-researched, and thoughtfully written biography." —*DownBeat*

"[An] exhaustive, definitive biography." —*Air Mail*

"Read it you must. . . . a remarkable read."   —*Marlbank*

"There's no doubt that *Saxophone Colossus* will be a great resource for future jazz scholars."   —*Nelson George Mixtape*

"A long book allows for a luxurious detail. . . . *Saxophone Colossus* does what the best biographies do: Gives you enough information to pursue your own lines of inquiry."   —*Point of Departure*

"Monumental."   —*WICN "Inquiry"*

"A memorable work that will become the standard biography of the saxophone giant and should be embraced by all jazz fans and general readers. Highly recommended."   —*Library Journal*

"[*Saxophone Colossus* is filled with] . . . precise and ravishing descriptions of Rollins' music, 'tireless work ethic,' inspirations, frustrations with the record industry, social and environmental activism, and surprising collaborations."   —*Booklist*

"[The] definitive account of a jazz icon."   —*Kirkus*

"Moving and meticulously researched."   —*Publishers Weekly*

"Scrupulous and exhaustive. . . Levy comes as close to the enigma of Rollins as any biographer could."   —*Telegraph* (UK)

"Rollins has never deviated from the obsessive nature of his calling. He's found a like-minded biographer, who paints pictures with words as adeptly as Rollins did with his saxophone. Subject and author deserve each other."   —*iPaper* (UK)

"Sonny Rollins told stories through his horn. His 'telling,' no matter how intricate or elaborate, was always pure, honest, and vulnerable, while the storyteller himself remained elusive and intangible. Until now. In Aidan Levy, Mr. Rollins has found his chronicler, an immensely talented writer whose lyricism, mastery, and dedication to truth matches that of his subject. The result is an opera, a calypso, a magnificent symphony that captures All of Him: Sonny, Newk, Theodore, Wally, Brung Biji, and the one and only Saxophone Colossus."

—Robin D. G. Kelley, author of *Thelonious Monk: The Life and Times of an American Original*

"When I was a boy, I knew nothing of Sonny Rollins, the man, but his music set me free. Now, forty-some-odd years later, this book has gifted me a profound, almost revelatory, appreciation of all it took for our singularly Great American Improviser to exist, to persist, to survive, to thrive, to comprehend, to transcend, to create, to liberate, to *be*—at once the towering, omnipotent, immortal Colossus and the humble, gentle, questioning, questing human. Sonny Rollins has always been the master storyteller of the jazz idiom. What an illuminative joy it is to finally read the story of his own life so exhaustively and engagingly told."

—Joshua Redman, Grammy-nominated saxophonist, composer, and educator

"Sonny Rollins is the most acclaimed and celebrated jazz musician alive. His fearless creativity and willingness to test his limits are the stuff of legends, as are his modesty, discipline, and self-criticism. With deep research and meticulous documentation, Levy, with the aid of Rollins, gives us a revelatory and richer picture of the man and his era. A colossus of a book."

—John Szwed, author of *Space Is the Place: The Lives and Times of Sun Ra* and *So What: The Life of Miles Davis*

"In this forensically researched biography of an American hero, the elusive Sonny Rollins stands revealed not only as the great Jazz Maker but a man of profundity and passions. By combining the story of his rise as a Saxophone Colossus with a picture of the Black artist in an age when social progress was not necessarily a given, Levy has produced a memorable book."

—Val Wilmer, author of *As Serious as Your Life:*
Black Music and the Free Jazz Revolution, 1957–1977

"The life and music of Sonny Rollins as chronicled by acclaimed author Aidan Levy is an insightful view into the daily struggles, achievements and spiritual journey of whom I like to refer to as the 'Maestro di Maestri,' Mr. Sonny Rollins. All I can say is:
II: READ LISTEN LISTEN READ:II
You will be enlightened as I am."

—Joe Lovano, saxophonist, composer, producer,
educator, and Grammy winner

"Aidan Levy has provided the jazz world and beyond an important documentation of one of the greatest musicians of all time. Sonny Rollins spoke his own language through the saxophone—just check out his solo on 'Alfie'! And *Saxophone Colossus* provides for us in words a portal to deeper understanding of this legendary jazz giant!"

—Terri Lyne Carrington, Grammy-winning
drummer, producer, and composer

"[The] authoritative book on Rollins...among the best-researched books ever devoted to jazz."

—Lewis Porter, Grammy-nominated pianist, composer,
educator, and author of *John Coltrane: His Life and Music*
and *Playback with Lewis Porter*

"I loved this book. What a dynamic life Mr. Rollins had. NEWK! One of the greatest musicians to ever walk the planet, always yearning, always growing, always REACHING for the cosmos."   —Flea

"One of the best books about jazz."   —Ishmael Reed

Saxophone
Colossus

Also by Aidan Levy

Dirty Blvd.:
The Life and Music of Lou Reed

Patti Smith on Patti Smith:
Interviews and Encounters (editor)

Saxophone Colossus

THE LIFE AND MUSIC OF
Sonny Rollins

AIDAN LEVY

hachette BOOKS

NEW YORK

Hachette Books
Hachette Book Group
1290 Avenue of the Americas
New York, NY 10104
HachetteBooks.com
Twitter.com/HachetteBooks
Instagram.com/HachetteBooks

First paperback edition: November 2023

Published by Hachette Books, an imprint of Hachette Book Group, Inc. The Hachette Books name and logo is a trademark of the Hachette Book Group.

The Hachette Speakers Bureau provides a wide range of authors for speaking events.

To find out more, go to hachettespeakersbureau.com or email HachetteSpeakers@hbgusa.com.

The publisher is not responsible for websites (or their content) that are not owned by the publisher.

Print book interior design by Six Red Marbles

Library of Congress Control Number: 2022943375

ISBNs: 9780306902796 (hardcover); 9780306902802 (paperback); 9780306902826 (ebook)

Printed in the United States of America

LSC-C

Printing 1, 2023

Dedicated to Kaitlin, Diana, and Isabel

Sonny's fingers filled the air with life, his life. But that life contained so many others. And Sonny went all the way back, he really began with the spare, flat statement of the opening phrase of the song. Then he began to make it his. It was very beautiful because it wasn't hurried and it was no longer a lament. I seemed to hear with what burning he had made it his, with what burning we had yet to make it ours, how we could cease lamenting. Freedom lurked around us and I understood, at last, that he could help us to be free if we would listen, that he would never be free until we did.

—JAMES BALDWIN, "SONNY'S BLUES"

The great work of the painter is not a colossus, but a "historia."

—LEON BATTISTA ALBERTI

CONTENTS

PART 1

PART 2

PART 1

Chapter I

ST. EUSTATIUS

(1864–1930)

The rhythm and the family name go back to Sonny's grandfather Steadman Rollins—but Sonny Rollins was almost Walter Berkel. Sonny's musical
inheritance is straightforward, but the name—the name is more complicated. "I had something about the name, I guess: Sonny Rollins," Sonny later
said. "It's just a name that...it sort of has a melody to it in itself, so that when
people begin to hear it...I mean, it sounds like somebody already."[1]

Sonny never met Steadman Rollins, but he felt his influence. "My father
told me that he played clarinet at one time. I never heard him play," Sonny
said, "but other than that I think it's probably further back. I think my
grandfather on my father's side was a singer. That's what I was told, and they
were from St. Croix. And my sister...had pictures, and she said I resem-
ble him very much.... He was also a lothario, and she gave me these stories
about him being chased out of—jumping out of windows when guys would
find him.... I'm not like that, but I may have gotten my musical thing from
him."[2]

Sonny's story, and the story of how he got his melodious name, begins
not on St. Thomas, but on the tiny island of St. Eustatius, a former Dutch
colony in the West Indies of only eight square miles. Sonny's paternal
great-grandmother, Martha Bennett, was born on St. Eustatius, or Statia, in
1864, the year after Emancipation in the Dutch West Indies.[3] By the time
she was fifteen, Martha worked as a teenage cook at Judith's Fancy, a plantation owned by a prominent Statia family, but traveled to the surrounding
islands for seasonal work.[4]

Martha's son, Steadman Rollins, or Rawlins, shared a name with a former governor of neighboring St. Kitts, a sugar plantation owner and slave
trader who had died in Nova Scotia in 1830. Sonny's grandfather was born

Steadman Warten Berkel on September 12, 1881—a birthday within a week of Sonny's—to Martha Berkel, née Bennett, in Statia.[5] For children born out of wedlock, no father was listed on the birth certificate. In 1885, when Steadman was a young child, Sonny's great-grandmother Martha gave up her nomadic lifestyle and moved them to St. Croix on a more permanent basis, where they lived in a beachfront property at 31 Strand Street in Southeast Christiansted, a short walk from Fort Christiansvaern and a block from the shore. Rather than seeking employment on one of the Crucian sugar plantations, Martha continued working as a cook, and the two of them attended the Moravian church. By the time he was eight, Steadman was going by Steadman Rawlins. By twenty, Steadman stood five-foot-nine and had become a carpenter in St. Croix, though he frequently traveled to the surrounding islands in the Caribbean for work, most commonly to St. Thomas. Eventually, Sonny's father, Walter, would follow in Steadman's peripatetic footsteps, enlisting in the navy; likewise, Sonny would also become a world traveler.[6]

Before Steadman's twentieth birthday, on June 27, 1903, Sonny's father, Walter William Rollins, was born to his carpenter-singer-lothario grandfather and Grace Ann Claxton, a servant from Nevis whom Steadman had met after she arrived alone and unmarried on St. Croix in 1900.[7] The relationship was not to last, and Grace returned to Nevis. She still maintained contact, though, eventually visiting Sonny and her other grandchildren several times in New York, but Sonny's father was raised by Steadman in St. Croix.

In 1908, Steadman married Helena or Helene Lyburt, and in 1911 they welcomed a son, Mathias, Walter's half brother and Sonny's uncle.[8] That year, Steadman was living in a rented property not far from the area Crucians call Contentment in a building named Perseverance with Helene; Mathias; Sonny's father, Walter; and Sonny's grandmother Martha, who at forty-four was still working as a cook. Martha would teach Sonny's father to cook, and he would eventually take it up as a profession. Medical care on the island was lacking; the first ambulance on St. Croix didn't arrive until 1917 after the transfer of power to the United States. In 1912, Helene gave birth to a second child, Sonny's uncle, who was stillborn.[9]

In St. Croix, music pulsated across the rhythmic topography, and it was not uncommon for a Crucian carpenter like Steadman to learn a trade while performing regularly.[10] The music of the Virgin Islands spans different traditions that are all communal and polyrhythmic, require an improviser's ingenuity, and are inextricably linked to dance. Steadman would have been familiar with quelbe (pronounced "quell-bay") and the various dances that were popular in the Virgin Islands: the cariso, quadrille, and bamboula. Quelbe, played by scratch bands, was an early calypso form emerging from St. Croix with a Taino influence that incorporated melodic improvisation, syncopated rhythm, and a storytelling thrust. Much of the repertoire has only three chords, but its nuances reside in the group interaction and the joyful mix of harmony, rhythm, melodic phrasing, and sexual innuendo.[11] As the music developed in the twentieth century, the flute was increasingly replaced by the saxophone. Scratch bands performed quelbe at masquerades, dance halls, and "moonlight excursions" at the parade grounds that were planned according to the almanac.[12] Quelbe would also be performed at impromptu gatherings on opalescent beaches or under the indigenous tamarind and baobab trees, the latter of which could live to be hundreds of years old and are often referred to as the "tree of life." This is the tradition Sonny inherited.

Forming a band required a resourcefulness born out of financial hardship.[13] If instruments were beyond their means, they fashioned them from whatever they could find: sardine tins, whittled mahogany, or fishing line, which gave a dual purpose to carpentry skills. It is a collaged art form, created out of disparate parts and pieces of the islands just as the musicians created themselves, not unlike the jazz tradition.

In addition to scratch bands, Steadman would have also been familiar with the Crucian tradition of cariso, a subversive West African musical form. It was sung in Virgin Islands Creole by all-female "Cariso Queens" in a code the slavers could not understand, accompanied by one or two goatskin barrel drums in a call-and-response with the singer never quite on the beat, a fugitive voice in rhythmic counterpoint to the drum's inexorable pulse.[14] Sonny would later adapt these West Indian forms to the jazz tradition—on the saxophone-conga duet "Jungoso" with Candido on his 1962 album *What's New?* and in "Duke of Iron," "Don't Stop the Carnival," "Brownskin Girl," and, of course, "St. Thomas."

This inheritance was part of a long-standing tradition of using music as a means of social protest. White plantation owners were wary of slaves using music for organized resistance, so laws were passed to prohibit it.[15] Yet in St. Croix, this free music galvanized rebellions nonetheless. In 1848, Moses "Buddhoe" Gottlieb, a twenty-eight-year-old free black who worked as a sugar boiler, led eight thousand slaves in a successful Crucian revolt that began with the ringing of bells and the blowing of conch shells, with cariso melodies and dances performed to the bamboula drum.[16] It happened again at the "Fireburn," a successful 1878 labor revolt on St. Croix orchestrated by David Hamilton Jackson that fought to end de facto slavery on the island. This was the musical tradition Steadman participated in and that would become Sonny's cultural heritage.[17]

As Sidney Bechet did before him, Sonny may locate his musical lineage through his grandfather and his peripatetic lifestyle, but he inherited his music at least as much from his mother's side. Valborg Solomon was born on St. Thomas on December 2, 1904, to Miriam Walcott, who gave birth to her before her twentieth birthday.[18] Valborg was a common Danish name, meaning "protector of the battlefield," a meaning that would be apropos later in life. Sonny's grandmother Miriam, who stood five-foot-four and projected a sense of inner strength and a canny intelligence, was also born in St. Thomas and worked as a domestic. Valborg's father and Sonny's maternal grandfather, Dr. Solomon, lived and worked in Haiti; he did not raise the children.[19]

In St. Thomas, Sonny's mother, Valborg, grew up in a full house. In 1911, she was living at 30 Norre Gade in Charlotte Amalie, the cosmopolitan center of the island, in a large multifamily town house, most likely of the colorful nineteenth-century terraced, painted-brick style, with scenic views of the lush countryside. Valborg lived with her stepfather, Adolph Victoria, a thirty-year-old Episcopalian blacksmith; her twenty-three-year-old mother, Miriam, Sonny's Lutheran grandmother, who worked as a washer; and Reuben Victoria, Valborg's two-year-old half brother who would become Sonny's uncle.[20] In the apartment next door lived Miriam's mother and Sonny's maternal great-grandmother, Eliza Walcott, who was born free in St. Croix in 1854 or 1855. Like Miriam, she was also Lutheran and, at fifty-six, was still working as a nurse on St. Thomas. Elizabeth Walcott, her daughter and Sonny's great-aunt, was nine years older than Miriam and took care of her own five children, Sonny's second cousins, aged two to fifteen.[21] Sonny's mother, Valborg, had only an eighth-grade education on St. Thomas, though she would eventually take night classes, and his grandmother Miriam had only a sixth-grade education, but their lack of formal education belied their fierce intelligence.

In 1922, Valborg, then eighteen, met nineteen-year-old naval steward Walter Rollins, who by that time had become "a friendly, polished individual who speaks French, Spanish, Norwegian and Danish," as he was later described.[22] Walter was five-foot-ten, muscular, and dashingly handsome, and he possessed the "dignity of an aristocrat" and "a New England accent." He was also a hell of a cook. Taking after Steadman's penchant for travel, Walter had decided to join the navy even sooner than was legally possible. It was common for Crucians to immigrate to the continental United States in search of employment, oftentimes through the military, and Walter enlisted on May 1, 1920.[23] To meet the age requirement, it seems Sonny's father bent the truth and listed his birth date as May 7, 1902, more than a year earlier than was actually the case. Becoming a steward was "sort of the highest a black could aspire to at that point," Sonny later explained.[24] Eventually, Walter would personally serve high-ranking government and military officials, including Admiral Ernest King in Seattle and President Warren G. Harding, one of the most corrupt conservative presidents in US history. Duke Ellington's father, James Edward Ellington, also worked as a butler for Harding. Walter was professional to a fault and never let his politics interfere with his work—he would vote for Franklin Delano Roosevelt three times.[25]

In 1922, when Walter met Valborg, he was stationed on St. Thomas on shore duty at the governor's mansion. He was a promising naval steward with a glint in his eye; she was a young music student.[26] She must have been impressed that Walter worked on Charlotte Amalie at Kathrineberg, the opulent governor's mansion. In 1923, their romance culminated in marriage, and they planned to come to the United States and settle in New York to raise a family.

The whole family would not arrive in New York immediately. On April 20, 1924, Sonny's grandmother Miriam traveled to New York for the first time, arriving with thirty dollars to visit a niece, Emelyn Steven, who lived at 49 La Salle Street in Harlem.[27] On November 3, 1925, Valborg and Walter welcomed their first child, Valdemar, Sonny's older brother, who was born on St. Thomas. In 1926, Valborg took a ship to New York with Valdemar, and they lived at 289 West 142nd Street at the corner of 8th Avenue in Harlem. On August 31, 1928, Valborg gave birth to her second child, Sonny's sister, Gloria, who was also born in St. Thomas. Nearly a year later, with Walter stationed elsewhere, Valborg, Valdemar, and Gloria made yet another journey to New York from the island.[28] "She really wanted more for us, and there was, you know, a limit to what she felt that we could achieve in the islands," Gloria later recalled, "and so she came in a boat across the ocean and there was a tremendous storm.... They were really pounded by waves."[29]

As Sonny explained of the decision to leave the islands, "I would imagine that it probably has to do with economics. Although my mother...was a person that always wanted to introduce us to culture.... So she might have been thinking about a better place to give her kids a chance to do whatever we do in this life—to be exposed."[30]

On April 18, 1929, they stepped off the ship *Domenica*,[31] and they made their way to 2773 8th Avenue between 146th and 147th Streets, a brick building in a predominantly West Indian neighborhood. Though they had moved around a lot, it seemed they were getting ready to put down roots in New York and would soon welcome the first and only member of the family to be born in Harlem.

Sonny would never meet the grandfather who passed down the music, though Steadman Rollins would also immigrate to New York City.[32] On May 4, 1923, Steadman, now forty-one, and his eleven-year-old son, Mathias, boarded a boat in St. Thomas heading to New York, where they took the five- or six-day journey to meet Helene, who had immigrated a year earlier and was living in Harlem at 265 West 136th Street, two blocks south of Strivers' Row.[33] Steadman was listed on the ship manifest as a shipwright, a carpenter who repairs ships. He arrived at Ellis Island, also with thirty dollars in his pocket and after a rigorous interrogation confirmed he was not a convict, a polygamist, an anarchist, or a "person who believes in or advocates the overthrow by force or violence of the Government of the United States."

He was labeled "Likely Public Charge," meaning he had no work prospects, then detained at Ellis Island for two days for further inspection due to what immigration inspectors deemed an unspecified "physical defect."[34] Steadman had no intention of becoming a US citizen—it seems he understood what it meant to be free and needed no new encumbrances—but he did intend to stay indefinitely. Steadman would never make it to fifty and would never meet his grandson Sonny, who was born seven years after his arrival.[35]

What's curious, though, about Steadman's immigration story is the multiple names he went by. When Steadman Rollins (or, as he was sometimes known, Stedman Rawlins, Stedmann Rollens, or Steadmann Rollings) arrived in New York in 1923, he was listed on his travel documents as Steadman Berkel, his birth name, married to Helena Berkel, with their son, Sonny's uncle—Mathias Berkel. So Sonny always would have been Sonny, but he was only a name change away from having been Walter Berkel.

Steadman Rollins and Steadman Berkel—two names, depending on the context—may sound unusual. Yet in the tradition of the West Indies, where the self was improvised, Sonny too would be known by many names—some inherited, some earned, and some taken. Though he only ever had one legal name, Walter Theodore Rollins, he would go by many: Walter Theodore, Theodore Walter, Sonny, Newk, Wally, Roundtree, Brung Biji, the Saxophone Colossus. This is the story of how he got each.

Chapter 2

HARLEM

(1930–1938)

Walter Theodore Rollins was born on Sunday, September 7, 1930, five blocks up from the Tree of Hope and half a block east of the Boulevard of Dreams. The Boulevard of Dreams—which was 7th Avenue—got its name for the joyful music that reverberated up and down the expansive promenade.[1]

Every Saturday at midnight, a few blocks from where Sonny was born, at 142nd Street and Lenox Avenue, the Duke Ellington Orchestra was broadcast nationwide from the segregated Cotton Club, thousands of miles across the color line, where for one hour a week Harlem's beating heart was also the nation's.

They called it the Tree of Hope because it stood "right on Seventh Avenue on the island in the middle of the traffic," Sonny recalled, between the Lafayette Theater and Connie's Inn, "and people would go there and just rub it for good luck."[2] It was chopped down in 1934.

Sonny was delivered by a midwife. "I was born Sunday morning... between two churches," he would recount during a 1993 concert at Carnegie Hall. "One on 138th, Abyssinian, and AME [African Methodist Episcopal] Zion, 137th Street."[3]

Sonny's birth was one of his older sister Gloria's first memories. Walter Sr. could not be there—he had almost no furlough opportunities. "We all lived at 121 West 137th Street," she said of their first-floor tenement apartment. The modest building has since been demolished, but the photographs that remain depict a five-story brownstone crowned by a cornice, with an arched entryway, fire escapes out front, and large windows; cars parked up and down the block, and people gathered on the front stoop. "I was looking out of the window and I was watching the people going into church, and all of a sudden when my godmother had come into the room and told me there was a new little boy up in the front room, I heard this carillon and...I had that kind of feeling inside me."[4]

Despite the preponderance of churches, Sonny would gravitate more toward finding the spiritual in the secular. "Harlem was a very vibrant place at that time. There was a lot of music, a lot of clubs, a lot of speakeasies, after-hours clubs," Sonny said.[5] "It was a perfect environment for someone like me who wanted to be a musician. All my idols lived nearby." The Harlem Renaissance began to decline during the Great Depression, he recalled, but the renaissance "extended beyond that from the nightclubs that were still in Harlem, which were part of the twenties but lasted through the thirties and were still going strong."[6]

Novelist and cultural critic Albert Murray, who lived in Harlem at that time, remembered it as the "golden era of jazz in Harlem": the Lafayette and Lincoln Theatres, Connie's Inn, Well's Place, the Rhythm Club, Smalls Paradise, the Savoy Ballroom, and the Cotton Club were all within walking distance.[7]

In 1932, illustrator E. Simms Campbell drew a "Night-Club Map of Harlem," packing as much of Harlem nightlife into two dimensions as he could: Earl "Snakehips" Tucker, Gladys Bentley at the Clam House, Garland Wilson tickling the ivories, Harlan Lattimore crooning at Connie's Inn, the Cab Calloway–immortalized Reefer Man, the Crab Man, the peanut vendor, conjure women, spiritualists, and Harlem's national drink, a "shorty of gin." Yet the rhythmic pulse of ballrooms, cabarets, and speakeasies from the Baby Grand to the Hot-Cha was tempered by the sound of God always within earshot.[8]

If New York was the Big Apple, Harlem was the stem; 125th Street was even known as the "main stem."[9] Harlem was a self-sustaining city within a city, full of urban strivers, with its own newspaper (the *Amsterdam News*), libraries (including the Schomburg Collection of the New York Public Library, where Sonny would go after school), and various labor organizations (such as the Brotherhood of Sleeping Car Porters).[10] Sonny grew up in a bustling neighborhood of rooftop playgrounds, Aaron Douglas murals, and the 7th Avenue Easter parade. Celebrities, day laborers, and numbers runners intermingled. Around the block was the 135th Street Y, known as the "living room of the Harlem Renaissance."[11]

During the Depression, central Harlem was not all serendipity, church bells, and the Home of Happy Feet. It was Sugar Hill, where Harlem's elite residents had an abundance of hope, and the Hollow, where there was little of it.[12] Harlem was a world of warring dualities: the church and the cabaret, abject poverty and the fledgling aristocracy of what W. E. B. Du Bois called the Talented Tenth, West Indians who came by boat and southern strivers who came by train during the Great Migration, Italians, Puerto Ricans, and Jews.[13]

The streets were syncopated: calypso, quelbe, African rhythms with Jelly Roll Morton's Spanish tinge, spirituals, blues, stride piano, Tin Pan Alley, a thousand songs from a thousand places.[14] Four blocks downtown from

Sonny's home was 133rd Street, the original Swing Street. This was the sound of Sonny's childhood.

In 1930, Sonny's family was living at 2773 8th Avenue. The rent was thirty-three dollars a month, and in addition to the immediate family, Reuben Victoria, his uncle, also lived with them. He worked as a lamp polisher.[15] Sonny's grandmother Miriam worked as a laundress and "had her own place," Sonny recalled, but she was always at their house if they were not at hers.[16] Miriam's was the apartment at 121 West 137th Street where Sonny was born.[17]

"They started to call me Sonny because I was the baby, the youngest," Sonny recalled. The first photo of Sonny shows him at eighteen months, posed on a plush cushion, wearing what appear to be white satin shoes and high white socks, dark shorts, white suspenders, and a stiff white shirt. His hair is well groomed, and he holds a ball nearly the size of his head with both hands. His world-weary eyes belie the rest of the Little Lord Fauntleroy outfit.[18]

Sonny grew up in a predominantly West Indian community in "Harlem proper," from the northern tip of Central Park at 110th Street to 145th Street—which he thought of as "the mecca" but sometimes referred to as the "lowlands."[19]

Life in Harlem during the Depression was tough. Winters were very cold, and summers were very hot.[20] The family spent periods on public assistance.[21] "I remember going to the home relief place and getting the boxes of food," Sonny said. "I think that the wartime was actually good in the sense that people began to practice thrift. There was rationing for everything. We saved tin-foil, along with pork fat, chicken fat—any kind of grease."[22]

When he was three, Sonny's family had to move to a new apartment at 69 West 135th Street. "The piano was left out on the street," Sonny recalled. "In those days in Harlem you used to see a lot of pianos on the street with the people's furniture that were being evicted."[23] After replacing the player piano, they could be entertained by an invisible James P. Johnson playing stride harmonies in the living room. "We moved around...for economic reasons," Sonny said.[24] During the Depression, they lived on every street from 135th to 138th.

The family loved animals, but one summer was so hot that Sonny's pet mouse Pete died of heatstroke.[25] The family also had a beloved Persian cat named Beauty. "I remember when Beauty got sick and transitioned my sister was very upset," Sonny recalled, "and I was, she thought, too anxious to have the cat transition, to put it out of her misery, so to speak. . . . As I look back on that, I had a not-so-tragic view of life and death."[26]

Sonny's father was rarely home, and meeting him when Sonny was two or three is one of his earliest memories.[27] Absence did not mean neglect. Walter Rollins Sr. "was a career Navy," Sonny said.[28] His father called and wrote often and sent frequent care packages—"these big dark red blankets from the United States naval station in Seattle," for example—but due to Walter's assignments, Sonny would sometimes not see him for two years.[29]

Sonny's stern father was a decorated naval steward known to many as Chief Rollins. He supervised up to 250 men, depending on the size of the ship. In 1935, his assignment was to serve Secretary of War George Dern during the independence negotiations in the Philippines.[30] When Walter came home to Harlem on brief furloughs, he supervised the family with the same insistence on military decorum that made his reputation and had little patience for independence. "He gave orders," Gloria recalled. "It was really tough to go from my mother to having my father in the house. We were all like midshipmen and he was in charge. It was something that I couldn't get accustomed to, my older brother could not get accustomed to, but Sonny really got accustomed to him, and Sonny became very attached to my father."[31]

As Sonny recalled, "My father was strict. . . . The house had to be spic-and-span." Meeting his exacting standards wasn't easy. Furthermore, Walter was embarrassed to discover that the family lived in an area resembling Catfish Row from George Gershwin's 1935 opera, *Porgy and Bess*. This was compounded when his close friend Admiral Arthur W. Radford, who would later become chairman of the Joint Chiefs of Staff, came to visit with his wife.[32] The neighborhood had "a lot of people running around, or sitting on doorsteps," Sonny recalled, "certainly something beneath the grandeur of an admiral in the United States Navy. It was a respect which transcended all of the racism which exists in America."[33]

As Sonny's future neighbor Doris Mason recalled, Walter "walked like he was proud, with that uniform on. I never saw the man in any civvies. The girls used to love his father. When he came home, we would swoon. We were like, 'Oh my god.' We had a crush on him."[34]

Valborg was more lenient than Walter, but just as hardworking. While her older children were at school, she would often take Sonny to jobs on Park Avenue, where he saw inequality firsthand. "She had nobody to take care of me, I was the youngest boy," Sonny said. "She used to take me down there and I'd have to wait in the closet or someplace while she cleaned the house."[35]

According to Gloria, Valborg's work ethic was tireless, but she doted on Sonny. "My mother raised us pretty much on her own, and she was an extremely brilliant woman, but she didn't have a chance to attend school in the islands," she recalled. "When she came to New York, she attended night school with all of us at home, godmother watching us. I still have the little mini diplomas that she got from every class that she attended."[36]

Sonny and Valborg were very attached to each other. When his mother entertained guests, Sonny would often stay out in the front room. She "would never make me go," Sonny said. "So I would sit there...till they finally left."[37]

Valborg also accommodated Sonny's distaste for West Indian food. "I didn't like rice, which my family ate a lot of," Sonny said. "I didn't eat what everybody else ate. I loved spinach and white potatoes mashed together. My mother really had to cook special for me."[38] At dinner, Gloria said, "My grandmother was very pious, and before we would eat, she would really say a lengthy grace, thanking god for this and that."[39] One night, "during her speech...Sonny said, 'Hold it, Gram,' and everybody stopped." Sonny turned on the radio, full blast, to the "William Tell Overture," the theme song from *The Lone Ranger*. "I was the baby in the family, so I got away with a lot of stuff," said Sonny.[40] Gloria called it "one of the funniest moments of my life."

The family sometimes went to Mother AME Zion or to hear future congressman Adam Clayton Powell preach at Abyssinian Baptist Church.[41] Though both were only a block away, most Sundays the family took the subway downtown to join the city's growing West Indian population at the Third Moravian Church, where Sonny went to Sunday school and was eventually confirmed.[42] "They are a Christian church, but...it wasn't gospelly or anything," Sonny said. "It was very straight hymns and Bach cantatas."[43]

Sonny was introduced to gospel by his grandmother Miriam, who took him to Baptist churches in Harlem.[44] "She used to take me to church right there on Lenox Avenue, and it was one of these real sanctified churches that had band instruments playing," Sonny said. "She took me to Mother Horn's church several times, and that made a big impression on me. I remember hearing a trumpet player...who was really swinging."[45]

Mother Horn's Church was on West 130th Street at the corner of Lenox Avenue, a flight up from a hardware store; it could fit eight hundred people in cheek by jowl when stretched to full capacity.[46] In the cramped sanctuary, crutches flanked the pulpit, left by congregants who had allegedly been healed by Mother Horn, who, in her white silk gown, was thought of by many as "God's right arm."[47] People regularly fainted as the congregation rolled along in call-and-response rhythm. She could lead a congregation through a riff like "God is unhappy," twisting the rhythm of the words and stamping her feet on the offbeat, as the congregation kept time with the refrain "These sins must go." Slowly, Mother Horn would then bring in the drummer, pianist, and a lone tambourine, culminating in a gradual crescendo as the tempo accelerated into a frenzy. It was at Mother Horn's that Sonny first learned to swing.

In addition to the black Pentecostal church, Miriam also exposed Sonny to radical leftist politics. She was a follower of Marcus Garvey, the West Indian founder of the United Negro Improvement Association (UNIA), known for popularizing the "back-to-Africa" movement. Another family hero was Ashley L. Totten, the secretary-treasurer for the Brotherhood of Sleeping Car Porters, who was born in St. Croix. "Everybody in the house was always talking about Totten, Totten, Totten," Sonny said. "He was one of the people who bridged the gap between native-born blacks and island-born blacks."[48] Sonny's mother took him to Lewis H. Michaux's African National Memorial Bookstore, which opened in 1932 and distributed Black nationalist literature.[49] "My mother wasn't an activist," he recalled, "but everybody went to that bookstore."[50] He and his grandmother marched for the Scottsboro Boys, Tom Mooney, and "anything that had to do with Black liberation.... We had a flag in the house for Black nationalism."[51]

The Jamaica-born Marcus Garvey arrived in Harlem in 1916. He began speaking on street corners and promulgating his ideas of black self-determination, anticolonialism, and Pan-Africanism. Garvey established his headquarters at Liberty Hall on Strivers' Row, around the block from where Sonny would soon come into this world; later, Sonny's grandmother took him to see the old UNIA headquarters on 135th Street.[52] "They didn't have megaphones, so no amplification," Sonny noted. "They said Garvey's voice was so strong, you could hear him almost to 125th Street."[53]

On September 6, 1930, the day before Sonny's birth, Garvey published an article in *Negro World*, arguing, "We must have a government of our own to satisfy the great inner urge for freedom, for self-respect."[54] Garvey's separatist politics were controversial, but that message of freedom and self-respect would set the tenor for the young musician's life.

In 1937, three years before Garvey's death, he laid out his ideas in what was eventually published as *Message to the People*: "See only yourself in everything. Make your nation the highest expression of human idealism. Then live up to it."[55] In works like "I'm an Old Cowhand," "Airegin," and, most significantly, "The Freedom Suite," Garvey had a profound impact on Sonny's conception of art and politics.

Social activism wasn't all that occupied Sonny's childhood: so did comic books, baseball and boxing, and, mostly, music.[56] In addition to a piano, Sonny's family had a banjo in the house, but his first musical expression was on the xylophone.[57]

One of Sonny's favorite musicians was Fats Waller.[58] The larger-than-life, cigar-chomping pianist and singer once accompanied silent films at the Lincoln Theater, just across the street from their apartment on 135th Street. Sonny heard the kinetic swing of Waller's plaintive "I'm Gonna Sit Right Down and Write Myself a Letter" on the radio: "one of my earliest memories of jazz."[59]

In a few years, Sonny would be attending school with the son of the clarinetist from that song, Rudy Powell. Waller's hit is "evocative of the whole Harlem scene," Sonny said. "It encapsulates the spirit of jazz."[60]

Waller was a revelation. It was then, Sonny said, that "I knew I wanted to play jazz.... It makes you feel that there is a God, and that things are okay." Waller "was the guy that... woke that up in me at an early age."[61]

The family also tuned in every Wednesday night for the WMCA broadcast of Amateur Night at the Apollo Theater.[62] They listened to the gospel group the Golden Gate Quartet and, on Sundays, *Wings over Jordan*, the nationally syndicated gospel program that championed civil rights, with Langston Hughes, Mary McLeod Bethune, and other African American luminaries discussing the issues of the day.[63]

The family also had a Victrola. Valborg played calypso records and sang Sonny the song he would one day call "St. Thomas." His brother introduced him to Duke Ellington, particularly "I Let a Song Go Out of My Heart."[64] Sonny was partial to tenor saxophonist Ben Webster on Ellington's "Cotton Tail," a contrafact or variation on the harmonic progression of George Gershwin's "I've Got Rhythm," or "rhythm changes." Nat King Cole became Sonny's favorite singer. Then there was trumpeter Bunny Berigan's 1937 rendition of "I Can't Get Started," and Louis Armstrong's "Sleepy Time Down South," which Armstrong first recorded in 1931. "Louis," Sonny said, "is everyplace and everywhere."[65]

The family also listened to Cousin Minnie Pearl and the Grand Ole Opry.[66] Gospel was on Sunday; Saturday was reserved for radio serials. Sonny dutifully tuned in for episodes of *Mr. Keen, Tracer of Lost Persons* and *When a Girl Marries*, unwittingly building his repertoire.[67] The theme to *Mr. Keen*, Noël Coward's "Someday I'll Find You," and "Serenade" by Drigo, the theme to *When a Girl Marries*, would become part of his set list.[68]

Sonny became an avid comics reader: Superman, Batman, Wonder Woman, Flash Gordon, Captain Marvel, Shazam, Steel Sterling, the Blue Beetle, the Human Torch, the Sub-Mariner. He read *Vault of Horror* and *Tales from the Crypt* and later became a lifetime subscriber to *Mad* after it launched in 1952. He particularly liked the work of Jack Kirby, who revolutionized comics, creating a new visual language through forced perspective, surrealistic urban landscapes, and three-dimensional characters who could seemingly reach outside the frame, much like the expanded harmonies and rhythmic vocabulary of Sonny's musical heroes.[69]

At one point, he hoped to pursue art professionally. As a child, Sonny started doing sketches and watercolors and eventually began making his own comic books. "I had a character called the Chain," Sonny recalled. "The biceps were bulging, and chains were breaking up all over him."[70]

The young Sonny's heroes also appeared on-screen: Tom Mix, Ken May-nard, the Durango Kid, Tim McCoy, Hoot Gibson, and Sonny's favorite, Buck Jones. "See, it was easy; there were guys who were good and guys who were bad," he said. "I bought the whole thing."[71]

Sonny also had his sports heroes: Joe Louis, his favorite boxer, and the Yankees; his favorite player was Joe DiMaggio. "When Joe Louis was fight-ing, the whole community would be listening on the radio," Sonny said, "and when he knocked the other guy out, as he usually did, people would pour into the streets with instruments and there would be an impromptu parade."[72] Later, there was Jackie Robinson, even though Sonny would stay loyal to the Yankees. "There was much hope and optimism abounding in society during those for me, formative years, and Jackie Robinson expressed it all, for all of us," Sonny wrote. "And he never once let us down."[73]

Valborg went to great lengths to bring up her children with a sense of cul-ture within and without Harlem, and her ecumenical taste had a deep impact on Sonny's future approach to repertoire.[74] She once took them on a train trip to Montreal,[75] but there was more than enough cultural activity in New York. They went to Radio City Music Hall, saw pianist-vocalist Bob Howard play stride piano at the Roxy Theatre "where there would be a movie and music on the stage," Sonny said, and "to City Center on Fifty-Fifth Street. They had a lot of operettas there," referring to the precursor to Lincoln Cen-ter that hosted all kinds of performances.[76] "I went to Broadway shows. As a matter of fact, I actually saw [the 1956 musical adaptation of] *Li'l Abner* on Broadway when I was older. I like all this music. I was very fortunate—I had a lot of music in my household, but specifically, I grew up listening to a lot of what you would refer to as popular music."[77]

During Sonny's childhood, Harlem theater flourished. Mayor Fiorello La Guardia's Works Progress Administration Federal Theatre Project offshoot, the Portable Theater Project, put six stages in each borough to broaden access to theater across class.[78] Sonny has vivid memories of the summer of 1935, when he was four years old, seeing a free open-air production of *The Pirates of Penzance* in Harlem's Colonial Park. Colonial Park also hosted twice-weekly dances, cordoning off two adjacent blocks.[79]

Jazz was unavoidable. "We used to pass by the famous Cotton Club on the way to school," Sonny said. "I remember walking by the Savoy Ballroom and seeing the pictures of all the celebrities appearing there, and many of them lived in our neighborhood."[80] Valborg took Sonny to calypso dances and sang songs around the house. "It was a very rhythmic music I loved as a little boy," he said.[81] He has memories of the Renaissance Ballroom and the Park Palace in Spanish Harlem, later the inspiration for his song "Park Palace Parade."[82] Locals called the stately casino and ballroom the Renny. It was an expansive theater on Seventh Avenue, just down the block from where Sonny was born, and featured calypsonians such as Trinidadian bandleader Gerald Clark, Macbeth the Great, and the Duke of Iron. Sonny would later dedicate a song to the latter.[83]

On their weekly trips to the movies, Sonny first heard songs that stuck with him for life.[84] In his early childhood, they went to the Lincoln Theater.[85] Sonny also saw movies at the Odeon. One of his early favorites was the 1936 film *Swing Time*, which introduced "The Way You Look Tonight," a song Sonny would record multiple times. "All through my life, I've remembered the scene with the song 'A Fine Romance,' where Ginger Rogers and Fred Astaire are up in the country in the snow," he said. To Sonny, the real star was composer Jerome Kern. "I still think of him as maybe my favorite," he said.[86] Another favorite was the Marlene Dietrich vehicle *The Blue Angel*, with composer Friedrich Hollaender's "Falling in Love Again."

"I liked people like Bing Crosby and I liked Louis Armstrong," Sonny recalled.

> I liked Frank Sinatra. Of course, I was getting a little older then. Everybody from Martha Raye—I think I first saw her singing "I'm an Old Cowhand" from my *Way Out West* album. So I liked her. I liked Jimmy Durante—anybody that was a performer, you know?
>
> I liked people like Nelson Eddy and Jeanette MacDonald—they were movie people and they sang operetta-like material. A lot of the songs that they sang became my standards. I liked Ginger Rogers and Fred Astaire. Fred Astaire, of course, we know how much the composers loved him as a singer, because he would give such an exact treatment to their songs. He would sing the words exactly like they wanted them

sung. And of course, Ginger Rogers. You know, every red-blooded American would have to say that they liked Ginger Rogers. Well, I'm a red-blooded American. So this is my background. I was born in Harlem, and people have to understand that just because you're black and you're born in Harlem doesn't mean that you just like black music. No, I like music, and in America, I was exposed to a lot of music in my household, and I listened to all of it. It's all part of who I am.[87]

For black actors, casting was often limited to minor, menial roles. It sent Sonny a clear message. "In those days, of course what could you do in movies except be a shoeshine boy or a Pullman car porter," Sonny later recalled. "We had aspirations beyond that. At that age and that time, we didn't realize all the things these people had to go through; that Louis Armstrong and all the other black actors and actresses who were doing that role...that was all they could do."[88]

Nevertheless, Armstrong made magic out of a cameo role. "It would be sort of a bland movie, but when Pops came on there to do his thing, boy, that lit up the screen!"[89] Sonny found other on-screen role models featured in more prominent roles. Onetime Ellington crooner Herb Jeffries became a leading man by acting in westerns with an all-black cast, such as *The Bronze Buckaroo* (1939). "The screen cowboys taught me about fairness, justice and improvising when you're alone," Sonny said.[90]

Paul Robeson, the black activist, singer, and star athlete, was Sonny's favorite. "Paul Robeson was a hero to Black America, and my super-hero," he said. "I saw his movies, I heard his recordings, I marched for his civil rights when he was targeted by American conservatives."[91]

Soon, Sonny started making his own music. "In a West Indian family, you were expected to do well in school, and if you didn't, there had to be a serious explanation as to why you didn't," Gloria said. "You also were expected to play a musical instrument.... Quite frankly, you had to play the piano or the violin or something to show that you were inclined toward the better things in life. I learned piano, and my older brother [was] an excellent violinist."[92]

Sonny looked up to his older brother and sister. He would see and hear Valdemar, Val for short,[93] practicing all the time, and Gloria played piano at church. When Sonny turned six, Valborg enrolled him in piano lessons. He took a few lessons, but it didn't take, and since he was the youngest, Valborg was more permissive with her doting son. "I was more interested in playing in the street," Sonny said. "It wasn't until I wanted to play the saxophone that I began. . . . But I never had the formal education that my older brother and sister had, so I always felt inferior to them."[94] He would need to find tools forged in Harlem.[95]

Sonny didn't exactly take to school, either.[96] He started Public School (PS) 89 at 135th Street and Lenox in 1936. Romare Bearden described it as "the school most of the tough street kids of the area went to."[97]

At the time, Harlem public schools were dilapidated, underfunded, and overcrowded. In a suppressed 1936 report from the Mayor's Commission on Conditions in Harlem, PS 89 was described as "probably the worst school in the Negro section of Harlem," close to "the center of vice and the hideouts of vendors of narcotics and other criminals."[98] Though the school served kindergarten through sixth grade, all the chairs were for kindergarteners. The brick building was only partially fireproof and had seen six fires in the previous four years. If anyone got burned, Harlem Hospital was across the street. The fire house was conveniently located around the corner, which punctuated classes with sirens and bells.[99] The school had no gym or library and, after much agitation, in 1936, finally secured funding to install indoor lavatories.[100]

The experience toughened Sonny up, but it also helped him develop his wry sense of humor. "When I was a kid, they used to call me Jester, because I was a bit of a jokester," he said.[101] The nickname stuck from around age seven until his early teens.[102]

It was across the street from this pressure cooker of a school that Sonny saw his way out of PS 89. One of the smaller saloons near the school, the Elks Rendezvous, opened in November 1937.[103] In August 1938, a silver-tongued thirty-year-old Arkansas-born saxophonist and singer named Louis Jordan booked his first residency at the Rendezvous.[104] The pay was thirty dollars per person per week, but it paid the rent and put his name on the map.[105]

Jordan lived a short walk from Sonny's apartment and could easily walk home from the Rendezvous.[106] His publicity billed him as "LOUIS JORDAN, HIS SILVER SAXOPHONE AND HIS GOLDEN VOICE." Louis performed three shows nightly, starting at ten—treating audiences to a dance show with his Tympany Four, soon expanded to the Tympany Five,[107] and a cabaret act replete with vaudeville dancers, multiple singers, and impressions. The Rendezvous was a "black and tan" club, so whites and blacks intermingled until the club closed at three or four in the morning.

When Sonny went back to school in the fall of 1938, right around the time of his eighth birthday, he passed by a glossy headshot hanging in the entrance: Jordan in a cutaway tuxedo and white bow tie, clutching a shining King Zephyr alto saxophone. "They used to have this picture outside— one of those eight-by-tens—and he had this great looking horn, shiny like a samurai's sword; and these sharp ties and tails the cats used to wear," Sonny recalled. "And I said, 'Man, this is it for me—I've got to go this way.'"[108]

Sonny saw Jordan before he heard him, but hearing him wouldn't take long. On December 20, 1938, Jordan recorded his first 78 as a leader for Decca, "Honey in the Bee Ball" and "Barnacle Bill the Sailor."[109] When Sonny's mother couldn't take him to work and his grandmother couldn't watch him, sometimes his uncle Reuben Victoria would take care of him at his girlfriend Lizzie's apartment. "Sometimes they'd leave me there, and I'd listen to all these records," he said. Lizzie was from Georgia, and she introduced Sonny to Lonnie Johnson, Arthur "Big Boy" Crudup, and Tommy McClennan. "She also had some Louis Jordan, who was like a bridge between the blues and jazz—he had a great big sound on the alto, and I just loved him," Sonny said. "Louis was more like city blues than country blues, I guess, although on some of the earliest band stuff like 'Outskirts of Town' he'd really be singing the blues in a more traditional manner; it was a slow blues and he was really hollering, which connected more to that country blues sound. Later on, Louis Jordan and the Tympany Five got more showbizzy. I followed everything they did really closely."[110]

Sonny took it upon himself to buy every Louis Jordan record that came out: "It's a Low Down Dirty Shame," "Caldonia," "Ain't Nobody Here but Us Chickens," "Is You Is or Is You Ain't My Baby," "Five Guys Named Moe," "Choo Choo Ch'Boogie."[111]

"His group the Tympany Five was the same quintet configuration that Bird and Dizzy used later, so that's the group I liked," Sonny recalled. "He was my complete idol, and he was an excellent musician. I used to look at the pictures of him and he always had a different saxophone. I've seen him playing the King Zephyr, I've seen him with Selmers, and I've seen him playing Conns. That attests to the fact that he was such a consummate musician. He probably played whatever he liked at that moment." Sonny also loved Jordan's vaudevillian persona. "People said if you're singing and having fun that you're not serious; but with Louis Jordan and Fats Waller, it can be both fun and serious. You can't deny the musical legitimacy of Louis Jordan."[112]

Between the photo outside the Elks Rendezvous and the records with Uncle Reuben, Sonny was hooked: "I was destined to play saxophone, and I knew it at that early age."[113]

Sonny pleaded with his mother repeatedly, but everyone in the family couldn't get past the nightlife stigma associated with his chosen instrument. His grandmother "had the impression of jazz musicians being no-good guys involved with drugs," Sonny recalled. "Everything negative that people would think about it in church."[114] Nevertheless, Sonny persisted. "He had his own frame of reference for music," his sister, Gloria, recalled. "While we were playing what our parents would like to have us play, Sonny was hearing something different."[115]

Valborg steeled herself, and when Sonny was eight, she scraped together enough money to buy him a used alto.[116] Sonny described the feeling years later in an unpublished draft.[117] The scene unfolds in front of Manny's Music, a store Sonny frequented that opened in 1935 on what was known as "Music Row."[118] Note the coda symbol.

A PICTURE (PHOTOGRAPH) OF MANNY'S WINDOW FOR THE FIRST PAGE/PICTURE, SHOWING THE "GLEAMING, SHINY, SHIMMERING, BRIGHT, GOLDEN, CURVED, BEAUTIFUL GLEAMING SAXOPHONES TO GOOD ADVANTAGE.

BOY, I WISH I HAD ONE OF THOSE........AND COULD PLAY IT! (OR ADD 'too' TO THE EXCLAMATION) PLAY IT TOO!

CONT. NOW AS IF IN ANSWER—DIFFERENT PRINT AND LOCATION ON PAGE (OF THE FOLLOWING IN DISTINCTION TO THE EXCLAMATION ON PREVIOUS PAGE):

THAT'S HOW 'SAX MEN' BEGIN. (OR END WITH 'Are Born' FOR 'BEGIN.')

FOR THE FIRST TIME THEY LAY EYES ON THAT CURVED SHINY BEAUTIFUL "LOOKING PIECE OF METAL" 2.) "BABY DOLL," IT MAKES THEM FEEL 1.) BIG AND PROUD AND STRONG AND IMPORTANT! 2.) BIG + WONDERFUL + PROUD + IMPORTANT. IF YOU HAD THAT SAX YOU WOULD REALLY BE SOMEBODY IMPORTANT [IN THIS WORLD.] YOU WOULD MAKE 1.) PEOPLE DANCE AND BE HAPPY 2.) PEOPLE HAPPY WITH IT AND MAKE THEM DANCE AND SING AND BE JOYFUL 2.) CHEERFUL

YES, YOU CAN SEE YOURSELF NOW, 1.) STANDING IN FRONT OF THE PEOPLE AND FILLING THEM WITH TONES, STRAIGHT FROM YOUR SAX ⊕, HANDSOMELY DRESSED AND GROOMED, HORN

GROOMED   DRESSED

GLEAMING LIKE THE SUN AS YOU PERFORM IN FRONT OF THE 1.) CROWDS 2) THRONGS,

SO YOU START PLAYING THE SAXOPHONE
MAYBE NOT THE ONE IN THE WINDOW
MAYBE EVEN YOU JUST BORROW ONE OR USE ONE

⊕ INTO THEIR HEARTS.[119]

Chapter 3

THE HILL

(1938–1944)

"When I got my saxophone...I went in the bedroom, shut the door, and I started playing, and I was playing, playing, playing," Sonny said. "My mother had to call me. 'Time to eat!' I just get into that zone, and it's a spiritual thing. And that's what has carried me through my life."[1]

Sonny's work ethic goes back to the beginning.[2] "I want to have my rudiments ready to go whenever the spirit hits me," Sonny recalled. "My part of the bargain—I want to get that right.... The other part, well that's up to a higher power... it just has to happen, because that's what jazz is. It's natural. It's like the sky—it's never the same two days in a row."[3]

After Sonny got his saxophone, homework was no longer a concern; he had found an all-consuming passion. "I was always shouting, 'Shut up, Sonny!'" recalled his sister, Gloria. "I was a few years ahead of him in school, so I had to do homework and I didn't want to hear all of this... stuff in the background, but he didn't pay any attention to me at all."[4]

This is not to say Sonny was being deliberately inconsiderate. "I would play in the closet so the sound didn't get all up and down the building," Sonny said. "I never thought about it as practice. I just loved to play and I would get in the closet and blow for hours—nine, ten hours, and I would get lost in my own reverie, in the sound. I really didn't practice any one thing, I'd just play songs and blow in a stream-of-consciousness way. Our neighbor, Mr. Mason, he would always encourage me.... I'll always remember his encouragement because, you know, the horn can be pretty loud."[5]

Matthew Mason Sr. was one of the first black supervisors in the post office. He was a pillar of the neighborhood on Edgecombe, known as Judge Mason, settling disputes on the block in a kind of people's court. His hobby was playing alto saxophone. According to his daughter Doris, Sonny practiced "all the time. Every day after school. We could hear through the walls. All the time!" Doris recalled eight decades later, singing the major arpeggio she still remembered being repeated ad nauseam. "My father was hearing this and saying to us, 'That kid really knows how to play a horn. That kid is going someplace.'... It was annoying, 'cause it was after school every day. [Sings arpeggio.] 'Oh, Sonny's practicing.' But his practice paid off."[6]

Some neighbors even practiced with Sonny. "Where we lived, there was a potpourri of cultures: the West Indians, Jamaicans, Bahamians, Haitians, Irish and all kinds," recalled bassist John B. Williams, whose family lived in the apartment below Sonny's after the family moved to Edgecombe Avenue. "He'd come down to our apartment.... I played drums while he jammed with my sisters. He told me once, 'When I make it, I'm gonna let you be in my band.'"[7]

Sonny knew where he was going. "When I was a young boy—I mean nine, ten years old—and I was playing the saxophone, studying, and all that stuff, I knew already—something inside of me—I knew that I would be a prominent musician. I knew...that was my big destiny."[8]

He was mostly an autodidact, but for embouchure, fingerings, tonguing technique, and basic scales, even the proper hand position to hold the saxophone, Sonny's mother brought him to the New York Schools of Music.[9] Located on 125th Street and Lenox Avenue, it was "just a little place upstairs over a store," Sonny recalled.[10] It was founded in 1921 by Arthur T. Cremin, a young red-haired Serbian Jewish violinist who'd graduated from the Prague Conservatory and believed that anyone, of any age, of any class position, could learn an instrument.[11] All they needed was a quarter. By the time Sonny began going there in 1938, the school had nearly twenty branches in the city.

Cremin, however, despised jazz. Four years earlier, in his Carnegie Hall debut as a composer, he premiered "The Storyteller," which the "crusader for musical censorship" intended as "a constructive substitute for the sexy tunes of the better-known Harlem bandleaders."[12] He had a particular vendetta against the saxophone, which to him symbolized the worst of modern dance music: "Just as demoralizing as the most pornographic literature."[13] He even publicly debated Duke Ellington about it in the press.[14]

Sonny's first teacher at the school was a white multi-instrumentalist named Mr. Bastien. "He was one of these saxophone players that played with a double embouchure," meaning he made tight contact with both lips on the mouthpiece, then considered an old-fashioned style favored by classical saxophonists that can lead to a less resonant sound.[15] Sonny bought Ben Vereecken's *Foundation to Saxophone Playing: An Elementary Method*, first published in 1917.[16] Vereecken's book had sections on "manner of holding the saxophone," "adjusting the reed," "sharps, flats, naturals, etc.," but also more advanced exercises on dominant and diminished sevenths, as well as on syncopated phrasing and ragtime.[17]

Sonny enhanced his studies with the Victrola. He played choice passages on loop, much to his family's chagrin. "We used to listen to records and slow the record down so we could get how...the guy was phrasing," Sonny said. Sonny himself would play the opposite way: "You speed Coleman Hawkins up," tenor saxophonist David Murray later said, "you've got Sonny Rollins."[18]

In 1940, when Sonny was in fourth grade, a new sound began to emanate from jukeboxes up and down Seventh Avenue: Coleman Hawkins's solo saxophone rendition of "Body and Soul," which he'd recorded on October 11, 1939.

"Body and Soul" was an unlikely success—Hawkins didn't even play the melody. Rather, over two majestic choruses, he creates a brilliant improvised countermelody, full of complex arpeggios outlining the underlying chord progression, only stating the original melody line in the first four bars. Technically virtuosic and deeply personal, in three minutes, Hawkins transformed the saxophone's vocabulary forever.

"I was standing outside the Big Apple Bar on the corner of 135th Street and Seventh Avenue, across from Smalls Paradise, and heard it on the jukebox through an open window," Sonny recalled.[19] To Sonny, Hawkins was "the epitome of the saxophone."[20]

As much as the solo sounded through-composed—legato phrasing, no hesitation in the attack—it came out of the blue. The thirty-five-year-old Missouri native had just returned from five years in Europe, and he expected some forward-looking soloists would have surpassed him in harmonic complexity, but "it was just like when I left," he said. "I didn't see nothing."[21]

During a stint at Kelly's Stables on West Fifty-First Street, Hawkins began using the old standard as an encore. "I never thought of 'Body and Soul' as being anything big for me," Hawkins recalled. When recording supervisor Leonard Joy asked him to record it, Hawk replied, "We don't even have an arrangement on it. Who wants to hear that!" The band made one take, and he "didn't even bother to listen to it afterwards." Hawkins thought of it as hackneyed, a throwaway. It turned out to be his signature recording.[22]

Hearing the record turned Sonny on his ear.[23] He couldn't articulate what Hawkins was doing yet, but had to find out. "Coleman was a guy that played chord changes in an up-and-down manner. He sort of played every change," he said. "He had a phrase for every change that went by. So in that solo, he was not only playing the changes, he was also playing the passing chords, which is another thing he was ahead of his time on," while effortlessly "building and building and building."[24]

Meeting Hawkins's standard, making changes with his acuity and panache, would be Sonny's lifelong goal. "A light went off in my head. If he could personalize a popular song like that without lyrics, any song was possible if you had that intellectual capacity," Sonny said. "Right after hearing the record, I bought a tenor reed and began using it on my alto mouthpiece to get that big Coleman Hawkins sound."[25]

Sonny's neighbor bought a transcription of the famous solo and practiced it over and over again. Sonny learned the solo too, but he also knew that only Hawk could play Hawk. "I never tried to copy Coleman Hawkins's solos," Sonny wrote. "I didn't think I would be successful, because his style was personal and he was doing difficult stuff. I tried to inhabit his soul, interpret music the way he did. Later, I tried to play more verbatim with Charlie Parker and Lester Young, but Coleman Hawkins's style defied copying."[26] Sonny would strive for a style that was just as personal. The bar had been set.

Sonny's two early saxophone idols, Coleman Hawkins and Louis Jordan, lived in the same neighborhood, but they could hardly have been more different.[27] Sonny would work to combine Jordan's "elemental" playing, as he thought of it, with Hawkins's "intellectual element and grandeur."[28] Sonny wore out the grooves on Hawkins's "The Man I Love"; "Stuffy" and its B-side, "It's the Talk of the Town"; "Bu-Dee-Daht"; and "Woody'n You?"[29] Sonny would also seek out the music of Hawkins's collaborators and eventually worked with many of them.

Soon, Sonny would see his new musical idol riding around Harlem. Jordan was inextricably linked to Harlem's main stem for Sonny, Hawkins with the erudite sophistication of Sugar Hill, the affluent enclave within Harlem that spanned 145th Street up to Washington Heights.[30]

In 1940, before Sonny's tenth birthday, his family moved up to "the Hill."[31] Walter Sr. had finally been reassigned as a steward at the Brooklyn Navy Yard, where he worked fifty-two weeks a year, seventy-two hours a week, for a respectable middle-class salary of $1,260 a year. Miriam was doing hand laundry, and they could afford the move. It was a positive time in Sonny's family life. One Christmas, the families of naval officers stationed at the Brooklyn Navy Yard were invited to a Christmas party there.

"I remember that one of my gifts was a book about Chinese outrigger boats," Sonny said. "I never forgot that."[32]

They moved to 371 Edgecombe Avenue, then settled a few doors over, at 377, by the corner of 152nd Street in a five-story, built in 1920. An expansive foyer on the ground floor opened to a narrow tiled hallway that led to a narrower stairwell. They lived on the third floor, in apartment 8, opposite two other units.[33] It was a peaceful block on Coogan's Bluff overlooking Colonial Park. Sonny had a beautiful view of the Bronx skyline. Across the viaduct were the Polo Grounds where the Giants played—Sonny recalls seeing pitcher Carl Hubbell walking to his car after the games. Not far off was Yankee Stadium, and down the Hill off in the distance loomed the Empire State Building, which had been built less than ten years earlier. There were benches and oak trees all along the park side.

Sonny's building had a Georgian front door with Ionic columns and decorative molding on the exterior windows. Photos taken the year they moved capture the front of the apartment, where two women in full-length mink stoles, hats, and kitten heels stand idly as a young boy in a newsboy cap plays nearby. Coupes are parked all up the block on Edgecombe. Walking south, a junkman with his wheelbarrow stands in front of the rubble of a demolished building at 335 Edgecombe as a woman passes by on her way to work, with a backdrop of a billboard with a flaxen-haired smiling woman holding a panhandle. Walking uptown from Sonny's, several men sit on a stoop shooting the breeze as a porter keeps his vigil in front of 385. Continuing east were the 155th Street viaduct and the Macombs Dam Bridge, connecting Manhattan to the Bronx via the Harlem River. To the north, a water tower loomed farther up on Edgecombe. Every weekend, a man named Frank arrived in a "horse-drawn vegetable wagon," Sonny recalled. "People would call out what they wanted," and Sonny's friend Tommy "had to get them and run upstairs."[34] It was a serene, almost pastoral, block, quite a change from the hustle and bustle of 135th Street down in the "valley" on the Harlem Plain.[35]

"I lived in apartment 7, and Sonny lived in apartment 8. We were next door to each other. We shared the same fire escape," recalled Doris Mason, who was the same age as Sonny. "The park benches across the street from where we lived, when we were kids, we could move the benches, and we used to move them up and down the park, wherever the group was gonna be that day. We'd sit, but we never put them back in place." Eventually, the city nailed them in place: "If you see those benches, Sonny and all of us, we're the cause of it."[36]

Parents looked out for other kids on the block. "If one of us did something, you can bet your life, they didn't wait to tell your parents; they'd chastise you right then and there," said Mason. "That's the way that block was. . . . Everybody got along." Mason recalled being able to look into Duke Ellington's kitchen window.[37]

Many of the Hill's houses had names. Around the block from 377 Edgecombe were the palatial Benziger House and the towering neo-Romanesque spires of the Bailey House. A short walk took you to the Roger Morris Apartments, where two of Sonny's heroes lived: Joe Louis and Paul Robeson, the latter of whom moved there in 1939.[38] "Joe Louis used to come after each fight," recalled Mason. "He had an aunt, lived in the next building from us, and he would come and rest, spend the night after his fight, and then leave in the morning, and all of us would be standing out waiting for him to come out the building. He had his training camp. He used to have buses to take all the kids on Edgecombe to go up to his training camp, spend the day."[39]

Marking their upward mobility, Sonny's family became proud owners of a new telephone number: EDgecombe 4-7013.[40] It wasn't the nicest apartment on the block, but it was a significant improvement that Sonny's mother found safer for her children.[41]

When he was eleven, Sonny started working on the Hill, as a delivery boy at a dry cleaners on the corner of Edgecombe and 155th Street. He would make deliveries in the neighborhood when he got off school. "I always wanted to work, and be a man, support myself."[42] He would also run errands for featherweight champion Chalky Wright. He could use the spending money to see shows at the Apollo on his own.

◄○►

Sugar Hill was not documented on E. Simms Campbell's map of Harlem nightlife, but it required its own map. Within a ten-minute walk of Sonny's apartment were Bowman's Grill, where regular jam sessions took place, the ribs were delicious, and bartender Charlie Davis would serve only two "White Zombie" cocktails per customer; the 721 Club, where in 1941 Ernie Henry played with singer Monette Moore; and the New Lamar Cherie, "Show Place on the Hill."[43] Louis Metcalf's Heat Wave was on 145th Street, and on St. Nicholas was Jimmy's Chicken Shack, the after-hours chicken-and-rib joint. "A little further up St. Nicholas, right on the same side of the street," Sonny said, was Luckey's Rendezvous, stride pianist Luckey Roberts's club. Sonny was too young to go in, but "Art Tatum and all them cats used to go in there and jam after-hours because it had a nice piano."[44] This was fast becoming Sonny's milieu.

During this period, Valborg introduced Sonny to his uncle, West Virginia–born saxophonist Hubert "Bumps" Myers, who was living at the time with Sonny's aunt Emelyn.[45] Uncle Hubert was a consummate professional; he'd played with Louis Armstrong, Big Sid Catlett, Jimmie Lunceford, and Benny Carter and was proficient on soprano, alto, tenor, and baritone.[46]

Another uncle, George Tapley Lewis, was an alto saxophone player born in Anguilla in 1910 who played briefly with Don Redman and Louis Armstrong before becoming a postal worker.[47] One day, Valborg took Sonny to visit Herbert Vanterpool, a family friend from St. Thomas, who played tenor, drawing Sonny's attention to the larger horn. "I remember very vividly how he had the saxophone under the bed," Sonny said, "and he pulled it out and opened it up, and there was this beautiful gold instrument, shining there in this deep red velvet case. That was the moment."[48]

Sonny discovered that though the majority of the clubs were closer to the main stem, his favorite musicians all lived up on the Hill. Duke Ellington had lived for a time a few doors from Sonny's apartment.[49] In 1939, Billy Strayhorn wrote the Ellington theme song, "Take the 'A' Train," based on the directions Ellington gave to his apartment at 935 St. Nicholas Avenue.[50]

In 1943, part of the third movement of Ellington's "Black, Brown and Beige" was called "Sugar Hill Penthouse." Sonny and his friends wouldn't just hear Ellington on the radio; they would see him in the streets. "Ellington was a very unusual dresser, perhaps *flamboyant* would be the word," recalled Bill Coggins, the younger brother of pianist Gilbert "Gilly" Coggins, who lived right across the street from Ellington. "He always had a word for the kids.... Of course, there were a lot of celebrities around." Not to mention future celebrities. "Harry Belafonte, he lived right around the corner," Coggins said. "Jackie McLean lived up the street. This was all before he was famous."[51]

Roy Eaton, a classical piano prodigy who made his Carnegie Hall debut at age six, lived at 375 Edgecombe and met Sonny soon after he moved to the Hill. "I was fortunate, as was Sonny Rollins also, to have come from a West Indian background. Our parents instilled in us the belief that anything is possible, that you do not let the world define who you are. You define yourself," Eaton said. "At the time we felt segregated.... But actually, the fact that we were in that confined community created a peculiar energy on which people like Sonny and myself thrived."[52]

Nevertheless, there was a cultural hierarchy to their respective musical interests. In music departments, Eaton said, "if you were caught playing jazz, you were reprimanded. You were not supposed to be playing jazz." Years later, he and others realized how myopic that perspective was. "Some of the things in our cuisine that we love the most were things that in Jamaica they looked at as poor food, like oxtail or curry goat—that was 'poor food.' The rich people, they ate steaks. But the good stuff is this poor food! And so this environment of segregation and degradation, it's not poor food at all. It was truly enriching." Eaton added: "The Jewish culture has a name for it—there should be a Jamaican word for it—*chutzpah*. That was the key."[53]

Sonny and his peers could take after the example of an older generation dotting Sugar Hill. "We had a chance at looking at people going about their daily business, famous figures at the time," recalled Sonny, "like drummer Big Sid Catlett, saxophonist Coleman Hawkins, bandleaders like John Kirby, Erskine Hawkins, Sy Oliver and Don Redman, bassist Al Hall, drummer Denzil Best, and trumpeter Red Allen, and all those other great musicians who lived on Sugar Hill. We'd see these guys out on the street in everyday life. They served as ideal role models for us."[54] Other major figures lived there, too: Harlem Renaissance artist Aaron Douglas, the tap-dancing Nicholas Brothers, pianist Mary Lou Williams on picturesque Hamilton Terrace, saxophonists Johnny Hodges and Budd Johnson, vocalists Dinah Washington and

Lena Horne, and bandleaders Andy Kirk, Count Basie, Lionel Hampton, and Fletcher Henderson.

"All the prominent black people lived up there," Sonny said. "Not only musicians, but also politicians."[55] One thirteen-story building at 409 Edgecombe housed "all the black dignitaries—W. E. B. Du Bois; Walter White, head of the NAACP [National Association for the Advancement of Colored People]; Thurgood Marshall; Roy Wilkins. It was the pinnacle building on that block."[56]

Coleman Hawkins was the one who excited Sonny the most. "He had an impressive Cadillac. He dressed well," Sonny said. "There were certain other people that acted more on the entertainment side. There was even a time in my life when I had a brief feeling about Louis Armstrong, that he was too minstrel-y and too smiley. That didn't last long. I was a young person at the time. But what impressed me about Coleman was that he carried himself with great dignity."[57]

In school, Sonny learned about earlier predecessors as well, such as bandleader James Reese Europe, which he later described in a draft of an essay: "As I grew up I learned of the Black American soldiers in W.W.I.; how they fought valiantly and courageously and were subsequently honored by France even as they were shunned by their own country. [*Strikeout in original.*] I learned about James Reese Europe and his extraordinary orchestra (part of that Black American contingent) and how their music heralded the new age. An age of democracy and against fascism."[58]

After the move to Sugar Hill, Sonny finished elementary school at PS 46, where a teacher named Mrs. Love "saw the promise in me," he said.[59] "I'll never forget her because she skipped me into a higher grade. I was doing the work, but... She was the first teacher that really inspired me to excel, and so I guess I began to like school a little better."[60]

Sonny spent seventh through ninth grade at PS 164, Edward W. Stitt Junior High School, a redbrick building named for the New York City superintendent (no relation to Sonny Stitt).[61] There was no school band, though the students did learn material like "I'm Called Little Buttercup" from Gilbert and Sullivan's *H.M.S. Pinafore*.[62] In the fall of 1943, an organization called the Youthbuilders invited Duke Ellington for a performance in front of two hundred Stitt students.[63]

The school provided rapid advancement classes for students like former Federal Reserve chairman Alan Greenspan, who attended a few years earlier. "It was the cusp of the new Jewish immigrants from the Holocaust from Germany and the African American community," recalled Roy Eaton, "and I would say relatively affluent African American community."[64] The school was integrated, but it was home to a number of youth gangs. Writer Gilbert Moore, who attended a few years later, remembered "swashbuckling names, the Royalistics and the Sabers and the Buccaneers. They roamed the streets and hallways with homemade guns and obedient switch blades, and with almost complete freedom to terrorize and declare war on each other."[65] In 1943, the Youthbuilders started a "juke box night club" where, according to the club chaperone, "they can congregate without fear of being attacked by rival gangs."[66]

Racial tensions remained high through legal and extralegal methods that kept black Harlemites as second-class citizens, sometimes in their own neighborhood—de jure segregation via racially restrictive covenants or de facto segregation enforced by racialized violence in the streets. In the spring of 1939, a youth gang from predominantly white Washington Heights, the neighborhood north of the border of Sugar Hill, was responsible for a wave of hate crimes. Groups of Stitt students had been violently attacked, resulting in forty policemen posted at and around the school during lunch and dismissal.[67] When Sonny began attending, it was still fresh in everyone's memory.

As a result, Sonny developed a keen street sense. "At that time blacks were living up as far as, maybe, 165th Street or something like that," Sonny said. "Then you got to the Heights and there were certain streets you didn't venture beyond, like past Amsterdam Avenue; there was a gang up there called the Rainbows, a bad Irish gang."[68]

Being West Indian meant facing double discrimination from kids in the neighborhood. "They would call us 'monkey faces' or 'black Jews,'" said Coggins. "The reason for calling us black Jews was that we'd work hard, save our money, and buy property. What the hell's wrong with that?"[69]

When Sonny was nine or ten, he experienced an "awakening" when his neighbor Doris Mason pointed out the distinction: "'Sonny, you're different than us,'" he recalled her saying. "I said, 'What do you mean?' She said, 'Oh, you're West Indian.'" Later, he discovered "the animosity between southern blacks and blacks that came from the Caribbean." At first, he struggled to accept his cultural heritage as a marker of difference, but eventually, he "came to embrace it." In the broader civil rights struggle, though, "it wasn't West Indian versus whatever," he said. "It was black versus antiblack.... [I]t's about color; it's not about place of origin. We were all [n-words] in the United States."[70]

Within Harlem, however, Sonny acknowledged that there was a distinction between African Americans with West Indian and southern roots: "They were brought up differently." According to Eaton, West Indian families subscribed to an uplift ideology that prioritized formal education. Sonny's sister, Gloria, later Roy's classmate at the High School for Music and Art, and his brother, Val, a future classmate at City College, went along with the plan.[71] Sonny was the prodigal son and spent more time in the streets than at the library.

Once he almost killed a man by accident. He and his friends would sometimes go to the roof, where they could watch passersby cutting through backyard shortcuts. "There was some loose mortar there, and as people were coming by...we'd drop the mortar down and scare people.... One day, I dropped this mortar—and this was a heavy piece of mortar—and I saw that it was going to hit this guy.... I prayed hard, man.... And bang, it fell next to him. It didn't hit him."[72]

Sonny played many of the games indigenous to New York: stickball, boxball, marbles.[73] His stickball team was called the Edgecombe Avenue Aces. "They had little jerseys," Gloria recalled, "and they beat everybody, so he made a lot of friends."[74] Stickball was an improviser's sport. A sawed-off broomstick with tape for a handle was the bat; manhole covers and fire hydrants were the bases; home-run boundaries could be the edge of a building; they used chalk when they had it. Once, from the manhole cover in front of 365 Edgecombe—which was home plate—Sonny "hit a pink Spaldeen from here onto the roof of 385," he said. "It was a prodigious feat that was never repeated. I still remember the impact, the sound, and the thrill of disbelief."[75]

Even though Sonny wasn't the oldest player, when he was thirteen or four-teen, he was appointed team captain. He seemed like a natural-born leader.[76]

———◄○►———

None of the intelligentsia on Sugar Hill expected Sonny and the Aces to amount to much. They played handball in front of Du Bois's building at 409 Edgecombe, where there was a good wall.[77] "I remember W. E. B. Du Bois coming home one time—and he's a very austere guy," Sonny recalled. "He looked at us like, 'Oh, what are these little ruffians doing playing up here?'"[78]

Sonny would have greater exposure to the ideas of Du Bois put into prac-tice at Camp Unity, an interracial, antichauvinist, anticapitalist summer camp in Wingdale, a sleepy town upstate.[79] During the summer of 1939 or 1940, Sonny recalls attending the camp, a formative experience of his youth. Initially, the majority of Unity's campers were from the radical Jewish Left, but by the time Sonny arrived it had become quite diverse. Sonny's grand-mother may have read about it in advertisements in the *Crisis*, the publication of the NAACP.[80]

"It was considered a communist camp at that time, and of course, *com-munism* was a bad word to some people," Sonny said. "It was a good word to the people in my community, because it afforded a lot of the black Ameri-cans intercourse with some of the other activities that you otherwise would be prohibited from engaging in.... Everybody that had any interaction with what would be called the liberal point of view were called communists at that time."[81]

For Sonny, it offered a summer escape. The camp spanned hundreds of acres in the foothills of the Berkshires, with stone fences, forests, and trails. Campers would congregate at a site affectionately called Lenin's Rock.[82]

Rates were proletarian: $22 per week or $3.75 per day. The camp's party affiliation was an open secret;[83] a bookstore on the grounds sold Soviet Union ambassador Joseph E. Davies's *Mission to Moscow* and *Soviet Russia Today*.[84] Campers—mostly adults, but sometimes as young as eight[85]—were referred to in camp brochures as "fellow-workers."[86] Abel Meeropol, a Communist Party member who in 1937 wrote the lyrics and eventually the melody to Billie Holiday's "Strange Fruit," was a counselor there. In the 1950s, Lorraine

Hansberry worked there summers. Even the notorious Harlem gangster Bumpy Johnson was safe there. He took several trips to Camp Unity, once to recover from "an operation"—gunshot wounds—"walk[ing] around with a big bucket filled with gin and orange juice."[87]

The camp hosted a number of musical acts in its thousand-person auditorium or open-air stage.[88] Huddie "Lead Belly" Ledbetter, Willie "the Lion" Smith with Sidney Bechet, trumpeter Frankie Newton, Max Roach, Tito Puente, and Pete Seeger all performed. In 1949, Paul Robeson spoke at the camp and gave a concert at nearby Peekskill, causing a riot.[89]

One of the camp songs was Paul Robeson's "Ballad for Americans," originally called "The Ballad for Uncle Sam." The song made a great impact on Sonny with its vision of radical egalitarianism. "The great voice—the great man—the great message of this song," Sonny later wrote of the piece.[90] The song was composed by Earl Robinson, with lyrics by John La Touche. Robinson was a card-carrying member of the Communist Party of the USA and also served as music director at Camp Unity. " 'I was a big fan of his," Sonny later said of Robinson.[91]

Sonny never performed at the camp, but his experience there was unforgettable. "Just the opportunity to interact with . . . different races of people and everything," Sonny said, "it was an opportunity not afforded by too many other places in our society."[92]

By contrast, when Sonny visited his father in Annapolis, Maryland, he came face-to-face with Jim Crow. In 1941, Walter Sr. was transferred to Trinidad and then to Seattle. In 1942, Walter finally landed at the North Severn Officers Club at the Naval Academy in Annapolis, where he became the chief steward at the club, supervising meals and weekly late-night dances. The family's hopes of living under one roof were dashed. "I remember my sister telling me one time that she was so upset about this," Sonny said.[93]

Sonny respected his father's position, even as he recognized the institutional racism that held him back. His father supervised the officers' mess and maintained the facilities for the servicemen. When Sonny visited, he worked at North Severn as a busboy.[94] "There's a lot of little incidents happened while I was [t]here," Sonny said.[95]

When Sonny wasn't working, he would take advantage of the music and movies that were part of the summer season. The experience was tempered by the fact that the theater in-Annapolis was segregated, and Sonny had to watch from the balcony. In the summer of 1943, he saw one of his favorites: *Cabin in the Sky*. With an all-black cast, the movie, which was a film adaptation of the eponymous 1940 Broadway musical, chronicles the journey of a gambler as he wrestles with angels, Lucifer, and temptation in an attempt to redeem his soul. "It had all my favorite people: the great Duke Ellington and his band; Ethel Waters; Lena Horne; Eddie 'Rochester' Anderson, everybody was familiar with him from the Jack Benny [radio] comedy show; and Buck & Bubbles—I used to see Buck & Bubbles at the Apollo Theater in New York."[96] Louis Armstrong even had a role opposite Mantan Moreland, Willie Best, and Moke and Poke as Lucifer Jr.'s "Idea Men" at the Hades Hotel. For Sonny, the songs were the stars: "Taking a Chance on Love," "Happiness Is a Thing Called Joe," "Things Ain't What They Used to Be," and the title theme, which Sonny later recorded. "It has a special meaning," he said. "I'm just not playing it as a piece of music. It represents my childhood."[97]

———◄o►———

On July 29, 1944, a balmy summer afternoon in Annapolis, Sonny was one of fifty-five hundred people who saw the Erskine Hawkins Orchestra at Sparrow's Beach, in a concert that set a wartime record for attendance on the Chitlin Circuit. Tickets were eighty cents apiece, and dancing took place from three to seven.[98] Sonny, at thirteen, was there for the music—Hawkins and Dud Bascomb on trumpet, Dud's brother Paul Bascomb, and Julian Dash on tenor—but he was also there for a girl.[99]

Marjorie Brown worked at the Naval Academy. "She was older than me, actually, but I had big eyes for her," Sonny said.[100] "They used to have people sitting on chairs on the stage, right next to the band. Sure enough, when I went there that day, there was Marjorie Brown sitting next to the Erskine Hawkins band. The implications were that she was friendly with the band. So that crushed my heart."[101]

To Sonny, the message was obvious. "Why would she mess around with a little squirt like me?" he thought. "I wanted to be like my idols. I wanted to be like Louis Jordan. I wanted to be like Coleman Hawkins. I wanted to be up there. I wanted to be a musician, playing."[102] If he got up there, it seemed, he might get the girl.

Sonny's father was not interested in such frivolous pursuits. "He did not take me to see Erskine Hawkins in Annapolis; I went there on my own," Sonny said. "He did not expose me to music. He did not contribute to my career choice."[103] Nevertheless, Sonny loved his father deeply and cherished these all-too-short summers in Annapolis.

Back at home, "a girl who didn't like me closed that heavy front door on my middle finger," he said.[104] A long scar would remain for life.

Meanwhile, Sonny had developed another crush. "I had eyes for Faith Ringgold," he recalled, "but she married an older guy and I'll never forgive her for that!"[105]

Born October 8, 1930, Faith Ringgold, née Jones, would eventually become a major American artist known for her intricate jazz-inflected quilts, but back then she was just Sonny's neighbor and classmate at Stitt.[106] In the fall of 1943, Ringgold had a birthday party at the apartment, and Sonny, who had also just turned thirteen, was invited. The party began at 5 p.m.; her mother, known affectionately as Ma Jones, was insistent that the party end promptly at 9, so Faith wanted to start early.

Everyone was told to bring a gift, and like some of the other boys, Sonny arrived with a twenty-five-cent bag of five candy bars from the drugstore. When the adults went in the kitchen and left the kids alone, they played Post Office in the dark coatroom. The classic kissing game consisted of a postman and a recipient. The postman would go into the coatroom and call out the recipient to receive her package. The postman would deliver a letter (one kiss), an airmail (two kisses), or a special delivery (three kisses).

"I had heard that Sonny thought I was cute and that he liked me, so I wasn't surprised when he called me in for Post Office," Ringgold wrote. "Sonny was good-natured.... We had a great time laughing before we finished our kiss, and Sonny bashfully went out to a roomful of teasers."[107] She then called in Earl Wallace, a hip, silver-tongued pianist who would become her first husband.

Faith and Sonny became lifelong friends. She witnessed his musical development; he, her artistic development. Guests would come to her apartment and hear Louis Jordan and others on the Victrola. Sometimes the Edgecombe Aces would bring their instruments. She'd even sing while Sonny played.

Mostly, Ringgold remembers Sonny's fierce dedication to his instrument. "Sonny was always serious about his saxophone," she wrote. "He could be heard practicing his horn above the street sounds and the boys' screams as they played stickball in the street below his window....Sonny knew he would become one of the great jazz saxophonists of his time."[108]

To get there, Sonny participated in his own after-school program every day, and then all day on weekends, at an institution that celebrated his ambitions: the Apollo Theater.[109] Sonny was there for the music, but he also took in the movie between sets.[110] "If I liked the band, I would stay there all day. They had about four or five shows a day. That means you'd have to see the movie four or five times," Sonny said. One memorable Apollo act was saxophonist, trumpeter, and bandleader Benny Carter appearing with Nat King Cole, who played to a record-breaking crowd in December 1944, but Sonny saw everyone.[111] The standard was high. "It was a place where you had to have something going, or they would let you know it in a minute," Sonny said. Once at a Thelma Carpenter concert, "They blew her off....Somebody didn't like her, and they heckled her.... That was the Apollo."[112] Yet, "By and large the Apollo was a neighborhood theater," said Coggins. "It was for Harlem. If you're restricted, you've got to develop your own culture."[113]

Sonny had the opportunity to meet his heroes in the streets where they lived. Val would be playing the Mendelssohn violin concerto with his sister accompanying him on piano; meanwhile, Sonny was hoping to catch a glimpse of Coleman Hawkins around the block.[114]

When Sonny was thirteen, he figured out Hawkins's address and sought him out. Sonny used to buy headshots of his favorites at a music store in Times Square and collected them in a scrapbook. He wanted Hawkins's eight-by-ten glossy by photographer James J. Kriegsmann signed.[115]

Hawkins lived on a tree-lined block in the King Haven Apartments, between St. Nicholas and Amsterdam.[116] "I waited there," said Sonny, "and waited and waited and waited; and finally, he came in and I said, 'Oh, Mr. Hawkins, would you sign this for me?'"[117] Of course, he said yes.

Later on, Sonny tried to meet Hawkins's drummer Denzil Best in the same way. Best was a "friend of a friend of my mother's," Sonny recalled.[118] Best lived only five minutes from Sonny's apartment.[119] He went after school one day at around four o'clock. For a musician, this was early. "You'd play till four—four or five o'clock [in the morning]. . . . [T]hree o'clock is early," Sonny said. "And this guy's trying to get some sleep." Best wasn't pleased to see an eager aspiring jazz musician on his doorstep. Sonny tried again with tenor saxophonist Eddie "Lockjaw" Davis, who lived in the Bronx. "He didn't answer at all," Sonny said, "so I never got a chance to disturb him."[120]

There would be more tenor players in Sonny's pantheon. From his association with Count Basie, Sonny had already heard Lester Young, the man they called the "President of the Tenor Saxophone," or simply "Pres," but he hadn't listened consciously.[121] In 1944, Sonny went out and bought his first Young record, "Afternoon of a Basie-ite," a Keynote date with pianist Johnny Guarnieri, bassist Slam Stewart, and drummer Sid Catlett. "It sounds very free and easy," Sonny said of the record, "but we know it's not, because what he's saying is deep as the ocean. There was a beginning and an end. He was storytelling all the way through."[122] Less than six months later, Young recorded another favorite: "Lester's Savoy Jump."[123] Hawkins was more arpeggios, a vertical player; Young was more horizontal, primarily a lyrical player. Sonny would soon try to marry the two styles.[124]

Pres was in the neighborhood, too. "Lester Young used to room with some people we knew up on Hamilton Terrace; so I used to see him frequently, walking around with his porkpie hat on, the whole silhouette and everything, and we'd whisper, 'Look, there's Lester Young, man.' And he was very cool and all by himself in a world all his own."[125]

Hawk and Pres were giants, but Sonny idolized others: Georgie Auld, Al Sears, Ben Webster, Arnett Cobb, Gene Ammons, Don Byas, Earl Bostic.[126] Sonny would strive to emulate their big sound, a quality that Webster himself came to admire in Sonny during the late '40s. "I always did dig Sonny because when he was coming on in the mid-'40s, most of the kids had a small sound, and Sonny always tried to have a bigger sound," Webster later recalled. "I've always admired him, because I think the tenor is a big horn, and you should get a big sound out of it."[127]

Another tenor player with a larger-than-life sound whom Sonny used to see walking around Sugar Hill was the Texas tenor Illinois Jacquet. On May 26, 1942, the nineteen-year-old Louisiana-born saxophonist performed what would become a legendary solo on the Lionel Hampton Orchestra's rendition of "Flying Home." Like Hawkins's "Body and Soul," Jacquet did not plan it out. "Marshal Royal, the first saxophone player, just reached over and put his hands [around] his mouth and said, 'Go for yourself,'" Jacquet said. "He knew I could play like all the saxophone players.... I had to go for myself."[128] As did all aspiring tenor players of the era, Sonny learned the solo note for note, but he too would go for himself.[129]

There were early signs he would. One night, Sonny started playing in front of a club on 133rd Street, Swing Street, "and the great piano player and bandleader Buddy Johnson said he really dug my playing—I was about twelve years old. That was a great feeling."[130]

Starting in 1943, Sonny began learning from two teachers—Walter Purl "Foots" Thomas and Joe Napoleon—in private saxophone lessons.[131] They had a reputation in the neighborhood; Jackie McLean studied with both, while Foots Thomas taught Bud Shank, tenor saxophonist Willene Barton of the International Sweethearts of Rhythm, and Ornette Coleman.[132]

Thomas's studio was around the block from Radio City Music Hall, on Music Row above Zimmerman's Budapest Restaurant. He shared the space with drummer Cozy Cole.[133] Foots was a seasoned veteran who started teaching when he tired of life on the road. Born February 10, 1907, he grew up in Muskogee, Oklahoma. He moved to New York in 1927, where he worked with Jelly Roll Morton and backed Cab Calloway; he arranged Calloway's hit "Minnie the Moocher."[134] Foots worked with and knew many of Sonny's favorites, from Hawkins to Webster to Eddie Barefield, who later taught Sonny clarinet.[135] Foots had the trifecta: he could double on clarinet and flute, he could orchestrate and read, and he could improvise. He was sometimes listed on records as "Sir Walter Thomas," but he also performed with "Walter Thomas and His Jump Cats." Foots would teach Sonny how to swing hard, with an air of royalty.

Thomas was one of the first to believe that improvisation could be taught.[136] He stressed the importance of repetition and variation—the idea of thematic or motivic development—a central concept later in Sonny's career. To Thomas, much could be expressed on only one note just by varying the rhythm. "Repetition!" he said. "You don't want to repeat a thing but over three times. If you do it over three times, it changes in some way."[137]

Thomas also taught Sonny about breath control and tone production, how to adjust his embouchure and his attitude to get the fullest sound from the bottom of the horn to the top.[138] His ideas were influential enough that twenty years later, Sonny made a note to himself of what Thomas called the "positive approach." Most of the principles were technical, but some were not. "Mentally adapt a positive attitude concerning production of these notes and to know that they will be hit when we go for them!!" Sonny wrote. "Imagine the notes as emanating from the bell of the horn."[139]

Sonny's other significant teacher, Joe Napoleon, had suite 37 in the same building (Thomas was in suite 41).[140] He advertised his services as "Tone Technician," offering saxophone and clarinet instruction as well as "chord-structure as applied to the instrument." In the September 1944 issue of *Metronome*, Napoleon and Thomas took out advertisements literally on top of each other.[141]

Napoleon was born Joseph Napoli on April 7, 1906,[142] and grew up in Brooklyn in a musical Italian family. According to one former student, he was "a slick Damon Runyon type character...impeccably well-groomed, Italian cat with a pencil-thin mustache, always clean-shaven, always a white shirt in suit trousers."[143] Napoleon was the younger brother of trumpeter and bandleader Phil Napoleon, and though he was never as well known as his sibling, he became a respected saxophone teacher, having taught Kenny Davern, King Curtis, and Sonny. With Sonny, Napoleon focused on embouchure, getting him to relax the jaw and let the force come from the diaphragm to get a big sound.[144] No one could teach Sonny how to get his own sound, but he could learn to play loud enough to make the walls shake.[145]

Napoleon demanded total commitment from his students. "One of his favorite sayings was 'Potentials are not credentials,'" recalled a former student. There was no piano in his studio, "so if he wanted to accompany you with some chords, he would pull out a ukulele."[146] Yet navigating complex harmonies was not the starting point. At first, Napoleon had students lie down with books on their diaphragm—the dictionary, the Bible—to learn how to breathe properly. Then he had them stand in front of a mirror for twenty minutes and slowly play a major scale with as much air control as possible: "Joe believed sound was everything."[147] Sonny kept one document from his time with Napoleon, which he signed to Sonny: "Saxophone Fingerings for Extremely High (False) Tones Above the Normal Range of the Saxophone."[148] When Sonny gained greater control of his diaphragm, Napoleon taught a thematic approach to improvisation, with an emphasis on learning the blues in all twelve keys. "Follow your phrases," he would say, meaning build a solo logically, starting with a melodic statement.[149]

Formal instruction was crucial, but Sonny suspected the best way to learn was on the job. He got his first paying gig when he was thirteen, in ninth grade, his last year at Stitt. To get paid on the books, anyone under eighteen needed working papers, with fourteen being the youngest eligible age. So Sonny lied about his age, claiming to be born a year earlier in 1929. "Like father, like son," Sonny said.[150]

His first professional gig was in a Bronx dance hall on Jerome Avenue. When he finished and went home at two in the morning, Valborg was there, a solitary figure waiting for him across the viaduct, the first of many bridges he and his saxophone would cross.[151]

"I didn't want her staying up for me, but I was glad she did," Sonny said. "I loved my mother very much . . . but maybe I didn't know how much she loved me."[152] Until Sonny began playing Carnegie Hall, no one else in the family would come.[153]

Family support notwithstanding, to his sister, Gloria, Sonny's entrance into the professional world of music was inevitable. "He had something within him that he expressed and it didn't matter; he didn't relate to what was on the written page," she said. "He had something that was coming out of him, that no matter what the music said, he interpreted for himself."[154]

Later, when jazz stars like Max Roach started pulling up in front of 377 Edgecombe, hollering for Sonny to come down, "he never forgot his friends who he grew up with," recalled Doris Mason. "Some people get famous, they don't know you. Sonny was Sonny. He *never* changed."[155]

Chapter 4

THE STREET

(1944–1946)

In 1944, Jackie McLean, who had recently moved up to the Hill, started as a seventh grader at Stitt. (He was less than a year younger than Sonny, but two grades behind, since Sonny had skipped a grade.)[1] Jackie didn't have a saxophone yet, but hearing this brash ninth grader made him want one even more. "That was the first time I saw Sonny. He was playing alto then," Jackie said. "Aw man, he was *bad*."[2]

Though Sonny was one of the baddest young players on the Hill, he had a lot to live up to at home. Gloria played piano and sang, but had decided to major in art at the prestigious audition-only High School of Music and Art (later the setting of the film and TV show *Fame*).[3] Violinist Val won spelling bees and had graduated from Music and Art as well, majoring in music. "He was being considered for the Pittsburgh Symphony, that's how good he was," Sonny recalled.[4] But Val went on to City College, which provided a tuition-free premed program and was within walking distance of their apartment on Edgecombe.

A 1951 article on Val noted: "During his undergraduate years he often expressed the hope that someday he would be able to make a contribution to Harlem and help relieve the suffering of the underprivileged."[5] After graduating from City College of New York in 1947, Val entered Meharry Medical College, where he was a member of the community service group the "Swanksmen." Eventually, Valdemar would struggle to be unexpectedly living in his brother's shadow. "He was the guy that everybody was looking to as the prime figure of the kids," Sonny said. "When I began to get famous and prominent, as Pres would say, I felt a draft."[6]

For the time being, though, Sonny's older siblings' scholastic achievements were so daunting that as the "black sheep of the family," it seemed hardly worth it to compete.[7] "Music and Art was a hell of a hard high school to get into in those days," Sonny said.[8] Even if he had gotten in, some of his peers, such as Kenny Drew, Roy Eaton, and bassist Bruce Lawrence, had classical backgrounds.[9] "I didn't play classical music," Sonny said. "I wasn't equipped to go to Music and Art."[10] He carried a "feeling of inferiority" with him for the rest of his life.[11]

Two years later, Jackie McLean applied to Music and Art in music but failed the test. "I was crushed. And instead of going to Music and Art, I went to Benjamin Franklin High School on 116th Street. And the reason that I went there was...Sonny Rollins."[12]

In the fall of 1944, Sonny enrolled at Benjamin Franklin High School, an integrationist forerunner to busing programs, founded in 1934 by progressive educator Leonard Covello. Students from Sonny's neighborhood on the West Side were bused over to Italian Harlem on the East Side, which also had a growing Puerto Rican population.[13]

The commute took an hour each way. The school was a block from the East River; getting home was an odyssey on the transit system. "We had to take the crosstown bus at 116th Street and Pleasant Avenue and travel west to the Eighth Avenue subway line, then we'd take the Eighth Avenue subway up to 155th Street. We would get out of school at three o'clock, and we'd be home by four."[14] Sonny also noted, "My group of students, coming from Edward Stitt Junior High School, were sort of the first black, integrated busing group really. We were the experiment. We met a lot of resistance from the neighborhood."[15]

That sometimes included physical violence. "They had all these race riots...like 'Oh, they're trying to send the blacks down in our neighborhood,'" Sonny said. "We had fights every day with the Italian boys, and the neighbors in the houses would throw stuff out the windows as we were walking back across town—the same old shit."[16]

Racial strife was not part of Covello's utopian vision. In 1942, the school moved to its newly designed building, with six Corinthian columns and a pediment with a bust of Benjamin Franklin at the center, projecting the neoclassical educational environment Covello hoped to foster for the all-male student body. Compared to PS 89, it was the School of Athens. There was a 1,250-seat auditorium where Italian American clarinetist Buddy DeFranco performed at one of the Friday-night concerts, two gyms where its championship basketball team practiced, a large cafeteria, a library, scientific laboratories, facilities for pottery making and photography, a woodworking and welding shop, and a rooftop playground with a greenhouse and weather observatory. Students had a choice of six majors: academics, a general course of study, commerce, art, music, and industrial arts.[17]

For those interested in music like Sonny, Benjamin Franklin had a school band, an orchestra, a record library, a functional organ, and training in instrumental music, choral practice, harmony, music theory, music appreciation, and piano.[18] Yet to Sonny, the state-of-the-art facilities went only so far. "I feel very bad about this, because I know I have a good mind, and if I had been taken in tow by counselors and teachers, I think I could have had a different life in many ways," Sonny said. "So this school they shipped us to was very weak in academics, but it wasn't really a vocational school, either. They gave you a smattering of academics—enough that it wouldn't do you any good—and kept you off the streets for a few years." Covello's experiment in public education worked for some, "but for me, it was a waste."[19]

Sonny's relationship with the music faculty ranged from superficial to adversarial.[20] One teacher, Bessie Carroll Redmond, the chair of the school's music department, became Sonny's nemesis.[21] "I was in the high school band, and I remember that I did study counterpoint and theory in high school," Sonny said. "But I had a very intimidating teacher who didn't really like me. She was a woman who looked just like George Washington."[22] Indeed, Redmond was a bona fide Daughter of the American Revolution, descended from a German immigrant who fought in the Revolutionary War.[23]

The curriculum at Franklin was based on classical theory. "I remember we had elementary harmony, and things like 'never write parallel fifths,'" Sonny said.[24] Redmond "had a very detrimental effect on me, because she really made a lot of things that should have been easy for me seem difficult." She would often single him out, which was discouraging. "I just couldn't get this stuff."[25] Redmond solidified the sense that Sonny would have to figure it out in his own way.

However opaque her pedagogy was, though, Redmond did have lessons to offer. Along with Raymond Burrows, a professor of music education at

Teachers College, she coauthored two books for Simon and Schuster, *Symphony Themes*, in 1942, and, in 1951, *Concerto Themes*, which reproduced the main themes of major symphonic works.[26] The introduction by music critic Deems Taylor called it a "godsend."[27] But Redmond had little interest in jazz—the closest she came in either book was Ernest Bloch's *America* with its "Negro Folk Song" and "Rhapsody in Blue."

Still, there may have been a kernel of significance to a single-line instrumentalist like Sonny: she insisted that more than harmony or form, "the best way to understand what music is talking about is to have a simple statement of the subject itself," that is, of the melody. *Symphony Themes*, for example, laid bare the theme of Tchaikovsky's *Pathétique Symphony*, which Sonny would later arrange and record.[28] In *Concerto Themes*, Redmond advocated for an approach to music based on "thematic listening," in which the musician "follows a theme through a network of structural, harmonic, and instrumental development."[29] Eventually, Sonny would do exactly that in his improvisations; decades later, he would also compose his own concerto.

Though Sonny was in the Franklin symphonic band, there was no opportunity for jazz there either. Band director Silas Birnbaum worked on Sousa marches for parades down Fifth Avenue. Leroy Brannigan, a fellow saxophonist in the band, recalled, "Every little chance that he got to play, if we had a little break or something, he was trying out different notes and constructing different chords. He had a strange way of playing. It was like he had a loose reed or something like that. There was a buzz on some of his notes."[30]

Most of what Sonny learned about music at Franklin came from his peers, many of whom passed through the school.[31] Among them were tenor saxophonist Percy France and drummer Sonny Payne;[32] trumpeter Red DiStefano and pianist Elmo Hope attended earlier at the old Franklin building.[33] Pianist Walter Bishop Jr. had been a student there but, by the time Sonny arrived, had dropped out to join Buddy Brown's band playing taxi dances.[34] There was a sense of camaraderie among them all. "I used to go to Gilly [Coggins]'s house after school and get him to teach me stuff," Sonny recalled of the pianist, who was six years older. "He [didn't] want to get into the... XYZ's of music, but I got something from him anyway."[35]

Two of Sonny's closest friends were trumpeter Lowell Lewis and drummer

Arthur Taylor, a classmate at Stitt known as A. T. Taylor was a year older than Sonny, Lewis seven months younger.[36] "His notes were clear and sharp," Brannigan said of Lewis. "He was quiet; he had nothing much to say to anybody. He played his trumpet and that was that." After school, they would go to Lowell Lewis's house, A.T.'s house, or to Sonny's.[37] Quietly, these three were preparing to change the sound of jazz.[38]

This group of musicians was a future Murderers' Row:[39] drummers Arthur Taylor, Rudy Lawless, Mark Fisher, and Roy Haynes, who was a little bit older; pianists Walter Bishop Jr., Kenny Drew, Gilly Coggins, and Little Lenny Martinez;[40] bassists Arthur Phipps and Connie Henry; trumpeter Lowell Lewis; and saxophonists Jackie McLean, Ernie Henry, Andy Kirk Jr., and Sonny. Not everyone became equally storied, but they all played a role in establishing the next vanguard: they were the original Sugar Hill Gang.[41] "They all had a respect for the masters, and they were—how can we say it for print?" saxophonist Johnny Griffin recalled. "Bad motherfuckers! They could *all* play."[42]

They absorbed as much music as they could, camping out at the Apollo every weekend and huddled around the record player.[43] From August 1, 1942, to 1944, the musicians' union strike limited record releases, but when it ended, a new sound was on jukeboxes and emanating from clubs—but didn't have a name yet.

It had begun in impromptu jam sessions, not just in New York, but across the country, at local watering holes where members of territory bands might test their mettle in friendly battle with their peers and elders.[44] The jam session became Sonny's primary form of schooling. He was there to find his voice.[45]

That competitive spirit was passed down to Sonny's generation. "It's the old business of everyone trying to outplay the next guy," Sonny said. "So I came up through that vigorous environment. You had to fight to win, and learn to take the defeats. But I had the stamina to stay."[46]

Jam sessions were often integrated. "You'd find, up in Harlem and the Harlems around the country, not only people like Lester Young and Roy Eldridge and Coleman Hawkins up there jamming," recalled drummer Max Roach, "but you'd also find Benny Goodman, Buddy Rich, and [Gene]

Krupa. All these folks would play together and hang out together. Martha Raye and all these folks were there at that time. They were the precursors, I guess, to Goodman hiring Charlie Christian and Teddy Wilson and Lionel Hampton, and 'breaking the color line'; and Duke Ellington hiring people like Juan Tizol and folks like that. During that period, it was verboten to cohabitate. But in these after-hours places, everybody got together and exchanged ideas, sang for each other, played for each other."[47]

According to Roach, there was music at "legitimate" houses from nine until three and "illegitimate" houses from four until as late as noon. In New York, sessions began at after-hours joints like Monroe's Uptown House and Minton's. Minton's opened in 1938 and would come to be thought of by many as the birthplace of the new sound, where it coalesced gradually around the iconoclastic ideas of Thelonious Monk, Charlie Christian, Kenny Clarke, Dizzy Gillespie, Howard McGhee, and others. All of it built on the past, but these were sounds never heard before: Monk's sui generis harmonies, his very *Monkishness*; Christian's lyricism that put the electric guitar on the map; Clarke's so-called magic ride cymbal; Dizzy's angular lines and breathtaking speed; McGhee's insouciant sense of broken rhythm. Together, they created a new language and what became known as bop required its own onomatopoetic lexicon to describe it in words, with its own mythology. Gillespie's "Oop Bop Sh'Bam (A-Klook-a-Mop)" is in part a tribute to Clarke, whose rim-shot and bass-drum combo sounded to Minton's manager, Teddy Hill, like "klook-mop." Clarke became known as Klook. The language came directly from the sound; sometimes the nicknames did, too.[48] Arriving at the tail end of this period of time, Sonny would be one of the language's first native speakers.

It would be a while before Sonny found himself in Minton's, though he would get there eventually. He and his friends first heard the new music downtown. By 1945, bop jam sessions took place at venues like the Lincoln Square Theater at 53 West Sixty-Sixth Street right off Broadway and at clubs all along Fifty-Second Street, in addition to clubs in the outer boroughs. On Saturday nights from nine to five, Charlie La Sister and Jimmy Butts presented a jam session and dance at the Lincoln Square, where for $1.50 at the door you could see, on one bill, Dizzy Gillespie, Charlie Parker, Ben Webster, Dexter

Gordon, Don Byas, Erroll Garner, and Stuff Smith.[49] The Renaissance hosted dances, where for $5, kids could see tenor saxophonists Dexter Gordon and Don Byas, trumpeter Buck Clayton, drummer Jack "the Bear" Parker, and vocalist Sarah Vaughan.[50]

Starting in the thirties, after Prohibition was repealed, the jazz scene began to migrate downtown; "Swing Street" gradually moved from 133rd to 52nd Street, between 5th and 6th Avenues. The move was partially motivated by white fear, which intensified after the Harlem Riot of 1943.[51] "It's funny the way segregation works," said Sonny. "When black acts played the Apollo and Smalls Paradise, white people would come uptown. Then, when integration allowed black acts to work downtown, that was good in some ways, but it spelled the demise of Harlem. The monied people weren't going there anymore."[52] As the scene expanded into downtown, some of what Sonny called "the energy that was Harlem" began to disperse.[53]

There were many factors that contributed to the formation of what some referred to as "52nd Street music." Though it was in part the next evolutionary step for the harmonic and rhythmic innovations that players like Coleman Hawkins and Lester Young had begun developing earlier, its origins were in part economic. In 1944, the federal government levied a wartime "cabaret tax" on all venues with live entertainment. Suddenly, many clubs couldn't afford to hire big bands anymore.[54]

It was in tight spaces that Prohibition-era speakeasies became jazz haunts.[55] It became known simply as "the Street"—a neon Art Deco tableau that was home to more than a dozen jazz shrines: Kelly's Stable, Jimmy Ryan's, the Three Deuces, the Onyx, the Yacht Club, the Downbeat, the Spotlite.[56] To Sonny and his friends, this was the only Street that mattered.

Sonny and his crew were still a little too young to get into the clubs. But the tight quarters and carnivalesque atmosphere—musicians, businessmen, tourists, pimps, prostitutes, and gangsters all crammed in like keys on a piano—made it easy to blend in. "I had to take a woman's eyebrow pencil," Sonny said, to paint on a Groucho Marx mustache. Wearing a khaki trench coat and a feathered fedora, he "tried to get the right swagger. It usually worked. I think the people who ran the clubs were more interested in the money than who was standing at the bar. So they let us in and I had the experience to

hear my idols up close and in person....At the Apollo Theater in Harlem...
you had to see them from the audience. On 52nd Street, you could be right
close to them. So it was great."[57] Gaining entrance on the Street felt like tres-
passing in Olympus. "We'd stand in the back," Sonny wrote of seeing Coleman Hawkins, "and it was like looking at a god playing."[58]

Since it was all happening on one block, it was easy to bounce from club
to club. "Art Tatum here, Billie Holiday there; Basie and his orchestra at this
club, Erroll Garner and his trio at that; Slam Stewart down here, and Coleman Hawkins at the Spotlite."[59]

It was on the Street that Sonny learned about the relationship between artist and audience. "It was a panorama, a pageantry," Sonny later recalled. "The
audience was there to *listen*. That's the thing with live music—everybody has
a role, even the audience. The guy nodding his head, the girl who's smiling,
the skeptic who's not impressed—they all make you play better."[60]

The explosion of jazz on Fifty-Second Street created an integrated atmosphere downtown, and the police were soon to follow. In July 1944, police told
the manager of the White Rose Inn to enforce a segregation policy to prevent
musicians from congregating there during set breaks. "'Why don't you keep
Negroes out of here? Let them stay up in Harlem where they belong,'" police
said. The manager refused.[61] At the White Rose, a quarter bought a drink;
Billie Holiday was a frequent customer, with her brandy Alexanders, her
chihuahua, and her boxer; down the bar might be Don Byas and Big Sid
Catlett.[62] These were the geniuses the cops wanted to keep out of midtown.

In November 1945, another police raid threatened to close the Three
Deuces, the Downbeat, the Onyx, and the Spotlite.[63] The four clubs' cabaret licenses were revoked—meaning no music could be played there—when
police made baseless allegations that marijuana was circulating in the clubs.[64]
The licenses were reinstated within a month, with police denying the raids
were racially motivated, but the patrons and musicians knew better.

On all sides were those wary of the new music. Many socially conservative
Harlemites felt it was exotic, marginal, or bohemian. Lucky Millinder, Cab
Calloway, and their ilk continued to headline the Apollo and Paramount.
"I don't think people would have foreseen the development of bebop and
what morphed from it," Coggins said. "Harlem was very restrictive. There

were definite boundaries. I mean, there was nothing holding you back from going beyond the boundary, but there would be consequences. I think a lot of people developed an internal ghetto without realizing it."[65] Sonny and his friends were creating not entertainment, but a new way of life.

The critical establishment was similarly slow to embrace the music being played on the Street. In December 1944, writer Barry Ulanov presented a concert of the "New Jazz" at Times Hall on Forty-Fourth Street: Barney Bigard, Stuff Smith, Erroll Garner, Pearl Bailey, and Don Byas performed.[66] The reviewer in the *New York Herald Tribune*, shocked by the deviation from New Orleans jazz, reserved his harshest criticism for Byas, who was singled out for his "manner approved by the jump addicts, a study in ceaseless scales devoid of phrasing."[67]

Sonny could not have disagreed more. He idolized Byas, a product of the swing era who became a bridge from swing to bop. His lightning-fast arpeggios up and down the tenor, replete with flatted fifths, upper extensions of the chords, and a rhythmic angularity, became another new yardstick. "Don Byas had the technical proficiency," Sonny said. "He was a bebopper who had roots in the earlier school." If he couldn't see him live, for seventy-nine cents, Sonny could hear Byas test how many notes could fit on one side of a ten-inch 78. "Those records he made with Dizzy Gillespie, 'I Can't Get Started,' 'Good Bait'—he was there already."[68]

As disc jockeys Symphony Sid Torin and Fred Robbins began playing this music on the airwaves, a name for it emerged along with several variants— bebop, be-bop, rebop, or ri-bop. No one could prove who coined the term. Whether it was Monk, who claimed it came from a tune he wrote called "Bip Bop"; Dizzy Gillespie, who claimed it as a nonsense expression that characterized the frenetic rhythm; or guitarist Charlie Christian, who allegedly would sing his solo lines as he played to the onomatopoetic phrase, the lack of a single-origin etymology emphasized that birthing the music had been a collective effort.[69]

Having a name allowed the new style several developments: bebop's commercialization (naming leads to marketing), a new crop of defenders and critics eager to define the new category, and the inevitable declaration that bop was hereby dead.[70] In 1946, *Time* pronounced it, "Hot jazz overheated with overdone lyrics full of bawdiness, references to narcotics and doubletalk."[71]

As soon as bop was named, its creators objected to being pigeonholed. "I don't like to think of my music as bebop—but as modern music," said Monk.[72] Ralph Ellison thought the term was "clownish."[73] In a 1947 issue of *Metronome*, Charlie Parker himself resisted the label. "Let's not call it bebop. Let's call it music," he said. "People get so used to hearing jazz for so many years, finally somebody said 'Let's have something different' and some new ideas began to evolve. Then people brand it 'bebop' and try to crush it."[74]

Yet *bebop* stuck. When Sonny first started taking the train downtown to experience the new music, he had not yet heard of the young alto phenomenon from Kansas City. But the word did provide a rallying cry and a name for the band Sonny had formed with his friends: the Counts of Bop,[75] befitting the royal status they felt the music deserved.

"The inner circle was comprised of people such as Gil Coggins, who was maybe five years older and already playing in clubs," Sonny said. "Gilly hung out with us a lot. The older guys often had families, while we were just guys interested in music twenty-four hours a day. Kenny Drew was in the inner circle, as were Lowell Lewis, myself, Arthur Taylor…Walter Bishop, and Andy Kirk Jr."[76]

The Counts of Bop were soon gigging, recruiting local kids from the neighborhood as they went. Arthur Taylor received a Slingerland kit with a twenty-eight-inch bass drum one year for Christmas and carted it on the subway to gigs.[77] Kenny Drew was a prodigy who took up the piano at age five and gave his first public recital at eight.[78] "Sonny Rollins took me and said, 'We're gonna go to this concert to hear Kenny Drew, 'cause…he's in the neighborhood. He can play,'" recalled Arthur Taylor. "I went to this concert, this guy was playing Bach and Beethoven off the top of his head!"[79]

Sonny himself had competition in the group. The young Jackie McLean was floored by alto saxophonist Andy Kirk Jr., the son of bandleader Andy Kirk. Part of the reason for Kirk's advanced style was his father's connection to Charlie Parker, who had briefly played in his band. Some of the other guys had not even heard of Bird yet. "Sonny sounded like Coleman Hawkins during this period," McLean said (only on alto). Kirk, though, "was the baddest cat around—everybody knew it. Even Sonny knew it."[80]

Walter Bishop Jr., who was three years older than Sonny and lived down in the valley, was also part of the inner circle and recalled Kirk as a saxophone prodigy. "He was the closest thing we had to Bird," he said.[81]

Sonny himself was still developing. "He could hear stuff that none of us could hear. In other words, when Sonny Rollins played, it was hip. I don't care what it was," Bishop said. "I remember, he used to come to me and say, 'B-b-b-b-Bish, how do you play such long lines, such long lines?' I didn't have a theory for it, but I said, 'Well, long lines are a series of short phrases that are connected. Like in speech. Connected.' And I showed him some little pivot points, some little connections. He took it and ran with it. He could play endless, almost without taking a breath. . . . Even in the course of another song, he managed to interweave melodies from other tunes into . . . like a collage. The Colossus of the Collage."[82]

Sonny sometimes spoke with a stammer, which appeared when he was trying to articulate a point of significance.[83] It was a broken rhythm he would translate to music—a stutter sounded hip over a beat—and eventually could speak on the horn with more fluidity and lyricism than anyone of his generation.

Improvisation was the cornerstone of their playing, especially for Sonny. "As far as improvisation, he's one of the most *improvisating* men I've ever heard," Taylor later recalled. "I don't think he plays the same thing twice in a year. . . . [I]t's the same as when we were kids."[84]

As they developed their own musical language, they also created their own slang and way of speaking. First came calling each other by their middle names sometimes as a term of endearment and a kind of code. Taylor was Stefan; Sonny was Theodore. "We were like avant-garde people," Taylor said. "We had our own language. . . . [W]e could talk English and you would hear what we were saying but you would not know what we were really talking about. . . . If you can have secrets with a group of people, it can be very powerful."[85]

As they gained fluency in this new language, Sonny made his first amateur recording—since lost—in a booth at a music store on Forty-Second Street. "I think it cost five cents or something," Sonny recalled. "I don't know how much it would be saying musically . . . probably not much."[86] He would cut his teeth at social functions in Harlem before he was ready for the studio.

The Counts of Bop played for dances and cocktail sips, usually in a quartet or quintet, with a nucleus of Sonny, Arthur Taylor on drums, and Lowell Lewis on trumpet—the "mainstays," Sonny said—alongside rotating personnel including Kenny Drew or Walter Bishop Jr. on piano and, on bass, Arthur Phipps, Connie Henry, or someone a few years older whom they knew simply as Carrington.[87] Gigs generally paid eight to twelve dollars total. Sonny was the leader. "They would call Sonny," recalled Jackie McLean. "He had work all the time on the weekends."[88]

"Dances, parties, Audubon Ballroom we would play," Taylor said. "We started out in St. Charles Church at 141st Street, playing for the kids on Friday evenings for two dollars a night. That was a lot of fun." It was, for the time being, a wholesome circuit: "Dance, and drink soda pop and have cake and flirt with the girls. You know, the regular stuff."[89] Soon, they began playing dances at the Renaissance or Smalls Paradise on Monday nights.

As bebop became synonymous with everything hip, dancers responding to what Duke Ellington referred to as the music's "terpsichorean urge" created a dance to fit the rhythm. "In our teens we did a solitary dance called the Applejack where you'd just do moves to the music," Sonny said.[90] Later on, Sonny would see Thelonious Monk dancing the Applejack on the bandstand. The dance had moves such as the Half Nelson and the Corkscrew; there was another dance for couples that was actually called the Bebop.[91]

"It wasn't like you were sitting there having a séance, like you know, you're getting some special messages from God," Taylor said of the introspective pose people increasingly struck in response to bebop. "It's like, whoa! People were having more fun, and they would dance."[92]

Sometimes the mood would get so hot that a dance became a brawl: "My mother had gotten me a beautiful herringbone overcoat from Barney's in New York," Sonny said. "I went out on my little gig there and had on my sharp coat and by the time we got through the first set, somebody called somebody something and the next thing the whole place was...everybody was throwing something at everybody else. So I went back to get my coat, and, of course, it was gone. And that taught me a good lesson—always keep your eye on your coat."[93]

After the dances, the first club the Counts of Bop played was Bowman's Grill, a neighborhood joint up the block from Sonny's apartment.[94]

Bowman's became a local hangout for Harlem gangsters. "That's where all the number runners and gangsters would go on the weekend, drinking and listening to jazz," recalled John B. Williams. "Gangsters and jazz musicians really were family."[95]

The Counts of Bop were deadly serious about the music. "During the war...society opened up a little bit," Sonny said, "and guys were a little more militant and didn't want to take these shoeshine jobs, using that as a metaphor. So I felt that bebop was speaking to that social issue. I felt that bebop was the language of the people who weren't going to take any more jive at home, we were going to now move away from that era—now we had to be viewed as one hundred percent equal musicians. So I heard about bebop musicians that wouldn't play 'Honeysuckle Rose' or take any crap from the audience; so the whole music had a sort of freeing aspect about it—it had a dignity. It appeared at the time as if the music stood for more."[96]

During this time, Sonny posed for a portrait with his saxophone. Unlike Louis Jordan in his eight-by-ten glossy, Sonny didn't crack a smile. He stood in front of a painted backdrop—Victorian staircase, ornate columns, alpine vistas—wearing a tweed jacket, a tie, and a dark button-down shirt, fingering his alto and staring directly into the camera like a gunslinger.[97]

After spending the summer of 1945 in Annapolis with his father, when Sonny returned to Benjamin Franklin High School that fall, racial tensions were high. According to a lengthy study of the Franklin student body by the school's founder and principal, Leonard Covello, one Italian American student expressed his supremacist views. "Why should I feel inferior when I know I am a better American than this bunch of Negroes, Puerto Ricans, Poles and Germans.... My father came here fifty years ago, and he is anyway more American than those _____."[98] Covello chose not to identify the derogatory term.

On September 27, 1945, tensions erupted into a riot when an Italian student and an African American student got into a fight over a basketball during a morning gym class. They agreed to settle the matter with a fight after school at the end of the day. News of the altercation spread, and when the bell rang, a group of Italian American students gathered in front of the school with sticks and began attacking African American students at random, blocking them from boarding the crosstown bus until police arrived. According to press reports, which sensationalized the incident as the Harlem Riots redux, knives flashed, rocks and bottles were thrown from rooftops, and clubs were brandished. The next day, some African American students approached the school, allegedly with weapons. Police then began indiscriminately searching the black students but not the white students.

Covello acted swiftly in response. "Race hatred is the most serious atomic bomb in our midst," Covello said later on during an Armistice Day program at the school, three months after the bombing of Hiroshima. "If we permit any group to stir up hatred against another group, we are helping to sow the seeds of destruction."[99]

A series of school- and community-wide assemblies followed, as well as an official resolution cosigned by Congressman Vito Marcantonio, who represented the school's district. Sonny's family was well aware of Marcantonio, who was "a big hero in our house," he said. "He was a Communist, and he came from...Italian Harlem. Vito Marcantonio was a very liberal person." In his proclamation, Marcantonio called for unity—the enemy of his working-class constituents was not race, he said, but capital. "When a Negro boy and a white boy got into a fight over a basketball, the spirit of Bilbo crept in," he said, referring to Mississippi senator Theodore G. Bilbo, then a national symbol for white supremacy. "This was the chance the dividers were looking for."[100]

Yet the man some knew simply as "the Voice" made perhaps the greatest impact in the aftermath of the Franklin riot.[101] Partnering with the national office of the NAACP, Covello arranged for Frank Sinatra to appear in the school's auditorium as an "Ambassador of Good Will," with a performance by the Nat King Cole Trio scheduled the following week.[102] "The minute some stuffed shirt or even a teacher gets up to tell kids about tolerance, kids say 'this isn't for me' and the speaker's a dead duck," Sinatra opined. "It won't cure, but it'll make kids think."[103]

Sinatra came on October 23, 1945. Just two months earlier, on August 22, Sinatra had recorded "The House I Live In" for Columbia in Los Angeles, and on May 8, he had acted in a short film of the same name for RKO Pictures.[104] The civil rights anthem, with music by Earl Robinson and lyrics by Abel Meeropol, both associated with Camp Unity, came from the 1942 musical *Let Freedom Ring*, which continued the message of Robinson's earlier work "The Ballad for Americans": "The children in the playground, the faces that I see / All races and religions, that's America to me."

The film would not be released for a few weeks after Sinatra's appearance at Franklin, but he preached its message off-screen. Sinatra's opening act was the school band, which performed Carmen Dragon's "I Am an American" and Karl King's "United Nations March"; it would be the only time Sonny opened for Sinatra.[105]

Speaking to a crowd of more than twenty-seven hundred spread over two assemblies, Sinatra broke the tension with a little levity: "Every race produces men with big, strong muscles—and guys like me," he said. He implored the students not to "go around calling names or indicating your racial preference" and asked them to serve as "neighborhood emissaries of racial good-will." He then performed "Aren't You Glad You're You?"[106] Perhaps he reached some of them.

"Then Nat King Cole came and he put on a concert," Sonny said. "It was really great, and it worked. The animosity stopped. We learned that you don't have to love everybody but you don't have to kill them either. I wound up becoming good friends with some of the Italian kids."[107] A decade later, Sonny would record "The House I Live In." But the civil rights struggle was about to come home.

Chapter 5

ANNAPOLIS

(1946)

The Street was buzzing on February 9, 1946, an ordinary Saturday for the Counts of Bop as they headed downtown.[1] Ella Fitzgerald, Red McKenzie, Red Allen, Stuff Smith, and Billie Holiday were all performing on Fifty-Second Street that night.[2] Sonny's hero, Coleman Hawkins, was appearing at the Spotlite for an extended residency,[3] and one of the architects of bebop was in Hawk's band: twenty-eight-year-old Thelonious Monk.

In Annapolis, Walter Rollins Sr.'s night was just beginning and was also filled with music and musicians. It was two in the morning when guests arrived in evening gowns and suits at the forty-three-year-old chief's basement quarters, a twelve-by-twenty-foot windowless basement apartment.[4] At the Naval Academy's North Severn Officers' Club, where Rollins was chief steward, the weekly dance ended at around one thirty, but the party often continued in Walter's cramped room. That night, he entertained five after-hours guests, all of them white: William R. Sima, the fifty-three-year-old Naval Academy bandleader who composed the "Navy Victory March" and "Gangway Song" and arranged the Coast Guard anthem "Semper Paratus"; his wife, pianist Rebecca Truman Sima; their son, musician first-class saxophonist William Sima Jr.; his twenty-three-year-old wife, Margaret Ann Sima; and Agnes R. Thompson, an Annapolis hairdresser.[5]

It was an ordinary party and not the first time it had happened. Rollins had a reputation among his colleagues as an impeccable host. They danced—Rollins taught them the rumba—listened to records on the phonograph, played poker for pennies, and drank whiskey.[6] The hairdresser got a bad headache, which Walter treated with a wet towel, and the remaining guests decided to spend the night and make sure she recovered.[7] At nine Sunday morning, the chief had a cook whip up some eggs and toast as a send-off.[8]

Two days later, on Tuesday, February 12, Sonny's father got an unexpected knock on his door. Lieutenant George Bruni, the treasurer at North Severn, stood imperiously outside with two other officers. When Walter opened the door, Bruni and his associates began a surprise inspection of the room. They found fourteen bottles of liquor, and without further explanation, Walter was placed under arrest and immediately transferred to the USS *Reina Mercedes*, a hulking prize of the Spanish-American War, where he and Naval Academy bandleader William Sima Sr. were detained in the brig without charge.[9]

When the inspectors returned to Walter's room later, they found the dregs of the party: more liquor, a deck of playing cards with Alberto Vargas pin-up renderings, and a framed photograph of Margaret Sima, the blonde wife of navy saxophonist William Sima Jr.[10] Sima and his wife had given Walter the framed photo, one of a dozen copies, as a souvenir from a Christmas party they recently hosted.[11] To the inspectors, the liquor and the cards were not the problem; it was the photograph of a white woman in Walter's room. Sonny's father had become the subject of a nationwide scandal.

"It was an officers' club which he ran, and there was a lot of fraternization going on," Sonny recalled. " 'There is this black guy and there are some white women,' you know the same old stuff. So my father got in trouble for that."[12]

As the Judge Advocate General's (JAG) Corps dissected every moment of the night of February 9, so did the press. Before long, opposite the headshot of a blonde, blue-eyed twenty-four-year-old woman, the *New York Daily News* was reporting on allegations that Walter "had a torrid love session with the blonde daughter-in-law of the Naval Academy bandmaster, in the basement of the officers' club."[13] The image of a philandering libertine that began to circulate in major media outlets coast-to-coast did not square with Sonny's austere vision of his father.[14]

Sonny and his family would soon find out that his father's friends in high places, who benefited from his three decades of dutiful service to the navy, had no compunction about throwing him overboard. Even if Walter didn't support Sonny's music, he taught him how to carry himself with dignity in all situations—friendly or hostile, on the Street or anywhere. But this new development demonstrated to Sonny that Jim Crow always lurked right around the corner.[15]

In 1946, miscegenation was illegal in most states, with the ban justified on sociological, psychological, and biological grounds. The Hays film production code prohibited as much as mixed-race hand-holding on-screen.[16] In 1946 in Oklahoma, an interracial couple served a one-year prison term on felony conviction for miscegenation, and both were banned from the state following their release.[17] In Mississippi, a twenty-eight-year-old African American man faced the electric chair on a miscegenation conviction for having sexual relations with a white woman. She refused to testify for fear of the backlash; he had been courting her for four years.[18]

Sonny had experienced the reality of Jim Crow firsthand during the previous summer at the North Severn Officers' Club, where his father held the small interracial gathering in his basement quarters that winter. In Annapolis, schools and public places were segregated. In 1924, miscegenation was ruled a felony in Maryland; until 1967, interracial marriage in the state carried a sentence of up to ten years. So in 1946, Walter Sr.'s predicament was not an anomaly.

Institutional racism pervaded the armed forces. The 1946 Meader Report, the result of an official Senate investigation into military conduct in Germany, amounted to racist propaganda.[19] With the Cold War just beginning, a fear began to spread insidiously that African American soldiers would feel more sympathy for Stalin than for a country that demanded the ultimate sacrifice in exchange for second-class citizenship.[20] Units were often segregated, and there were reports of African American soldiers being barred from whites-only dining halls that welcomed white prisoners of war. The Double V campaign—a civil rights push for "Victory Abroad, Victory at Home"— saw black soldiers return home to the white supremacist rhetoric they had just supposedly defeated abroad.[21] Yet in the wake of World War II, racially motivated military court-martials were on the rise.[22]

During peacetime after a devastating war, instead of a de-escalation of military intervention, the navy was pressing for an expanded international fleet and preparing for a major nuclear test. This conflicted with President Truman's February 1946 call for austerity through a unification of the army and navy.[23] To make the case that the navy was running a tight ship morally and fiscally, they made Walter Rollins a scapegoat.

Walter Rollins Sr. was forty-three at the time of the party, but some reports listed him as old as forty-seven to exaggerate the age gap with the woman in question. He was guilty until proven innocent; all the court wanted to know was whether he could dance and if he was dancing that night. The cards were stacked against him, but Sonny's father believed an acquittal was possible.

The navy's top brass were closely involved in what turned out to be a monthslong investigation and court-martial. Secretary of the Navy James V. Forrestal, the driving force behind the push for naval integration, personally appointed the chief prosecutor to ensure a conviction.[24] "Naval officers receive a minimum of commendation for the things they do well," Forrestal wrote that April, "and the maximum for their shortcomings."[25] Forrestal selected Jesse R. Wallace, a veteran navy attorney who had served as counsel to Admiral Thomas C. Hart in the investigation of the attack on Pearl Harbor. The general public would be excluded from Walter's trial, but members of the press would not, making the proceedings effectively open to the whole nation.[26]

The nationwide media frenzy meant that the details of the case would be sensationalized on a near-daily basis. The *Washington Post, Brooklyn Daily Eagle, Chicago Tribune, New York Daily News*, and papers reaching from Cincinnati to Lubbock, Texas, all reported the developing story over hundreds of articles, oftentimes accompanied by photos. Valborg commuted every Sunday to be by her husband's side, returning to New York on the weekends. Sonny and his siblings stayed in New York, but they read every painstaking detail of the trial in the papers.[27]

The court-martial for Naval Academy saxophonist William Sima Jr. began in mid-March. The charge was that he had "willfully, knowingly and without proper authority introduced his wife into the quarters of Walter W. Rollins (Negro)."[28]

Many of the prosecution's witnesses were Walter's subordinates: African Americans who worked under his supervision and had cultivated a jealousy compounded by the toxic notion that he had little interest in fraternizing with those of his own race, and bigoted whites resentful that a black man was above their rank and class position. One witness attested to rattling poker chips, another to eggs on a platter, another to toast. When breakfast was delivered, there was no sign of a raucous party, just the six people seated, bed made at military standard. Witnesses denied that Rollins had danced with any of the women, but the court doggedly pursued the allegations.[29] "My father had the opportunity to interact person to person with white officers," Sonny recalled. "That was the beginning of the end right there."[30]

On March 19, the prosecution called an unlikely star witness to the Sima trial—Walter himself. He appeared at Bancroft Hall in full navy regalia, with six gold hash marks on his left sleeve to represent twenty-four years of service with good conduct. Rollins seemed unconcerned with what to him was a simple misunderstanding.

"Did you dance?" asked the prosecutor.

"I think I danced once or twice," Walter responded, inadvertently incriminating himself and contradicting other witnesses' previous testimony. "I showed the girls—the ladies—how to dance the rumba." Burke then inquired about the drinking charge. "They were drinking something," Walter replied, clarifying that he had served soft drinks, but there was whiskey in the room.[31] That was enough evidence to seal Walter's fate. At the end of Sima's eleven-day trial, Sima was found innocent of drinking and gambling, but guilty of bringing his wife to the party and was given six months' probation.[32]

Still, Rollins continued to believe that his sterling naval record and reputation for hospitality would outweigh the court's racial bias. On April 5, 1946, he was interviewed by a reporter from the *Baltimore Afro-American* on board the *Reina Mercedes*, where he was held without charge for seventy-eight days. "This is the first time during my 26 years of Naval service that I have been accused of wrongdoing by officers," Walter told the reporter, adding that he kept liquor in his room for such occasions. The article portrayed Walter as a hardworking family man and described his three children: twenty-year-old Val was graduating from City College that June, seventeen-year-old Gloria was at Music and Art, and fifteen-year-old Sonny was "a pupil of the Franklin High School"—Sonny's first mention in print.[33]

Walter remained confident. "The Navy recognizes a man by his abilities and because of this I have very high hopes of being exonerated," he said.[34] "The whole thing was just a little unfortunate." He intended to move forward with plans to open a nightclub in Annapolis that would specialize in local Maryland foods, "one of the best places in this area with an orchestra and the type of service for which I have gained a reputation throughout the Navy." But the story dragged on for weeks, then months, and the dream began to dissipate.

Congressmen were worried about their own potential incrimination in the case. On April 13, Senator David Walsh, chairman of the Naval Affairs Committee, and Representative Philip Philbin visited Walter for a private meeting in his holding cell on the *Reina Mercedes*.[35] They had likely attended several of the parties in Walter's quarters. They claimed to be friends, but soon the real reason for the visit emerged: they were there to pressure Walter to resign.[36] But Walter clung to his pride and his belief that a just outcome would be reached.

The JAG Corps had three options for a court-martial: deck, summary, and general, each with increasing levels of severity. A general court-martial consisted of five to thirteen officers with a dedicated prosecutor who prosecuted the worst offenses: mutiny, treason, desertion, destruction of property, and murder. There was no maximum sentence, with conviction leading to a possible death penalty.[37] All Walter had done was host interracial parties, but the charge was tantamount to high treason.[38] In total, the charges carried a maximum sentence of 180 years.[39]

Walter's fate was to be handed down by an all-white seven-member court-martial.[40] Walter's defense counsel consisted of Captain Franz Otto Willenbucher, a thirty-one-year veteran turned civilian lawyer who had served with him on a destroyer for two years in the '20s.[41] Cautioned that Walter might need a civilian defense attorney, Valborg arranged an appointment with Evelyn Baker Richman at her office downtown.[42] Richman was a partner in a law firm with her husband, at the time a rare case of gender parity.[43] Years later, in 1960, after being named the first female city magistrate in New York history, she would acquit Miles Davis when he was unjustly charged with assaulting a police officer outside of Birdland.[44]

Richman studied the case files, then arranged to meet the Rollins family, which she called "one of the most charming and talented families I have ever met."[45] She then took a train to Annapolis to meet with Walter himself, still confined to the brig. Following her meeting, she was "completely sold," Richman said later.[46]

On June 6, 1946, the trial began in Bancroft Hall, an ivy-covered block-long dormitory building for midshipmen. The kangaroo court was converted from a basement visitors' lounge.[47] On the cusp of his graduation from college, Valdemar took the train to see his father one last time before the trial. "Wish you the best of luck, Dad," he said, grabbing his father's hand, his face ashen.[48] Walter was going to need it.

The first day of the trial was quickly adjourned when it emerged that the navy stenographer had no knowledge of shorthand and had missed large chunks of the proceedings.[49] The next day, the charges were finally read. The court insisted that all women, including Valborg, who had made the trip from New York, leave the courtroom for the recitation of the "morality" charges, but members of the press were allowed to stay and reported it in minute detail the next day.[50]

The court intended to strip Walter of his dignity, as he quickly realized. When North Severn treasurer George Bruni testified that it took Walter a suspicious four minutes to unsuspectingly answer the door the Tuesday of his arrest, Walter responded, "Mr. Bruni, please, don't you know what this means to me? I've got twenty-seven years' service." Then the prosecution called club janitor Frank Stallings, a white man whom Sonny recalled as a virulent racist, a "deep redneck" resentful of his father's position, to attest to Walter's alleged theft of navy property.[51] Stallings claimed that Walter regularly mailed large packages weighing up to forty pounds to the same address in New York. It didn't occur to the court that Rollins was sending care packages to his family.[52] Walter testified that he had allotted himself a bottle of whiskey a week, which he drank sparingly in his room. He "earnestly believed that I was quite within my rights," he said, owing to his long hours and rare furloughs.[53]

The adultery charges were even more unsubstantiated. Margaret Sima, the woman in question, was finally called to the stand and flatly denied that she had ever even been alone with Walter.[54] Then her mother-in-law testified that she and Margaret had sent Walter postcards from a vacation in New Hampshire. The prosecution claimed that the postcards were a link in "a tremendous chain of circumstances,"[55] but as he began to read the innocuous notes, they only pointed to Walter's innocence. Finally, the hairdresser from the party admitted that she had lied previously about the headache that extended the party because she did not realize "the seriousness of the whole thing,"[56] that a man's livelihood and the well-being of his family were hanging in the balance.[57]

More flimsy evidence came from the "knot-hole gang," a group of three African American steward's mates who had served under Chief Rollins, so named by the press for all claiming to have witnessed Walter's infidelities that past summer from a one-and-a-half-inch slit in the ceiling or a hole in the wall. One night, one of them allegedly saw Sonny eating dinner as his father paced the floor. Later in the evening, he heard Walter introduce his son to a woman obstructed from view who sounded like she had a "reasonable amount" of education.[58] One member of the gang was kept on the stand for 234 questions,[59] totaling five and a half hours, almost a whole day in court.[60] The coup de grâce came when the prosecution claimed that Sima referred to Walter as "Othello."[61] Their testimony, which was unsuccessfully coached by the prosecution, was quickly discredited. One began visibly falling asleep while on the stand.[62] Another had recently been dishonorably discharged after a theft conviction. All admitted to resenting Walter for excluding them from the parties, not realizing that the whites-only guest list was beyond his control.[63] Later, the defense called an expert witness, a navy civil engineer who testified that it was physically not possible that any of them could have seen what they claimed to have seen from the hole in the wall.[64]

In light of the case resting almost entirely on perjured or irrelevant testimony, the court decided to take a recess.[65]

When the trial was turned over to the defense, Walter's lawyer began with a character witness, Vice Admiral Arthur W. Radford, deputy chief of naval relations and an old friend of Walter's. Radford took the stand, testifying that as far as he was aware, Walter had built an "excellent" reputation and always acted with integrity.[66] Letters of support from two rear admirals were read to the court.[67]

Closing arguments were lengthy. The prosecution read a 35-page, 13,650-word document to the court, reiterating their call for Walter's conviction on all counts.[68] The defense's closing statement was less than half as long, claiming that the case was open-and-shut—there was simply no credible evidence. To conclude the trial, Walter was permitted to read a written

statement. "If I may address the court, all I would like to say is that I conscientiously state that I don't believe I am guilty of the charges," he said. "That
is all."[69] He still believed he would be exonerated, but the months of investigation and the three-week trial had shaken him and his family to the core.

On July 1, Secretary Forrestal was on his way to Bikini Atoll to survey the
devastation of the atom-bomb test that day.[70] Meanwhile, the fallout from
Annapolis had just begun to settle over Sugar Hill.

First, there was a verdict in the court of public opinion.[71] On July 6,
1946, the *Pittsburgh Courier* published three separate articles about the case,
accompanied by individual headshots of Walter and the entire Rollins family.[72] Valdemar, the "brilliant son," is listed as the twenty-year-old president
of the Interracial Society at City College, with a "reserved but nonetheless
strong distaste for the lurid accounts which the papers have carried." Gloria echoed his sentiments. "I think she has felt the effects of the case more
than the others," said Valborg of her daughter. "She's not too appreciative
of the publicity and particularly dislikes the way the *Daily News* has angled
the story." The *Daily News* had published more than a dozen stories covering
the case, to wit: "Rollins Denies Hot Love with Blonde."[73]

In Sonny's portrait accompanying the *Pittsburgh Courier* story, his
first-ever photo in the paper, he is wearing a suit and tie, a solemn look on
his face. "Youngest of the Rollins children is exuberant, re-bop-loving Walter
Jr., a senior at the Benjamin Franklin High School," read the caption. "A
light-hearted youngster of fifteen, Walter wants to be a popular musician,
has organized an orchestra in his neighborhood. His reaction to the case has
been confined to eagerly buying the daily papers and being very relieved on
days when nothing has been printed about the case."[74]

Valborg insisted on her husband's innocence and reaffirmed her loyalty.
"Why shouldn't I be loyal? Mr. Rollins has been a wonderful husband and
father. He is devoted to his family," she said. "His duties at the officers' club
kept him so very busy that he has been forced to live there. When he accepted
the job, we thought he would be able to get home often because it is so close
to New York. But my husband is conscientious as his twenty-seven years
with a perfect record will show." She articulated what the court would not. "I
think the main thing in the case was the race issue," she continued. "Walter

has been friends with the Simas as long as he has been at Annapolis. Visiting their home occasionally was his only form of recreation. He never went to town because of the jim-crow conditions there. When it was brought out that he had been entertained by whites, Negro-haters and jealous subordinates of Walter's combined to get him into trouble."[75]

Yet her attempt to speak truth to power did not reach Annapolis.[76] The court returned a unanimous guilty verdict,[77] sentencing Rollins to six years in prison. Evelyn Baker Richman planned to take the case to the Supreme Court, but the chances of a successful appeal looked dismal. Walter's last hope rested with the reviewing authority in Washington, which would determine his final sentence. In the meantime, he continued languishing in the brig.[78]

The naval authorities in Washington concluded their deliberations in late August. Walter's sentence was read during the trial of William Sima Sr., who would ultimately face a conviction as well. Walter's sentence was reduced to two years, with a permanent demotion to steward's mate, third class, the lowest rank, and a Bad Conduct Discharge.[79] After twenty-seven years of honorable service underneath a concrete ceiling, he would eventually become a cook at a Long Island restaurant.[80] Walter was to serve his sentence along the Maine–New Hampshire border at Portsmouth Naval Prison,[81] a massive building commonly referred to as "the Castle" or the "Alcatraz of the East," known throughout the navy as hell on earth.

The article detailing Walter's sentencing in the *Pittsburgh Courier*[82] ran adjacent to another news item: "Coroner's Jury Frees White Lynch-Slayer." In Barnwell County, South Carolina, William Craig, a white man, was acquitted for the lynching of James Walker Jr., a thirty-five-year-old black man, with a verdict of "justifiable homicide."[83] Craig had shot Walker in the back from his front porch and claimed self-defense; he was fully exonerated. The juxtaposition of the two articles made it abundantly clear—a white man could murder a black man in cold blood and walk free, but a black man could go to prison for dancing.[84]

In the first week of September, Valborg, Valdemar, Gloria, and Sonny went to visit Walter one last time before his prison sentence began.[85] It was the last chance they had to see their father for a long time. A few days later, Sonny turned sixteen.

It was hard to accept that the vision of a more just society was restricted, in part, to that tiny sliver on Fifty-Second Street. "Jazz has always been a music of integration," Sonny later said. "In other words, there were definitely lines where blacks would be and where whites would begin to mix a little bit. I mean, jazz was not just a music; it was a social force in this country, and it was talking about freedom and people enjoying things for what they are and not having to worry about whether they were supposed to be white, black, and all this stuff....A lot of times, jazz means no barriers."[86]

Through the ordeal of seeing his father be publicly shamed, the slow violence of witnessing the military's failure to uphold justice communicated unequivocally to sixteen-year-old Sonny what it meant to be black in America. It deepened his growing distrust of authority, and his natural tendency to have his guard up, to become someone whom few people really knew, who later in life might change his phone number, or not have a phone at all. It proved that when the chips were down, you couldn't necessarily rely on your friends. Sonny's periods of intense collaboration would be followed by periods of intense solitude.

Yet to a teenager who was raised in a community that instilled a sense of hope for change and the possibility of racial uplift, and the grandson of a Garveyite who had him marching in the streets of Harlem, the bleakness of his father's verdict seemed to confirm still a deeper truth. Sonny was a born perfectionist, made more so by a disciplinarian father. Now he would have to work even harder to prove himself. "Don't ever shrink from the belief that you have to prove yourself every minute, because you do," Sonny later said.[87]

To Sonny, proving himself meant no margin for error, even when improvising in the moment—it meant perfection. By perfecting himself, perhaps he could perfect the world around him. "I am naïve enough to feel that there is such a perfect world possible...*content of your character more than color of your skin*," Sonny later said. "I always naturally felt that."[88]

The saxophone would be his means of piercing the veil of indifference and outright hate. Sonny would let his guard down onstage, but the instrument would also be his buffer, a third arm to keep an imperfect world at arm's length. Sonny would never be closer to anyone than he was to his instrument.

It was during that summer of family heartbreak, with Louis Jordan's

"Choo Choo Ch'Boogie" in the background on radios everywhere,[89] that Sonny's mother bought him his first tenor. It was a King Zephyr, the same make as Jordan's alto from the photo at the Elks Rendezvous. The family could not have been in good financial shape after the costly trial, but for about $200,[90] Sonny finally had a saxophone to fit the tenor reeds he'd tried to play on the alto.

Having finally grown into the larger horn, figuratively and physically, Sonny had a story to tell, more urgent than Jordan's. He would speak on the saxophone in a grainy, pugilistic voice, enunciating with a rough-hewn attack that favored tonguing almost every note, unlike the legato phrasing that characterized the cool sangfroid of Coleman Hawkins and Lester Young.[91] If Sonny squeaked, and he did early on, it was not because he misspoke, but because he had spoken perhaps too emphatically. It was the insistent cadence of Marcus Garvey, or a Joe Louis jab, translated to the saxophone. Sonny would create himself as a voice that could not be pinned down, captured, or locked up in the brig. "A lot of people and a lot of musicians have tried to transcribe some of my works," Sonny later said, "and they've come back to me and said, 'Sonny, you know we can't write down your solos, they can't be written down.'"[92]

Soon thereafter, Sonny posed with his new tenor in front of the same Victorian backdrop from the earlier portrait with the alto. Older, more mature, bearing the weight of the heavier horn, Sonny stands resolute, dressed in oxfords, gray slacks, and a sport jacket with a folded pocket square, Hawkins-esque, fingering the keys with a thousand-yard stare. This is no grinning high schooler—he has seen some things, and he has a story to tell.[93]

Sonny had seen firsthand that his father played by the unjust rules of white society and had been taken down by Jim Crow. So why would Sonny volunteer to play a game so clearly designed for him to lose? There was another game, maybe even more serious, where breaking the rules was not only encouraged but also required to succeed. Down on the Street, Sonny heard the antithesis of the ideology that had devastated his family and put the hypocrisy of the nation's democratic ideals on public display. It was a sound Sonny himself could not yet give voice to, but that spoke undeniably and with great velocity: "Now's the Time."

Chapter 6

THE MONASTERY OF
SAN JUAN HILL

(1946–1947)

During the trial, Sonny found a much-needed distraction in a new 78 that had just hit record stores. In April 1946, tenor saxophonist Don Byas released his rendition of "How High the Moon" with his quintet.[1] Sonny collected Byas, buying the record despite its having only one side by the brilliant tenor player. The B-side had the recording debut of an alto saxophonist he had never heard of by the name of "Chas. Parker."[2]

"I actually bought that record for Don Byas, because I didn't really know Charlie Parker," Sonny recalled. "It was interesting, but after playing it for my friends at school, I realized this guy has got something going here, and I began to become a devotee of Charlie Parker."[3]

The mysterious Chas. Parker was also a student of Byas, having heard him at the jam sessions at Monroe's Uptown House, "playing everything there was to be played."[4] Spinning Byas's rendition of "How High the Moon," Sonny had a sudden shock when he turned it over and played "Ko Ko." It came at him even faster than Byas. It had two other names Sonny was not familiar with, trumpeter Miles Davis and pianist Hen Gates, plus Max Roach on drums and Curly Russell on bass. "Ko Ko" was a "contrafact,"[5] based on the structure of Ray Noble's "Cherokee," with its sixty-four-bar form and complex bridge of descending two-five-one turnarounds testing the mettle of any improviser—even Miles Davis, who claimed it was so difficult he laid out and let Dizzy Gillespie play both the trumpet and the piano parts.[6] Charlie Barnet's 1939 rendition of "Cherokee" was a pop hit; Parker's "Ko Ko" would never grace the charts, but it was destined to be far more influential— a Promethean blaze of harmony and rhythm that opened a new frontier.[7]

"Parker sounded radical," Sonny later recalled. "He was an individual innovator." Listening to the standard harmonies, Parker heard something deeper, nested within the changes. "I kept thinking there's bound to be something else," Parker told *Down Beat* in 1949. "I could hear it sometimes, but I couldn't play it."[8] Eventually, he did.

When Sonny first heard "Ko Ko," Bird's landing seemed out of the blue, yet as he learned, "Bird didn't come out of nowhere—he had to come up the hard way, through the ranks."[9] Around the time Sonny moved up on the Hill, Parker worked a few blocks away as a dish hand at Jimmy's Chicken Shack, where Art Tatum played. By the time Sonny heard him, Parker had been paying dues on Fifty-Second Street for a while, but it wasn't until the end of 1945 that he got his break. Even then, it wasn't so big.[10]

"Ko Ko" was recorded by Savoy owner Herman Lubinsky and producer Teddy Reig and would constitute Parker's modest debut as a leader. "Hen Gates," it turned out, was a pseudonym for Dizzy Gillespie.[11] On trumpet, instead of Dizzy, Parker hired Miles Davis, a nineteen-year-old recent Juilliard dropout from St. Louis.[12] Lubinsky bought four tunes from Parker for fifty dollars each—"Billie's Bounce," "Now's the Time," "Thriving from a Riff" (later renamed "Anthropology"), and "Ko Ko"—and intended to get his money's worth. Due to the complications with "Ko Ko," it seems Lubinsky packaged it with what was ostensibly Byas's least commercial track from his session that day. Instead, "Ko Ko" announced a revolution in jazz.

Bird was ahead of his time—a 1946 *Metronome* review of "Now's the Time" and "Billie's Bounce" described it as "a sound that's nothing short of miserable."[13] When Parker finally gained critical acceptance, many would consider "Ko Ko" his greatest recording, the bebop equivalent of Louis Armstrong's rendition of "West End Blues." When Sonny first heard "Ko Ko," he didn't know what to make of Parker's fusillade of notes, but he kept on listening. First, it was much faster, too fast for vibrato.[14] "At the time, we had 78 RPM records and 45 RPM records," Sonny recalled. "We'd speed up a Coleman Hawkins record, play it real fast, and you could hear Charlie Parker."[15]

"Now's the Time" was the new "Body and Soul."[16] "It took a minute to get into Bird when I heard that—I didn't realize what was going on. I didn't comprehend it," Sonny said, "but then there was a rumor that Charlie Parker had died, and I remember hearing 'Now's the Time' and 'Billie's Bounce' on every jukebox in Harlem—and by that time I'd gotten the message and real-ized how heavy he was."[17]

The message came faster than anyone could understand it, but it came from within the tradition. Right in the middle of Parker's solo on "Ko Ko," he quotes an arpeggiated line from New Orleans clarinetist Alphonse Picou's classic "High Society." It is at once an homage to the past and a bold restatement—this is *our* high society, a changing of the guard. More than a gauntlet thrown, though, Parker thought of his music as "another concep-tion" played "in the vernacular of the streets." As Parker told Paul Desmond, he wanted to play a "*beaucoup* of horn" without alienating the people.[18]

Parker, like Ellington, was decidedly beyond category. He demonstrated to Sonny that anything was fair game—from Bartók and Beethoven to Byas and Ben Webster. Sonny, like Parker, recognized that the Great Man theory was a myth. There would be no Bird without Earl Bostic, Johnny Hodges, and Willie Smith, or Stravinsky for that matter—but it was Bird who pulled it all together. "He bought records of Kay Kyser's 'Slow Boat to China,' which he played often, and Mario Lanza singing 'Be My Love,' which he would imi-tate, singing in an exaggerated, fractured tenor," recalled Chan Parker, Bird's common-law wife, of his eclectic taste. "The only record he bought which was even close to being hot was Peggy Lee's 'Lover,' which he would play over and over until my mother would freak out." One day, he visited Sheila Jordan in her loft and he "turned me on to Béla Bartók and Stravinsky."[19]

Bird subverted the toxic notion of the primitive genius. In Kansas City, he cultivated his preternatural ability by practicing eleven to fifteen hours a day, studying the Klosé method book in tandem with jam sessions.[20] Even when Parker finally rose to a level of prominence, he remained his own worst critic. In 1951, when he was asked to contribute to the "My Best on Wax" feature in *Down Beat*, he pulled no punches. "I'm sorry," he wrote, "but my best on wax has yet to be made."[21]

To Sonny, Parker represented the antithesis of the injustice that went down in Annapolis. Even in his personal life, Bird stood for the most radi-cal inclusivity. His common-law wife, Chan, was a half-Jewish jazz-loving dancer from Westchester whose birth name was Beverly Berg.[22] Bird played progressive music, both aesthetically and politically. "If you saw him in performance, he was very dignified, so he was going against the grain," Sonny said. "Highly intricate, involved, complicated, intellectual...he had to be recognized as not just great music but as a person that was an artist, not an entertainer, and that was very important for us because we were coming up after the war. A lot of people wanted to be treated a little better in the American mainstream. Charlie Parker to us represented that."[23] Some heard Parker and saw only drugs—he had a notorious heroin habit—but Sonny and his friends saw Parker and heard only dignity. Eventually, they would come to see the multitudes and contradictions he contained.

Sonny began to internalize Parker: his spirit of protest, his indefatigable work ethic, his unrelenting self-criticism, his storytelling, his penchant for playing musical quotes in improvised solos, his broad musical palette, his ambition to strive for a fuller totality of expression in blazing rhythm, to never repeat himself. "Charlie Parker was our God," Sonny said. "He was our prophet."[24] In that tradition, Bird already had the qualities of martyrdom. "We saw him as a Jesus Christ figure who got crucified for standing up for freedom. And even the fact that he used drugs—that was a sacrament. When we were coming up, he was the man."[25]

Before Sonny met Bird, he was brave enough to show up at his doorstep at the Dewey Square Hotel. "I was like just one of his fans at that time," Sonny said. "I knew he was in there, but he didn't answer the door. But I remember knocking on the door. I mean, what was he going to say to me anyway?"[26] Sometimes Bird just flew the coop. "I remember one time, Bird was at Minton's and we saw a lot of guys and his girlfriend, Doris," Sonny said. "He found out we were all running after him, so he and his old lady were able to escape us and go into the Dewey Square Hotel."[27]

Soon, Bird welcomed them to his flock. "In those days, there used to be a group of us who would follow Bird around—to me he was just a larger-than-life figure," Sonny recalled. "We would wait until he came off the stand at the Three Deuces, just so we could hang out with him. We were like this flock following him around, and Bird had just finished playing, but he had the patience of a saint with all these people he didn't really know."[28] These encounters with Bird in the club led to encounters off the bandstand when Sonny would visit him at the Dewey Square. To Sonny and the Counts of Bop, he became "a father figure to us all."[29]

Eventually, Bird had a chance to actually hear Sonny play through saxophonist Budd Johnson. "Budd took me, he said, 'Okay, man, I'm going to take you around to play for Bird,'" Sonny recalled. "And then I played...so Bird said, 'Hey man, that's me!' So, Bird knew that he had a disciple then, for sure."[30] It was more a compliment to Bird than to Sonny.

A quintessential nonconformist, Bird wanted them to find themselves, and he was always supportive. "He always had something positive to say," recalled Walter Bishop Jr., who was part of Sonny's inner circle. "Maybe the guy wasn't too swift with his changes but he had a big sound, and Bird would compliment his sound. The guy would feel ten feet tall. It took me years to figure it out. The thing was that I was looking at what they *couldn't* do. He was looking at what they *could* do, and he inspired them."[31]

When they couldn't catch Bird in person or missed live broadcasts on the radio, they would try to find bootleg recordings. "It was almost like military intelligence," Jackie McLean said. Luckily, their neighbor on the Hill had a wire recorder. "The guy made these wire recordings and you could go to his house and buy them from him for two dollars each. So, the night that Bird made 'Be-Bop' and 'Big Foot' and 'Groovin' High' and so much of this stuff, I went over and bought that stuff, man...took it back to my house and listened to it, man....I said 'Oh, shit, man.' So, I started transcribing this stuff...and working on it. Then I'd go to sessions outside my neighborhood and I would be playing this stuff.... [T]hey'd be listening, thinking that it was my stuff. Sonny had it, all of us on the Hill had those recordings. It's like we had a secret weapon."[32]

One of Bird's trade secrets: "Learn the lyrics to all the standard songs we play and learn to sing all the original pieces, and try to sing them in tune... and that way, you won't play anything uncouth," he told Arthur Taylor. Bird knew all the lyrics, and sometimes referred to songs by lyrics instead of their proper title: "All the Things You Are" became "YATAG," an acronym for his favorite line, "you are the angel glow."[33] Sonny, too, would always learn the lyrics to the songs he performed.

The Counts of Bop didn't pick up only on Bird's licks; they also picked up on his mannerisms, from the licorice-scented Sen-Sen breath freshener he used to the pocket watch he kept in his shirt pocket.[34] "We were all trying to emulate Charlie Parker," recalled Art Taylor. According to Taylor, they even copped Bird's walk. "He had an accident when he was a child which gave him some kind of affliction where he had a limp, so everybody was walking around limping like Bird, thinking it was a hip walk."[35] Bird was like Papa Legba, the Afro-Haitian *orisa*, or spirit guide, who walked with a limp because he walked between two worlds—he had one foot in the human world and one foot in the world of the gods.[36] Parker was an *orisa* to Sonny and his friends.

At that time, the line between Bird and Sonny was not as wide as one might think. Though Bird was an artist, not an entertainer, he still played at the same kind of dances the Counts of Bop played, at venues like the Lincoln Square Center. "Charlie Parker would be playing 'Cherokee' at a tremendous rate of speed and people would be dancing in halftime. That's when people had rhythm," Taylor recalled. But being able to dance to it doesn't mean people fully understood its mystique. "Like Charlie Parker used to say, man, 'If the audience knows what you're doing, they don't have to come and see you—if they know how you do it. Always have that mystery. There's always got to be some mystery.' "[37]

In his senior year of high school, Sonny met a brilliant pianist many considered jazz's most mysterious man, Thelonious Sphere Monk. Sonny had first heard Monk in 1944 when he bought a Hawkins ten-inch 78 with "Drifting on a Reed" and "Flyin' Hawk" as the B-side: Monk's recording debut.[38] "I got this record and rushed home to play it," Sonny recalled. "It had a pianist on there who had...a little different style."[39] Monk immediately stood out. His staccato accents to Hawkins's lyrical vibrato created a beautifully dissonant counterpoint, connecting the stride-piano tradition of James P. Johnson and Willie "the Lion" Smith with the sweeping improvisational vision of Art Tatum: artful and restrained, bracingly new, but not wholly detached from the past. To Sonny, there was a straight line from Fats Waller to Monk. "Everything about Monk's playing—the harmonies, the rhythmic sense, the fact that he played stride-style piano," Sonny said, "that's right up my alley."[40]

Monk didn't play a lot—spread across the two tracks, Hawkins scarcely gave him forty-five seconds of solo time—but when he did, it made an impression.

Monk had endured a tumultuous year himself.[41] After Coleman Hawkins disbanded his quartet to join Norman Granz's Jazz at the Philharmonic, Monk was out of a job. He joined Dizzy Gillespie's big band, only to be publicly fired onstage at the Apollo when he lost track of time at a nearby bar. By the end of 1946, Monk was so out of work that he let his union membership lapse. Yet Monk's ill fortune was Sonny's kismet. Monk continued frequenting jam sessions: Club 845 on Prospect Avenue on Sunday afternoons, at Minton's on Monday nights, or at pianist Mary Lou Williams's apartment. On one of these occasions, a sixteen-year-old saxophone prodigy from Sugar Hill caught the ear of the twenty-nine-year-old Monk.

"I played a little job when I was starting out at a club in Harlem," Sonny recalled. He was opening for the man known as the high priest of bop, so the pressure was on. Sonny rose to the occasion. "Monk was a very unassuming guy," Sonny said. "He indicated to me that he liked my playing. I think that was the first time I met Monk."[42]

Not long afterward, trumpeter Lowell Lewis was invited into Monk's bedroom studio. "While we were still in high school, Thelonious Monk somehow found out about Lowell and gave him a job to go to Chicago," Sonny said. "So Lowell went with Thelonious to Chicago for a week while we were still in high school. And after that, he said, 'Come on, I'm going to get you in Monk's band.'"[43]

When the last bell rang at school, Sonny's classes truly began. They'd make the pilgrimage downtown from Franklin High School in East Harlem to Monk's monastery all the way on the West Side. "So somehow [Lowell] worked it out so they finagled this other tenor player out of the band, and he brought me by his pad to play, and Monk liked me and hired me." The feeling was mutual. "Monk was great to me. He was older than me, maybe thirteen years older or so, and I looked up to him as a father figure—a guru, really."[44]

Sessions began informally. "He used to sneak me into bars after school," Sonny later recalled.[45] But when they migrated back to Monk's apartment, Monk taught Sonny about "the geometry of musical time and space."[46] The lessons were not didactic. "I don't think he was particularly trying to mold me," Sonny said. "He was the type of guy who would never tell you what to play; he wouldn't try and make you do it this way or that way. If he liked you, here was the music, and that's that."[47] Monk immediately liked Sonny's originality. "Monk would say, 'Yeah, man, Sonny is bad. Cats have to work out what they play; Sonny just plays that shit out the top of his head.'"[48]

By the time Sonny began showing up at his informal rehearsals, Monk had begun to distance himself from bebop, the form he helped create. "Mine is more original," he said in 1948 of the countless bebop imitators who had flooded the scene. "They think differently, harmonically. They play mostly stuff that's based on the chords of other things, like the blues and 'I Got Rhythm.' I like the whole song, melody and chord structure, to be different. I make up my own chords and melodies."[49]

Sonny quickly became a fixture at Monk's bedroom jam sessions, where he rehearsed his complex compositions. Monk lived with his family in San Juan Hill, in the Phipps Houses between Amsterdam and West End Avenue.[50] The neighborhood had been a hub of African American bohemian life, where Monk's idol James P. Johnson birthed the Charleston in Jungle's Casino after witnessing longshoremen from South Carolina doing the dance. Charlie Parker, Dizzy Gillespie, and Max Roach regularly played at jam sessions at the Lincoln Square Center; up the block, Bird sometimes played dances at the St. Nicholas Arena. Yet some of the most innovative music in San Juan Hill was emanating from Monk's humble tenement apartment.

Sonny routinely walked through the building's entrance court with his tenor, past the steam pipe and the inlaid star mosaic on the floor.[51] Monk insisted on a dapper style regardless of the occasion—bespoke suit, horn-rimmed glasses, well-manicured goatee.

It was always a family affair. "When Monk took me under his wing," Sonny said, "I used to go down to his house and hang out with [Monk's wife] Nellie and the family."[52] The Monks lived in a cluttered two-bedroom apartment on the ground floor, with a tin ceiling, faded linoleum, and a pristine refrigerator.[53] Sonny would walk through the kitchen to Monk's spartan, dimly lit bedroom and studio. A Klein upright took up as much space as Monk's worn-out cot, barely large enough to accommodate the pianist's large frame. The inner sanctum was a jazz shrine with a kind of visual syncopation: on the ceiling, next to a naked red lightbulb, Monk plastered a 1939 letter-size portrait of Billie Holiday, white flower in her hair, hung at a canted angle. Sarah Vaughan commanded a spot on the wall; Dizzy Gillespie's headshot hung proudly over the piano, signed "To Monk, my first inspiration. Stay with it. Your boy, Dizzy Gillespie." Framed photos and tchotchkes took up all the available real estate atop the piano. A lone window looked out on an alleyway.

Completing this cramped collage, musicians would jockey for space between the dresser, cot, piano, and chair. Sonny and Lowell Lewis would regularly see Idrees Sulieman, Kenny Dorham, Julius Watkins, and others.[54] Sonny brought along other members of the Counts of Bop, especially Jackie McLean, who lived across the street from Lewis, and Arthur Taylor, to absorb as much of Monk's influence as they could. Others from outside their group, such as pianist Randy Weston, also joined in.[55]

To Sonny, Monk was "the old master painter," and the musicians who gathered at his apartment were the canvas.[56] "Monk would have what seemed to be way-out stuff at the time and all the guys would look at it and say, 'Monk, we can't play this stuff...' and then it would end up that everybody would be playing it by the end of the rehearsal," Sonny mused. "It was hard music."[57]

Some sessions were more like lessons than rehearsals. Despite Monk's admonition against using established harmonic structures, it was not as though he didn't know the Great American Songbook. If a young musician really wanted to learn standard repertoire, Monk was the authority. "He knew the changes to all the songs," recalled Arthur Taylor. "Like Rollins and McLean. When they want to know a song, they go to Monk's house, and Monk can give you the right chords. When you get the chords from Monk, it's right. . . . You can improvise on it or whatever you want to do, but he'll give you the right stuff." In performance, though, Taylor recalled, Monk would "play only his own stuff."[58]

Some people heard all that dissonance in Monk's playing and thought he didn't know the standard tunes. But to those who knew, they heard the opposite: Thelonious broke all the rules because he knew them better than anyone.

Two of Monk's favorite mantras were "Always know" and "Play yourself."[59] His message was clear: If you didn't "always know" the tune like the back of your hand, even the melody could sound wrong. Before you could "play yourself" on a standard, it had to become a part of you. And in order to write your own standards, you had to know all the others first. Sonny took this lesson to heart.

Later, when Sonny was asked what Monk had taught him, he said, "Nothing." What did he learn from him? "Everything."[60]

As Monk was sketching out what would come to be standards—"Ruby, My Dear," "In Walked Bud,"[61] and "Off Minor"—Sonny and his crew were some of the first to workshop these brilliant, beguiling compositions, with their intervallic leaps and dissonant resolutions, vexing rhythms and charged silences. Monk epitomized the sound of surprise.

At these after-school sessions, Monk defied his mythic public persona. "Monk was an enigmatic guy, but he was one of the best people I've known—completely honest," Sonny said. "He really helped me out, took me under his wing, so to speak. He's a beautiful person. I get so upset when people try to depict Monk as being some kind of a weird guy or a crazy guy. It's so completely opposite from reality."[62]

Monk mostly led by example, but when he did speak, he imparted his wisdom in homespun adages, some of which were later taken down by saxophonist Steve Lacy, another acolyte. "Those pieces were written so as to have something to play, and to get cats interested enough to come to rehearsal"; "A genius is the one most like himself"; "What should we wear tonight? Sharp as possible!"; "A note can be as small as a pin or as big as the world, it depends on your imagination"; "What you don't play can be more important than what you do play"; "Just because you're not a drummer, doesn't mean that you don't have to keep time"; "Pat your foot and sing the melody in your head when you play. Stop playing all those weird notes, play the melody."[63] He would often remind his protégés that "Know" was a palindrome for Monk, with the *M* flipped upside down. When Sonny played a phrase, he learned to examine it from all perspectives.

For Sonny, Monk's approach to music became a secular religion. "Anything was possible with Monk," Sonny said. "That's why we called him the

High Priest . . . because the spiritual element was of a high order."[64] Sonny was a monk in Monk's temple, and everything Monkish, from the focus on the melody to the rhythmic angularity to the staccato attack to the fine threads, he absorbed into his own original style, translating San Juan Hill to Sugar Hill, piano to the saxophone. He learned the meaning of originality from one of the most original artists of the century, any century. And he learned it from an artist who had been unfairly portrayed as disconnected from reality. Nobody was realer than Monk.

"When you're around those musicians, man, they make you understand without conversation that your story is as important as every story told," said drummer Perry Wilson, who later played in Sonny's band. "Sonny used to tell us stories and there was a little bit of humor in it. He'd say, 'Monk and I, man, I could go by his house, man, and we could sit for eight or ten hours, and never say a word to each other. Be in the same room. And after ten hours, 'Hey, man, I'm gonna cut out.' 'All right, Newk, I'll see you man.' Just that energy in the room . . . and you know when they got together and made some music it's way the fuck up *here*. Right? . . . They know how to call and answer; they know how to finish each other's sentences, so to speak."[65]

At one of these rap sessions on Sixty-Third Street, Monk said, "'Man, if there wasn't music in this world, this world wouldn't be shit,'" Sonny recalled. "It was sort of an oversimplification, but the way he said it, I said, 'Wow, exactly.'" Nietzsche had said the same thing.[66]

For Sonny, Monk provided a sense of belonging during an alienating time in his life. He helped him become himself. As Sonny's sound crystallized, many of Monk's principles—melodicism, space through sound and silence, sartorial flourishes, a Sisyphean work ethic, an encyclopedic knowledge of the tradition, all of that ugly beauty—deeply informed his artistic development.

Soon, Sonny was applying his lessons with Monk to his own practice sessions. "I remember one moment that I had when I was playing with some of my friends," Sonny said, recalling one of the many times he rehearsed with Lowell Lewis after school. "I was rehearsing with him one day and was taking a solo in which I was able to manipulate the time in a way that drew his attention. He made a remark about it, and then I realized, oh, I must really have something."[67]

In late June 1947, Sonny's father was released from prison. The navy's clemency rules allowed for pleas after one-third of the sentence was served; Walter had served nine months of his two-year sentence. That spring, Sonny graduated from Benjamin Franklin High School. "Most of the guys didn't finish it, but I felt I had to finish it," Sonny said of his high school experience.[68] Arthur Taylor, for one, dropped out when he was fifteen and never looked back. Pursuing an advanced degree meant playing by the same set of rules that led to his father's demise, so Sonny would graduate and be done with the system.

In the Franklin yearbook, every graduating senior got two or three lines next to their photo. Lowell Lewis, smiling, self-assured behind his glasses, listed his activities—band and office squad—that he intended to become a musician, and a nickname, Sweet and Low. On Sonny's page, opposite his slightly bemused photo, is a classmate, John Reid, a member of the school orchestra, who wrote simply "Good balance for Rollins." (Though Sonny never discussed him, they remained in touch until Reid passed away fifty years later.)[69] On Sonny's page, there was a would-be crime photographer and a lawyer, and Sonny:

WALTER ROLLINS
Musician
A second Paul Robeson[70]

It was an impossibly lofty goal. Sonny wouldn't have it any other way.

As a new high school graduate, Sonny could have gone to college as his siblings had done. Many musicians of his generation joined the armed forces: saxophonists John Coltrane, Von Freeman, and Lou Donaldson all served in the navy;[71] John Lewis and Kenny Clarke played in army bands together; Donald Byrd performed in an air force band. Instead, Sonny decided to enter the workforce.

Through his older brother, Sonny began working at a "place that made these little ornamental pictures of European people from the Middle

Ages—queens and kings, well-dressed people and carriages. That was a good job," he said. Along with some guys from the block on Edgecombe, he got a job in the midtown Garment District "pushing clothes through the street, going from one factory to the next." He worked as an office courier, as a factotum at a candy factory on Canal Street, and as a runner at a hat factory, where "the people were glad to have us. When I got that job, I realized why they were glad to have us, man. You had to be on your feet all day. You had to really hustle and get that hat and take it to another part of the factory, and give it to another guy who was waiting there to do something with the felt. 'Hat here!' You had to go and take it up to another guy who was waiting to put the brim on. 'I've got the brim!' Another guy's up there with the steam.... We learned what working was. I don't think we lasted more than two days." In addition to amplifying his legendary work ethic, these arduous full-time jobs served as a reminder of the fate that awaited him if he couldn't make his side hustle his main hustle. "A lot of guys had nothing else, no other type of job they were capable of doing," he said.[72] Not Sonny.

So as soon as he could, he joined the American Federation of Musicians (AFM) Local 802, which had officially integrated in 1886.[73] This was the musicians' union that Miles Davis, Kenny Dorham, Thelonious Monk,[74] and Bird all belonged to. It negotiated contracts with all the clubs on Fifty-Second Street. "I believe workers need the protection of a union," Sonny later said. "I'm a big union man and I'm proud of it."[75]

Soon after graduation, Sonny and Lowell Lewis applied to become members of Local 802. Lowell was first; he applied on July 3, 1947. A week later, Sonny went down to the AFM union hall in the RCA Victor Building, where he was called to appear before the Examining Committee with about thirty-five other applicants.[76] That day, the younger Walter Rollins's application was approved, and, at sixteen, Sonny was officially a professional musician. Arthur Taylor was last to join, but on December 18, 1947, he was in, too. The Counts of Bop were legit.

Chapter 7

GOOF SQUARE

(1947–1948)

Donnellan Square sits between 149th and 150th Streets, a triangular sliver
of green space fenced in and dotted with benches, separating St. Nicholas
Avenue from St. Nicholas Place. On one side were Jimmy's Chicken Shack
and Luckey's Rendezvous, where Art Tatum's dazzling arpeggios once reverberated through the walls; on the other was the Bailey Mansion, its imperi-
ous spires bearing down on the street below. Around the block was Sonny's
apartment, and in the summer, sparrows were always singing. The square was
dedicated to a fallen World War I soldier, but Sonny and his friends knew it
by another name: Goof Square. This, in a sense, is where hard bop was born.

———◦———

In the summer of '47, after Sonny graduated high school, Charlie Parker
became an even more powerful influence. That summer, Bird made his
first commercial recording on tenor.[1] It was Miles Davis's debut as a leader,
recorded on August 14, 1947, with Davis's tunes "Milestones," "Sipping at
Bell's," "Little Willie Leaps," and "Half Nelson." Sonny memorized Bird's
tenor solo on "Half Nelson."[2]

"Bird made a deep impression on me on tenor," Sonny said. "I heard him
play it very seldom, but his ideas, his drive, the way he could create moved me
very much. As soon as he started to play on tenor or alto, he'd create the complete mood and would carry everyone, including the rhythm section, along
with him. That's the mark of a true soloist."[3]

Yet he carried Sonny and his friends along in other, more harmful ways.
Sheila Jordan had a vivid memory of Bird on tenor and why he picked up the
bigger horn. "I heard Bird play tenor. He played great, but it wasn't his horn
of choice," she said. "The only reason," she said, "was that he pawned his alto,
and then somebody would give him a tenor, 'cause they didn't have an alto...."

He had that cunning, baffling, powerful disease of heroin addiction—and it is a disease."[4] Bird's towering virtuosity and his deadly disease would inspire Sonny and his crew to reach the greatest heights and lowest depths.

Jackie McLean recalled Sonny's rapid development during this period. McLean had followed Andy Kirk Jr., the most precocious of their group, to Theodore Roosevelt High School in the Bronx after Sonny graduated from Franklin. But around the time Miles Davis's debut record came out, McLean recalled, Sonny all but vanished. In the summer of '47, he "dropped off the scene during the entire summer and autumn."[5]

Sonny hadn't disappeared into the woodshed, but was in fact on tour for the first time. "When I was a young aspiring musician just out of high school, I got my first job away from home playing with a group in Montreal," Sonny later wrote.[6] He and Lowell Lewis were hired by trumpeter Al Bryant. Five years older and raised in Springfield, Massachusetts, Bryant was a plunger-mute specialist who went on to play with Lionel Hampton, Dizzy Gillespie, and Jaki Byard.[7] "We used to go up to his house, and then we made gigs with him. It was before we really were playing with anybody else. He was one of our early people," Sonny said. "An older guy used to drive and would drive very slow."[8] Bryant was not ego driven and never publicly touted his connection to Sonny—but his modesty belied his outsize presence on the bandstand.[9] Al "was a forceful player...an extroverted player," Sonny said. "He was a good musician then, and I always had respect for his playing."[10]

When Sonny reappeared on the New York scene months later, he had gone through a metamorphosis. "His sound had been like a Coleman Hawkins on alto saxophone," McLean said, "but when he returned late in the winter of 1948, he was more like a Charlie Parker playing a tenor saxophone."[11]

Charlie Parker set the standard they all aspired to, but many of his acolytes associated Bird's eminent brilliance with the habits he epitomized, and Sonny was among them. "We can't talk about the musicians identified with the Hill without addressing 'the scourge,'" Sonny said. "As everybody became addicted, each and every one of us, we ended up having something else in common. First it was music; then it became the search to satisfy our drug habits. That brought us into other spheres of hell. But...it was a shared experience."[12]

What Sonny refers to as his "drug deviant years" were the result of a perfect storm.[13] In 1948, two major developments shook bop: the arrival of the long-playing record, or LP, which liberated jazz musicians from the three- to five-minute playing time of 78s, and the arrival of heroin in Harlem, which had them in thrall to addiction. That year, the drug flooded the neighborhood, and the Mafia was a key player. On February 10, 1946, two days before Sonny's father's arrest, mob boss Lucky Luciano had his prison sentence commuted and was deported to Italy in exchange for his sub-rosa aid in the war effort. In short order, Luciano embedded himself in the Sicilian Mafia and established a drug trade with Lebanon, Turkey, and the Golden Triangle, importing opium and processing it in Italy. Luciano then used his connections in the organized-crime world to ship the heroin elsewhere in Europe and to the United States, primarily to New York. The drug hit the waterfront in New York, where it would then be cut, distributed to local dealers, and funneled into the streets with the aid of crooked cops willing to look the other way.[14]

"In 1948," Sonny said, "heroin was just getting out into the neighborhoods; it was cheap and it was plentiful. That's when I got hooked."[15]

"It came on the scene like a tidal wave," recalled Jackie McLean. "I mean, it just appeared after World War II. I began to notice guys in my neighborhood, nodding on the corner, you know, and so we all began to find out that this is what they were, they were nodding because they were taking this . . . thing called 'horse.'"[16]

Though it was most prevalent in Central Harlem, heroin was also sold in Italian Harlem, near Benjamin Franklin High School.[17] "The ethnic lines started to be crossed with the introduction of heroin," recalled Edwin Torres. "All of a sudden, mothers of some of my friends wanted to know why their sons were stealing clothes, appliances, anything. They didn't know what heroin was. Even hip guys like me had never seen a street junkie."[18]

Soon, Harlem Hospital noticed a surge in young addicts. "The problem has become acute in recent years," concluded one study. "It is especially noteworthy that youngsters are the ones in whom there is a dominance of symptoms." In 1948, the hospital admitted no addicts between the ages of fifteen and twenty; by 1950, there were thirteen. In the same period, the total heroin addiction cases jumped from four to forty-two. The data was incomplete, though. Most addicts either stayed on the street or never made it to the hospital, and those who survived usually wound up in prison.[19]

To Sonny and his friends, it seemed to be part of living the life. "When we found out that Billie Holiday used drugs, and Charlie Parker used drugs, we figured it can't be all bad—and maybe that's the key to creativity," Sonny said.[20]

While Sonny's friends glorified it, the government had criminalized it and made an example of Billie Holiday. Ironically, Sonny and his friends found out about Parker and Holiday from the papers, which sensationalized their perennial battle with addiction and federal law enforcement.[21] In May 1947, just as Sonny was about to graduate from high school, Lady Day was arrested by federal narcotics agents; after a very public trial, Holiday was sentenced to a year and a day at the Federal Reformatory for Women, a minimum-security prison in Alderson, West Virginia.[22] Parker was arrested in June 1948 at the Dewey Square Hotel.[23]

More than any other opioid, heroin was so potent that exposure quickly led to addiction. Holiday's first husband, trombonist Jimmy Monroe, got Billie hooked; Bird was driving to a gig at Charlie Musser's Ozark Tavern in Missouri in 1936 when a tragic car accident killed bassist George Wilkerson. Bird suffered three broken ribs and a fractured spine. During his three-month recovery, the doctor prescribed a highly effective painkiller: heroin.[24]

To Harry J. Anslinger, the barrel-chested, bullheaded commissioner of the Federal Bureau of Narcotics, heroin was the key to criminality.[25] He used his media savvy and the support of William Randolph Hearst to spread the notion that marijuana induced brutal violence almost immediately upon inhaling. In 1937, his propaganda campaign led to the passing of the Marihuana Tax Act—playing on racist fears by substituting the Spanish slang term *marihuana* for the more commonly used *cannabis*—which led to more drug convictions.[26] But it was still not enough to match his ambition. As the Mafia ramped up heroin production and distribution, Anslinger, who was also obsessed with investigating international organized-crime syndicates, had the department ready to crack down. The new policies and an effectively militarized narcotics bureau led to the mass incarceration of African American drug users.

In 1945, there were three times as many white heroin users as black, but Anslinger, by all accounts a virulent bigot, had devised a way to focus attention on the black minority of addicts by stoking white fears.[27] With a monomaniacal obsession, Anslinger fixated on jazz musicians as emblematic of the moral turpitude he saw sweeping the nation, with heroin as the fuel behind it. For Anslinger, the enemy in the War on Drugs needed a public face, and it seemed almost no one could be better suited for his cause than Lady Day and Bird.[28]

Anslinger's private notes suggest he was as opposed to jazz as Joseph McCarthy was to communism. "Music hath charms, but not this music. It hails the drug," he wrote.[29] Another note refers to the music as "a series of wild melodies and vulgar variations, that sounded like the jungles in the dead of night."[30] Anslinger kept a typewritten article detailing the effects of drug use, citing an expert's response to the publication of Mezz Mezzrow's *Really the Blues.* "Especially," it read, "will it gather a bountiful harvest of recruits among so many of the young people who right now are prostrating themselves before the altar of jazz, swing, boogie-woogie, jive, and all the other drivel that comes only too frequently from the radios and phonographs of the nation." The case descriptions he saved document how the legalistic language of the drug war became the dominant understanding of drug culture: probationary periods, weights, small buys, and violations.[31] Complex artists were reduced to a paragraph detailing their history of drug use, their fates sealed in their rap sheets.

As drugs ripped through Harlem "like a tornado," as Sonny would later recall, Bird of all people spoke out against drug use. As early as 1947, he did everything he could, short of quitting, to negate the myth that heroin was the source of his genius. "It all came from being introduced too early to night life," he said in 1947. "When you're not mature enough to know what's happening—well, you goof."[32] Bird referred to his addiction as an "eleven-year panic" that culminated in his stay at Camarillo State Mental Hospital in California in 1946, immortalized by his song "Relaxin' at Camarillo," a title Dial Records founder Ross Russell insisted on despite Parker's objection.[33]

"I didn't know what hit me," Parker said. "It was so sudden. I was a victim of circumstances.... High school kids don't know any better. That way, you can miss the most important years of your life, the years of possible creation. I don't know how I made it through those years. I became bitter, hard, cold. I was always on a panic—couldn't buy clothes or a good place to live."[34]

In 1949, when Parker was widely considered the "world's greatest living jazz musician," he said that anyone who deals heroin or gives it to kids should be shot. "Any musician who says he is playing better either on tea [marijuana], the needle, or when he is juiced, is a plain, straight liar," he said. "When I get too much to drink, I can't even finger well, let alone play decent ideas. And in the days when I was on the stuff, I may have thought I was playing better, but listening to some of the records now, I know I wasn't. Some of these smart kids who think you have to be completely knocked out to be a good hornman are just plain crazy. It isn't true. I know, believe me."[35]

Despite Bird's prodigious accomplishments, he thought of himself purely as an example of how not to be. " 'Everybody says I'm this, that and the other, but that's not as important as maybe showing to a lot of people that I'm here for another purpose,' " Max Roach remembered him saying. " 'That's to say, don't throw your life away using dope and drinking and doing all this bullshit that I'm involved in, that I just can't seem to break away from.' " Sheila Jordan recalled Bird passing the same antidrug message to her husband, pianist Duke Jordan. "He saw Duke on the couch, nodding out, and said, 'Man, didn't you learn anything from me?' "[36]

With Parker lacking the fortitude or the treatment options to kick his overwhelming habit, whether it was opiates or stimulants—dope, reefer, nutmeg, Benzedrine, alcohol—his exhortation fell on deaf ears.

The stars of the generation ahead of Sonny all seemed to be doing it: Art Blakey, who ran the weekly "Three O'Clock High" series at the Rockland Palace and Audubon Ballroom; Miles Davis, whom Lowell Lewis idolized; and Dexter Gordon, nearly seven years older than Sonny, who was altering the tenor vocabulary. Sonny met Gordon at a dance at the Hunts Point Ballroom in the Bronx soon after he got his first tenor, and Gordon's tenor was in hock. "Dexter was strung out at the time, and I was a young cat whose mother had just bought me my brand-new tenor. He didn't have a horn, so I lent it to him," Sonny said. "He was already an established star; I was just a kid. But he didn't steal my horn!"[37]

As a result of heroin use, some of bop's creators were early casualties of the scourge. On April 1, 1947, trumpeter Freddie Webster, a key influence on Miles Davis they called "Web,"[38] died at the age of thirty in the Strode Hotel in Chicago. Yet this early warning did not dissuade Sonny and his generation from living the life.

There were other attempts to stem the tide. In 1950, *Ebony* ran an editorial titled "Who Killed Bop?"—or, more accurately, what? "It is no secret that some of the younger bop musicians held the stupid opinion that to play like the really great jazzmen they had to ape their vices," the editorial said.[39]

Different drugs were used at different hours. To prevent themselves from nodding off, many musicians began taking Benzedrine. "I would take Benzedrine so that I could practice...so that I wouldn't sleep," said Max Roach. "So did Miles. Everyone did. We didn't want to sleep, 'cause we didn't want to miss nothing during that period. You know, there was music 24 hours a day."[40]

Marijuana was the gateway.[41] "I smoked reefers before I messed around with drugs, but the feeling of heroin is so much more intense than reefers, so if you're an impressionable kid, why there you are—you end up hooked," Sonny recalled. "This cat first turned me on by snorting. So I tried that, man, and I got so sick, throwing up all day, that I said, 'Oh, I'll never do that shit again.' But still, you go back to it, because the pressure's so great to be one of the guys and hip; and I did it again, and probably got sick again. Then finally I didn't get as sick. It took a while before we got into shooting."[42]

For many, dope was a kind of pact between musicians and the music that nothing else mattered, that in fact the music mattered almost more than life itself. "The drugs were just a way to get into the music more, I believe," Sonny said, "to shut out everything else but the music."[43]

To Sonny and his peers, "It was our way of having something apart from a hostile society. It wasn't us being hostile; it was a society being hostile to us, and this was our way of having our thing."[44] Yet it was a barrier that society also used against them. "It wasn't so much the drugs themselves as much as the fact that black musicians couldn't use drugs and get away with it," Sonny said. "I mean, Billie Holiday was a big drug addict; but even though white artists were big drug addicts, too, they as a rule could get away with it. So black musicians felt that this was a way to penalize them more."[45]

By 1948, the tide was turning and bebop was gaining some popular acceptance, but many still considered it a pariah art form. Later, in a scathing 1963 editorial, Max Roach railed against the injustices that meant that instead of celebrating America's jazz royalty, they were degraded and dehumanized. "The royal family of 'jazz' is a joke. No other 'Duke' has ever reigned so nobly and gotten such ill and paltry (monetary) compensation. No other 'Count' has been so nobly used. No other 'Lady' has died so friendless and under such dire circumstances, (and in jail, yet). No other 'Pres' (ident) has been so ill abused or condemned to die so torturously slow. No other 'King' has been so ignobly detested by sight. Since our aristocracy is held in such low esteem, can the plebeian hope for God to save us?"[46]

Beyond the indignities suffered by the jazz aristocracy, even within Harlem they had not yet accepted the music that Sonny and his peers based their lives around. This became undeniably clear to Sonny at the Apollo Theater. "They would maybe be there for somebody like Erskine Hawkins's Band or something like that...Tiny Bradshaw...Lionel Hampton, he would have the place packed," Sonny said. "I remember feeling bad when Coleman Hawkins was there...that there weren't a lot of people in there. That kind of hurt me a little bit. Also, when Charlie Parker was there, there weren't a lot of people then. But then I realized that...the kind of music that they played and that I was trying to get into, it was a thing which you can't depend on a lot of people. It might just be a small group of people who appreciate it. So you just have to not expect big houses screaming and hollering. It just wasn't that universal a thing."[47]

By the summer of 1948, the fault lines in the bop wars had only deepened. That July, a *New Yorker* profile of Dizzy Gillespie simply called "Bop" described bebop as a "manifestation of revolt," with the beboppers as self-proclaimed progressives and the old guard as reactionaries. Boppers were "'the left wing' and their opponents 'the right wing,'" with the "moldy figs" dismissing Sonny and his ilk as "dirty radicals" and "wild-eyed revolutionaries" relegated to the underground. "Such is the bitterness that bebop has stirred up in the jazz world that some of its detractors say that the new music is a product of heroin, cocaine, and marijuana," read the article, "a charge that [Gillespie arranger Gil] Fuller, a college graduate of impeccable morals, denounces as 'a gross and gratuitous libel.'"[48]

Heroin was not just a dangerous bop accessory, but a way to make life bearable. Sonny later explained it this way: "I think the main thing is that it's the way *you* like to feel; I don't think it makes a person play any better. I just think some people like to be high, so *they* feel better about what they're doing, but actually it's not sounding any better. And if a guy gets really messed up it can sound worse."[49]

The titular character of James Baldwin's short story "Sonny's Blues" exemplified this. "'It's not so much to *play*. It's to *stand* it, to be able to make it at all. On any level.' He frowned and smiled: 'In order to keep from shaking to pieces.'"[50] Was Sonny Rollins the basis for Baldwin's Sonny? Probably in part. Before writing the story, Baldwin used to listen to Rollins while living as an expatriate in Paris in the early 1950s.[51]

Like Baldwin's Sonny, for a while, Rollins felt that music and drugs were inextricably linked. "The life of a jazz musician is a difficult life," Sonny said. "You want to get to the inner spirit and sometimes you drink, or you do drugs, or you smoke a lot and you do all these things to try to get the spirit out."[52] Yet drugs were ultimately a spirit suppressant. "There was a time when I would say that I would never stop getting high because I liked it and it made me feel good," Sonny later said, "until it began to kick my ass."[53]

It was not long before the Counts of Bop were all hooked. Jackie McLean was one of the last holdouts. "The guys that I admired in my neighborhood were all doing it...Sonny Rollins, Andy Kirk Jr., Walter Bishop, Arthur Taylor, Kenny Drew, Mark Fisher," McLean recalled. "They were all messing around, except for me and Lowell Lewis....Consequently, we were thrown together, because those guys are very clannish, and if you're not doing what they do, you ain't in, ain't going to be around them. Even when they practiced, they had rehearsals and stuff, we were lockouts. One day I went to [Lowell's] house. He told me—he said, 'You're all alone, man.' He said, 'I went down there yesterday to Sonny's house and tried a little of that thing. It's happening, man. I'll see you later.'"[54]

McLean was forced to play with musicians a tier below. Then he caved to the peer pressure, snorting some heroin in the bathroom at a cocktail sip. "When I got on the stage and picked up the saxophone about a half hour later, I felt very relaxed. I just felt as though I was all right. . . . I had no idea that it would get a grip on me at any particular time. I mean, you never think it could happen to you."[55] Immediately, Jackie was back in the inner circle. "It was like a club of Draculas," McLean said.[56]

McLean started buying one-dollar caps of heroin, thinking he could use it in moderation, but soon he was buying five-dollar bags. "I started doing it over the weekends, like Friday, Saturday, Sunday. Then trying to lay off Monday, Tuesday, Wednesday, like that. Slowly but surely . . . I begin to add on days, like Friday, Saturday, Sunday, and Monday. I would try not to do nothing Tuesday and Wednesday. Before you know it, I was doing it all the way up to Tuesday. The next thing you know, I was doing a little bit of it every day."[57] Pretty soon, they were spending all their gig money on drugs.

"There was a cat named Sonny, I know we used to cop from him," Rollins recalled of a connection. "He used to be around 140-something Street and St. Nicholas."[58] Sometimes, they would go to a house on Hamilton Terrace where a dealer named Willie Gordon lived; they could cop any time of day or night, though usually during the day. A ten-dollar bag "would keep me high for a week," Arthur Taylor recalled. "His stuff would put you out." Gordon was a few years older and a "very light-skinned cat . . . like a gangster type. Talked gangster shit," Taylor said, and he was known for "that strong dope." Gordon dealt "the inside stuff from uptown. That was like the inside, 'cause this cat didn't deal with everybody. He more or less dealt with a few choice people."[59]

One of their favorite places to get high, especially in the summer, was the aforementioned Donnellan Square or, as Sonny knew it, "a little park we called Goof Square."[60] They liked it so much they wrote at least two tunes about it: Sonny's "Goof Square" and Kenny Drew's "Donnellon [sic] Square."[61]

The Counts of Bop became the mayors of Goof Square. "We used to sit on the benches in there," McLean recalled. "When I left my house, and I would be going out after dinner or something . . . that's where I would walk to, from 158th Street all the way down there to see if anybody's in the square. Sometimes it would be nobody. Sometimes be a lot of cats in there." "We used to be pretty wild," recalled Arthur Taylor. "The cats was getting high... intravenously."[62]

Across the street from Goof Square was Luckey's Rendezvous, the posh club owned by pianist Luckey Roberts. They never went in, but "would stand outside, 'cause when Art Tatum was coming up to hang out," Taylor said, "we would all go out there and stand and look just to get a glimpse of him."[63]

Sometimes they would pick up new members of the band in the square. Bassist Percy Heath, a former Tuskegee Airman, moved from Philadelphia to New York, just a block south of the square. Heath's reputation preceded him, and soon he was in the mix with the Counts of Bop. "I could take little jobs, one nighters," Heath said. "That's where I would play dances, those ten-dollar gigs, with Sonny Rollins and Kenny Drew."[64]

Many older musicians met them passing through Goof Square on their way to the 145th Street subway. Vocalist Earl Coleman, five years Sonny's senior, was one. "A young tenor player by the name of Sonny Rollins came through. I said, 'Man, he's bad! He plays the tenor like Bird!'" he recalled. "Next, I met Jackie McLean and we all became friends right away. I call them 'The kids up on the Hill.' One day I called Miles and said, 'Say, man, there are some bad little ol' kids up here!'"[65]

Drummer Joe Harris, a few years older, lived in the neighborhood and often saw them congregating in the square on his way to work with Dizzy Gillespie. Harris was known as the "cleanest-living drummer in New York," so he wasn't using. In Goof Square, he usually saw Sonny, Arthur Taylor, Jackie McLean, Kenny Drew, Andy Kirk Jr., and Lowell Lewis shooting the breeze, and other things. "They were all sitting there, and then they were only about three or four years younger than me, so I was really in their groove," Harris recalled, "because they hadn't established themselves yet, but they knew me, since I was a young guy with Dizzy's big band."[66]

Harris's employer, Dizzy Gillespie, also stayed clean. Sonny met him at the Rockland Palace when Dizzy was about thirty years old; he also saw Dizzy dance the lindy hop at "the Track"—the Savoy Ballroom.[67] "I was just beginning to mature as a player and Dizzy was like a god to me," Sonny said. "He was on such a high celestial level. He looked down and said, 'Sonny, you've got big feet.'" Sonny began collecting a scrapbook, and Dizzy was a part of it. "He was always an exciting, inspirational figure to all of us."[68]

Not long before, Sonny also met drummer Roy Haynes, five years older than Sonny, who'd been gigging with bandleader Luis Russell, Sarah Vaughan, and bop vocalist Babs Gonzales. "I was hearing a lot about Sonny Rollins up on the Hill," Haynes recalled.[69] One day, Sonny paid Haynes an impromptu visit with his friend, pianist Little Lenny Martinez.[70] "I didn't know that Sonny was playing an instrument until one night shortly after that visit, when I saw him with an alto at a restaurant on St. Nicholas Avenue where we used to eat after gigs on Saturday night," Haynes said. "I said, 'You play saxophone?' and he said, 'Yeah, I have a little gig.'"[71]

When he was not in Goof Square or down on Fifty-Second Street, he was with Harriette Acosta, his first serious girlfriend. She was a month younger than Sonny, beautiful, with a plucky persistence.[72] Growing up on Edgecombe Avenue, "Harriette would always be begging for...like we had candy, and she'd be begging for it, and we said no," recalled Doris Mason. "She said, 'That's all right. Every dog will have his day.' She used to say that to us all the time." Sonny and Harriette were young lovers in Harlem. "I had my first sexual experience with her when I was a teenager," he said. They had a rocky romance. "If we were fighting about something, she'd come down to the place I was playing at, and I'd leave my horn there, and she'd mess up my horn," Sonny said. "I'd come back... 'Damn, there's something wrong with my horn!' 'Oh, Harriette was here.'" As Sonny recalled, "I don't think she was really a fan of the music. I think she was more a fan of the environment... the clubs, the musicians. She was more a fan of the scene."[73] Unlike Sonny, Harriette did not have music to support their shared habit. "She became a heroin addict, and therefore she had to become a prostitute, and therefore went through a hard, hard, *hard* life." She was not a sex worker when they first met, "but that came not too long after," Sonny said. "I'm not demeaning her in any way by saying that. What she did to get drugs...she didn't have anything."[74] They were on again, off again for years.

In late 1948, Sonny met his next major influence—Bud Powell, then in his early twenties.[75] "I think he was a genius," Sonny said. "His improvisations were definitely on a par with Charlie Parker. If you're thinking of the bebop style, Bud Powell was supreme. In fact, some people put him above Charlie Parker."[76] Sonny particularly liked Powell's short but dazzling solo on the 1946 recording of Sonny Stitt's "Good Kick."[77]

Powell was a prodigy; he came close to Art Tatum technically, while assimilating the stylistic and harmonic advances of his mentor, Thelonious Monk, whose "In Walked Bud" was dedicated to him. Bud knew those pianists well; Tatum "used to take me out for a drive in his big [sky-blue] Lincoln," Bud recalled, while he and Monk "used to hang out all day and all night at after-hour joints."[78] Sonny had heard his staggering virtuosity on Powell's first date with Bird on the Charlie Parker's All-Stars session recorded on May 8, 1947, alongside Miles Davis, Tommy Potter, and Max Roach.[79]

By 1948, Powell's mental state had deteriorated and he had undergone extensive electroshock therapy at Creedmoor State Hospital. This was the latest treatment attempt in a series of encounters with the mental health-care system triggered by a 1945 police brutality incident that ostensibly left him brain damaged.[80] No matter what traumas and injustices were inflicted on Powell at the hand of the state, though, no one could ever touch the genius he had in his fingers. "What can you say," Sonny said, "except when he sat down and started to play, that was it."[81]

It was during Powell's stay at Creedmoor that Jackie McLean was the first of the Counts of Bop to meet Bud, after a chance encounter with his younger brother, pianist Richie Powell. McLean's stepfather, Jimmy Briggs, who ran the numbers on the Hill, owned a jazz record store where Jackie worked the counter.[82] One day, Richie came into the store wearing a housepainter's smock. When Jackie played a Charlie Parker tune, Richie told him it was his brother on piano.[83] Jackie didn't believe him until that Sunday, when Richie took him around the corner, where Bud lived on the second floor with his mother, his partner, and their infant daughter.[84] There McLean encountered a vacant-looking figure.

"I was frightened to death," McLean recalled. "I'd never seen Bud Powell, so I didn't know what he looked like anyway. And Bud was coming home from a mental institution on a weekend furlough. So Bud was out to lunch anyway."[85] And then the mysterious figure spoke. "'You don't believe

I'm Bud Powell?' " said the man. "And man, I almost lost it. I said, 'Uh, I don't...' He turned around and walked over to the piano and opened it, and sat down, and the minute he hit those keys, man, I said 'Oh my god.' Then he looked around, he said, 'What have you got in that case?' " McLean took out his horn. "He played an introduction, and I played 'Buzzy' with him, and he said, 'Hey, you can play a little bit! How old are you? And I said, 'I'm fifteen.' He said, 'Oh, wait, I want my wife to see you.'... He told me that I could come down anytime."[86]

Jackie was at Bud's house every week, and soon, Arthur Taylor, Walter Bishop Jr., and Sonny were invited as well. At the time, Powell was not that well known.[87] To Sonny and his band, though, Bud was a local celebrity.

Sonny referred to Powell as the "great professor of the music," but his lessons were delivered entirely through the piano—he taught theory through practice and everything by ear. "Playing the piano, he was able to articulate so much of the bebop language, and of course we all looked up to Bud Powell. He was one of the gods," Sonny said. "We used to go by and stand outside of Bud's house. He lived on the second floor one flight up and we used to listen to Bud practicing.... He was like a mad genius. I mean he was like Beethoven, you know.... This cat, he was really one of the people that defined bebop."[88]

Sonny and Jackie used to pass each other coming to and from Bud's apartment. "I remember one day I was walking up, and I ran into Sonny, and Sonny said, 'You coming from Bud's?' I said, 'Yeah.' And he said, 'Uh-huh.' He said, 'Who's the baddest, Bud or Bird?' And I said, 'What do you mean, man?' ... He said, 'I asked you a question. Who's the baddest, Bud or Bird?' I said, 'Bird.' And he said, 'Yeah? You sure of that? See you later.' And he split. And that's when a bulb went off in my head. I said, 'Of course, man! It's Bud, too. The two of them! It's like spring or fall.'"[89]

Like Bird, Bud took them under his wing, recalled Arthur Taylor. "'Arthur, he's like one of my children, he's just like Sonny and Jackie,'" Bud once said. "'They're my children, you know.'"[90]

Around this time, Sonny also met drummer Art Blakey. Blakey had a group called the 17 Messengers, a precursor to the Jazz Messengers, with Kenny Dorham, Idrees Sulieman, and bassist Ahmed Abdul-Malik. Blakey had converted to Islam and adopted the name Abdullah Ibn Buhaina or "Bu," and many of the 17 Messengers were Muslims. Sonny was not a part of that group, but he did visit Blakey at his apartment in Harlem.[91] Consistent with the ethos that would drive the Jazz Messengers, Blakey regularly welcomed new up-and-comers to 117th Street and Lenox Avenue.[92] "Art was serious when he needed to be, frivolous when the situation called for it," Sonny recalled. "We were down there one night to hang out, and there happened to be a flood in his apartment building. The rats from the basement were coming up and trying to get into Art's bathroom. So everybody took turns with a baseball bat going into the bathroom trying to knock these rats back down to the basement.... Like a carnival game, except it was real!"[93]

The lessons Sonny absorbed from these giants were complemented by on-the-job training. Sonny began going to rehearsals with George Hall and His Hotel Taft Orchestra, so named for their long tenure at the hotel's Grill Room at Fifty-First Street. Critic George T. Simon once claimed the band was "about as musical as a submerged submarine," but Sonny was "trying to get big band experience," he said.[94] The band was mostly white, but integrated; trombonist Ferdinand Lewis Alcindor Sr., Kareem Abdul-Jabbar's father, also played with them.[95]

Everything Sonny learned was road-tested in the jam sessions. "It was more about the music than about becoming a household name—especially the type of music that was making the break from swing," Sonny said. "The guys that were doing that felt marginalized anyway, so they had a community and it was a very close-knit community." There was the Heat Wave, where Sonny saw saxophonist Lucky Thompson.[96] There were the Blue Monday jam sessions at Smalls Paradise, an expansive basement club, its singing waitstaff on roller skates. For $1.25 at the door they would participate in impresario Johnny Jackson's sessions with guest artists including Leo Parker, Serge Chaloff, Duke Jordan, Conte Candoli, Flip Phillips, and Art Blakey. Eventually, they went to the Paradise Club, where tenor saxophonist George Walker "Big Nick" Nicholas held court.[97]

Sometimes they would go to Brooklyn. There were the Monday sessions at the Putnam Central Club.[98] There were the Friday sessions in Bedford-Stuyvesant at the Chess Club, a place run by Fred Brathwaite Sr., a close friend of Max Roach and the father of Fab 5 Freddy.[99] "In those days Max Roach was like the Godfather of Brooklyn," recalled Jackie McLean. There, they met Roach, Duke Jordan, saxophonists Ernie Henry and Cecil Payne, bassist Michael Mattos, drummer Willie Jones, Randy Weston, and Kenny Dorham, who had recently moved to the Hill with his family and started hanging out with Sonny and the band.[100] Kenny was short for McKinley; Sonny knew him as "Kinney," and they were "really tight."[101]

"Sonny would come with us, and everybody would be really excited, because wherever he played he dominated. It was incredible," said McLean.[102]

Though sessions were technically informal, they dressed to slay. Sonny usually wore an Ivy League suit and tie with a marcel hairdo. He sometimes pegged his pants in the style of the zoot-suiters. The conk or marcel hairstyle, which called for kinky hair to be straightened with lye, was popular at the time. "I used to go to a cat over on 145th Street near Broadway, a cat named Duke," Sonny recalled. "He used to marcel over there. And then there was a guy who used to do Ray Robinson's hair right down the street here."[103]

Finally, Sonny felt he was ready for the legendary jam sessions at Minton's Playhouse, where bop's foundations were laid; it was still going strong. The club was run by saxophonist Teddy Hill and located on the ground floor of the Cecil Hotel, where musicians sometimes stayed. The sessions took place on Mondays, when Fifty-Second Street was dark, so it attracted top talent.[104] Bird may not have been a presence there anymore, but his spirit persisted, and players like Gilly Coggins, trumpeter Idrees Sulieman, and tenor saxophonist Eddie "Lockjaw" Davis kept it alive. "That was church, man," recalled Sheila Jordan of the after-hours jams at Minton's. "You got out, it was daylight."[105]

Minton's was a no-frills kind of place; a beer was 50 cents, and top-shelf liquor was $1.50.[106] It held about seventy-five people: bar in front, bandstand and tables in back.[107] Sonny had a vivid memory of the brightly colored mural, depicting Charlie Christian, clarinetist Tony Scott, trumpeter Hot Lips Page, and an unknown drummer huddled together in hot pursuit of the new sound as Billie Holiday lies facedown in a brass bed, wearing a sultry red dress and nursing a hangover.[108] Painted in 1948, it was still relatively new when Sonny got there. "There used to be a white cat that played clarinet named Tony Scott, and I remember that he was running the sessions there,"

Sonny said.[109] It was a cutthroat scene, and weak players might call a familiar tune only to be weeded out when the band played it in an unfamiliar key. "If you were playing a gig and weren't cutting it," Sonny recalled, "they might leave you alone on the bandstand."[110]

Between the jazz aficionados mixed in with the tap dancers, hustlers, and pimps, Sonny never knew who was listening.[111] One night in the fall of 1948, a promoter in the audience approached him. "You want to come up to play intermission at this club up in the Bronx?"[112] He was referring to the Club 845, which opened in 1945 in the Morrisania section.[113] It had a semicircular bar, plastic-covered seats, and an elevated stage.[114] At the 845, Johnny Jackson, who also ran the sessions at Smalls, hosted a "Matinee Jam Session" on Sundays from four to nine for $1.50 at the door. "Miles Davis would be there, Eddie 'Lockjaw' Davis, Dexter Gordon, Bud Powell," Sonny said. "The big boys were there." And Sonny was hired to play during their set breaks.[115]

For Sonny's gig at the 845, he brought a trio.[116] On this particular Sunday, twenty-two-year-old Miles Davis happened to be on the bill. "We played intermission, and Miles was one of the stars...with the main group, and Miles heard me playing, and said...'Sonny, I want you to join my band.'...I said, 'Yeah, of course.'"[117]

There was another reason the gig at Club 845 was memorable. "I'll never forget that night, because I never got paid for that job," Sonny said. "The guy ran out without paying me my money. Of course, it turned out great because I had a chance to meet Miles."[118]

Sonny and Lowell Lewis dug Miles from the moment they heard him solo on Parker's "Billie's Bounce." Miles could play fast, though not as fast as Parker, and, perhaps partially in response to the speed of Bird and Diz, emphasized lyricism over virtuosity. "I thought it was very interesting that Miles Davis played a slightly different role than the great Dizzy Gillespie," Sonny said. "Whereas Dizzy Gillespie and Charlie Parker were sort of doing the same in a sense...Miles came up with a contrasting way of playing."[119]

It was more a deliberate stylistic choice than a response to creative limitation. "I heard Miles Davis and Fats Navarro get into it one night at Birdland, and boy, I'm telling you, Miles was playing like Fats," Sonny recalled. "They played some high note passages and everything. Fats's articulation was like a machine gun playing. It was marvelous to behold....A lot of people liked Fats better than anybody."[120] Miles could never beat Fats at his own game, so he changed the rules.

Sonny idolized Miles. "He was a god," Sonny said, "but he was only four years older than I, which is why I think my relationship with him was more like one of a peer."[121]

Sonny kept an undated draft of a letter that underscores the life of extreme highs and lows they were living.[122] Sonny supported his friends who tried to kick the habit, even if he did not intend to himself at the time. The drug threatened to eclipse the music, but for Sonny, it never would.

Dear Don,

I heard that you were in town. Instead of you getting in touch with me you and Normy didn't even come by. Whether or not you had any stuff or not you could have dropped by and said hello. Speaking of stuff I wanted Norm to cop for me that night because my connection had been busted and he froze after I had did him a good turn like that not more than a week before. Good luck to you in your kicking. Hoping to see you soon.

Sonny Rollins[123]

Written on music manuscript paper, on one side was the letter, on the other a handwritten lead sheet for "Darn That Dream."[124]

"We both went through bad times," said Jimmy Heath of Sonny, whom he met during this period. "We got through it...and that's a gift from God, because a lot of our friends died...early."[125]

Some would not make it to the other side of the scourge. Others, like Lowell Lewis and Andy Kirk Jr., barely survived, but lost their music careers in the process.[126] Far on the other side, four decades later in 1993, Heath would arrange "Darn That Dream" for Sonny's *Old Flames*, and they would perform it at Carnegie Hall. But they would go through hell to get there.

Chapter 8

PROFESSOR BOP

(1948–1949)

When Sonny registered with the Selective Service two weeks after his eigh-teenth birthday, he was still living at home.[1] He was six feet tall, soon to be six-foot-one, 180 pounds, and fit, but he would do whatever he could to avoid the draft. "I had to go down to Whitehall Street to be examined for the Army," Sonny recalled. "I was already profoundly alienated from American society, to the extent that I did not want to go. We put pinpricks in our arms so we could say that we were drug addicts and be exempted. I guess the ordinary American kid was glad to fight in World War Two. But I was so alienated that I did not want to fight for this country."[2]

On his Selective Service form, he listed his occupation as "Musician" but claimed he was "unemployed." Soon, though, that would change. Sonny was still booking twelve-dollar cocktail sips and small clubs with the Counts of Bop. In November 1948, he was backing crooner Carl Van Moon with Kenny Drew and Arthur Phipps at Tondaleyo's Melody Room, which had just opened above Bowman's earlier that fall, billed as "Sonny Rawlings" with "the latest progressive jazz and bebop."[3] He learned to project while work-ing with rhythm-and-blues groups: guitarist Jimmy "Baby Face" Lewis and trumpeter, vocalist, and bandleader Milton Larkin, who came from Houston and helped codify the "Texas tenor" sound. Yet some of Sonny's gigs could hardly have been more wholesome. On Monday, December 27, 1948, he per-formed at the Audubon Ballroom with "John Stoney's Big Band featuring Sonny Rollins" at a function billed as a "Yule-Tide Frolic," where frolickers danced the applejack and the bop.[4]

Gradually, they started getting called to go on the road. "I think Kenny Drew was the first guy that began playing with other people that were really traveling," Sonny recalled. "We were getting picked off by the older musi-cians who began recruiting us."[5]

One of the first to hire Sonny was Roy Haynes, who used him on a Sunday-afternoon dance gig at the Audubon Ballroom with Kenny Dorham.[6] Then Art Blakey began using him in pianoless trio gigs with bassist Curly Russell at Birdland.[7] Sonny would don a white dress coat, but he had no compunction about breaking a sweat. Pianist Paul Bley was at the Open Door in the Village for one of these pianoless trio gigs when Sonny and Blakey got into a game of one-upmanship. "Blakey's forte," Bley recalled, "was playing thirty choruses, each one louder than the next. Rollins knew this and started climbing slowly with Blakey until they got to the top of Art's volume. Then Sonny climbed about twenty more choruses volume-wise."[8]

The older musician who gave Sonny his first taste of the road, though, was Babs Gonzales.[9] Babs was only twenty-nine when they met, but he had a lifetime of experience. He was a hip-hop forefather, small-time hustler, onetime drug pusher, and the self-proclaimed "Creator of the Be-Bop Language."[10] Later on, when Babs self-published *Movin' on Down de Line*, one of his two memoirs, he reserved what may have been his highest praise for Sonny: "He's cool."[11]

"Babs heard about me through the grapevine—well here's this young guy that really sounds good," Sonny later recalled. "So he approached *me*, actually."[12]

Gonzales took a syncopated path before he wandered into Goof Square. Born Lee Brown, he grew up in Newark, where he graduated salutatorian of his class at the famed Newark Arts High School, where Ike Quebec, Sarah Vaughan, and Wayne Shorter got their start.[13] He could also play piano and drums, but ultimately settled on the voice as his instrument of choice—as much wordsmith as tunesmith.[14] He was a little guy with a loud voice and even coined his own term to describe himself: *expubident*.[15] Babs had made it by age twenty, when, in 1939, he formed a sextet with Dizzy Gillespie and Don Byas. In 1941, he did a six-month stint with Charlie Barnet. While on the road with Barnet, Babs changed his name to Ricardo Gonzales and quickly picked up enough Spanish to pass.[16] After his hustle got him in trouble with a Harlem gang, Babs bought a one-way ticket to Hollywood. He bought a turban and went by the name Ram Singh, figuring correctly that he would face less discrimination. After stints as a wardrobe attendant at a Beverly Hills country club and as Errol Flynn's chauffeur, in 1943, he organized a vocal group in Los Angeles with Nadine Cole, Nat's first wife, and composed the hit "Oop-Pop-a-Da."[17] Before leaving Hollywood, Babs claimed, Ava Gardner replaced their signature tam berets with four novelty hats that she had crocheted herself.[18]

Originally in the mold of Billy Eckstine, Babs soon sought to translate the lightning-fast, chromatic language of bebop into vocals. He was one of the first practitioners of what would later be known as vocalese—putting lyrics to complex musical phrases. The style built on the nonsense syllables of Leo "Scat" Watson's Spirits of Rhythm and Slim Gaillard, but it was Babs who really codified bebop vocals and slang.[19] In 1945, he opened at Minton's with his new group, Three Bips and a Bop, conceived as "a vocal bridge to the people."[20] A four-week gig turned into nearly a year. Despite the fact that there was still "no bread" in bop, Babs successfully built a reputation as a bop iconoclast; the Bips were even invited to perform at Carnegie Hall.[21]

To the bebop scene, "Babs was like a Walter Winchell; he was a news reporter about music," said saxophonist Lou Donaldson. "He knew everything about musicians—where they played, where they came from...their girlfriends. Anything you wanted to know, he could tell you."[22] Via his Expubidence Publishing Co., he printed and self-distributed his *Be-Bop Dictionary and History of Its Famous Stars*, known to some as the jive "boptionary," a slang lexicon in the tradition of Cab Calloway's *Hepster's Dictionary* (1938) and Gaillard's *Vout-o-Reenee Dictionary* (1946). Unlike Sonny's heroes, Babs did not hesitate to define bop: "Hundreds of people have asked me to define Be-Bop. The only answer your author has is, 'Be-Bop is symphony with a modern beat.'"[23] Yet like many of his peers, Babs preferred the term *progressive music*. In a 1949 editorial, he opined that "bop has been a dominating factor toward racial harmony, not only among musicians and show-people, but also among the general following. Therefore, a lot of biased critics and writers have always panned it."[24]

Gonzales was always living large or flat broke, but from Babs, Sonny got his first up-close lesson in controlling his own business. Even though some claimed that Babs's business practices were at best shady, he called for more financial literacy so artists could liberate themselves from exploitative industry practices.[25] He was litigious when record labels ripped him off, and he had an effective line for club owners who didn't pay up: "Get my bread or I take your head."[26] When Sonny met him in 1949, Gonzales claimed his ambition was to bring up the next generation by imparting his "knowledge of what's really happening so they can be prepared to pay their dues."[27]

He didn't have to look hard to find Sonny: Babs lived within spitting distance of Goof Square, at the Douglas Hotel.[28] Furthermore, Babs had already used Sonny's older friends Arthur Phipps and Roy Haynes on record dates, so one way or another, he would have come across Sonny. Sonny recalled the Douglas as a "show-business hotel."[29] It accommodated "transient, single or couple By Day or Week." Babs fit into all of those categories, depending on the time of day. Charlie Parker stayed with him once, and walked off with a few of his suits, but Bird always paid him back.[30]

Almost immediately, the association with Babs led to Sonny's recording debut, which, as it happened, was on a major label.[31] Since the early days of the bebop generation, the art form had gone from an underground movement to the lingua franca of cool, and Capitol Records music director Paul Weston wanted to hop on the bop bandwagon. The transition from swing to bop was complete—what was once perceived as a threat to the status quo was now seen by the establishment as a source of profit. Stan Kenton arranger Pete Rugolo, the label's bop talent scout, signed Babs to a one-year contract in early January 1949, alongside a raft of talent—Lennie Tristano; Miles Davis, who would record the first tracks from *Birth of the Cool*; Tadd Dameron; and vocalist Dave Lambert.[32]

Babs asked Sonny to be on his first record for Capitol, with horn arrangements by J. J. Johnson. "I wanted to try something different so I went into rehearsal with a nine-piece group," Babs wrote. In addition to Johnson, he hired trombonist Bennie Green, pianist Linton Garner (Erroll's brother), drummer Jack "the Bear" Parker, bassist Arthur Phipps, saxophonist Art Pepper (under the pseudonym Jordan Fordin), and "a new cat from on my block uptown, 'Sonny Rollins' on tenor. While rehearsing, one day a cat with a 'French Horn' named 'Julius Watkins' came by so I eased him in too. (Why not?)"[33]

On January 20, 1949, at the age of eighteen, Sonny made his recording debut. They recorded two sides: "Capitolizing," an onomatopoeic tune full of "boopareenees," signifying on the mutual capitalizing between Babs and Capitol, with the label of course taking the lion's share of the profits, and "Professor Bop," a humorous vocalese paean to the rise of bop.

The record's personnel list used Babs's bop slang, listing the trombones as "Bones," Linton Garner's guitar as "Box," and Jack "the Bear" on "Tubs."

The two songs have the two most common chord progressions in bebop. "Professor Bop" is an altered rhythm changes, a common thirty-two-bar song form based on Gershwin's "I Got Rhythm."[34] Babs gave Sonny only sixteen bars for his solo—half a chorus—splitting the rest of the solo time with Bennie Green, Johnson, and Watkins, though Sonny made it count, playing with a rhythmic flair and creating a cohesive lyrical statement. "Capitolizing" is an up-tempo twelve-bar blues, with a melody or "head" emphasizing the tritone or "devil's interval."[35] Sonny played two choruses, with Babs singing background vocals on the second. Sonny's sound was big and resonant like Hawkins, if not as polished as it would later become. Bird's influence was clear, especially in the phrasing and harmonic language, but Sonny managed to hold his own opposite the track's other soloists, Johnson and Watkins.

On both solos, Sonny had under a half minute to get in and get out; this required an economy of language and a grace under pressure while improvising. In order to play long later in his career, he first had to learn to play short.[36] Babs singing syncopated scat backgrounds under his thirty-second solo would be enough to ruffle the feathers of most eighteen-year-olds. But Sonny kept his cool.

The record got favorable reviews. "*Capitolizing* is Babs at his best," read the May 1949 *Metronome* appraisal.[37] Sonny was not happy with his performance, though, beginning a lifelong tendency toward the harshest self-criticism. "It sounded very derivative," Sonny later said of his solo work. "It was very much in Charlie Parker's bag. It was sort of, 'Hey, who's that? Wait a minute, is that me?'"[38]

With his star on the rise after his Capitol debut, Babs played a show at New York's Town Hall and appeared on television on Perry Como's *Chesterfield Supper Club*. When a certain "great impresario" approached him to ask about joining a tour—most likely Norman Granz's Jazz at the Philharmonic—Babs "told him 'coloredly' what to do with his gig," after "he had 'drug' me like I was 'dirt' a year earlier."[39] This was to Sonny's benefit; if Babs had joined the tour, Sonny would have missed out on a whole series of gigs.

Instead, Babs cut out the middleman and organized his own tours.[40] After getting a settlement from RCA-Victor for a protracted copyright infringement lawsuit over "Oop-Pop-a-Da," Babs was left with $2,700 and bought a Ford. He began renting concert halls in Connecticut or New Jersey "for thirty or forty dollars," he recalled, and hired someone to advertise the show for a 10 percent cut. He would then assemble a quintet in New York, cram them all into his car, and play for two consecutive weekends.[41]

Though Sonny was uncowed by established musicians like Dexter Gordon and Fats Navarro, whom Gonzales also hired, he considered it a learning opportunity. Navarro "had so much command, and his technique...was so outstanding."[42]

Fats Navarro was born in Key West and came up in territory bands along with stints with Billy Eckstine and Andy Kirk, where he was in the trumpet section with future collaborator Howard McGhee.[43] Fats was *the* influence on a young trumpeter neither he nor Sonny had yet met: Clifford Brown. By the time he was squeezing into Babs's Ford, Navarro had performed and recorded with some of Sonny's idols: Coleman Hawkins, Eddie "Lockjaw" Davis, Illinois Jacquet, and Dexter Gordon. He was known as Fats, Fat Boy, or Fat Girl, due to his waistline and high voice, though he had already begun to dissipate due to his heroin addiction.[44]

On April 27, 1949, Sonny was back in the studio on another Gonzales date for Capitol, with Wynton Kelly, Bruce Lawrence, and Roy Haynes in the rhythm section. The front line was J. J. Johnson, flautist Alberto Socarrás, violinist Ray Nance, Babs on vocals, and bandleader Don Redman on soprano saxophone. "The great Don Redman—that was something, to cross that historical line," Sonny said.[45] The group recorded "Real Crazy," "Then You'll Be Boppin' Too," "St. Louis Blues," and "When Lovers They Lose," an original Gonzales ballad. Sonny plays brief solos on all but the ballad, with Haynes goosing him with his signature "Snap Crackle" sound. On "You'll Be Boppin'," Babs sets up Sonny's solo with an ensemble quote of the melody to "Flying Home," but just as Jacquet did when he played the famous solo, Sonny goes for himself.[46]

Sonny's brief turn on wax sent a ripple through a small but vocal subculture. The ears of Ira Gitler, a young jazz fan, critic, and soon-to-be record producer, pricked up. "His reputation actually predates that first studio visit," Gitler wrote. "It began in his Harlem neighborhood and filtered down to midtown jazz circles. Other musicians began to talk about him and so did the kind of listeners who seemed to be on all the scenes in those days. They mentioned his name with the kind of implied message that said 'something's happening' without actually spelling it out."[47]

Savoy producer Teddy Reig also took note of Sonny. Reig was thirty, a Harlem-born, Brooklyn-bred freelance jazz producer, promoter, and full-time hustler with an ear for bop.[48] He was a snappy dresser who looked sort of like a Jewish Fats Waller and was "tall in the belt," in his own euphemism.[49] He covered the scene in Manhattan and Brooklyn and knew every scheme in the book, but regardless of his methods, he made good records. And according to a future colleague, Teddy was "crazy about Sonny Rollins."[50]

On May 11, 1949, Reig was at Harry Smith Studios by Times Square recording J. J. Johnson's Boppers,[51] with pianist John Lewis (fresh off of arranging Miles Davis's *Birth of the Cool* sessions), bassist Gene Ramey, drummer Shadow Wilson, and Sonny. Less than a year earlier, Bird had recorded "Parker's Mood" in the same studio. Johnson had developed the virtuosic technique to translate Charlie Parker's harmonic language, as well as the streams of eighth notes and double-time lines, to the trombone. It was near impossible with a slide instrument, but Johnson could make the trombone sound the way crushed velvet felt.[52]

The saxophone was better suited to what would one day be called "sheets of sound," but the trombone was closer to human speech. Johnson could do both, with style.[53] Johnson strove to bring the lyricism of Lester Young to the trombone, he said. A Pres solo "started someplace, it went someplace, and it ended someplace; and all of the places that it started and went were wonderful and articulate...it's like speech...placing, using, and choosing the right words to go with other words." To Sonny, Pres "would be more of a guy who was singing than speech," he later said. "In a sense, I play in a speech-like way." If Sonny was a speech-like player, would a solo replicate verbal repartee on the stand? "No, it would not," Sonny explained. "If anything, it would come the other way around."[54]

Whereas Johnson brought a peerless fluidity to his articulation on an instrument prone to choppy phraseology, it was more natural for saxophonists to slur their "words." Sonny, on the other hand, imposed an artificial impediment, forcing himself to tongue almost every note, even at great speed, bringing a crisp, trombone-like articulation to the saxophone.[55] Critics used to the prevailing legato tenor style of Georgie Auld or Stan Getz would describe Sonny's clipped notes and "tendency to reed squeaks" as "undistinguished" or "poor,"[56] but it was in reality a distinctive and technically challenging rhythmic vocabulary still early in its development. Like a trombonist, who needed the deliberate intentionality to coordinate slide and embouchure to "speak," Sonny's syncopated runs were not just in his fingers, which in lesser players had a way of getting ahead of the mind's ear as they flew up and down the body of the saxophone—he too was speaking. His elusive style of phrasing, impossible to transcribe with any degree of rhythmic accuracy,[57] was akin to moving from the undifferentiated wail of vowel soup to a soliloquy of fricatives and glottal stops. This propensity for a speech-like style is in part why throughout Sonny's career, so many of his interlocutors were brass players—and J. J. Johnson was one of the first.[58]

"Sonny Rollins was a very outgoing, fun person," Johnson recalled. "Sonny had his own way of playing, his own style of playing that really caught our fancy, and it was just great just to be involved in his…bursting onto the scene. And burst onto the scene he did."[59]

Johnson gave Sonny the opportunity to record his first compositions. Of the four tunes they recorded, two were Sonny's. "Audubon" takes its name from the Audubon Ballroom, and perhaps Audubon the ornithologist in a sly reference to Bird.[60] The other was a blues: "Goof Square." Also on the session were Johnson's "Bee Jay," another twelve-bar blues, and Jimmy McHugh and Dorothy Fields's "Don't Blame Me," taken as a medium-ballad trombone feature.

Though this was the first recorded evidence of Sonny the composer, he had already been writing for years. "Everything is really about setting things up for me to improvise on," Sonny said. "I loved melody, so I always had melodies in my mind."[61]

On "Aubudon," Sonny took just one chorus; the other tunes had shorter forms, so he took three choruses each on "Bee Jay" and "Goof Square." His harmonic vocabulary is still mostly in the Bird mold, but his sound is eminently Sonny Rollins. The Johnson quintet recorded multiple takes that day, of which two survive for "Audubon," three for "Goof Square," and two for "Bee Jay." The consummate improviser even then, Sonny hardly repeats himself in each take.

Multiple takes were not unusual for Savoy. "You may notice that there were a lot of good extra takes from the Savoy sessions. That was Mr. Lubinsky being cute," Reig said of Herman Lubinsky, the founder of Savoy.[62] "He knew he could eventually cash in on all those takes he didn't pay for. That's why he would often tell us, 'I don't like that, let's do something else.' As the years went by, he accumulated extra tunes. He was a shrewdy." Reig later elaborated: Lubinsky was a "*gonif* and without a doubt the cheapest bastard on the planet."[63]

Two weeks later, on May 26, 1949, Sonny returned to the studio with Johnson's Boppers, this time for a session produced by another early fan of Sonny's, Bob Weinstock.[64] The tyro producer was a larger-than-life eccentric—in his waistline, his thick New Yorkese, and his passion for the jazz business. He grew up in a Jewish family on the Upper West Side, the son of a shoe salesman.[65] His father and uncle, who sold chemicals to the film industry, supported his passion for jazz, and when he was still a teenager, Weinstock started selling records out of his parents' apartment by placing ads in *Record Changer* magazine.[66] In January 1949, when he was only twenty, Weinstock branched out into producing records, recording the Lennie Tristano Quintet and selling 78s for seventy-nine cents under his fledgling New Jazz label, a precursor to Prestige.[67]

For the May 26 session, Johnson expanded his quintet to a sextet, with Kenny Dorham on trumpet, John Lewis on piano, Leonard Gaskin on bass, and Max Roach on drums. "I met Max, but I wasn't hanging out or anything with Max, because I was just a new kid on the block," Sonny recalled. "It was just great to meet him....I just made a record with him, but...he was way above my pay grade."[68]

They recorded four tunes: "Elysees," "Opus V," "Fox Hunt," and Sonny's composition "Hilo," another twelve-bar blues.[69] The 78 with "Hilo" and "Opus V" marked Sonny's first substantive mention in *Down Beat*, but it was damningly indifferent. "Six well-known boppers play two middling good sides," read the review in the September 9, 1949, issue. "Tenor man Rollins, credited with scoring *Hilo*, solos to no great effect, while Kenny Dorham's trumpet solo, as always, starts out well, ends up without climax due to the lack of force and authority in his phrasing and attack."[70] It established what would become a pattern of early critical rebuke for Sonny in the pages of jazz's publication of record.

——◇——

As Sonny's career gained momentum, Fifty-Second Street was at the end of a long decline. The Street had gone through a "jazz drought" that began in 1947, and according to an article in *Down Beat*, other than Jimmy Ryan's, one of the only stalwart clubs, "the rest of the joints tossed out the tooters and brought in strippers."[71] Bop City opened in mid-April 1949,[72] but even there, bop was hardly featured.[73] That May, the Royal Roost closed.[74] Attempts to bring bop to the Village stalled. By the end of 1949, the Clique Club would become Birdland, named in honor of Parker and known as the "Jazz Corner of the World," and there bop flourished.[75] There were still plenty of places to play, and a growing audience with a voracious appetite for the music, though still little money to be had.

The Three Deuces reopened on July 14, 1949,[76] and by Tuesday, August 2, Sonny was playing there as part of Leonard Feather's "Tuesday Nite Bop Sessions," where bebop was alive and well.[77] "Believe me when I tell you that when I arrived—at a mere 10:45 p.m.—I couldn't get in myself!" wrote a *New York Age* columnist. "Fortunately, Leonard plowed a way through the mob for me, and though I couldn't possibly get a table, at least I stayed long enough to realize why these affairs are such hits."[78] The reason was self-evident: Sonny, Miles Davis, Buddy DeFranco, Bud Powell, Max Roach, Tommy Potter, John Lewis, and Charlie Parker were all there on the same night.

On August 9, 1949, a week after the Three Deuces session, Sonny had an opportunity to record with Tommy Potter and Bud Powell, for Bud's Blue Note debut. Powell, now twenty-four, had been in and out of Creedmoor, where he was subjected to more electroconvulsive therapy (ECT) treatments. On April 16, 1949, he was discharged as an outpatient, pending continued sobriety and mandatory monthly check-ins at the hospital.[79] However, Powell began using heroin again. He was performing with Fats Navarro, and making brilliant music, but Navarro's heroin addiction had begun to take a serious toll.

At this time, Sonny had one of the more harrowing experiences of his life. Soon after Bud came back on the scene, he and Sonny went to shoot up on the roof of a tenement building. So soon after his most recent hospitalization, Bud had not rebuilt his tolerance for the drug. Yet there they were, "with the needles and all of this paraphernalia," Sonny recalled. "I was younger than Bud, so I was okay, but after Bud took his, he passed out. I ended up cradling his head and trying to get him to revive. My whole life came before me and, God, 'if Bud Powell dies and he and I are together using drugs'—it was just a nightmare scenario." No one was there to help, so Sonny turned to prayer, and "as providence would have it, he came back to consciousness."[80]

So Bud Powell lived to play again and, as fate would have it, to record with Sonny. That July, Alfred Lion and Francis Wolff paid Bud a house visit. Lion and Wolff, whom some musicians called the "Animal Brothers,"[81] though they were unrelated, were German Jews who met at a popular skating rink in Berlin and bonded over their mutual love of jazz. Lion cofounded Blue Note Records with Max Margulis in 1939; Wolff joined them later that year, escaping Nazi Germany. Eventually, saxophonist Ike Quebec, who acted as an informal A&R (artists and repertoire) representative for the label, recommended Thelonious Monk and Bud Powell. In 1947, Blue Note had recorded Monk, and in 1949, they finally got the chance to record Bud.

Bud began teaching Sonny and Jackie McLean the music that would be on the record. There were two tunes recorded with the Be-Bop Boys, a quintet led by Sonny Stitt and Kenny Dorham in 1946, "Bouncing with Bud" by Powell and Gil Fuller, originally known as "Bebop in Pastel," and Powell's "Wail," originally known as "Fool's Fancy."[82] They also rehearsed Powell's "Dance of the Infidels," an altered twelve-bar blues with an intro culled from

Prokofiev's *Love for Three Oranges*, and "52nd Street Theme" by Bud's mentor, Thelonious Monk.

Jackie worked hard to learn the material, but Bud leveled with him. "'Look, Jackie, you won't be on this record date,'" McLean recalled him saying. "'Not this one. You're not quite ready yet, you know?...It's okay.'"[83]

Sonny was excited to record with the other Professor Bop and his sidemen as Bud Powell's Modernists: Fats Navarro, bassist Tommy Potter, and drummer Roy Haynes. "Very fast company," Sonny said. "The top of the line."[84]

Yet it took Alfred Lion time to catch on to bop. "I didn't dig it all the way. I'm sorry, I didn't, and I'm not the only one who didn't," Lion recalled. He was a nonmusician who could never read a note but "went by my ears and by my feeling." In part, it was Monk and Bud Powell who opened his ears to bop. "Ike [Quebec] and I went to see Monk, and when I heard him I keeled over," Lion recalled. "I said, 'That guy's so different. Everything is different—the compositions, the beat.' I loved him, and that's how we started with Monk and bop. Then Bud came up the same way. He was fantastic, and I went for that."[85]

In contrast with other label owners, Lion paid for rehearsal time. "I didn't care about overtime. I didn't care about how much money it cost me. I wanted to get the thing right. So I never rushed them into the studio and rushed them out," he said. "When we went into overtime—which was double for everybody and triple for the leader—forget all this, let's make the records, right? The musicians didn't do it just for the money. They wanted to do it right, too."[86] The money wasn't much; at around this time, union scale for a three-hour session was eighty dollars for the leader and forty dollars per sideman, with any overage going into double time.[87] But the record would sound great.

At one point during the Powell session, Sonny made a mistake he never forgot. "Bud looked over at me...I mean, he really gave me a look," Sonny said. "That was the last time I made that mistake—I played it perfectly after that." But Sonny also inspired Bud. "There was this riff he played in one of his songs, and he said, 'Hey, Sonny, I got that from you—hahaha.'"[88]

The quintet arrived at WOR Studios in Times Square, probably in the wee hours of the morning.[89] "I always liked to record late at night," said Lion. "I never liked to record during the day because I feel better at night, and I know the musicians are more with it at night."[90] As always, Francis Wolff photographed the session. For his Blue Note debut, Sonny dressed to impress; even though only the producers, engineer, and fellow musicians would see him in the studio, he always made sure to look his best for a recording session. He wore black-and-white gingham pants, a black leather belt, a loose-fitting button-down, and a silver wristwatch. Navarro wore a baggy short-sleeve button-down with the first few buttons undone. He'd already begun to lose weight, but you would never know it from the size of his sound. Roy Haynes wore a white fleece shirt and sunglasses. Bud kept it casual in a dark T-shirt and slacks.[91]

With the exception of "52nd Street Theme," of which only one take survives, they recorded at least two takes of the other three tunes. On "Wail," a fast rhythm changes, Sonny was tasked with playing the first solo, leaving him no time to recover after the head, but he played one of his most inspired to date. The arrangement of "52nd Street Theme," another rhythm changes, is taken even faster, but Sonny locks in with Haynes, playing breathless lines of eighth notes. Bud remains the star of the session—sometimes singing in unison as he solos—but Sonny is given a solo spot on every tune. Sonny was speaking the language his own way, not like Bird, Hawkins, Byas, or Pres, but a synthesis that was sui generis—like Sonny.

Other saxophonists on the scene quickly took note. "When I heard Sonny on that record, you know, that was startling, because his rhythmic concept was so strong," said Jimmy Heath. "His rhythmic concept, the way he put his lines together rhythmically, was attractive to everybody that heard it."[92]

Down Beat didn't hear it, though, writing of "Bouncing with Bud"/"Wail," "Both sides are distinguished mainly by the presence of a Mr. Fats Navarro," with not a word about Sonny. *Metronome* was damning with faint praise. "Sonny solos vigorously, Fats and Bud are good," read the review, adding that "Fats' tone is rounder than ever, Sonny's is poor." But the small community of serious jazz fans knew that a new voice had arrived. "In the short span of eight months," wrote Ira Gitler, "Rollins served notice on the jazz world at large that he was an emerging force."[93]

In the summer of '49, Sonny had another opportunity to play in Miles

Davis's band, with Roy Haynes on drums, at the club Soldier Meyers in Brooklyn.[94] Located in Brownsville, the club was run by a Jewish former lightweight boxer, army veteran, and Coney Island concession worker; Soldier Meyers was his boxing name. His son Norby Walters was a jazz buff and convinced him to start presenting bebop. In short order, they presented Thelonious Monk, Stan Getz, Lester Young, and Miles Davis, who decided to recruit someone from the Counts of Bop. Even though many considered Andy Kirk Jr. the strongest player in the group, Miles enlisted Sonny. "All of them used to look up to Andy Kirk Jr.," Miles recalled. "[Illinois] Jacquet said, 'Wait till you hear Andy Kirk Jr.' But I said, 'Newk is enough.'"[95]

Soon, consensus began to emerge that Sonny had eclipsed Kirk. One day that summer, Kirk came to Jackie McLean's house in a state; he had heard Sonny with Miles in Brooklyn the previous night and insisted that McLean go and check it out.[96]

> It was a hot August night, I'll never forget...burning up... humid...hot, you know, coming out of the subway, walking down the street towards the club. And the door of the club was open. And I listened. I said 'Oh, man, Bird is sittin' in with them!' Just listening, you know....I didn't even think of Sonny, because the last time I had heard Sonny he sounded, you know, very much like Coleman Hawkins.... And I got to the door and there Sonny was, man, standing out there in front of the mic, playing....It just turned everybody around.[97]

Sonny's development shook Andy Kirk Jr. to the core. "It drove Andy nuts," McLean said. "Andy just stopped playing and started getting real... like a derelict, you know, not taking care of himself....I just said, 'So, I gotta get into Sonny's band.'"[98]

Playing with Miles gave Sonny an early sense of validation. "Miles was the guy that brought me out of my shell in certain ways," Sonny later said. "I felt that I couldn't really play as well as certain other guys that were big at that time and Miles said 'No man, you can do it. That's why I have you instead of some other guy.'"[99]

Later that year, Sonny connected with another influential trumpeter.

In December 1949, he played a series of shows with thirty-year-old Howard McGhee at the New Chancellor in Utica. Billed as McGhee's All-Star
Boptet, the entire band at the time was part of Sonny's crew: Sonny, Kenny
Drew, Percy Heath, and Arthur Taylor. It was Arthur Taylor's first gig on the
road.[100] McGhee, often stylized Maggie, was once described by *Metronome* as
"the middle-register virtuoso," and was one of the key voices in the early days
of Minton's.[101] McGhee could run changes with the best of them, but he
also had a gentle side. "I used to go all out to excite people, but I believe that
pretty music is just as important," he later said. "I think that music without
beauty ain't sayin' too much."[102]

Utica had a thriving industrial economy and a population of about a hundred thousand, and musicians from Fats Waller to Billie Holiday included it
as a stop on the way to or from New York.[103] When McGhee and the band
arrived at the Hamilton Hotel in Utica, it was so cold that they had to leave
the hot water running to heat the room. There may not have been a bathroom in the hotel room, but there was definitely a sink. "I had to turn the
hot water on. Fortunately, there was hot water, and that hot water provided
the heat, and you can imagine it wasn't much, but it was essential. That's how
cold it was," Sonny said. "I'll never forget that."[104] Sonny learned quickly that
on the road, you had to be prepared for anything.

On the bandstand, though, Maggie brought the heat. The New Chancellor was a supper club on Utica's commercial hub on Bleecker Street and billed
itself as the "Home of Artists," with a jam session every Sunday. Maggie's
Boptet was so well received that they were held over another week.[105] Despite
the cold, there was a silver lining: the Duke Ellington Orchestra was in town,
playing at the Stanley Theatre a few blocks away. "I met a lot of people like
[trumpeter] Al Killian and a lot of . . . musicians I admired," recalled Arthur
Taylor, "never dreaming that I would ever meet them on a social basis."[106]

The gig was exciting to Utica's tight-knit jazz scene. Trumpeter Sal Amico
saved a piece of errant sheet music Sonny left behind and held on to it for
decades.[107] On the front was a tune called "Night Blindness," never recorded;
on the back was a brief sketch of a line that would become Sonny's "Mambo
Bounce," which he would record in 1951.[108]

Shortly after the gig at the New Chancellor in Utica, Maggie was named as the top trumpeter in the 1949 *Down Beat* poll, with Charlie Shavers and Miles Davis taking second and third place.[109] To Sonny, the opportunity to play with Maggie deepened his connection to Charlie Parker and Coleman Hawkins. "He was one of the guys that I looked up to," Sonny said.[110] Years later, Sonny would write the tune "McGhee" as a tribute.[111] And he never forgot the Hamilton Hotel.

Yet just because Sonny was in such illustrious company—Miles Davis, Howard McGhee, Bud Powell—did not mean that he was above playing dance gigs. On December 16, 1949, a social group called the Top Hats presented a dance at the Lincoln Square Center,[112] and Sonny provided the music.[113] The *New York Age* described it as "Sonny Rollins blowin' like mad backed by an excellent array of musicians."[114] We know who they were: the Counts of Bop. Sonny was ready to blow wherever and whenever he had a chance.

Chapter 9

CHICAGO VIA MONTREAL

(1950)

On July 6, 1950, Fats Navarro died.[1] That June, Art Blakey and Percy Heath had driven the twenty-six-year-old trumpeter, once large in girth and amplitude, now gaunt and unconscious, to Bellevue. They sent him over to Metropolitan Hospital on Welfare Island, where he languished until he died a month later.[2] His official cause of death was reported as tuberculosis—the death certificate read "Died of natural causes"—but everyone on the scene knew what truly caused his demise.

"Fats Navarro didn't have to die," read an editorial in *Down Beat*. "Other musicians of his age and talent will not have to die, either—if they cease and desist now. This may sound like Calvinism of the grimmest kind—but most unfortunately is the glaring truth."[3]

Navarro's death sent shockwaves through the scene. He died penniless, so the senior Andy Kirk, one of Fats's early employers and a surrogate father, surreptitiously covered the funeral and burial costs. The funeral was held in Harlem on July 12 at Butler's Funeral Home with the burial the next day at Rose Hill Cemetery in Linden, New Jersey; the funeral procession stopped in front of Birdland.[4] Sonny was there, along with Charlie Parker, Dizzy Gillespie, and Bud Powell. Seeing Navarro's promising career cut short by drugs was too much for Bud to take, it seemed. "We were in the church at his funeral," Sonny said, "and it was all quiet and everybody reading, and Bud jumped up and made a commotion in the proceedings."[5]

To Sonny, it was a tragedy, but Fats's premature death did not cause him to change his habits; he was in too deep to get out without help. "[Fats] got into drugs like a lot of people did and just wasted himself away," Sonny said. "I'm a blessed guy, man, and I know it. I know what playing with Fats Navarro meant."[6]

Yet there were pockets of joy amid the grief. On August 6, 1950, Sonny played at the reception for the wedding of Joseph Knight and Barbara Jones, the older sister of Faith Ringgold, Sonny's childhood crush. Ringgold herself would marry Earl Wallace November 1 that year.[7] Barbara's ceremony at Abyssinian Baptist Church and reception at Bowman's Rainbow Room were lavish; Faith hand-embroidered the veil. Madame Willi Posey, Ringgold's mother and an accomplished fashion designer, designed the gowns for the entire wedding party.[8] At the reception, there was "enough food to feed an army," Ringgold wrote: southern cooking, an eight-tier wedding cake, and a barrel of beer.[9] Sonny provided the music, with Arthur Taylor on drums, Kenny Drew on piano, and Jackie McLean on alto.[10] According to Ringgold, they kept the repertoire conservative and danceable: " 'April in Paris,' 'I'm in the Mood for Love,' 'Moonlight Becomes You,' and some fast tunes like 'Flying Home,' 'A Train,' and 'Tuxedo Junction.' We danced till the last lingering notes of 'Home Sweet Home.' "[11]

That August, Sonny was back on the road with Babs Gonzales, this time in Philadelphia.[12] "I got too big for my pants," Babs wrote. "I let a guy in 'Philly' talk me into bringing down a group of all stars. This guy didn't have any money, but I thought it might work so I invested my last six hundred dollars."[13] Babs got Sonny, tenor saxophonist Wardell Gray, trombonists Bennie Green and J. J. Johnson, and trumpeters Joe Newman and Russell Jacquet, Illinois's brother, packing as many as he could fit into the Ford. Ten days before showtime, Babs drove to Philly to make sure everything was copacetic and discovered that a package tour he referred to as the "Steam-rollers" was booked for the same day.

The competing all-star lineup at Philadelphia's nearly three-thousand-seat Earle Theatre had "Queen of the Jukeboxes" Dinah Washington headlining, the Ravens, Eddie "Cleanhead" Vinson's band, Foxx and White, the comedy duo of Redd Foxx and Slappy White, roller-skating novelty act Harold King, and Arnett Cobb's band. For her twenty-sixth birthday on August 29—the same day as Bird's—Dinah had the Earl Bostic band as special guests.[14]

Lines went out the door at the Earle, and Babs lost his shirt. "We went down and played the job to only one hundred and ten people," Babs wrote. "Dinah came by and laughed her ass off, saying, 'You ought to know better than to buck 'The Queen.' However, she gave me fifty dollars so I could have two hundred to split between the fellows."[15]

Next, Babs was booked in Montreal at the Café St. Michel opposite St. Louis–born trumpeter Louis Metcalf, a club resident since 1946.[16] Located in the Little Burgundy neighborhood, the St. Michel was one of the premier venues in Montreal's robust jazz scene, which boasted at least a dozen clubs presenting live music nightly.[17] According to the Montreal *Gazette*, Café St. Michel was "home of the best in colored entertainment."[18]

For the better part of a decade, Metcalf was a fixture on the scene and hosted a Sunday jam session that prominent Montreal musicians such as Oscar Peterson would attend.[19] Souvenir cards on the club's tables proclaimed Metcalf's band "Canada's greatest jazz band"—they were the first in the city to play bebop—and word had spread among American bop musicians on gigs up north that Café St. Michel was the hippest place to be.[20] Art Pepper, Conte Candoli, and Maynard Ferguson sat in with Metcalf's band, while others would just come by to listen before heading to an after-hours jam session.[21] But Sonny was booked there all night.

Sonny stayed with thirty-two-year-old saxophonist and pianist Harold "Steep" Wade, who grew up in Montreal. Wade worked in Metcalf's band

and would sometimes sub for Oscar Peterson when he couldn't make a gig; several years later, he played with Charlie Parker when he came to Montreal. His technique was not as polished as Peterson's, but his rhythmic and harmonic sensibility made him a distinctive voice on the piano.[22] During his time with Metcalf, Wade, along with drummer Mark "Wilkie" Wilkinson, picked up a debilitating heroin habit, which would eventually end Steep's life in 1953.[23] But in 1950, he was still a vital part of the Montreal bop scene. "Steep's girlfriend was using heavy drugs at that time," Sonny said. "I remember her very well. And Steep might have been himself." Sonny was, too. "Everybody was doing some kind of drugs."[24]

When Babs left Montreal, Sonny stayed "around town looking for work," according to *Down Beat*.[25] But then Sonny caught wind that Metcalf's Texarkana-born bassist Al King and his wife were driving back to Texas in his brand-new '49 Mercury and were passing through Chicago.[26] Sonny snapped up King's offer.

"He had a French white lady with us, and the three of us in the car, driving from Montreal to Chicago. It might have been considered something dangerous to do at the time probably, but, you know, we do foolish things when we're young."[27]

It was a rare sight on the road in 1950. "A black guy, a little white French girl, driving to the United States all the way to Texas.... I wasn't thinking about the racial problematic that would be involved," Sonny said. "I didn't think about that very much. I wanted to go to Chicago."[28] They arrived unscathed. "I do not recall any serious incidents along the way," Sonny said, "just dirty looks and that sort of thing."[29]

Chicago in 1950 was a freewheeling jazz cornucopia, and Sonny was anxious to visit for the first time.[30] In 1938, an eighteen-year-old Charlie Parker made his way to Chicago from Kansas City, so Sonny, who had recently turned twenty, was in a way following in Bird's footsteps. The Windy City had entered a second golden age of jazz. The confluence of Prohibition and the First Great Migration led to the music flourishing at speakeasies like Kelly's Stables on the North Side and the "black and tan" Sunset Café on the South, where Al Capone drank and Earl Hines, Cab Calloway, and Louis Armstrong played all night. The Second Great Migration fueled an industrial economy that spurred the Chicago Black Renaissance. While 52nd Street had become a pale shadow of its former glory, on 63rd Street in Chicago, music went till dawn, then continued right on past it. When Sonny arrived, this was the case at clubs across the city, like the Blue Note, the Rhumboogie, and the DeLisa, which would have a Monday-morning breakfast dance at 5 a.m. after the last show at 4. Chicago was known as a tenor town, with Gene Ammons, Johnny Griffin, Clifford Jordan, Claude McLin, and Eddie Harris on the scene. Sonny fit right in.[31]

"Guys would be playing 24-7, all over town," Sonny recalled of this first visit. "Every place you went, there were jam sessions, venues, guys playing all day, all night."[32]

There was a looser atmosphere, more jam sessions than in New York, though not more money, and drugs were cheaper. "When I got to Chicago, I was using heroin, and...it was an introduction in a way to the jazz scene in Chicago," Sonny said. "A lot of the guys, of course, were using heroin, and so I happened to meet a lot of people."[33]

At the end of 1950, the scene was flush. The Red Norvo Trio with Charles Mingus and Tal Farlow was at the Hi-Hat, the George Shearing Five was at the Blue Note, Buddy Rich was at the Capitol, and the next day Count Basie hit the Brass Rail, where Dave Brubeck, Wardell Gray, Joe Williams, and Benny Carter were supposed to be on one bill.[34] And these were just the musicians passing through. What Sonny initially thought would be a short stay turned into two months.[35]

Chicago had its own homegrown talent. One of the musicians Sonny met who would be important in his life was twenty-four-year-old trumpeter Robert Gay, known in Chicago as Little Diz.[36] "His name speaks for itself; he sounded exactly like Dizzy," recalled Chicago pianist Junior Mance. Little Diz actually met his namesake in New York after moving there in 1945 with composer George Russell and alto saxophonist Henry Pryor, but by 1950 he was back in his hometown.[37] Gay and Sonny were both the black sheep of their families: jazz-loving sons who got involved with drugs. Gay came from a family of gospel singers known professionally as the Gay Sisters, along with their child-prodigy brother, who at four years old was known as Preacher Donald Gay. When Sonny met Little Diz, the Gay Sisters were performing at Carnegie

Hall opposite Mahalia Jackson and Clara Ward and had just signed with Apollo Records.[38] Sonny would meet the whole family eventually, but not on this trip.

Another influential Chicago musician Sonny met at this time was drummer Ike Day, who was also four years older.[39] "I played with Ike, who was also strung out," Sonny said.[40] Amid the frigid Chicago winter, Sonny and Ike had a gig together on the North Side. Day was a local legend. He was about five-foot-four, weighed scarcely more than a hundred pounds, and had a serious heroin habit, but when he sat down at the drums, he had the power and speed of the Chicago L.[41] In one of the few photos of Day, Max Roach and Kenny Dorham can be seen standing dumbfounded over Day's drums at the after-hours Macomba Lounge, where "he was so bad on the drums that he set up two drums," according to Johnny Griffin, "and then any other drummer could come and sit in." Buddy Rich tried, but nobody could outplay Ike Day.[42] "He could come around with just a snare, a sock cymbal [hi-hat] and a ride cymbal," recalled drummer Steve McCall. "You'd never miss the bass drum. He'd play on a radiator or the wall and it wouldn't seem a gimmick." It wasn't; he never owned a full drum set. Papa Jo Jones, who was one of the greatest drummers who ever lived, said that Day was "one of the greatest drummers who ever lived."[43] Max Roach called him "just a terror."[44] Art Blakey said he sounded "like nothing you've ever heard."[45] And outside of Chicago, no one ever heard him. His sole recordings with Chicago tenor saxophonists Tom Archia and Gene Ammons were not miked properly, and the drums are mostly inaudible. Day had offers to leave the city from bands passing through, but he always turned them down.[46]

Day seamlessly blended polyrhythmic counterpoint with hard-driving swing, typified the art of the perfectly placed snare fill, and we know from his few surviving recordings, always got the last word. "It's hard really to remember what he was doing compared to the drummers today," Sonny said. "Art [Blakey] and Max Roach used to come by and hear him, and I can hear a lot of Ike's music in their playing."[47] And, we can surmise, Ike's music became a part of Sonny's.

Ike "was a nice guy," Sonny said. "He wanted to get off of drugs, and he was on drugs, as we all were as a matter of fact, and he wanted to, you know, get himself straight, and he wrote me a letter…when I came back to New

York...that was what he tried to do. Of course, it never happened."[48] Day would not survive the '50s.

Ike shaped Sonny's rhythmic sensibility, but Sonny also credits him for cultivating more unusual repertoire. "We were playing the repertoire of the day," Sonny said, "some of the Parker things and some older. It was Ike who got me interested in playing songs that were a bit before my time, like old Duke Ellington arrangements." Day's four years on Sonny gave him "familiarity with the Lunceford things, the older jazz arrangements. He used to berate me for not knowing them, so I had to bone up."[49]

According to Arthur Taylor, their gig on the North Side was in a trio[50] with Day and pianist Vernon Biddle, who had toured Paris in 1948 with Howard McGhee.[51] Taylor was in Chicago on tour with bassist-turned-cellist Oscar Pettiford, and seeing Ike Day perform with his old friend was a wake-up call.[52] "When I heard him, I had to revamp my thinking. I thought about giving up music right then and there," Taylor said. "He sounded like Buddy Rich, Tony Williams, Art Blakey, Max Roach, and Kenny Clarke, and all of them rolled into one. I'm telling you, I never heard anything like that in the history of music. In my experience I never heard anyone play that much drums."[53]

Other musicians would stop by the gig, Sonny said, such as bassist Wilbur Ware and trumpeter Danny Blue, formerly of the Georgie Auld Orchestra.[54] "Wilbur was in the club. He might have played with us, just sat in on the bandstand, you know, but I met Wilbur when I was in Chicago at that time, for sure."[55] Seven years later, they would record *A Night at the Village Vanguard* together.

Sonny had other gigs during that two-month stay. On November 11, he was at the Rhumboogie for "Façade," a concert presented by Chicago disc jockey Norm Spaulding, with Sonny, bass trumpeter Cy Touff, pianist John Young, drummer Tiny Kahn, and pianist Lou Levy. The Jimmy Payne Dance Group interpreted the music.[56] The performance was "an unprecedented appearance of Modern Dance and Jazz in a simultaneous presentation," according to the *Chicago Defender*. "The Jimmy Payne dancers have worked in every medium of dance, but their interpretation of modern rhythms has been foremost. They appear ideal in a concert with Sonny Rollins."[57]

And then there were the jam sessions. Every Saturday afternoon, jazz impresario Joe Segal began hosting sessions at Seymour's Record Mart, a record store in the Loop abutting the campus of Roosevelt College.[58] The at-capacity sessions were held on the second floor, eighty in the audience; admission was a dollar, the proceeds going to the musicians. Each week alternated between Dixieland and bop. The store's owner, trumpeter Seymour Schwartz, hosted the trad days; Segal hosted the bop.[59] At the latter, some of the players from "Façade" were regulars: John Young and Cy Touff, as well as vibraphonist Hal Russell and on at least one occasion, preserved on record, Sonny—on alto.[60] "I'd have all the modern guys up there," Segal recalled. "People like Al Cohn came up, [drummer] Tiny Kahn, even Sonny Rollins when he was hangin' out here in town, playing an alto." As for the alto, despite Chicago being a tenor town, "That's all he had then," Segal said. "I don't have a recording of it but I was there, I remember."[61]

Yet a recording does exist. It's hard to make out the rhythm section, though a bass, drum, and piano are present. Sonny takes a two-bar solo break, then blows for three choruses on a thirty-two-bar form. It's ninety-six measures of Sonny, weaving in and out of the chords with bop chromaticism, going into double time, and sounding more like Charlie Parker and less like Sonny than he ever would again.[62]

During this time, Sonny rented a room at the South Central Hotel in Bronzeville just north of Washington Park, where musicians often stayed.[63] Arthur Taylor was staying there with Oscar Pettiford's band. Then on November 17, the Dizzy Gillespie sextet started a three-week gig at the Silhouette.[64] It was Gillespie, Jimmy Heath (who still played alto and was known as Little Bird), bassist Percy Heath, vibraphonist Milt Jackson, drummer Charles "Specs" Wright, and a player Sonny had never met or heard of, a twenty-four-year-old North Carolina–born tenor saxophonist who came of age in Philadelphia named John Coltrane.[65]

"I knew Jimmy," Sonny recalled, but "I don't remember meeting Coltrane before that."[66] It's tantalizing to speculate that Sonny and Coltrane played at a Chicago breakfast jam at this time, but Sonny has no memory of hearing him play, and it's unlikely that Coltrane, always laconic offstage, made a strong impression, not until later at least. Innocuous as it may have been, the South Central Hotel on the South Side of Chicago in the fall of 1950 is almost definitely where Sonny met Trane.

Sonny had one more significant performance during his stay in Chicago. On December 21, Billie Holiday debuted opposite Miles Davis at the Hi-Note on the North Side, and Sonny was in Miles's band. Lady Day had been all over the news not long before, when she was on tour at the Longbar Showboat and Breakfast Club in San Francisco and her $5,000 royal-blue Lincoln Cosmopolitan was impounded after her chauffeur was arrested for narcotics possession. After a spell in the hospital, Holiday got booked into the Hi-Note, but the managers reportedly hired a "singer sitter" to make sure she showed up.[67] Miles had also made headlines recently, when he was arrested in Los Angeles that September for narcotics possession. At the trial in November, he was acquitted with a ten-to-two vote, but the whole debacle had already done irreparable damage to his reputation; until then, he had been known for clean living.[68]

The negative press didn't stop the Hi-Note from presenting two notorious stars on one bill.[69] The club was prepared for at-capacity crowds, removing half of the bar and clearing most of the tables to make room.[70] Not even the subzero temperatures—fifteen below—could stop people from packing the Hi-Note, among them Anita O'Day, who preceded them at the club.[71] Miles enlisted a local band led by tenor saxophonist Claude McLin.[72] Every night after they got paid, Miles and several of his bandmates would buy as much heroin as they could afford, at a dollar a cap. With Miles's seventy-five-dollar weekly allowance from his father, even after covering the bill for a nice hotel, he could afford a lot.[73]

Despite the potential complications, the gig was a huge success.[74] Though temperatures continued to hover in the negative double digits, Sonny couldn't resist making the trek to the North Side. "I remember I played opposite Billie Holiday with Miles one time," Sonny said. "That's what I remember. I was so messed up on drugs that it's not clear…but the salient points I do remember."[75]

There were more than a few salient points to Sonny's first trip to Chicago: he also played with Day, turned Seymour's Record Mart on its ear, and met John Coltrane. There was one more unforgettable moment. Walking home just before dawn, Sonny passed "this club on 63rd Street and Cottage Grove, and it had windows so you could look in as you passed by on the street," he said. "You could look in and see the bandstand, and there was Pres playing, man—steely moment."[76] Chicago at that time was a place where you might have a Lester Young sighting while wandering home at five in the morning.

"It was just one of the greatest times I've had in my life," Sonny said. "Chicago I consider my second home."[77] Sonny felt the pull of Harlem, but he would be back.

Most significantly, performing at the Hi-Note may have secured him a spot in Miles's band.[78] After the arrest and the public shaming, Miles had hit rock bottom. It had been "the worst year of my life," he said.[79] But back in New York, Bob Weinstock was looking for him. Undeterred, Weinstock wanted to sign jazz's most notorious young trumpeter to his new label, Prestige. During a business trip to St. Louis, Weinstock dialed down the Davises in the phone book until he reached the right one, who informed him that Miles was in Chicago.[80] Weinstock got in touch and offered Miles a $750 advance for an exclusive three-year contract, payable as soon as he returned to New York.[81] It wasn't a great contract, but with the Holiday gig at the Hi-Note ending January 7, and an expensive habit to feed, Miles took Weinstock up on his offer. "I spent the rest of the time in Chicago thinking about who I was going to record with," said Miles.[82] And he knew just who to get on tenor.

Chapter 10

BIRDLAND

(1951)

When Sonny got back to Harlem from Chicago in January 1951, his mother welcomed him home, despite and perhaps because of the clear signs of addiction.[1] Chicago had pushed his harmonic and rhythmic conception to the next level, but beyond his fellow musicians and a minority of serious bop devotees, relatively few jazz fans knew about him. That was about to change. Sonny hadn't made a recording in nearly a year and half, but he was going back into the studio—with Miles Davis.

After working with Babs Gonzales, whose outré persona often relegated him to the periphery, playing with Miles "was a career boost," Sonny said. "Miles was...one of Charlie Parker's, and Charlie Parker was our prophet at that time. So when Miles asked me to play with him, it was you know, wow."[2]

Despite the bad press surrounding him, in the 1950 *Metronome* All-Star Poll, Miles supplanted Dizzy Gillespie to take the top spot in trumpet, which led the magazine to conclude that "this was the year in which Miles Davis took over."[3] With a tone and a style likened to "the sound of a man walking carefully over eggshells," that year saw a bumper crop of Miles imitators.[4] As for the tenor poll, Sonny, who had been largely absent from top clubs and recordings, would never have cracked the top ten. Stan Getz, three years Sonny's senior, was the overwhelming favorite, with Flip Phillips, Lester Young, and Warne Marsh trailing behind—four of the top five were white.

But, Miles said, "People loved Sonny Rollins up in Harlem and everywhere else. He was a legend, almost a god to a lot of the younger musicians. Some thought he was playing the saxophone on the level of Bird. I know one thing—he was close. He was an aggressive, innovative player who always had fresh musical ideas."[5]

Miles never told him what or how to play. "When I first started playing with Miles, if it was necessary to tell somebody what to play, then they would not have been there in the first place," Sonny recalled. Together, they made it new. They would "take a cliché riff," Miles said, and "break it up...you would just dart in and out of the rhythm, especially if you had a good drummer." And between Art Blakey, Kenny Clarke, and Roy Haynes, they *always* had a good drummer. They called it *peckin'*. "We used to play a style called peckin', broken phrases...nobody does that anymore," Miles said. "That was one of Charlie Parker's styles, because his father was a tap dancer. Ba-ba-bip da-dah-d'n-da dee-da-dee-deh—like tap dancers dance! That rhythm, you hadn't heard no shit like that!"[6] And Prestige Records wanted to capture that bird- or Bird-like style.

According to Sonny, peckin' "was my thing," he said. "It was part of my style. It was one of those things that just came to me. I don't think I practiced it at home or anything. It was part of improvising." Miles may have gotten peckin' from Sonny, but Sonny "took everything from Miles," he said. "*Soul* is not descriptive enough a word....He didn't just play something that had great dexterity to it. Whatever he played, there was meaning behind it. . . . He wasn't just playing a good riff. There's nothing wrong with that, but Miles was telling a story."[7]

Prestige was still a ragtag operation being run out of Bob Weinstock's storefront on Tenth Avenue. Ira Gitler was technically in the publicity department, but was a "jack-of-all-trades" who "packed and unpacked the 78s, made trips around the neighborhood to the many distributors of other labels to pick up records for Bob's mail order business; wrote label copy; composed ads for the mail order biz that ran in *Down Beat*; did promotional work with disc jockeys and columnists; and swept the floor," he said.[8] He also supervised some sessions. Prestige was a far cry from a major label, but in the jazz world, it was rapidly becoming a driving force by recording visionary artists the majors would never touch.

On the frigid, slush-filled night of January 17, 1951,[9] Sonny arrived at the independent Apex Studios on the second floor of the Beaux Arts Steinway Building on West Fifty-Seventh Street, around the block from the Plaza Hotel. It was a cavernous space with good acoustics; Prestige did most of their recordings there until the studio went bankrupt in the early 1950s.[10] At Apex, Sonny met Miles, trombonist Bennie Green (a familiar face from the Babs Gonzales date), pianist John Lewis, bassist Percy Heath, and drummer Roy Haynes.

Apparently, Weinstock had reservations about having Sonny on the date—the Prestige logo was a tenor sax, so the stakes were high—but Miles prevailed upon him. "He liked Sonny Rollins, as crude as Sonny was at that time," Weinstock said, "and also John Lewis. On his first date, you can hear a very different Miles Davis than on the Capitols."[11]

"Morpheus," composed by John Lewis, prominently featured Roy Haynes in a cymbal-heavy polyrhythmic mode that suggests free time, laying the foundation for a choppy trumpet-tenor melody line on top of trombone counterpoint. It sounds outlandish, but it's actually a twelve-bar blues.[12] Sonny takes two succinct choruses, playing with an earthy ballast, and showing off the "pecking" style, staging a playful call-and-response with himself.

Sonny took only one chorus on Miles's drowsy "Down." Miles took the standard "Blue Room" as a ballad, with Sonny playing a relaxed sixteen-bar coda on one of the two takes, which was spliced in, bending the time while demonstrating that Coleman Hawkins was never far from his mind.[13] "Whispering," the Paul Whiteman hit that became the basis for the chord progression of Dizzy Gillespie's "Groovin' High," is taken at a medium tempo and has a certain irony to it; "Groovin' High" was so overdone at that point that maybe it was hipper to go back to the source. Sonny took one chorus, playing with Hawkins-esque filigree and legato phrasing.

The highlight, for Sonny at least, was his own impromptu recording debut as a leader. Weinstock never went to jazz clubs; his roster of artists recruited new talent. "So at the end of the session, Miles had been talking to Bob Weinstock, saying, 'You've got to sign Sonny,'" recalled Gitler. In between takes, Miles "had talked Bob into letting Sonny be featured. And John Lewis, who was Mr. Punctuality, had to hit at 10 p.m. at Birdland with Lester Young, so he was gone."[14] Not one to be dismissed, Miles sat down at the piano himself. As the tape rolled, Miles played an eight-bar piano intro to Charlie Parker's "Confirmation" as Percy Heath pedaled and Roy Haynes slapped the hi-hat. When Sonny entered, instead of stating the melody, he launched right into a lyrical solo, a move borrowed from Hawk's "Body and Soul." Sonny explored the full range of the horn, by turns honking and playing vibrato, effortlessly articulating double-time lines with an offbeat rhythmic inventiveness that pulls from Hawk, Pres, Bird, and Byas. At two and a half minutes, the track feels oddly truncated.

With the exception of the standard "Blue Room," which Prestige billed as "introducing" Sonny Rollins, Ira Gitler named the other tunes.[15] "Morpheus" was named for the god of dreams; "Down" was not named for the downward thrust of its melody but "for the fact that 'down' was an expression of approbation amongst jazz musicians at the time," Gitler said. "If you were 'down' you were really taking care of business and Miles impressed me with his solo that felt as if he was talking to you, telling a story."[16] "I Know" was for the cognoscenti: "Sonny played the changes on 'Confirmation,' no head," Gitler said, "and so 'Confirmation' I called 'I Know.'"[17]

The arrangements are strong, but by his own admission, this was not Miles's most inspired session. He played with feeling, but flubbed notes and lethargic phrasing make him sound more behind the beat than usual. The other sidemen joked that he played better piano than trumpet on his own session. Earlier in the day, Miles had been recording with the Charlie Parker Quintet and was exhausted by the time he got to the studio for his Prestige debut. "I had started to shoot heroin again and so my body and chops weren't in the best shape," Miles recalled. "But I think everyone else played well—especially Sonny on a couple of tracks."[18]

Not everyone would agree. *Down Beat* wrote of "Morpheus" that it "isn't very cleanly played," while *Metronome* gave the track a B– and "Blue Room" a C+, singling Sonny out for being "still out of tune."[19] The next 78, with "Down" and "Whispering," was released later in 1951 and was given a B and a B–, respectively, by *Metronome*.[20] *Down Beat* dismissed it as "two very bad sides from Miles," in which "no one seems at all interested in playing and a completely lifeless and uninspired performance results."[21] It may not have been the most auspicious beginning, but nonetheless Sonny had made the big leagues.

After the January 17 session, Sonny and Miles made their way back uptown to score heroin. By 1951 "it was everywhere," said Arthur Taylor. Miles, always an impeccable dresser, kept his hair perfectly coiffed, but otherwise he was starting to slip. He had started hanging out with the guys from the Hill, in Goof Square or, if it was warm enough, Colonial Park, and now Miles had joined Sonny's inner circle.[22] Likewise, Sonny had more control of the horn than ever, but had completely lost control of his heroin habit. Walter Bishop, Kenny Drew, Art Taylor, Jackie McLean, Art Blakey, and Miles—they were all using. "I was spending a lot of time in Harlem, chasing down that heroin," Miles recalled. "Heroin was my girlfriend."[23] It was becoming Sonny's, too.[24]

Beyond their mutual self-destructive habit, Sonny and Miles forged an unshakable bond. "We became very good friends," Sonny recalled. "We had a lot of the same musical tastes." They did not come from quite the same background, though. "Miles's family was very black middle-class, so Miles was always into very sharp dressing, very fine cars, and all that," Sonny said, "which was a little bit different than what I was experiencing."[25] Yet they came to really understand each other. To Sonny, Miles was a shy guy. "As an artist Miles is just trying to learn like everybody else was," he recalled. "Miles would turn his back on the people to play. And people would say, 'Look at this arrogant guy.'...Miles would do that 'cause he was being shy—that's why he was doing that."[26] As for his macho persona, "that's how he wanted to be known, but actually he was a really gentle guy, man. He was like a pussy-cat, really....It was just posturing. And when the rumors began to build up, then he wouldn't...He wanted to have that image, so he got it."[27]

In those heady days in 1951, they were still having fun. "I'm a big fan of these guys, Bob and Ray," Sonny later recalled. "That informs my playing, I think."[28] Bob and Ray were the comedy duo of Bob Elliott and Ray Gould-ing, who brought their quick-witted call-and-response comic timing to tele-vision and radio in New York that year. They would lovingly satirize radio programs—for example, Sonny's childhood favorite, *Mr. Keen, Tracer of Lost Persons*, became *Mr. Trace, Keener than Most Persons*.[29] "Whatever happens to me, all I have to do is think about one of these characters," Sonny said. "My sense of humor is important to me as a human being and carried me through so much of this life."[30] Bob and Ray's off-the-wall banter, pulsating with spontaneous comic asides, was the kind of dynamic Miles and Sonny had, only they did it through the language of bebop.[31]

Miles and Sonny patronized Bell's Restaurant and Bar in Harlem, a res-taurant, bar, and ice cream parlor that opened in 1943. Sonny knew it previ-ously from Davis's song "Sippin' at Bell's," which Miles recorded with Bird. At Bell's, Miles said, "Everyone that came there was clean."[32] Well, almost everyone.[33]

Sometimes, Sonny and the guys would wander over to Bud Powell's to sit at the master's feet.[34] At around this time, Miles floated through vari-ous hotels—the Hotel America and the University Hotel—but the group avoided hotels. Whichever apartment they went to, they would usually get high and nod off.[35] At Sonny's on Edgecombe, "we would get high and look at that beautiful view he had of that park across from where he lived," Miles recalled. "You could see Yankee Stadium from there."[36] After they copped from Willie Gordon, they would often go back to Arthur Taylor's house to shoot up; Art's mother, Amy, was beloved by all of them and probably didn't know what they were doing.[37]

Some musicians came out publicly against drug proliferation on the scene. In February 1951, Cab Calloway published a scathing editorial in *Ebony* titled

"Is Dope Killing Our Musicians?" Calloway invoked Marx—"A spectre is haunting the American music industry: the spectre of narcotics." Though Calloway did not include any names in the editorial, in a sidebar, most likely written by the editors, eight musicians were called out by name and pictured: John Simmons, Miles Davis, Eddie Heywood, Gene Krupa, Billie Holiday, Howard McGhee, Art Blakey, and Dexter Gordon: "If all of the most gifted musicians who have been arrested, convicted and imprisoned for being found with dope were assembled in one place, one of the greatest all-star orchestras in the history of the band business could be organized."[38]

The "Reefer Man" himself, who apparently had sworn off reefer, was particularly disappointed in Miles. "One young trumpeter, recently picked up on the West Coast for possession of heroin, happens to be one of the most brilliant minds in contemporary jazz. He has contributed mightily to the growth of the modern jazz movement and is widely admired for his talent. Music needs this man, the country needs to hear his music, we all need the joy and beauty his playing can bring into our lives." To Calloway, he could play even better sober.[39] Surprisingly, Calloway praised the Federal Bureau of Narcotics, but he did offer an alternative to the criminal justice system: the "cure" offered by the US Public Health Service in Lexington, Kentucky. Ultimately, he wrote, "the road to reality is not paved with narcotics."[40]

When Sonny and Miles weren't on the bandstand, they were listening, sometimes to Louis Armstrong, despite the perception that the younger generation had turned its back on Pops.[41] Once when they were playing at Birdland, Sonny recalled, "Louis Armstrong was appearing a few blocks down on Broadway at a big show bar. When Miles Davis and I got through with our sets, Miles would say, 'Come on, man, let's go down and catch Louis.' So we hustled down Broadway to this place where Louis Armstrong was playing. They knew Miles, so we went up and got a chance to catch a Louis Armstrong set. And believe me, that injected us with so much musical inspiration that we came back to Birdland and blew our whatcha-call-its off."[42]

To Sonny, Armstrong transcended style and period. "When I think of the spiritual, I think of Louis Armstrong," he said. "For me it was not so much hearing Louis Armstrong, although of course I used to listen to him— that '27 to '28 music is some real bad stuff—but when I used to see Louis

Armstrong, that did a lot for me. . . . So seeing Louis Armstrong, that gave me a feeling, made me feel uplifted. The music is great; man, Louis Armstrong did everything; but just being in his physical presence, you could feel the music and depth of his musical personality. I love him."[43]

Miles found some decent work, though not consistently.[44] On February 15, the Miles Davis All-Stars were booked for a week at Birdland opposite trumpeter Joe Thomas and vocalist Wynonie Harris.[45] Miles hired Sonny, J. J. Johnson, Kenny Drew, Tommy Potter, and Art Blakey.[46]

The basement club at Fifty-Second and Broadway had a canopied entrance at street level; out front stood barker, occasional jazz vocalist, and Birdland emcee Pee Wee Marquette, who was about three and half feet tall. He was known "for mispronouncing musicians' names if they didn't lay a tip on him (i.e., bassist Teddy Kotick became 'Teddy Kotex')," wrote Ira Gitler. Admission was ninety-nine cents, and if patrons didn't ask for a penny back the ticket taker would keep the change. "Moving a bit further into the club you became aware of a long bar on your left," wrote Gitler, "most often inhabited by a mixture of visiting musicians, an assortment of hustlers (pimps, ladies of the evening, garden-variety thugs, et al.) and jazz aficionados who couldn't get a seat in what we called 'the bullpen,' an enclosed area with chairs that ran parallel to the bar and ended at the left side of the bandstand."[47] Jazz aficionados generally couldn't afford to pay the cover for a white linen tablecloth and avoided a drink minimum, though salted nuts were on sale for a quarter, more to make them thirsty than to hark back to "Salt Peanuts." On the other side of the "bullpen," leather banquettes led to a glass radio booth where disc jockey Symphony Sid Torin held court for his weekly fifty-five-minute live Friday-night broadcast on WJZ.[48]

On February 17, the broadcast featured Miles playing Sonny's "Evans,"[49] a contrafact for "Get Happy," retitled "Out of the Blue" by Ira Gitler later that year;[50] Miles's "Half Nelson"; Bud Powell's "Tempus Fugit," which Powell pronounced "Fugue-it"; and Denzil Best's "Move." Miles had defined himself more by lyricism than as a virtuoso trumpeter, but on this night, the up-tempo material would silence any detractors who claimed that he played so pretty because he couldn't play as fast as Fats Navarro or Dizzy Gillespie.[51] Sonny sounded more at ease at quick tempos than previously and broke up his phrases, exemplifying the "peckin'" style as opposed to the unbroken eighth-note runs he had recorded earlier. Sonny had learned to be in conversation with the rhythm section, on this night especially Art Blakey, who had a penchant for "dropping bombs," using the bass drum as an accent to respond to the soloist during a rest. On "Tempus Fugit," Sonny took the first solo, playing a combustible four-bar break, leaving a big rest at the end punctuated by a crash of Blakey's cymbal as Sonny took off. Symphony Sid commented on the song's minor progression. "That sounds like one of those old bar mitzvah tunes. Are you for hire for bar mitzvahs?" he said. "Are you making bar mitzvahs?"[52] Miles and Sonny needed to support their habit—even Bird made the occasional bar mitzvah[53]—but they weren't exactly playing the bar mitzvah circuit right then.

Miles soon added a new experimenter to his laboratory, a close friend of Sonny's. He wanted to test out an alto player with the group to fill out the horn section, and Bud Powell recommended Jackie McLean sit in. On Monday, February 19, Jackie made his debut with Miles.[54] He had practiced all day for two days to prepare, but when he arrived, the combination of performance anxiety and heroin forced him to leave the stage during a solo to vomit and he didn't make it to the bathroom.[55] Nevertheless, Miles invited him to hang out the next day and asked if McLean had any tunes. Jackie showed him the second song he had ever composed, "Dig," which put a bop spin on the changes to "Sweet Georgia Brown." From then on, Jackie was part of Miles's coterie.[56]

That year, a pianist and student at the New England Conservatory heard Sonny for the first time when he was playing with Miles. His name was Cecil Taylor. "He was marvelous," Taylor recalled. "Not only was he marvelous, but I learned so much from him about what I wasn't able to accept."[57] According to Taylor, it was around this time that Sonny connected with an early incarnation of the Modern Jazz Quartet when it was led by Milt Jackson.[58] "Sonny was hanging around, not doing much," said Kenny Clarke. "So I got [Minton's manager] Teddy [Hill] to hire Sonny."[59]

Taylor: "I was up in Minton's one Saturday night, I was about twenty-one years old, and Milt Jackson was leading a band with Sonny in it. Saturday night! In Harlem! Everybody's, 'Hey, hup, ho.' Then all of a sudden, Milt and

Sonny played this piece, and you could hear everybody breathe. I said, 'Oh.' That, to me, is what it's about. You play from the heart. If that's what you really love, it doesn't matter if there's one person there or 10,000."[60]

Sonny soon shared the bandstand with another new voice on tenor Miles decided to try out—John Coltrane. On Sunday, March 11, Miles was booked into the Audubon Ballroom for a "3 o'clock high" dance, a regular event headlined by the likes of Art Blakey and Roy Haynes.[61] Admission was seventy-five cents from 3 to 4 p.m. and ninety-eight cents after that. Coltrane was between gigs with Gillespie, so he was available to make the Audubon.[62] Though Sonny and Trane had met several months earlier in Chicago, they had never played together.

"It was a great gig, and we became friends after that," Sonny recalled. "It was brotherhood; it was love. He was like a preacher in a way. Coltrane didn't waste time. He didn't do things frivolously. Everything he did was important. Whenever we got together, it was always a communion, talking about things that mattered. There was no jive. It was always meaningful."[63]

Before the Audubon, Sonny had barely heard of Coltrane. Conversely, Coltrane must have known about Sonny. Years later, when asked which musicians he respected most, Coltrane listed Sonny as one of the "great soloists," alongside Monk, Charlie Parker, Miles Davis, Dizzy Gillespie, and Benny Golson. "Some guys, you know, you call great, man, you know? Sonny, he's one," Coltrane said. "He just reached that great status, man."[64]

Coltrane was the son of a preacher who had gone into the navy; Sonny was the son of a navy man who became a kind of preacher.[65] And what they each had to preach was different.

The meeting marked the beginning of a friendly rivalry. "Although Coltrane eventually emerged as the number one man, we had quite a few sessions together," Sonny recalled. Sometimes, "I outdueled him," Sonny said, "then I guess that sometimes we had a standoff."[66]

It was a band for the ages playing a low-key dance gig: Miles, Coltrane, Sonny, Powell, Percy Heath, and either Art Blakey or Kenny Clarke.[67] Sonny had played with everyone else, but he didn't know what to expect from Coltrane. It wasn't anticipated to be an evenly matched tenor battle—Coltrane was unknown, while Sonny was on the rise—but Miles did stoke the fire.

"Sometimes when I played with Miles and Coltrane," Sonny said, "John would be taking a solo and Miles would sidle up to me and whisper something into my ear about how good I was. A little later, when I was playing, I would notice Miles whispering in Trane's ear."[68]

Miles wanted to hire Jackie McLean as well, but didn't have the budget for four horns. Jackie figured Coltrane would be playing alto as he often did with Dizzy, but Miles clarified that Coltrane would be playing tenor. Despite leaving McLean off the gig, Miles insisted that he come to watch.[69]

Jackie expected a bloodbath. He gathered "all my people in my neighborhood" to come witness it: "I said, 'Hey, Sonny Rollins is playing tomorrow night with Miles and they bringing some dude from Philly, some gun from Philly named John Coltrane. I said, 'I wanna be there for the slaughter.' At that time Sonny was untouchable." Of course, hindsight is twenty-twenty. "It's like comparing soup with salad," he said.[70]

According to McLean, Sonny did outblow Trane on that day. "It was awesome, man, because Sonny Rollins... he was unmatchable at that time." Miles concurred with McLean's verdict—as Miles said of Trane that night, Sonny "set his ears and ass on fire."[71]

That wasn't Sonny's reaction, though; he was caught off guard by Trane. "I really had to listen carefully to him. I often wondered, what was he doing, where was he going?" Sonny said. "I didn't think it would be proper to ask, but I listened harder, and eventually I began to understand his music. Later, we became good friends. Good enough friends for me to borrow money from him, and Coltrane and Monk were the only two people I would ever ask for a loan."[72]

Coltrane was ready to leave Dizzy, but he would not join Miles until later. "During this period, [Miles] was coming into his own, and I could see him extending the boundaries of jazz even further," Coltrane wrote. "I felt I wanted to work with him. But for the time being, we went our separate ways."[73]

Jimmy Heath, who knew Coltrane from Philly and toured with him in Dizzy Gillespie's band when they were both playing alto, recalled that Coltrane "had rhythm, too, but he was working very differently—hard—on the harmonic concept of music. Sonny had both." At the time, Heath and

Coltrane "were thinking about harmonic connections in the music, the melodic connections, but Sonny was always—and that is the most important thing about him—he was a leader in rhythmic playing on the tenor saxophone.... [H]e set the pace for rhythmic playing as a jazz improviser." To Heath, this extended to Sonny's songwriting. "Sonny Rollins never wrote a song like 'Giant Steps'—half notes," he said. "He's like a drummer on the saxophone."[74]

To Heath, Sonny represented the total package: "His rhythmic concept and his sense of humor, his intensity, his sound, his romantic touch in his playing, when he's playing a ballad or something, he has all the expressions of life," said Heath. This isn't to discount what Coltrane was doing—far from it. "We all came from different areas of the country, and we all played differently," Heath said. "It wasn't 'Send in the Clones'!"[75]

Some of the gigs Sonny played with Miles were explicitly in support of political causes. On Friday, May 11, Sonny performed with the Miles Davis All-Stars at an event prior to the convention of the New York State Labor Youth League, the state branch of the youth-centric arm of the Communist Party USA.[76] The convention's goal was to build "the unity of Negro and white youth in the fight for peace."[77] The "LYL Peace Dance" was held at the Rockland Palace; Miles hired Sonny, J. J. Johnson, and vocalist Earl Coleman, playing opposite the Vicente Sigler band, which appealed to the current mambo craze.[78]

The LYL dance took place only days after Harlem had taken to the streets to protest the May 8 execution of Willie McGee, a World War II veteran and father of four who was wrongfully convicted of raping a white woman in 1945.[79] Miles was profiled in the *Daily Worker* in advance of the dance and said, "How can they sentence a man to die like that? I sent a telegram about the Martinsville Seven. This country is beginning to make me neurotic." As for the LYL, he said, "They're on the ball. They know what's happening." Miles was on the ball, too. He described the liberating experience of being in Europe, where you could "feel like a man for once in your life."[80]

From May 31 to June 13, Sonny was back at Birdland with the Miles Davis All-Stars: J. J. Johnson, Kenny Drew, Tommy Potter, and Art Blakey, with bassist Earl May subbing for Potter on some gigs.[81] On June 2, with

Potter on bass, they were featured on the live broadcast with Symphony Sid on WJZ, playing "Move," "Half Nelson," "Down," and others.[82] The group had jelled enough that each successive player, especially Sonny, tends to start his solo with the concluding phrase of the previous solo, as though passing a baton.

That summer, Sonny got his nickname. Lester Young was Pres, Coleman Hawkins was Bean, Charlie Parker was Bird, Diz was Diz, and Miles dubbed Sonny "Newk." One day Miles and Sonny got in a cab, and the white cabbie did a double take: "Damn, you're Don Newcombe!" Though they had never thought about it, the resemblance to the Brooklyn Dodgers pitcher was uncanny. "I may have had a baseball hat on," Sonny said, "and so Miles sort of picked up on that and began putting the cab driver on, talking to me as if I was Don Newcombe."[83] He began describing how that night, he would strike out Stan Musial, the all-star St. Louis Cardinals hitter, and promised to leave tickets for the driver at Ebbets Field.[84] "The cab driver was thrilled of course, so I went along with it, and from then on people began calling me Newk," Sonny said. The joke was as much on Sonny as the cab driver. Miles was "razzin' me, you know, because I wouldn't do that 'cause I was a Yankee fan."[85]

Still, as Dodgers go, Sonny could do worse than Don Newcombe. The original Newk, who stood six-foot-four and weighed 250 pounds, was the 1949 Rookie of the Year and played on the National League All-Star team for the '49, '50, and '51 seasons.[86] The two Newks wouldn't formally meet for fifty years.[87]

As the summer heated up, Miles would go to the pool at Colonial Park with Max Roach. His addiction was escalating, though. "He went down to the bottom," Art Taylor recalled of Miles at this time. "From beautiful dressed, down to a bum."[88] Miles had bounced around different addresses, living for a time with drummer Stan Levey on Long Island, and at around this time moved in with Jackie McLean. To afford drugs, Miles began doing transcription work for music publishers, pawning his instrument, even turned to pimping. The goal was to find some relative moderation, going through periods of detox off the drug and then back on, but over time, the heroin had won out, and Miles was becoming more and more of a derelict.[89] And so was Sonny.

Late that summer Sonny performed at an event in Newark presented by WNJR disc jockey Carl Ide and proclaimed as "Modern Jazz Day" by Republican mayor Ralph Villani. On the bill were pianist and vocalist Barbara Carroll with her trio and a group composed of Lennie Tristano, Lee Konitz, Gerry Mulligan, Terry Gibbs, Sonny, and an unknown local drummer.[90] However, Sonny couldn't support his habit on the little money he made from gigs, so he turned to crime. "During this period, I became a truly despicable person," Sonny recalled. "I had no friends. I was really a rough cut. I stole all kinds of stuff from my own home. I stole other people's horns. If musicians saw me coming, they'd go the other way."[91]

Sonny would never rip off anyone from his inner circle, only "guys who couldn't play, guys you might consider squares. I only ripped off people that were outside our life." He would also pick pockets. "I hung out with a guy who had a method for pickpocketing. There is kind of an art to pickpocketing. I would be the guy who distracted our mark. Then this guy would go to work. The person we stole from was usually some poor woman returning from a day job someplace. Maybe coming home to feed her kids. We'd be finding ways to distract her on the bus. And he would slip into her pocketbook. I've been through all these things. I wasn't proud of it. And I got away from that life as soon as I realized what I had become."[92]

Just as Sonny's career was gaining momentum, things were not looking good—Miles Davis was a pimp, and Sonny Rollins was a pickpocket.

Meanwhile, Sonny's brother, Valdemar, had given up a violin chair in the Pittsburgh Symphony to take the Hippocratic oath, was now almost finished with medical school, and was imminently getting married. The wedding was Sunday, September 9, at St. Luke's Episcopal Church at 141st and Convent, and "numerous collegiate friends attended" to celebrate the union of Val and his bride, Doris Jones, a graduate of the Oberlin Conservatory of Music and the Eastman School of Music and an accomplished classical pianist who had become an assistant professor of music at Fisk University, a historically black college in Nashville.[93] Sonny pulled himself together enough to serve as the best man at the wedding.[94]

The following month, Sonny was back in the studio with Miles.[95] There was little money involved. For thirteen years, from 1946 through 1958, the

American Federation of Musicians sideman rate remained at $41.25 for a three-hour session, with the leader getting double. Of that amount, $8.66 went to the Music Performance Trust Funds. Only composers received royalties, so this meant that on many of the classic Prestige sessions, take-home pay for sidemen was a flat fee—$32.59.[96] Prestige was an indie label and didn't have the vast resources of the major labels that would eventually lure Miles away with more lucrative offers, but it didn't stop Miles from negotiating.

"We'd get into these staring sessions," said Prestige owner Bob Weinstock. "He'd ask for more money and I wouldn't answer. Then I'd look at him and he'd look at me; we'd just stand there. We went through this a lot. I'd give him the money, but I'd always say, 'Okay, that means we have to do another album.' He'd say, 'I don't want to do another album.' I'd say, 'And I want better people than the last!' "[97]

For his second album with Prestige, which would eventually be released as *Dig*, Miles hired Walter Bishop Jr., Art Blakey, Tommy Potter, Jackie McLean, and Sonny. On October 5, they all convened at Apex Studios, the same studio as the "Morpheus" session. The album was to be an experiment in the still-nascent "microgroove" technology. The LP format had been used for live recordings, primarily to record long classical works, but not on many studio albums.[98] "Before the LP era, you were bound by three-and-a-half minute 78s at the most," said Weinstock, who considered it a "monumental" recording session. "I sensed that we were going to have LPs. I heard rumblings."[99]

Weinstock was already known for what might be termed an economical, laissez-faire approach. No rehearsal to keep it spontaneous, but also to save money; not many takes; if a take went awry, they would usually record over it immediately to save tape; little to no editing or splicing—but tracks still had to be tight enough to fit on the records. The LP format allowed musicians to really stretch out. With the possibility of recording longer tracks, Miles also invited Jackie McLean for his recording debut at the age of twenty.[100] Nevertheless, it would initially be released as a series of singles.

McLean was the first to arrive at the studio. Then one by one, his musical heroes began to show up, two of whom were not on the date: Charles Mingus and Charlie Parker. "I was nervous," he recalled. "Bird saw that.... After we started running down the heads and stuff, he came out and said, 'Hey, look. You sound real good, man. You're playing great. Keep it up. It sounds good.' That's all I had to hear. Once he gave me that encouragement, I wasn't as nervous anymore. But he was there for that whole recording that day. It was incredible, the kind of pressure that I was under."[101]

Even having Sonny there, despite their closeness in age, added to the stress. "By that time I thought Sonny was the greatest...tenor saxophone player around," McLean said.[102] But Sonny was experiencing his own stress—a bad reed, the bane of a saxophonist's existence, and probably a leak in the horn— and he conspicuously squeaks throughout the session.

As intimidating as Art Blakey could be to an unseasoned player, he had a way of setting people at ease in comparison to, for example, the technical high-wire act of Max Roach. "Max had all this technique and he was very busy," said Walter Bishop Jr. "Blakey changed the whole feel. On the fast tempos, I didn't have to fight to try to get through, because he gave me space."[103]

With Bird sitting in the control room to avoid psyching McLean out too much, they laid down seven tracks that day rather than the usual four—"Conception," "Denial," "Out of the Blue," "Bluing," "Dig," "My Old Flame" (the lone ballad), and the standard "It's Only a Paper Moon," the opposite of the perfectionist approach to recording Sonny would later take. George Shearing's "Conception," which Miles had recorded earlier as "Deception," was the shortest track, at just over four minutes.[104] Every other song exceeded the five-minute mark, with "Bluing" running for ten. "Denial" was another Gitler title for a "headless" tune, this one based on the changes to "Confirmation," just like "I Know." Fed up with his bad setup, Sonny takes only one chorus. "As his horn was giving him some trouble that day, he grabbed the tenor offered by J. R. Monterose (another studio visitor) just before his solo," recalled Gitler, "but the horn was out of tune and he drops out after one chorus."[105]

Sonny's technical difficulties notwithstanding, the energy in the room was palpable on the recorded tracks—McLean's jitters, Sonny's sangfroid leavened by the frustration of a stale reed, Miles in his own estimation playing more trumpet than he had in the studio for a long time, Blakey's sibilant ride cymbal ever present as he drops bombs on the bass drum in all the right places.

Sonny and Jackie were shut out of royalties. Miles would take the composer credit for "Dig," but in reality McLean had written it. Sonny wrote "Out of the Blue," which was also credited to Miles.[106] Independent labels like Prestige and Blue Note had their own publishing arms and built a 50 percent publishing split into the contracts with their artists. They would promise to use their business savvy to collect and in exchange would take half the royalties.[107] Miles claimed that Weinstock tried to get his publishing rights when he signed the contract but that he refused.[108] Jackie gave them both the benefit of the doubt and assumed it was all a miscommunication, speculating that Weinstock "assumed that those tunes that were played there that day were Miles' tunes." However, Miles didn't correct the error, and years later the royalties still went to him.[109]

The critics did not love it. Of "My Old Flame," Barry Ulanov gave it a B− rating and wrote that "Miles just wanders aimlessly," though he said that Sonny "makes the most of his tenor sax bridge."[110] Of "Dig," *Down Beat* gave it two stars and wrote that "Miles, altoist Jack McLean, tenor Sonny Rollins are not helped a bit by the rude, unswinging drumming of Art Blakey."[111]

To Sonny, the *Dig* session drew a line in the sand for hard bop. "When Miles was coming out with a lot of the 'cool' sounds, it was sort of alarming to many people in the jazz community because of the emphasis on the softer side of the music," Sonny said. "Then, when Miles came out with Jackie and myself, we really asserted the hard-bop element, which was a relief to many in the community" who were concerned with "what was threatening to be a movement of 'coolness' in jazz."[112]

Bob Weinstock did not love Sonny's tendency to squeak, but his rhythmic flair and natural lyricism shone through. "Sonny Rollins was too much!" said Weinstock. "At that time, Sonny was a joke to all of the musicians. They loved him because he was a bebopper and he knew everybody....But he hit so many clinkers that they would crack up when he played. They would tease him, but his ideas were so great. Despite the clinkers, they all knew, just like I knew...because I signed him to a contract...that he'd be a force someday."[113]

Weinstock was so impressed by Sonny's playing on the session that he offered him a contract with Prestige that day. Just past his twenty-first birthday, Sonny was signed to the same label as Miles Davis.

Yet a contract with Prestige was not enough to feed his addiction. Four days after the *Dig* session, on the night of Monday, October 8, Sonny was with Kenny Drew and their friend Lenny Martinez,[114] a pianist from the Hill who had served in the US Air Corps, and they had a half-baked plan: armed robbery. Kenny Drew had procured a gun. "We decided to go downtown and stick up some place. I don't think we had any specific place in mind," Sonny said. "It was such a stupid thing to do. But it wasn't like I was one of the guys sitting down and planning it. I was sort of the dumb guy who was just going along. I was the big dope who took the gun. I didn't really know anything about guns. I have never fired a gun in my life."[115]

At about one in the morning on October 9, the three of them took a taxi downtown to Fifty-Ninth Street and Lexington Avenue.[116] They weren't doing anything suspicious, but seeing three black men pull up in a cab on the Upper East Side late on a Monday night was enough to rouse the suspicion of Detective William Mulligan of the Burglary Squad, who approached the vehicle. After searching them, Mulligan saw that Sonny had a concealed pistol in his trench coat; apparently, some hypodermic needles were in the cab.[117] Attempted robbery was off the table, but carrying a concealed firearm was illegal. Mulligan arrested all three of them on the spot. The gun was Drew's, but Sonny took the blame; he wasn't about to implicate his friends.

What followed was the worst night of Sonny's life up to that point. The police took him to the Manhattan House of Detention for Men, a hulking high-rise known as the Tombs, located downtown at 125 White Street.[118] To Sonny, it was "like a living tomb."[119] Convicted felons were housed there, but the Tombs was primarily a dismal purgatory that held prisoners who were awaiting trial and the inevitability of incarceration.[120] The guards were known for corruption and harsh treatment of inmates.[121]

The facility had a capacity of 951, but that October, the inmate population had ballooned to 1,266.[122] On October 5, days before Sonny's arrest, the Tombs came under fire when the New York State Commission of Correction officially asked the prison to demonstrate why it should not be closed.

Members of the Prison Association of New York inspected it and found there were not nearly enough prison beds, with "inmates sleeping on floors and in corridors, and 'an atmosphere of demoralization.'" This was just the official report.[123] Two months earlier, when Bud Powell and Thelonious Monk were arrested for narcotics possession following a similar search of a car without probable cause, they were brought to the Tombs. When Powell got agitated and started screaming in protest, guards poured buckets of ammonia solution on him.[124]

When Sonny arrived at the Tombs, it wasn't long before withdrawal symptoms set in. It was so severe that the guards threw him in a straitjacket. "Can you understand what it would feel like to be in a straitjacket?" Sonny recalled. "I couldn't either, but I was, and it was brought about by sort of a drug psychosis in prison."[125] Thus began Sonny's odyssey through the circle of hell they call the US criminal justice system.

After being arraigned on October 9, Sonny was left to fend for himself in the Tombs for three days. On October 11, Sonny and his accomplices— Kenny Drew and Lenny Martinez—appeared before Magistrate Ambrose J. Haddock at City Magistrates' Court at 100 Centre Street.

Martinez had a prior conviction, but Haddock dismissed all charges against him and Drew.[126] For Sonny, bail was set at $1,500, which his family posted that day.[127] On October 17, after *The People of the State of New York Against Walter Rollins* was brought by District Attorney Frank S. Hogan, an indictment was filed on two counts: "criminally carrying concealed a loaded pistol" and "criminally possessing a pistol," "without a written license." Indictment hearings have no defense, and, as the adage goes, "a grand jury would indict a ham sandwich."[128]

On October 22, Sonny's lawyer, forty-two-year-old defense attorney Joseph Panzer, entered a plea of not guilty.[129] As Sonny had no prior record, he reasoned, maybe they could beat the charges. The trial was scheduled to begin in a month.

By November 29, though, Panzer had reconsidered. Sonny was a twenty-one-year-old black man in a city that was predisposed to find him guilty, and though he had no drugs on him at the time of arrest, and there was no probable cause for a stop-and-frisk, he did have a gun. So copping a plea for a misdemeanor was probably the best he could do.[130] That day, Sonny appeared before the Court of General Sessions, with the Honorable Louis J. Capozzoli presiding. Capozzoli served in the New York State Assembly and as a Democratic congressman from New York's Thirteenth District from 1941 to 1945. He was elected to the Court of General Sessions the previous year, so he was concerned about seeming tough on crime. He was also a member of the New York Rifle Club.[131]

After getting arraigned at the bar, Sonny's lawyer, Joseph Panzer, and Assistant District Attorney Eugene Leiman approached the bench. Panzer told the judge that Sonny wanted to withdraw his not-guilty plea in exchange for the court dropping one charge.

"Rollins, did you understand what your lawyer said to me?" Capozzoli said.

"Yes, sir," said Sonny.

"Did you wish to plead guilty to the possession of a firearm as a misdemeanor?"

"Yes, sir."

"Did you have in your possession on October 9, 1951, an automatic pistol?"

"Yes, sir."[132]

Sentencing was scheduled for December 20, two months later, with bail continued.

As Sonny's life came crumbling down, it was likely that his cabaret card would be revoked as well due to the city's unjust Prohibition-era policy, so playing for more than two consecutive nights in a New York City club that served liquor—any club in the city—would be impossible for the indefinite future.[133] Sonny's reputation, welfare, and livelihood were all at stake due to a gun that probably never would have been fired. His family was heartbroken.

After Bud Powell and Thelonious Monk were convicted that August, Powell was deemed mentally unstable, taken to Bellevue, and then sent on court order to Pilgrim State Hospital in Brentwood, Long Island, for sixty days. Monk was sentenced to two months at the workhouse, probably on Rikers Island, and lost his cabaret card.[134] So within a span of two months, Powell recorded "Un Poco Loco," one of the masterpieces of the bebop era; Monk first recorded the standards "Straight, No Chaser," "Four in One," and "Ask Me Now"; and Sonny recorded "It's Only a Paper Moon" and "Dig" with Miles Davis. During the same period, they had all been brutalized, Monk was sent to prison, Powell was recommitted, and Sonny was thrown in a straitjacket and locked in the Tombs.[135]

Before Sonny's sentencing, when Monk was released, he and Sonny went to visit Bud at Pilgrim in Islip. After being admitted on September 4, the Pilgrim staff decided following an observation period to extend Powell's stay indefinitely and subjected him to more shock treatment. Fortunately, they had a piano there. Sonny and Monk took the hour-and-a-half drive out. "I felt very close to Bud, and Monk did, too, of course, and we'd go to visit him in the mental hospitals, several times," Sonny said. "We used to go way the hell out to Central Islip, all the way out on Long Island. . . . All the cats used to dress in street clothes; there were no uniforms or hospital outfits. And we went in to see Bud, trying to talk to him: 'Well, how do you feel, man, how are you doing?' Suddenly I saw this guy closing the doors, and I said, 'Whoa, man! We're just visiting.'"[136]

Sonny also had a contract with Prestige. On December 17, three days before his sentencing, he was back at Apex Studios on West Fifty-Seventh Street for his first-ever full session as a leader with *Sonny Rollins Quartet*.[137] It was what would likely be Sonny's last time in a recording studio for a while. He got Percy Heath, Art Blakey, and, perhaps to show there were no hard feelings, Kenny Drew.

The session was off to a disastrous start. Bob Weinstock had been diagnosed with manic depression by the end of 1950, and he would sometimes have Ira Gitler fill in for him when he couldn't make it to the studio.[138] On this occasion, Gitler was in the engineer's booth for his first time as session supervisor; it was also the night before his twenty-third birthday.

"Like true love, the course of true jazz seldom runs smooth," wrote Gitler. "It was a miserable, sleety night,"[139] and conguero Sabu Martinez, who was supposed to be on the record, couldn't make it from the Bronx. When Sonny took out his saxophone to warm up—his own instrument was sometimes in hock—he found he was missing a neck strap. He jury-rigged one out of a coat hanger and a piece of rope that he hung around his neck in baleful foreshadowing.

It was a strung-out session, with Sonny recording eight tunes: "Time on My Hands," "This Love of Mine," "Shadrack," "Slow Boat to China," "With a Song in My Heart," and the originals "Mambo Bounce," the twelve-bar blues "Scoops," and "Newk's Fadeaway." Kenny Drew nodded off between takes, and each time Art Blakey woke him up with a snare roll.[140] Sonny began the recording session with "Time on My Hands" by Vincent Youmans, with lyrics by Harold Adamson and Mack Gordon. Sonny was having more reed problems that day, but he managed to imbue the song with a deep vibrato and a pathos that was unprecedented for him on record.

On "Mambo Bounce,"[141] after stating the danceable theme, in which Sonny is echoed by Kenny Drew in a playful call-and-response, Sonny played over blues changes, with an insouciant swagger and a huge sound, exploding into double time on his fourth and final chorus. As Gitler recalled, the band had trouble segueing from the melody to the blues solo section amid the drug-induced haze, but after some false starts, they finally got it straight.[142]

On "This Love of Mine," a ballad made popular by Frank Sinatra, Sonny sings through the horn with legato phrasing and a vibrato reminiscent of Coleman Hawkins. He may have recently seen Louis Armstrong perform Robert MacGimsey's "Shadrack" in *The Strip*, a 1951 film released that past August. "This tune took quite a while to get together," Gitler said. "Like so many small-group arrangements of this period, it was not written out in advance, but worked out on the spot by Rollins and Drew."[143]

The night ended with a blowing session on the "rhythm changes" progression, and Sonny really cooked that night. He quoted the melody to Bud Powell's "Wail," fresh in his mind since he had just seen Bud at Pilgrim. Gitler titled the track "Newk's Fadeaway," an ominous double entendre referring to Sonny's nickname and his namesake's screwball, known as a fadeaway, as well as the song's fade-out ending. "I always had a mysterious air about me, and even in the old days would disappear for different reasons," Sonny later said. "That's why there's a song on my first session called 'Newk's Fadeaway.' But Monk and Max [Roach] knew where I was. Art Blakey, Al Haig, Miles—all my boys knew where to find me."[144]

On December 20, Sonny appeared in the Court of General Sessions before Judge Capozzoli for sentencing with his attorney, Joseph Panzer, and Assistant District Attorney Harold X. McGowan. The case was *The People of the State of New York Against Walter Rollins.*

"Walter Rollins, what have you now to say why judgment should not be pronounced against you according to law?" asked the clerk.[145]

Before Sonny could answer, Capozzoli interjected. "Why didn't you keep your appointment to visit the psychiatric clinic?"

"I was ill," Sonny replied.

"You were ill?" said Capozzoli.

"Yes."

Sonny's lawyer interceded. "Judge, this boy has no prior record," said Panzer. "In this particular instant, when he was found with the gun, he was also found in possession of some hypodermic needles, for which there is a case pending in the Court of Special Sessions. The boy has told me and his mother has told me he would like to go to Lexington, Kentucky, for a cure. He is a drug addict and he is unfortunate in that respect. I don't know what this court can do for him. With reference to Lexington, I think he can enter there himself, and in view of the fact that he has no prior record and lives at home and has not been a bad boy, I ask your honor to be as lenient as possible."

"Counselor, a drug addict with a pretty loaded revolver is a bad combination," said Capozzoli.

"I understand that," said Panzer.

Capozzoli had a busy day, and he had heard enough. "Penitentiary."

Panzer then tried twisting the story, which he bungled. "Before you sentence him, judge, may I say one thing?" said Panzer. "The boy never had any prior conviction. This revolver he said he found in a lot with the needles. He was going, he says, in a cab with two other boys to a police station to give this revolver because he said at the time he was in a lot and found this revolver wrapped up with some needles."

This got Capozzoli's attention. "Wait a minute. Let me understand you," said the judge. "You say he found the needles?"

"I said he found the loaded revolver. He had the needles on him. He used to use them."

"I thought you also said he found the needles."

"If I said that, I didn't mean it," said Panzer. "He said he found this revolver and was going to give it to the police station and report it. I don't think—"

"Let me show you, counselor. If that were so, then obviously, it was unjust to prosecute this defendant. It was unjust to arrest and unjust to indict him and unjust to sentence him, but I don't think that is so. I am quoting now which is in effect what he told the Probation Department: 'He claims he found the pistol early that night in a lot on West 147th Street and St. Nicholas Avenue, and although he knew it was illegal, he retained possession of the weapon in the belief that he might sell it.'"

At this point, Panzer was grasping at straws. "Well, that may very well be, judge. I want to point out to the court that this boy is a narcotic addict."

"Listen," said Capozzoli.

I know that and, listen, I wish there was a way of taking these unfortunates, who are in the throes of such a vicious habit, and submit them to the proper scientific care and treatment to the end that they might be cured and be given a chance to join society. The problem is beyond me. I am sorry. I wish there was some way of doing it. I cannot establish these clinics. I cannot establish the institutions. We spend so much money for so many other things which, in comparison, is trivial, and yet we have hesitated to recognize this problem as a real nationwide serious problem. For some reason or other, that has not been done. I am faced with one or two alternatives; either I send him out to mix with society again with this background and my knowledge of his conduct and his behavior, or else I have got to put him out of circulation. Now, what can I do? I wish there was some way I could send these fellows to some institution to be treated. What can I do about it? I have no way of controlling it. Here he is in a taxicab with a sweetheart.

"He is not a vicious boy," Panzer said. "He lives with his mother. He is a musician."

"Counselor, I will leave it to the parole board to decide what they will do with him."

"Can you send him to Lexington?"

"I cannot. I wish I could," said Capozzoli. "I have no control over Lexington."

"Suppose you see that he admits himself to Lexington?"

Capozzoli was frustrated at this point. "No. If it were a question of petit larceny, I would take my chance. But let us be fair. I have been a lawyer too, and I have been in your place for years—"

"I know that."

"Suppose I should let this fellow go out and, God forbid, he goes out for drugs and shoots somebody. What will happen to Judge Capozzoli? Penitentiary. I am sorry."

So with that, Sonny was put "out of circulation" and handed a sentence of one to three years.[146] Sonny's family was gutted. They had watched the family patriarch go to prison only five years earlier, and now so was Sonny. Sonny would later become an advocate for decriminalizing drugs; he knew that the health-care system was better equipped to deal with an "epidemic" than the criminal justice system.[147]

Miles Davis's fate was not as dire. One night, Miles was playing with Jackie McLean at the Downbeat Club on Fifty-Second Street, strung out.[148] Miles looked down from the bandstand where, to his surprise, stood his father, Miles Dewey Davis Jr., wearing a raincoat and scowling. They finished the set, and father and son went to the greenroom, where they had a stern chat. Dr. Davis insisted that he was leaving that night and Miles was coming with him.[149] He wrote the club owner a check for Miles's outstanding pawn tickets, then they left the club and boarded a train to East St. Louis where Miles would kick his habit cold turkey, at home.

Before Sonny left for Rikers Island, he got in touch with Jackie McLean and entrusted him with the gigs that were still coming his way.[150] The Counts of Bop would have to continue without their leader. Soon thereafter, Sonny was packed into a van, hurtling headlong into the fiery furnace.

Chapter 11

CARVIN' THE ROCK

(1952)

In early 1952, Sonny was getting noticed in the press. He didn't know it, but that February he made his first appearance in a jazz poll. In the tenor saxophone category of the *Metronome* All-Star Band poll, he tied for twenty-fifth place with Tex Beneke, Allen Eager, Eddie Miller, and Gene Cedric. The overwhelming favorite: Stan Getz.[1] That April, Sonny had multiple mentions in *Down Beat*. In a profile of Roy Haynes, the drummer identified Sonny and trumpeter Clifford Brown as underrated musicians who had been "unjustly neglected."[2] Then Sonny had his first *Down Beat* review of a record he was the leader on, "Mambo Bounce" with "This Love of Mine" as the B-side, albeit a tepid four-out-of-ten rating. "After going through the motions of pretending to be a real mambo, *Bounce* soon removes its disguise and turns out to be just another record of just another tenor man playing just another blues," read the damning appraisal.[3] In addition to these press notices, Miles was back from St. Louis and wanted Sonny for a gig at Birdland, but, as Miles found out, Sonny wasn't available.[4]

On Rikers Island, Sonny was languishing in a five-by-eight cell with a metal bed, a foot-and-a-half-wide table that folded against the wall, and a prison-grade toilet.[5] They called inmates by number, not name.[6] A handbook, printed at the Rikers printshop, was given to all inmates when they were admitted, explaining "how to get along in this Institution."[7] After checking their money, valuables, and clothes, inmates showered and then were given a medical exam. Then they received their prison uniform, bed linen, and ID card with their name, number, and sentence, which they were required to carry at all times. One of the only saving graces was the library, which held thousands of volumes inmates could take to their cells on loan. They were allowed to write one letter per day and could receive one visitor for an hour every two weeks.[8]

"Every visiting day, my mother would be there," Sonny recalled. "She really pulled me through. My sister came by one day when my mother couldn't make it, and I vowed then that I would always keep her in my best wishes and do everything I could to take care of her." His girlfriend, Harriette, never visited. "She sent me her picture...and I guess it helped me a little bit, reading her letters and looking at her. It was that picture that in a way got me through it."[9]

The Rikers rules were stringent and the schedule enforced with metronomic precision. The handbook was clear: "OBEY these rules," and "if you feel an order is not proper or just, obey it regardless."[10] There would be a block count at least five times a day, in which inmates stood and faced their own cell gates—after breakfast, at 8 a.m., 3:30 p.m., 4 p.m., 7:30 p.m., and at any time that a correction officer blew his whistle and demanded a count. Before the 8 a.m. count, beds had to be made according to the prison standard. At 7:30 every night, a lever would be pulled, and the prison's mechanical locking system would clink the cell doors shut in unison; they could read until lights out at 9.[11] After lights out, talking, whistling, or singing was strictly prohibited. Spitting was not allowed.[12] Laundry was done weekly, except for underwear and socks, which had to be handwashed daily in the cell's tiny sink, a habit Sonny maintained for years.[13] To walk from place to place, inmates were required to walk in twos to the right of a brass line on the floor. No other pattern was allowed.

"There were no cellmates," Sonny said. "It was hard, especially since I'm claustrophobic."[14]

Compounding the sense of isolation, until 1966, when the Rikers Island Bridge went up, you couldn't get there by car, train, or bus—only by ferry. Rikers Island is a 400-acre penal colony in the East River between the Bronx and Queens, not far from LaGuardia Airport where planes could be heard roaring overhead. Within weeks of Sonny's arrival, a plane botched its landing and crashed 300 yards from the island shore, but miraculously there were no casualties.[15] Originally a fraction of its size, the once "115-acre plantation" was expanded to 400 acres by inmate labor with refuse and debris from subway excavations; the island was, by some accounts, mostly garbage. A 25-acre plot was used as a landfill, until Robert Moses had the bright idea to replenish the city's greenery by converting it into a nursery where inmates tilled the smoldering soil.[16]

New vanloads arrived every day with upwards of ten thousand short- and long-term inmates admitted annually.[17] To the four hundred guards and civilian staff who worked there, it was known as City Penitentiary; to those who lived in one of the 1,887 prison cells, it was "the Rock."[18]

The prison was notorious. First there was the stench, what one former inmate described as "a devil's mix of shit, urine, and disinfectant."[19] Then there was the de facto segregation. More than 90 percent of the inmates were black, but Cell Block 5 was predominantly white and nicknamed the "Waldorf Block," which housed inmates like infamous bookmaker Harry Gross, probably the best-known prisoner at the time. Then there was the corruption. When Sonny arrived, there was a thriving narcotics ring being run by guards and staff, including the penitentiary chef.[20] Guards would shake down inmates or extort exorbitant fees from their families at up to three times the black-market rate for marijuana, cocaine, opium, and heroin, diluted heavily. When the operation was busted by undercover cops soon after Sonny arrived, one of the indicted guards hanged himself,[21] but the sting mostly targeted black pushers and the practice continued unabated. Guards and inmates alike were always looking over their shoulders.[22]

Inmates with no access to drugs had other options. "They used to use nutmeg," Sonny said. "Nutmeg in a certain way would produce a hallucinatory thing and people would get nutmeg in jail."[23]

Then there was the work. Generally, white inmates had the cushiest work details: laundry, library, clerical work, or the infirmary. The dirty jobs, like digging graves for the potter's field on Hart's Island, mostly went to the black prisoners.[24] Yet thanks to jazz-loving chaplain Armen D. Jorjorian, Sonny was assigned a job better suited to his abilities: arranging hymns for the Protestant chapel. "That was our job," Sonny said. "We would spend all week in the Protestant chapel, rehearsing and playing our music. Whereas other guys were mopping floors or whatever, but we had a clique of guys which saved my life."[25]

The Protestant Mission House and Chapel, one of two religious institutions at Rikers, was a modest trapezoidal brick building, and every Sunday at 8:30 a.m., it offered inmates one of the only pleasures to be found on the island.[26] "Those guys could play," Sonny recalled. "We were there every day. That was a great gig."[27] The Salvation Army donated instruments. The hymns were played straight, not swung; at Easter, Sonny took the melody on tenor to Bach's Baroque cantata "Jesu, Joy of Man's Desiring." He would remember it for life.

Musicians were in and out, like Randy Weston, who was only at Rikers for a day and therefore wasn't in the band, but "some guys were there for a long time," Sonny said. "A really good young white guy... There was an Italian trombone player, Mario... he was a top-notch player."[28]

Sonny's closest friend at Rikers was pianist Elmo Hope,[29] then twenty-eight and in the middle of serving a one-year sentence on a larceny conviction.[30] Hope was a piano prodigy and also of West Indian heritage—his parents had immigrated from Antigua and Barbados in the British West Indies. Like Sonny, he grew up in Harlem and attended Benjamin Franklin High School, but did some of his most important self-directed studies of classical theory while advancing bop harmony alongside Bud Powell, who was a year younger.[31] As Bertha Hope, Elmo's wife, recalled, Monk and Powell recorded before him, so "Elmo made a concerted effort to change how he sounded" so he wouldn't be dismissed as a "Bud Powell imitator... but people like [saxophonists] Johnny Griffin and Paul Jeffrey told me that rapid-fire right hand and the harmonic elements—the growling left hand—that those were all Elmo Hope inventions more so than Bud."[32] Within the hopeless confines of the Rock, Sonny continued his own studies—and cultural resistance—with Hope.[33]

At Rikers, Sonny and Hope composed two tunes together: "Carvin' the Rock," combining Charlie Parker's "Carvin' the Bird" and the song's place of origin, with an unconventional thirty-six-bar form,[34] and "Bella Rosa,"[35] named by Sonny for Hope's friend Rosemary, with its medium tempo meant to evoke her carefree gait.[36]

Father Jorjorian was thirty-two when Sonny met him, having grown up in Chicago before moving to New York to pursue his PhD at Columbia University.[37] While writing his dissertation, a chaplain position opened on Rikers, and he applied, figuring it would temper the monastic life of doctoral study.

He got the job in 1947 and expected to stay until he obtained his PhD, but ended up staying until 1955. "The attractiveness and challenges inherent in this very 'live' ministry were so enticing as to prompt me to lay aside the abstract concerns of theory in favor of the practical and immediate needs of people in stress," Jorjorian wrote.[38]

As Sonny recalled, "Father Jorjorian championed...really protected us.... That's where we had a chance to have an oasis within the confines of that institution."[39]

That February, Jorjorian published an article reflecting on his experiences with a thousand drug addicts on Rikers.[40] In the article, he outlined a therapeutic approach to counseling addicts antithetical to the punitive model Sonny had encountered up to that point. Jorjorian rejected the black-and-white thinking of figures like Harry Anslinger, that "the addict is a monster—some kind of moral throw-back for whom any hope of redemption is utterly out of the question." He also dismissed the persistent theory that "an addict is merely the victim of his environment, and that the problem's solution lies in removing the addict from a bad one to a good one." Though environment was a significant factor, Jorjorian had discovered through experience that addicts cut across socioeconomic status and race.[41]

Many of the addicts Jorjorian counseled were musicians. "It is no accident, I believe," he wrote, "that the most recent expression of modern music, Bop, lends particular enchantment to addicts. The uninitiated thinks of Bop as a meaningless conglomeration of musical forms, bent upon obscuring the function of the original theme. But, the devotee thinks of it as the all-in-all ultimate musical expression of his own fantasies and inconsistencies. The 'flatted fifth,' a completely indecisive musical expression, serves as an adequate illustration of the basically abstract nature of this pursuit. It is the Bop artist's subtle and passive effort to bring the discordant world around him into harmony with his discordant self."[42] Whether he had been hip to bop before he got to Rikers or not, Jorjorian had become one of the initiated.

Jorjorian had found that most addicts he counseled felt "separated from the world," and he sought to make them feel connected, even if that connection was not spiritual.[43] He knew that many in his flock were atheists or agnostics and that filling the void with God was not necessarily the goal.

Sometimes they filled it with music, which as far as he was concerned was another form of God. Thus, it was not his approach to "chain addicts to a chair and proceed to preach to them the evils of narcotic drugs," but to employ "the spiritual equivalent of shock therapy": "They must be shown at least the possibility of conclusions about themselves and their potentialities other than those they have consistently accepted and acted upon; conclusions that are positive and encouraging, rather than something that is completely disheartening. They must be given something to live for!" Ultimately, what was most unconventional about Jorjorian's approach was that he viewed the inmates not as numbers on a prison log, but as human beings.

Jorjorian recognized that overcoming addiction was a matter of mental health and that the path to recovery did not end after the withdrawal period; it began there. However, this radical shift in drug treatment from punishment to rehabilitation was slow to garner widespread support at the level of policy.[44]

On September 7, 1952, Sonny's twenty-second birthday passed behind bars. On September 11, the city's parole commission held its regular meeting at 10:30 a.m. on the sixteenth floor of 100 Centre Street: who would serve out the rest of their sentence at the penitentiary and who at the reformatory, who would be rearrested, and, finally, who would be released. Those granted parole had earned the requisite "merit marks" in prison.[45] Thirteen inmates were granted parole that day, including Sonny. And on October 14, 1952, Sonny had regained his freedom. They gave him a bologna sandwich and his gate money—a quarter.[46] This would get him home; subway fare cost a dime.

"The worst part was being in this fucking institution... not having your freedom," Sonny said. "I was playing music, so it was cool, but even with that—not having your freedom, man. I persevered, and I think it made me strong in a way I never thought I'd be tested. But it was pretty rough." Seven decades later, he said, "I cannot take an MRI, and being in jail may have something to do with it.... It faded in a way, but in another way, it hasn't faded."[47]

After ten months, Sonny had finally regained his freedom, but back on the street, old habits die hard.

Chapter 12

COLLECTORS' ITEMS

(1953–1954)

When Sonny left Rikers, he quickly got hooked again, and his reputation was as low as it would ever be. "I had stolen from my best friends—I didn't have any friends. I had taken everything from my house," he said.[1] Max Roach had only one admonition to new arrivals in New York: "'Stay away from Charlie Parker, and stay away from Sonny Rollins.'"[2]

There were two people who pulled him through. "The person that gave me pride to overcome it—besides Bird—was my mother, who stood by me after I had nobody. After I had ripped everybody off," Sonny said. "People would see me coming down the street, they'd run. But my mother stayed with me all the way. And Charlie Parker."[3]

Almost anyone who didn't run when they saw Sonny coming was chasing a fix. Sonny reconnected with Miles Davis, who had also gotten hooked again when he got back to New York. Miles hired Sonny for a session for Prestige in January 1953, which was later released as *Collectors' Items*. The other sidemen were pianist Walter Bishop Jr., bassist Percy Heath, drummer Philly Joe Jones, and Charlie Parker. Bird played a rented King tenor and used the pseudonym "Charlie Chan," a reference to his common-law wife, Chan, more than the eponymous film character, which he used to duck a contractual obligation to Norman Granz at Verve.[4]

It was going to be another strung-out session. To avoid any complications and due to the excitement of recording Bird on Prestige for the first time, session supervisor Ira Gitler called a rehearsal a week prior to the date, anathema to the Prestige model of maximum spontaneity, maximum frugality. Parker showed up, but everyone else was a no-show. Bird himself was trying to quit heroin by replacing it with enormous quantities of alcohol, but almost everyone else on the session was still hooked.[5]

The following day, Bird came to the Prestige offices to request advance payment.[6] Sonny would also sometimes go to Prestige looking for an advance, where he would encounter Sol Weinstock, Bob's father, "an irascible character," Sonny recalled, who was loath to write a check. "During that period, I was very much involved with drugs, and often we would go by there...not really having an idea of what I was owed or what I was due....I just went by there trying to get some money."[7]

On January 30, 1953, the session was off to a rocky start at WOR Studios. Gitler had booked studio time at 2 p.m. He would ordinarily provide sandwiches or sodas as victuals, but, knowing the personnel's proclivities, "here I ordered a fifth of Gordon's gin and twelve bottles of beer to be shared among the six musicians and myself," he said.[8] When Gitler arrived early, he discovered that recording engineer Doug Hawkins, his main collaborator at the studio, was off, with a replacement he barely knew, Bob Lee. Walter Bishop Jr. and Percy Heath showed up on time. The rest trickled in late. First came Bird, then Sonny. Philly Joe Jones showed up next. Then Miles, the leader, finally showed up, more than an hour late. It was past 3 p.m.

Bird decided to set him straight. "Miles was messing around a lot at the time, and he just wasn't taking care of business," Sonny later recalled. "So Bird was really dressing him down like a father to a son. 'Why'd you do that? What's the matter with you, you can't have a band and come in late.'...This was the relationship they had even though Bird was doing it under Miles's name....Bird was explaining to him how a leader was supposed to do it."[9]

Gitler was surprised when "Bird appropriated the Gordon's and in two chug-a-lugs left the bottle virtually empty. No chaser." Miles recalled, "By the time the engineer was running the tape for the session, Bird was fucked up out of his mind."[10]

To some extent, for the musicians on the date, it was primarily a payday. "Being in the throes of addiction, what you have to realize is...the way the forces change," said Walter Bishop Jr. "First was the music, dope was the last. And then it changed—dope, music, because you had to play music to make the money. So a lot of times you're on a record date, and you're looking at your watch, because you might be sick or halfway sick...so it's almost like getting through the date so you can get paid, so you can get <u>paid</u>, so you can get <u>paid</u>!"[11]

It was Sonny's first session with Philly Joe Jones.[12] Jones was a musical polymath; in addition to the drums, he was a tap dancer, pianist, and composer, and he had a stand-up comic's wit and timing.[13] "I used to play with Bird all the time, off and on," Jones later said. "We had a good time together because we were both into the same thing at that time.... He was strung out and so was I, and I had it all the time. So he would hang out with me during the day and tell me, 'C'mon, play some with me tonight.' So he'd be with me in the afternoon; we'd play chess, get high, and I used to cook all the time. I was living on 52nd Street, right off Broadway. So Bird would come down to my house, have dinner when he was working at Birdland, and would go right from my house to work."[14]

Only on this day, Philly Joe was hanging out with Sonny before going to work.

"Bird at that time was not a happy man," Sonny said. "He was getting into all sorts of stupid things, like getting put out of Birdland, if you could imagine something as ridiculous as that. And I guess he was needing money, and he was in pretty bad shape during that entire period. And I perceived that one of his biggest problems was that all of these kids were getting high because of him, and there was nothing he could do about it—because he was hooked himself and couldn't stop, and all his disciples were using. That was one of the biggest hurts in his life."[15]

In the studio that Friday, Bird was happy to see Sonny; it had been a while, and it seemed that Sonny's ostensible sobriety brought Bird some satisfaction that not all of his flock was lost. "'Well, Sonny, how are you doing? Are you cool?'" Sonny recalled Bird asking. "And I said, 'Yeah, man, I'm straight, now.'"[16] It was a white lie.

Miles handed out the sheet music for "Compulsion," an up-tempo rhythm changes he had written for the date. The challenge wasn't the blowing section but the head, which was intricate and could have benefited from the rehearsal they had missed. Bird was passing out, which only made matters worse, and in the run-through, Miles was missing notes. They rolled the tape, but couldn't make it past the melody on take after take. When they finally got it down, Miles was cracking notes on his solo and stopped the tape again.

Gitler was starting to get worried. He left the engineer's booth and came into the studio. "Man, you ain't playing shit!" Gitler said, hoping to motivate Miles. Miles did not respond well to this. He packed up his trumpet and started to leave. "Cat says I'm not playing shit," Miles said. Afraid that if the session were a failure it would be his last as supervisor, Gitler pleaded with Miles to stay, and the band eked out a complete take.[17]

The next tune was another rhythm changes, this one by Jimmy Heath, who was originally slated as the second tenor on the session until Weinstock got the opportunity to record Bird and bumped him.[18] They took it at medium tempo, and the resulting takes were much smoother. Miles peppers his solo with quotes from 1952 pop hits—"The Blacksmith Blues," by Ella Mae Morse, and "Heart and Soul," which landed vocal quartet the Four Aces on the charts. Sonny offers a quote of his own, from "Anything You Can Do (I Can Do Better)," from *Annie Get Your Gun*, which had been adapted for film in 1950.

"'Anything You Can Do (I Can Do Better)' was just one of the riffs that we played. It had nothing to do with my attitude about Charlie Parker. I would never say that to him," Sonny later clarified. "I might have been a foolish young boy playing that to his guru. If there was a little of that, it was sophomoric. I was ignorant."[19]

The well-timed quote would become one of Sonny's trademarks. "Sonny Rollins has the best recollection of the American Songbook of anybody that improvises," Jimmy Heath said. "He'll come up with a song that is so out of the jazz world, but an American popular song, and he'll throw that in his improvisation, and he'll make you laugh." According to Heath, Sonny could "take it and make it his own."[20]

On the second take of the tune, Sonny opens his solo by quoting "Autumn Nocturne," Bud Powell's "Wail," and "Anything You Can Do" again. On the trading section, Sonny had to nudge Bird to alert him to his turn. Gitler called the tune "Serpent's Tooth," named for a line in Shakespeare's *King Lear*: "How sharper than a serpent's tooth it is to have a thankless child!"[21]

They only had two tunes in the can, and at 5:30 engineer Bob Lee announced that he had to leave at 6 p.m. sharp. They attempted to record Monk's "Well, You Needn't," but Miles's chops were giving out. Hearing the Monk tune, Gitler "had a brainstorm," he wrote. "''Round Midnight,' and the nature of its tempo, would give us some more minutes toward an LP and be less taxing on Miles. Bird and Miles would be the main soloists and Sonny would cross the opening and closing bridges."[22] With the clock ticking, there was only enough time for one complete take. They played with great feeling—Bird on obbligato under Miles's plaintive rendition of the melody, Sonny wailing with the weight of a man who had just been released from prison. "Miles, Bird, and Sonny rose to the occasion, as great musicians will do, and taped a masterpiece," Gitler said. "At the last note of 'Midnight' the clock on the wall hit 6:00."[23]

After this climactic moment, there was still more drama between Miles and Bird as they were packing up. "When we were moving out of the door, Miles said to Bird, 'I never did that to you on your dates' and Bird, calling after him down the long hall, countered with 'All right, Lily Pons,'" referring to the soprano, "and followed it with, in booming tones, 'To produce beauty we must suffer pain. From the oyster comes the pearl.'"[24]

Yet the most dramatic moment of the date would be an unspoken exchange between Sonny and Bird. At the end of the session, "Philly Joe told [Bird], 'Yeah, Sonny was over there getting high,'" Sonny said. Hearing this, Bird was speechless. "Bird's whole attitude towards me changed; and he never spoke to me again," he said. "Then I went and said, 'Well, I'm going to show Bird that I can be cool.'"[25] The path to recovery would be an arduous journey, but Sonny had taken the necessary first step of acknowledging the problem. Sonny would come to think of this moment—seeing Bird's crestfallen face—as one of the pivotal turning points in his life.

As he struggled to get out from under his addiction, Sonny's star was on the rise. In the 1952 *Metronome* poll, published in February 1953, he secured the last spot in the tenor saxophone category—twenty-second place—behind Arno Marsh, Herbie Steward, and Jimmy Heath. Stan Getz took the top spot, with Miles Davis winning the trumpet category.[26] Despite his critical acclaim, there weren't many gigs to be had, in part because his prior conviction led to problems with his cabaret card. The cabaret-card policy, which was enforced by the NYPD, branded convicted musicians so they couldn't get hired when they rejoined society—an ineffective deterrent to drug abuse that belied the purported goal of reducing recidivism rates. The racist policy targeted jazz musicians, who were far more likely to perform in cabarets since their music was not accepted by the elite establishment.[27] Billie Holiday, Charlie Parker, and Thelonious Monk were all victims of this unjust policy, which Sonny thought of as "racial subjugation." In order to keep working, for years Sonny had to navigate the Kafkaesque bureaucracy—"a bunch of crooked politicians," first at the Department of Licenses at 300 West Forty-Third Street, then elsewhere. "It was absolutely corrupt," Sonny said.[28] At one of these visits, he ran into Diahann Carroll, though it was unclear why she was there. According to Sonny, Monk had to pay, too.

"I, of course, was one of the victims," Sonny recalled. "I had to pay off... maybe Lieutenant Milligan or Gilligan.... I paid him off, paid him off, up to a certain period. Then...I had to go down to a business place down on Chambers Street, another city building down there, and so this was not exactly the police now....I had to go down there next and I had to buy Broadway tickets to shows for the people down there, and that went on for a while, and then it ended...it all ended so...I didn't have to pay anybody off anymore." The cabaret-card policy remained in effect until 1967. "It was all so under the table that I can't remember exactly how often I went...Eventually, Maxwell Cohen broke it up," he said, referring to the attorney who led the fight to overturn the policy, "and everybody saw how corrupt it was."[29]

Bribing police was not unusual. Art D'Lugoff, who later owned the Village Gate in Greenwich Village, recalled that officials in charge of enforcing the law would look the other way if their palms were greased. "Either they paid somebody off or they got a good lawyer to get them off," D'Lugoff said. "First of all, many of them couldn't afford a lawyer. If they could, the fee was so astronomical that—to pay a lawyer in order to get a job that didn't pay very much didn't make any sense."[30]

As part of the terms of his parole, Sonny "had to have a day job—a nine-to-fiver," he recalled. "I wasn't just free to roam around and get into mischief." It was at the Columbus Circle offices of the Timken Roller Bearing Company, which manufactured roller bearings for railroad lines nationally. He settled into a daily routine: "I used to go to work, and then after I'd get off of work, I'd walk around the corner and stop by Monk's house." His parole officer was satisfied, but there was one problem: "I was strung out," he said, "so my days there were not long. It could have been as short as a month."[31]

With his parole officer breathing down his neck and the cabaret-card policy preventing him from gigging in his hometown, Sonny had developed a wide-enough reputation that he began to get booked outside the city, beyond the cabaret card's reach. In February 1953, twenty-year-old Canadian pianist Paul Bley booked Sonny at the Jazz Workshop, a jazz collective he had started in 1951 along with two other Montreal pianists, Keith White and Art Roberts. Bley had left Montreal in 1950 to enroll in Juilliard, but he would return for Workshop concerts; his exposure to the New York scene allowed him to book leading artists to come for a week, backed by a rhythm section of Workshop members.[32] On February 5, the Workshop had Charlie Parker and Brew Moore as guests on their short-lived half-hour CBC television show, *Jazz Workshop*, which ran every Thursday for three months starting that past December.[33]

"When Sonny Rollins came to the Jazz Workshop," Bley recalled, "he sat down at the table at ten o'clock at night and chugalugged a whole bottle of Gordon's Gin before the first set."[34] Maybe it was pure coincidence, but it was the same brand Bird had downed at the recent *Collectors' Items* session. There was a high level of enthusiasm for Sonny's performance, which was one of the last in the Workshop's series, which ended that June; the organization broke up soon thereafter.[35] Sonny had made a new friend and musical ally in Paul Bley.

Otherwise, the gigs were still few and far between. Sonny was booked with Miles for a week in Baltimore at the Club Tijuana opening on April 28, 1953, though it seems Jimmy Heath deputized.[36] When Sonny went to Philadelphia with Miles,[37] he got a warm meal at the Heath home, where Percy, Tootie, and Jimmy grew up. "If I'd go to see Sonny and somebody, I'd invite him down to my house and my mother would cook," recalled Jimmy Heath.[38]

Either in Philly or Baltimore—Sonny can't recall which—he and Miles got busted. "It happened kind of a stupid way, copping something from somebody," Sonny said. "It was probably doing something obvious that somebody that was checking us could see that those cats were doing something wrong....We were at the hotel room or something, getting high. But that's probably one of those things I blocked out."[39] Not long thereafter, it seems, Miles realized he had to get straight and returned to East St. Louis, again hoping to quit cold turkey. This time he would be successful. He wouldn't be back in New York until February 1954.[40]

On June 9, 1953, Sonny paid a visit to WOR Studios to see Elmo Hope record "Carvin' the Rock" and "Bella Rosa." Sonny wasn't on the session, though. Hope was joined by Percy Heath, Philly Joe Jones, alto saxophonist Lou Donaldson, and a twenty-two-year-old Fats Navarro disciple Sonny had never met named Clifford Brown. It would be several years before they intersected again.[41]

Donaldson, who lived up on the Hill, knew Sonny but kept his distance from his scene as he had a young family and "wasn't into that kind of living," he recalled.[42] Sonny hired him for a dance gig and had Lou recruit the band; Sonny knew his reputation was too unreliable.[43] "He gave me all of these stock arrangements, and told me to get these guys together," Donaldson said. "So I got them together and rehearsed them, and then he came up at the day of the gig...with an alto instead of a tenor. He done borrowed a guy's alto. And I knew that because I saw the guy sitting out there in the audience.... He said, 'Yeah, well I'm here because Sonny got a reputation of pawning people's horns.'" At intermission, Sonny went behind the big white sheet that served as a curtain and gave Donaldson all the money for the gig to distribute at the end. When the gig ended, Sonny "never came out, and the guy, he came to me and said, 'Where's Sonny, where's Sonny?' I said, 'Well, I hate to tell you, but I think Sonny headed for the pawnshop.'"[44]

Brown and Donaldson were clean and as a result were never at the hang at Philly Joe's, where Sonny would often be. Philly Joe, himself a notorious addict and sometime dealer,[45] had a room at the Bel-de-Bue Hotel, a seven-story elevator building on Central Park West.[46] The telephone was in the hallway, and tenants had access to a communal kitchen. Jimmy Heath lived with Philly Joe on and off, initially to establish residency for his union membership. To support his habit, Heath stole shoes from his part-time job at Macy's and sold them to his musical compatriots until he got busted for petty larceny. One Tuesday in October 1953, as Heath recalls it, Sonny came by Philly Joe's and "told me that he had to make a recording the following day and wanted to borrow my horn," he said.[47] Heath lent him his tenor, expecting to get it back, especially considering his brother Percy was on the date. He had no such luck; Sonny pawned it immediately.

The following day, October 7, 1953, Sonny had a recording date for Prestige with Kenny Clarke, Milt Jackson, John Lewis, and Percy Heath—the MJQ—for what would become *Sonny Rollins with the Modern Jazz Quartet*.[48] Since Sonny's borrowed saxophone was already in hock, Ira Gitler rented one for him.[49] Yet they were otherwise on top of it. They had even booked a rehearsal, since "John Lewis was unwilling to go into the studio unprepared," Gitler said, "and [Bob] Weinstock had to respect the wishes of the musical director of probably his fastest-rising group."[50]

At the studio that Wednesday, Sonny sounded his most at ease yet on record. The session began with Duke Ellington's standard "In a Sentimental Mood," with Clarke's subtle brushwork, lush voicings from Jackson and Lewis, and Heath's rock-steady bass line. The tight arrangement has the quartet playing mostly on one and three, with Clarke's snare accenting two and four. On solo breaks at the end of the bridge, Sonny explodes upward but maintains an air of restraint, his dewy vibrato reminiscent of Ben Webster. Next was another standard, "Almost Like Being in Love," a hit from the Broadway musical *Brigadoon*, which Charlie Parker had also recorded in 1952.[51]

The standout tracks are Sonny's originals, though. Gitler named an up-tempo stop-time tune "The Stopper," which foregrounds Sonny's sophisticated rhythmic sensibility. "No Moe," a rhythm changes, is a sly reference to Elmo Hope's nickname, Mo (not Moe).[52] Sonny moves effortlessly from quoting "A Tisket, a Tasket" to a furious double-time line and ends the solo with a playful growl.

Jimmy Heath wasn't able to get his horn out of hock. Right around this time, he was arrested after federal agents caught him selling heroin to various musicians, including Buddy Arnold, a former saxophonist with the Buddy Rich band. Heath was sentenced to take "the cure" in Lexington, Kentucky. Sonny wrote Heath a letter explaining what had happened. "Man, me and Miles and Trane and all of us at that time, we'd take things from each other,"

Heath recalled. "He sent me this letter, saying 'I know I'm a low dirty moth- erfucker and all this stuff, but I couldn't help myself' and here's the pawn ticket."[53] The letter somehow made its way to Heath's mother, who took the pawn ticket, got his horn out of hock, and sent it to Lexington. It was the last thing Sonny ever took from his close friend and later became a kind of joke between them. "He's given me so much since then," Heath said.[54]

As for the record, Nat Hentoff gave the 78 release of "In a Sentimental Mood" and "The Stopper" a cool two-star review in *Down Beat*. "Sonny's a good musician," he wrote, "but he adds about as much to the Modern Jazz Quartet as I would on my recorder."[55]

It was around this time that Sonny began performing with Monk again. Without a cabaret card, Monk was relegated to performing in the outer boroughs, under the radar of the police and the union, and the Brooklyn scene was thriving. That August, Monk played at the Putnam Central in Bedford-Stuyvesant, where for ninety cents at the door listeners could hear "Thelonius Monk" with "Art Blakley" from 10 p.m. until 5 a.m.[56] Max Roach was running the Friday sessions and brought Kenny Dorham, Charles Mingus, J. J. Johnson, Walter Davis Jr., and Miles Davis to the club. Jazz fans in Brooklyn knew how to get down; when Monk played there, he wasn't the only one dancing to his music.[57] It's likely that Sonny took part in some of these sessions, but it was a foggy time. "I was definitely in a stupor during that period," he said.[58]

In November, Sonny had his first opportunity to record with Monk, who hadn't made a studio recording since December 1952, nearly a year, despite his contract with Prestige. Contrary to Sonny's most recent record, only a month earlier, Bob Weinstock had finally decided that LPs were the wave of the future. Monk had met a number of musicians in Brooklyn, in part through Randy Weston, the towering young pianist whose father owned a luncheonette that was a favorite haunt of jazz musicians. Monk hired Sonny, Percy Heath, and Brooklyn natives trumpeter Ray Copeland and drummer Willie Jones; it would be Jones's debut recording.

The session was scheduled for 2 p.m. on Friday, November 13, and the date seemed doomed from the start. Ray Copeland called in sick with the flu, so French-horn player Julius Watkins, whom Sonny knew from his very first recording with Babs Gonzales, was brought in as a last-minute replacement.[59] That Friday, Watkins and session producer Ira Gitler arrived first. Then Percy Heath and Willie Jones showed up, but no Monk or Sonny. Gitler was sweating bullets.[60]

At around 3 p.m., Monk and Sonny strolled in, an hour late, apparently with Monk's three-year-old son, later known as T. S. Monk, in tow.[61] It turned out their cab to Fifty-Seventh Street had a fender bender with a motorcycle; no one was injured, but it slowed them down. When Monk handed out the music, Watkins's part was written for trumpet.[62] The first piece was a medium shuffle with a thirty-two-bar form based on the standard "Sweet Sue,"[63] with a tricky sixteenth-note line on the bridge. Just as Sonny did back in the sessions in Monk's bedroom, they rose to the occasion. Gitler asked for a title. "Let's call this...," Monk said, trailing off. Gitler marked the title as "Let's Call This." The arrangement for the next tune called for Watkins to harmonize with Sonny in an unusual dissonance; he may have wondered if he was playing the part right, but of course he was. It ends with a sixteenth-note machine-gun burst that resolves into a tritone—what Monk called ugly beauty. When they finished the tune, Gitler asked for a title. "Think of one," Monk said, asking Gitler to come up with it himself. Ira marked it down as "Think of One."[64]

They had time for—and needed—one more tune to fill out the desired LP. Monk wanted to record "Smoke Gets in Your Eyes," but they didn't have time to work out an arrangement, so Monk wrote the last tune on the spot.[65] With a four-bar chromatic piano intro, the melody is a simple four-bar ostinato line repeated four times—an auditory equivalent to Escher's staircase.[66] Sonny managed to play an eighty-bar solo without running out of ideas as Jones's ride cymbal just kept swinging and Percy Heath kept walking down that staircase, sometimes in contrary motion to the others. When Gitler realized that the piece had legs, he grabbed a piece of paper, wrote "MORE" in big letters, and held it up to the control-room glass. So the band began trading fours, and the resulting track was nearly eleven minutes long. Gitler had just the name for it: "Friday the Thirteenth."[67]

For their efforts, *Down Beat* gave them a two-star review, giving the "unlucky Friday" a withering critique. "On the seemingly endless *Thirteenth* almost everybody plays as if he were on the brink of tears," wrote the reviewer. "Thelonious, I remain convinced, has a great deal to say but he needs direction. That's what a recording director is for—to give minimal guidance when needed: it was sure needed here."[68]

Meanwhile, Sonny and Monk had trouble booking gigs. Oscar Goodstein, the punctilious manager of Birdland, wouldn't book Monk at the club and likely felt the same way about Sonny, given the cabaret-card situation. Goodstein, who had become Bud Powell's "manager," wanted the musicians in a "glass enclosure." However, there were Monday-night jam sessions at Birdland, where according to French jazz pianist Henri Renaud, who visited New York for four months that winter, Sonny, Kenny Dorham, and Walter Bishop Jr. stopped by, and on at least one occasion, Monk did, too; Goodstein tried to ban Monk from the club.[69]

That winter, though, Monk finally managed to land a regular weekend gig, Friday through Sunday at Brooklyn's Fiesta Room at Tony's Club Grandean. Tony's was an unassuming bar at 562 Grand Avenue at the corner of Dean Street; the name was a portmanteau, which management felt added a touch of class to the former Tony's Bar and Grill. Vincent Jones, a dancer who went by Zandoo, had an act with his partner, Dajaa, in which he entered in a coffin; it was Zandoo's idea to start presenting jazz.[70] Tony's was owned by an Italian family—the Bordellos—but it had a mostly black clientele. That December, jazz fans Freddy Brathwaite Sr. and Jimmy Gittens decided to produce a Monk concert at the bar.[71]

Monk hired Sonny and Willie Jones on drums, with the rest of the band lost to history.[72] That night, Tony's emcee, Jimmy Morton, a jazz-loving law-school dropout, was working the door when some local gangsters showed up. "They wanted to come in without paying and I wasn't going to allow that," recalled Morton. "So we got into it at the door, and it grew and grew until the chairs were flying."[73] Randy Weston was there for the fracas; so were Henri Renaud and his wife, Ny.

"There must have been only two pale faces (my wife's and mine) in this club frequented by many young blacks who danced wonderfully to the sound of Monk's music," Renaud recalled. That night was "like out of a western, and the club emptied out in just a few minutes. Thelonious and Rollins didn't stop playing during the fight and when everything was back in order, Monk swore he had not noticed anything, he was so engrossed in his piano. He was a being who lived on another planet."[74]

Despite the furor, Monk was asked back, possibly as soon as the next night, where, unexpectedly, all the damage had already been repaired.[75] Monk's residency continued to the following May, and Sonny was often with him, along with Brooklyn-based musicians such as bassist Michael Mattos, Gary Mapp, or Sam Gill.[76]

Tony's didn't advertise Monk's residency due to his cabaret card having been revoked, but the Brooklyn scene was robust enough to draw a crowd by word of mouth.[77] Getting the musicians back into the club after intermission was sometimes a challenge, though. "Most of the famous jazz people were almost all into drugs," Morton said, "so what would happen at the intermission, I couldn't find anybody....I'd be running up and down Dean Street looking in hallways."[78]

Yet Bob Weinstock of Prestige was under the impression that drug use was waning. "I'm glad to see that what I call the junky era of recording is almost over," said Weinstock in January 1954. "That's when a man would need forty or eighty dollars and would do a date just for the money. Musically he just went through the motions of his capabilities. It's a good thing for jazz that's over with."[79]

For Sonny, it wasn't over yet, but Weinstock, the founder of what many musicians thought of pejoratively as the "junkie label," didn't care. He recorded two types of artists: those that "hit me emotionally, not because I feel like studying their music," like Gene Ammons and Sonny Stitt, Weinstock told Nat Hentoff, and "those who are trying to advance jazz. Serious musicians like Teddy Charles, Hall Overton, George Wallington, Jimmy Raney, Lee Konitz, the Modern Jazz Quartet, and, in terms of bop, Sonny Rollins."[80]

On Wednesday, January 20, Sonny was hired to play on twenty-five-year-old trumpeter Art Farmer's sophomore album for Prestige.[81] Farmer hired an all-star group for his quintet: drummer Kenny Clarke, bassist Percy Heath, pianist Horace Silver, and Sonny. At the time, Farmer "wasn't getting rich, not in the pocketbook, but in the head."[82] Sonny wasn't getting rich either;

as *Down Beat* reported that February, union scale for a three-hour recording session was still $41.25, with no royalties or residuals.

They recorded four tunes: Farmer's "Confab in Tempo," "Soft Shoe," and the ballad "Wisteria," along with a standard, "I'll Take Romance." Sonny took brief solos on all but the ballad and played well despite continued reed trouble. Given his state at the time, it's entirely possible, likely even, that he just didn't always have access to fresh reeds during this period.[83]

The session was not remarkable, save for one thing: a twenty-nine-year-old optometrist moonlighting as a recording engineer in his parents' living room in Hackensack, New Jersey. His name was Rudy Van Gelder, and it was Sonny's first time working with him. Over the years, Sonny would come to think of him as "very much an artist," he said. If Van Gelder was the engineer, "We knew [the recording] would be impeccable, and perfect."[84] It would eventually be known as the "Van Gelder sound."[85]

Van Gelder was a sonic alchemist who insisted on precision. He was "very neurotic," said Prestige art director Don Schlitten. He didn't want "people playing before it was time for the session. The session was booked for 1 o'clock, and if the piano player began playing at a quarter of 1, he would get very upset and close the piano."[86] The compulsive behavior produced results, though. No one knew how he did it; Van Gelder never revealed how he got his sound to any of the labels he worked for. So it came to pass that the music made in a Hackensack living room, venetian blinds and all, would redefine what it meant to listen to jazz.[87]

Though Van Gelder had begun working with Alfred Lion and Francis Wolff in 1952 and the "Van Gelder sound" would become most synonymous with Blue Note, he was not exclusive to any label. Starting in January 1954, he began working with Prestige. Bob Weinstock was impressed with what Van Gelder did for Blue Note; Weinstock idolized Alfred Lion and bought every Blue Note record. So Weinstock was familiar with Van Gelder when he stumbled upon his optometry practice one day in Teaneck.[88]

Prestige became one of Van Gelder's biggest clients. Weinstock would go out to Hackensack with Miles Davis on April 3, 1954, with Dave Schildkraut on alto; with Miles again on April 29, this time with Lucky Thompson on tenor; and on May 11, with Monk, who hired tenor saxophonist Frank

Foster. Earlier that February, Miles had returned to New York, having kicked his habit, and he wanted to start working with Sonny again. Yet when Miles appeared at Tony's Grandean with Monk, Charles Mingus, and Max Roach, he used alto saxophonist Gigi Gryce.[89] That February, Sonny had risen in the annual *Metronome* poll, tying for sixteenth place with Brew Moore, Georgie Auld, and Arno Marsh.[90] But there was a reason for his conspicuous absence on these sessions and gigs—Sonny was back on Rikers Island.

Chapter 13

HACKENSACK

(1954)

So there he was, carvin' the Rock again. That past September, Elmo Hope had also been rearrested on larceny charges and pleaded guilty in October.[1] Walter Bishop Jr., who was in and out of Rikers, was in.[2] On March 9, 1954, Sonny was rearrested for parole violation and, at twenty-three and a half, was sent back on that ferry to the underworld. The Parole Commission gave him four months. Three days later, Harriette gave birth to Sonny's stepdaughter, Sonya, named after him. Though Sonny didn't believe he was the biological father, he would be involved throughout her life, "as much as is possible in all these years."[3]

Sonny had turned himself in on the recommendation of his parole officer, who remained in contact with Sonny's parents and had "prevailed upon them and also the parolee that if he became addicted to drugs again, he should surrender himself to this office to be committed to the Penitentiary for a 'cure.'"[4] Turning himself in, Sonny's parole officer told them, would result in a maximum ninety-day sentence, but he failed to include that promise in his report so another month was tacked on. There would also be no "cure" at Rikers.

In a meeting on May 20, the Parole Commission considered reducing

Sonny's sentence from four months to the promised ninety days. Fortunately, the three-member commission took a progressive approach to correction.[5]

Sonny's parents, they noted, had been "quite cooperative and appear to be very intelligent people." And the commissioner was sympathetic to Sonny's situation. "Now, this inmate surrendered himself here with his father and he admitted that he had been using drugs just for about one or two months prior," he noted. "He said he was spending about six to nine dollars per day.... He had been out about eight months and was living with his parents. He reported for a short while and he worked at two or three jobs during that short period. I spoke to the Parole Officer about this case. He said he knew of his drug addiction through the parents. He told the parents that in accordance with our rule that if he surrendered himself, in all probability, he might get no more than ninety days. He prevailed upon him to do that. His father accompanied him here."

The commission chairman agreed. "I think we should live up to the so-called indirect promise that he made to the parolee," he said. "I take it for granted that he did come in with his father and he threw himself on the mercy of the Commission, and I think we should go along with it."[6] So Sonny's sentence was reduced.

In 1954, Rikers was in crisis. The problem was overpopulation.[7] Rikers cells were doubled up, and some prisoners slept on bunk beds that filled large dormitories. Inmates were meant to eat in a mess hall with rows of long steel tables with welded steel benches all facing the same direction, but now sometimes they were fed in their cell or the prison corridor.[8] Prisoners were intermingled, the young and the old, career criminals and addicts, thieves and sex offenders, and there were not enough guards. In 1954, police began cracking down on drug trafficking and use even more; that year saw a 10 percent increase in major crimes.[9] When Sonny returned, of the system's $8.5 million annual budget, only half of 1 percent went to psychiatric, psychological, and social welfare programs for the incarcerated. The combination of a stronger police presence and a lack of rehabilitation efforts compounded the recidivism rate, and the prison population continued to snowball.[10] So Sonny reexperienced what Commissioner of Correction Anna M. Kross called the "lock-'em-up-and-forget-about-'em policy of the old era."[11]

Fortunately, Father Jorjorian was still chaplain at the Protestant chapel.

In addition to arranging the hymns, Jorjorian made it possible for Sonny to compose three songs: "Airegin," "Doxy," and "Oleo," all of which would become jazz standards.[12]

On June 8, Sonny had served his ninety days, and the Parole Commission lived up to its promise.[13] He had passed through the crucible, but he would remain on parole for years.

———————◦———————

Back on the outside, Sonny just couldn't quit. "I didn't finally decide to quit," he said. "I had to quit."[14]

Sonny's mother took him in as always, but back on the scene, he was bombarded by the same old temptations. Two weeks after his release, on Tuesday, June 22, Sonny had a reunion with Miles Davis. Miles was living at the Arlington Hotel near Madison Square Park and was still using, if not heroin, then cocaine.[15] Yet Miles was as prolific as ever and was working and recording steadily. He was booked for a week in Baltimore at the Club Tijuana, the hottest jazz club in the city's black cultural hub, and Sonny was the featured tenor. After closing on June 28—the Art Blakey Quintet came in the following day—Miles went back to New York, where he had a record date for Prestige and hired Sonny for his quintet alongside Percy Heath, Horace Silver, and Kenny Clarke.[16]

On June 29, the quintet drove out to Hackensack to record at Van Gelder Studio. Sonny had recorded with everyone on the session before except for twenty-five-year-old Horace Silver, who played both piano and tenor saxophone until the ivories won out.[17] For Kenny Clarke, working with Miles during this period was in stark contrast to the meticulous preparation of the Modern Jazz Quartet. "We'd all walk in the studio and then Miles would say, 'What are we going to play?' And then right away something would come up in my stomach," said Clarke. "It was such a thrill."[18]

Sonny composed three of the four compositions, but they weren't all finished when the band got to the studio. Sonny "would be tearing off a piece of paper and writing down a bar or a note or a chord, or a chord change," Miles recalled. "We'd go into a studio and I'd ask Sonny, 'Where's the tune?' And he'd say, 'I didn't write it yet,' or, 'I haven't finished it yet.'"[19]

Miles brought liquid cocaine to the session, but the music was subdued, with Miles and Sonny pecking and strolling across the sky on top of Kenny Clarke's clouds of rhythm.[20] Sonny's "Oleo" is a B-flat rhythm changes with offbeat accents. It was smooth like butter, the title a reference to oleomargarine.[21] It marked Miles's first recorded use of his iconic Harmon mute, complemented by Sonny's breathy subtone. To add to the freewheeling mood, Miles had Silver and Clarke lay out on the melody except for the bridge, which was improvised by Silver. On the solo section, Silver also laid out outside of the bridge, a technique of opening up the form by removing the chordal instrument, which Sonny and Miles called "strolling."[22] Sometimes Sonny laid out, too. On his pithy solo, he rests long enough between two lines in the first chorus that one of the guys can be heard saying, "Yeah, man."[23] Playing with negative space was key; the effect was like an auditory silhouette.

"Doxy" has a sixteen-bar chord progression similar to Bob Carleton's standard "Ja-Da." The rumor that "Doxy" refers to a European bread spread is false.[24] Rather, the title is a double entendre—"sacred and profane," Sonny said. "Religious doctrine and/or prostitute, loose woman/liturgical."[25]

George and Ira Gershwin's "But Not for Me" was the sole standard they recorded that day, in part as a tribute to pianist Ahmad Jamal, one of Miles's favorites, who had recorded it that past January.[26]

The final tune was Sonny's "Airegin," on which Silver lays out on the melody. "I saw a photograph of some Nigerian dancers in a magazine and it thrilled me very much to see," Sonny later explained. "So the next song that I wrote I dedicated to the dancers, and I titled it 'Airegin,' which is Nigeria spelled backwards."[27] *Airegin* and *origin* also have a homophonic connection. "It was an attempt to introduce some kind of black pride into the conversation of the time. That was my history," Sonny said. "I felt it was time for black people to not feel embarrassed or...ashamed of Africa...but...I wanted to be slick about it. Maybe I felt I *had* to be slick about it."[28]

"Airegin" was the most complex tune Sonny brought that day, with an atypical thirty-six-bar form that unexpectedly shifts from a mostly minor progression to arrive at a major resolution. The bridge is similar to Billy Strayhorn's "Day Dream," with its chromatically descending two-five-one patterns.[29]

Prestige packaged it with three previous Miles Davis sessions as *Miles Davis with Sonny Rollins*, with cover art by Don Schlitten, who reproduced several photographs of Miles playing in a checkered shirt and newsboy cap superimposed on a black background. In the three-star review in *Down Beat*, Nat Hentoff continued hurling brickbats at Sonny, writing that "Rollins to this ear is no particular asset to the session, hence the rating. In contrast to Miles, Sonny's tone is undistinguished and his conception almost never comes freshly alive. It's too bad Sonny's considerable personal force can't be concentrated into less cliche-like patterns. Everybody else is fine." As for the compositions, he commented that "the lines aren't exactly memorable, although *Airegin* has promise if developed."[30]

Sonny's peers could hear what the critics couldn't. He marked July Fourth with a freer kind of independence, alongside Thelonious Monk at the Open Door in the Village, returning to the club July 25 with Art Farmer, Horace Silver, Curly Russell, and Art Taylor. That summer, eighteen-year-old saxophonist Don Menza heard Sonny live for the first time, when Sonny played opposite Count Basie and Sarah Vaughan at Birdland.[31] "I was blown away . . . I couldn't comprehend all the things he was doing, and I never tried to analyze what he was playing. I wanted to absorb it emotionally and spiritually." When he went home to Buffalo, he was still in awe. "I remember going back home and just staring at the saxophone for a week! I couldn't touch it." Despite everything that was going on musically, Menza noticed that Sonny never moved when he played, a stoic stage persona he inherited from Bird. "He looked like a statue," Menza said. "He was immobile."[32] For Sonny, the theatrical yogic contortions he would become known for came later.

On August 18, Sonny was back with Prestige at Van Gelder's for what would become *Moving Out*, his first date as a leader in nearly a year.[33] He hired Elmo Hope, Percy Heath, Art Blakey, and his close friend, trumpeter Kenny Dorham, who phrased like a tenor player on trumpet because he used to be one.[34] Bob Weinstock and Prestige art director Don Schlitten were there to produce the session. Weinstock was the only one with a car, so, Schlitten recalled, "I met Bob and Newk at Bob's office and we rode out to Van Gelder's together." As always for recording sessions, Sonny, ever the clotheshorse, was nattily dressed.[35]

Schlitten's approach to studio recordings was to simulate the immediacy of a club performance. Sessions would begin at 1 p.m. and last four or five hours. To lay down enough material for a ten-inch LP in one day was not such a great feat, he explained. " 'What do you mean in one day?' " people would ask. " 'You know, 'Why don't you take three days to do a session?' They don't understand that those four guys that are in the studio on Tuesday are not gonna be in the same frame of mind on Wednesday. So what is the point? Jazz is of the moment." There would not be many takes. "That's a waste of time and energy. You either play it or you don't play it," Schlitten said. "That's why Prestige was put down, because they did that. They didn't rehearse. People would complain, but that was all a bunch of junk. You don't need rehearsal if you're going to play jazz. You know how to play the tune and you know the chords."[36]

That approach makes sense for standards, but on that August day, all four tunes were Rollins originals, albeit with familiar chord progressions. What's more, Art Blakey didn't have his hi-hat, but he made up for it with his ride cymbal.[37] And they didn't all know the tunes; all four were Rollins originals. On "Moving Out," a twenty-four-bar form full of two-five-one progressions, the written melody line is brief; a two-bar opening tag leads into a two-bar solo break for Sonny. His improvisation is the melody, lyrical and full of rhythmic surprises, and the title, according to Ira Gitler, refers not to physical movement, but to figuratively moving out, far from home.[38] "Solid" is a blowing session on a twelve-bar blues with some solid trading, and "Swingin' for Bumsy" shows off everyone's playing over rhythm changes.[39]

"Silk 'n' Satin" is Sonny's take on Henri Herpin's "(All of a Sudden) My Heart Sings," which Sonny probably knew from Kathryn Grayson's performance in the 1945 film adaptation of *Anchors Aweigh*.[40] "We used the chords of an existing song and added our own changes to compose our own melodies," Sonny later recalled. "The guys used to do it in order to make money because of course the rights to all the original songs were registered with music publishers." The tender ballad was inspired by Harriette.[41]

Sonny's sound had matured, and for the first time in a long time on record, he wasn't plagued by reed trouble.[42] To Ira Gitler, who wrote the liner notes, the album was the fulfillment of Sonny's early promise.[43] "Sonny Rollins has come to the front as the most important reedman in the tradition of Charlie Parker," he wrote. Sonny was already known for self-deprecation. "Sonny will probably shake his head when he reads this and say, 'nothing was happening,' but his modesty is exceeded only by his talent."[44]

Some listeners did conclude that nothing was happening. Nat Hentoff, writing in *Down Beat*, liked the group and Van Gelder's recording, but dismissed Sonny as "unimaginative, however rhythmically powerful, and the overfamiliar lines of the 'originals' don't help either."[45]

It seems that Hentoff's caustic review affected sales. "I was at Prestige one day, and a truck rolled up and started bringing boxes of records," recalled Don Schlitten. "I asked Bob... 'What's all that?' He said, 'That's Sonny Rollins records coming back. They didn't sell.' And there was talk about the 10-inch LP. But Weinstock kept faith in him. He liked the way he played, he thought he was a great player, and he felt that he would eventually be recognized. And he was right."[46] Prestige had developed a reputation as the "junkie label," part of a system that exploited artists, but Schlitten insists that there wasn't much money in it for anybody at that time. "They didn't make money," he said. "It was survival and belief, really."[47]

For Sonny, gigs remained scarce. On September 23, he was billed with Thelonious Monk and Willie Jones at the Club Baron in Harlem to inaugurate a new Thursday-night "cool jazz" series. The show started at 8:30 p.m. and ran to 1 a.m. and was advertised as "The Greatest in Modern Jazz."[48] Evidently, the superlative didn't attract a large crowd, but the next Thursday, they were back for a second edition.[49]

A month later, on October 25, 1954, Sonny was back in Hackensack again for another leader date with Prestige. He wanted to use Art Taylor, stalwart bassist Tommy Potter, and Elmo Hope. Hope was not available—he may have gotten busted again and been sent back to Rikers since the August 18 session—so Sonny called in a last-minute favor from Monk. Sonny hesitated to call someone of Monk's stature for a sideman gig, but Monk immediately agreed and did it for a sideman rate.[50]

They recorded three tunes. Sonny had first heard Jerome Kern's "The Way You Look Tonight" in *Swing Time*, the 1936 film he loved as a child. On the record, he took enough liberties with the melody that on the British edition of the LP, it was titled "The Way You Blow Tonight."[51] They then cover Vincent Youmans's "I Want to Be Happy," from *No, No Nanette* at a medium tempo. Finally, they stretched out on the ballad "More Than You Know," another Youmans standard, sung memorably by Mildred Bailey.[52]

The resulting album, *Sonny Rollins and Thelonious Monk*, was issued some months later and featured Sonny with a pencil mustache in a white button-down shirt and tie on the cover, his eyes closed in a moment of rapture.[53] Ira Gitler's effusive liner notes were a subtle jab at Nat Hentoff, who had panned Sonny's previous album.[54] In the then forthcoming *Encyclopedia of Jazz*,[55] which relied on questionnaires solicited by Leonard Feather and Gitler, they asked for a list of favorites on each musician's instrument. Many listed Sonny: Allen Eager, Hank Mobley, Jimmy Heath, Charlie Rouse, Billy Root. "In addition, people like Milt Jackson, Miles Davis, Percy Heath, Elmo Hope, Billy Taylor, Phil Woods, Teddy Charles, Thelonious Monk and Art Farmer have all concurred on his tremendous blowing," Gitler wrote in the liner notes. "The critics may be a bit slow (didn't they give 'Now's The Time' and 'Billie's Bounce' C ratings?) but musicians are quick to perceive those in their ranks who have something to say. Now it is up to the jazz public to bridge the gap."

Hentoff responded by upping the ante. "Ira Gitler's argumentative notes fail to convince me that Rollins possesses particularly 'individual ideas' or that his blowing is 'tremendous,'" he wrote in his rebuke. "Rollins swings hard, and he plays with considerable warmth, but as has been stated here before, he lacks freshness of conception and his imagination is not individually distinctive enough to raise him to the top level of jazz improvisers."[56]

Yet Sonny's growing influence was undeniable. Five days after the recording, on October 30, Sonny was scheduled to appear at the all-star "Great Moderns in Jazz" concert at Town Hall produced by jazz promoter and critic Bob Reisner, "featuring the outstanding Jazz Groups of '54," a "fabulous history making musical event."[57] The lineup was staggering: Charlie Parker, Sonny Rollins, Art Farmer, Thelonious Monk, Horace Silver, Hall Overton, Jimmy Raney, Addison Farmer (Art's twin brother), Art Taylor, Gigi Gryce, Will Bradley Jr., Teddy Kotick, Phil Woods, Michael Mattos, and Willie Jones. However, the concert was so badly promoted that almost no one showed up, and at intermission, a union representative arrived to collect Bird's pay, which was owed for an earlier missed gig.[58] He "was in such a drug-induced stupor during those times," Sonny said, that he can't remember if he was "one of the multitude" that night.[59]

By the end of the year, Sonny made his first appearance on the final list of the annual *Down Beat* critics' poll. He was in thirtieth place in the tenor saxophone category, after Gene Sedric, with 15 votes. For comparison, the top vote getter, perennial favorite Stan Getz, had 1,318 votes.[60]

Yet in what was becoming a pattern—getting professional recognition and then retreating from the spotlight, either by choice or by force—Sonny decided it was time for a change. Whatever he was doing in New York may have been successful musically, but he was still addicted and wanted to finally live up to Charlie Parker's hope for him. So the timing was perfect when Sonny got a call for a gig at the Beehive Lounge in Chicago. Joe Segal, who ran the jam session at Seymour's when Sonny was there in 1950, was managing bookings for club owner Sol Tannenbaum and wanted Sonny at the club for a one- or two-week stand.[61] He would be gone for a lot longer.

Leaving his hometown signified a commitment to finally part ways with his self-destructive lifestyle, but it also meant losing his first great love—Harriette. She was still hopelessly hooked. "I was close to Harriette when she was really messed up, and she would come by the club, and we weren't having any kind of relations, but I would give her money because she needed it," Sonny said. He imagined a different life for Harriette, but it was not to be. "I don't know how she would have been...I didn't know that Harriette. That Harriette never got to exist." She died in 1978.[62] Sonny hoped that a healthier, sober version of himself would have that second chance.

It was time for Sonny to move out.

Chapter 14

THE BEEHIVE

(1954–1955)

When Sonny returned to Chicago to headline at the Beehive Lounge, he was still strung out—a lot of the Chicago scene was—and he had nowhere to stay. "I was doing what we used to call carrying the stick," Sonny said. "In the old days, the hobos were drawn in cartoons, they all had a stick with their belongings in the bundle tied onto the stick, and so that's why when you saw guys who were carrying the stick, you know they had no lodging themselves."[1] There, Sonny shed all of his baggage and hoped to bury his habit in the Chicago winter.

He was shedding as much as he could. Soon after he arrived, Sonny reconnected with Robert Gay, the prodigal son of the gospel-singing Gay family who went by the moniker "Little Diz," whom he had met on his first trip in 1950. When Sonny finished at the Beehive, sometimes he and Little Diz would sit in at jam sessions organized by local disc jockey and promoter McKie Fitzhugh. "He and Sonny would go and sit in at different places around town," recalled Little Diz's brother, Donald Gay, "and that's how that went down."[2] When the sessions would end, though, they had nowhere to sleep. Fortunately, Little Diz knew how to carry the stick in his hometown. "We were sleeping in all different parked cars and stuff," Sonny said. If it got really cold, Sonny would ride the L all night long.[3]

The Beehive was a midsize club on the South Side of Chicago where the whiskey and beer flowed freely and the music was wide open. The club was located right off Jackson Park, the once-majestic home of the World's Fair of 1893.[4] It was a square brick building with baby-blue double doors and large placards advertising the current and coming attractions on the windowpanes in place of a marquee.[5] Above the signs hung a neon beehive; the club promised "CONTINUOUS ENTERTAINMENT" in neon lights, and at all hours of the night the joint buzzed with honeyed tones and stinging dissonances. There was no cover and no minimum, so anyone could come in.[6] The no-frills lounge seated 150 or 160 people at tables opposite a long bar; a cramped bandstand large enough to accommodate two or three horns, a drum set, a piano, and a bass rose eight inches behind the bar, just high enough for the musicians to be seen above the bartenders' heads. There was a bare-bones sound system, a couple of microphones, and no bass amplifier.[7] When Sonny was invited to play there in the winter of 1954, as Chicago-born saxophonist and trumpeter Ira Sullivan recalled, "everybody wanted to work there."[8]

The Beehive's success was surprising, at least to its owner, Sol Tannenbaum. The money was in the Loop, but all the action on the jazz scene was on the South Side.[9] Tannenbaum did not know contemporary jazz, but he did know about the drug scourge and drilled a peephole into the basement green-room so he could monitor the musicians' activity between sets.[10] Yet Tannenbaum had faith in Joe Segal to curate a contemporary jazz series at the club, starting with Coleman Hawkins, Charlie Parker, and Lester Young, and it became a hit.[11] More acts followed: Gene Ammons, Sonny Stitt, Wardell Gray, Howard McGhee, Eddie "Lockjaw" Davis, and, finally, Sonny.

The visiting headliners would play with the house rhythm section, which at the time was pianist Norman Simmons, bassist Victor Sproles, and a rotating drum chair.[12] According to Simmons, when Sonny arrived, he "didn't really completely discover who he was," he said. "When I met him at the Beehive, that particular confidence was not there yet."[13] It would be by the time he left Chicago.

Sonny relished the opportunity to return—and when his gig at the Beehive ended, he decided to stay.[14] And Sonny was accepted as an honorary Chicagoan. It was a city with a "unique small-town feeling," where Lake Michigan got at his "sub-sub-sub-conscious."[15] To Sonny, New York had become inextricably linked with his addiction, and he thought it might be easier to get clean on fresh soil.

In 1954, Chicago was still a jazz cornucopia. Drummer Leroy Williams recalled, "Sixty-Third Street was almost like Fifty-Second Street in New York. There was clubs on both sides of the street—music everywhere."[16] North Side musicians flocked to the South Side, where the bands were integrated. There was so much to hear—Johnny Hodges, Roy Eldridge, and Ben Webster at the Blue Note at the corner of Madison and Clark in the Loop; King Kolax at the Crown Propeller on Sixty-Third Street; Billie Holiday was headlining through New Year's at the Rodeo on Forty-Seventh Street.[17] On Wednesdays, Joe Segal booked local artists at the Beehive: Ira Sullivan; saxophonists John Gilmore, John Jenkins, and Eddie Harris; trombonist Julian Priester; pianist Kenny Fredrickson; trumpeter Red Rodney; and others. Monday there were jam sessions where Sonny could have encountered saxophonists Johnny Griffin or Harold Ousley, bassist Richard Davis, or pianist Junior Mance. "Eddie Harris and I used to drive out to the Selmer factory in Indiana," Sonny said, "and bug those guys about what they should be doing on the horns."[18]

From Bronzeville to the Loop, there were more gigs to be had and more camaraderie than on the cutthroat scene in New York. For musicians, it was a Wednesday-to-Sunday workweek, with jam sessions and off-night gigs on Monday and Tuesday. "We were around the clock in Chicago. The music never stopped," Simmons said. "We'd go to restaurants, and we would all be hanging out together, you know, and then after the restaurant we would be going to after-hours clubs, we'd come out of the after-hours clubs in broad daylight and go with our tennis racquets and play tennis, and by the time I got home it was noon the next day."[19]

Musicians played across genre, and so did Sonny. "We played all kind of gigs, shows and everything going on in Chicago," Simmons said, "and that's why everybody could work all the time, 'cause all the musicians playing all of these gigs were jazz musicians. It wasn't divided like it is in New York where everybody's specialized." Sonny heard Muddy Waters and Howlin' Wolf on Forty-Seventh Street, absorbed the rhythm-and-blues sound of saxophonist Tommy "Madman" Jones, and got enmeshed in the blues, gospel, and jazz scenes.[20] "Being in Chicago, I wanted to hear everything, dig everything, soak up as much atmosphere as I could," Sonny said. "I got to hear a lot of different things, including sanctified church groups. I never made a conscious attempt to incorporate any of this into my playing; it all seeped in by osmosis."[21] In the span of one week, Sonny could encounter musicians on the jazz avant-garde, in blues bands, and at strip joints—it was all one continuum.

"He was warm. He was a wonderful musician. And being who he was, he helped the musicians out to learn," recalled Chicago pianist Chris Anderson, "but he worked all the same kind of gigs that we worked. He worked gigs that you wouldn't believe he'd be on, for his stature. But he was in the salt mines. He worked the blues gigs, rhythm-and-blues gigs.... There was a place outside Chicago called Calumet City that had a bunch of strip joints. We worked those even; we had to. He worked them, too."[22]

Sonny got a ride fifteen miles outside Chicago to the Illinois-Indiana line, where segregated Mafia-controlled gambling houses and neon strip clubs lit up the State Street strip, a result of the postwar manufacturing boom in northwest Indiana. Unexpectedly, the Cal City burlesque gigs at the Whiskey-a-Go-Go or Babe's Safari Cruiser offered yet more rigorous training in the

Great American Songbook. Sight-reading was a must, and ten-dollar gigs ran from 8 p.m. to 4 a.m., sometimes 5, with musicians hustling down the strip to play other clubs during set breaks. The dancers didn't want just anything to bump and grind to, but "Rhapsody in Blue" and standards like "Bésame Mucho" or "There's No Business Like Show Business." So thrill-seeking factory workers unknowingly caught Sun Ra, Norman Simmons, Von Freeman, or Sonny playing behind the velvet curtain by mob fiat.[23] This trial by fire in Jim Crow strip joints was part of the raw material that forged his next album—work time would become *Work Time*.

One memorable gig Sonny played was at a West Side blues club, booked by a smooth-talking guitar player named Little Leo Blevins.[24] "He hired Sonny, himself on guitar, Chris Anderson on piano, Wilbur Campbell on drums," recalled Wilbur Ware, who played bass. "[Blevins] would say, 'We got to play blues now.' And that means fast blues, slow blues, shuffle blues—that's all they want to hear. Okay, a gig is a gig. I think we made ten dollars a night. But it was worth it. We'd go over there, and oh, we thought we were playing some blues. We got funky—Leo even fell on his knees; he could do that... fell on his knees bending them strings, you know; something like T-Bone Walker would do."[25]

The next night, Sonny might play a gig with Sun Ra at the Rhumboogie, co-owned by African American entrepreneur Charlie Glenn and boxing legend Joe Louis. "I knew him as Sonny Blount," Rollins recalled. "I was tight with John Gilmore. I used to go by his house a lot in Chicago. John was a beautiful guy."[26] On one occasion, through an association with Chicago trumpeter George Brown, whom Sonny had met in New York, he got an opportunity to sit in with Gene Ammons. "They let me play, and...I was a young lion, I must have sounded good. So Gene Ammons told George, 'Hey man, why didn't you tell me that guy could play that good? Why'd you bring him up on my show?'"[27] Sonny was grateful that Ammons even gave him a look. "Gene was very nice to me as an unknown, somewhat decrepit looking young saxophonist in town....He was one of the best saxophonists that we had."[28]

More than anything, Chicago meant community. "When we came up, we got together to practice, the drummers, everybody got *together* to go over their stuff," Simmons said. While the younger generation was coming up, the older generation would come down to meet them, "passing information down and telling us which way to go...all of us stood on somebody's shoulders."[29]

Bassist Victor Sproles, who played in the house band at the Beehive with Sonny, was a key figure in fostering a sense of solidarity on the Chicago scene. He and his wife, Janis Sproles, lived right by Washington Park on the South Side. It was a one-bedroom garden apartment with a basement. "Our home was the hang-out for musicians who came to the city to play at different venues, when they finished their gig," recalled Janis Sproles. "We had a Ping-Pong table in the basement. On Tuesdays, we had chess night. Some of the fellows would cook. Wardell Gray loved to cook, his specialty was spaghetti with mushrooms....Sonny would come by our house and sit and talk for hours with my husband, Victor Sproles. He was known to go outside early in the morning to just blow his horn for hours and hours."[30]

Yet Sonny was still hooked. He began to realize that if he didn't do something major, he would never be free. On May 4, 1954, while Sonny was still in Rikers, Ike Day had died in a tuberculosis sanitarium.[31] "The doctor told him he had TB and told him if he didn't stop playing, it would kill him, and Ike said, 'Well, I been playing all my life and that's the way I'm gonna die.'"[32] Even if Day's death was not caused by drugs, heroin hastened his demise. Day had written to Sonny that he wanted to get clean, but he passed before that ever happened.[33]

"Very few people were getting away from heroin at that time, very few people," Sonny said. "Most guys ended up...dying from an overdose...or just destroying their life."[34]

Many musicians passed through Chicago after leaving the United States Public Health Service Hospital (USPHSH) in Lexington, Kentucky. "That period we were living through the dope scene," recalled Norman Simmons, "and so a lot of cats, when they came out of the hospital, they came to New York through Chicago and just kind of boned up and sharpened themselves up on the way back to New York."[35]

In January 1955, Sonny and Little Diz decided to voluntarily check themselves into Lexington.[36] Four hundred miles from Chicago to Lexington, they were ready to commit themselves to what was then called "the cure."

———◇———

In Lexington, they had to find their way to the facility; no public transportation went there. Boxing champion Barney Ross came in a plane;[37] William S. Burroughs, who was there in 1948, took a taxi to the gatehouse. "All the taxi cab people know when they see guys coming off the train," said one former patient. "They say, 'You're going to Lexington.'"[38] It was located seven miles outside the city, in the middle of farmland. Perched on a hill, rising out of the Kentucky bluegrass like a mirage, it was a hulking, unfathomably large Art Deco–style building with wrought-iron gates and brick archways, on a lush thousand-acre campus.[39]

The facility was a New Deal–era project spearheaded by the Bureau of Prisons and the Public Health Service. The result was, as one doctor put it, "more like a prison than a hospital and more like a hospital than a prison."[40] The first modern rehab facility, the Narcotic Farm opened in 1935.[41] The official name had changed to the USPHSH, but those who lived and worked there always knew it as "Narco" or simply "the Farm." Everyone in the treatment program—inmate or volunteer—was there as a patient.[42]

Voluntary applicants, known as "vols" or more commonly as "winders"— for the frequency they wound in and out of the institution—were generally admitted to Lexington using a legal loophole known as the Bluegrass Law.[43] This required going to the police in Lexington and effectively turning yourself in as an addict with the intent to go to the US Public Health Service Hospital. Winders were then brought before a magistrate and given a one-year sentence that would be commuted once the addict took the full cure. It's not clear how much this policy was enforced; most people went directly to the facility when they got to town. After completing their intake papers, it was explained that winders, who took up about one-third of the thirteen hundred beds, could check out whenever they wanted—knowing they would probably be back. The relapse rate was between 90 and 99 percent.[44]

"It was a place where you were able to treat addicts, something like the Betty Ford Clinic in later years," Sonny said. "Anyway, you were treated in a humane manner, as a sick person, not as a criminal." He was going into the lion's den, even though he thought he "might have a better chance with a lion than with some of these substances."[45]

When Sonny and Little Diz got to the station in Lexington, they encountered Jim Crow. "Kentucky had been neutral in the Civil War, but it was totally segregated, and not until the Civil Rights Movement did that ever change," said Marjorie Senechal, whose father, Abraham Wikler, worked at the Addiction Research Center (ARC), which was part of the facility.[46] "The schools were segregated; the buses, black people had to sit in the back; the fountains at the courthouse, there were two, one for colored, one for white; everything was completely and totally segregated." The Farm was distinct as one of the only places in the city that was integrated.[47] Beyond that wire fence, segregation was outlawed; it was a federal property, and under federal law, they weren't even allowed to grow tobacco there.[48]

When Sonny and Little Diz got there, they filled out their applications for admission detailing their history of addiction, daily fix, and emergency contacts. The hospital assessed patients a fee of $8.50 per day, which was waived based on financial necessity.[49] Then they put their civilian clothes in a basket, showered, and were given a medical examination. After the doctor determined the state of their addiction, they were given standard-issue pajamas, a bathrobe, and slippers and then sent to dry out in the detox ward. Men and women were housed separately. To mitigate the worst of the withdrawal symptoms, the hospital used tapered doses of Dolophine, the brand name for methadone.[50] Detox lasted between ten days and two weeks, at which point they would be sent to the general population for four months. This was "the cure."

The Farm was rife with contradictions. To the winders, it was a port in a storm; to the scientists at the Addiction Research Center, which was part of the campus, it was an endless pool of human and animal test subjects that would lead to the most comprehensive study of addiction in history; to the pharmaceutical industry, it was a gateway to market approval for potentially addictive drugs like Demerol and Thorazine; and to the CIA, it was a highly classified part of the MK-ULTRA program that ran experiments with LSD.[51] Yet it was also thought of as "a country club as prisons go," wrote William S. Burroughs Jr.[52] There were softball, tennis, bowling, pool, even golf. On its working farm, patients cultivated Kentucky corn. The rooms were small but livable. And still, it was a prison. But everyone agreed on one thing: Narco was a jazz utopia.[53]

In addition to Sonny and Little Diz, a partial list of musicians who went to Lexington includes Dexter Gordon, Sammy Davis Jr., Jimmy Heath, Chet Baker, Elvin Jones, Tadd Dameron, Red Rodney, Howard McGhee, Wilbur Ware, Sonny Stitt, Jackie McLean, Lee Morgan, Stan Levey, and Bennie Green.[54] In 1964, a band of patients from Lexington played on *The Tonight Show* with Johnny Carson.[55] While Sonny was there, some musicians were well known in the jazz world, some not: saxophonist Buddy Arnold, "a guy named Raphael that played bass" who experimented with odd time signatures, and Chicago saxophonist Clifford Jordan, a year younger than Sonny.[56]

The program took a multipronged approach to rehabilitation. There was talk therapy, and then there was jazz therapy.[57] Musicians couldn't take their instruments in—the staff couldn't risk contraband[58]—but the hospital had its own supply. Musicians were allowed to practice, rehearse, and compose for five or six hours during the day, with two hours reserved for evening rehearsals with groups ranging from small combos to big bands.[59]

Practice rooms were adjacent to the auditorium. When guitarist Wayne Kramer of iconoclastic proto-punk band the MC5 did two years at Lexington in 1975, "I found chord changes penciled on the walls," he wrote. "They were sophisticated substitutions, and I wondered who might have written them: Tadd Dameron? Lee Morgan? Gerry Mulligan?"[60] Maybe Sonny.

But the real excitement took place in the expansive Art Deco–style auditorium, where weekly concerts, sometimes featuring dancers, were held on the proscenium stage, and patients filled the auditorium up to the balcony.[61] When it was warm enough, musicians could play outside.[62]

At Narco, Sonny was thinking about Charlie Parker.[63] On March 9, Bird stopped by Baroness Nica de Koenigswarter's room at the Stanhope Apartment Hotel on the Upper East Side, where he began vomiting blood. Dr. Robert Freyman was called and determined that Bird had stomach ulcers, lobar pneumonia, and cirrhosis of the liver.[64] He refused medical advice to go to the hospital but agreed to stay with Nica until he was able to make it to his gig at Storyville in Boston. On March 12, according to one report, he was watching a juggler on television when he laughed, gasped for air, and died soon thereafter of heart failure. After the ambulance came, the morgue mistakenly tagged Bird's body as "John Parker," and there he lay for forty-eight hours, unclaimed, necessitating an autopsy. The coroner who performed it concluded that Parker appeared to be between fifty and sixty years old.[65] Some would say their prophet was just too good for this world. Jesus was thirty-three; Bird was thirty-four.

"Boy, wait 'til I see Bird and let him know that I got his message," Sonny recalled thinking, "and I was so happy, but it wasn't to be. But I'm sure in another world he'll know that people got his message."[66]

Bird's death sent shock waves through the jazz world. Dizzy Gillespie famously said that Bird was "the other half of my heartbeat." His funeral was March 21, 1955, at Abyssinian Baptist Church, a block from where Sonny was born. At 12:15 a.m. on April 2, a memorial concert was held in his honor at Carnegie Hall, described as the biggest jazz concert yet produced in New York, 2,760 mourners filling the hall.[67] Dozens performed: Dizzy, Monk, Mingus, Art Blakey, Kenny Clarke, Stan Getz, Roy Haynes, Billie Holiday, J. J. Johnson, Clifford Brown, Tommy Potter, Horace Silver, Mary Lou Williams, and Lester Young. It didn't end until after 3:30 in the morning.

Sonny played at a Bird memorial documented only in the *Blue Grass Times*, Narco's patient-run newspaper.[68] "The jam session held Tuesday night, March 15, was one of the best presented here in a long time," read the article. "The music department has been sparked by new personalities." That night, they played songs that were part of Bird's repertoire. Robert Orville "Sonny" Gibson—a young saxophonist who aspired to be "half as great as was Bird!"—played "Crazeology" and "Whispering," the latter being the basis of "Groovin' High." Clifford Jordan played alto on "Just You, Just Me" and "Sweet Georgia Brown," setting "a relaxing mood by his seemingly effortless execution, and his sounds circulated all through the auditorium. More could be done with him!" Drummers Maurice Lyles and Eddie Robinson played a drum duo.[69] Sonny was the final act, starting with "I Can't Get Started."[70]

But now I'm broken-hearted[71]

Sonny closed the night with "How High the Moon."[72] Bird had performed the tune with Miles, but he also cowrote his own version based on the chords: "Ornithology."[73] Sonny wanted to remember Bird as he lived, not how he died—by taking flight. The choice of material did not elude the jazz cognoscenti at Narco: "Every true enthusiast here understood the depth of the feeling Sonny was trying to express—no doubt!" And Sonny must have felt that Bird had taken flight himself. Bird was their prophet, and everyone there, especially Sonny, was there because of him, not in spite of him.[74]

At the end of Sonny's four and a half months, he felt ready to reenter society sober. "That place served me well," Sonny said. "If I didn't have the determination to stop, it would not happen, because there are people that went there, that still used drugs when they came out."[75] Sonny was the rare Lexington success story.

On May 5, 1955, Sonny and Little Diz left Lexington for Chicago.[76] When they set foot outside the fenced-in institution, they were immediately greeted by the cold stare of Jim Crow.[77]

———◁◦▷———

Back in Chicago, Sonny had almost no possessions. He didn't even have one consistent tenor he was playing. "I always had access to have a horn 'cause I was Sonny Rollins," he said, but "there was no one horn that I had all the way through these experiences."[78] All he had was his resolve—it would take all his determination to slay the dragon.[79] "So then I said, 'Oh wow, this is it now. I have to be out here and...I have to break this habit now. Nobody around, I'm not in jail, I'm not in Lexington and...it's up to me.'"[80]

Sonny's reentry wasn't entirely solitary. He found strength in community through the helping hand of the Gay family. After they got back from Lexington, Little Diz invited him to stay at the Gay family home at 5639 South Cottage Grove Avenue. There, Sonny rediscovered his gospel side. The family matriarch, Fannie Parthenia Gay, had founded the nationally known Gay Sisters gospel group. She hoped to bring her son Robert back into the fold and Sonny along with him.[81]

The Gay family were leading figures in Chicago's gospel community.[82] Evelyn, the oldest, would one day be known as the "First Lady of Gospel Songs"; Millie was the middle daughter; Robert strayed and became a jazz musician; Geraldine was the youngest daughter, about six months younger than Sonny, and would later be known as the "Erroll Garner of gospel."[83]

The youngest son, Gregory Donald Gay, born in 1945, was a child-prodigy evangelist known as the "Boy Preacher," who was sermonizing by age three and leading tent revivals at four.[84]

When Sonny first came to Chicago in 1950, the Gay Sisters were performing at Carnegie Hall with Mahalia Jackson and Clara Ward.[85] In 1951, they had a hit on Savoy with "God Will Take Care of You."[86] They toured all over the country.[87]

Sonny was surprised they let him stay there at all. "I was, you know, a guy who uses drugs," Sonny said. "How nice it was for them to let me stay there, because it was a very small house." Mother Gay, Sonny said, was "a very spiritual person. She knew Mahalia, she knew Sister Rosetta Tharpe, all those people. And it was really nice, she used to pray for me to get my life together." And when she prayed, Sonny said, "she prayed in tongues."[88]

They restored Sonny's sense of belonging. "The Gay family was my home away from home," he said. "I fell in love with Geraldine. She was a great pianist who composed some nice gospel songs."[89]

Geraldine was as beautiful as she was talented. Before she was born, Fannie had Sister Rosetta Tharpe's mother, the turbaned revivalist Katie Bell Nubin, known as "Mother Bell," pray for her daughter to be "a gifted child like Rosetta."[90] She was. When Geraldine was a toddler, she started playing piano all on her own. Soon it became apparent she could pick out any tune she wanted. When she was six or seven, her older sister Evelyn began taking piano lessons, and Geraldine could play her practice material by ear.[91] Geraldine heard Sister Rosetta Tharpe and had a word for her brilliance, *fly*, and added that you were singled out "if you showed any kind of flyness with your music."[92] Geraldine was fly, and Sonny knew it.

"I really had a nice relationship with Geraldine," Sonny said.[93] Geraldine's first boyfriend was the Reverend James Cleveland, a gospel star who would go on to collaborate with Aretha Franklin on *Amazing Grace*, the best-selling live gospel album of all time. (Years later, when Sonny was asked to list his favorite ten albums, *Amazing Grace* topped the list.)[94] Cleveland told Geraldine her "hair and clothes" were his favorite things about her; Sonny loved her music.[95] "He said, 'You have perfect pitch,'" she recalled Sonny telling her.[96]

For a brief period, Sonny used to attend the church regularly. "I used to go there every week, which I enjoyed because the music was so animated," Sonny said.[97] Donald Gay could hear the gospel influence in Sonny's music, and the experience made it stronger. "He's got the spirit," he said.[98] The Gay family attended Elder P. R. Favors's Church of God in Christ Church, the "sanctified church of the West Side," where Geraldine played the piano; Malachi Favors, the bassist and cofounder of the Art Ensemble of Chicago, was part of the congregation.[99]

Outside of church and family meals, Sonny and Little Diz practiced together every day. "My brother and him would go out every morning to Jackson Park at about seven o'clock to get their chops together," recalled Geraldine. "I didn't know what 'chops' meant! And I said, 'What do you mean?' And he said, 'Geraldine, chops means get your lips together to play your horn.'"[100]

Getting his chops together also meant finding a place of his own, but there were rules. The first rule was that he had to avoid the clubs at all costs. He began living like a Buddhist ascetic. And he got a day job. Sonny took whatever he could get.[101] One day, Sonny bumped into guitarist George Freeman on the job when he knocked on his door. "I was surprised to see him, and I guess he was surprised to see me," Freeman recalled. "But he was selling lady's stockings. That was my last time seeing Sonny. After that he became totally famous."[102] He did a stint as a porter, as a janitor at a typewriter repair shop on the North Side on Ohio Street, and at a restaurant supply business in Greektown loading and unloading trucks for deliveries in Chicago and nearby in Gary and Hammond, Indiana.[103] At the truck-loading job, Sonny befriended some of the workers and disclosed his secret identity, but at the typewriter factory, they had no idea. "It was about ten guys in there fixing typewriters, and I was like the janitor," Sonny said. "I think they called me Wally, see, 'cause my name is Walter.... I used to put up signs on the wall saying, 'Please don't throw your paper towels on the floor.'"[104]

Quickly, he earned enough money to move into the YMCA in Bronzeville. One morning when he headed out for work, he passed a record store on State Street, and in the window display was his picture on the cover of the recently released *Sonny Rollins and Thelonious Monk*.[105] The irony was not lost on him. "I think I went in there and told the cat, 'That's me, I'm Sonny Rollins.'"[106]

Sonny also sat in on some music classes at the University of Chicago. "I didn't have the money for tuition so I had to leave," he said, "but because I'd made a few records, I was fortunate to come into contact with teachers who were willing to instruct me. I wanted to get a thorough foundation because I was very depressed about the records I'd made. I knew now that music was sacred to me."[107]

He committed to a monastic existence—a sabbatical—until he had the fortitude to return to the scene. "I used to buy a loaf of whole wheat bread, I used to get Oscar Mayer...liverwurst," he said. To drink, "they had these tomato juices, these little cans. So I got as much of those as I could...'cause then I could keep them in my room."[108]

During the day, Sonny would practice in his room, where people would listen from outside. "He had a BB gun," according to one future band member, "and if he would catch guys hanging outside his door, he'd shoot their asses with the BB gun."[109]

At night, Sonny would practice in the basement of the Y, where they had a piano.[110] One night, he heard someone playing a Clifford Brown record on repeat who turned out to be trumpeter Booker Little.[111] "I was playing it over and over again, and I guess I was driving him mad, because he was trying to practice himself," Little recalled.[112] At the time, Little was a seventeen-year-old sophomore at the Chicago Conservatory who had come from Memphis and was also living at the Y.[113] Finally, Sonny decided to approach him. "He asked me what I was doing, and I told him I was trying to learn the melody," Little said. "He told me that it was probably best that I go buy a sheet on it, because if I kept listening to the way he played it, it was going to rub off, and I was going to play it the same way. I never forgot what he said, though I did continue listening to Clifford Brown records."[114]

Sonny immediately recognized Little's talent and seriousness. "I think that he was defining his style but it was certainly evident that he had all of the chops and everything," Sonny said.[115] They began practicing together in the basement of the Y.[116] Sonny was always working things out in writing, and he recorded some of his interval studies on music manuscript paper. At this time, he was focusing on the ninth interval and writing out exercises that he would master in all twelve keys, a practice of documenting his autodidactic study of music theory that would remain a lifetime habit.[117]

Sonny was like a boxer in training. "He loved boxing," recalled pianist Harold Mabern, a hometown friend of Little's, who was one of the few people who had the temerity to approach Sonny at the YMCA, evidently avoiding the BB gun. They ran into each other at boxing matches at the Chicago Stadium.[118]

By the middle of the summer, Sonny decided to venture back into the Beehive, which he recalled as straight out of *Cabin in the Sky*, where Lucifer's minions battle for the protagonist's soul. He wasn't ready to bring his horn; it was purely a test of strength, and damn it all if he was going to succumb to temptation.

"So I went by there one night—'Hey Sonny, how you doing man? Hey, man, I ain't seen *blah, blah blah*. Hey man, I've got some good stuff. I've got some good stuff, man, come on.' And that's what I was afraid of," Sonny said. "My hands got sweaty.... So a while I went through this and finally I said, 'Okay, let me get out of here.' So I said, 'Okay, man, see you cats later, man.' And I got out, went back, got back into my life of being an honest person doing a day job."[119]

That September, right around the time he turned twenty-five, Sonny decided to go back into the Beehive a second time. Art Blakey and the Jazz Messengers were headlining.[120] The quintet was Blakey on drums, Kenny Dorham on trumpet, Hank Mobley on tenor, Doug Watkins on bass, and Horace Silver on piano; Silver and Watkins were the only members who were clean.[121] "I just remember sitting in the car with Horace, and then I went inside to pal around with Art and everybody, and I was able to withstand the temptation again," Sonny said.[122] This time, Sonny stayed for the whole night, hanging with the band in the dressing room during set breaks.

At the end of the night, Sonny handed Horace a handwritten note:

Dear Horace,

You are the living (in flesh) representative of all that modern progressive musicians should be. Continue to play and to live the life that your talents are worthy of.

(Signed) S.R.[123]

For Sonny, living a life worthy of his own talents seemed closer than ever. On September 15, 1955, the week after his twenty-fifth birthday, Sonny was finally and officially off parole.[124]

On October 2, Norman Granz's fifteenth annual Jazz at the Philharmonic tour was passing through Chicago's palatial Civic Opera House, in the Loop.[125] Ella Fitzgerald, Dizzy Gillespie, the Oscar Peterson Trio with Ray Brown and Herb Ellis, and Stan Getz, in his JATP debut, were all part of the package. "That was the crème de la crème of the presentations of that day," Sonny said. He decided to go to the concert and see if he recognized anyone. "I was standing outside looking to see if we saw anybody that knew us and we knew them—of course we were in different strata at that time." Sonny saw Peterson and approached him. Peterson must have known of Sonny's reputation, because he "put ten dollars in my hand," Sonny said, not a small amount of money at that time. "He knew what the deal was. And I never forgot that." Rather than be insulted, Sonny was moved. Years later, he told Peterson's manager "how much I appreciated his act of kindness to me at a time when I needed it."[126]

Sonny was feeling stronger, and by the third time he went to the Beehive, "I really felt it," he said. "'I got it whipped.'" The temptation was still there, but he decided it was finally time to start playing out again. Sonny had survived, not just for Bird, but for everyone else who didn't make it through: for Fats Navarro and Ike Day; for his mother, who supported him through it; and for himself. After spending the better part of a decade hooked, he said, "I cheated the serpent demon here in Chicago."[127]

Sonny went back to the Beehive, where the Max Roach–Clifford Brown Quintet was booked from September 30 to October 13.[128] This time, he brought his horn.

Chapter 15

BROWN-ROACH INCORPORATED

(1955–1956)

"I really met Clifford when Roach and Brown Incorporated passed through Chicago in 1955," Sonny said.[1] *Brown and Roach Incorporated* was the title of an LP they had just put out on EmArcy, but it was also a philosophy; they were dead set against artist exploitation, businesslike in their demeanor on- and offstage, and committed to being taken seriously as artists of the highest order.[2] The Brown-Roach Quintet was signed to a major label—EmArcy was a phonetic spelling of the initials for the Mercury Record Company—and they were represented by a major agency, the Associated Booking Corporation (ABC), run by the notorious Joe Glaser.[3] They were true coleaders; on albums, the group was generally billed as Brown-Roach and on gigs as Roach-Brown.[4] They dressed impeccably for performances, always in suit and tie, usually with a pocket square. Their cerebral brand of hard bop was harmonically and technically complex, and behind Max's relentless ride cymbal, they played faster than anyone. They were not entertainers, but artists. Theirs was the sound of the civil rights movement to come.[5]

Sol Tannenbaum, who owned the Beehive, didn't even know their names when they arrived, but the Max Roach–Clifford Brown Quintet was so popular that their initial two-week run, which began September 30, 1955, was extended to November 10. The group broke the club record and was so hot that Tannenbaum began to worry that people were staying the whole night and preventing the tables from turning over. The quintet was Roach and Brown on the front line, George Morrow on bass,[6] pianist Richie Powell (Bud's brother), and Harold Land on tenor.[7] Like the Modern Jazz Quartet, they were committed to staying together and developing a group sound, but that was about to change.[8] Harold Land's grandmother was gravely ill, and when she died while he was still on tour, he went back to California.[9] What was planned as a temporary leave became permanent. Suddenly, there was an opening for a tenor that needed to be filled, and Sonny was newly available.

Clifford Brown—everyone called him Brownie—was from Wilmington, Delaware, and was only a month younger than Sonny.[10] They were both prodigies and encountered many of the same giants coming up: Dizzy Gillespie, J. J. Johnson, Fats Navarro, and, of course, Max Roach.[11] A car crash in June 1950 put him out of commission for almost a year, but he continued his assiduous practice.[12] After he recovered, Charlie Parker hired him for a week in 1951. Bird "took me into a corner and said, 'I don't believe it. I heard what you're saying, but I don't believe it,'" Brown recalled.[13] By the time Sonny heard him in Chicago four years later, Brown had found his voice.[14]

Sonny knew of Richie Powell; they both came up under Bud's wing. Though Richie would be overshadowed by his older brother's peerless genius at the piano, he made an important contribution to jazz piano vocabulary in his own right. "McCoy Tyner got his harmonic style from Richard Powell," said pianist Harold Mabern, who saw him with Brown and Roach at the Beehive in 1955. "What you call fourths—[Tyner] got that from Richard Powell."[15] Powell's comping style came through on his plaintive bitonal introduction with the sustaining pedal on "Delilah" from the 1954 album *Clifford Brown and Max Roach*.[16] "He was really on his way to becoming a harmonic genius...because if you've got Bud Powell for your brother, you're not going to compete with Bud overall, so he found another way."[17]

The quintet showcased a clean-living alternative to the strung-out lifestyle that pervaded the jazz scene. Sonny and Clifford had "nothing in common, besides our music," Sonny said. "We evidently came up in different milieus, because when I got out of high school, I was sort of getting into the life...the jazz life." For a long time, Sonny thought that "to be a great jazz musician, you had to sort of come up in the life, and Clifford of course did not.... But having come up in the life and been burned, I realized...what Clifford was.... He was a great, great human being, and that influenced me a lot because...not only did he have a great influence on keeping me on the straight and narrow...but it also made me realize.... You just needed to be dedicated to your horn—your instrument. That was enough."[18]

Brown and Roach represented a new clean-living, middle-class lifestyle that would redefine what it meant to live the jazz life. Max lived in New York with his wife, Mildred, and their young children, Brown in West Philadelphia with his wife, Emma LaRue Anderson. LaRue inspired "Joy Spring"—in fact, was his "joy spring."[19] "Clifford was like a professor. Smart guy. He was a mathematical genius and a chess champion," recalled Lou Donaldson.[20] Max Roach played chess, too, but Clifford was on another level.[21] He was a ringer at pool; his only vice was that he loved to bet on horse races.[22] "If you didn't see him with his horn, you wouldn't realize he was a musician." Brown subverted the stereotype of a jazz musician, as did Max. "Max was messed up," Donaldson said, "but after he got the group with Clifford Brown, he kind of changed and turned more . . . into a gentleman."[23]

By the time Sonny met Brownie, the scene was changing. "The whole atmosphere is getting healthier and healthier," Clifford said in 1954. "At one time you weren't anywhere if you weren't hung on something, but now the younger guys frown on anyone who goofs."[24]

Anyone who heard him knew within two seconds that Brownie was *bad*. He had an ear-to-ear smile and a short, squat frame, but when he put that trumpet to his lips and closed his eyes, he spoke with the articulation of a double-action revolver. Clifford Brown was the exact type of serious, sober musician Sonny was hoping to meet.

The meeting was kismet. Brown and Roach Incorporated was always on the road, traveling the "Baltimore-Washington–St. Louis–Cleveland-Detroit-Boston-Toronto circuit."[25] Earlier that September, when they played the Rouge Lounge in Detroit, they had been successful enough to pick up new cars in the Motor City.[26] "Brownie bought a new Buick and I bought a new Oldsmobile," said Roach. "Richie bought a new Pontiac too, and there we were, five guys on the road with three cars."[27]

They played the tightest, most challenging music in hard bop. "Our own policy," said Brown, who did most of the group's arrangements, "is to aim for the musical extremes of both excitement and subtle softness whenever each is necessary, but with a lot of feeling in everything. . . . We're trying more and more to have our solos built into each arrangement so that it all forms a whole and creates emotional and intellectual tension."[28] In Chicago, though, things were more open.

Word had spread that Sonny was living in seclusion at the YMCA, so Max and Clifford decided to pay him a visit.[29] Sonny was in the basement with Booker Little and Harold Mabern.[30] Sonny came up with Booker, and Max gave him the proposition: Would Sonny join the quintet until Harold Land came back from California? Sonny said yes, pending an audition.[31]

On November 7, 1955, Sonny had his trial run with Brown-Roach, Inc., at the Beehive. "Go baby, go!" shouted members of the audience. And they did. True to Chicago's inclusive ethos, it wasn't just the quintet either. They invited pianist Billy Wallace, Chicago tenor saxophonist Nicky Hill, and guitarist Little Leo Blevins. Sonny didn't have the best reed, but no reed could stop him. Everything he had absorbed during the ordeal of the past year— deep-dish Chicago blues, the pent-up emotion and dissonance, the divine spirit of Mother Gay's glossolalia, even some Monk quotes—came pouring out.[32]

Recorded and eventually released as *Live at the Bee Hive*, it was the kind of legendary blowing session Chicago was known for. They played the standard "I'll Remember April" for a sprawling half hour, Richard Carpenter's "Walkin'" and "Cherokee" each for twenty minutes, and Dizzy Gillespie's "Woody'n You" and Tadd Dameron's "Hot House" each nearly fifteen minutes. Max exhibited an uncharacteristic lack of restraint on his solos as he unleashed rhythmic fusillades on the snare; Clifford played virtuosically even for him. It was probably "Cherokee" that clinched it for Sonny. They played it at a clip faster than Charlie Parker's "Ko Ko," which was based on the song's famously difficult changes, and Sonny made sure to throw in a quote or two from Bird's iconic solo. The twenty-minute jam culminated in a ferocious trading section. It was clear Clifford was standing next to a force of nature.

This was not how Sonny felt, though. "I had big shoes to fill, because they had a really tight-knit, singular sounding group," Sonny said. "It was a very formidable task, and I did it with some concern that I would be able to live up to the high standard of the band as a sideman." He did more than that: "As it turned out, I changed the character of the band."[33]

Sonny didn't quite jell with the group sound. It was one of the cleanest groups out there, both socially and musically. Harold Land didn't have the same grit as Sonny, who pushed the band beyond the right angles and precision they were known for. With his sense of rhythmic displacement and the tendency to linger over a melody line and pull it apart with a biting sarcasm that somehow maintained its reverence, Sonny was quintessentially hip. In the Brown-Roach Quintet, he was the grain of sand that found itself inside the oyster.

"It was *very* tough following Clifford's solos. It was so tough that I decided I *couldn't* really follow—Clifford was a very fiery player," Sonny later recalled. "But I didn't play in quite that style....I was the sort of guy who built a solo up as he went along."[34]

Brown and Roach offered Sonny the gig, but Sonny had options. He could have formed his own band and picked up where he left off. Also, Miles was looking for him.[35] Miles was making a comeback: he'd signed to two labels at once—Columbia and Prestige.[36] He was getting major bookings in Sonny's hometown—twenty weeks a year at Birdland starting that October.[37] His new quintet was top-shelf—drummer Philly Joe Jones, bassist Paul Chambers, pianist Red Garland, and, as Nat Hentoff had just reported in *Down Beat*, Sonny himself. "Miles has been trying to convince Sonny to leave Chicago and go on the road with him," Hentoff wrote, "and finally, to Miles' great delight, he has succeeded." Miles fans hoping to see Sonny were sometimes disappointed when they showed up and saw a more obscure tenor saxophonist in his stead: John Coltrane.[38]

As Miles envisioned it, the transition to a major label—Columbia—included Sonny by his side. He was dismissive of the Brown-Roach Quintet: "Actually, Brownie and Max are the whole group. You don't need anybody but those two."[39]

Headlining at Birdland with Miles would allow Sonny to come home, compared to the punishing touring schedule of Brown-Roach, barnstorming the circuit—"rough-rough-rough all the way 'round," Sonny said.[40] Yet Sonny saw that rejoining Miles would lead him straight back to the life he had led. Brown-Roach would lead Sonny to the life he wanted. So Sonny turned down Miles and suited up for Brown-Roach, Incorporated.[41]

At first, there was a steep learning curve.[42] Complex tunes like "Joy

Spring," "Daahoud,"[43] and Duke Jordan's "Jordu" all had precise arrangements, and Sonny had joined them midtour. "We'd be rehearsing as much as possible," Sonny said. "We'd get there early enough to do a long sound check or something like that, or we'd go by there in the daytime to rehearse, and sometimes we'd rehearse right in the hotel."[44] Like one of his idols, Louis Armstrong, Brownie traveled with a portable tape recorder and taped many of the rehearsals and performances for later review.[45]

After leaving Chicago, the quintet continued its rigorous touring schedule with Sonny in tow. "In those days, it was not that nice being out on the road, 'cause when I joined the band…we had to stay in some funky hotels," Sonny said. "This was the '50s, so…it's segregation, Jim Crow." They had to rely on *The Negro Motorist Green Book* to find accommodations that would allow black travelers.[46] Living in hotels was mitigated by the fact that there weren't many one-nighters. "We'd stay in a club two, three, four weeks in each city," Roach said. "It's not like we'd come only a week or one night."[47]

On November 15, they were at Music City in Philadelphia.[48] Then they were at the Showboat in Philadelphia Thanksgiving week, through November 26;[49] at Olivia Davis's Patio Lounge in Washington, DC, starting November 28;[50] at the Las Vegas club in Baltimore, December 13–18;[51] at Basin Street in New York from Christmas to New Year's;[52] at Philadelphia's Blue Note through January 7, 1956; back at the Las Vegas in Baltimore from January 10 to January 16;[53] at George Wein's Storyville in Boston starting January 23; and at Basin Street January 27 and 28 opposite the Erroll Garner Trio.[54] Perhaps most exciting to Sonny, before they headed to Boston they were booked on January 20 for a few days at the Apollo Theater in an all-star revue with Dinah Washington, tap dancer Teddy Hale, and comedian Slappy White.[55]

In between touring, Sonny also found time to honor his contract with Bob Weinstock at Prestige. On December 2, 1955, Sonny went out to the Van Gelder Studio in Hackensack with his Conn tenor to record *Work Time*.[56] EmArcy agreed to let Roach do Sonny's record; George Morrow was the bassist. Richie Powell was not available, so on piano, Sonny got Philadelphia-born pianist Ray Bryant, whom Sonny had recently met in Philadelphia, to round out the quartet.[57] The session was quintessential Prestige. "One session, no rehearsals," Bryant recalled. "My biggest memory from that is the memory of playing fast.'"[58] Keeping the pace would be difficult, Bryant said, because Sonny was known for "unlikely" material.

The first tune they recorded was Irving Berlin's "There's No Business Like Show Business," the theme song of the eponymous film released earlier that year starring Ethel Merman.[59] Sonny had rehearsed it in Chicago with Booker Little and chose it for its melody and chord structure, though the title had an undeniable resonance for Sonny.

"Okay, fellas," Sonny said in the studio as the rhythm section noodled. Nearly every tune was taken way up, but Sonny tongued almost every note like a tuned snare drum. He took "No Business" at a brisk clip, soaring on the first solo chorus with just the bass as accompaniment, closing with an authoritative cadenza. Cole Porter's "It's All Right with Me" is also taken up-tempo, but amid the torrential downpour of notes, Sonny was not afraid to sustain one note for several measures or embellish with some light vibrato. On the lilting ballad "There Are Such Things," popularized by Frank Sinatra in 1942, Sonny conjured the influence of Coleman Hawkins.[60] Sonny's "Paradox," the album's sole original, had a bit of the Latin tinge, and Roach played an extended solo. Billy Strayhorn's "Raincheck," which Bryant learned on the date, opens with Sonny in playful call-and-response on the melody, with Sonny trading with Max later on in the piece. Sonny revered Ellington, and by extension Strayhorn. "Monk is an extension of Duke, I think, and Duke is the unsung giant of American music," Sonny later recalled. "Duke said that he had heard some of my records and liked the way I played. Can you imagine how I felt about Ellington saying something like that? I've recorded as many of his songs as I could. Perhaps he heard one of those."[61]

As far as the public was concerned, Sonny had all but vanished, and the album constituted a dramatic reentry. It was quickly apparent that Sonny was a leading tenor in the post-bop school.[62] Ira Gitler was more laudatory than ever in his liner notes. "Perhaps he has not reached the 'giants' category yet," he wrote, "but he is certainly one of the few eligibles."[63] Even Nat Hentoff, an erstwhile Sonny Rollins detractor, gave *Work Time* a glowing four-star review in *Down Beat*. "Rhythmically, no tenor today swings any more authoritatively than Sonny and few are as sustainedly driven as he," he wrote. "His ideas erupt from the horn with bullet-like propulsion."[64]

When Brown-Roach came to New York, Sonny hadn't played in public in his hometown for a long time, and fans packed Basin Street to hear him go toe to toe with the man who was said to be the second coming of Fats Navarro. The Brown-Roach Quintet was on a double bill with George Shearing's quintet, and everyone from EmArcy producers to high school kids flocked to the club with eager anticipation.[65] For Sonny, it was a triumphant homecoming, and to mark it, he picked up a new tenor. "When I came to New York with Max and Clifford, I didn't have a Mark VI," Sonny said, referring to the Selmer saxophone developed in Paris and manufactured in Elkhart, Indiana, known to some as the saxophone gold standard.[66] One night at Basin Street, Johnny Acea, a thirty-nine-year-old pianist who played with Dinah Washington, Illinois Jacquet, and Roy Haynes, said, "'Oh, Sonny, why don't you get a Selmer? Why don't you get a Selmer?'...Because having a Selmer was sort of the top-shelf instrument to get....So I thought about it, and...I finally got a Selmer." Sonny preferred American brands—he knew that Bird and Pres did, too—but owning a Mark VI was a status symbol, and Sonny bought one.[67]

Back in New York, Sonny began hitting the scene immediately. One of the musicians he met and performed with was a wildly creative Jewish French-horn player named David Amram. Dave, as Sonny called him, was two months younger than Sonny and just shy of his twenty-fifth birthday.[68] After completing his military service, Amram moved to Paris, where he took part in the city's bohemian jazz scene before relocating to New York to enroll in the Manhattan School of Music on the GI Bill in September 1955. An artist friend suggested he move to the East Village, which had some of the freewheeling spirit of the Latin Quarter. Amram found a railroad-style sixth-floor walk-up in Alphabet City, within walking distance of Café Bohemia.[69] Rent was only forty-two dollars.[70] That Christmas Eve, Amram met Sonny.[71]

Sonny "had his whole life together in a whole new way," said Amram. "He was starting a new approach and a new life, and refreshing himself, and he came back just looking like a million dollars, as they used to say, and played magnificently, and was so positive to be around and such a terrific artist."[72]

That winter, Amram began hosting jam sessions at his apartment, and

Sonny was among the artists who came "to play music, cook an improvised omelet, read a poem, show everyone their latest sketches for a new series of paintings, read from the outline of a new play, or just hang out to schmooze."[73] The fact that it was six flights up was no deterrent. "Thelonious Monk, Sonny Rollins, Kenny Dorham, Mary Lou Williams, Charles Mingus, Dizzy Gillespie, Oscar Pettiford, Thad Jones, Bill Evans, Pepper Adams, Julius Watkins, Cedar Walton, and Randy Weston used to climb all those stairs of my East Village walk-up and spend time, jamming and sharing musical ideas."[74]

At this time, Amram booked one of his first gigs as a bandleader, at Sarah Lawrence College.[75] The concert was so well received that Amram was asked back. When he called Sonny for the second concert, Sonny agreed to do it for very low pay.[76] They drove up to Bronxville with Charlie Parker alum Teddy Kotick, pianist Cedar Walton, drummer Phil Brown, and Sonny. "There we were in the car, with Sonny Rollins, and he spent the whole trip out not talking about himself, but all the wonderful people that had inspired and influenced him," Amram said. He spoke of Coleman Hawkins, Lester Young, and unsung players like Wardell Gray and Arnett Cobb. "When he spoke about Miles, he used to say 'Mr. Miles Davis' and when he spoke about Bird he would say 'Mr. Charles Parker.' So beautiful."[77]

It was then that Sonny taught Amram a lesson about the craft. "Around the second chorus [of "I'll Remember April"], Sonny leaned over to Cedar Walton and said, 'What was that chord you played in the third bar of the bridge?' Cedar... just looked blank... as we were playing away, so [Sonny] said, 'Keep on playing. I'll catch it the next time.'" So he did. "And then of course when he played his choruses, he got to that part and did something fantastic." Amram was shocked by Sonny's musical curiosity. "He taught me the great lesson: if you don't know, ask."[78]

To Amram, Sonny immediately became a kind of guru. When Amram criticized a honking saxophonist who soloed only on one note, "Sonny said, 'Don't put that guy down.... That's the best he can do.... That's how he feeds his family. That's his thing.'" Once, Amram called Sonny and interrupted a practice session. "He said, 'Hold it, Dave, hold it,'" Amram recalled. Sonny hit one note in octaves on the piano, hitting the sustaining pedal so it rang out for forty-five seconds, then played over it on his saxophone. He did this for three minutes, then said, " 'What's up, Dave? How's it going?'...He was searching for what he felt were the correct notes to tell that story."[79]

Sonny also taught him to play at the highest-possible level, regardless of the environment. "So much great music was created in what Lenny Bruce referred to as the 'toilets,' those clubs with out-of-tune pianos, no sound systems, run by people who weren't smart enough to sell dope or be pimps. The lowest echelon of the bottom of the crime scene was just to run a jazz club. That was the first thing before you became an informant or something, so that wasn't what you call a great environment. But when Sonny would play, when Max Roach would play, they would turn them into temples of art, which showed that the music was so beautiful."[80]

Sonny also imparted his tireless work ethic. Amram began living with Ahmad Basheer (sometimes spelled Bashir), a scat singer from Detroit who was a mutual friend of Sonny's and had known Charlie Parker.[81] One day after playing at the Rockland Palace, Amram and Basheer were wandering around Harlem, "having a good time, eating up a storm and everything, and we ran into Sonny," Amram said. "Basheer said, 'Man,' he said, 'can you give me a dollar so we can get the subway fare to get back?'" They ate so much they ran out of cash. "Sonny looked, he said 'Of course,' he went and handed Basheer two dollars, then he said, 'Have you guys ever thought about getting a job?' That was after he gave him the two dollars, and he said it in a humorous way...maybe you're great philosophers, but you've got to take care of the realities of life as well."[82] As Sonny recalled, Basheer "was a somewhat heavyset guy, and he liked to eat, but he wasn't always employed in a way that would give him the wherewithal to satisfy his appetite."[83]

At one point, Basheer got a job at a carwash in New Jersey, and Sonny asked if he could come by and work with him. "You had to work your behind off washing those cars," Sonny said. "You got to five o'clock, you could hardly walk. I don't think I lasted more than one day."[84] At night, of course, Sonny could outlast anyone on the stand.

During this period, Amram also saw Sonny at the jam sessions at Kenneth Karpe's East Side loft, which began that fall.[85] Ken and his wife, Sylvia, hosted the sessions, which ran all night; individual tunes would be played sometimes for upwards of an hour. Karpe's loft attracted the city's best players: Oscar Pettiford, Thelonious Monk, Charles Mingus, Philly Joe Jones, and Art Farmer among them. The members of the band for Sonny's next album stopped by: Doug Watkins and Tommy Flanagan. The entire Brown-Roach group were frequent visitors when they were in town.[86]

This time was doubly sweet for Brownie. Not only was the new Brown-Roach Quintet's New York debut a hit, but during the Basin Street run, his wife, LaRue, also gave birth to their son, Clifford Benjamin Brown Jr., on December 28. Brown had taken the train to and from Philadelphia every day they were at Basin Street, and he rushed home after they closed on New Year's Day.[87] It was short-lived; soon, the quintet would return to the studio and then went back on the road.[88]

The quintet was popular enough at Basin Street that EmArcy decided to name Sonny's debut album with the group *Clifford Brown and Max Roach at Basin Street*, even though it was recorded entirely at Capitol Studios in New York.[89] Producer Bob Shad's approach to recording was diametrically opposed to Bob Weinstock's; while Weinstock was one and done, Shad seemed to favor as many takes as were necessary. On January 4, 1956, in between performances at Philadelphia's Blue Note, they hit the studio in New York to record Richie Powell's galloping "Powell's Prances" and "Gertrude's Bounce," named for the buoyant gait of Chicago artist and jazz aficionado Gertrude Abercrombie, a friend of the band's, and Benny Golson's "Step Lightly," which was renamed "Junior's Arrival" to commemorate the birth of Brownie's son. Powell did most of the arrangements. They had to cut it short—they were booked in Philadelphia, Baltimore, at the Apollo, in Boston, and back at Basin Street, so the album would have to wait.

On January 31, 1956, the Brown-Roach Quintet drove to Detroit, where the quintet was booked for a week at the Rouge Lounge, a club at the end of a bowling alley on the outskirts of the city.[90] It was probably at this time that Sonny met Richard "Prophet" Jennings. An artist, journalist, and hustler who ran the concession stand at the Flame Showbar, Jennings knew all the jazz musicians in Detroit and just about every musician passing through. His product was in high demand: a variety of marijuana he called "Chicago Light Green."[91]

Jennings was blown away by Sonny's new composition "Valse Hot," and Sonny came to see him at the YMCA, where he lived. "He had so much grease in his hair, that the way his hat was blocked [shaped], he would take his hat off and his hair would be in that block," Jennings recalled, adding, "That man played the keys off the saxophone."[92]

Detroit was home to a thriving jazz scene.[93] On this trip, Sonny made an instant connection with another Detroiter—pianist Tommy Flanagan, who was six months older than him and getting ready to move to New York, a move drummer Elvin Jones had made the previous year.[94]

Before leaving Detroit, Max took some time to expound on his vision for jazz as a vehicle for the civil rights movement. "It's a form of social protest," Max said. "The artist reveals sometimes the smoldering anger and impatience with existing conditions that are unfavorable to him. This unconscious quality is the soul that makes it a pure art form. It's a militant expression that reflects the thinking and feelings of Negroes today."[95]

After closing at the Rouge Lounge, they left on February 6 and drove to Cleveland, where the quintet opened at the Loop Lounge.[96] Through Associated Booking agent Bert Block, Max and Brownie had it in their contract that they would always receive equal billing. For the whole week, the band made $1,150; Sonny was probably making $25 or $30 a night, minus the hotel and food expenses—a 25-cent breakfast, $1.25 for dinner, $25 for the week at the hotel.[97] This was standard. Every night when they finished at 2:30 a.m., they went back to the sixty-room Carnegie Hotel, where the racist manager charged musicians rent in advance because "too many of them checked out via the fire escape to duck paying their bills."[98] They checked out of the Carnegie Hotel at 3:49 a.m. on February 15 and drove back to New York.[99]

On Thursday, February 16, they returned to the studio to finish *At Basin Street*. They recorded two takes of the Cole Porter standard "What Is This Thing Called Love," arranged by Tadd Dameron, who was in the studio for the session.[100] Sonny and Brownie traded eights, then fours, leading up to a blistering tag. They then recorded three takes of "Love Is a Many-Splendored Thing," the theme song of the eponymous 1955 movie starring William Holden and Jennifer Jones. It was a radical departure from the hackneyed Four Aces hit version with the Jack Pleis Orchestra, also released that year.

In Richie Powell's arrangement, the head began with a 5/4 time signature, an unusual meter later made famous by Dave Brubeck's "Take Five," three years later.[101] On February 17, they laid down three takes of "I'll Remember April." They then did one take of Richie Powell's ballad "Time," Powell on celeste for the melody to capture "the time a man spends just sitting in jail, wondering when he's going to get out."[102] They recorded one take of Tadd Dameron's "The Scene Is Clean," which Dameron wrote with Sonny in mind,[103] and several of Dameron's "Flossie Lou," which were left off.[104] By the end of the session, they had produced a classic album.[105]

Starting Monday, February 20, the quintet was booked upstate at the Town Casino in Buffalo for one week: three shows nightly, a Sunday matinee, and a radio broadcast from the hall.[106]

The Town Casino was a cavernous thousand-seat restaurant and lounge with a neon marquee, a proscenium stage, and white tablecloths, run by impresario Harry Altman.[107] The club was billed as the "Copacabana of upstate New York," and the jazz acts were integrated into the floor shows, but during Sunday matinees, jazz was the highlight. On Sunday afternoon at 2:30 p.m., they performed for the second in the series of weekly broadcasts hosted by WEBR disc jockey Joe Rico.[108] They played "Daahoud," followed by a brief live radio interview with Max. When asked about the recent recording session, Max explained that they were "very, very happy about the whole set."

They played their arrangement of Monk's "'Round Midnight,"[109] followed by the burning "Blues Walk," a blues written by Sonny Stitt. Rollins started his solo slowly, hanging on a few notes, then began seamlessly building a series of fluid eighth-note lines, playing through the bar line, marrying virtuosic technique with a startling lyricism.[110] The band began playing syncopated background hits, and Sonny just kept pushing; the idle chatter in the audience ceased as listeners began to hoot, cheering him on, but Sonny was on another plane.

After closing in Buffalo, there was the matter of getting paid. The band's contract stipulated that payment would be made "at the end of engagement," which sometimes resulted in club owners trying to stiff them.[111] Brown-Roach, Inc., had a secret weapon to make sure this kind of treatment wouldn't happen: Clifford Brown.

"Everybody says Clifford Brown was soft. He was hard and tough," said Max. "Many times when we were on the road, and we'd run into situations where the money would get funny, Clifford would be just the opposite from what most of the people say about him. I mean, he was really, really, really heavy, and I wouldn't have put it past him whether he would shoot somebody." In Buffalo, Max explained, some clubs were money-laundering schemes run by the Mafia. "So the guy at the end of the week, he came up short with the loot. Clifford went into his office, stayed for a while while I was packing up my kit and everything, and when he came out, he came out with the money."[112]

Brownie was the group's enforcer, but he also had a great sense of humor—necessary for life on the road. One day before a show, Sonny announced in the dressing room that he no longer wanted to be called Newk. "So Brownie looked at him and said, 'Well what should we call you?'" Max recalled. "And he said, 'Call me Roundtree.' So Clifford very quickly responded to this. He said, 'Oh, I know why you want us to call you Roundtree. I read a story about a fighter who could never get past the third round, so they called him Round-*t'ree*!'"[113]

Vibraphonist Terry Gibbs, another EmArcy artist whose quartet opened at the Town Casino the day after the Brown-Roach Quintet closed, would periodically meet them along the highway at Howard Johnson's, then the largest restaurant chain in the United States.[114] "We'd meet for about an hour, eat, laugh a little bit, then go onto our jobs because it was always early in the morning," Gibbs recalled. Sonny, he said, "was the tenor player of the day. He knocked me out.... You know when you can always tell a good player? You'll hear a record, and you can remember the solo. You can sing the solo after a while."[115]

After Buffalo, the quintet was booked in Boston from February 27 through March 4 at George Wein's Storyville at the Copley Square Hotel.[116] A twenty-six-year-old Japanese pianist named Toshiko Akiyoshi was a recent arrival at the Berklee College of Music and began making the jazz scene.[117] Richie Powell couldn't make the gig, so a sub came in and asked Toshiko to sit in.[118] She was ready for the challenge. "Max had a lot of original tunes and original arrangements," Toshiko recalled, "but I knew them all from the record."[119]

Sonny and Brownie had only really known each other for four months, but friendships got close fast on the road. "He and I were getting tight," Sonny said. "We were getting to phrase together."[120]

While working with the quintet at Basin Street in Manhattan, on a triple bill with the Don Elliott Quartet and the Matt Dennis Trio, on Friday, March 16, Sonny rode out to Hackensack to record with Miles Davis in what turned out to be their final studio session together.[121] Still beholden to Prestige and Columbia, Miles was laying down as much as he could at Van Gelder's to satisfy his contractual obligation to Bob Weinstock.[122] For this pickup quintet session, Miles hired two musicians from Detroit and two from Harlem: pianist Tommy Flanagan and bassist Paul Chambers,[123] drummer Art Taylor, and Sonny. They recorded three tunes: "No Line," a blues named for its lack of a head or melody; Miles's "Vierd Blues," a slow blues shuffle; and Dave Brubeck's "In Your Own Sweet Way," which had not been recorded before, even by Brubeck.[124] To complement the subdued timbre of Miles's Harmon mute, Sonny played much of the session in a subtone. On "Vierd," Sonny played a counterpoint to the shambling melody that would presage the improvised head to "Blue 7" a few months later.

Tommy Flanagan had just moved to New York and was fresh off recording with Thad Jones and Kenny Burrell earlier that week.[125] "It was my birthday; that's how I remember. My twenty-sixth birthday. March 16," Flanagan recalled. "He had the date and I got the call. We just cooked. All except that one Brubeck tune. That came about strangely. Miles had that tune in his back pocket—a sketch of the chords. I remember him telling me how to voice the intro. He always knows exactly what he wants. It makes him easy to work with. If you don't play what he wants, he tells you like this [whispering hoarsely]—'Play block chords, but not like Milt Buckner. In the style of Ahmad Jamal.'"[126] So that's what Flanagan did on the intro.[127] At the very least, the recording showed Sonny that Tommy Flanagan could think on his feet.[128]

The following Thursday, March 22, Sonny was in the studio to record *Sonny Rollins Plus 4* for Prestige, where he was still under contract.[129] The Brown-Roach Quintet agreed to do the album under Sonny's name, but Sonny felt the title Prestige gave it was unfair to Max and Brownie—it may have been Sonny's record, but they were the bandleaders. Max would later answer with *Max Roach Plus 4*.[130]

Sonny chose three covers and two originals. The up-tempo "Kiss and Run" was a Sam Coslow tune recorded in the 1953 film *Affair with a Stranger*. The similarly brisk "I Feel a Song Coming On" by Jimmy McHugh was part of the soundtrack for the 1935 film *Every Night at Eight*.[131] The Irving Berlin ballad "Count Your Blessings (Instead of Sheep)" was sung by Bing Crosby in 1954's *White Christmas*. Everyone cooked on the fast tunes, and Sonny played Bing with confidence. Yet the originals were the highlights.

The first was an experiment in waltz time. There had been Debussy's "Valse Romantique" and Tchaikovsky's "Valse Sentimentale," and now there was Sonny's "Valse Hot." He brought handwritten lead sheets for "Valse Hot" in pencil to the session. It was based on the changes to Harold Arlen's "Over the Rainbow," with a different melody of course, and done in three.[132] There weren't many jazz waltzes—it would be more than a year before Dave Brubeck would cover "Someday My Prince Will Come." "When I began playing jazz," Sonny said, "I associated it automatically with 4/4 time. But then I heard Fats Waller's 'Jitterbug Waltz' [from 1942], and I guess this planted the idea in my mind that there were many meters adaptable to jazz that hadn't yet been fully utilized."[133]

Sonny had just the right group of musicians to test the theory—Brownie had a perfect combination of a mathematical mind and emotional depth, and Max had been behind the polyrhythmic beat of Bud Powell's "Un Poco Loco" and Thelonious Monk's 6/4 "Carolina Moon."

On "Valse Hot," the accents fall in unlikely places, though, and to make the swing feel light and effortless would be difficult for anyone. "Max said he'd never really played a jazz waltz before," Sonny said. "He didn't have any trouble with it, but he told me later that he went home and sat in the basement all night practicing. Sometime after that we began experimenting in waltzes with different tempos and accents, switching the pulse around from the first to the second or third beat, and getting as much variety out of the idea as we could."[134]

The other Sonny original was "Pent-Up House." "It had nothing to do with incarceration," Sonny said. "I felt pent up," and the melody and arrangement evoke that feeling.[135] The melody has a cross-rhythm, three against four, suggesting a vertiginous 3/4 time signature with a syncopated chromatic line. On the solo section, Richie Powell lays out, allowing Brownie to stroll and release the pent-up energy that builds throughout the head.

Ira Gitler's ecstatic liner notes for *Sonny Rollins Plus 4* proclaimed Sonny a key contemporary progenitor of modern tenor, demonstrating his impact through a chart that showed his influence on the styles of Jimmy Heath, Charlie Rouse, Allen Eager, J. R. Monterose, Hank Mobley, John Coltrane, Phil Urso, and even Sonny's own early influence, Dexter Gordon.[136] Sonny would later claim it as one of his personal favorites from his own catalog.[137] With this record, Nat Hentoff's doubts about Sonny were put to rest. He gave the album four and a half stars, Sonny's best review to date.[138]

Yet for Sonny, the recording date was just one day in an endless tour.[139] In late March they went to Rochester; Toronto; Miami University in Oxford, Ohio; and finally the Esquire Club in Trenton, New Jersey, before a brief mid-April respite.[140]

The quintet was booked at Basin Street from April 26 to May 9 on a triple bill with the Chico Hamilton Quintet and the Erroll Garner Trio, but in order to play for an extended run in New York, Max needed to have his cabaret card restored.[141] The State Liquor Authority had granted him permission to work in the city, but the police department flatly denied his request. On April 23, he filed a petition in the state supreme court for an order directing the police commissioner to grant him a license. His lawyer was Harold Lovett, a successful African American attorney who also represented Miles Davis.[142] Max hadn't been arrested since 1946, when he did time for drug possession.[143] He'd since cleaned up and become one of the most prominent leaders in contemporary jazz, with a family to support.[144] His hearing was scheduled for May 31, after the Basin Street gig ended, but it seems the city allowed him to perform in the meantime. That Saturday and then again on May 6, the quintet was part of a thirty-minute live national broadcast on WCBS radio's *Basin Street Jazz*, though Max was laid out with a stomach bug for the latter date and Willie Jones subbed.[145]

When they closed at Basin Street, the quintet was booked at the Showboat in Philadelphia, inside the Douglass Hotel. They were contracted to open

Monday, May 7, and play through the next Saturday for $1,450, but it's not clear how much of the gig they played.[146] After one of the nights, Max drove home to Brooklyn,[147] leaving the rest of the band in Philadelphia for a day. Almost as soon as he got home, he got a frantic call from Brownie. Sonny and Richie Powell had been in a car crash. Even though Sonny didn't drive, Powell had him drive his '55 Pontiac, and Sonny drove it into a ditch, totaling the car. "He'd just gotten that car," Sonny recalled. "I messed up my mouth... and wasn't able to play much, and I hit my knee.... I'm forever praying to Richard, always asking for forgiveness, because that was my fault."[148]

Max "jumped into my car and went down to Philadelphia, and in those days, it was almost like Bessie Smith: they would not take Sonny Rollins and Richard Powell in the hospital," Roach said.[149] When he arrived, they were recovering at Powell's mother's house in suburban Willow Grove, with "Sonny's teeth hanging out of his head."[150] Both fully recovered, but it was a cautionary tale of what could go wrong on the road.

With the two injured band members healed enough to play, the quintet was booked at the Patio Lounge in Washington, DC, from May 21 to May 27 opposite the Paul Bley Trio.[151] During this gig, Sonny found time to head back to Hackensack for what would turn out to be one of his most important record dates: *Tenor Madness*.

The date was Thursday, May 24, 1956. Sonny hired the rhythm section from Miles Davis's First Great Quintet: Paul Chambers, Philly Joe Jones, and Red Garland. They also brought John Coltrane, who wasn't hired for the session but came along to show support for Sonny.[152] There wasn't much money in the Prestige dates, and three hours was usually all they needed. Union scale in 1956 was still $13.75 an hour for sidemen, or $41.25 for a three-hour session, with the leader usually getting twice that.[153] Bob Weinstock and Rudy Van Gelder worked quickly and didn't talk much.[154]

When the band arrived at Van Gelder's, everything was precisely placed. They trusted Van Gelder implicitly. "We never cared what he was doing," Weinstock said. "The great musicians like Miles, Rollins, Coltrane, Gene Ammons, they didn't want to hear playback."[155] At Van Gelder's, they just drew the blinds and blew. It was first take, best take.

Sonny chose lesser-known standards: "When Your Lover Has Gone" by

Einar Aaron Swan; the plangent "My Reverie," Larry Clinton's setting of Debussy that had been covered by Bing Crosby, Tony Bennett, and Mildred Bailey; and "The Most Beautiful Girl in the World," a Tommy Dorsey hit from Rodgers and Hart's *Jumbo*. He included one original, the breezy "Paul's Pal," dedicated to Chambers, with Philly Joe Jones showing off his subdued brushwork.

Sonny was searching for a sound that day, and he did not like what he was hearing. "When Your Lover Has Gone" and "My Reverie" have some of his most lyrically sophisticated playing, using a vibrato à la Coleman Hawkins, who kept the former in his repertoire.[156] "The Most Beautiful Girl in the World" began as a waltz and transitioned into 4/4, and Sonny played like Lester Young, scooping notes and hanging on them, hewing close to the melody. "Sonny was in his usual pessimistic form," Ira Gitler wrote in the liner notes. "After each number he would shake his head and say 'Nothing's happening.'"[157]

Then he made something happen.[158] Someone suggested that Sonny invite Trane to play on a track. Coltrane had evidently fallen asleep in the car;[159] fortunately, he had his horn. They settled on a twelve-bar B-flat blues well known on the scene at the time. Kenny Clarke, who had composed it, recorded it in 1946 as "Rue Chaptal" and alternatively as "Royal Roost."[160] Hank Mobley[161] had recorded it as "Sportin' Crowd" with Art Blakey's Jazz Messengers at a live date in November 1955 at the Café Bohemia.[162] When Sonny and Trane recorded it as "Tenor Madness," it would become the definitive version of the song.

It would be something of a rematch, albeit a friendly one, from the time at the Audubon with Miles a lifetime ago.[163] That Thursday in Hackensack, Coltrane wasn't *Coltrane* yet. The cognoscenti knew him from his recent live performances with Miles Davis in San Francisco and elsewhere, but *Down Beat* wouldn't review a Davis album with Coltrane until May 30. Ira Gitler described Coltrane as "a mixture of Dexter Gordon, Sonny Rollins, and Sonny Stitt," but as Hentoff noted, "so far there's very little Coltrane." To Hentoff, he suffered from a "general lack of individuality."[164] And Coltrane was still struggling with addiction. In the liner notes for *Tenor Madness*, Gitler pointed out that "Coltrane takes the first solo and also leads off on the chases." It was a necessary detail: Trane's sound was not yet recognizable enough for listeners to figure that out themselves.[165]

That's not how Sonny felt, though. "You could tell it was him instantly," he said. "When you were around him you felt like you were with a genius. A genius and a serious, energetic player. He had a sense of humor, but he was serious. His humor wasn't about cracking jokes. He was more droll, or wry. Almost like a minister, a minister of music."[166]

For the time being, Sonny was king. "The funny part about this whole thing with Coltrane is that I am four years his junior, and I was famous before Coltrane," Sonny said. "He was a guest on *my* record."[167] Coltrane himself wouldn't make a record under his own name for another year.[168]

On "Tenor Madness," Sonny's playing was more horizontal, focused on melodic and rhythmic development, Coltrane's more vertical and focused on outlining harmony through arpeggiated runs; Sonny's sound was throaty, the musical equivalent of tree bark, Trane's diaphanous, like quicksilver; Sonny was the Marianas Trench, Trane up in the stratosphere.

At the end of the third chorus of fours, Coltrane played an arpeggiated lick, and Sonny responded by inverting it. It was as though Coltrane did a 360 dunk, and Sonny did a reverse 360, effortlessly. "Because of the humor in my music, people have accused me of not really playing, of just playing around. In fact, John told me that about 'Tenor Madness.' He said, 'Aw, man, you were just playing with me.' "[169]

Decades later, Sonny admitted that Coltrane was right. "I wasn't really playing," Sonny said. "Coltrane was playing. I was only playing halfway, because I thought that I was the guy and that Coltrane was this young whippersnapper. That was my mindset. It was immature."[170]

Nevertheless, it was impossible for most to tell who had won the tenor battle. But that was not the point. "They're both storytelling," tenor saxophonist Mark Turner explained, "but Sonny feels more like a novelist and Trane is taking a journey to the top of a mountain and then coming back down with information to give us all. They're two different paradigms, but both of them are necessary."[171]

Not everyone saw it that way, though. Nat Hentoff gave the album a tepid three and a half stars in *Down Beat*, and the reason for it was Coltrane.[172]

Hentoff concluded that Coltrane "appears to be pressing and lacks Sonny's compactness of impact." Sonny was commended for leavening his angular playing with a sense of lyricism. It was Coltrane, Hentoff wrote, who "mars what should have been an interestingly balanced all-Rollins LP."

Saxophonist Don Menza was stationed in Frankfurt, Germany, with the army when *Tenor Madness* was released. At the time, he was a Stan Getz acolyte and had been listening to Coleman Hawkins, Gene Ammons, and Sonny Stitt. "When *Tenor Madness* came out, I said, 'God, I hear all of those people in him. I hear all of that sound,' and it really confused me," Menza recalled, "so I took and actually transcribed Sonny's tenor solo from 'Tenor Madness' and I heard Bird, I heard Lester Young, I heard Coleman Hawkins in him. But what really touched me was his beautiful ballad playing."[173]

To Sonny, *Tenor Madness* was just another day in the life. Later, Menza helped repair Sonny's tenor, and Sonny asked him to play it to make sure it worked. "I played the first two choruses of the 'Tenor Madness' solo," Menza recalled. "And then I stopped and I looked at him and I said, 'You recognize that?' He said, 'It sounds familiar.' And I told him what it was. He says, 'Really!'"

After the quintet closed at the Patio Lounge in Washington, DC, on May 27, they checked out of the New Dunbar Hotel at 2:23 a.m. on May 28 and drove the nearly four hundred miles to Cleveland to open at the Cotton Club that night.[174] They arrived road-weary and looking for a good night's sleep.[175] That night, they were on fire.[176] They stuck mostly to standards: "Take the 'A' Train," "Nice Work If You Can Get It," "What's New," "I'll Remember April," and some new standards, "Jordu," "Valse Hot," and "Daahoud." Sonny played beautifully on his ballad feature, Jimmy Van Heusen's "Darn That Dream," sustaining a high D on the tenor for fifteen seconds on the cadenza before concluding to raucous applause.

Around this time in New York, Richie Powell married Nancy Welch, a white woman from Broomall, Pennsylvania, a small suburb of Philadelphia. She was nineteen and Richie twenty-four.[177] Shortly after the wedding, they all attended an all-night party, leaving at seven or eight the next morning.[178] Max had a policy that he would never let his wife behind the wheel, but Richie was more progressive. Nancy was having trouble making a U-turn at the cul-de-sac at the end of the road. Roach admonished him for letting his wife drive. "Richie looked at me and said something that disarmed me. He said, 'All you old guys are the same.'" Max got the message, but to him, it was a bad sign.

As an unmarried man, Sonny would sometimes be teased by Max for being too serious about women. "I would always be involved with a girl, and Max would say, 'Oh, Sonny, come on, man. Just have fun. You're getting deep and dramatic,' which I did," Sonny said. "That's what Max called me, because I generally would say goodbye to these girls at the airport." Sometimes, Sonny was not "deep and dramatic" enough. Probably in Cleveland, he met model Bonnie Jean Pleasant, a beautiful, tall, and intellectually serious twenty-three-year-old black woman born in Alabama.[179] Before long, Bonnie Jean moved to New York to be with him, but the courtship was short-lived.[180] "Unfortunately, she came by my hotel just at a time when another woman that I was semi-involved with had come to my room," Sonny said. "She was knocking on the door, and this girl was about to leave, and here is Bonnie Jean coming in....I didn't do that to hurt her....I wasn't ready to get into real marriage."[181]

When the Brown-Roach Quintet left Cleveland on June 5, they drove to Detroit, where they opened in the Rouge Lounge that night and played for a week.[182] Starting June 15, the quintet was double-booked at Tutz's in Milwaukee for ten days at $1,800 and at the Continental Restaurant in Norfolk, Virginia, for a week at $1,150. Somehow, they ended up playing the gig in Norfolk, a few blocks from the water.[183]

It was the band's first time performing in the South. That past December, Rosa Parks had started the Montgomery bus boycott when she refused to relinquish her seat to a white woman. The previous August, in Mississippi, fourteen-year-old Emmett Till was lynched in Mississippi in a town called Money.[184] Norfolk wasn't Mississippi, and it wasn't Alabama, but the civil rights movement was overwhelmingly opposed all throughout Virginia. The Continental, ten miles from the world's largest naval base, was a segregated club. From June 15 to 21, they stayed at the Plaza Hotel, listed with a star in the *Green Book*, and owned by black entrepreneur Bonnie McEachin, who made sure guests were treated with respect.[185]

Max had been born thirty-five miles from Norfolk where Virginia borders North Carolina in a community of sharecroppers in the Great Dismal

Swamp that they called New Land. He still had relatives nearby and invited them to the club. The club owner, Ben Dobrinsky, who was Jewish, allowed them to attend as long as they sat right next to the bandstand.[186] There was only one microphone for Brownie and Sonny, and the crowd talked loudly through the whole set. The experience was degrading for the quintet, but as always, they carried themselves with dignity and played through it; their motto was "a way out of no way."[187] To add insult to injury, not many people showed up.

On Monday, June 18, they were featured on a live broadcast from the Continental on Norfolk's WNOR station, which aired a regular "Modern Music Show" from the restaurant.[188] Throughout the run, they maintained an air of wry levity; Max even joked to the audience at one point that he was early New Orleans jazz drummer Zutty Singleton.[189]

As diners talked over him, Max introduced Sonny's ballad feature, "Someone to Watch over Me."[190] After a lyrical double-time line during his solo, Sonny hung on a high F-sharp, the highest note on the horn, letting it ring out like a siren or a freedom bell. The rest of the band dropped out. The audience conversation did not abate, but everyone heard it, and maybe it made them all think for a moment as they applauded. When Brown picked it up on his ballad feature, "What's New," the chatter grew even louder. George Morrow played his feature "These Foolish Things," a wistful bass solo as the rest of the band mostly laid out, with Richie Powell adding a few flourishes.

The last tune of the broadcast, "I Get a Kick Out of You," went out at a blistering three hundred beats per minute.[191] Brownie and Sonny played brilliantly, with Richie dropping out on Sonny's solo, leaving Sonny to take them as far out as he could go. The tune lasted twenty-five minutes, as the chatter continued. Finally, Max played a thunderous drum solo that built to a rumble until they were all in the eye of the storm, drowning out the din of the crowd. People began to lose their composure, shouting out in recognition of the arresting rhythm. Sonny came in, pushing Max on; they weren't in Virginia anymore.

"All of a sudden we both heard it," Sonny said. "We were phrasing, attacking, breathing together."[192] After they finished, they still had to go out the back door.

Chapter 16

SAXOPHONE COLOSSUS

(1956)

On Friday, June 22, 1956, Sonny recorded *Saxophone Colossus*. It was just another day for Sonny, and probably not even the most memorable one that month.[1]

He assembled a stellar pickup band: on bass, a twenty-two-year-old sharply dressed Detroiter named Doug Watkins who was equally comfortable playing arco or pizzicato;[2] on piano, Tommy Flanagan, another Detroit native Sonny had played with on the Miles Davis session three months earlier; and on drums, Max Roach, who had driven to New York with Sonny from Norfolk the day before. "I remember that we [were] all working, we were all very busy at that time, recording other places with other people," Sonny said.[3] They had never played together as a band, so it was anyone's guess if the session would be greater than the sum of its parts.

Flanagan would remember the session as a kind of happy accident.[4] "Whether people want less accompaniment or want you to play right along with them isn't necessarily discussed. With Sonny Rollins, it didn't need to be. You know when you feel like you're being crowded out," Flanagan said jokingly. "There's less room for you to play."[5] For Flanagan, though, developing a "sympathetic interplay" took time, and they had only a few hours. "I've made an awful lot of dates where I played with people for the first time.... You're lucky when something like that comes out good."[6]

They drove out to Rudy Van Gelder's in Hackensack with Bob Weinstock, and Sonny brought his Mark VI tenor and the sheet music for a set of new tunes he had been working on but had not yet workshopped with Brown-Roach, Incorporated.[7] "Moritat," the German word for the medieval tradition of the murder ballad, was originally known as "Die Moritat von Mackie Messer," with music by Kurt Weill and lyrics by Bertolt Brecht from *The Threepenny Opera*, but most people in the United States knew it as "Mack the Knife." Sonny was very familiar with the tune, which was popular at the time. "I had seen the opera, heard the song. Louis Armstrong's version. Heard Lotte Lenya's version. Then, of course, Bobby Darin had a big hit with it [in 1959]. It was quite ubiquitous at the time."[8]

"Moritat" began with Max on the hi-hat and Watkins playing half notes on the bass, as chorus after chorus, Sonny showed he was a killer on the saxophone. Next was the Gene de Paul ballad "You Don't Know What Love Is." It had been covered by Miles Davis in a 1954 quintet session with Dave Schildkraut on alto saxophone.[9] Sonny leaped from the tenor's lower register up to the altissimo range, manipulating the rhythm so he was perfectly behind the beat but always right on time. "Strode Rode" was the only original Sonny brought into the studio. "I might have written that one in Chicago," he recalled. "It was named for a legendary place there called the Strode Hotel, which is where Freddie Webster died. I never even saw the Strode Hotel when I was in Chicago, but I wanted to dedicate something to Freddie Webster."[10] Sonny had never met Webster—he died of a suspected heroin overdose in 1947—but his playing was hugely influential on the bebop generation, especially Miles Davis. "Freddie Webster was one of the mythical people to us," Sonny said. "That was a big loss in my life, and I wanted to commemorate that."[11] The song has an unusual forty-bar form—two twelve-bar sections, a four-bar improvised bridge, and a final chorus of the A section. Sonny played his first chorus with bass only, which Watkins handled effortlessly.

Then there was an impromptu original, later titled "Blue 7," a B-flat blues, on which Sonny improvised the melody.[12] The piece was more than eleven glorious minutes in total and would eventually become one of Sonny's most studied recordings. The eminent composer, jazz historian, and French-horn player Gunther Schuller would write an essay canonizing "Blue 7"—"Sonny Rollins and the Challenge of Thematic Improvisation"—but not for a few years. Sonny, Schuller would claim, had created a new style of "thematic improvisation," a kind of spontaneous composition with linear development, which had fundamentally altered the jazz language. On that particular day, though, Sonny was just playing the blues as best he could. "I guess it's true, but I had never thought about it," Sonny said. "I was just playing it."[13]

Bob Weinstock was digging what he heard in the studio. "This was like a ball game," recalled Weinstock. "The team's either hot or cold. . . . I was in the middle of a Stanley Cup, seventh game, with Mario Lemieux playing against Wayne Gretzky." To Weinstock, "Blue 7" was the game-winning goal. "If I saw Sonny Rollins was playing his ass off like on 'Blue 7,' which to me is a classic, I'd just give him a sign, like you wind your fingers around in a circle. That meant 10-4. Other times, I'd show him the stop watch and throw [it on] the couch. That meant, 'No more time. Play, man.' . . . I showed him the stop watch, and I threw it on the couch. He just nodded, closed his eyes and kept playing and playing."[14]

Tommy Flanagan wasn't as overwhelmed. "I'm sure all the acclaim about 'Blue 7' didn't mean that much to him," Flanagan said. "I've heard him play much better than that."[15]

As influential as "Blue 7" would become in the critical canon, it was still not the session's most iconic song. That would be the calypso Sonny knew as "St. Thomas." "I was just beginning to introduce my Caribbean songs that I knew from my family," Sonny said. "I was just beginning to sort of drop them on my colleagues."[16]

The song was the Creole product of the Afro-Caribbean diaspora. "It's called 'Roll, Turn, Spin' or 'Run, Come, See' or about a million thousand things," said Taj Mahal of the song. "Every island and every guitar player down there has a version of it and every island has a different version from the other island, and sometimes four or five different versions exist on one island. You have to understand that these were people who didn't have anything. They were not allowed to have anything, so when they did have something, everybody figured out millions of ways of making it work."[17]

Sonny first heard it as a child when Valborg sang it to him and then later at West Indian dances in Harlem at clubs like the Park Palace, which she took him to see. Some claim it was originally known as "The Lincolnshire Poacher," a traditional English folk song.[18] In 1945, Sonny heard Danish opera star Lauritz Melchior sing "Vive l'Amour," also known as "Vive la Compagnie," in his first film role, *Thrill of a Romance.*[19] "When I listen to that song, it's the same as 'St. Thomas,' and the native people there probably took their version listening to that song, 'Vive la Compagnie' and turned it into 'St. Thomas.'"[20]

Sonny had no pretensions of having written it himself. "I sort of arranged the melody; that's the most credit I ever take," Sonny said. "But the record company was more than happy to ascribe composing to me—so that they could take the proceeds."[21]

The version Sonny's mother heard in St. Thomas growing up was syncopated, with a quelbe bounce that had an air of joyous resistance, the kind of revelry reserved for carnival days. What Sonny called "St. Thomas," Valborg probably would have known as "Fire Down There."[22] Dripping with sexual innuendo, it had been recorded several times even in the previous few years. The famous calypsonian the Duke of Iron, one of Sonny's favorites, had a version.[23] Then in 1954, a twenty-one-year-old Bronx-born calypsonian recorded it under the stage name the Charmer, billed as "Trinidad's newest sensation." His name was Louis Walcott or, as he would later be known, Louis Farrakhan.[24]

Me mama done tell me, boy, there's fire down there

Just that February, Brooklyn-based West Indian pianist Randy Weston released "Fire Down There" on his trio album *Get Happy*.[25] "He was my idol," Weston said of Sonny. "I love Sonny so much because I'm a sound freak. See, with the music, it's the sound. That's why, Coleman Hawkins and Pres and Louis, that's why those people are beyond category, as Duke would say. Sound they got, and Sonny Rollins has the most incredible sound on the saxophone." To Weston, Sonny had internalized the music's Afro-Caribbean origins. "I call it African American classical music—I don't call it jazz. Sonny's got the Caribbean roots. I've got the Caribbean roots. I've got the Virginia roots. To me, it's just an expression of mother Africa."[26]

To Weston, Sonny understood the legacy of the ancestors. "We knew the ancestors were the bosses," he said.

They created something that never happened before. They took European history and they got a sound of Africa in those instruments. Sonny Rollins, he expressed that sound, that combination of Jamaica and New York, Jamaican food, dances, way of life. And the black audience would know whether you played well or not. You didn't have to look at *The New York Times* to see whether you played well or not. You better play well, I don't care whether they call it the black church or the blues or jazz—that audience would know exactly when it's right. And when it's not right, you in trouble. So Sonny was a big seller in the black community, African American community, because some of the artists are just known downtown. And he kept the humor, he had that beat in the music, because to me all the giants have a sense of humor when they play, because that's some healing. Now as a musician in the African tradition, you have to be able to play something to make people laugh, because laughter is the best healing the creator gave us when things are bad. So if Sonny played "St. Thomas," man, you laugh. That's the tradition of Africa that remains with us, and Sonny Rollins is a spiritual giant.[27]

To Jamaican pianist Monty Alexander, "St. Thomas" was as old as time. He was twelve when *Saxophone Colossus* was recorded, and soon it could be heard in Jamaica. "Every note he played, it was life," Alexander said. "'Sonny, blow! Blow, man!' Like a large wind coming from all over the universe." For Alexander, "St. Thomas" really did it. "When you hear him not only play a calypso song, a riddim like that...he owns it. He ain't just playing it. He's owning it. He's reliving it. That's why it takes off. He'll move an audience even if they're not jazz fans. He's beyond jazz." The song evoked the sound of musicians "way up in the bush that played on bamboo saxophones with little matchboxes for reeds, and they fashioned a bell out of a condensed milk tin can...and they had a sound that was totally indigenous....So when Sonny's playing, I'm hearing a guy that's coming from the raw earth."[28]

For Sonny, recording "St. Thomas" was a natural coming to consciousness, but it wasn't so surprising that he recorded a calypso in 1956. That year was the beginning of Elvis Mania, but it was also the year of the Calypso Craze. Some even speculated that calypso might supplant rock as America's pop music of choice.[29] Harry Belafonte, who was three years older than Sonny and also grew up in Harlem, had become a national star. Earlier in 1956, his sophomore album, *Belafonte*, with the calypso "Matilda," became the first to top the newly created *Billboard* pop album chart.[30] It stayed there for six weeks.[31] That May, Belafonte released *Calypso*, with the hit "Banana Boat Song (Day-O)." By September 8, *Calypso* claimed the top spot on the chart, becoming the top-charting album of 1956 and the first album of the LP era to sell more than a million copies.[32] That July saw the release of *High Society*, starring Frank Sinatra, Bing Crosby, and Grace Kelly, which became one of the top-grossing films of the year. It opened with Louis Armstrong singing "High Society Calypso," written by none other than Cole Porter.

Calypso got its name from the Greek goddess who enchanted Odysseus with her improvised melodies and imprisoned him on the Island of Ogygia, thought to be somewhere in the Atlantic Ocean. Traditional calypso is based in improvisation, with folk melodies and lyrics created extemporaneously to tell a story, and the art form's reigning raconteurs had their own royal titles: Lord Invader, Duke of Iron, King Radio. In 1957 came *Miss Calypso*, the debut album by Miss Calypso herself: Maya Angelou. As the craze launched everyone from poets to cruise-ship singers into major label contracts practically overnight, the Trinidadian calypsonian Mighty Panther was wary of pretenders to the throne who couldn't improvise. Calypso, he told *Down Beat* in May 1956, is "the voice of the people in Trinidad. It is called the newspaper of the common man....A Calypsonian in Trinidad has no respect for rank or station; he'll sing against the governor or anybody if he has something to say. An element of humor holds the listener while the Calypsonian drives across his deeper purpose."[33] Sonny brought to jazz the calypsonian's radical egalitarianism, storytelling impulse, wit, and improvisatory spirit.

Sonny's "St. Thomas" leads off with a sixteen-bar solo drum intro—tuned toms and the clink of the hi-hat on two and four—to establish the feel. Tommy Flanagan comps sparsely and rhythmically as Doug Watkins plays mostly half notes on the bass line. Sonny's syncopated phrasing of the melody combines the humor, depth, and narrative thrust that define both calypso and swing. His solo all stems from a two-note motif. The first eight bars of the solo consist mostly of only four notes twisted around rhythmically, and the first two notes of the solo are the same as the first two notes of the melody. "St. Thomas" was simple, but the way Sonny played it revealed hidden depths.[34]

Max ends his solo with a ride-cymbal crash, and Sonny erupts in an all-out swing. "There's a connection between those grooves, and definitely in my own playing, it's consolidated in a natural way," Sonny said. "But in playing 'St. Thomas,' I think I had to make more of a differentiation to prove the point."[35]

Sonny was telling a story of roots and fugitive flight: there was his childhood, his mother singing to him, the West Indian dances in Harlem, and embedded in the song's DNA, Martha Bennett at Judith's Fancy, Sonny's grandfather Steadman Rollins, Valborg and Miriam in St. Thomas, all of that island rhythm streaming out as he proudly claimed his West Indian heritage. When Sonny restates the melody to take it out, Max keeps the ride cymbal swinging relentlessly. But on the final chorus, Max returns to the calypso feel, as if to say, it all goes back to the islands—to Africa. On "St. Thomas," Sonny took flight. He knew what the calypsonians knew: "If you surrendered to the air, you could ride it."[36]

When Ira Gitler heard the album, he knew just what to call it: *Saxophone Colossus*. "One of the Seven Wonders of the World was the Colossus of Rhodes, a bronze statue of Apollo, 100 feet high," Gitler wrote in his liner notes. "The use of the word colossus brings to mind its adjectival derivative colossal, a word which has had its share of buffeting about among Hollywood's celluloid hucksters in their press releases regarding many of the empty epics which pass across the screens of the nation. The dictionary says colossal is gigantic; huge; vast. When applied to Sonny Rollins' talent it also signifies depth."[37]

Designer Tom Hannan took the idea and created a cover befitting the title.[38] For Sonny's albums, he designed the variegated cover for *Sonny Rollins Plus Four*, the geometric abstraction of *Sonny Rollins and Thelonious Monk*, the stark black-and-red lettering of *Tenor Madness*, and others. For *Saxophone Colossus*, Hannan used a blue background, then cropped and darkened a photo of Sonny in sunglasses, looming with his saxophone: the Saxophone Colossus.

When the album was released the following April, it got widespread acclaim. *Billboard* touted Sonny's "architectural logic."[39] "Rollins is in his fearful prime," wrote Whitney Balliett in the *New Yorker*.[40] Ralph J. Gleason gave Sonny his first five-star review in *Down Beat*.[41] The *Saturday Review* touted it as Sonny's breakout album.[42] Yet *Saxophone Colossus* never cracked *Down Beat*'s biweekly "Jazz Best-sellers" list.[43] When it was released, the top-selling jazz albums were Shelly Manne's *My Fair Lady*, Erroll Garner's *Concert by the Sea*, and *Ellington at Newport*.

However, the album exerted an outsize influence on Sonny's peers. "He may play something that sounds like a car running down at a high speed, and you'll say 'Whoa!' in the middle of his solo, and if you know anything and you lived any and you heard any music in your life, you know what he's talking about and where he's coming from," said Jimmy Heath. "Expressions of life—Sonny always had that. And the island life is his forte."[44]

Soon, tenor players began studying the minutiae of what Sonny and Coltrane were doing, including their fingerings and finger positions. "The first thing a teacher will tell you is to look in the mirror and keep your fingers close," said Wayne Shorter. "Bird did, Trane did, Hank Mobley kept them close. Sonny Rollins can do both, keep his fingers close *and* far away. Make a note *pop*. But Trane made his notes pop with keepin' them close. With Sonny Rollins, it's his West Indian shit—he hits the keys like they were steel drums."[45]

By mid-1957, when *Saxophone Colossus* was released, the Calypso Craze had reached the jazz world.[46] At around the same time *Saxophone Colossus* came out, J. C. Heard released *Calypso for Dancing*, Sarah Vaughan covered "The Banana Boat Song," and Herbie Mann recorded "Oi Vay, Calypso." Mal Waldron recorded "Blue Calypso" with trumpeter Bill Hardman; Sonny's childhood friends Jackie McLean, Julian Euell, and Art Taylor; and, of all people, John Coltrane.[47] So Sonny was not unique in recording a calypso, and he was not the first; it was purely a testament to how deeply he had internalized the art form that he would be widely credited for introducing it to jazz.

Yet by the end of 1957, the craze vanished almost as quickly as it arrived.[48] Maybe mainstream American culture couldn't figure out how to dance to calypso. However, *Saxophone Colossus* would outlast it,[49] and in 2017, the album was selected for preservation in the Library of Congress's National Recording Registry.

Decades later, when tenor saxophonist Joshua Redman asked Sonny about the album, which Redman called "probably the most influential record for me of any record in any genre of music," Sonny was characteristically self-deprecating. "It was just another record date, you know?"[50]

Chapter 17

I REMEMBER CLIFFORD

(1956)

The end of June 1956 would be seared into Sonny's memory, but not for the *Saxophone Colossus* session.

On June 27, the Brown-Roach Quintet was booked to open in Chicago at the Blue Note in the Loop opposite the Oscar Peterson Trio.[1] "When we got to Chicago, we had barnstormed around the country about a year and a half or two," Max said. "We were working on the South Side and we were finally in the Loop."[2]

The quintet generally traveled together on the road, but had split up. Max, George, and Sonny were in New York, while Richie and Brownie had gone to be with their families in Philadelphia. A trumpet company in Elkhart, Indiana, asked Clifford to try some new instruments in the hope of getting an endorsement. He and Richie would leave on the night of June 26 and make a pit stop in Indiana. They would all meet at the Mansfield Hotel in Chicago.[3]

On June 26, Max, George Morrow, and Sonny drove from New York to Chicago, stopping only for gas.[4] They arrived at the hotel late that night and waited for the rest of the band to arrive. It was a reunion of sorts, too; the Miles Davis Quintet was playing at the Crown Propeller and was also staying at the Mansfield.[5]

The week off with family and friends had been a good one for Brownie and Richie. Before he left, Brownie had caught a fish, which his sister Geneva fried for a soul food dinner. LaRue and Clifford Jr. were on a trip to Los Angeles, and Brownie missed them terribly—June 26 was her birthday and their second wedding anniversary—but he would have to wait until after the Chicago engagement. He couldn't bear to leave the calm and warmth of home, but a gig was a gig, so he drove his Buick to Philadelphia to meet Richie and his wife, Nancy, at the Showboat Lounge, where Cannonball Adderley's group was booked for the week.[6] Adderley asked Richie and Brownie to sit in, and they happily obliged.[7] Afterward, the three of them stopped by the Philadelphia Blue Note to meet Chico Hamilton and his wife.

It was pouring when they got on the road at about 9 the night of June 26. Brownie was tired, and so was Richie, but they had to get to Chicago. When Brownie thought he would pass out, he had Richie take the wheel. Then Richie did the same and changed seats with nineteen-year-old Nancy, who, like Richie, wore thick glasses.[8] Nancy drove on, through low visibility, while the men napped. It was dark on the Pennsylvania Turnpike, and the road was winding and slick with rain. Freight trucks were out on the highway making their weary haul. Suddenly, Nancy lost control of the car, which veered off the road at Bedford Interchange and into a guardrail, skidding into a bridge abutment, and plummeting down an eighteen-foot embankment before it came to a final resting place against a utility pole below. All three were killed instantly.

A truck driver found the wreck and reported it to the police. The death certificate listed the time of death as 1:15 a.m. on June 27, 1956.[9] Clifford Brown was twenty-five, Richard Powell twenty-four, Nancy Powell nineteen.[10] One of the only things to survive the wreckage was a reel-to-reel tape of the quintet at the Beehive that past November—Sonny's audition tape. It would be a long time before Max could bring himself to play it.[11]

After Sonny survived the scourge, between the Miles Davis Quintet and Brown-Roach, he had chosen the group most likely to live through the rigors of touring—and then this happened.

The Brown family in Wilmington found out quickly, but in Chicago, the tragic news didn't reach the rest of the quintet immediately. At the hotel, George and Sonny were on the second floor, two doors apart, not far from Coltrane's room. Max was on the third floor. When Coltrane got home from the Crown Propeller at about 5 a.m. on June 27, Morrow recalled, the telephone rang and it was Naima, Coltrane's wife, "telling him there was an accident but they didn't know who."[12]

At around 9 that morning, Sonny got up early and decided to go out and buy a new set of matching ties for the quintet's momentous opening at the Blue Note. Only a year earlier, Sonny was working as a janitor in Chicago; now he was back, working at the same club where Duke Ellington played when in town.

Later that morning, Max got a call from Joe Glaser at Associated Booking. "Max, brace yourself," he said. Before the news could sink in, Glaser announced that if Max was willing, he could still go on that night. Perhaps Miles Davis or Roy Eldridge, who were in Chicago, could fill in for Brownie. Max refused. The Blue Note engagement was canceled; Dorothy Donegan agreed to take their place.[13] "None of us could have made that gig," Sonny said. "Everybody was in shock, days after the incident....I'm ashamed of Joe Glaser. I thought he had more sense than to even suggest we do the gig after that."[14]

When Max got off with Glaser, he called Sonny and George in their rooms. Sonny had just gotten back with the new ties. On the third floor, Morrow recalled, "Max dropped it on us—'I have something very tragic to tell both of you—there's been an accident and Brownie and Richard and his wife were killed instantly,' and that's the way he said it. It still didn't register on me. On a strip of paper next to the telephone there was a notation of the funeral home it was in, it said 'Bodies at such and such a place' and just to see 'Bodies at such and such a place' it began to register. Neither of us said anything but went back to our respective rooms."[15]

The initial shock of their deaths was overwhelming. "When Brownie and Richie died, George and Max and me just bawled like babies," Sonny said. "It was too much."[16]

Sonny was speechless. "All I could do was go back to my hotel room and practice all night long," he said. "I was so stunned that at first it did not seem real and the only way to deal with it was to practice."[17]

Recorded only days before the accident, *Saxophone Colossus* was suddenly a kind of elegy. The ballad "You Don't Know What Love Is," as it turned out, was the last song Richie Powell ever played.[18] Everything Sonny played on the session attested to the depth of his musical relationship with Brownie, and now Clifford Brown was gone. "I came to terms with his death on an emotional level by rationalizing that he was too good a person to be in this world," Sonny said. "He was really a beautiful human being."[19]

After Max broke the news, George Morrow told Coltrane, who connected it to the call that morning from Naima. "It had been reported in Los Angeles I was dead, too," recalled Morrow. "Others reported the death of Bud Powell instead of his brother.[20]

When Max told Sonny and George, he called each respective family from his room. Then he locked the door, opened a bottle of liquor, and drank until he was numb.[21] Beyond the grief, Max felt responsible for their deaths. Why had he agreed to let them go separately? Then Brownie, Richie, and Nancy appeared to him in a hallucination and told him that "Everything's all right."

That night, Sonny, Max, and George went to see the Miles Davis Quintet at the Crown Propeller,[22] where they told anyone who didn't already know. Among them was the Ghanaian percussionist Guy Warren, living in Chicago at the time.[23] On their way back to the hotel, "Max was driving, Sonny was sitting in the front seat, and I was in the back," Morrow recalled vividly. "We were approaching our turn off on Lake Shore Drive at about 10 o'clock that evening and Max had turned on his left-hand turn signal rather than his right." Only they were turning right.

"No, don't!" George called out. "A car was barreling down on us and Max turned around and it hit the front," he said. If Morrow didn't yell and Max didn't hit the brakes, they could have joined the rest of the quintet in heaven. "All I could see was headlights. We were so scared from then on, we went straight back to the hotel. We parked that car till we got ready to leave Chicago."[24]

The following day, the remaining members of the quintet, Guy Warren, Miles, and other musicians had an informal gathering to mourn, "discussing Clifford, and the business, and everything," recalled Warren. Warren offered Max what solace he could. "He saw the look and my whole demeanor," Max said. "I was just crushed. He said, 'You know, Max, Brownie said what he was supposed to say and he's on his way.' For some reason, that lifted me out of that. It lifted me up from something."[25]

"It took me a long time to be able to reconcile that," Sonny said. "And it took Max a long time, too. He might not have ever reconciled it....With George Morrow and myself, it was just losing our soul mates, but Max had all of the dreams that they had for the band—the whole thing he lost."[26]

Around midnight on Thursday, June 28, they checked out of the Mansfield Hotel. Maybe in part as a tribute to Brownie, Sonny was listed as "S. Rollins—Roundtree" on the bill, the nickname he and Brownie had joked about. As Sonny recalled, the band passed through Detroit on their way to

Wilmington for the funeral, stopping at the home of Prophet Jennings, a close friend of the band. "We were all in Prophet's house bawling like babies," Sonny said. For everyone, "that accident was hugely traumatic."[27] Friday night, hundreds of mourners drove to Bell's Funeral Home in Wilmington to pay their tearful last respects to Brownie.[28]

Three separate funerals were held at the same time on the same day—June 30 at 1 p.m. Richie and Nancy had only been married for one month; as an interracial couple, they were not allowed to be buried in the same cemetery.[29] Sonny, George, and Max could go to only one funeral, and they decided it would have to be Brownie's.

Clifford Brown was interred at Mount Zion Cemetery, in his hometown of Wilmington, following a three-hour funeral service at Wilmington's Mount Carmel Methodist Church, filled to capacity. There were three carloads of flowers, condolences from all over the country as well as France and Switzerland. Sonny, George, and Max were honorary pallbearers. A reporter accosted a visibly shaken Max Roach to ask what was next for the quintet. "The suddenness of the accident has given no time to think of other plans," he said.[30]

A photo of Sonny, George, Max, Max's mother (Cressie Roach), and his wife, Mildred, was taken at the funeral. Max wore sunglasses; they all wore matching suits and ties, most likely the ties Sonny had bought for their opening at the Blue Note.[31] During the service, none of the surviving members of the quintet could hold back tears.[32]

———◄○►———

After the funeral, the remaining members of the quintet took a break. "Subsequently, I drove all the way back to New York," recalled George Morrow, "and we didn't do anything for about a week or two."[33] Sonny plunged into practicing to cope with the grief and also sat in at clubs around the city. Saxophonist Zoot Sims was debuting a new quintet as part of a broadcast series; Gerry Mulligan sat in on one session, Sonny at another.[34]

What was now the Max Roach Quintet was booked in Detroit at the Graystone Ballroom in early July and needed two new members. Max enlisted a pair of Detroit natives: twenty-three-year-old trumpeter Donald Byrd and twenty-six-year-old pianist Barry Harris.[35] Byrd was a Clifford Brown aco-lyte who shared not only Brownie's precise articulation but also his intel-lectual curiosity; he was gifted in math, was well versed in the Schillinger System, and would go on to earn a doctorate in education and a law degree, but his most important degree came from Minton's.[36] If Bud Powell was the professor in New York, Barry Harris was the professor in Detroit, mentoring a whole generation of Detroit pianists, Tommy Flanagan, Kirk Lightsey, and Hugh Lawson among them. Touring musicians would stop by Harris's place, including Sonny and Coltrane, bassist Paul Chambers, and just about any-one passing through the Motor City.[37]

It was through listening to Bud Powell's "Dance of the Infidels" and "Bouncin' with Bud" that Harris first encountered Sonny. "I thought the best of him. I thought he was the greatest tenor player ever," Harris said. Harris thought Sonny's work with Powell was "some of the best records. Even when he made that record with Bird, where Bird played tenor.... Sonny Rollins was the man, brother. He always was the man, and I never stopped thinking of him as the boss." Harris had positive memories of his brief time with the quintet. "I don't think we ever recorded," he said, "but we had a pretty good time, 'cause we played Sonny's tune 'Valse Hot.'"[38]

The Graystone Ballroom was an expansive neo-Gothic dance hall, built in 1922, and it could accommodate three thousand dancers—four thousand if they danced close.[39] The quintet was booked on a bill opposite the Drifters, the Orioles, the Turbans, the El Dorados, and the Moonglows, along with Miles Davis and Lester Young, probably part of the series of "Jazz vs. Rock 'n' Roll" concerts that presenter Frank Brown began booking earlier that year. It's not clear if Miles made the gig—his name was dropped from the newspa-per ad on July 7—but it seems Pres was there.[40]

At first, the rowdy crowd was disrespectful. "I heard guys in the audience shouting out, 'Blow, Clifford!'" recalled Detroit jazz fan Jerry "Tiger" Pearson. "I and my friends knew all about Clifford's tragic death. But these guys' rude comments finally compelled Max to get on the microphone and announce: 'Ladies and gentleman, I don't know if you know or not, but Clifford died in a car accident about a month ago. We are respectfully trying to keep the band going. This young man is from Detroit—this is Donald Byrd.'"[41]

The night ended on a high note for Sonny—jamming with Pres. "Lester was there and he came up on stage and we played together," Sonny said.[42] It would be the only time they'd share a stage.[43]

From Detroit, they played their next gig in a more pastoral setting than their usual circuit.[44] It was in the "Concerts for Connoisseurs" series, part of the Lenox Jazz and Folk Festival in Lenox, Massachusetts, in the Berkshire Mountains.[45] In 1950, Stephanie and Phil Barber bought a small piece of the 380-acre Wheatleigh property and converted the outbuildings into the Music Barn and Inn.[46] In 1955, the hay barn became the Music Barn, a six-hundred-seat auditorium, but it still retained its pastoral roots—the green-room had a dirt floor.[47]

Tickets for the July 12 show were only $1.65.[48] They made it clear to the small crowd that showed up that the concert was a memorial for Clifford Brown and Richie Powell, who played at the Music Barn the previous summer with the Brown-Roach Quintet. According to a review, Byrd and Harris had already established an "extraordinary" rapport with the band.[49]

However, Max didn't find the rapport so strong. No one could fill the void left by Brownie and Richie, and he wouldn't have it any other way. Donald Byrd "played Clifford's solos off the record verbatim and I explained to him that this wasn't the reason he was there," Max recalled.[50] "He was to play Donald Byrd," as Barry Harris was to play Barry Harris.[51] On August 13, after a week in Atlantic City, they moved on to the Colonial Tavern in Toronto, where for maybe the first time they took a plane.[52] On August 21, they were back at the Rouge Lounge in Detroit, where Harris and Byrd had a supportive hometown crowd.[53] Shirley Carter, a twenty-two-year-old Detroiter who lived and breathed jazz, was one of the most ardent supporters at the Rouge.[54] "If they hadn't had folks supporting them, they wouldn't have made it. It was not a time of a lot of money flowing," she recalled. "But we knew that we were getting the best."[55]

It was on a Friday night at the Rouge Lounge that Sonny met Shirley, who had majored in music at the famed Cass Technical High School. She had also been in the fencing club, and Sonny had to stay on his toes to keep up with her rapier wit. Cass Tech was the breeding ground for many jazz stars, and Carter grew up alongside Kenny Burrell, Barry Harris, Paul Chambers,

Doug Watkins, and the Jones and McKinney families. She was closest to Donald Byrd, her "adopted big brother," going back to intermediate school, she said. "I was his chauffeur and his everything when he would come to town. He'd call me and I'd just get in the car and go to where he had to go." As platonic friends, Byrd thought of Carter as his "protector"—"he had to take me along to visit his girlfriend so they wouldn't chase him out of the neighborhood," she recalled. She would help him see the women he wanted to see and avoid the ones he didn't. "There were probably a lot of females that wanted to chop my head off because they were trying to get to Donald." On this particular night, though, Byrd was responsible for her meeting Sonny.

First, Sonny noticed her car—by chance, she recalled, "the same make, model, and color that Clifford Brown and them died in." It was a two-door Buick Super, black with a white top and a burgundy interior. "It was like he was looking at a ghost or something. . . . I told him, 'Well, I'm a safe driver.'"[56]

It was not just her car that made an impression on Sonny. Carter was a trained classical violinist, the daughter of a hardworking father who, when he came north to Detroit from Shreveport during the Great Migration, brought his two violins with him. "He loved it, and he was good," she said, "but it's just like me. There was no place to go as a violin performer because there was no place that I would be hired." She would major in violin at Cass Tech, as well as studying saxophone. She graduated high school early and enrolled as a music major at Wayne State. With limited opportunities for a female musician of color, Carter set the violin aside.[57] She pursued a successful career in human resources, but she spent every weekend at the Blue Bird, Frolic, Flame Show Bar, the Rouge Lounge, and the West End.[58] She was a dyed-in-the-wool jazz fan.

Shirley must have been the kind of girl Sonny was hoping to meet. But alas, the road was the road. After Detroit, the quintet drove back to New York, where they had a moment to catch their breath. On August 28 or 29, Sonny stopped in at Lester Young's gig at the Café Bohemia to wish him a belated happy forty-seventh birthday.[59] The Count Basie Orchestra stopped by, too. On the set break, "Lester came over to Sonny and gave him a big hug and said, 'So nice of you to come down. Come on up, won't you come up and play with me?'" recalled pianist Bill Triglia. "But Sonny Rollins said, 'I just want to listen. It's so nice to listen to you, I don't want to play.'"[60]

Then Max, George, and Sonny returned to Lenox sans Harris and Byrd. The summer festival at the Music Barn and Inn featured concerts and discussion panels, part of the seventh annual Jazz Roundtable. Not far from Tanglewood, the summer home of the Boston Symphony Orchestra, Stephanie and Phil Barber decided to program a festival that took jazz as seriously as the European classical tradition. From August 27 to 31, five panels took place at the Music Inn, and all but one of the participants were musicians. Each of these engrossing discussions lasted three to four hours and sought to pair two warring schools of thought—for example, the traditionalist moldy figs versus the modernists.[61] Panel discussions on improvisation, composition and instrumentation, rhythm, and developing an audience for the music featured such luminaries as Charles Mingus, Milt Jackson, Oscar Pettiford, Quincy Jones, Ray Brown, Dizzy Gillespie, Willie "the Lion" Smith, George Wein, Nesuhi Ertegun, Marshall Stearns, and Langston Hughes.[62]

Sonny's panel was "Instrumental Tradition and the Development of Instrumental Techniques," with Rex Stewart, Wilbur de Paris, Bill Russo, John Mehegan, Dizzy Gillespie, Oscar Pettiford, and Max Roach. They discussed sound, phrasing, and technique. "I'd like to point out that there are more different styles of saxophone than any instrument with the possible exception of the piano," Sonny said. "Things that will be stressed in the future are going to involve better articulation of tone, a clearer tone and a general increase in overall technique."[63] The roundtables were so successful that there was unanimous support to expand the program the following year for the summer of 1957 to a three-week workshop with sixty students called the Lenox School of Jazz. Sonny had participated in one of the formative events of formalized jazz education.[64]

That night, on August 30, a jam session–style concert at the Music Barn was taped for Willis Conover's *Voice of America* broadcast.[65] Sonny played with Dizzy and a rhythm section of Pettiford, Mehegan, and Max. Then Sonny and Max stayed onstage, joined by Morrow for a pianoless trio rendition of "Valse Hot." It all came to a finale with Dizzy, Jackson, Brown, Max, John Lewis, and Sonny.[66]

Back at the Blue Note in Philadelphia starting September 10, simmering tensions bubbled over.[67] Max claimed he wanted Byrd and Harris to play themselves, but sometimes he felt the absence of Brownie and Richie on the stand. This was especially true on their arrangement of "A Night in Tunisia," which ended with Brownie climbing to the top of his range, a difficult feat for any trumpeter. "Brownie'd go all the way up and hit that high F and that's the only thing Max heard," recalled George Morrow. "And that's the reason Donald Byrd was scared Max was going to hurt him. Max wanted to hear that high F and say, 'Give me that high F' and Donald Byrd say, 'I can't.' 'Give me that high F.' 'I get a headache.' 'Get you some aspirins then, but I want that high F.'"[68] Finally, it got to be too much. In Philadelphia, Byrd walked off the bandstand.[69] Kenny Dorham was there the next night. Dorham had his own group—the Jazz Prophets—but decided to disband it and join the Roach Quintet instead. With Byrd out, Harris left, too, and went back to Detroit.[70]

The timing for their departures was unfortunate, as Max had his next studio recording for EmArcy slated imminently for September 17 and 19. Luckily, Max had sheet music.[71] Dorham was more than capable of handling it, even though he had just come in. On piano, Max called Ray Bryant, who had proved himself on Sonny's *Work Time* session that past December.[72] Adding to the pressure on Bryant, Thelonious Monk was watching in the studio with drummer Osie Johnson. The album would be called *Max Roach Plus 4*, in part a tongue-in-cheek response to *Sonny Rollins Plus 4*.[73]

The album introduced the quintet's more percussive direction with George Russell's "Ezz-thetic," based on Cole Porter's "Love for Sale" and dedicated to heavyweight champion Ezzard Charles, and two Roach originals, "Dr. Free-Zee," in which Max overdubbed tuned tympani on top of the drum set, and "Mr. X," named for Malcolm X.[74] " 'Just One of Those Things' was one of the fastest tunes I have ever played," recalled George Morrow.[75] The tune was played at such a bracing clip that Sonny's streams of eighth notes made it seem almost as though the record was a 33 played at 45 RPM. And despite the tempo, in a kaleidoscopic stop-time chorus, Sonny manages to make the whole thing swing. A four-star *Down Beat* review noted that "it is a case of matching Rollins' musical virility or being overpowered by it."[76] Far from dismissing him, the critical establishment finally knew Sonny was a force to be reckoned with.

On September 17, after Sonny left the studio the first day of the *Max Roach Plus 4* sessions, he met an up-and-coming drummer who idolized Max: Paul Motian.[77] Pianist Bill Triglia, whom Sonny had just seen with Lester Young that August, called Motian for a Monday night at Birdland. When Motian showed up, he found Triglia and bassist Curly Russell and, on the front line, trumpeter Tony Fruscella and Sonny. "I was kind of scared at the time, when I saw it was Sonny Rollins and all these people," Motian said. "But I did my best, tried to play my best, tried to play with them, and learn...I don't know, just play!"[78]

As it turned out, Zoot Sims was in the audience. He was in a desperate situation. He had been called earlier that evening by Sam Firsten, who owned the Cotton Club in Cleveland. Art Tatum was sick—he would die November 5—and canceled his run at the club, which was supposed to begin that night. Having heard that Motian could hold his own with Sonny, Sims asked him to come to Cleveland with his quintet immediately. They opened the next day.[79]

Around this time, Max Roach recruited twenty-two-year-old pianist Wade Legge for the quintet. He was born in West Virginia, grew up in Buffalo, and was good enough on bass to play it in Dizzy Gillespie's band—starting when he was eighteen—until he switched to the instrument he would be better known for.[80] Legge was a quiet musician who kept his own counsel; everything he had to say, he said on the keys.

On September 26, the Showboat hosted a Richie Powell memorial concert for the benefit of Pearl Powell, Bud and Richie's mother.[81] More than a thousand people showed up to see leading figures perform in Richie's honor: the Roach Quintet, Oscar Pettiford, pianist Bernard Peiffer, Sahib Shihab, Kenny Burrell, Willie Jones, David Amram, and Cannonball Adderley's group. Even Babs Gonzales showed up.[82]

On October 5, the day the Roach Quintet opened at Greenwich Village's Café Bohemia, Sonny rode out to Van Gelder's in Hackensack to record his first album as a leader after the accident and his first-ever concept album. He was still under contract with Prestige and planned to make a record in tribute to his mentor, Charlie Parker. For *Rollins Plays for Bird*, Sonny hired the Roach Quintet with Kenny Dorham and Wade Legge. Sonny,

Max, Kenny, and Wade had all played with Parker.[83] In addition to Sonny's twenty-seven-minute Bird medley, the record included two other tunes, Sonny's nearly twelve-minute waltz, "Kids Know," and "I've Grown Accustomed to Your Face," the ballad from the chart-topping *My Fair Lady* 1956 Broadway cast recording.

"When Clifford died, when it came to looking for another trumpeter to replace him and Kenny Dorham was selected, I tried to do a 3/4 jazz song again," Sonny said of "Kids Know." "The title refers to a certain innocence that children have; they have a natural intuition, special affinities when it comes to spiritual things before they grow up and get jaded."[84]

The medley covered seven tunes from Bird's repertoire. It opens with Sonny summoning the spirit of Bird with a quote from "Parker's Mood" before transitioning into "I Remember You." It's full of the electric double-time lines Parker was known for and Sonny's playful quotes.[85] Dorham handles "My Melancholy Baby" himself; the rhythm section plays "Old Folks" as a trio; Sonny then plays "They Can't Take That Away from Me," rhythmically stretching the first note; Dorham takes "Just Friends"; Roach, Legge, and Morrow cover "My Little Suede Shoes"; and Sonny and Kenny close it out with "Star Eyes."

Parker's absence was felt keenly, but his legacy was still alive. At around this time, Sonny was interviewed for his first profile in *Down Beat*, written by Nat Hentoff, a staunch critic turned supporter. "After I understood what he was doing," Sonny said of Bird, "I realized it was a combination of everything up to that point, plus himself. He added something without taking away from what had come before."[86] Likewise, on *Rollins Plays for Bird*, Bird was in there, side-slipping in and out of the chords. But Sonny had found his own voice.[87]

With the Montgomery bus boycott still ongoing amid attempts to dismantle the NAACP, Sonny felt it was time to make music with a message. At the *Rollins Plays for Bird* session, he also recorded "The House I Live In," the socially conscious Earl Robinson tune Frank Sinatra made famous when he recorded it in 1945 in the short film of the same name. Sonny closed the song with a coda from "Lift Ev'ry Voice and Sing," the black national anthem with lyrics by NAACP leader James Weldon Johnson and music by his brother J. Rosamond Johnson. Rather than resolving into a major chord at the end, as the song normally does, Sonny ends with the song lingering, unresolved. (It would not be released until 1961 on *Sonny Boy*.)

"I learned it just growing up in Harlem. Everybody knew it," Sonny said of "Lift Ev'ry Voice." "That's when I had a chance to do my thing, which I was commissioned to do in my own mind—to keep bringing up these civil rights matters. W. E. B. Du Bois recommended that anybody that got any kind of prominence that could make use of their knowledge of the civil rights struggle should do so."[88]

Next, the Roach Quintet was booked at Sugar Hill, a jazz club on Newark's Broad Street. The club opened in October 1956: in addition to Roach, Mingus, Dizzy, and Howard McGhee were some of the first to play there.[89] A young Newark-based trombonist named Grachan Moncur III led a group that played when the marquee acts weren't performing and sat in with the Roach Quintet, forging a relationship with Sonny.[90]

During this gig, Sonny also met an unknown tenor player who would become one of the iconic figures in jazz: Wayne Shorter.[91] The Newark-born Shorter was three years younger than Sonny and was in the middle of his army service in Fort Dix, New Jersey. Whenever he could get free, he made the jam-session circuit and had built up a reputation; Max Roach knew him as the Newark Flash.[92] On a weekend furlough, Shorter decided to see the new Roach Quintet with Kenny Dorham. He walked in to the sound of "Love Is a Many-Splendored Thing." "Max saw me come in with my Army suit on," Shorter recalled. "He waved his drumstick at me, saying, 'Come on up, come on up.' So I pointed to my uniform and then pointed to the door, indicating that I was going home to change into civilian clothes."[93] When he came back in his street clothes wielding a Martin tenor, Max called him up.

Just like when Sonny auditioned for the Brown-Roach Quintet, they "started off with 'Cherokee'... REAL FAST," Shorter said.[94] That was the only tune he played with them, but he made the changes, and a strong impression. After the set, Sonny suggested that Shorter get a custom-made metal Otto Link mouthpiece, at the time the mouthpiece of choice for Sonny and Coltrane, with its distinctive golden glint and characteristically bright tone. To Shorter, Sonny "had that full sound all the way up and down the horn... and only a few people had that." Sonny also had "a lot of rhythm...and he would leap out at things and take it and express something. So you would see the actual force, you'd feel that statement that Sonny made; in a certain way like Charlie Parker did, too. . . . Sonny's content was always like a full meal—the meat and potatoes and salad and everything there."[95]

Then Thelonious Monk enlisted Sonny to record what would become the classic album *Brilliant Corners*. The session was at Reeves Sound Studios at 1600 Broadway, right by Basin Street. It was Monk's third album for Riverside Records, the independent label founded by Bill Grauer and Orrin Keepnews. In 1954, they signed their first artist, Randy Weston, and then in 1955 they bought out Monk's contract with Prestige for $108. As Keepnews said, Monk soon became "the real magic in the launching of Riverside."[96]

The first session for *Brilliant Corners* was on October 9, in the midst of the Roach Quintet's Café Bohemia run.[97] *Brilliant Corners* immediately proved challenging for Keepnews. "Basically, dealing with Monk in full-scale action meant that it was my job to supervise and control the creative flow of recording sessions that involved a perfectionist leader driving a group of sensitive and highly talented artists beyond their limits," Keepnews wrote.[98]

Riverside sales manager Robert Richer "spent hours in the studios with Monk and was privy to a lot of his craziness," he said. "Monk was a genius, and he marched to his own drummer. . . . When he was recording, nothing else was there. He was by himself, and I mean, the building could have been on fire and it wouldn't have bothered him."[99]

Just like old times, Sonny had the opportunity to rehearse with Monk before the session. Monk was spending a considerable amount of time with Baroness Kathleen Annie Pannonica de Koenigswarter, the black sheep of the Rothschild family who had decided to use her fortune to support jazz musicians, most of all Monk. It quickly became a common sight to see Monk and the baroness rolling up to jazz clubs in her Bentley S1 Continental Drophead Coupe.[100] To those who didn't know her well, she was known as the Jazz Baroness; to those in her inner circle, she was Nica. After Charlie Parker died in her room at the Stanhope in 1955, the management asked her to leave, and she relocated to the Bolivar at 230 Central Park West on the Upper West Side. She had a Steinway grand, and after Monk's piano was destroyed in a house fire earlier that year, the Bolivar became his second home.[101]

It was there that Sonny and Monk rehearsed *Brilliant Corners*.[102] Nica had begun recording the goings-on in her room on her Wollensak reel-to-reel recorder, and she documented the rehearsal.[103] As was often the case at Nica's, others were there to absorb Monk's genius by osmosis. David Amram witnessed Monk teaching Sonny his new compositions "Brilliant Corners" and "Ba-Lue Bolivar Ba-Lues-Are," a modified B-flat blues written in response to Nica's ongoing battle with hotel management over her "unruly" guests. Monk didn't provide a lead sheet; he *imparted* a new tune, and Sonny imbibed it. "It was like two guys working the way it is when I work on my farm or you're building a house and just putting in the nails," Amram recalled. "They would play one measure, then say, 'No, wait a minute. Hold it, hold it, hold it!' And then they'd stop and go back and forth and back and forth. They worked out every single measure. Sonny wanted to be positive that he knew Monk's fantastic chord structure, and Monk wanted to be sure that Sonny was comfortable doing that, and they really worked on that. And I remember sitting there for about an hour and forty-five minutes, and then they had it down. And then of course when they recorded it, it just sounded beautiful."[104]

Like all Monk tunes, they were complex. "He had that thing almost like Albert Einstein or an atomic scientist," Amram said of the compositions. "He could make variants on exactly what it was, and he always knew where he was. So when you hear Monk records, you listen really carefully, you can see he's right in time, and he's right harmonically."[105]

Yet no amount of groundwork could prepare even the best musicians for *Brilliant Corners*, which would be recorded over three grueling sessions spanning two months. And Monk had the best musicians: Oscar Pettiford, Max Roach, Ernie Henry (the newest member of Monk's sporadically working quartet), and Sonny.[106]

"I always had to be alert with Monk," John Coltrane later said, "because if you didn't keep aware all the time of what was going on, you'd suddenly feel as if you'd stepped into an empty elevator shaft."[107] That was *Brilliant Corners*.

On October 9, things got off to a relatively easy start with minor hiccups. Monk arrived at the studio in a suit, tie, and pocket square.[108] Bill Grauer had just booked Reeves as Riverside's new recording studio home, within

242 | Saxophone Colossus

walking distance of the Riverside office on Fifty-First Street, much closer than schlepping out to Van Gelder's in Hackensack.[109] Keepnews, who was supervising, didn't know engineer Jack Higgins, who was "lacking in jazz experience."[110]

The first tune, "Pannonica," a ballad dedicated to Nica, wasn't so difficult, despite its unconventional chord structure. Complicating matters, though, Monk noticed a celeste in the studio and decided to butt it up to the piano so he could play the bell-like instrument with his right hand and the piano with his left. On one of the first takes, Monk cuts off the band after Ernie Henry misses a note at the end of the melody. "Hold up, hold up," said Monk. "You messed up on that, on that...what you call it...tag. When you play it, man, keep it in mind. There's a tag on the song, you know?"[111] Henry didn't make that mistake again. On the completed take, Sonny leads off on the solos, improvising confidently through the form. Monk plays what is probably the only dueling celeste-piano solo in jazz history. The other tune that day was "Ba-lue Bolivar Ba-lues-Are," the album take featuring a lengthy solo by Ernie Henry and Sonny. Monk turned thirty-nine the next day.

"It was always different playing with Monk because you had to play like him," Sonny said. "You couldn't play something that didn't have anything to do with his style, his approach and the things that he laid down, which meant that you couldn't get away from them while you were playing. And also, those things couldn't help but influence you."[112] This meant, for Sonny, a propensity to growl through the bell of the horn, a reminder of Sonny's roots in the sanctified church, as well as Monk's.

On October 15, they returned to Reeves to record the album's title track, "Brilliant Corners." Though they recorded twenty-four takes, they never finished a single one. Unlike conventional thirty-two-bar forms, "Brilliant Corners" was twenty-two bars with unusual changes; leave it to Monk to create a form divisible by eleven. It was metrically and harmonically complex, full of triplet quarter-notes that stretched across the bar line and, in the third measure, a sixteenth-note line at the bottom of Sonny's register that required double-tonguing; every other chorus went into double-time. Complicating matters further, Monk didn't provide any sheet music; they would have to play it by ear.

Roach recalled Monk's amusement that day. "I have all the stars on my session," Monk gloated, "and they can't play my music."[113]

The session lasted four hours. "It was one of those sessions where we were not getting paid, or I should say we were not getting paid enough," recalled Roach. "That record date had a lot of volatility," Sonny said.[114] Monk tested everyone's patience, not least Pettiford's. After Monk delivered a harsh rebuke and the two almost came to blows, the bassist was so irate that on the next take he laid out altogether and pantomimed his part, thinking it would only go better. By the end of the four hours, they managed to eke out each section of the song correctly. At the end of the session, Monk "pulled the music out of his suitcase and put it up in front of us, but by that time we had learned it by rote," Roach said.[115] By withholding the sheet music, Monk made sure they really learned the tune, and he added an extra hour of overtime, as well as a whole other day at the studio.

"Brilliant Corners" would have to be "welded together" by Keepnews into one seamless take. Yet it would become, as Roach put it, "one of the landmarks of that period."[116]

The Roach Quintet's rigorous touring schedule meant that Monk's band wouldn't make it back to the studio for nearly two months. On October 16, the day after the "Brilliant Corners" session, the quintet was booked at Club Marina in Washington, DC, for a week. To solidify the new band and make sure they were performing in style, they all bought matching new suits at Joseph A. Bank in Baltimore.[117] On October 24, a two-week booking at the Preview Lounge's Modern Jazz Room in Chicago fulfilled the group's deferred dream of being booked in the Loop.[118] Impresario Joe Segal was "gassed" by Sonny when he caught the quintet at the Modern Jazz Room. "Not since Bird at his peak have I heard a saxophonist with such instrument control, fecundity of ideas and inspiration, and a sound that fills you to tears with its fullness and richness and beauty," Segal wrote.[119]

On November 5, they opened at the Cotton Club in Cleveland. They arrived road-weary and looking for a good night's sleep, and Sonny was not willing to put up with the dump they were staying in. "That was the funkiest hotel I've ever stayed in my life, and I've stayed in some funky hotels. But this one was so bad that I wrote a song, 'Funky Hotel Blues' about that hotel," Sonny said.[120]

"So I said, 'Man, let's try to stay somewhere downtown. . . . Anyway, the guys said no, so I said, 'Let me go, I'll go. You cats wait in the car, let me go in there and see if . . . they'll accept us staying here.'" The Olmsted Hotel let them stay. "It was really great. I mean, guys had a chance to stay in a decent room, and get some room service and all this stuff. I remember my steak. . . . You know, just a decent room which everybody else would take for granted."[121]

From November 12 through 18, they were at the Showboat in Philadelphia.[122] To fill the piano chair—Wade Legge may have already left the group—they recruited a seventeen-year-old recent high school graduate named McCoy Tyner, who used to practice with Richie Powell.[123] Local trumpeter Cal Massey called Tyner and said, "'Well, Max is looking for a piano player,'" Tyner recalled. "And I said, 'Really? What if I'm not ready for that?'"

Max felt he was ready. "Max wanted me to go out of town, but I had just graduated from school and I didn't want to go on the road right away, and I had other plans at the time," Tyner said. "I was really tempted to go, but I just couldn't."[124]

They returned to New York for a month, November 30 through New Year's Eve, at the Café Bohemia opposite Lester Young.[125] Finally, Orrin Keepnews was able to schedule time at Reeves to finish *Brilliant Corners*.

What he hoped would be the album's final session took place December 7 at an optimistic 10 a.m. There were personnel changes; Paul Chambers was called in to replace Pettiford. Ernie Henry had joined Dizzy Gillespie's big band, which toured more consistently than Monk. Standing in for Henry was thirty-five-year-old trumpeter Clark Terry, a veteran of Count Basie and Duke Ellington.[126] Monk had hired Terry the night before, after seeing him perform with Basie at Birdland. Monk added kindling to the fire until dawn, never discussing the record.[127]

Terry still arrived on time for the 10 a.m. session. So did Chambers and Keepnews. But there was no Sonny, Monk, or Max.[128] When Monk, Max, and a bearded Sonny finally arrived, Monk began working through "Bemsha Swing," the puckish sixteen-bar tune he cowrote with Denzil Best, who was of Barbadian ancestry and infused the song with island rhythms.[129] Max found some timpani drums in the studio, and Monk had Max play that as well as the drum kit, adding to the rhythmic tapestry and to Max's side-man rate.[130] With a good take completed, Monk still had some time left to fill. "I turned to Monk and I said, 'We got about twenty minutes of studio time left. I need another five minutes to have a respectable, useable length on this thing,'" Keepnews recalled. "'Can you give me, in one take hopefully, a five-minute solo piano tune? Preferably a standard?'" Monk whipped out a solo rendition of "I Surrender Dear," and the session was complete.[131] *Down Beat* gave *Brilliant Corners* a rare five stars.[132] It was a masterpiece.

Sonny had his own recording session with Prestige later that day, and he and Max drove to Rudy Van Gelder's together for what would become *Tour de Force*.[133] It was the final album on his Prestige contract. Sonny hired George Morrow, Max, and his old friend Kenny Drew. Sonny also got Earl Coleman, a thirty-one-year-old crooner in the tradition of Billy Eckstine, who sang on Bird's "This Is Always" in 1947.[134]

Coleman knew Sonny from the Goof Square days. While serving a prison sentence in the South, Coleman wrote to Bob Weinstock about recording for Prestige. "A letter came right back and he said, 'Sure, man, you can have your own album.' Then he said, 'And Sonny [Rollins] is always buggin' me because he wants to do something with you.'" Sonny then wrote Coleman directly, "so I knew I wasn't forgotten," Coleman said.[135]

The album was an exercise in the limits of tempo. "B. Swift," based on the changes to "Lover," the Rodgers and Hart waltz but set in 4/4, and "B. Quick," based on the changes to "Cherokee," are purely solo vehicles with no melody, intended to break the sound barrier. Poet Ed Dorn would later remark upon hearing it that "Rollins was the first man in space."[136]

They also recorded "Ee-Ah," a medium-tempo blues, and "Sonny Boy," a rhythm changes that didn't make it onto the album. "Two Different Worlds," rendered by Coleman with a tentative grace, was a ballad by Al Frisch with lyrics by Sid Wayne. Written just that year, the song was a contemporary hit by Don Rondo, selling more than a million copies. This was one of its first covers.[137] It is a tale of embattled lovers à la Romeo and Juliet, and Sonny and Coleman politicize the vanilla ballad implicitly.[138] Coleman handled "My Ideal" with the same sensitivity, with Sonny revealing his tender side, in stark contrast to his take-no-prisoners approach to "B. Swift."[139]

The album wasn't released until February 1958.[140] "To utilize an understatement," read the review in *Down Beat*, "Rollins clearly has emerged as a vital individualist."[141] Yet more meaningful to Sonny was getting the approval of Coleman Hawkins. In an interview, Hawk listed some of his favorite tenor players: Al Cohn, Zoot Sims, Budd Johnson, Sonny Stitt. "Yes, I like Getz. And there's Sonny Rollins."[142] Three weeks later, in the *Down Beat* readers' poll, Sonny saw his name right next to Hawkins's. Stan Getz, the perennial favorite, took the top spot, followed by Lester Young, Zoot Sims, Bill Perkins, Hawkins, and, in sixth place, Sonny.[143] "Sonny Rollins is the first major influence on a significant number of young tenors since the Stan Getz of the late '40s and early '50s," wrote Hentoff in a profile shortly afterward.[144] Sonny told Hentoff he had no imminent plans to leave the Roach Quintet, but he hoped to one day lead his own band, not only on records.[145]

Sonny went back to Hackensack a second time on December 16.[146] He was now able to record for other labels, and Blue Note called. It would be released simply as *Sonny Rollins* (later designated volume 1). He hired Roach, Byrd, pianist Wynton Kelly, and bassist Gene Ramey.[147]

To Sonny, Kelly perfected the art of comping. "He was the perfect accompanist because he was unobtrusive," Sonny said.[148] "Whenever there was something to be played, he played it. Whenever there was the correct sequence to be played, he was there. So he was like the guy who was there and wasn't there at the same time."[149]

As was standard Blue Note practice, they got paid rehearsal time; during the session, they listened to playback, and if the artist felt it was necessary, they did another take. Sonny respected Alfred Lion's "unquestionable integrity," he said. "He loved the music and definitely loved the musicians... and he wasn't out to make money."[150] Francis Wolff would listen from the control room at Van Gelder's, and if he thought it was swinging, he would do a Monkish dance in a circle. If he wasn't dancing, there was a problem.[151] On this day, he must have been dancing.

Sonny recorded four originals: "Decision," a minor blues with a thirteenth bar that hangs in abeyance; "Bluesnote," a twelve-bar blues; the angular "Plain Jane"; and "Sonnysphere," a rhythmic send-off that segues into a blowing session over rhythm changes, with a bridge from "Honeysuckle Rose." Sonny also included "How Are Things in Glocca Morra?"—the ballad from the 1947 Broadway production *Finian's Rainbow*, which had a successful revival in 1955.

According to Leonard Feather's liner notes, the album exemplified "the student who has turned teacher, the scholar who became a school."[152] After years in the salt mines, the critical establishment was firmly behind Sonny. *Metronome* called him "undoubtedly the boss."[153]

Sonny rang in the New Year at the Café Bohemia, and what a year it had been. Just prior, he was a Chicago janitor named Wally. After an arduous year on the road, he was universally proclaimed a leading voice on his instrument— the Saxophone Colossus. In 1956, Sonny made ten albums, six as a leader and four as a sideman—*Clifford Brown and Max Roach at Basin Street, Sonny Rollins Plus 4, Tenor Madness, Saxophone Colossus,* and *Brilliant Corners* among them.

Yet with critical acclaim came a wave of self-criticism. "Next year I may take some time off, go back to school, and stay away from the scene completely until I'm finished," he told Nat Hentoff that fall. "I've just started. I've just scratched the surface. That's an honest appraisal of myself, so I don't dig this being an influence. I'm not trying to put myself down or anything.... I've got a lot of work still to do, a lot of work."

He would get there one day, he hoped. "I'm not satisfied with anything about my playing," Sonny said. "I know what I want. I can hear it."[154]

Chapter 18

WAY OUT WEST

(1957)

Much to Sonny's chagrin, the acclaim kept coming. In the 1956–1957 French jazz critics' poll in *Jazz Hot*, Sonny won the tenor category. In the January 1957 *Metronome* all-star poll, he tied for fifth-place tenor with Al Cohn.[1] Max Roach came in second on drums after Shelly Manne. But the Roach Quintet couldn't afford to rest on their laurels—barely even for a day.

On Tuesday, January 8, they were back at the Rouge Lounge outside of Detroit.[2] At this time, Sonny had a legendary run-in at an after-hours jam session at the West End Hotel with saxophonist and flautist Yusef Lateef, a Detroit native.[3] "This was on a Monday, a typical off night, so it turned into a kind of jam session," recalled jazz fan Jerry "Tiger" Pearson. "That evening Yusef out-played Sonny." The two would remain lifelong friends.[4]

After Detroit, the Roach Quintet was at the Midway Lounge in Pittsburgh for a week, a capacity audience every night,[5] at the Loop in Cleveland starting February 4,[6] and then back in Chicago's Modern Jazz Room starting February 13 for two weeks.[7] Pianist Billy Wallace, then living in Chicago, had been one of the last people to play with Charlie Parker and one of the last to play with Clifford Brown.[8] At the Modern Jazz Room, Max decided to give Wallace a two-week audition, also enlisting bassist Bill Lee, and hired Wallace after opening night.[9]

It was probably at the Modern Jazz Room that Sonny met Lucille Pearson, his future wife. Born Ethel Lucille Pearson on July 5, 1928, in Kansas City, Missouri, she was a twenty-seven-year-old secretary at the Tuberculosis Institute of Chicago and Cook County. She grew up an only child in a little house in Kansas City, a world away from the part of the city synonymous with jazz, a baptized and confirmed Lutheran who'd grown up taking piano lessons. Her father, Leonard J. Pearson, was a World War I army veteran who worked as a meat inspector; Lucille inherited his shrewd intensity. Her mother, Nanette, was a conservative homemaker. When Leonard died in early 1949, Lucille and Nanette moved to Chicago, where at forty-eight Nanette took a civil service job as a tax examiner with the Internal Revenue Service (IRS) that she would hold for fifteen years.[10]

Lucille was the type of person who kept handwritten recipes for sweet potato pie and "light fruit cake,"[11] but just like her mother, nothing got past her; Lucille Pearson did not suffer fools. At the Tuberculosis Institute, she mastered shorthand, took dictation, helped manage the budget, arranged meetings, and made travel plans, a skill set that would one day have an unlikely application in jazz.

Lucille "might have seen me a couple of times there," Sonny said, but after that first meeting in Chicago, they struck up a correspondence.[12] There was instant chemistry.

The meeting was not pure kismet; jazz geography was in play. "There was a musician that I was rehearsing with at the time, and this musician had a girl-friend who was a girlfriend of Lucille's," Sonny recalled, referring to Booker Little.[13]

The woman "had told me a lot about Sonny, and so she sort of wanted us to meet," Lucille said. "And when I met him, I knew right away that this was going to be something special. I don't believe he did, but I did. And I was determined that this was the guy. She told me not to do this, because she said you're gonna get hurt. . . . Just have a good time, but don't get involved. But I did."[14]

After Chicago, the quintet played the University of Wisconsin-Milwaukee on February 25, then flew to Los Angeles, where they opened at Jazz City on March 1.[15] It was Sonny's first time on the West Coast.[16] The quintet's three-week stand, though successful, would mark the end of the club.[17] The LA scene on Central Avenue and beyond was robust, but the clubs were not breaking even.

The quintet stayed six miles from the club at the Watkins Hotel.[18] The Watkins opened in 1946: the first black-owned hotel on the West Side.[19] There was both a beauty shop and a barbershop on the ground floor, as well as the Rubaiyat Room, an elegant lounge that hosted bop acts. Everyone from Duke Ellington to the Harlem Globetrotters stayed there.[20] "In fact," Sonny said, "I met my wife there."[21]

No, not Lucille: her name was Dawn Noreen Finney, an eighteen-year-old student at Los Angeles High School and pageant queen who had already landed professional modeling gigs. In the May 19, 1955, issue of *Jet*, she was featured, bikini clad, in a beachside centerfold photo: "Kicking up her heels and displaying a shapely leg, piano-playing Los Angeles high school student Dawn Finney does backward push-ups on a California beach. She plans to study voice, play and sing her way to fame."[22] She was born in Los Angeles on May 23, 1938, and grew up in a musical family.[23] A grandmother, Marvina Finney, was an opera singer; her brother Leonard became a dancer and dress designer. Her mother, Lillie, hoped Dawn would become a concert pianist.[24] But she felt the pull of dance and modeling.[25]

"Every time I'm on the stage," she said in 1958, "I get a boost—as if I were meant to be there." Dawn seemed headed for stardom—she sang in the alto range, played piano, and was five-foot-eight with an hourglass figure. Within two years, she would appear as a cover model for Les Baxter's *African Jazz*—she was in demand and fetched $250 per cover—and had a cameo in *Imitation of Life*. She was serious, with a work ethic to go along with her natural abilities. "I've learned that you have to work very, very hard if you want to be a star in show business," she said. "It's nothing to play with."[26] So she and Sonny had ambition and self-discipline in common.

Dawn's fastidious lifestyle was not necessarily conducive to the jazz life. She woke up at 6 a.m., stretched, bathed, and brushed her hair a hundred strokes. She always completed this morning ritual to music. Then she ate a wholesome breakfast of orange juice, toast, and eggs—never any pork.[27] After dinner, she would relax with a bubble bath, then "curl up in bed with a newspaper, half-listening to the soft strains of music from her hi-fi set" and read a book of poetry. The whole routine was finished with a hundred more strokes of the hairbrush, then to bed by 9:30 p.m.[28] She wasn't ever at the club.

Yet one fateful night, she found herself at Jazz City. "When I met Sonny at the jazz club in Hollywood I thought he was so masculine and played the sax out of this world," she later recalled. "However, he was going through tremendous pressure, always traveling all over the world, writing and playing music wherever he could.... He is a genius."[29]

It seems they met through LaRue Brown, Clifford's widow, who was from Los Angeles and, like Dawn, worked as a model.[30] But for Dawn, the entertainment world was full of players. "There are so many propositions from men," she said wearily. "Sometimes it is difficult to know who is right, or what is right for me. It's a tough job separating the phonies from the honest, sincere people. I get so many promises and advances. But I always try to make the right decisions, or I always want to be a lady."[31] But Sonny's proposition seemed genuine. And Dawn lived only a ten-minute walk from the Watkins, so it was not hard for them to immediately start spending a lot of time together.[32]

Within a week of arriving in LA, Sonny was offered a recording date. Lester Koenig, the blacklisted screenwriter turned owner of Contemporary Records, got in touch with him and hastily scheduled a session.[33] Sonny wanted to try playing with a pianoless trio—no chordal instruments—just strolling.[34]

The choice to record without a piano "wasn't for economic reasons," Sonny said, but musical ones. "I just liked the sound, because I liked the freedom. I love playing solo," Sonny said.[35] He was also thinking of Don Byas's duet with Slam Stewart on "I Got Rhythm."[36] "A pianist by definition leads the horn players, because of the chords and volume and everything," he said. "I like more freedom, so that if I wanted to go from this chord to that chord, I didn't have somebody dictate to me, 'You have to go from a B to an E here, and I'm going to make it so loud and prominent that you'll have to do it.' To me that was a little constricting. I always loved the idea that if I could get a rhythm section—a drummer for the rhythm and the bass player for the basic harmony—then I had the freedom to do what I wanted to do. Which was perfect for me."[37]

There was perhaps still another motivation for dropping piano. After Clifford Brown and Richie Powell passed, according to Max Roach, "We had been booked beyond that, of course...so we—Sonny Rollins and George Morrow and myself as a trio—honored some of the things that had been committed, without Brownie and Richard, and I guess that might have been the beginning of what I began to hear...out of that tragedy, as we worked these trio things, and it was almost like in memorial to these two very wonderful musicians....Sonny and George and myself, we both began to adapt to just that sound, and tried to compensate for the fact that the piano and trumpet wasn't there, and I began to hear something else, and so did Sonny."[38] To Sonny, they were not gone, but in a sense, the pianoless trio carries the ache of a phantom limb.

For *Way Out West*, the top poll winners from the 1956 *Down Beat*, *Metronome*, and *Playboy* jazz polls happened to be in Los Angeles: drummer Shelly Manne and bassist Ray Brown.[39] Sonny loved Shelly on Coleman Hawkins's "The Man I Love," and Ray Brown he had just seen the previous summer in Lenox. "Ray and Shelly both realized that [*Way Out West*] was somewhat different than what was being done," Sonny recalled. "They loved it. They accepted the challenge."[40]

The timing was tight. Brown was playing next to Jazz City at the Peacock

Lane with the Oscar Peterson Trio, and Manne's Shelly Manne and His Men were at the Topper.[41] Sonny was playing with Max from 9 p.m. to 2 a.m.[42] Brown and Manne also had packed recording schedules.[43] So the session was called for March 7 at 3 a.m. It would give everyone enough time to make it to Contemporary Studios after their respective gigs and Brown enough time to catch his breath and make it to his recording session with Stuff Smith later that afternoon.

"They were young, virile guys. They could play long hours," Sonny said. "It went until we could get it done."[44]

At first glance, what would become *Way Out West* promised an East-meets-West-style showdown, but in reality the difference was more geographic than musical. Koenig and Nesuhi Ertegun, his right-hand man, marketed artists like Shorty Rogers, Jimmy Giuffre, Barney Kessel, and Shelly Manne as part of the "West Coast" sound. "We invented it for publicity purposes," Koenig said of the term.[45] "The truth is," Sonny said, "East and West Coast musicians all knew each other personally or by reputation, and were friends."[46]

Koenig's approach was "partly influenced by John Hammond and partly influenced by [William] Wyler," said his son, John Koenig, "in terms of, to use a trite expression, capturing the magic, which is really what you're trying to do when you make a live jazz recording."[47] So this album would attempt to combine Hammond's sense of finesse with Wyler's cinematic scope.

"Les Koenig left the choice of material completely to me," Sonny said. "I was out west and had all these Western songs in mind from my youth. The album is merely a tribute to independence and being self-sufficient, which is what the West really means—at least in Westerns."[48] He would call it *Way Out West*, a reference to the 1937 Laurel and Hardy film. One key touchstone for the album was Herb Jeffries, the singer who lent his husky baritone to the 1940 hit "Flamingo" with the Duke Ellington Orchestra. Sonny had first encountered Jeffries as a movie cowboy in *Harlem on the Prairie* (1937) and *The Bronze Buckaroo* (1939), with his ten-gallon hat and six-shooter proclaiming the kind of radical black Americana Sonny would strive to embody.[49]

Despite Shelly Manne's accolades, he was nervous to face Sonny in the studio. "I went into making that album with a little trepidation," Manne later recalled. "I respected and admired Sonny Rollins so much—I still do—and I knew he hadn't been playing with this kind of set-up—with the bass and drums, just a trio. I was a little worried, but Sonny was so beautiful, and played so great, it was just enjoyable."[50]

Contemporary was in an industrial area adjacent to dance and interior design studios and "was basically a warehouse," said John Koenig. "It was a law office for a while; it was an antique store." In the back, a cramped shipping room doubled as a bare-bones studio; recording sessions took place with stacks of records on shelves ready to be shipped out to distributors. They set up a makeshift control room next to the Contemporary publicist's office, until the publicist moved to the building next door. "It had high ceilings and it had a concrete floor, which I didn't like the sound of the reverberation off of, and there was a carpet taped to the floor, so that cut down a little bit of the harsh reverb."[51]

Nonetheless, Contemporary's studio produced great sound. Koenig invested in high-fidelity microphones—Telefunken condensers, Neumanns, and the AKG C-12—and hired audio engineer Roy DuNann away from Capitol. DuNann was the audio engineer behind Tennessee Ernie Ford's "Sixteen Tons" and Dean Martin's "That's Amore." He was a master tinkerer who'd built a tube amplifier from scratch. To cut masters in-house, he repurposed a Western Electric cutting lathe originally used on Al Jolson's *The Jazz Singer*, which he found at a junk shop.[52]

Contemporary launched Stereo Records to experiment with stereo sound, and *Way Out West* would be the new label's and Sonny's first release in that format.[53] Sonny was on the left channel, Brown and Manne on the right, with some spillover due to the close quarters.[54] This made it easier to hear Sonny's overtones, the glottal growl through the bell, the thunk of the pads against the saxophone, the sound of the tongue clipping each note, Brown's fingers gliding up and down the fretboard and his singing in octaves as he solos, the frisson of Manne's Zildjian cymbals, the skins of his Leedy drums, his guttural grunts, and individual strands of the wire brushes. You can hear the sweat. Sonny made a dank shipping room in the back of a shabby office building on Melrose Place sound as wide open as the Mojave Desert at dawn.

There was no rehearsal in advance, so they began rehearsing immediately.

The first tune Sonny called was based on "After You've Gone," the Turner Layton standard, but without the head. It was a little loopy to start. "Before we start, I'd like to know one thing before you spin 'em," Sonny said. "Can I name this 'After You've Come? Is it all right? I mean, it doesn't have to be suggestive if you don't think that way…"

"Are you gonna give this album to your pastor?" came the retort.

If the song was listed under a different name, and Sonny didn't play the melody, he could claim composer's credit. Later, he'd muse further: "After You Vacated?" They settled on something less suggestive: "Come, Gone."[55]

Bing Crosby did "After You've Gone" as a ballad, but Sonny counted it off way up, and took the first sixteen bars unaccompanied. "Here's how we do the rest," Sonny said, referring to the half-time blues tag that concludes the piece.[56] As Sonny let loose in the studio, riffing on the blues scale, the guys began singing like Joe Williams imitators.[57] Between takes, Sonny worked things out—certain intervals, patterns he wanted to explore—concentrating intensely, even after his five-hour gig earlier that night.[58] One probing take of "Come, Gone" lasted ten and a half minutes. Two minutes into the take that ended up on the album, Sonny seems to express his frustration by quoting the opening to "I Can't Get Started" five times in direct succession, twisting it around rhythmically, like a skipping record or a stutter. By the sixth take of the night, they moved on to Ellington's "Solitude," which Sonny imbues with a bit of a country drawl and a Hawkins-esque vibrato. He cuts it off when he returns to the melody. "Fellas, fellas," he says, then sings the opening. "All right?"[59]

By the eighth take, they're onto Johnny Mercer's "I'm an Old Cowhand." Bing Crosby sang the tune in *Rhythm on the Range* (1936),[60] which Sonny saw as a child.[61] Sonny told Manne that he wanted a "loping along in the saddle feeling.…I want that cat out on the range all the way." It would be a challenge for any drummer; the beat had to sound like horses' hooves and be hip at the same time. "If we can't get it," Sonny said, "we'll do something else."[62] As it happens, Manne was the perfect choice for *Way Out West*; he had been living on a functional horse farm in the San Fernando Valley, and he knew just the sound Sonny was looking for. All it took was a wood block, a snare rim, and a bass drum, and suddenly he conjured a horse in the studio—Sonny had a swinging canter to ride on.

To Sonny, learning the lyrics was especially important to conveying the sensibility of "Cowhand." "You know what, you've got to dig the lyrics to these songs to really dig it, man," Sonny said in the studio. "You know what I mean? This is a cat... really," and then he began singing. "'I'm an old cowhand on the Rio Grande.' You know, that kind of shit." He chanted the rest like a rap. "'Sure ain't fixin' to start in now. My cheeks ain't tan. I'm a cowboy who never saw a cow.' That's me. 'Never roped a steer 'cause I don't know how. And I sure ain't fixin' to start in now.' You dig? Yippie-yi-yo-ki-yay!"[63] Sonny sang a few more bars of the melody sans lyrics, snapping on two and four to set the mood. "You spinnin'?"

Still, it wasn't coming together. The sixteenth take of the night was aborted. Seventeenth—another breakdown. Eighteenth—same result. "This is gonna be a hit," someone said in the background. "Mark my words."

"Number nineteen," came the voice from the control room as Sonny worked out an intervallic pattern—5-1-3-6-5-3-4-3-1-5—transposed into a few different keys.

"Ready, Sonny?" says Brown.

The nineteenth take was going well, then... breakdown. Between takes, Sonny began experimenting with overtones, playing two notes simultaneously. On take twenty-two, it seemed that Sonny found what he was looking for. Shelly clippity-clops along for the first eight bars, making his bass drum hit for Sonny's seamless pickup to the melody. Brown plays beautiful obbligato lines under the melody, then walks on the bridge as Shelly moves to the ride cymbal. Sonny builds up to a sure-footed swagger on the solo, never steering far from the melody. Brown plays an eloquent, subdued two choruses, and Manne heats things up, grunting along as he solos. After two choruses of drums, he comes to an abrupt stop and for an idle moment, the bottom seems to drop out. But Sonny comes back in and takes it out, departing from the melody, rhythmically playing on one note, as they ride, somewhat literally, into the rising sun.

By now, it was 7 a.m. They had made only half the album, but Sonny was still cooking. "I'm hot now," he said. Manne had been awake for an entire day, but his energy was unflagging: "Man, I feel like playing."[64] Brown had to make it to his session with Stuff Smith that afternoon, but he just smiled. A half hour later, they'd be done.

"Wagon Wheels" was another Tin Pan Alley tune, written by Peter De-Rose and Billy Hill, sung in the eponymous 1934 film; Sonny may have seen it sung by cowboys, but probably heard his hero Paul Robeson sing it as well. Sonny's take was more polyrhythmic, in part due to Manne's three-over-four beat. They rehearsed it for a few minutes and laid it down in one take.[65]

They finished the session with a series of takes of Sonny's original "Way Out West." There was a bit of confusion about the form, and a slightly delirious conversation followed. "A round robin," said Ray Brown. "Now listen, you're gonna play the first and the last on both choruses. In other words, he's gonna play ten the second time."

"Now he plays five, five, five, five," said Shelly. "Five, he starts it again. In other words, he plays ten, and we're already in the second chorus."

"Right," said Sonny.

"Crazy."

Sonny eventually had to sing it to them to get what he wanted. They recorded one more track—"There Is No Greater Love"—track thirty-three of the session. "Ready?" said Sonny. "Then let's get out of here."

"Yeah, let's do it," said Brown. "I want to get home to my old lady." They all wanted to go home, but in their predawn delirium, "No Greater Love" just wasn't coming together: two false starts, then a third take that only made it through the first minute, followed by a fourth flubbed track. "Oh shit!" someone shouted. Sonny wanted this one to be "melancholy," he told Brown, singing the melody.

"You don't want it to sound like a society band," Brown replied.

"No!" said Sonny. "Okay, let's do one more."

Finally, on about the forty-third take of the session, they completed their final take, and walked off—into the sunrise.[66]

———◦———

Soon after the session, Sonny met photographer William Claxton for the cover photo.[67] "Sonny said, 'I've never been to the West before, so let's do something Western,'" Claxton recalled. "And I said, 'Do you want to wear a cowboy hat?'"[68]

At Western Costumers, a costume shop on Melrose, they rented a ten-gallon hat, a holster and pistol, and a steer's skull. Claxton knew the Mojave Desert well enough to find "a patch of wonderful Joshua trees and cactus and set him up there posing like he's a famous cowboy that was just standing there with his kill."[69] They didn't need the pistol; Sonny had his saxophone, which he brandished like a six-shooter. He kept his suit and tie on.

When the album was released, Sonny caught some flak from New York musicians who found the whole gunslinger gimmick corny.[70] "I heard that Sonny Rollins was quite angry with me for setting him up in that stupid way because he's a serious musician," Claxton said, adding that they didn't speak for years. Over time, however, it became one of the most iconic photos in jazz history, and Sonny changed his tune. Before Claxton died in 2008, he and Sonny reconciled. " 'Sonny, have you forgiven me?' " he asked. "And he said, 'Oh, yeah, man. You know, of course I have. That picture worked out wonderfully.' "[71]

Way Out West came out that summer, a critical and commercial success. Ralph J. Gleason gave it five stars in *Down Beat*, Sonny's second, after *Saxophone Colossus*.[72] For the first time, Sonny had an album on the jazz best-seller chart.[73] *Way Out West* debuted on the list at number fifteen—Miles Davis's *Cookin'* was at twelve and Shelly Manne's *My Fair Lady* was still number one. The label was happy enough that Contemporary asked Sonny to record at least one new album a year for the next three years, and Sonny agreed.[74]

During this trip, Sonny met a future Contemporary artist who embodied the frontiersman's aesthetic: Ornette Coleman. The Texas-born saxophonist was six months older than Sonny, but he hadn't yet made an album and wouldn't record *Something Else!!!!* for nearly a year. He played a plastic Grafton saxophone, compared to Sonny's beautiful Mark VI tenor, but Sonny did not discriminate. Coleman was already working with trumpeter Don Cherry and drummer Billy Higgins, both twenty, and they all came to see the new Max Roach Quintet at Jazz City.[75] Cherry and Coleman began practicing with Sonny in parks or on the beach in a Malibu cove. "It was beautiful," Sonny said. "You could play with the sound of the ocean as accompaniment. . . . It would be 98 percent playing and maybe 2 percent talking." And what did they practice? Something similar to what Sonny was playing in between takes on the *Way Out West* session. "Patterns."[76]

Hearing Ornette for the first time, Sonny was not as shocked by his approach as the critical establishment would be. "The same quality I heard in Ornette, I heard in Louis Armstrong and in Charlie Parker. It was the same thing I heard when I heard Coleman Hawkins play," Sonny said. "I don't know how people compartmentalize music, but to me, jazz is jazz is jazz is jazz!"[77]

Sonny met another up-and-coming saxophonist at Jazz City: "When I was working with Max, Eric Dolphy came by one time in California and he wanted to sit in with the band," Sonny said. The original members of the Brown-Roach Quintet had met Dolphy in 1954 when they did jam sessions and rehearsals in his family's garage-cum–practice studio, but Sonny "didn't know Eric Dolphy." To test the mettle of anyone who dared sit in, "What we would do is we'd say sure, and when the guy comes up we'd stomp off the tempo real fast... and then see if the guy could handle it. It was sort of a dirty trick to play on people. But Eric did all right. We said, 'Okay, this guy can play.' That's how I met Eric Dolphy."[78]

Beyond appearing nightly at Jazz City, recording *Way Out West*, practicing with Ornette Coleman and Don Cherry, and spending time with Dawn Finney, Sonny went back into the studio with the Roach Quintet for Max's next EmArcy recording, *Jazz in 3/4 Time*. This time, Max decided to extend Sonny's experiment on "Valse Hot" to an entire album, the first waltz-only album in jazz history. The idea was hatched by EmArcy founder Bob Shad and presented to the "dean of modern drummers," who initially "didn't dig it." But after reconsidering, "I began to enjoy it more," recalled Max. Yet even to the dean, playing comfortably in three posed a challenge. "It's awkward at first, but after a while, everything fits right into place."[79]

The group still consisted of Max, Sonny, Kenny Dorham, George Morrow, and Billy Wallace. The recording for *Jazz in 3/4 Time* was spaced over three (of four) days: March 18, 20, and 21. They entered Capitol Studios and laid down eight tracks, five of which ended up on the album: Max's "Blues Waltz" and "Little Folks," dedicated to Roach's kids, Daryl and Maxine; Sonny's "Valse Hot," which they rerecorded; "I'll Take Romance"; and "Lover." The album was rounded out by "The Most Beautiful Girl in the World," which Sonny recorded on *Tenor Madness*; the quintet recorded it on

September 19 as an outtake from the *Max Roach Plus Four* session with Ray Bryant on piano.[80] *Jazz in 3/4 Time* did well with the critics; it got four and a half stars from Leonard Feather in *Down Beat* that fall.[81]

On March 27, less than four weeks after they met, Sonny and Dawn Finney got married. Sonny was "so captivated by the beautiful scenery—and she was a very beautiful girl—that the whole thing got me," he recalled. "Not only did I make *Way Out West*, but I also put a ring on a woman's finger."[82] The ceremony was held that Wednesday at the courthouse.[83] Sonny was twenty-six; Dawn was eighteen.[84] When the quintet returned to New York, Dawn came back with Sonny.

Sonny's touring and recording schedule continued unabated. On April 14, he returned to Van Gelder's to make his next album for Blue Note, *Sonny Rollins, Vol. 2*. He got trombonist J. J. Johnson, Paul Chambers, Art Blakey, and dueling pianos to round out the sextet: Horace Silver and Thelonious Monk. Sonny wore a dark suit and white button-down to complement his manicured goatee. One of Francis Wolff's photos has Sonny closing his eyes in contemplation like Rodin's *The Thinker*, his horn in his lap; the shot that became the cover photo captured him taking a drag on a cigarette and staring into a far-off point. We see Monk closing his eyes with monastic intensity, cigarette hanging out of his mouth, as he pounds the keys, with a wide-eyed Horace Silver taking it all in as the master plies his craft.[85]

The blinds were drawn, and they got down to business. They recorded Sonny's own "Why Don't I" and "Wail March," the standards "You Stepped Out of a Dream" and "Poor Butterfly," and Monk's "Misterioso" and "Reflections." Blakey "was a very earthy drummer . . . more so than a technical drummer like Max," Sonny said. "Art had an extraordinarily strong rhythmic beat. It was elemental, and that meant it sort of went with everything."[86] Blakey's influence was inescapable, as was Monk's, like two powerful currents towing them along.[87]

The highlight of the session was "Misterioso,"[88] on which Monk and Silver share piano duties. When Monk finishes his solo, the piano drops out as he and Silver trade places for J. J. Johnson's solo. It establishes a playful counterpoint, which develops into a trading section that has Blakey using his tuned toms to good advantage. It was in no way a piano battle; Silver clearly deferred to Monk, who was already considered an elder statesman of the music. "I remember that Monk was originally supposed to be here and Horace also came by or was there or was invited or something," Sonny recalled. "But in those days, it was a tremendous feeling of camaraderie among those that were playing and doing the recordings, so everything worked out beautifully...no ego problems."[89]

The album was released that October.[90] Dom Cerulli gave it five stars in *Down Beat*, calling it "the wailing set of the year."[91]

Meanwhile, Sonny kept on gigging with the Max Roach Quintet: two weeks at the Café Bohemia starting mid-April, on the bill for two Town Hall concerts presented by jazz impresario Bob Maltz, the Showboat in Philadelphia May 6–12, plus a concert presented by Baltimore's Interracial Jazz Society at the Famous Ballroom on Charles Street at 5 p.m. on May 12.[92] McCoy Tyner came in to see them at the Showboat, "and around the corner at Pep's Bar, was Billie Holiday," Tyner recalled.[93] Sonny decided to see her on his set break. "So Sonny asked me during intermission, he said, 'Can I borrow your coat? I'm going to go down and meet Billie Holiday.'" Tyner gave Sonny his coat and "blew my opportunity."[94]

After the Showboat, they played the Colonial Tavern in Toronto for a week, then returned to New York, where Kenny Dorham had a record date.[95] On May 21 and 27, Sonny was at Reeves Sound Studios recording as a sideman on Dorham's Riverside debut, *Jazz Contrasts*. Dorham hired pianist Hank Jones, bassist Oscar Pettiford, Max Roach, Sonny, and for several tracks harpist Betty Glamann.[96] They recorded the standards "Falling in Love with Love," "I'll Remember April," "My Old Flame," and "But Beautiful," as well as Clifford Brown's "LaRue" and "La Villa," cowritten by Dorham and Gigi Gryce.

Jazz Contrasts would not be a best-selling album, but it had a significant impact on those who did buy it—especially John Coltrane. Coltrane evidently studied the record and hung on every note Sonny played. In the eleventh and twelfth bars of Sonny's solo on "My Old Flame" (at 3:21 to be exact), Sonny improvised a laid-back diminished pattern that he hadn't played on record before and never played again. Coltrane took that ten-second riff and turned it into a melodic tribute—"Like Sonny."[97]

On May 23, the Max Roach Quintet returned to the Café Bohemia in the Village, where they were booked through June 2, then extended to June 9.[98] It was there that Sonny played his final engagement with the Max Roach Quintet. From June 10 to 16, the Roach Quintet returned to Cleveland to play the Loop Lounge, but Sonny didn't go with them to the city that inspired his "Funky Hotel Blues."[99]

Sonny had another opportunity to go with Miles, and he took it. Playing with the Miles Davis Quintet meant not as much travel along the circuit he had been on for more than a year. Sonny was now a married man, and being out on the road was simply not conducive to the stable lifestyle he aspired toward.

With the Roach Quintet in Cleveland, Sonny would have to hire an entirely different rhythm section for his next recording session, his first as a leader on Riverside.[100] As an unlikely business model for an independent record label, Riverside's jazz catalog was in part supported by sports-car racing. "I don't think they ever figured they would ever have a genuine, bona fide record company, but they did," said Robert Richer, the Riverside director of sales. Richer was an ABC radio disc jockey who hosted a jazz show that played Riverside records when Riverside cofounder Bill Grauer hired him to run sales and promotion. A sports-car aficionado, Richer contributed his Le Mans Replica Frazer Nash for the cover photo to Randy Weston's *Trio and Solo*. Grauer, a fellow racing buff, bought a retired Greyhound bus and converted it into a mobile recording studio. In 1956, they drove it to Sebring, Florida, then a hub for sports-car racing, and recorded *The Sounds of Sebring*, the first in a series of albums featuring a mix of interviews with race-car drivers and the thrum of actual race cars.[101] Riverside sold it by mail order and made a killing.[102]

The Riverside offices were at 553 West Fifty-First Street, a "derelict tenement" whose chief virtue was its private parking lot. "The lot was worth more than the building was," Richer said. "I mean, it was an absolute fire trap." This didn't deter Sonny, though. "I used to see him around the office all the time," Richer said. Bassist Wilbur Ware was the Riverside house bassist and worked in the shipping room to make extra money.[103]

As for their broader business strategy, Riverside "was not nearly as well-managed as Blue Note was," Richer said. Label cofounder Orrin Keepnews thought of Grauer as "one of the most hard-driving, goal-oriented business executives I have ever known,"[104] but to Richer, Grauer's management style was "nonexistent." Grauer "could charm the birds out of the trees, but there was not the fiber, there was not the steel that you needed to deal with a lot of real eccentric people," Richer said. "And Orrin wouldn't know a balance sheet from a dinner plate."[105]

What Keepnews did know was the music itself, even if it didn't immediately increase the label's profit margin. Despite its modest digs, Riverside had a vision, with an eye toward the long view. "Riverside's policy and its philosophy was not to sell records instantly," Richer said. "Rather than like a rock 'n' roll record, which had a life span of maybe thirty days, Riverside's hope was to have a catalog life span of thirty years." As a result, "there never seemed to be enough money to pay the artists."[106]

Sonny struck an unusual deal with Riverside, Keepnews wrote. "He insisted on being paid in full, rather than accepting any form of advance against royalties. That really seemed self-defeating, and I tried to talk him out of it, assuring him that the immediate payment would be the same in either case and noting the sad truth that jazz albums rarely sold enough to reach a positive royalty-earning position," Keepnews wrote. "His logic was unforgettable. 'I like you guys,' he explained, 'and I think of you as friends, but if we had a royalty deal, sooner or later I would be convinced that you were cheating me—and I don't want that to happen.'"[107]

On June 11, Sonny recorded *The Sound of Sonny*, alongside Roy Haynes, Percy Heath, and Sonny Clark. The same band returned June 12 for a second session, and Paul Chambers replaced Heath on June 19 when Heath had a prior engagement with the Modern Jazz Quartet.[108] They began the first session with "Just in Time." They did four takes, and in an atypical move, Sonny asked for playback.[109] They did at least five takes of "Ev'ry Time We Say Goodbye" and four takes of "Toot, Toot, Tootsie," which he knew from the Eddie Cantor version. In the middle of the third take of "Cutie," Sonny cut the band off. "No, no, no, no," he said. "No, no, no, no, no, no, no, no...NO!"

Sonny was grappling with freedom within limitation. "Almost every album I've been on so far has been blowing eight choruses each on four or five tracks," he said, so on *The Sound of Sonny*, he aimed for "more sense of form,"[110] with or without the rhythm section. Sonny strolls on "The Last Time I Saw Paris," with Clark laying out on piano, and takes the first solo chorus in stop time. He goes into stop time again toward the end of "Toot, Toot, Tootsie" and on "Dearly Beloved." On "Mangoes," he eschews the legato double-time lines that predominate the rest of the session for rhythmic accents. Sometimes he drops the time altogether, as he does on his cadenzas on "Just in Time" and the ballad "What Is There to Say?" Sonny's playful "Funky Hotel Blues," commemorating his year on the road with the quintet, was left off the album.[111]

Notably, "It Could Happen to You" marks the first time Sonny played unaccompanied tenor on a studio album, in the tradition of Coleman Hawkins's landmark "Picasso."[112] "My ultimate goal," Sonny said not long after, "is unaccompanied tenor."[113] He wanted to be the Segovia of the tenor. "This I *know* I will do. I've got to get at least *this* out of music."[114]

It may have seemed unlikely that Miles Davis would disband the First Great Quintet, but that's exactly what he did.[115] Miles felt compelled to fire Philly Joe Jones and John Coltrane after their substance-abuse problems got out of control.[116] To replace Philly Joe, Miles tapped Sonny's old friend Art Taylor. "I said, 'Miles, I don't want to be in your band,'" Taylor recalled. "'I'd rather be just good friends...You know, make a record sometime or a gig or something. But I don't want to take Philly Joe's place, 'cause I know how much you love him.'"[117] Finally, Miles offered Taylor "so much, I couldn't refuse it."[118] Along with Red Garland and Paul Chambers, the remaining members, Miles had a new quintet, and Sonny reconnected with his childhood friend from the Counts of Bop.

From June 17 to June 27, Sonny opened with the new Miles Davis Quintet at Café Bohemia.[119] The reunion of Sonny Rollins and Miles Davis was big news in the jazz world, and people turned out to see it. "I mean, the lines are around the block," recalled Taylor.[120] The new quintet packed the place, even on weeknights. Miles, whom Sonny claimed was a shy guy, never announced a tune.[121]

Reuniting with Miles had a social dimension—Sonny was newly married to Dawn, and Miles was in love with Frances Taylor, a Katherine Dunham dancer and actress who had recently appeared in *Mr. Wonderful on Broadway*.[122] "Miles invited us for dinner with he and Frances," Dawn recalled. "He cooked red beans and rice and it was delicious." Meeting Miles, Max, and Sonny's other associates was enriching in many ways. "I gained a lot intellectually," she said.[123]

Sonny and Dawn led parallel lives—Dawn began taking classes in psychology and French, Sonny was out all night working in the booze-soaked atmosphere of the club—but she came with him on tour. "The road was tiring, if exciting," she later said. "Being married to a musician, I found out that some phases of show business can be a rugged, hard mental hassle. You have to keep your thinking high, keep yourself in a good mood and have faith . . . or else you'll break up. It's just that tough."[124] It seemed Sonny was ready to settle down into married life, though. He thought of himself as the black sheep of the family, and his sister, Gloria Anderson, certainly was settled. Sonny had a niece, Vallyn, born in 1956, and a nephew, Clifton, would be born that October.

When Sonny and Dawn first came to New York together, life in the city was exhilarating. "We were part of the in-group," she said. "That's when New York is really exciting. I loved it."[125] They didn't have an apartment, and Sonny didn't want to bring his new wife to live with his family up on Edgecombe, so they stayed at the "most expensive hotels until we could not afford it," Dawn said. But the honeymoon phase was short-lived. Staying out until early in the morning for work meant that Sonny didn't know what Dawn was doing while he was gone. The music industry had already given him understandable trust issues, Dawn recalled. "Sonny was very serious," she said, "and had been hurt by financial managers, agents and others."[126] To cope with the stress, he had begun drinking heavily.

One night, Sonny lost control of his emotions. "I will never forget this night," Dawn said. "One night when we were staying in Manhattan, Sonny had left for work. I got hungry for Chinese food, and as I went to the front desk, I told the clerk if he called, tell him I went to pick up some food. When I got back they said Sonny had called at least twenty times that night and I said, 'Did you tell him I went to pick up dinner?' They said he did not give them a chance. Well, when he came home that morning back to the hotel he kicked the door in. I was terrified. His explanation is that a woman heckled him all night."[127] Sonny was perhaps expecting the beatific figure of his mother waiting for him across the viaduct when he came home from the club in the early-morning hours, a standard of unconditional love and self-sacrifice almost no one, save his own mother, could meet.

Despite the red flags, they decided to make their union more permanent by moving into an apartment. Yet Sonny could not find a landlord that would rent to a black man, even one of his stature and reputation. "It was before I moved onto the Lower East Side that I began experiencing a lot of discrimination in trying to find someplace to live," Sonny later said. "I had the money, but I couldn't live…and that was the reason they wouldn't sell me an apartment.…I wasn't naïve about the situation, but it just hit me in a different way when I thought that I had reached a certain place in society. People were writing about me…and I thought, 'Hey, I can get a decent place to live that I could afford.' And so the sting of discrimination arose in a different sense."[128]

Sonny channeled his feelings about the experience—and what it meant to be black in America—into his music. "That's when I wrote 'The Freedom Suite,'"[129] he said. He wouldn't record it until 1958.

Sonny finally found an apartment through a fellow musician: Edward Hammond Boatner Jr., the son of the noted composer and arranger of spirituals. The world knew Boatner Jr. as Sonny Stitt. In addition to introducing Sonny to his father's work, Stitt knew of an apartment down on the Lower East Side at 400 Grand Street, above a fruit and vegetable market. "Sonny Stitt got me that apartment down there," Sonny said.[130] There was a neighboring apartment building on the other side of Grand Street. Walter Page of the Count Basie Orchestra and Eddie Durham lived in the other building, and Sonny began seeing them around. Immediately, he found that in the melting pot of the Lower East Side, discrimination was not as ubiquitous as it was elsewhere below Harlem.

On June 18, 1957, one day after Sonny began his summer engagement with the Miles Davis Quintet at the Bohemia, he signed a two-year lease for 400 Grand Street, apartment B: red-tile entryway wedged between ethnic storefronts with multilingual lettering, garden level in the rear of the building, perfect for the cats that would soon frequent the backyard.[131] Loyalty Group Realty listed him as "Sunny Rollins," but the terms were not disagreeable otherwise. The rent was set at $85 a month, or $1,020 a year, and after laying out an $85 security deposit, Sonny and Dawn moved in.

Chapter 19

A NIGHT AT THE VILLAGE VANGUARD

(1957)

As the green-eyed monster flared up at home, Sonny was getting reacquainted with Miles. After the initial run at the Bohemia, they went to the Cotton Club in Atlantic City, where the Davis quintet played from July 1 to 7 opposite pianist Hampton Hawes's trio.[1] To get back to their romantic partners and "to cop drugs," Sonny and Miles would hightail it to New York every night before dawn. "We get off the gig—Atlantic City—and go back to New York. And Miles is zooming. This cat is doing like seventy-five, eighty, eighty-five, ninety."[2]

Miles had graduated from the 1948 Dodge convertible known as the Blue Demon to a Mercedes 190SL coupe.[3] "We're going along trying to get back, so finally, at that rate you have to get stopped sometime," Sonny said. "The cat stopped Miles—'Okay, pull over.' Come to find out Miles doesn't have no driver's license, don't have nothing, man." That was Miles Davis in 1957: pedal to the metal at four in the morning in a Mercedes sports car, no license.

Miles had some fast-and-furious competition. On one occasion, he was driving down Seventh Avenue at three or four when he rolled up next to Nica de Koenigswarter at the wheel of her "Bebop Bentley" with Monk and his wife, Nellie, as well as Hawes. Miles pulled up and rasped, "Want to race?"

Hawes recalled. Nica calmly nodded, then announced to her passengers, "This time I believe I'm going to beat the motherfucker."[4]

Sonny also got close to Nica at this time.[5] "I always likened her to the great royal patrons of Mozart or Wagner's day," Sonny recalled. "She realized that jazz needed any kind of help it could get, especially the musicians. She was monetarily helpful to a lot who were struggling. But more than that, she was with us. By being with the baroness, we could go places and feel like human beings."[6]

As Sonny gained some stability in his life, he was likewise in a better position to pay it forward to other musicians who were struggling with the same inner demons he had conquered. Hawes, a self-taught Los Angeles native who would become a bright light at Contemporary Records, had won "New Star of the Year" in the 1956 *Down Beat* critics' poll, and commanded a $1,500 weekly booking fee. But by the summer of 1957, he was in the throes of heroin addiction.[7] Hawes went broke in Washington, DC; left all his clothes in the hotel room to skirt the bill; and somehow made it back to New York with fifty cents in his pocket before opening in Atlantic City at the Cotton Club opposite Miles.[8]

One day, Hawes was nodding off on a bench overlooking Central Park when the Bebop Bentley pulled up with the Jazz Baroness and a familiar face. "Man, get in this car." It was Monk. "A good musician ain't supposed to be sittin' on no bench lookin' like you look."[9]

Nica drove them back to Monk's apartment, where they gave Hawes a meal and put him in the bathtub. Then they took him to the kitchen and propped him up next to the piano. Sonny was there for the intervention.[10]

"You're an important figure in jazz and you ought to set a better example," someone said.

"Okay."

"You got to straighten up and get yourself together before you die or something."

"You right."

More was said, then this: "We heard about you just like you heard about us, we knew there were brothers out there trying to do it. We're all in it together and you're too important to fuck up like this."[11]

Monk handed Hawes some cash to help him "get yourself together," and they left. Within two days, Hawes was back on the needle. Like Sonny, no one could help him until he helped himself.[12]

The intervention was a way to pay it forward. "A couple years earlier, I would have been Hampton Hawes, having to get myself together," Sonny said.[13]

From July 8 to August 11, the Davis quintet packed the Bohemia for a five-week run, where Marlon Brando and Ava Gardner mixed with fans from up on Sugar Hill.[14] On three consecutive Saturdays starting July 13, they were broadcast live on Mutual's "coast-to-coast" *Bandstand U.S.A.*[15] During the Bohemia run, John Coltrane had joined Thelonious Monk's quartet with bassist Ahmed Abdul-Malik and drummer Shadow Wilson; they had just begun their legendary run at the Five Spot. When Miles and Sonny weren't on the stand at the Bohemia, they came to see Monk, often sitting at a table with Nica, nearby the likes of Jack Kerouac, Frank O'Hara, and David Amram.[16]

At the time, Sonny was engaged in a friendly rivalry with Coltrane; Sonny came to the Five Spot to hear Trane with Monk, and Trane came to the Bohemia to hear Sonny with Miles. At the Five Spot, Sonny recalled, "I happened to be in the house and everybody wanted us to play at that time and I didn't want to. So... I didn't feel like taking him on at that time.... But then he ran in on me one night at the Bohemia, and I cut him that night."[17]

Jimmy Cobb recalled that Miles "would just get them up there and see what they was going to do to each other. For a long time, Sonny Rollins [was] a saxophone colossus. Everybody in the world wanted to play like Sonny Rollins.... So every night he used to get up there, and Sonny used to tear him up. So [Coltrane] said, 'Oh, I'm getting tired of this whipping.' Said, 'I got to figure out something else to do here to get across this.' So he got to working on what he was working on. He went in—and I think, in the end, it confused Sonny, because Sonny didn't know what it was."[18]

On Sunday, July 21, the Davis quintet appeared at the inaugural Great South Bay Jazz Festival in Great River, Long Island.[19] According to a review, the majority white crowd, most of whom "had not even to this day accepted Charlie Parker," found Miles's turning his back on the audience condescending. Miles and Sonny would never pander to the audience.[20]

The Bohemia's acoustics made it hard for Arthur Taylor to blend with Miles, who began hovering by the drum set.[21] "It just kept goin' on and goin' on, until one night he said to me, which I knew it was gonna happen to me at some time—like you have a premonition that something's gonna happen. . . . We were playing whatever song we were playing, and he said, 'Goddamn it, motherfucker. Don't you know how [Philly] Joe makes that break on that?' I said, 'Man, you can kiss my ass.'" Taylor got up in the middle of the set, packed up his drums, caught a cab, and went home. "Miles never said a word about it. We never discussed it. Never changed our relationship. Nothin' like that. And the next night he got Jimmy Cobb." (Miles would replace Cobb with Philly Joe again soon afterward.)[22] Later, Taylor realized there was a valid lesson there. "It's not supposed to be like one of these instruments is supposed to stand out above the other ones," he said. "They're supposed to blend together for an overall sound."[23]

In the August 1957 issue of *Down Beat*, Sonny was named "New Star" in the tenor-sax category of the International Jazz Critics Poll. Sonny had fifty votes; John Coltrane came in second, with thirty. Sonny also came in second in the overall tenor rankings. Stan Getz topped the poll, with seventy-four votes, followed by Sonny with forty-seven; it must have been strange to see his idol, Coleman Hawkins, in third with forty votes.

On August 23, the Miles Davis Quintet performed in front of a crowd of twelve thousand at the Second Annual New York Jazz Festival on Randalls Island under the Triborough Bridge.[24] On Monday, August 26, the Davis quintet opened at the Crawford Grill in Pittsburgh, where they were booked for the rest of August.[25] However, Miles had to cut it short. On August 30, news reports circulated that Miles had been hospitalized for surgery. During the previous two years, he had begun to suffer from benign nodes or polyps on his vocal cords, hence his raspy voice. He was out for all of September.[26]

With Miles recovering, Sonny decided it was time to form his own band, and on September 11, *Variety* reported he'd done it.[27] Sonny signed with Associated Booking, Joe Glaser's agency, which still represented Max Roach. As Sonny later recalled, unscrupulous booking agents often skimmed 30 percent off the top and took their cut of the remainder.

"In this music business, everyone is a slave: white and black are a slave to the industry," Sonny said. "But of course, black people are more prone to get taken advantage of. In my case—and in many cases—they tell you how many records you've sold, and you have to agree with them. Some people have been really ripped off in music. One kid I used to be with, Joe Glaser, a very famous entrepreneur, used to be Louis Armstrong's management." Glaser, who was born in 1896, was not exactly a "kid" when Sonny was represented by him. "I was with his agency one time when I first left the Max Roach band, and I was working there with one of his agents. I had actually caught them ripping me off with a deal, and one of his agents was a very honest guy: 'You know, Sonny, I have been in the boxing business and I have been in the music business, and the music business is worse than the boxing business.' "[28]

On September 22, Sonny went back to Hackensack to record *Newk's Time* for Blue Note. He hired Doug Watkins (the bassist from *Saxophone Colossus*), pianist Wynton Kelly,[29] and Philly Joe Jones.[30] "Philly Joe had an urbane way of playing that was sophisticated," Sonny said. "I just knew that if he was there, whatever I needed him to do, it would be done. I knew I could expect more than just good-feeling swing."[31]

Two weeks past his twenty-seventh birthday, Sonny showed up at Van Gelder's wearing a white button-down with black cuff links, tan slacks, sunglasses, and shiny black shoes.[32] He picked Kenny Dorham's "Asiatic Raes," recorded elsewhere as "Lotus Blossom"; "Tune Up," which Sonny and Philly Joe had just recently been playing with the Miles Davis Quintet; and Sonny's "Blues for Philly Joe."[33] From the Great American Songbook, Sonny chose "Surrey with the Fringe on Top," "Namely You," and "Wonderful! Wonderful!" The latter was a hit for Johnny Mathis in 1956.[34] "Namely You" was a ballad from *Li'l Abner*, a Broadway musical that opened in 1956, which Sonny had recently seen in the theater.[35] "Surrey with the Fringe on Top" was from *Oklahoma*, adapted into the 1955 Academy Award–winning film.

"I like 'Namely You,' and 'Surrey with the Fringe on Top' I probably saw in the movies or something," Sonny said, "so it was a natural part of what I did—of what I heard. I heard that music and I liked it, so I played it....I had the freedom to choose my repertoire, which I always did, even with producers.... So for me, it was just a normal thing to play 'Surrey with the Fringe on Top.' "[36]

"Surrey" was a groundbreaking saxophone-drums duo. Miles Davis had recorded the song in 1956 with the First Great Quintet, so Philly Joe knew it well.[37] The version in the 1955 film has a fully orchestrated string and brass section, but little to no percussion; Sonny's rendition had everything the original didn't, down to Philly Joe's feathering (lightly playing) the bass drum.[38] "You're not hearing a bunch of streams of eighth notes," tenor saxophonist James Brandon Lewis later said of the track. "It's broken up rhythmically. So many different ways of articulation going on within this piece. You hear different accents, you're hearing slurring, smearing of notes—it's like he's talking." The album wasn't released until mid-1959, and only got a three-and-a-half-star review in *Down Beat*, but its influence would eclipse its initial lukewarm reception.[39]

Sonny was booked with his new group at the Village Vanguard for two months starting October 15, playing opposite Anita O'Day.[40] The club was founded in 1934 by Max Gordon, a Jewish Belarussian immigrant and Columbia Law School dropout. To break even, Gordon primarily booked folksingers, comics, and poets, as most bohemian clubs in Greenwich Village did. In 1935, Gordon moved to the space previously occupied by the Golden Triangle, a subterranean speakeasy so named as a riff on its triangular shape, and converted it into a nightclub with a stage at the triangle's apex. As television increasingly eroded his talent pool, in May 1957 Gordon saw an opportunity to expand the club's jazz programming. "He began reinventing the Village Vanguard as a jazz club exclusively, more out of necessity than anything else," his wife, Lorraine Gordon, wrote. "Only in retrospect does this seem brilliant."[41]

Sonny was feeling the pressure. That past June, *New Yorker* jazz critic Whitney Balliett called him "possibly the most incisive and influential jazz instrumentalist since Charlie Parker."[42] Sonny would cement the Village Vanguard's rebranding effort and his solo career simultaneously. "There's sharp disagreement among critics and jazz buffs about the playing prowess of some jazz musicians, but not about Sonny," Gordon wrote, adding: "Sonny's the greatest of them all—no two ways about it."[43]

Finding musicians capable of meeting Sonny's exacting standards proved difficult, especially for drummers: Larry Ritchie, Frank Gant, Roy

Haynes—nothing clicked.[44] "I used to be pretty ruthless. I didn't spare any-one's feelings," Sonny said. "I used to hire and fire with regularity—that was my trait. I was constantly auditioning guys. It was like, 'Okay, good, next!' I'm not proud of that period. I think I might have been able to handle it bet-ter but at that time I was really intense about things coming out right."[45]

Eventually, he settled on a group: Haynes, bassist George Joyner (later known as Jamil Nasser), Gil Coggins on piano, and Donald Byrd.[46] They began rehearsing as much as possible, with sessions going beyond the music.[47] "We used to have long philosophical conversations on a wide range of sub-jects," Joyner recalled. "The sun rose over a few of them."[48]

Yet all seemed for naught. "When we got to the Vanguard, he didn't play anything he'd rehearsed," recalled Haynes. And then, "he fired everybody."[49]

"Time to hit, 10:00 p.m.," Joyner wrote of the night. "Sonny is warming up backstage. We're on the bandstand ready to play. At 10:45, he stepped out and played near the entrance door for ten minutes. Then he reached the bandstand at 10:55 and played some more. Finally, we grew tired of posing with our instruments and segued into an F blues. The crowd screamed their approval." In the backroom kitchen, which musicians used as a greenroom, Sonny voiced his disapproval. "After the first set, Sonny called a meeting and upbraided us for not respecting his leadership. He said, 'I am the leader. You cats should follow me.' Donald Byrd spoke first. 'What are you doing?' Sonny said, 'You can leave!' One by one we posed the same question and received the same answer. Rollins fired each one of us."[50]

Sonny had to find a new rhythm section, fast. He had arranged with Blue Note to record a live album at the Vanguard on November 3, his first live album and the first to be recorded there. He called Donald Bailey—the bass-ist, not the drummer—who was available.[51] It was likely at the Tijuana in Baltimore, where Bailey was in the house rhythm section, that he met Sonny and Miles. Bailey was a first-call bassist in Baltimore, having performed with Parker, Monk, and Roach. He "played like he's singing," as his children remembered it.[52]

Bailey was a family man, with five children,[53] and life on the road was not conducive to his responsibilities. He worked for the US Postal Service in Bal-timore for thirty-three years, but his daughter said, "His real job was music.

Every night, he would get home at two o'clock in the morning, and get up at six to be at the post office. He did that every day."[54]

As for the drummer, Philly Joe was with Miles, Art Blakey had the Messengers, and Art Taylor was unavailable. So Sonny called Max Roach for a recommendation. Max suggested that he try a nineteen-year-old drummer named Pete "La Roca" Sims, a Harlem-born graduate of the High School of Music and Art who got his stage name when he started playing in Latin bands.[55] At a recent Monday-night jam session at Birdland, La Roca got so into the music that he broke Roach's drumheads. Rather than chewing him out, Max recommended him to Sonny. La Roca thought of Sonny as "one of my favorite players well before I had the opportunity to play with him."[56]

To Sonny's relief, he didn't have to break him in. "He was one of those people who you don't have to tell what to do. This is very important," Sonny said of La Roca. "You find a lot of musicians who are always asking the leader, 'What about this? What should I do here? How should I hit that?' ... The person who's asking you how to do everything, that person is not ready."[57]

To complicate matters for La Roca, Sonny decided not to call a pianist, just like *Way Out West*. "I wanted to create the harmonic sequences that might be necessary for me to be me and show what I could do as an individual player," Sonny said.[58]

This was a challenge for La Roca, but ultimately rewarding. "It was his pianoless trio period and the interaction was intense," La Roca said. "What I love about Sonny's playing is that he is so inventive within the mainstream jazz vernacular. Because he knows so many ways to deal with musical material, he is never repetitive and hasn't had to invent a new language. Also, he never asked me to do anything but swing!"[59]

As the recording date for *A Night at the Village Vanguard* rapidly approached, Sonny was called to be a sideman on *That's Him*, Abbey Lincoln's debut album on Riverside, recorded October 28, 1957, at Reeves Sound Studios.[60] Lincoln had made a splash in 1956 when she appeared as herself in the film *The Girl Can't Help It*, singing "Spread the Word" with Benny Carter's band. She fell in love with Max Roach and decided to leave Hollywood behind.[61] "She felt like, 'What the hell am I doing?' " Roach said. "Especially when she came to see people like us, I guess, when she would hear the way that we'd play, and I would become engaged in the music, and meeting people like Sonny, and the way we were serious about it."[62]

"I've wanted to do something like this for a long time," Lincoln told *Metronome* after the album came out, "but could never interest the right people."[63] Max introduced her to Orrin Keepnews, and suddenly, Riverside had a movie star frequenting its shabby offices.[64]

Lincoln hired Kenny Dorham, Wynton Kelly, Paul Chambers, Max, and Sonny. She chose her own material, with a new song, "Strong Man," that Oscar Brown Jr. composed especially for the date. "Happiness Is a Thing Called Joe," from *Cabin in the Sky*, was familiar to Sonny from childhood. The five-hour session had no rehearsal. "Everybody was exhausted by the time we had cut eight tunes, but then we find out that one more tune is required to fill out the LP," Lincoln said. "Wynton picked up the bass and was showing Paul the changes on 'Don't Explain,' and everybody told Wynton how good he sounded. So we decided to omit the piano and let him play bass on the last tune."

The spontaneity gave Lincoln a new thrill. "I knew I was never going back to doing what I had been doing," she said.[65]

Less than a week later, on Sunday, November 3, it was Sonny's Blue Note recording date for *A Night at the Village Vanguard*. Anita O'Day had recently set an attendance record at the Vanguard at 240 for one set, but it was Sonny who solidified the Vanguard as *the* place in New York for progressive jazz.[66]

The recording actually began during the Sunday matinee. Rudy Van Gelder made a rare appearance outside his parents' living room for the occasion, recording equipment in tow.[67] "Good afternoon everybody, boys and girls, this is Uncle Don," Sonny said drolly, referencing the erstwhile popular children's radio show and setting the jocular tone. He then introduced the band properly and began with "A Night in Tunisia," with La Roca and Bailey keeping the pace. La Roca, in his recording debut and understandably over-eager, exploded with drum pyrotechnics; it was as though he played everything he knew. There was no set list; Sonny called tunes from the bandstand. "'I've Got You Under My Skin,' okay?" he said discreetly to his bandmates.

After the afternoon set, though, Sonny decided to replace Bailey and La Roca with Wilbur Ware and Elvin Jones.[68] "I was trying to get them for the entire session but they did not arrive until after the matinee had ended," Sonny recalled.[69] Wilbur "was terra firma, and that's one of the requirements of playing in the trio."[70] At the time, Ware was playing at the Five Spot in Monk's quartet with Coltrane and Shadow Wilson; he and Sonny had met in 1950 in Chicago.[71]

As for Elvin Jones, "There was something that he did with a 6/8 rhythm that other people weren't doing," Sonny said. "Once you heard Elvin play it, you said, 'Why isn't everybody playing like that?'"[72] Jones could swing harder than almost anyone. "His beat was so liberating, so free, and universal."[73]

Ware and Jones have differing accounts of how they ended up on the record. According to Ware, he came down to the Vanguard the previous day, and Sonny asked him to come on Sunday to "'do a track on my date.' And he said, 'but I'll pay you for the whole date.' It wasn't that much...it was fifty or seventy-five dollars or something like that—one side. And two sides, LP, was a hundred and a quarter, I believe...and he said, 'And you don't have to bring your bass,' and he said to Don [Bailey], 'Will it be all right if he uses yours?' And he said, 'Yeah, that'd be fine.'"[74]

Jones was not aware that Sonny wanted him. He had recently returned from a three-month northern European tour with J. J. Johnson's group, and soon after, Johnson fired him, apparently on November 2. When he got back to New York the next day, Jones had to cool off. "I used to carry a pistol all the time and I said, 'Shit, I don't want to be bothered with this motherfucker.'"[75] Jones's nonmusician brother Tom was visiting, and said, "'You look funny! Let's go out and get drunk,'" Jones recalled, "so we start walking around going to these bars and we got up to Seventh Avenue, and there's Wilbur Ware. I didn't even know what it was and it was the Village Vanguard. And Wilbur says 'Where have you been? Sonny has been looking for you all night!' And I said, 'Wilbur, please don't tell him. You know I don't believe this. Sonny ain't looking for nobody.' And he says, 'C'mon down. I'll prove it.'"[76]

When Jones and Ware walked down the stairs to the Vanguard, Sonny was getting ready for the evening set, and Sonny asked Jones to sit in.[77] Jones had walked into the Vanguard half in the bag, packing heat, still seething that J. J. Johnson had fired him; a few minutes later, he was recording *A Night at the Village Vanguard*.

As Ware tells it, Bailey and La Roca began the set, and Sonny called him and Elvin up for their one tune. Yet once they took the stand, they never left.[78] Jones had some apprehension about sitting down at La Roca's drum set. "I was afraid to play," Jones said. "I hate playing on somebody else's drums, 'cause I am prone to put a hole through somebody's bass drum."[79] Ware, on the other hand, was used to playing on a borrowed bass.[80]

A pickup gig with no set list: not the most auspicious beginning for a live recording. Jones didn't even realize he was being recorded at first. "I finally came to my senses and I see there's Frank Wolff and the Blue Note executives. They were recording!" Jones said. "I didn't know this was a recording, and Sonny said, 'Oh man, thank you,' and I said, 'Oh man. Shit!'"[81]

So Ware and Jones could follow, Sonny mostly stuck to standards, but there was instant chemistry. The evening set began with "A Night in Tunisia," taken at a slower tempo than Sonny had played it that afternoon. A minute in, though, Sonny darted into a take-no-prisoners four-bar double-time solo break and didn't let up until he reached the screaming cadenza. Next, he called "Softly, as in a Morning Sunrise," with Jones on brushes, then "Four"[82] and "Woody'n You."

Then came a curveball. "Thank you very kindly, ladies and gentlemen," Sonny said. "We'd like to carry on now with a composition, I think it's from *Finian's Rainbow* if I'm not mistaken. Either *Finian's Rainbow* or *Kiss Me, Kate*..." The audience chimed in. Finally, Sonny announced, "So we will now give you 'That Old Devil Moon' from the hit show *Li'l Abner*."

Sonny may not have remembered which musical "Old Devil Moon" was from—*Finian's Rainbow* was correct—but Ware didn't know the changes at all. "I had heard it, but I hadn't played it to remember it well enough to record it, and he said, 'Oh, you can hear it.' So I said, 'Okay, let's take it.'"[83] It would be one thing for an experienced bassist to play a tune cold and follow the pianist, but with no piano, Ware would have to intuit the chord progression from Sonny's single line, a difficult task for anyone. But Wilbur Ware had uncommonly big ears. In the middle of Sonny's solo, he threw in a quote from "Three Blind Mice,"[84] a wry peak in an exhilarating performance. Following it, Sonny introduced the band: "Elvin Jones on drums, formerly of the great J. J. Johnson Orchestra, now appearing with Stan Getz, and tonight of course, he's appearing with myself, Sonny Rollins. And on bass, the very great Wilbur B. Ware." His middle name was Bernard, but the double entendre was intentional.[85]

After blowing through a fourteen-minute "What Is This Thing Called Love?" and a faster version of "Softly, as in a Morning Sunrise," Sonny unveiled an original composition to the audience—and the band. It was a B-flat blues he called "Sonnymoon for Two," written for his wife, Dawn. During the applause for the previous tune, he sang part of the head to Ware and Jones and then counted it off. That would have been enough; it consists of a syncopated four-bar riff, based primarily on five notes and stemming from the "blues scale," repeated three times. Then, over sixteen choruses, Sonny gradually builds a solo, slowly developing a motif. "If you're going to play 'Sonnymoon for Two,'" Sonny recalled, "I always felt that my solo should have been included as part of the melody."[86]

Sonny then shifted to the ballad "I Can't Get Started," with Jones taking part of the tune in double time. Before playing "I'll Remember April," Sonny sang the opening to give a sense of the Latin feel he was aiming for and counted it off. After that, Sonny said, "Let's do 'Get Happy,' okay? Wilbur, in F?" The next tune, a Sonny original called "Striver's Row," was named after the block in Harlem and based on "Confirmation" with an improvised melody.[87] On "All the Things You Are," Sonny called the tune but never played the melody.[88]

Something so unplanned yet close to perfection was exactly what Sonny wanted. "Elvin and I thought...since it wasn't rehearsed, it was spontaneous, a good feeling, thing, 'Oh, this ain't nothing,'" Ware said, "but Sonny seemed to sense something; he felt real comfortable with what he was doing, because he asked us, he said, 'Look, man, I'm going on tour and I'm going out to the West Coast and from there I'm going to Paris, and I want you all to stay with me. I'll take care of this, and anything you need, I'll get for you.'" It would have been Ware's first journey overseas, and Sonny's, too, but Ware didn't want to give up his position as the house bassist at Riverside. Jones had gigs of his own. The trio never performed again.[89]

As for Donald Bailey, not long after his time with Sonny at the Vanguard, "Miles Davis came to our house," recalled his son Derrick Bailey, "and he had a conversation with my mother and father about going on the road. My mother said no. Miles called her a name, and my father said, 'Get the fuck out my house.'" Bailey would stay in the Baltimore-DC area for the rest of his career, working at the post office by day and gigging by night. When he died in 1995, Keter Betts played the funeral; Sonny called the Bailey house that day to offer his condolences. Humble to the end, some of his own children did not even know he played on *A Night at the Village Vanguard* until they were thirty years old.[90]

Blue Note cut the album down to six tunes and released *A Night at the Village Vanguard* that February.[91] The reviews were positive but not stellar. *Metronome* felt that Sonny was "noodling" on part of the album, though "much like any given night of blowing, side one warms us up for the exceptional side two, which, incidentally is worth the minimum, er, price of the LP."[92] *Down Beat* commented that Sonny was a "tempest of his own," "sacrificing melodic content for the sake of virile drive."[93] *A Night at the Village Vanguard* never cracked the *Down Beat* jazz best-seller list—the top twenty jazz albums listed in every biweekly issue—but over time it would come to be considered a classic. It established the club's reputation and launched Sonny's solo career.

The day after the recording, Monday, November 4, Sonny was in Beltone Studios recording *Sonny Rollins Plays* for Leonard Feather's Period Records.[94] Having seen Sonny at the Vanguard leading up to the Blue Note date, Feather wanted to capitalize on Sonny's "unexpectedly swift" ascendancy.[95] Sonny hired Gil Coggins, the pianist and childhood friend he had just fired at the Vanguard the previous month; trombonist Jimmy Cleveland, who had recently played on *Miles Ahead*;[96] Wendell Marshall, a first-call bassist who, like his cousin Jimmy Blanton, was known primarily for his tenure with Duke Ellington;[97] and Philadelphia-born drummer Kenny Dennis, who had recently subbed for Shadow Wilson with Monk and Coltrane at the Five Spot.[98]

Jimmy Cleveland had fond memories of the session. Sonny was "doing something that's interesting all the time. If he's just standing there playing the saxophone, it's interesting to watch him. He has personality, he has character. He'll raise his saxophone, it's not anything new, Lester Young used to do that, it's just something that brings a little something different that makes you look at him. And the way he puts his notes together is another thing. If you're really listening, Sonny Rollins is gonna say something to you, because he is different, and his harmonies, his chord structures, the way he handles his structures is so different. It's so original. The things that he does with the meter in his solos. I mean, even if it's a standard tune, I heard him playing 'You Are My Sunshine,' something like that...And, man, he turned that tune inside out."[99]

According to Kenny Dennis, "He could play one note and make it sing. When I say sing, he could expand on it in a way that he could touch on all of the principal elements of music: harmony, melody, and rhythm."[100]

They recorded only three tunes: "Sonnymoon for Two," with Sonny playing two stop-time choruses; "Like Someone in Love"; and Tchaikovsky's "Theme from Symphony No. 6 Pathetique," which Sonny had been playing not long before at the Vanguard. To Dennis, the juxtaposition of songs meant that "all of us are a melting pot."[101]

It was probably at this time that Sonny introduced Elvin Jones to a young Philadelphia bassist named Jimmy Garrison; they would later play together in the John Coltrane Quartet. Sonny had a concert in Philadelphia, and Garrison wound up sitting in.[102] The bassist was "scared to death," he recalled. "The cats around Philly were good, but not of that stature. Sonny Rollins and Elvin Jones, man! Anyway, I made the gig, terrified, and got through it. Even then I had no problem playing with Elvin, and he never forgot."[103]

Sonny's next major date was his Carnegie Hall debut, on November 29, 1957. The all-star concert was billed as "Thanksgiving Jazz at Carnegie Hall," with the Sonny Rollins Trio, Billie Holiday, the Dizzy Gillespie Orchestra with Austin Cromer and Lee Morgan, the Thelonious Monk quartet with John Coltrane, the Chet Baker and Zoot Sims quartet with Mose Allison, and in his New York concert debut Ray Charles with drummer Ed Blackwell. The concert was presented by Ken Karpe, the friend of Richie Powell's who used to host jam sessions at his loft.[104] Proceeds went toward the Morningside Community Center, which provided day care, mental health services, recreation, and camp programs to more than four thousand Harlem families.[105] There were two sets, at 8:30 p.m. and midnight, and tickets were $2 to $3.95. It was at capacity for the early show, 60 percent full for the late show.[106] It was taped for *Voice of America*, which was hosted by the disc jockey and presenter Willis Conover.[107]

Sonny used bassist Wendell Marshall and drummer Kenny Dennis from *Sonny Rollins Plays*. On the opener, "Moritat," Marshall walked with half notes, with Dennis only on snare with brushes. Sonny played the second solo chorus in stop time. Dennis came in on the ride cymbal and Marshall started to walk, as Sonny showed all he could do up and down the horn, then hung on a G for half a chorus, varying the syncopated rhythm.

At the midnight show, Dennis was nowhere to be found, forcing Conover to fill time by showering Sonny with praise: "A man with a sound on tenor saxophone which all the young men of that instrument are hoping to emulate." After a few bars of "Sonnymoon for Two," Dennis showed up at the drums. "'Some Enchanted Evening,' then let's get out of here," Sonny said to the band. He embellished on the melody of the *South Pacific* ballad before exploding with quadruple-time lines, finally returning to a full-bodied vibrato. The rhythm section dropped out, and Sonny was all alone for his cadenza, taking the melody as far out as he could.[108] Wild applause. Yet Sonny was already gone.

"Sonny Rollins! Sonny?" said Conover. "Acknowledge your public, will you? He's already in the cab."[109]

Sonny's transition to bandleading had gone well; only three months in, he'd made it to Carnegie Hall. But at home, the Sonnymoon was over.

Dawn wrote of what she called her "breakdown," which began one night when Sonny came home in the early-morning hours after work. "I knew I was in trouble one night he came home and I was in my gown and walked outside," she wrote. "I should not have, but I was so lonely I needed some air. He never believed me. We broke up three times."[110] That November, they separated, but this, it seems, was only the first of the breakups.[111]

To Dawn, their short marriage was an education in music—she loved the art, even if it didn't work out with the artist. "I love the classicals," she later said: Victor Young, Max Steiner, and Debussy. "I love some jazz, too. Mostly progressive, modern"—Monk, Miles, Lena Horne, and Sarah Vaughan. "And," she said, "I do appreciate Sonny Rollins as a musician."[112]

"I was studying the piano when I met Sonny, and felt we had a lot in common," Dawn said. "Everything seemed all right in the beginning because there was all this traveling with different bands and the two of us never really got a chance to know each other. Then we settled down...did get to know each other, and found out we had nothing in common at all. He lived only for his music, for nothing else, for nobody else."[113]

"We weren't married too long, unfortunately," Sonny later said. "I'm not proud of that period in my life. We were both young, and she was a wonderful, wonderful woman...we were living in New York together, and then we broke up. She went back to California."[114] Ending the marriage was devastating to Sonny. "It took me a long time to get over that breakup," he said. "Neither of us were prepared for marriage. We were both young...but boy, having to break up was hell."[115]

Almost as soon as Sonny's marriage to Dawn dissolved, Lucille Pearson decided to move from Chicago to New York to rekindle her bond with Sonny. Moving on December 1, 1957, she rented an apartment in the Village at 815 Greenwich Street, a five-story walk-up building.[116] Having left her position at the Tuberculosis Institute with a recommendation from the executive director for being "utterly reliable," she secured a job as secretary to R. H. Ritchings, the head of patent development at Research Corporation in New York.[117]

Yet Sonny didn't have much time to reflect on his failing marriage or the possibility of future romance.[118] He was called for one more record date in 1957. It was with Dizzy Gillespie, who had a session for Jazz at the Philharmonic with impresario Norman Granz. "I like Norman Granz a lot," Sonny said, "and Norman Granz, well, he liked me a lot."[119]

For *Sonny Side Up*, Dizzy wanted Sonny, but not just Sonny Rollins; he also wanted Sonny Stitt.[120] Dizzy tried to summon the spirit of the cutting session when he called them. "'Rollins is going to be there and he says he's gonna carve your ass,'" Stitt recalled him saying. He said the same thing to the other Sonny. They said, "'Let's get him.'"[121]

In reality, the two Sonnys were good friends, so any battle that ensued would be congenial. "I've always loved Sonny's imaginative mind," Stitt later said. "He's inventive. Sonny's a free liver, he doesn't give a damn about nothin' but music, his mama probably, and himself. He's a beautiful man."[122]

Rollins had never recorded with Dizzy, but he had with the pianist on the session, Ray Bryant, who had been working with Dizzy's big band, and for the recording session, "he just took the nucleus out of the band. He had Charli Persip on drums and he asked me to come and play the piano, Sonny Rollins and Sonny Stitt were gonna be the guests, so he said, 'Now who do you want on bass?' I said, 'My brother.' "[123]

On December 11, 1957, the two Sonnys met Dizzy, Ray and bassist Tommy Bryant, and Persip at Nola Studios. "Dizzy was always on time, never late," recalled Persip. "I got to the record date, he was there already!" Persip thought the record date was with the big band, and was surprised when Stitt walked in, followed by Rollins. "I was quite nervous," Persip said. "Terrified, as a matter of fact."[124]

That day, Rollins and Stitt recorded separate duets with Dizzy; an album was eventually released as *Duets*. Rollins played on Dizzy's "Wheatleigh Hall," a burner named for the estate in Lenox that housed the Music Inn, and a slow blues Dizzy simply titled "Sumphin." Yet what made Rollins's collaboration with Dizzy stand out was the blowing session with his Lower East Side neighbor. On December 19, the week before Christmas 1957, the two Sonnys returned to Nola Studios to see if the place was big enough for the both of them.[125]

"On the Sunny Side of the Street" has a marvelous Dizzy vocal, with Stitt going into double time on his solo; Rollins swings hard, saving something for later. "The Eternal Triangle" was Stitt's up-tempo "rhythm changes" for the session. He taught it to Rollins by ear, but Dizzy had to practice the melody line in another room for an hour to get it up to speed.[126] Rollins starts the fourteen-minute tenor battle with five choruses of high-octane blowing. His sound is huge, and he tongues almost every note, a challenge at such a fast tempo. It feels like he's speaking on the horn—sometimes growling, sometimes bellowing with laughter. Stitt plays eight choruses. The two tenor heavyweights then traded for six choruses until it seemed they exhausted all possibilities, but they were just getting started. Ultimately, it was a draw, though some disagreed. There was no bad blood between Sonny and Sonny—one photo even shows them kissing platonically.[127]

They also recorded Avery Parrish's "After Hours," a slow blues. But where Rollins really distinguished himself was on Vincent Youmans's "I Know That You Know." They played it at a blistering 320 beats per minute. And Sonny burns through three stop-time choruses, without swallowing any notes or dragging. It would be difficult to play Sonny's solo from a transcription, looking at the sheet music, but to improvise it whole cloth demonstrated a peerless level of virtuosity.

Sonny's appraisal: "It was okay."[128]

As 1957 wound down, there was one more accolade: Sonny was voted the number two tenor saxophonist in the *Down Beat* readers' poll, behind only the perennial, Stan Getz. Down at number eleven, John Coltrane was beginning to get himself together.

Sonny, at twenty-seven, had established himself as the young tenor to watch. He had been on the scene for nearly a decade and had earned his place in the jazz firmament. The year 1957 alone was prolific enough for a lifetime. Sonny played on ten albums as a leader or sideman—many becoming classics—toured with the Max Roach Quintet, reunited with Miles Davis, went out on his own, and debuted at Carnegie Hall.

But Sonny's personal life was out of balance. His marriage had fallen apart, and he also grieved the loss of his beloved grandmother Miriam.[129] Sonny's pace was so intense, and life on the road and in the woodshed so demanding, he barely had time to process everything that had happened to him during the previous decade in a meaningful way. It was time to look inward.

Chapter 20

THE FREEDOM SUITE

(1958)

In 1958, as the civil rights struggle gained steam, Sonny and his peers began "thinking that music could change the world," he recalled. "I thought that this world could change and get more peaceful, with everybody loving each other and all this hope. But then I learned, and I lived a little longer."[1]

In early February, Sonny played Birdland for two weeks opposite vocalist

Jeri Southern and guitarist Johnny Smith's group.[2] Some in the audience did not appreciate Sonny's stoic stage persona; he didn't announce the band or the set list. "I think the jazz musician owes a little something to his audience, even if we are mere laymen," wrote one frustrated fan from New Jersey. "After all, who pays his salary?"[3] To Sonny, this demeaning attitude nullified any social contract.

At Birdland, Sonny's quartet probably had bassist Henry Grimes, drummer Frankie Dunlop, and pianist Dick Katz.[4] Grimes had recently turned twenty-three. A Philadelphia-born, Juilliard-trained bassist, Grimes initially met Sonny when George Morrow let him sit in with the Brown-Roach Quintet in Philly. He'd worked with Anita O'Day, Gerry Mulligan, Al Cohn, Zoot Sims, and Lennie Tristano before Sonny hired him.[5]

Dunlop, twenty-nine, was from Buffalo and had been recommended by Charles Mingus.[6] Mingus prepared Dunlop for Sonny's high expectations, particularly of drummers. "All of the geniuses are like that," said Dunlop. "They may be eccentric, but deep down inside, they're concerned about their music. Monk, Mingus, Rollins, Miles Davis—they didn't want any substitutions for what it was really supposed to be." Sonny got Dunlop into the union and "took a chance on hiring me to play with him at Birdland, when I still had three weeks to go to complete my residency requirement."[7]

Pianist Dick Katz's tenure with the band was short-lived; after Birdland, Sonny decided to return to the pianoless trio format. "The guys I liked on piano were with other people," Sonny explained at that time. "I'd like to use Bud Powell, for example. But I couldn't seem to find a guy who could contribute. They got in the way. They played too much. Their chords interrupted my train of thought. I ended up getting bugged at all piano players." Playing without a safety net, Sonny said, would force musicians to "listen to each other."[8] Finding a capable drummer and bassist would always be tough, though. That February, Sonny had a Riverside recording date for *Freedom Suite*, the first prominent civil rights–themed album of the modern jazz era.[9] Fortunately, he was able to hire two musicians who aligned with him politically and musically: Max Roach and Oscar Pettiford.[10]

The first session was on February 11 at WOR Studios with recording engineer Sam Morse. "It was important to Riverside, very much a newcomer and still struggling to establish itself, that Rollins (being willing to record for us rather automatically), gave the label a certain amount of status," recalled Orrin Keepnews, who produced the session.[11]

At the first session, more than an hour passed and still no Sonny. Keepnews asked Roach and Pettiford to record a duo; they played "There Will Never Be Another You."[12] When Sonny finally showed up, he "remained impatient and unsettled; for a while we had to deal with an unusual number of false starts and abruptly interrupted takes," Keepnews recalled. That day, Sonny stuck entirely to standards—Noël Coward's "Someday I'll Find You," Tom Adair and Matt Dennis's "Will You Still Be Mine," and Al Dubin and Harry Warren's "Shadow Waltz"—and didn't mention anything to Keepnews about "The Freedom Suite," which would be the album's centerpiece.[13]

They did several takes of Meredith Willson's "Till There Was You," effectively as a bass-saxophone duo, with Max playing only on Pettiford's solo. "Till There Was You" eventually became a standard, but at that time, it was very new. Willson's *The Music Man*, where it originated, had opened on Broadway only two months earlier, and Sonny was only the sixth jazz artist to record the song in a studio.[14]

After the first day, Keepnews was fed up. His Riverside partner, Bill Grauer, would have to supervise the next date in March, with Keepnews "insisting that scheduling complications made it impossible for me to handle control room supervision on the second date," which he later regretted.[15]

Between sessions for *Freedom Suite*, Sonny's trio with Grimes and Dunlop was booked opposite Billie Holiday for Valentine's Day weekend at Joe De Luca's Red Hill Inn in Pennsauken, New Jersey, outside of Camden.[16] They alternated forty-minute sets from 9:20 p.m. until 2 a.m.[17] Lady Day had been on the bill at the Carnegie Hall Thanksgiving show, and Sonny had also been on the double bill with her in Chicago in 1950.

" 'She's so evocative; I've gotten so much training listening to Billie Holiday. Just listening to 'Lover Man,' " Sonny later said, "it evokes the song: This is what it is and this is how to play it. Not note for note, but this is the feeling you're supposed to have when you play it."[18] Sonny could do anything he wanted on the horn, but Holiday taught him how to imbue every note with feeling. "Her range was so narrow, but it's amazing that she could create so much emotion and so much musicality in that narrow range. She was pure music.... I think she could feel my love for her. She was a very sensitive woman. I didn't have to tell her. She knew. She just needed kindness."[19]

At the Red Hill Inn, Sonny and the band stayed at the Walt Whitman Hotel in Camden, as did Holiday. "It was tragic what the press did to her. How they vilified her," Sonny said. "It was really, really tragic." Part of that tragedy included her husband, Louis McKay, who notoriously beat her and stole her money. "He was okay to me," Sonny said, "but I saw Billie abused by some of the people she was working for."[20]

Sonny managed to befriend her. "She was sort of down on her luck at that point. She was still addicted and she had lost her cabaret card," Sonny said. On one occasion, probably after the Carnegie Hall concert, they shared a cab home. She took out a copy of her autobiography, *Lady Sings the Blues*, "and she autographed it and gave it to me, but she didn't really know me—know my music or anything. I was just a good guy, a good musician who revered her, but I didn't think she knew much about me.... It was a great honor for me to bring her home."[21] Holiday would pass away the following year; Sonny would always have that cab ride.

Sonny had previously recorded "Airegin" and "The House I Live In," but "The Freedom Suite"—not unlike Holiday's "Strange Fruit"—would be a far bolder statement.[22] It was for his Garveyite grandmother who took him to protests as a child, for his father, for Brownie, and for American culture as a whole. "It was an attempt to introduce some kind of black pride into the conversation of the time," Sonny said. "That was my history."[23]

"I think W. E. B. Du Bois once said that, 'It's the obligation of artists to be political,'" Sonny said. With the 1903 publication of *The Souls of Black Folk*, Sonny's childhood neighbor stated that "the problem of the Twentieth Century is the problem of the color-line."[24] Du Bois later admitted that he did not fully grasp at the time that unconscious bias was so powerful that it would remain a problem more than a half century later and beyond.[25] "There certainly was a racial divide problem in the Twentieth Century and there still is in the Twenty-first," Sonny later said.[26] His inability to rent an apartment in 1957, the inciting incident for "The Freedom Suite," exemplified Du Bois's concept of "double-consciousness"—"this sense of always looking at one's self through the eyes of others" that made it impossible "for a man to be both a Negro and an American without...having the doors of opportunity closed roughly in his face."[27] Sonny's "Freedom Suite" extended the tradition of the "sorrow songs," as Du Bois referred to them, James Reese Europe, Alain Locke, and James Weldon Johnson to the hard-bop era.[28]

That past September, Louis Armstrong—"Ambassador Satch"—had canceled a State Department tour of the Soviet Union in response to the government's refusal to enforce desegregation policies in support of the "Little Rock Nine." In an unprecedented show of public outrage, at least for Armstrong, he called President Eisenhower "two-faced," with "no guts," and described Arkansas governor Orval Faubus as "an uneducated plow boy," adding that "the way they are treating my people in the South, the government can go to hell....It's getting almost so bad a colored man hasn't got any country."[29] What was not evident to the State Department was evident to Armstrong—they had deployed jazz to fight oppression abroad, but they hadn't fought it at home. Six months after Armstrong rebuked Eisenhower, Sonny publicly joined the fight. "Outside of my specialty—music," Sonny said, "I was also in the whole world."[30]

Duke Ellington had composed a series of suites from *Liberian Suite* to the 1957 release of *Such Sweet Thunder*, and Sonny's "Freedom Suite" was also in that tradition. It heralded Sonny as a major composer in the jazz idiom. "It is my belief," wrote Benny Golson, a great composer in his own right, "that his compositions are worthy of being classified with those of Horace Silver, Gigi Gryce, John Lewis, George Russell, and Thelonious Monk."[31]

The piece is a nearly twenty-minute thematic work consisting of four movements developing from a four-bar motif. The first movement begins in 4/4 time and a major key; the second goes into 6/8 meter in a minor key, ending on a cadenza with an unresolved chord.[32] The other movements include a ballad and a final up-tempo theme that alternates between major and minor chords, culminating in a repeating four-bar drum fill. The effect is a synthesis of the first two movements' moods, all leading back to the essential rhythm; just because the arc of the moral universe bends back and forth in a dialectical dance doesn't mean it can't bend toward justice.[33]

Most of the piece was through-composed, but there was ample freedom, Sonny explained: "We had a lot of space to extemporize in the music."[34]

Sonny was surprised that Riverside supported the album. "I gained a lot of respect for Orrin Keepnews because he allowed me to do it at a time when there were no albums that I know of that put the music and the conditions of the black man together," Sonny said, despite the fact that Keepnews missed the recording session for "The Freedom Suite." "I don't think the other labels would have given me that freedom, so I respect him."[35]

On March 7, Bill Grauer met Sonny, Max Roach, and Oscar Pettiford at WOR Studios to record the title track. Max and Oscar had to sight-read the music. "We didn't know what was happening," Roach said. "The date simply grew organically. It's not something we planned or foresaw. The piece itself dictated what was supposed to happen at that particular moment. We were conscious of the piece as a vehicle that has input so that its personality and character would inspire us. You cannot just come in and do what your technique, no matter how great it is, feels like doing. You must respect the personality of a composition. Like Trane says, 'Sometimes it works, sometimes it don't.' And when it works you are the first to know. That day it worked."[36]

Sonny treated the packaging as an extension of the music. The high-contrast cover photo, taken by Riverside photographer Paul Weller with a design by Paul Bacon, depicted Sonny in profile, shirtless, like a regal African bust.[37] Lest anyone miss the message in the music, Sonny composed a pithy liner-notes statement: "I remember that I worked so hard to make sure that my syntax was correct, and yet I wanted my feelings to be clear," he said. "I really sweated over writing it!"[38] Sonny was as much of a perfectionist in writing as he was in music. He writes, crosses out, and rewrites the same passages over and over again, playing with the word choice and order as he goes.[39] Finally, he arrived at this polished piece of prose: "America is deeply rooted in Negro culture: its colloquialisms, its humor, its music. How ironic that the Negro, who more than any other people can claim America's culture as his own, is being persecuted and repressed, that the Negro, who has exemplified the humanities in his very existence, is being rewarded with inhumanity."[40]

Orrin Keepnews's liner notes were much more extensive—about fifteen hundred words—but not as piercing. He wrote that "The Freedom Suite" is "the heart of the record," a piece that "could turn out to be a jazz work of massive and lasting significance."[41]

On the completed album, "The Freedom Suite" took up side one; the standards were on side two. The Great American Songbook and "The Freedom Suite" were two sides of the same LP.

To Keepnews, "The Freedom Suite" was "not a piece about Emmett Till, or Little Rock, or Harlem, or the peculiar local election laws of Georgia or Louisiana, no more than it is about the artistic freedom of jazz. But it is concerned with all such things, as they are observed by this musician and as they react—emotionally and intellectually—upon him."[42] Yet Keepnews qualified his statement: "It is probably possible to enjoy the suite very much merely as nineteen minutes of fascinating variations on a theme by a superior improviser and two of the finest rhythm men in jazz."[43] To Sonny, the music and the struggle were inextricably linked, but he would soon find out that this oblivious listening practice was not uncommon.

When *Freedom Suite* came out that May, Riverside "took a lot of heat," Sonny said. He "took some heat for it as well." Of the seven-line statement on the back, Keepnews "even had to say at one time that he wrote the statement"— which Keepnews claimed on several occasions—"which is ridiculous."[44] In the *New York Times*, John S. Wilson characterized it as a "risky tour de force."[45] Other critics ignored the message altogether. "The meaning of freedom here," wrote Jack Maher in *Metronome*, "is something like free verse."[46]

The album did not sell well. "It was something that both Bill and Orrin wanted to do, because they were very, very liberal guys and they thought that that kind of thing would be great for the artists," recalled Robert Richer, who ran sales and promotion for the label. "Not particularly great for Riverside Records, but they felt that was something that needed to be done."[47]

The sales did not reflect its impact. "It wasn't like something that nobody knew about; it was a controversial record," Sonny said.[48] In 1962, Bill Grauer remastered the album and released it under his Jazzland label as *Shadow Waltz*, after a song on the initial release. On *Shadow Waltz*, Keepnews's liner notes, which Marxist critic and jazz historian Frank Kofsky referred to as a "virtual sea of equivocations and circumlocutions taking up about 1,500 words and almost three entire columns of print," remained intact, but Sonny's fifty-three-word statement was omitted. "The Freedom Suite" was side one of *Freedom Suite*, side two of *Shadow Waltz*. Keepnews explained that

Freedom Suite had "been withdrawn solely because it was not selling well," Kofsky wrote, and "it was re-released subsequently as *Shadow Waltz* in hopes that it would do better in the new format."[49] *Shadow Waltz* also got a new cover. Gone was the vibrant color, replaced by a black-and-white portrait of Sonny in a tuxedo. Yet the new cover, depicting Sonny staring solemnly into the distance, was reminiscent of another freedom writer who preceded him: Frederick Douglass.[50]

However, many got the message of *Freedom Suite*. To Art Farmer, it signified that "you can do anything in music so long as it sounds musical: instead of regarding melody, harmony, and rhythm as prisons, they use these elements for freedom. These three have reached the level of jazz musicianship where they are not imprisoned anymore."[51]

To Sonny, the album was never about sales, just sending a message, and there was a ripple effect.[52] Songs like Charles Mingus's 1959 "Fables of Faubus," Nina Simone's 1963 anthem "Mississippi Goddam," and John Coltrane's "Alabama" would follow. "The Freedom Suite" directly inspired Max Roach and Abbey Lincoln's *We Insist! Max Roach's Freedom Now Suite*, recorded in 1960. Recording *Freedom Suite* with Sonny, Roach said, "gave me the strength to keep on keepin' on."[53]

The album fulfilled a dream: as Sonny had foretold in his high school yearbook, he had finally become "A second Paul Robeson."[54]

During an interview for the *New York Age* at the Continental in Brooklyn, Sonny mused on some of the themes that enlivened *Freedom Suite*.[55] "Jazz isn't widely accepted, because it signifies freedom and democracy," Sonny said. "Jazz is integrated. Many people just won't accept this, so they reject the music."[56] The interview closed with Sonny enumerating the pitfalls of being a contemporary jazz musician. "Jazz is an unstable business. You've got to do a lot of cross-country hopping; you have to keep late hours; your diet is mainly black coffee, and sometimes you don't even know where you will open next."

On Sunday, March 16, Sonny performed at an all-star benefit at the Black

Pearl on the Upper East Side[57] for drummer Mel Zelman, who was injured in a car crash.[58] During an interview on a set break in Rochester's Ridge Crest Inn,[59] Sonny discussed what he would one day refer to as his search for the "lost chord"[60] and his intention to take a sabbatical from performing to find it. Sonny was not satisfied with his playing and planned to go to Europe that spring to focus on technique, writing, and overall presentation. He hoped to study at the Paris Conservatory. "I'm searching for a sound, a certain sound," he said. "I've got it up here, but I've got to get away and work it out."[61] Sonny would return to the United States, and to performing, he said, if and only if he found what he was looking for. Eventually, he would make good on this promise.

Sonny reconnected with someone who'd helped him get closer to that sound: Monk. Sonny was part of a sextet on a recording session for Riverside on February 25, with Art Blakey, Wilbur Ware, Johnny Griffin, and Donald Byrd. However, Monk apparently never booked Sonny and Blakey. "Both later insisted to me quite convincingly that they never had been told," said Orrin Keepnews.[62]

Sonny also searched for a sound at Baroness Nica de Koenigswarter's Bauhaus estate on top of the Palisades, which she purchased from film director Josef von Sternberg.[63] "When she first bought that house, I played my horn in every one of the rooms to see the sound," Sonny said. "To know which room jelled, sound-wise." Nica dubbed it "the Pad," but soon it had another name, "the Cat House," a double entendre for the jazz musicians who frequented it and the overwhelming preponderance of actual cats there. "The Baroness loved her cats. I love cats, too," Sonny said. He saw Coleman Hawkins, Monk, and other pianists like Garland Wilson and Eddie Heywood: "It was like a boulevard of great artists."[64] There was a Steinway upstairs and a Ping-Pong table in the dining room, where Monk demonstrated his mastery of rhythm by playing for long stretches and beating almost anyone audacious enough to take him on.[65]

Nica's relationship with Sonny was not always purely platonic. "I had a brief relationship with the baroness," Sonny said.[66]

At around this time, she began asking the denizens of the Cat House what their three wishes would be if they could have anything in the world. Sonny's response would prove prescient:

1. Money.
2. To be able to do what I want to do on the horn.
3. To have a closer affinity with nature.[67]

The Rollins trio opened at the Showboat in Philadelphia on March 31, then on April 17, they returned to Birdland for a week opposite Maynard Ferguson.[68] Soon thereafter, Ferguson offered Frankie Dunlop a job, and he took it.[69] For Sonny, a series of festival appearances and all-star concerts followed: a weeklong stint as part of the Spring Jazz Festival at the Black Pearl on the Upper East Side, a "Cavalcade of Jazz" at Philadelphia's Town Hall headlined by Dinah Washington and the Modern Jazz Quartet, and at Carnegie Hall opposite Ferguson, Helen Merrill, Billy Taylor, Art Blakey and the Jazz Messengers, and the Max Roach Quintet.[70]

As critical consensus began to build around Sonny (*Down Beat*'s Dom Cerulli wrote a major profile, while Whitney Balliett identified Coltrane as "a student of Sonny Rollins"),[71] he reiterated that he was contemplating a sabbatical. "Maybe what I need is some rehearsals to snap me out of the doldrums," he said. "I think I react better to adversity. I like to fight, in a way of speaking. Right now, I feel I just want to get away for a while. I think I need a lot of things. One of them is time...time to study and finish some things I started a long time ago." One of these things was a concerto for tenor, a project he put on hold when he joined the Brown-Roach Quintet; it would take another three decades.[72] "I think if I could go to Europe...or even get away from the New York scene for a while, I could assess things, judge myself more objectively."[73]

There were simply too many distractions for Sonny to practice how he wanted. "If you can take ten minutes and study with complete concentration, it's sometimes worth more than a longer time of less intense concentration," Sonny said.[74] "I practice chords, tonguing exercises, tone exercises. I try to do a little bit of everything. I find that if I practice exercises, it helps whatever

I'm doing. Exercises are no different than playing at Carnegie Hall. It's all the same."[75]

That spring, with Sonny's career on the rise, he reconnected with Lester Young, who was in decline, having sunk deep into drink and depression. "He kept drinking because of the reputation and the attitude that they had towards him and the promoters had towards him," recalled drummer Willie Jones. Harold Lovett, Miles Davis's lawyer, told Jones that Pres wanted to move into the Alvin Hotel, where he could "look down Broadway and look at Birdland."[76] Jones took Pres to Max Roach's house on Willoughby Avenue in Brooklyn, and from there they went to check Pres into the Alvin.[77] Max, Miles, Papa Jo Jones, and Sonny paid the rent.[78]

At the Alvin, Pres waxed philosophical. "If you can think of a godly person, and you're drinking some Gordon's gin, if you could put those two together, then you've got Lester Young," Sonny said.[79] "We would talk about his career and the things that went against him because of his color. I said to myself that I don't want to end up like Pres, drinking, you know, and have people taking advantage of me—not being able to take care of my affairs. I was determined to do a lot of positive things in life because of being around Lester. I learned life isn't just about music, that you really have to know what to do when you are off that bandstand. It's not just about being a gifted artist. It's also about being a person that stands up."[80]

On Sunday, July 6, Sonny made his debut at the Fifth Annual Newport Jazz Festival in Freebody Park.[81] Sonny's performance was not included in Bert Stern and Aram Avakian's classic concert film *Jazz on a Summer's Day*, which captured the convivial atmosphere, in which seersucker suits and America's Cup yachts met the sound of Thelonious Monk.[82] General admission tickets cost only $1.50.

The festival presented a wide range of artists: Louis Armstrong, Duke Ellington, the new Max Roach Quintet, Benny Goodman, Anita O'Day, Mahalia Jackson, Chico Hamilton, Ray Charles, and Chuck Berry among them.[83] The 2:30 p.m. Sunday-afternoon concert, billed as "An Afternoon of Modern Jazz," featured the Rollins Trio with Henry Grimes and Roy Haynes, the Thelonious Monk trio, the Horace Silver Quintet, the

Tony Scott Quintet, Anita O'Day, Billy Taylor, Sonny Stitt and Sal Salvador, J. J. Johnson, and Lee Konitz.[84] Demonstrating his versatility, the twenty-two-year-old Grimes played with six groups: Monk, Sonny, Benny Goodman, Lee Konitz, Tony Scott, and Gerry Mulligan.

Despite the heat, Sonny came out in a suit and tie and sweated through two tunes: "Moritat" and "I Want to Be Happy," the latter of which was recorded.[85] "Happy" came at 320 beats a minute. Still tonguing most of his notes on his frenetic eighth-note runs and wailing in the upper register, Sonny played chorus after chorus, taking it way out but always returning to the melody with Grimes and Haynes following him wherever he went, culminating in a tempestuous trading section with Haynes.[86]

On July 10, Sonny made his major label recording debut as a leader on MetroJazz, a new division of MGM Records, which had signed him that June. Leonard Feather handled A&R; the first two artists he signed were Sonny and pianist Toshiko Akiyoshi.[87] "I still like the idea of a trio, but I would like to make records with a larger group," Sonny said earlier that year.[88] *Sonny Rollins and the Big Brass* gave him the opportunity to do both.

The first session at Beltone Studios in Manhattan began with the trio. Henry Grimes was on bass; on drums, Sonny got Specs Wright, whom he had heard at Philadelphia's Town Hall earlier that May. Instead of his usual Mark VI, Sonny played a King Super 20 Silversonic on the session, which gave his tone more bite. Sonny recorded "What's My Name?"—a Latin tune that was part of the repertoire of Jeri Southern, with whom Sonny had recently shared a bill at Birdland. The trio also recorded "If You Were the Only Girl in the World," a standard that had recently been performed in *The Bridge on the River Kwai* (1957), which had just won the Oscar for Best Picture. The last tune they played as a trio that day was "Manhattan." Sonny then played "Body and Soul" on unaccompanied tenor in a clear homage to Coleman Hawkins.

On July 11, this time at Metropolitan Studios, Sonny returned for the big-band session, orchestrated by thirty-eight-year-old saxophonist and arranger Ernie Wilkins.[89] "I knew I would never become another Sonny Rollins or John Coltrane," Wilkins said, but he could arrange for them.[90] Sonny was backed by a twelve-piece big band: Nat Adderley on cornet; Reunald Jones, Ernie Royal, and Clark Terry on trumpet; Billy Byers, Jimmy

Cleveland, and Frank Rehak on trombone; Don Butterfield adding ballast on tuba; and a rhythm section of Grimes, Roy Haynes, pianist Dick Katz, and guitarist René Thomas.[91] Thomas was "a Belgian guitar player that I like better than any of the Americans I've heard," Sonny told Leonard Feather when they were discussing the personnel.[92]

There were four big-band tunes—"Who Cares," "Love Is a Simple Thing," Sonny's "Grand Street" (named for his current address), and Wilkins's "Far Out East," a playful response to "Way Out West." On Sonny's part, which was labeled "Sonny" instead of "Tenor," before each solo section it read "Blow!"[93] And Sonny blew![94]

As Sonny sought more solitude in his professional life, he wanted more stability in his personal life. Earlier in the year, he reunited with Shirley Carter, whom he had met in Detroit in the summer of 1956. She would periodically come to New York to visit her cousin who was a student at Columbia University, her "adopted big brother" Donald Byrd, and Byrd's wife. It was probably when the Rollins trio was back at Birdland for the last two weeks in July that he met up with Donald Byrd and saw Shirley again. Soon, they were romantically involved. Carter recalled that Donald Byrd would "be coming to the club checking on me...to see if I was really where I said I was going. It was really funny. I used to just harass him: 'Daddy's gotta take care of me, huh?'"[95]

On August 4, Sonny took Shirley to see the Duke Ellington Orchestra play on a boat cruise and dance on the Hudson.[96] It departed the 125th Street pier in Harlem at 9 p.m. and returned at 1:30 a.m.[97] "Now you're talkin' about a sound," Carter recalled of the band. "It was absolutely magical... and Sonny was so thrilled....He was so excited to be able to go on this boat with Duke Ellington, it even surprised me! But that's how humble he was. He wasn't arrogant."[98]

Soon they were in love. "He's a very nice, warm person if you know him. He's not nasty or mean," she recalled. "Some people get their heads out of whack when they get too much attention....He's a gentleman, and he's absorbed in his music, but not to the point that he's obnoxious. Some of them just didn't see anything else. He saw *everything* else, but he stayed on course for what he wanted." She thought of him as a great example to others, but despite having gotten clean, exercising regularly, and keeping a healthy diet, Sonny felt resigned to the fate of Bird. "He used to talk about some of the things he did when he was younger: 'I'm probably going to die young because I abused my body when I was younger.' "[99]

A week after the Ellington boat cruise, Sonny got a call from Art Kane, the art director at *Seventeen*. He wanted Sonny to meet him and some other jazz musicians at 17 East 126th Street in Harlem at 10 a.m. on August 12 to pose for a group portrait for *Esquire*'s "Golden Age of Jazz" issue. Kane had never worked as a professional photographer—he didn't have a studio, and his assistant had never loaded a camera—but he had an idea to "start the story off with a gigantic spread whereby we get together every jazz musician we can possibly assemble."[100]

It was ambitious. Gather several generations of jazz musicians, same time, same place: from Luckey Roberts, born in 1887, to Sonny, the youngest pictured, born more than four decades later. To art director Robert Benton, it was "like planning D-Day."[101] It seemed unlikely that any working jazz musicians would show up for a group photo at a Harlem brownstone on a Tuesday morning at 10. One musician claimed facetiously that he was "astonished to discover that there were two ten o'clocks in each day."[102] "I still don't know how he called all of those guys and got them together, and they all came," Sonny said of Kane.[103] The fifty-seven musicians sensed history in the making, or at least an early-morning block party.

" 'I remember that day,' " he later told his childhood neighbor Doris Mason. " 'You see I'm on the end? I almost missed that picture, 'cause I got there late.' "[104] Fortunately, almost everyone else did, too. "It was an honor," Sonny said. "It was my saxophone idol Coleman Hawkins. Then there was also my other idol, Lester Young. There was Art Blakey, the great drummer. And the women who were represented—there was Mary Lou Williams and Marian McPartland. Miles Davis was out of town, and John Coltrane was out of town. And I think Duke Ellington was out of town. But everybody that was in New York seemed to be there."[105]

Kane turned the day's *New York Times* into a megaphone and stood across the street as everyone got in formation. It wasn't until about 2 p.m. when the kibitzing finally stopped and the stragglers returned from a corner bar; Willie "the Lion" Smith came but was still at the bar when the shutter finally clicked.[106]

Most people smiled; Sonny did not. It was hot and humid—temperatures in the eighties—but everyone was dressed to the nines for posterity's sake.[107] Mingus stared down the camera, a cigarette hanging out of his mouth. There was Pres in his porkpie; Blakey wore a bow tie; Monk and Sonny are the only ones in sunglasses.[108] "After the picture was taken," recalled Buck Clayton, "we all went to Minton's Playhouse and hung around there until 3 o'clock in the afternoon. Then we went home."[109]

To Sonny, it had broad social significance. "Jazz had been seen as a bunch of ghoulish characters that came up after it got dark, like Dracula-type people who went into these night clubs," Sonny said.[110] "Suddenly, we were being seen the way we saw ourselves."[111]

"A Great Day in Harlem" led *Esquire*'s January 1959 "Golden Age of Jazz."[112] John Clellon Holmes contributed an essay called "Time Present," Ralph Ellison contributed a now-classic essay titled "Golden Age, Time Past," and an array of musicians gave their thoughts in "Time Future"—Monk, Brubeck, John Lewis, Roger Sessions, Willie "the Lion" Smith, Gerry Mulligan, Duke Ellington, and Sonny.

"The man who is most influential at this point is Sonny Rollins," said Mulligan. "Rollins has evolved a very individual approach to rhythm. It is interesting to observe how he has developed because he used to be a much, much harder player, and I have noticed in the last year or so, especially, he is playing much more gentle and soft."[113]

To Sonny, the future was in the past. "Nothing is new," Sonny said. "At the same time there are new things...it's paradoxical." Of those making it new, he named Monk, Bud Powell, John Coltrane, Frank Foster, and Lee Morgan; John Lewis, Gil Evans, J. J. Johnson, Benny Golson, and Nelson Riddle as composers. On a social level, Sonny had expected jazz to be "taken out of the night clubs" by 1958. "I would like to see it on a concert stage represented with the same dignity with which classical music is being represented today," he said. At the time, jazz concerts generally restricted each act to two or three tunes. "The force of the music itself is breaking it down."

On August 14, Sonny went to the Five Spot to see Thelonious Monk receive an award for his recent win in the piano category of the *Down Beat* International Jazz Critics Poll; Erroll Garner, Miles Davis, and Art Blakey were also in attendance.[114] Sonny came in second in the tenor category, with fifty-nine votes, as Stan Getz continued his reign with sixty-four; Ben Webster and Coleman Hawkins followed; in fifth place was John Coltrane.

After leaving the Five Spot that night, Sonny played Birdland, where he began a three-week stint, initially opposite vocalist Chris Connor, then Maynard Ferguson.[115] On Friday, August 22, Sonny also donned a tuxedo for the third annual New York Jazz Festival on Randalls Island, playing for a crowd of twelve thousand.[116]

On Sunday, August 31, Sonny was the guest soloist with the Modern Jazz Quartet—Percy Heath, John Lewis, Milt Jackson, and Connie Kay—at the Music Barn in Lenox, Massachusetts,[117] their first meeting since *Sonny Rollins with the Modern Jazz Quartet*.[118] The concert concluded the fourth season of the festival and also the program at the School of Jazz, whose faculty included Bob Brookmeyer, Kenny Dorham, Jimmy Giuffre, Lee Konitz, and Max Roach.[119] For twenty-three-year-old pianist Ran Blake, one of the thirty-three students at the school, the concert, and the whole summer in general, was transformative.

"It really was a profound experience being there," Blake said. "Everybody was one large family."[120] To Blake, "Sonny Rollins and Coltrane were in a special shrine." Later on, he had a brief meeting with Coltrane at Gunther Schuller's apartment; they spoke for three minutes. "'Oh, it's so good to meet you, sir,'" Blake said. "'You and Sonny mean a lot to me.' And he said, 'But what about our fathers? Don't forget about Ben, Hawk, and Pres.' I just remember Trane's warmth talking about Sonny."[121]

Hundreds came out for the Music Inn concert. The performance was recorded and subsequently released on two albums by MetroJazz and Atlantic.[122] Milt Jackson, who went by Bags, naturally played on "Bags' Groove," and also on "A Night in Tunisia," in which you can hear Sonny shouting, "Yeah, Bags!"[123]

On September 19, Sonny reunited with Monk at the Five Spot, a burgers, fried chicken, and coleslaw saloon right next to Cooper Union. It was run by brothers Joe and Iggy Termini; their Sicilian father, Salvatore Termini, opened the no-frills dive, which was originally called the Bowery Café, in 1937. When the Termini brothers took over, they changed the name to the No. 5 Bar; in August 1956, they applied for a cabaret license and renamed it the Five Spot.[124]

The cramped stage barely rose off the ground; a cluttered bulletin board advertising Village happenings served as a backdrop. Sounds bounced off the tin ceilings, wooden bar tables and chairs, smoke curling through the room.[125] Waiters in white shirts and black bow ties served drinks, and a clamp light on the piano illuminated the performers. The club had no cover and no minimum; anyone in the Village could wander in. Pitchers of beer were only seventy-five cents.[126] It could accommodate only seventy-five people, but it was often at or over capacity.[127]

That November, the Terminis booked their first act: Cecil Taylor. The club became a haven for avant-garde experimentation and soon became "the center of the jazz world!" wrote Amiri Baraka, then LeRoi Jones.[128] Baraka and the Beat Generation luminaries Allen Ginsberg, Gregory Corso, Jack Kerouac, and Ted Joans rubbed elbows with abstract expressionists Willem de Kooning, Larry Rivers, and Grace Hartigan. The Jazz Baroness and her Bentley were a ubiquitous presence. The club was open nightly, but the headliner usually had Monday nights off. So Mondays at 9:30 p.m. they had regular poetry readings backed by a jazz band; Langston Hughes read there once with Charles Mingus.[129]

In July 1957, Thelonious Monk began a six-month residency, starting his set somewhere between 9:30 p.m. and midnight.[130] The Terminis couldn't afford to pay much, but better-paying clubs were loath to book experimental jazz. "Nobody had money in those days," recalled Termini. "[Local] 802 gave us a low scale—seventy-six dollars a week for a sideman, ninety for a leader. The Monk quartet got eight hundred a week. That was a lot for us."[131] In reality, Monk only earned $600 a week, taking $225 for himself and giving each sideman $125.[132]

In the spring of 1958, Monk returned to the Five Spot with bassist Ahmed Abdul-Malik, Roy Haynes on drums, and rotating saxophonists.[133] When Johnny Griffin quit in September—he claimed the money wasn't good enough—Monk hired Charlie Rouse, but there was a two-week gap before Rouse was available.[134] At that point, Sonny wouldn't ordinarily work for just shy of $21 a night, but he did it for Monk, playing in the band September 19 to October 1.

Monk often performed with a cigarette hanging out of his mouth, a cocktail and a glass of water perched on the piano. The club had no dress code, but Monk expected his band to have style; Sonny wore a suit and tie with a pocket square. "We played together with Monk for a minute at the Five Spot," recalled Roy Haynes of this time with Sonny. "I remember one night, Monk said to me, 'Roy Haynes. You play better when you wear that suit.'"[135]

One night, twenty-one-year-old trombonist Grachan Moncur III, who had first played with Sonny at Sugar Hill in Newark, sat in with Monk. "Sonny told Monk to let me sit in," Moncur recalled. "I played a couple of notes with him, and I remember after, me and Monk was standing outside and I said, 'Monk, you mind if I sit in on the next set?' Monk says, 'No, not this time. You don't know the arrangements, man.' I said, 'Man, this is a nice guy. He's just letting me down nice. He knows I don't have the experience.' I knew I wasn't as good as these cats, but I knew I wanted to be as good as these cats, and I just wanted to get my feet wet, see how it felt, or how long I could last with them."[136]

On September 20, Sonny and Monk played a benefit concert at Carnegie Hall for Mary Lou Williams's nonprofit Bel Canto Foundation, planned as a rehabilitation center in the country to help musicians struggling with addiction.[137] She booked as much jazz star power as she could, Lester Young, Ben Webster, and the Monk Quartet among them. However, the concert was a flop; Williams's dream of a retreat for musicians was never realized.[138]

Around this time, Sonny proposed to Shirley Carter, and she said yes. He was still legally married to Dawn Finney, but he intended to finalize the divorce on his upcoming California tour.

Having finished his run with Monk, Sonny flew to the West Coast for the inaugural Monterey Jazz Festival.[139] It took place from Friday to Sunday, October 3–5, at the Monterey County Fairgrounds, a twenty-acre plot in the small seaside city of about twenty thousand. The population boomed temporarily as the festival welcomed about twenty-one thousand attendees to the outdoor six-thousand-seat amphitheater.[140] The intergenerational lineup included Dizzy Gillespie, Louis Armstrong, the Max Roach Quintet, Billie Holiday, and Sonny.[141]

Yet for some, the festival highlight took place outside the fairgrounds, only a ten-minute drive away at the historic Mission Ranch in Carmel.[142] It usually hosted events like a "Hillbilly Hoedown" or a lecture by conservative congressman Charles Teague at a Young Republicans dinner.[143] But on October 4, it hosted a jam session with Sonny Rollins and Gerry Mulligan.[144]

Sonny and Gerry shared a mutual admiration. Mulligan had recently named Sonny as the pinnacle of modern jazz in the *Esquire* article that accompanied "A Great Day in Harlem." Sonny sent Gerry a congratulatory letter on his "beautiful collaboration" with Thelonious Monk on *Mulligan Meets Monk*, their 1957 album on Riverside.[145]

The jam session at Mission Ranch began with Mulligan, tenor saxophonist Brew Moore, and trumpeter Dickie Mills in a take-no-prisoners blowing session with drummer Ernie Sheriff anchoring the local rhythm section. After Mulligan outblew Moore, he announced that Sonny was "in the house," according to drummer Richard Barker, who was there. A moment later, Sonny took the stand.[146] They played an up-tempo blues, and Gerry and Sonny started trading twos, fours, sixes, then eights. Sonny then took over, playing so fast "you expected his saxophone to explode and spray shiny brass keys across the room," Barker wrote. "He was as impassive and as assured as a statue of Buddha. Around the room the whisper ran, *Sonny knows*."

Gerry could hardly keep up—few could. He answered Sonny's feverish choruses with a "semi-Dixie-honk-cum-Bud-Freeman style." Sonny just smiled, but Gerry was shaking his head. Sonny then "showed him some neglected ideas. 'See,' his choruses seemed to say, 'you forgot this, and this, and this.'" Someone in the audience started yelling and clapping, and Mulligan gave him the middle finger in time with the beat, then "Sonny blew two more incredible choruses in time to the moving finger." Then Gerry walked offstage with the baritone and returned with Brew Moore's tenor, where "for a few minutes Gerry Mulligan did not exist; he was a tenor saxophone with fingers."

Sonny called "Anthropology," Charlie Parker's "rhythm changes," and counted it off way up. This time, Gerry didn't even accept the challenge. He picked up a trumpet, to no avail. As if emphasizing the point, Sonny quoted "Doin' What Comes Natur'lly" from *Annie Get Your Gun*. Sonny then called "Will You Still Be Mine," the standard he recorded on *Freedom Suite*. After Sonny played six choruses, Mulligan answered, but then Sonny came back in even stronger; he was just getting started. Mulligan gave up. He walked off the stage behind a partition, "sprawled out on the floor on his back, his legs drawn up, the baritone on his chest. His hands were under his head, his eyes were shut and he had a big smile on his face. Somebody leaned over him. . . . Mulligan answered him without opening his eyes. 'Man, will you please get the hell away from me? Let me listen to the music.' "[147]

Gerry would have another opportunity. The next night, Sunday, October 5, the festival closed with an all-star jam session at the fairgrounds as planes passed overhead.[148] The climactic jam began at 12:20 a.m., three and a half hours into the concert.[149] The group consisted of Dizzy Gillespie, Benny Carter, Gerry Mulligan, Buddy DeFranco, Ray Draper on tuba, and Gillespie's rhythm section—pianist Junior Mance, bassist Sam Jones, drummer Lex Humphries, and guitarist Les Spann. Sonny took the mike. "Benny Carter. The very great Benny Carter," he said. "Benny Carter!"[150]

Sonny called "I Want to Be Happy," stood in front of the mike in his three-piece suit, counted it off at a brisk pace, and closed his eyes. No other horns jumped in at first. It was a chilly fall night, but as Sonny threw in quotes from "St. Thomas," he was giving off heat. He played continuously for nine and a half minutes.[151] Mulligan then entered for a few bars, followed by Dizzy. It was a free-for-all until Benny Carter entered the fray, and in three lyrical choruses brought everyone home. It ended gloriously just after 1 a.m.[152]

Sonny found it all invigorating. "The energy at Monterey is great, man!" Sonny later recalled. "I remember so many instances there when it was like being carried on an ocean, lifted up. When I play there I tend to get engulfed in something."[153]

From Monterey, Sonny was booked from October 7 to 19 at Art Auerbach's Jazz Workshop in North Beach for his San Francisco debut.[154] Sonny used a pickup band—always a gamble—but Elmo Hope was available, so it was a nice reunion with an old friend. Sonny also had drummer Lenny McBrowne, who had recently relocated to the Bay Area when he landed there on tour with Paul Bley, and twenty-two-year-old bass prodigy Scott LaFaro.

LaFaro was a Sonny Rollins nut and honed the lucid upper-register playing, harmonic inventiveness, and rhythmic bounce he would become known for by transcribing Sonny's recorded solos. "I think horn players and pianists have probably influenced me the most," LaFaro said. "Miles Davis, Coltrane,

Bill Evans, and Sonny perhaps deepest of all. Sonny is technically good, harmonically imaginative, and really creative. He uses all he knows to make finished music when he improvises."[155] LaFaro would die in a car crash at twenty-five, less than three years later, but would become a widely influential voice on the bass.

Sonny himself was "trying not to be too much aware of being an influence, but it's sometimes disconcerting and it's an added responsibility," Sonny said. "I do have some friends, I know, but it puts more pressure on me and I feel I have to produce. Much more pressure than when I was a sideman."[156]

Also at the Jazz Workshop was saxophonist Kermit Scott. Scotty was an unsung hero of the bebop generation regarded by Dizzy Gillespie, Dexter Gordon, and Thelonious Monk as foundational to the art form, though he eventually became a Bay Area longshoreman.[157] Sonny was aware of Scotty through his stately solo on Billie Holiday's 1940 recording of "Falling in Love Again." Scotty could play forever—like a whale never coming up for air—using a technique called circular breathing.[158] Scotty "was known at that time as 'One-Note Scotty,' because he would use that circular breathing during his performances," Sonny recalled. "So I said, 'Hey man, teach me how to do that, man!' So he taught me how to circular breathe. We really got to be good friends."[159] In his notes, Sonny referred to it as "Scotty breathing."[160]

Next, Sonny went down to Los Angeles, where he had a recording date at Contemporary for *Sonny Rollins and the Contemporary Leaders*.[161] Sonny got bassist Leroy Vinnegar,[162] drummer Shelly Manne from *Way Out West*, pianist Hampton Hawes, guitarist Barney Kessel, and British vibraphonist Victor Feldman.[163] The album was recorded at Contemporary's Melrose studio from Monday to Wednesday, October 20–22, 1958. Since the band was formed exclusively for the record, Sonny chose all standards, albeit obscure. If they didn't know a song, Sonny brought lead sheets.[164] The first session began with "I've Found a New Baby," the standard made famous by Bing Crosby, Ethel Waters, and Charlie Christian, whose brief solo on the Benny Goodman version was canonical. They recorded at least eight takes, not all complete.[165] On one take, Manne was struggling to contend with Sonny's booming tone in the shipping room/recording studio. "You got any more earplugs left?" Sonny asked the engineer.

"Every time Sonny starts blowing," said Manne.

"That sounds like the people I play for every night," Sonny retorted. But this gentle ribbing was all in good fun, and continued into the virtuosic trading—never released—between Sonny and Barney Kessel and then Sonny and Shelly on the next take. The take that made it onto the album was shorter than the others (three and a half minutes) and had no trading. Sonny plays more than a whole chorus hanging almost entirely on one note, demonstrating how much he could do with rhythm alone.

Next, Sonny turned to what must have been another lead sheet from the sheaf in his case, an original that didn't make it onto the final album—it would later become known as "Alfie's Theme." Barney Kessel tore through the descending minor-chord progression before the take eventually broke down into idle conversation. The tune would not materialize on any recordings until 1965.

Sonny then recorded "The Song Is You," associated with Frank Sinatra, though he probably knew it more from Charlie Parker's repertoire.[166] The first take was done at about 240 beats per minute. "Hold it, hold it, hold it!" Sonny yelled after three minutes. He counted it off at about 280. Sonny wasn't getting into it, though. He began quoting "Bewitched, Bothered, and Bewildered," another Sinatra tune, to perform his bewilderment. Kessel and Feldman played fine solos until Sonny wrapped it up with one final chorus. The thirteen-minute take never caught fire. "Well, that's not it, I know," Sonny said. They decided to call it a day.

On October 21, not everyone showed up on time, so Sonny warmed up with a low-key "How High the Moon," which wound up on the record.[167] When everyone arrived, they started with a ten-minute take of "I've Found a New Baby," then moved onto "I've Told Ev'ry Little Star," another Jerome Kern song, doing several takes. "Rock a Bye Your Baby with a Dixie Melody" was an odd pick—the minstrel song was popularized by Al Jolson, who sang it in blackface in the 1918 Broadway production of *Sinbad*. It was a top-ten hit for Jerry Lewis in 1956, later performed by Nat King Cole, Sammy Davis Jr., and Aretha Franklin. Sonny thought of it as a "humorous sort of thing."[168]

They then recorded several takes of "Alone Together," before returning to

"The Song Is You." There were many more takes—one at 300 beats per minute, another at a dizzying 420 beats per minute—and one of the faster takes made the album.[169]

Sonny then turned to "In the Chapel in the Moonlight," the album's sole ballad. Manne sat this one out, perhaps to give his arms a rest after "The Song Is You." Sonny wasn't satisfied with how it was coming off; he kept saying, "One more."[170] They did more than ten partial and complete takes, all unsatisfying to Sonny.

They came back the next day and recorded at least eight takes of "You," from the soundtrack to *The Great Ziegfeld*, the 1936 Oscar winner for Best Picture. This was Victor Feldman's only appearance on the album.[171] There were yet more takes of "Alfie's Theme" and "I've Found a New Baby" before calling it quits.[172] At the end of the session, Sonny wasn't satisfied. His perfectionism in the recording studio would persist for the rest of his career.

Amiri Baraka dismissed *Contemporary Leaders* as "shallow and superfluous."[173] Yet for Sonny, sometimes good press could be even worse than bad. That November, the inaugural issue of the *Jazz Review*, edited by Nat Hentoff and Martin Williams, featured Art Farmer's rave review of *Freedom Suite*. But it was the lead story that caught his attention: "Sonny Rollins and the Challenge of Thematic Improvisation" by Gunther Schuller.[174]

According to Schuller, Sonny was the next in a lineage including Louis Armstrong, Coleman Hawkins, Lester Young, Charlie Parker and Dizzy Gillespie, Miles Davis, and the MJQ—Sonny's heroes. "Today we have reached another juncture in the constantly unfolding evolution of improvisation and the central figure of this present renewal is Sonny Rollins," Schuller wrote. "With Rollins thematic and structural unity have at last achieved the importance in *pure* improvisation that elements such as swing, melodic conception, and originality of expression have already enjoyed for many years."

Schuller took as his case study "Blue 7," Sonny's improvised blues from *Saxophone Colossus*. The bitonal theme became a "fountainhead" that was developed on that day in 1956, and the recording itself would become a fountainhead for generations of musicians trying to figure out how he achieved such a clear sense of thematic unity on the spot.[175] To Schuller, Sonny's ability to offer theme and variation on the melody for more than a dozen choruses was indicative of his genius. "Such structural cohesiveness—without sacrificing expressiveness and rhythmic drive or swing—one has come to expect from the composer who spends days or weeks writing a given passage," Schuller wrote. "It is another matter to achieve this in an on-the-spur-of-the-moment extemporization." He compared Sonny to "Mozart, Shakespeare, Rembrandt..." and concluded Sonny's thematic approach was ultimately more significant than Charlie Parker's or Lester Young's.[176]

To Sonny, being described in such exalted terms deepened his insecurity that he was not living up to his burnished reputation.[177] "When I read that I was sort of taken aback, because I didn't know what I was doing!" Sonny later said. "Of course, now I understand more about what improvisation is. But back then, it was like, 'So this is what I'm doing?' It made me self-conscious about playing. It took me a while to get over that....People like Gunther Schuller are analytical, which is fine, but I'm a little bit more of a primitive!"[178]

Sonny understood better than anyone the exhaustive practice that was necessary to do what he did, but what he did not understand, and what could not be dissected through analysis, was where the creative spark came from. "When I play, what I try to do is to reach my subconscious level," Sonny later said. "I don't want to overtly think about anything, because you can't think and play at the same time—believe me, I've tried it. It goes by too fast. So when you're into yoga and when you're into improvisation, you want to reach that other level."[179] High-level cognition was necessary to reach that level, but when Sonny hit the stage he entered a flow state and needed to have anything technical under his fingers to avoid getting tripped up, the saxophone a direct extension of his consciousness.[180]

Sonny was playing so much during this period that he had little time to think. While debuting in Los Angeles at the Jazz Cabaret in late October, Sonny also had to attend to his divorce and his proposal to Shirley Carter.[181] After closing in LA, he flew back to the East Coast, where he could barely catch his breath before embarking on his highest-profile tour to date.

Chapter 21

THE ROAD

(1958)

The third annual "Jazz for Moderns" tour in November 1958 had one tour bus, four groups, and thirty concerts in twenty-four days, spanning Toronto, the Northeast, the Midwest, and the South.[1] When it was possible, Sonny drove his new Cadillac with the classic fishtail fenders, just like he had once seen Coleman Hawkins drive through Sugar Hill.[2] "It was like driving a feather," Sonny said.[3] Mostly, though, he rode the bus. "I made good friends on that tour," Sonny recalled. "Paul Desmond and I became good friends. I remember he was the guy that introduced me to Pepto-Bismol, because when you're on the road, you eat all sorts of crap, so he said, 'Oh man, here, try this.' And it actually worked, so to this day I carry Pepto-Bismol in my briefcase."[4]

The four acts were represented by Joe Glaser's Associated Booking—the Dave Brubeck Quartet, Maynard Ferguson Orchestra, the Four Freshmen, and the Sonny Rollins Trio. Leonard Feather emceed, and the producer was Ed Sarkesian, "an amiable, honest, nervous man from Detroit" who owned the Rouge Lounge.[5] Sarkesian's business partner, "Honest John" Srabian, sold glossy souvenir programs for a dollar.[6] The program had bios of every bandleader in the order in which they would appear: Rollins, Ferguson, Brubeck, and the Freshmen. Sonny got two pages; Ferguson got three; the Freshmen got six; Brubeck got eight. Sonny's bio concluded with his future plans: "Find a place to settle, study, and work for my bachelor's degree in Music"—a world apart from life on the road.

Sonny hired bassist Henry Grimes and drummer Kenny Dennis. "The smaller the group, the more difficult the blend, because you only have a few voices, so you've got to make those voices really connect," recalled Dennis.[7] Being on the road was never easy. "Even if you have a plush bus or custom-made transportation, one-nighters are one-nighters," Dennis said. "That's wear and tear on mind, body, and soul."[8]

Though Sonny mostly kept to himself, others brought what levity they could onto the bus. "There was a general laugh-it-up atmosphere during the long days on the bus, as if it were tacitly admitted that the one-nighter grind is tough and the only thing to do is pretend it isn't happening," wrote Feather.[9] Maynard Ferguson read reviews aloud with sarcastic asides; Ferguson arranger and saxophonist Willie Maiden revealed himself to be "the world's foremost authority on beer and the liquor licensing laws of every state"; Henry Grimes "exchanged about ten words in the first twelve days and earned himself the nickname Loudmouth." Paul Desmond played chess with drummer Joe Morello or Scrabble with Leonard Feather and usually won; Eugene Wright played pinochle. In a running joke, the musicians rated any and all aspects of the tour from one to five stars, the rating system for Feather's vaunted "Blindfold Test"—"everything from a bowl of soup to a men's room." One day, Ferguson said jokingly, 'We've got to get some hate going around here. There isn't enough good, healthy hate around the bus.'" They would find it on tour.[10]

The package tour was integrated, but of the approximately thirty people involved, only seven were black. "Since it was such a mixed tour and there were these top-flight people on the tour—Brubeck and the Four Freshmen," Sonny said, "we all stayed at the same hotel. And I stayed at some of those hotels with everybody." Decades later, Sonny would remember the exact hotels, like the Croydon in Chicago or the Fort Pitt in Pittsburgh, "which to me was outlawed, off-limits for black people. I never stayed there, and nobody I knew of stayed there."[11]

However, there were intragroup problems. "Everybody was a white guy— Brubeck and Maynard Ferguson—though the young Slide Hampton was in that band," Sonny said, "and Eugene Wright, 'the Senator.' He was another black guy, and then all the guys in my trio were black, of course. So within that group of artists, I experienced a little tension, because I was all of a sudden put on the same social level with them."

The tour kicked off on Halloween, when the bus picked everyone up at Columbus Circle and headed for Boston, where they were playing at Symphony Hall.[12] "Sonny Rollins is not too well known a figure to the general public," wrote Newport Jazz Festival impresario George Wein in advance of the show, which he was copresenting. "I imagine that Leonard's introductory remarks will explain quite clearly how important a figure Rollins has become in modern jazz, both as an influence on other musicians and as a fantastic virtuoso on the tenor saxophone."[13]

Feather's remarks did explain. "Jazz in general may be said to be the product of four main components—the individual soloist, the small unit or combo, the large orchestra, and the vocal element," he said. Sonny was the soloist, Brubeck the combo, Ferguson the orchestra, and the Freshmen the vocal. If Sonny was hoping to avoid Gunther Schuller's article, he had Feather bringing up thematic improvisation every night onstage. "Rarely, until the arrival on the scene of the soloist you will be hearing in a moment, did [jazz] have what you might call a structure and thematic unity—that is to say that each solo tells a story and tells it with authority. Accompanied by Henry Grimes on bass and Kenny Dennis on drums, here is the man who's been called the most important saxophonist since Charlie Parker—Theodore 'Sonny' Rollins!"[14]

As the opening act, Sonny was allotted only three tunes in the program, usually playing "I Can't Get Started," "After You've Gone," and a blues.[15] "I often wondered why he was the opening act," recalled Ferguson pianist Bob Dogan. "He should have been the feature, because he was the standout musician on the tour, for sure. Everybody was in awe of him because he was one of the all-time greats—then. It was always kind of a let-down after him, because his performances were so sterling, and so captivating. They should have had Sonny Rollins last because the intensity of his performance was just so great." Dogan always watched Sonny's set before the Ferguson band went on, heading backstage during Brubeck. "I'd go all the way to the top, in the crow's nest, and his sound would just penetrate all the way up there."[16]

Every night, the Four Freshmen's Bob Flanigan told the same joke: "Did you know that Lawrence Welk makes Guy Lombardo sound progressive?"[17] Sonny made the Freshmen sound like Lawrence Welk.

After Boston, they went to Smith College in Northampton, where Sonny played with the Ferguson band as well, in part because one of the Freshmen was out sick.[18] After a stop in Worcester that Sonny and the trio missed,[19] the tour drove to Allentown, Pennsylvania, where they were appearing on

November 3 at the city's Fairgrounds in Agricultural Hall, "compared with which the Holland Tunnel would be a model of acoustical perfection," Feather mused. The out-of-tune upright piano was a problem for everyone else, but not for Sonny's pianoless trio. A crowd of two thousand gathered, not the largest in the hall's history, but, as one reviewer wrote, "it may have well been the most appreciative."[20] It was a far cry from where Sonny was exactly a year earlier—recording *A Night at the Village Vanguard.*

The next day they were at the Zembo Mosque in Harrisburg, then drove to Pittsburgh after the show, arriving at 5 a.m.[21] Early the next morning, they drove more than three hundred miles to Massey Hall in Toronto, almost missing the start of the show due to a customs delay.[22] Then they took an all-night ride back to New York, where they had two packed shows the night of November 7 at Carnegie Hall.[23]

Right before going on at Carnegie, Sonny found out that earlier that day his mother had died suddenly of a heart attack, just shy of her fifty-fourth birthday.[24] At the beginning of the concert, there was a kind of visitation. Before the house lights dimmed, Sonny walked onstage alone. "A woman in the front row began screaming full-throat in shocking snap-brain madness," wrote poet Clark Coolidge. "She was obviously and instantly in some closing chamber of her own mindpain and the audience froze. Seemingly without pause for thought Sonny began to play with her, duetting with whatever demons were striking these crazed sounds, imitating her screams and turning them around, reflecting and shining them anew."[25] The woman was escorted from the concert, and Sonny counted off "Cherokee." Sonny practiced in his hotel room after Brownie died, and he played after his mother died—only this was at Carnegie Hall.

Sonny eked it out and played what *Variety* called the "standout performance of the night,"[26] which ended at 2:30 a.m. Sonny was learning what it truly meant to succeed in a cutthroat business—playing Carnegie Hall the night of your mother's death without shedding a tear or missing a beat. He knew he would have to choose between attending his mother's funeral and continuing on tour. With the bus leaving for Charlottesville at 6 a.m., Sonny had three and a half hours to decide.

Little did he know, his mother intended to be at Carnegie Hall that night.

"She came over to my apartment, and all she talked about was Sonny," recalled Doris Mason, Sonny's next-door neighbor. "She came in, she said, 'Oh, I'm gonna surprise Sonny tonight! I'm going to see him play...' And she left the apartment and went into hers, and after she opened the door, she collapsed, and she never regained consciousness. At the time, Sonny's brother was studying to be a doctor, and he told my mother, 'I tried everything to save my mother.' It was such a sad thing, and she never got to go to see him play that night."[27]

Though Valborg's sudden death sent Sonny reeling, he felt compelled to press on. Through the ups and downs of endless hours in the woodshed, his fall from grace, and eventual rise to fame, Valborg never abandoned him, and he was not about to abandon his biggest break to date when she had sacrificed everything for him. His late grandmother had instilled in him a deep social consciousness, and there were thousands of people down south he had an opportunity to reach; he could dazzle audiences as he had done on the first week of the tour or have the only black bandleader on the program appear to be a no-show. At 6 a.m., Sonny was in Columbus Circle, sitting bleary-eyed on the bus, quietly mourning, hurtling headlong into the South.

"My mother came back to me after she passed away and it was such a great day,"[28] Sonny later recalled. "I woke up and I was in tears because I was sort of arguing with her before she passed. When she died suddenly, and I wasn't there, I really felt guilty. But she came back to me in sort of a dream while I was sleeping. But it was more than a dream. She came back and talked to me."[29]

"Jazz for Moderns" had two shows on November 8, an afternoon show at the University of Virginia (UVA) and an evening show at Virginia Polytechnic Institute (later Virginia Tech), a dramatic departure from Carnegie Hall.[30] In Charlottesville, all the public schools had been closed since September 1958 in protest of the 1954 *Brown v. Board of Education* decision, in a standoff between the state and municipal governments and a federal court order mandating integration. But the colleges were open. With *Freedom Suite* still fresh, the scene in the city was an affront to everything it represented.

In the fall of 1958, twelve black students in Virginia were expected to transfer to all-white schools. In response, segregationist Virginia governor

J. Lindsay Almond Jr. mandated that all public schools be closed immediately and mounted a legal challenge at the state level to reinstate segregation.[31] The action, known as "massive resistance," would bar thirteen thousand students from classes. That past September, President Eisenhower had publicly weighed in, hoping the schools would reopen; to no avail.[32] When Sonny arrived in Charlottesville seven weeks later, the schools remained closed.[33] Sonny would mount his own individual act of massive resistance.

Robert Bland was a senior at UVA and destined to be the first black undergraduate to graduate from the school that spring. "There had been some African American students who attended law school, med school, and grad school, but in general, they had not admitted undergraduates until the time that myself and a couple of other students of color came in," he said. "I was in that first graduating class. The other two gentlemen who came in with me, they transferred out to other schools before they graduated."[34]

Bland would not attend the concert. "We didn't participate in a lot of campus activities, because for the most part, we didn't really feel welcome and there were some that we were downright excluded from, so we who were attending school there at that time usually went into town to socialize."[35]

At the 4 p.m. concert in Memorial Gymnasium, sponsored by the PK-German Dance Societies, Sonny looked out at the crowd and saw a sea of white faces sitting on rugs and blankets covering the floor. According to the student newspaper, they "greeted each of the four groups with increasing enthusiasm,"[36] but as Leonard Feather saw it, the students were all "trudging in from a football game" and were "noisy and restless. Many of the students brought in bottles or checked them at the door."[37]

As soon as Sonny and Brubeck finished their sets, they immediately hopped on the bus and took off for Blacksburg, 150 miles away. They had a show at 9:30 p.m. that night at Virginia Tech's three-thousand-seat Burruss Hall, sponsored by the German and Cotillion clubs.[38] The tour chartered a second bus to take Ferguson's band and the Four Freshmen in the hope they would arrive midconcert.[39] "I'm not just sounding you, man—they were *here*, here in (ugh) Blacksburg!" read a review in the student newspaper. "First, Sonny and his studs came on swinging. I know you've eared this cat, but have you ever *seen* him. His long chin is lengthened even more by a magnificent growth of underbrush—I mean, man, he looks like an Ethiopian prince! Well, Sonny wasn't cool; he was frigid! That cat latched onto his horn and blew himself an ice castle on the far end of Cloud 7; in fact, most of the time he was so far out that most of the audience couldn't even see him!"[40]

According to Feather, the two campuses were "150 miles apart geographically and a million miles apart in every other respect." With the Virginia Tech audience "a sober, quietly attentive crowd," Feather wrote, "our faith in the future of America was restored."[41]

Yet to Sonny, neither concert restored his faith. At one of the shows, Sonny met some fans of his music but not his politics who did not take kindly to *Freedom Suite*.[42] "I remember being confronted—not in a hostile or violent way, just verbally—about why I made this record," Sonny later recalled. "The controversy was slightly scary—but not too much, because I was a big, strong guy, and when you're young you think you're indestructible. But in retrospect it was a little scary, yes. And it was also one of these situations where some people talked with me about it and some people didn't, but it was always there, hanging over everything."[43]

It wasn't the music they objected to, but the message. "Several fans, white fans, confronted me and wanted to know what I had meant in my comments that accompanied the album. Some of them were obviously upset. I felt pressure to rescind my statement, but of course I did not do that."[44] Sonny discovered firsthand "how the world moves," as Ralph Ellison's Invisible Man asserted. "Not like an arrow, but a boomerang."[45]

Sonny wasn't the only one to notice the chill of the South. "A ghostly camp follower on parts of this tour was Jim Crow," wrote Feather. "We ran into him several times in a few days, notably when seven of the thirty of us were unable to check in at the same hotel." After playing Indianapolis, he recalled, "we stopped at a diner for breakfast. The waitress, after keeping Gene Wright and me waiting a long time before taking our orders, finally gave Gene a sidelong look that said, 'I'm sorry, but we can't serve *you*.' . . . When a soft-drink machine outside a St. Louis diner failed to cough up a bottle, somebody cracked, 'Even the machines down here discriminate.'" The organizers concluded that "the South must be eliminated from future tours."[46]

After St. Louis, they went on to Iowa City, Minneapolis, Madison,

Chicago, and Detroit, where they played at Masonic Auditorium on November 16, outdrawing Erroll Garner.[47] In Detroit, Sonny saw Shirley Carter for the first time in months; she hadn't heard from him since before he left for California. Given his long absence, she had developed cold feet about the prospect of uprooting her life in Detroit, moving to New York, and getting married. That Sunday night, Sonny had his performance and would be gone the next day; she had to work on Monday.[48] She left him a note on his music manuscript paper.

> Dear Sonny,
>   Sorry, I couldn't wait any longer for you, but you know I'm a hard working girl. I hope you have a safe trip to Buffalo and I'll be looking forward to your return trip here.
>
> Love, Shirley
>
> p.s. Don't get angry at my writing on the back of your music, but I couldn't find anything else.[49]

The spark was still there, but the timing was not. "I didn't realize exactly who he was at that particular time," she said, "or I would have responded differently. But I hadn't known him long enough, and I wasn't at ground zero where he would start and leave and come back to—I was in Detroit—so it was already a strange situation. And with him going back and forth to the different obligations that he had, you know, I wasn't fully aware of it. I could have maintained it. It wouldn't have been a problem. I just didn't understand it."[50] They parted ways.

On November 22, the Jazz for Moderns tour went to Buffalo. Between the constant travel and sleep deprivation, friction between Sonny and Kenny Dennis ignited, it seems over a musical disagreement.[51] Sonny got physical with him; after the altercation, Dennis left the tour.[52] "One of the things that I came away with was to be involved and to be committed," Dennis said. "If you're going to get involved with this music we call jazz and self-expression, do not by any stretch of the imagination take it lightly, because it is a very strong force."[53]

Sonny had high standards, but "looking back at it, that's a good thing," Dennis said. "Sonny Rollins is a perfectionist, and he knew what he wanted for his music. . . . Many times, you start out playing something, and you know how you started, you don't know how you're going to end up, and that's some of the beauty and the pain of it all. . . . I don't want to sound corny, but nothing ventured, nothing gained."

There were no hard feelings. "Throughout the years I've seen him, and we're always cordial, we're always very nice," Dennis said. "There's an ongoing good relationship between the two of us." For the rest of the tour, Frankie Dunlop filled in on drums, playing with both the trio and the Ferguson band.[54]

The tour rolled on to Rochester, Erie in Pennsylvania, and Louisville's Freedom Hall, Sonny's first time in Kentucky since Lexington.[55] At the end of the tour, Ed Sarkesian announced, facetiously, "During the last three days of the tour, a psychiatrist will be on the bus for reorientation." It ended with an overnight ride from Cleveland to Buffalo and two final concerts on November 23, a matinee and an evening show, at the Philadelphia Academy of Music, before the final stop at Columbus Circle. After thousands of miles on the road, everyone was ready for a rest. Even Maynard Ferguson, with his legendary "granite lip," had busted his chops.[56] Sonny came off the tour with a broken engagement and having missed his own mother's funeral. It was the toll of the road.

There were no more tours in 1958, but Sonny kept on pushing. After Jazz for Moderns, he hired Pete La Roca, who, at twenty years old, felt ready for more "intense interaction" a year after *A Night at the Village Vanguard*. It was a young band: Grimes was twenty-three, Sonny the oldest at twenty-eight.

On November 30, Sonny performed in a "Battle of the Saxes" at the Sheraton Park Hotel in Washington, DC, opposite the Gerry Mulligan and Ben Webster quartets. Then there were two shows at Town Hall in New York on December 27, with the Miles Davis Sextet, the J. J. Johnson Quintet, Art Blakey and the Jazz Messengers, and Anita O'Day.[57] Outside of these one-off concerts, Sonny was booked at the Five Spot on a double bill with Charles Mingus. Fans squeezed into the smoke-filled room, sitting close enough to catch Mingus's sweat.[58]

On New Year's Eve, the scene in New York was offering up an embarrassment of riches, yet there was no hipper way to ring in 1959 than with Sonny and Mingus at the Five Spot.[59]

Sometimes, Sonny watched Mingus from the Five Spot phone booth.[60] As captivating as Mingus was, he had a tendency to make a double bill a single bill, and some nights Sonny avoided the awkward situation of waiting for Mingus to leave the stand and didn't show at all. "It was great to hear [Sonny] when he came because sometimes he didn't show up," recalled alto saxophonist John Handy, who was in Mingus's quintet. "I'm sure it was because Charles would go on and play so long, and I was embarrassed to be there because it was really rude.... Charles would simply get on and not get off."[61]

On one night when Sonny didn't show, Handy sat in for Sonny with La Roca and Grimes, borrowing Booker Ervin's tenor.[62] That night, John Coltrane, who was in between gigs with the Miles Davis Sextet, came in to hear what Sonny was working on. "It was bad weather, and the place was practically full, and people pushed John to get his horn and sit in with Sonny's group," Handy said. "He played a couple tunes, and one was okay. John wasn't gonna sound bad on anything at that point, and then the world almost came to an end when he played the second tune—'Well You Needn't.' "[63] It was strange foreshadowing: with Sonny in absentia, Coltrane took his place.[64]

Eventually, Sonny got back at Mingus for bogarting the stage. As Sonny recalled, Mingus "did to me what Max would do to Charli Persip when he played opposite him at the Jazz Gallery, which was play all night. Not let them get on the bandstand. Mingus did that to me at the Five Spot. The thing is this. They were pulling rank. At that time, I couldn't rank with Charles Mingus.... You might not think so, but I wasn't as famous. I didn't feel I was on par with Charles Mingus." Later on, he said, "I got back at Mingus. Mingus was working at the Vanguard...and he got into some kind of trouble with Max Gordon. I don't know what it was, but Mingus was a volatile cat. I was not working in town, but Max called me and said 'Mingus's band is here, but they won't play. You want to come down here and do the gig?' And I went down there and did the gig. And there was nothing Mingus could say, 'cause he knew what happened a long time ago. So Charles McPherson, Lonnie Hillyer, they were all just sitting down in the club. Mingus wouldn't play. I got a couple guys and played the gig the rest of the night. After that, we were close friends."[65]

Sonny may have downplayed his own level of fame, but he was not entirely wrong. At the dawn of 1959, Stan Getz was still the king of the tenor, though Sonny and Coltrane were coming up. In the annual *Down Beat* readers' poll, Sonny came in second, with 999 votes to Getz's 1,722; Coltrane came in third with 597.[66] In the German critics' poll in *Jazz Podium* and the French poll in *Jazz Hot*, however, Sonny came in first.[67]

It seemed Sonny was truly appreciated in Europe, where he had never been. After facing Jim Crow at home, he decided it was time to cross the Atlantic.

Chapter 22

FINDING THE BRIDGE

(1959–1960)

Sonny began 1959 in New York and ended it in New York, but there would be a whirlwind in between. After closing at the Five Spot, Sonny played at the Half Note in the Village, then the Village Vanguard opposite Anita O'Day from January 13 to 18.[1] On January 23, Sonny realized a childhood dream when his trio opened a long weekend at the Apollo Theater with Dinah Washington, Maynard Ferguson, and Gerry Mulligan. He had played at the Apollo with the Brown-Roach Quintet, but having his name on the marquee was different.[2] The trio returned to the Vanguard on January 27.[3]

Preparations for Sonny's upcoming European tour—his first—were complicated when booking agent Bert Block couldn't reach him to finalize the paperwork. On February 10, less than two weeks before, Block finally sent Sonny a letter at the Vanguard.[4] Sonny's evasiveness was probably due to the fact that he hadn't yet settled on a drummer. He held revolving-door auditions at the Vanguard, finally settling on Pete La Roca.[5]

Outside the Vanguard, Sonny was a hard man to find unless you knew where to be. He frequented jam sessions in low-rent bohemian artist lofts, a fertile atmosphere free from market forces that served as proving ground, incubator, grapevine, and performance space. There was 821 Sixth Avenue, a fifth-floor walk-up with no heat or hot water where painter David X. Young, photographer W. Eugene Smith, and composer Hall Overton lived. Everyone came through: Monk, Rahsaan Roland Kirk, and Sonny, too.[6]

Sonny could sometimes be found at 335 East Thirty-Fourth Street, where trombonist Clyde Cox, trumpeter Ralph Hughes, and bassist Paul Worthington, all southern transplants, hosted late-night jam sessions starting in 1956.[7] It was on the second floor of a three-story building; woodworking shops were on the first and third, but the loft was a different kind of woodshed. Mostly white musicians gathered there: Al Cohn, Zoot Sims, Al Haig, Steve Swallow, Dave Frishberg, and Mose Allison among them, but "the whole idea of the loft was not to exclude," recalled Cox.[8] Bud Powell came by, as did Henry Grimes and Sonny. Up to twenty musicians crammed into the tight space.[9]

The organizers had a strict anti-hard-drug policy. It was "pure love with maybe a taste of gin and vodka or something and maybe a little joint of grass," recalled regular Bob Dorough, who later recorded a vocal version of "St. Thomas."[10] One night, Mose Allison "was playing the piano, and I said, 'Let me have a turn, and so I'm playing the piano now, and suddenly I hear a new trumpet sound, and I look around, and it's Mose. 'Son of a gun!'" Dorough met Henry Grimes there, and Sonny "caused a furor if he showed up."[11]

After some rare time at home, Sonny flew to Europe, where the tour began on February 21 in the Netherlands opposite the Horace Silver Quintet with drummer Louis Hayes, bassist Gene Taylor, trumpeter Blue Mitchell, and tenor saxophonist Junior Cook.[12] The first concert was at the Singerzaal in Laren.[13] For the televised performance, the trio wore dark suits and ties—Sonny had black horn-rimmed glasses. They played "I've Told Ev'ry Little Star," "I Want to Be Happy," and "Weaver of Dreams."[14]

Sonny received a royal welcome in Amsterdam from one of America's leading jazz ambassadors and a hero: Don Byas,[15] who "was waiting for me there on the steps of the Concertgebouw," tenor in hand, Sonny recalled.[16] Byas had heard about Sonny and wanted to see if he lived up to his reputation.

"We went down to my dressing room and we began playing," Sonny said, as Byas was saying, " 'Let me see what you know.' We played and played and were there for quite a while. Fortunately, I was young and strong, 'cause we almost played up to the time that I should be getting ready for the concert that night."[17] Sonny began to wonder if Byas was trying to bust his chops before his Amsterdam debut, but realized by the end of the blowing session that it was a rite of passage. Byas could wear out most tenor players, but no one could wear out Sonny Rollins.[18]

The sold-out midnight concert polarized critics.[19] "Lots of Noise, No Jazz," read one headline.[20] Yet the fans were enraptured, giving several standing ovations.[21] "Rarely have I been so fascinated by a single musician during a concert," wrote leading Dutch jazz presenter and journalist Michiel de Ruyter.[22]

They flew to San Remo, the Italian resort city not far from the French border, where on February 22, the Rollins Trio and Silver Quintet were headlining the fourth annual Festival Internazionale del Jazz di Sanremo at the stately art nouveau casino theater. The two-day festival was known for its cosmopolitanism; the first iteration featured pianist Romano Mussolini, the son of the dictator, in a legendary rebuke of fascism. The 1959 lineup included German trombonist Albert Mangelsdorff with Serbian trumpeter Dusko Goykovich, Jamaican saxophonist Joe Harriott, French saxophonist Barney Wilen, Swedish saxophonist Lars Gullin, and Italian guitarist Franco Cerri and his International Trio.[23]

Sonny's appearance was well received, but according to bassist Coleridge Goode, a member of the Joe Harriott Quintet, Sonny "became unhappy with Henry Grimes' playing and was extremely rude to him, on stage in front of everyone. I talked to Henry afterwards and the guy was nearly in tears."[24] Grimes was not surprised by Sonny's "pressure makes diamonds" approach. Sonny was "striving for perfection," Grimes said.[25]

The next stop was Paris, where Sonny showed the French what it meant to be chic. He was booked from February 23 to 28 at the Club Saint-Germain-des-Prés in the Sixth Arrondissement.[26] Anticipation had mounted in *Jazz Hot* for the French debut of the recent poll winner in the tenor category, and Sonny did not disappoint.[27] Many bohemians steeped in existentialist philosophy made expatriate jazz musicians their idols. Kenny Clarke led the house band at Le Blue Note on rue d'Artois abutting the Champs-Élysées, where Lester Young began an extended residency in mid-January; Count Basie, Donald Byrd, Stan Getz, Cannonball Adderley, Bud Powell, and Louis Armstrong would all perform in the City of Lights within a span of three months.[28]

Sonny stayed at the six-story Hotel Crystal at 24 rue Saint-Benoît, down the block from the Club Saint-Germain.[29] During Sonny's stay, one of his childhood idols, Lucky Thompson, was there for a run at Le Chat Qui Pêche.[30] Only a five-minute walk away, Lester Young was staying on the rue de Seine at the Hotel la Louisiane, where Billie Holiday, Charlie Parker, and Miles Davis had once stayed.

For Sonny, it was also Saint-Germain-des-*Pres*. When he saw Lester Young every morning at the boulangerie, Pres would doff his porkpie. "He would be seen in the morning getting his French loaf of bread like everybody did," Sonny recalled.[31] The Club Saint-Germain was a jazz cellar at 13 rue Saint-Benoît, whose signature cocktail, the Saint-Germain, fueled the bibulous atmosphere: one-eighth Cointreau, three-eighths dry vermouth, half vodka.[32] When it opened in 1948, it gradually became Paris's late-night jazz hot spot. Music booker Marcel Romano transformed it into the Parisian Birdland: Coleman Hawkins, James Moody, the Modern Jazz Quartet, Bud Powell, and Roy Eldridge played there, with local musicians like Barney Wilen and Roger Guérin filling out the rest of the programming. Like Birdland, the club attracted celebrities—actors Alain Delon and Nicole Berger were frequent visitors.

Amid the tables with dim lamps and a small dance floor, "There was always that war—it was a war between the people who came to listen to music who knew who was playing, and the others who came to spend an evening and try to get the girl," recalled pianist René Urtreger. The music was nonpareil; after jazz concerts at theaters like L'Olympia, Club Saint-Germain was the place for late-night jam sessions.[33]

Yet Paris was not a jazz utopia, as imagined by Martin Ritt's 1961 film *Paris Blues*.[34] The Algerian War was still being waged, and the recent reelection of Charles de Gaulle perpetuated the fight to continue French colonial rule. With the French military's hopes of victory dwindling, de Gaulle faced a double bind—concede defeat to the revolutionaries and recognize Algerian independence or integrate the Algerians into French society, both outcomes unacceptable to the government.[35] Some jazz musicians, Kenny Clarke and Art Blakey most prominently, were Muslim converts and when they performed in Paris, had more in common with the Algerian revolutionaries than the majority white dancers who flocked to the jazz cellars to hear them.[36] "The French are as racist as anybody in the world, but their racism was more against the Arabs, and there was the war in Algeria and Morocco, and anti-Semitism," said Urtreger.[37]

However, jazz was more appreciated in France than at home, and Sonny saw that the jazz scene at least was more progressive in its politics. "This tour proved to be most educational in many ways," Sonny wrote of the experience in a 1961 letter. "For not only did I realize for the first time (and first hand) the genuine respect and appreciation with which jazz is received, but I also learned an important biological lesson: That being that there is in reality a true brotherhood of all people! Hearing these words spoken and actually seeing the truth of them is another thing. I actually realized that external physical characteristics and even environmental cultural traits are just so external and superficial as compared to the real being underneath."[38]

One friend Sonny made at the Club Saint-Germain was Basile Drossos, a chemical engineer and jazz collector. "He was a very, very interesting man. We were talking about politics and everything mostly, and the ambience in Paris," Drossos recalled. "It was not just about jazz music. It was more than that." They became close friends and frequent letter writers. When Basile and his wife had a son, Alexis Theodore Drossos, his "Uncle Sonny Theodore," as Sonny referred to himself in letters, sent some flutes and, eventually, an alto saxophone. Alexis would become a professional saxophonist like his adopted uncle.[39]

On February 28, Sonny headlined *Naissance d'Une Musique*, a live French television broadcast from the Club Saint-Germain, hosted by American expatriate jazz presenter Sim Copans. Sonny hired Kenny Clarke, who led the house band at Le Blue Note alongside guitarist Jimmy Gourley, bassist Pierre Michelot, and pianist René Urtreger. Clarke suggested to Sonny

that he use Gourley, Henry Grimes, and Urtreger, despite Sonny's morato-
rium on piano.[40] Urtreger made his reputation in 1957 when he collaborated
on Miles Davis's mostly improvised score for Louis Malle's *Ascenseur pour
l'échafaud*, and later backed, among others, Dexter Gordon, Sonny Stitt, and
Ella Fitzgerald; he had just finished a monthlong stint with Lester Young.[41]

Urtreger had heard all of Sonny's records. "I was twenty-four, and it was
the day after my little girl was born," Urtreger recalled. Sonny asked him if
he knew "Ornithology" and counted it off. "He didn't like to have a pianist
with him. Maybe he had some bad experiences with other pianists. He was
very surprised to hear somebody out of New York, out of the United States,
playing like I was." Urtreger was even more surprised. "We have a word
in French, *inouï*; it means 'never heard before.' I think I had never heard
here somebody playing like that. My favorite musician of all time is Charlie
Parker. So I found him the equivalent, the same level—not almost—he was
the same level as if I played with Charlie Parker."[42]

From Paris, the trio then flew to Stockholm. From March 1 to 3, they
performed at the Nalen jazz club. Sonny was described in the concert poster
as "currently the world's best-publicized jazz star," and received more standing ovations.[43] On March 4, Sonny was part of radio and television broadcasts from Södra Teatern in south Stockholm. For the Swedish performance,
Sonny replaced La Roca with Joe Harris in a Sugar Hill reunion. Harris emi-
grated in 1956, "in the heyday of jazz in Stockholm," he recalled. "Sweden in
those days was paradise on earth for me. No racism, no discrimination—the
people were honored to have us."[44]

When Sonny called, "It was like a homecoming," Harris said. "There was
nobody in Europe playing like Sonny." On the gig, Harris used Norwegian
Swedish drummer Egil Johansen's drums, with the initials E. J. on the bass
drum. "That was about three years since I'd been away from New York. I'm
playing and practicing, so I'm still in shape."[45] He would have to be.

Swedish jazz presenter Olle Helander hosted the television broadcast.
"Somebody told me that you are not particularly fond of being looked upon
as the creator of a new style of jazz. Is that true?" he asked Sonny.[46]

"Oh, well I don't really feel that I deserve the title of a creator in any
respect," Sonny said. "There are many other jazzmen who should precede me,

actually. You know? I am just in the experimental stage, and I have lots more to do."[47]

Sonny counted off Duke Ellington's "It Don't Mean a Thing (If It Ain't Got That Swing)" with an eight-bar drum intro. "Not every guy could make the tempo, but Sonny could," Harris recalled. "Sonny had a phrase if you couldn't make it—'Get out of the hole!' "[48] Chorus after chorus, Sonny navigated the minor progression up and down the horn, then traded with Harris, swinging ferociously.[49] After playing Sonny's "Paul's Pal," on "Love Letters," the Academy Award–nominated Victor Young ballad from the eponymous 1945 film, Sonny closed his eyes and began telling a story. He began a rubato cadenza, caressing each note with a lithe vibrato reminiscent of Lester Young, then a triplet arpeggio à la Coleman Hawkins, interspersed with double-time chromatic lines evoking Charlie Parker.[50] He was standing onstage in Stockholm, but his heart was back on Edgecombe Avenue. All of his influences were there onstage with him, each saying their piece, but as the rhythm section came in and brought Sonny home, it was as though Hawkins, Pres, and Bird left the stage one by one until all that remained was Sonny Rollins. He repeatedly quoted Rimsky-Korsakov's "Scheherazade"; this was just one of Sonny's *One Thousand and One Nights*. The familiar melody enlivened *Balalaika*, the 1939 musical drama, but also one of Sonny's favorite radio serials growing up, *The Green Hornet*. As far as he had ever been from home, he was only a song away from Harlem.

March 5: Radio Studio Zurich, with La Roca back in the drum chair, performing opposite the Silver quintet.[51] March 6: Stuttgart Liederhalle,[52] as part of the "Treffpunkt Jazz" series.[53] March 7: Back to Paris, at the famed Olympia Hall.

Sonny arrived at the Hotel Crystal to find his luggage damaged during travel, with François Postif, a French jazz journalist, waiting for him in the lobby. When they got to Sonny's room, Postif peppered him with questions. Why did his reed squeak on early recordings? "Some critics believe I created a new style with that!" Sonny replied. "But who can say where the line is between what you want to play and what you play?" What was Sonny's favorite Sonny Rollins album? "Generally, I listen to my records very little. In reality, I will listen when I can't do otherwise; when friends come to the house, or when listening to the radio and I'm too lazy to go and turn the button." What is hard bop? "A term that was invented by a journalist from the West Coast of the United States. It's like 'rock 'n' roll' for 'rhythm and blues': the same with a new suit." Then he asked about Sonny's alleged rivalry with Coltrane. "Coltrane is the sort of man that makes me play better and give the best of myself," he said. "With him, every time we meet, it is a kind of . . . competition to see how far I can go." How did Sonny feel about his own playing? "I feel for some time I've been running in circles and treading water—maybe it's the calm before the storm."[54]

Sonny performed two concerts at the two-thousand-seat Olympia. Much of the audience loved it, but critics were divided.[55] Aris Destombes wrote that "Sonny Rollins is undergoing an evolution; he still seems to be exceeded by the turbulence of the creative forces bubbling in him and a profound lack of unity, full of internal contradictions." There seemed to be a lack of unity in the band as well; when Sonny quoted "Alouette," the children's song about plucking a lark's feathers, the lark was La Roca.[56]

Sonny was having problems with La Roca's playing, and it seems after the midnight concert he may have literalized his musical allusion—"je te plumerai la tête."[57] "I did knock Pete La Roca on his behind," Sonny later confirmed, but "Pete La Roca was a good drummer."[58] La Roca left the tour soon thereafter. After the Olympia, the trio played in Brussels on March 8, and in Frankfurt on March 9, but after the altercation at the Olympia, on March 10, La Roca flew back to New York.[59]

For La Roca, touring with Sonny was the experience of a lifetime, and there seemed to be no bad blood between them. "Sonny was, and still is, one of my very few heroes!" La Roca later said.[60] When La Roca died in 2012, Sonny recalled in his remembrance that during the tour, "he did his job. That's why he was working with me, and I have only high praise for him."[61] La Roca would go on to perform with John Coltrane, lead his own groups, and in 1965 record *Basra*, a classic album for Blue Note. But he and Sonny would not work together again.

With La Roca gone, Sonny hired Kenny Clarke. "Every record that I made with Kenny Clarke, I don't even remember him being there," Sonny said. "When he's there and you don't know it, that's perfect. He was there, and he was not there."[62] On March 11, the Jazz Club Sud-Est hosted the trio in Marseilles at the Théâtre du Gymnase, a 695-seat theater built in the early nineteenth century.[63] After the show, they continued at the cellar at the Hot Club d'Aix in Aix-en-Provence.[64]

As March 11 became March 12, time became elastic. They played only three tunes during the hour-long set: "Woody'n You," "But Not for Me," and "Lady Bird."[65] "Stretch out!" Sonny shouted, as Grimes took a bass solo. On Tadd Dameron's "Lady Bird," Sonny quoted "Four," "Joy Spring," and Ponchielli's "Dance of the Hours," but the most significant homage came in the first chorus. Sonny began his solo with the melody to Miles Davis's "Half Nelson," a contrafact of "Lady Bird," then quoted Charlie Parker's 1947 two-chorus tenor solo note for note from memory.[66] He must have known— March 12 was the fourth anniversary of Bird's death.

At the end of the night, as Clarke played a snare roll, the free soloists climbed higher and higher to their invisible summit, and then Sonny went a half step beyond. "That was a ball!" he said. As the bohemian masses cried out for an encore, Sonny knew he had already given them everything he had. "Je suis fatigué!"

After the Aix performance, Sonny stayed on in Paris, right as Pres was getting ready to leave. While Sonny was in Aix, Pres was in a radio studio with René Urtreger and several others, then later that night at Le Blue Note, and he was "very tired," Urtreger recalled, "very diminished."[67] Pres was supposed to join Jazz at the Philharmonic after closing at the Blue Note a week later, but he was in such poor health that he decided to end his residency at the club and cancel the tour with Norman Granz. Before going home, he had to take care of some business with Sonny, though.

François Postif had interviewed Pres that past February, intending to publish the Q&A in a forthcoming issue of *Jazz Hot*.[68] To decipher what Pres said, Postif consulted Sonny as he worked on the transcription. As Postif played the tape back to Sonny, Sonny told him that Pres had just come to see him and insisted on settling a twenty-dollar debt, saying it was his last chance to repay him.[69] Yet Sonny could never repay his debt to Pres.

On Friday, March 13, Blue Note manager Ben Benjamin threw Pres a farewell party at the club. On March 14, Pres flew home to Idlewild Airport in New York, where Elaine Swain insisted he go to the hospital.[70] Pres instead went to the Alvin Hotel, where Sonny used to visit him. Lester Young died at 3 a.m. on March 15, 1959, looking out at Birdland, age forty-nine.[71] The police arrived and immediately repossessed his saxophone, $500 in travelers' checks, a ring, and his wallet as collateral to cover his hotel bill. This was how the authorities treated the President.

The day before Pres's death, Sonny was quoted in *Melody Maker* from a brief interview conducted during his February run at the Saint-Germain: "Great jazzmen never die musically."[72]

It seems that after Pres cut his Blue Note run short, Sonny played the rest of it with Kenny Clarke and Henry Grimes. By March 18, news of Pres's death had reached Paris, when *Le Monde* published an obituary. Sonny and Grimes returned to New York the next day.[73] Pres's funeral was the same day as Sonny's return flight, but Sonny had already said goodbye in Paris, and in a way would never say goodbye.[74]

Sonny didn't want to go down the path that led to Pres's demise. On March 18, the day before Sonny left Paris, he thought of Lucille Pearson and sent her a postcard with an image of the Luxor Obelisk in Place de la Concorde.

A special card for you.
Dig?

Yours truly[75]

———◄○►———

After Europe, Sonny began strategizing to scale back his relentless touring schedule. He got signed to BMI as a writer, along with Miles Davis, Dinah Washington, Billie Holiday, and Ahmad Jamal.[76] Licensing tunes like "Airegin," "Doxy," "Valse Hot," and "The Freedom Suite" could open up a passive income stream, but Associated Booking still had him booked through the summer.[77]

First was a string of dates in San Francisco and Los Angeles. Sonny planned to use his trio, but then he heard a twenty-year-old trumpet prodigy from Indianapolis who convinced him to expand it to a pianoless quartet: Freddie Hubbard.[78] He was classically trained, but the sounds of Indiana

Avenue beckoned, and soon Hubbard and his fellow Jordan Conservatory students, bassist Larry Ridley and trombonist David Baker, were expelled for playing too much jazz.[79] Hubbard immediately matriculated into another local institution—the Montgomery Brothers: bassist Monk, vibraphonist Buddy, and, best known, guitarist Wes.[80] In 1958, Hubbard hitched a ride to New York with a reporter from the *Indianapolis Recorder*. There, he would become Sonny's first unofficial student.

Hubbard first lived in the Morrisania section of the Bronx; then he moved to Brooklyn, which became his true conservatory.[81] He sometimes got hair-cuts at Kenny Dorham's house on President Street. "Sonny, Max, and K.D.," Hubbard recalled, "were hang-out partners in Brooklyn."[82]

At after-hours hangs with Arthur Taylor, Paul Chambers, Wilbur Ware, and Duke Jordan at a sausage stand by the Blue Coronet in Bed-Stuy, Hubbard "learned how they swung." Once, he and Jackie McLean walked six miles from McLean's apartment on Houston Street to 116th Street, just talk-ing, which Hubbard called "the most fun I ever had." The endless hangs led to jam sessions, which led to sessions at Count Basie's on Seventh Avenue in Harlem.[83] "You couldn't sit in if you couldn't play," Hubbard recalled. "You have a suit and tie and you get up there and the motherfuckers change keys."[84] One night, Donald Byrd approached the stand and immediately introduced Hubbard to John Coltrane.

Coltrane invited Hubbard to practice with him at the apartment he shared with his wife, Naima, and his stepdaughter, Syeeda, at 203 West 103rd Street. Coltrane was developing the "Coltrane changes" that culminated in "Giant Steps."[85] "I'd go to his house and wake him up," Hubbard said.[86] At Coltrane's, he learned what it meant to have a work ethic. "I'd take the sub-way to Trane's house every day he was in town. I had a headache when I left there because he was practicing so much."[87] This culminated in Hubbard's first recording session in New York, on Coltrane's *The Believer*.

Hubbard got his first regular gig playing four nights a week at Turbo Vil-lage, a club in Bed-Stuy run by brothers Mike and Nat Catanzano—"some gangsters in Brooklyn."[88] The Freddie Hubbard Four had shifting person-nel, but by early 1959, it was pianist Cedar Walton, bassist James "Spanky" DeBrest, and drummer Albert "Tootie" Heath.[89] One night Philly Joe Jones came by and sat in, and he was so impressed that he started taking others. First he brought Bud Powell. And finally, in walked Sonny.[90]

"He'd pop in the door and he'd listen and disappear," Hubbard recalled. "Those were his disappearing days. But he started coming by my house, picking me up. He'd say, 'Let's go for a ride.' So he'd take me, and we'd ride around town in his car, and he always had his mouthpiece, blowing on it."[91] Life lessons in Sonny's Cadillac led to practice sessions on the Lower East Side. Suddenly, Hubbard was practicing with John Coltrane and Sonny Rollins, sometimes on the same day.

On April 1, 1959, during the first *Giant Steps* session, Coltrane recorded three tunes—the title track and two tunes dedicated to people who helped him take those "giant steps," "Naima" and "Like Sonny"; the latter was not on the final album.[92] The tune was more than just "like" Sonny; it was lifted directly from Sonny's solo on "My Old Flame" on Kenny Dorham's *Jazz Contrasts*.[93] Later, Sonny would write his own tribute to Coltrane, "John S.," "private code," Sonny said, for "John and Sonny," not *New York Times* jazz critic John S. Wilson, as some mistakenly thought.[94]

"The difference between him and Coltrane was that Coltrane worked his harmony out very scientifically," Hubbard said. "He studied Nicolas Slonimsky's *Thesaurus of Scales and Melodic Patterns*. Sonny was different. Spontaneous. There was no fear in him—not of the saxophone, not of the music. He was like Bird, because he wasn't thinking about practicing intervals and scales and all that stuff, like Coltrane. All he needed was a song and he could hear the freedom of the music through his own personality."[95]

Sonny *was* practicing intervals and scales—constantly—but he wasn't thinking about it on the stand. In practice sessions with Sonny, Freddie would work on everything from the cycle of fourths to ways to approach a chord from unexpected intervals, always in all twelve keys; developing complex rhythms, conversational phrasing; and, Freddie said, how to "keep it melodic as much as I could."[96] Sonny wrote out hundreds of exercises in pencil on manuscript paper dealing with interval studies and harmonic patterns. As a challenge, they often practiced in difficult keys: "G-flat concerts and Bs, funny keys. He'd be runnin' all over them motherfuckers. He would practice some straight-up scales, and he would start up the top and come down through it, and he would just try all the different kind of ways of playing the chord—so that you would learn it." When Hubbard got home, he would soak his lips.[97] That April, Sonny asked him to make his trio a quartet.

On April 7, 1959, Freddie's twenty-first birthday, the new Sonny Rollins Quartet began a four-and-a-half-week residency at the Jazz Workshop in San Francisco. In addition to Hubbard, Sonny had Henry Grimes and a pickup drummer, twenty-six-year-old Lenny McBrowne, a Brooklyn native and student of Max Roach who had relocated to the West Coast. Up against Gerry Mulligan at the Blackhawk and Earl "Fatha" Hines at the Hangover, Sonny's opening was still the biggest in the Workshop's history—exceeding even his own record-setting 1958 run at the club.[98]

To Hubbard, it was trial by fire. "We were in San Francisco, and we were playing 'Cherokee' way up, and he had a way of doubling that up," he said, "and I look at this motherfucker, I said, 'Wow.' But his timing was immaculate."[99]

On April 29, they appeared on a televised broadcast from the Jazz Workshop on KQED, hosted by Ralph J. Gleason. Sonny had been calling rehearsals several times a week, and his group was beginning to coalesce. "When things happen right," he said, "everybody swings and the group gets together and everyone, the house and the guys on the stand feel it and it's a wonderful thing that I wish I could do more often.... It just makes life worthwhile."[100] Before they closed at the Workshop on May 3, Billy Eckstine stopped by after he finished his set at the Fairmont Hotel and ended the night by singing a couple tunes with the quartet.[101]

In California, Sonny hoped to reconcile with Dawn, whose career had taken off.[102] She had just booked a monthlong modeling gig in New York, Canada, and San Francisco and was going to London with the Harlem Globetrotters that fall. She had just bought a new home in luxurious Baldwin Hills, known as the "Black Beverly Hills." On the San Francisco leg of her tour, she and Sonny reunited.[103] To prove he was serious, Sonny apparently flew to Dawn's brother's birthday party in Los Angeles.[104] By early May, a gossip column reported "model Dawn Finney and her famous hubby, Sonny Rollins, hand-in-hand and house-hunting."[105]

Sonny had two more concerts in the Bay Area, both May 8. In the morning, he appeared opposite the Dizzy Gillespie Quintet at a rally for the Irwin

Memorial Blood Bank that also featured an early performance by comedians the Smothers Brothers. At night, the Rollins Quartet was at the Oakland Auditorium Theater with the Horace Silver Quintet and the Mastersounds.[106]

It seems Dawn accompanied Sonny back to Los Angeles, where she was modeling at the "Fashions at the Watkins Hotel" show with LaRue Brown, Clifford's widow.[107] After a protracted negotiation over Sonny's booking fee—he demanded nearly $2,000, nonnegotiable—the management at Jazz Seville in Los Angeles finally agreed.[108] From May 13 to 26, the Rollins Quartet played opposite the Chico Hamilton Quintet featuring multireedist Eric Dolphy on tenor, baritone, clarinet, and flute.[109] The reviews were tepid, the crowds sometimes scarce.[110] "There were many nights when there were two to four people in the entire club!" Sonny later wrote. "L.A. is a weird town and people don't come out unless something is extraordinary."[111]

During Sonny's Seville residency, he introduced Hubbard to Ornette Coleman and Don Cherry, and they had a jam session at the Watkins Hotel.[112] The Coleman group "had rehearsed so much, it sounded like one horn," Hubbard recalled. "I respect Ornette, 'cause Ornette can play straight. But when I came out here to play with him and Don Cherry, he had me over at the hotel, I said, 'Man, what the fuck is this?' He had it written out, but he had no measure lines." The key, bassist Charlie Haden told him, was "playing off a sound."[113] Not long after this session took place, on May 22, Coleman, Don Cherry, Charlie Haden, and Billy Higgins went into the studio at Radio Recorders in Los Angeles and recorded *The Shape of Jazz to Come*.

Sonny could have recorded his own album at the time, but refused. Soon, he made Dorothy Kilgallen's column: "Sonny Rollins, one of the biggest names in modern jazz, bids fair to become one of the biggest problems to his record company."[114] Despite Sonny's various record label commitments, he had no interest in recording. Lester Koenig wanted another album for Contemporary, to no avail.[115] Then Leonard Feather wanted to make a follow-up to *Sonny Rollins and the Big Brass* for MetroJazz, and, to Feather's surprise, Sonny agreed. "Come on out," Sonny told Feather over the phone. "It's nice and sunny here, and I'm ready."[116]

The day of the session, Henry Grimes and Lenny McBrowne showed up, but not Sonny. "We waited a half-hour, an hour; his phone did not answer,"

Feather wrote. He took a taxi to South Central where Sonny was staying, and Dawn answered the door.

"'I'm sorry,' she said, 'Sonny just doesn't feel like recording.'" Feather "could not even get inside the door to talk to him. Back at the studio, I told the men; we packed up and left, and the next day I flew back to New York." Sonny would never make another album for MetroJazz.

As for the rekindled romance with Dawn, it didn't take, and their relationship soon ended for the final time.[117]

Following two nights at the Senator Hotel in Sacramento on June 3 and 4, he stayed out west, missing a booking at the Half Note in New York.[118] He sent two Western Union telegrams to Lucille Pearson. On June 20:

> GREETINGS WILL BE IN NY NEXT WEEK SO HAVE
> THINGS READY
> STAY WELL SINCERELY
> SR[119]

Then on July 1:

> CANNOT CONTACT YOU BY PHONE WILL CALL 12:00PM
> TONIGHT URGENT
> SR[120]

It's not clear what happened, but Sonny arranged for Lucille to pick him up at Idlewild Airport.

Lucille:
Here is the mail box key and the ignition key. Come out to Idlewild Airport. My license number is (W.P. 7614) there is a dent in my trunk. After getting car place the little white tag which will be in the sun visor, back in the ignition key and return to garage. Please wash those 2 pots and don't use the toilet, it's broken.

> Best wishes
> Sonny[121]

Back in New York, Sonny's romance with Lucille blossomed. Lucille was not in show business and brought into Sonny's life the kind of stability he was looking for. They could hardly be more different. She was a shy midwesterner, fiercely independent, a lifelong Republican, he a son of Harlem who grew up with a black nationalist flag in the house; she was a secretary who was good at accounting, he a jazz musician who accounted only for flatted fifths; she dressed plainly, while he had a pharaonic beard and was typically the most striking person in the room. But the chemistry was real. Soon, Lucille gave up her Greenwich Street apartment and moved into Sonny's three-room flat at 400 Grand Street.[122]

The summer festival season was gearing up, and Sonny was booked at Randalls Island, the Playboy Jazz Festival in Chicago, the Music Barn in Lenox, and Monterey, with more in between.[123] There was a brief window to relax, but Sonny kept practicing. One day, Freddie Hubbard knocked on the door. "He had his barbells and sweats and a Christmas tree," Hubbard recalled. (Sonny had gotten Freddie into bodybuilding as well.)[124] "And I said, 'Sonny, what's the Christmas tree for? Man, it's July. What are you doing? It's hot in here.' He kept the place hot, too...'cause he wanted to sweat....That motherfucker came to the door with a water pistol. He said, 'Hey!' He'd pick his horn up and was walking around the house, practicing."[125]

Starting July 22, Sonny was booked for two weeks at the Sutherland Lounge in Chicago.[126] He brought Freddie and used a Chicago rhythm section: drummer Wilbur Campbell, pianist Jodie Christian, and his old friend Victor Sproles on bass.[127] It was a hazing for Hubbard. During one set, they played "Confirmation" for twenty-eight minutes; Sonny soloed for more than twenty-five. Hubbard tried to get a note in edgewise, but Sonny boxed him out. Then he finally gave him a chance. "Too long!" Sonny bellowed in the middle of Hubbard's first chorus. He then cut him off, taking the head out. After this rite of passage, he let Hubbard in on "I Can't Get Started," making it a trumpet feature. Sonny prohibited any bootleg recordings, but he made an exception in Chicago for a former Juilliard student who had loaned Sonny his tenor in 1954 before Sonny went to Lexington. Sonny had pawned the loaner, but eventually returned it. Remembering this, Sonny allowed him to record the gig on his reel-to-reel recorder.[128]

The Sutherland stretch marked the end of Freddie Hubbard's 1959 run with the Sonny Rollins Quartet. Sonny had helped him find his voice and launched him into the spotlight.[129]

Sonny stayed on in Chicago for the inaugural Playboy Jazz Festival at the air-conditioned twenty-thousand-seat Chicago Stadium, on August 9.[130] Yet Sonny had no stable trio at the time. One of Sonny's biggest shows to date, and he risked it with a pickup band, but that was how Sonny rolled.[131]

Sonny didn't mind the risk, especially in Chicago. He enlisted twenty-seven-year-old Chicago-based drummer Walter Perkins and twenty-six-year-old Evanston-based bassist Bob Cranshaw; Coleman Hawkins was using them for his set as well, with the addition of Eddie Higgins on piano.[132] Cranshaw had played with Max Roach, Association for the Advancement of Creative Musicians (AACM) cofounder Muhal Richard Abrams, Wynton Kelly, Sonny Criss, and the MJT Plus 3 (Modern Jazz Trio) alongside Frank Strozier, Harold Mabern, and Perkins.[133] Yet this was the highest-stakes gig of their lives, with the least preparation.

Luckily, Cranshaw had big ears. "We formed a groove that was just incredible, the two of us," Cranshaw said of Perkins. "We could play with anybody, anywhere." But this wasn't just anybody. "I said, 'Yeah. I'll do it.' All of a sudden, after I hung the phone up, I started to think. I said, 'Oh shit. I don't know whether I'm up for that,' because the Wilbur Wares and the Victor Sproles, they were the more experienced bass players in Chicago. And there was no piano," said Cranshaw. "I said, 'Aw, man. I may be biting off more than I can chew.' But I followed through."[134]

On August 9, Cranshaw and Perkins arrived at the stadium at noon; Sonny had told them to come at one.[135] Yet at two, when the concert started, Sonny was nowhere to be found.

"The guy came to us and said, 'Where's Sonny?' I said, 'I have no idea. I haven't met him yet. I don't know. Maybe he's here. I have no idea,'" Cranshaw said.[136]

Stan Kenton, the Four Freshmen, and June Christy played. Still no Sonny. Then came the Austin High Gang.[137] They "played twenty minutes, half an hour," Cranshaw said. "We were next, and everybody was waiting for Sonny."

Sonny arrived in the nick of time—shaved head, goatee, suit, and sunglasses.[138] "Sonny had probably been in the auditorium since eleven o'clock, just casing everything," Cranshaw said, "but he picked his time to want to come out. And we just tore the place up.... No rehearsal, we just played."[139] Perkins, like Cranshaw, never put himself first. "Like I tell everybody who I play with, 'This is a team. We're a team,'" Perkins later recalled.[140]

Cranshaw and Perkins knew "Oleo," but they had never played it at 300 beats per minute. "When I got through," Cranshaw said, "I couldn't bend my fingers."[141]

Sonny introduced the band with characteristic brio, then counted off "Without a Song."[142] Following Sonny was tough. "He's playing in and out of things," Cranshaw said, "but it can become confusing. So, if a guy didn't know him, he'd say, 'Where the fuck are we? Where are we in this tune? Where is he?'" Cranshaw said. "I've seen him turn the time around. Now where do you go? Do you go with where he is, or do you stay where you are?"[143] Cranshaw decided to stay put—he was the anchor, Sonny the kite.

Sonny played an unaccompanied cadenza, but when he came back in on the melody, he unexpectedly changed key. Cranshaw caught it immediately. In that moment on "Without a Song," Sonny found his new bassist. "I realized that he had the ears," Sonny said. "I said to myself, 'Wow, I wish I could get this guy to play with me.'"[144]

It would have to wait. "I told him then," Sonny said, "'Look, I'm going to retire for a while, but when I come back I want you to join my band.'"

"So I said sure," Cranshaw said. Cranshaw thought Sonny was just humoring him. For the next two years, it would seem he was.[145]

————◁○▷————

Back in New York, Sonny returned to 400 Grand Street, where he was living with Lucille, and they were soon engaged. In the dog days of summer, life was idyllic. His growing fame did not impinge on his need for privacy. "Nobody really knew who I was down there," Sonny said.[146] Furthermore, the predominantly immigrant community meant less discrimination. This allowed him a sense of both anonymity and belonging. "I used to go to Ratner's to pick up pastries for my wife, Lucille," he recalled. "On her way home from work, she used to visit a man named Izzy and his wife, who ran a pickle store on Suffolk near Grand. We bought our chickens at a kosher butcher next door. We were welcomed on the Lower East Side as an interracial couple. The rest of the world isn't like that."[147]

Uptown it certainly wasn't. Around midnight on August 25, 1959, Sonny turned on the radio and was shocked out of his summer reverie. That night, Miles Davis had been beaten and bloodied by police outside Birdland. "When it came over the radio that this happened, I went up there with my starter pistol," Sonny said. "To do something like that today, I'd be asking to be killed. . . . I wanted to fight next to Miles."[148]

Miles was arrested for assault and disorderly conduct, taken to the hospital for stitches, and then escorted to the precinct on Fifty-Fourth Street.[149] The officers were acting in self-defense, they claimed, but there wasn't a scratch on them. A week later, Miles was still having headaches. Then he was stripped of his cabaret card.[150] Not until the following January was Miles acquitted of all charges. Justices Benjamin Gassman, Arthur Dunaif, and Evelyn Richman presided: the same Evelyn Richman who represented Sonny's father in Annapolis in 1946.[151]

The police-brutality incident only reinforced Sonny's decision to back away from the scene altogether. He canceled any remaining gigs.[152] On September 6, his was the culminating concert at the Music Barn's summer festival in Lenox. At the last minute, Sonny sent a telegram notifying them he would not be performing.[153] The next day was his twenty-ninth birthday. On October 3, he was booked at the Monterey Jazz Festival as part of a premiere by Quincy Jones featuring Sonny's idols Ben Webster and Coleman Hawkins. He canceled that as well, replaced by Ornette Coleman.[154]

Almost anyone with a saxophone was copying Sonny or Trane, but not Ornette. When Ornette blew into the Five Spot on November 17 with his white acrylic plastic Grafton saxophone, it was like a bomb went off.[155] The Grafton tied Ornette to Charlie Parker, who also used the Grafton, which was not a toy—making it seem all the more explicit that Ornette was the Bird of the New Thing. Soon, Sidney Poitier, Leonard Bernstein, Sandra Church, Gunther Schuller, Virgil Thomson, Miles, Max, Monk, Mingus, and Coltrane came out for what was heralded as *the* jazz event of 1959.[156] "Sonny would come in and hide in the phone booth," recalled Tootie Heath.[157]

Ornette "was bigger than Trane, bigger than Sonny at that time," recalled Hubbard. "He had them motherfuckers in a mist. . . . Something new. Around

New York, Ornette is it."[158] From a purely technical perspective, Sonny was superior, but Ornette communicated something beyond technique. "I remember one night going to see Ornette when he first came to New York and was playing at the Five Spot," Sonny later recalled. "After catching him and his group, I went to the Jazz Gallery and the group over there sounded so hackneyed after hearing Ornette. The music had no real life."[159] To Sonny, Ornette found a way "to communicate with the higher forces...to get that sense of the *real* music."[160]

Yet it wasn't just Ornette taking off. With Sputnik in orbit, jazz was in the midst of its own space race. It was going out into the stratosphere (Trane's *Giant Steps*), to the moon (Miles's *Kind of Blue*), zero gravity (*The Shape of Jazz to Come*), bending time (Brubeck's *Time Out*), and for an excursion on a wobbly rail (Cecil Taylor's *Looking Ahead!*). It was going further, in many directions at once. Sonny had learned that a body in motion stays in motion, but it doesn't necessarily get closer to its destination. He was "the king of the hill," as Harold Mabern recalled, but he didn't know where he was going yet.

"I was feeling the pressure of being number one a great deal," Sonny recalled, "because I had a lot of work and I've never felt myself a fully adequate musician. I've always felt there's more that I could do—in terms of technique and musical knowledge. So I wanted to get away and...go back to school and study piano and...composition."[161]

There were those who warned him that at the peak of fame, such a rash move was career suicide. "I was cautioned by some people, 'Sonny, don't leave the scene; they'll forget about you! It's a highly competitive field of music and...if you leave the scene you are going to destroy the fan base you've built up.'" But Sonny didn't care; he believed it was paramount to "really make sure that what you are doing is what *you* want to do. Don't get caught up in what other people expect of you [or else] you're lost when they don't like you; you're just out there all alone."[162] Counterintuitively, the solution to being comfortable in his own skin was to go out there—really all alone.

One gig in Baltimore with Elvin Jones stuck out.[163] "Elvin," Sonny wrote in a note, "While I'm playing rubato, don't look all around the audience or look offstage or look in any direction but mine."[164] Yet to Sonny, Jones was not the problem. "People didn't really get it, so I said, 'Man, I'm not really doing it. I got to get myself together. First of all, I'ma go back and woodshed.'"[165] The gigs would still be there whenever he came back, but if he kept taking them, he would never get past the plateau. "I felt that my name was bigger than my talent at that time," Sonny said. Despite the hard-won critical acclaim he'd finally gotten, "The problem was that I really wasn't good enough for myself."[166]

So he left.

◆◇◆

Despite appearances that Sonny had gone AWOL, his retreat from public life was not so sudden. He had discussed it with journalists for at least a year. Many would speculate that "Trane threw Sonny under the bridge."[167] However, Sonny consistently ranked ahead of him in all major polls. And *Giant Steps* was still months away. "The idea of two tenors tangling was a media hype—it always is," Sonny said.[168] "It goes back to the big band horn battles. But it was overdone; John and I were close personal friends, and the music was paramount." Pitting Sonny and Trane against each other was "what they were doing in slavery days," Sonny said. "I noticed that you could never have more than one person up there at a time."[169] Yet the sense of competition was undeniable.[170] "These young guys like Ornette Coleman and Coltrane were coming up," Sonny recalled. "I told myself, 'Sonny, you better get your shit together, because these cats have something to say.'"[171]

Ultimately, it was a confluence of forces that led to Sonny's decision. He later gave three reasons: "so I could 1) experiment with my music, 2) study my horn, and 3) end a drinking habit which had become serious."[172] Sonny had conquered his heroin habit, but other temptations loomed, and alcohol was unavoidable in the clubs. The Bridge had no distractions. "Music aside, the Bridge presented a way for me to clean myself up in a physical way," Sonny said. "Musicians playing in these clubs and being around drugs and cigarette smoking, alcohol, we needed to have a parallel to that."[173]

Then there was Sonny's long-held ambition to go back to school and follow in his siblings' footsteps. "I always wanted formal music training, which my brother and sister had. I didn't," Sonny later said. "I was always trying to catch up on my education."[174] And Sonny was striving for a more perfect sound, a sound that only he could hear. But more than anything, he just needed a break. It had been a rough decade.

"I'd lost the ability to play what I wanted to play every night without the interference of emotionalism," Sonny recalled. "I was filled with question marks."[175]

Financially, it was a devastating move. He was passing up $2,000 a week for club bookings and $1,000 a night for concerts.[176] Quarterly royalty checks and his advance from BMI wouldn't go that far; most of Sonny's income came from live appearances. In the quarter from September through December 1958, Prestige sold more than twenty-five hundred Sonny Rollins records, but it earned him only $357.24 in royalties, and at that time, Sonny still had to make an additional $548.25 in royalties before he had earned out his advance.[177] He was probably in the black by the fall of 1959, but even with his other albums, income from royalties alone would put him at the poverty line.[178] So for Sonny to take a sabbatical, Sonny and Lucille would have to stretch her steady paycheck as far as they could. Sonny was giving up the financial security he had fought so hard for, but he was gaining peace of mind.

"The problem was that I had no place to practice," he said. It was a perennial problem facing instrumentalists in the city—neighbors. According to Sonny, his neighbor was pregnant. "The horn I'm playing, it's loud," Sonny said. "I felt really guilty."[179] Sonny tried practicing in the closet to muffle the sound, like he did growing up in Harlem, but it was still too loud.[180] He needed a bigger woodshed.

In the spring of 1960, "I was sitting at home on a Sunday afternoon and all of a sudden the urge came to me to get out of the house—I'm somewhat of a mystic, by the way, but not in the weirdo sense—and walk," Sonny later recalled.[181] Sonny walked over to the corner paper stand on Delancey, and then, like a vision, he saw the steps leading up to the Williamsburg Bridge, and he ascended.[182] "Here was this big empty space and nobody there," Sonny said. "So I walked across the bridge and I said to myself, 'Wow! I can come up here and practice. There's nobody here!'"[183]

"It was a beautiful, perfect place," Sonny said. "I had the view of the river and all the boats going back and forth and I was able to be on a part of the walkway where I wasn't visible to the subway trains and traffic, which were crossing. I felt like it was God-sent."[184]

Chapter 23

THE BRIDGE

(1960–1961)

In the climax to the 1948 film *The Naked City*, police pursue the harmonica-playing murderer across the Williamsburg Bridge. He bounds up the stairs to the esplanade, shoots a Seeing Eye dog, dodges games of double Dutch, and whirls past roller skaters and baby strollers amid the relentless rush of cars and subway trains. He gets to the pedestrian footpath, sweating profusely and rapidly losing momentum. With police closing in on him from the Manhattan and Brooklyn sides, he climbs a tower before plunging 150 feet to his death.

The plot characterized how most New Yorkers felt about the Bridge. When Sonny first went out there in the spring of 1960, the nearly sixty-year-old structure was covered in potholes and widely considered the most hazardous bridge in the city.[1] The congestion caused regular car accidents, some fatal and explosive.[2] It was mostly mentioned in the press as a site of suicide attempts—despondent schoolteachers, jilted husbands, an out-of-work artist—some prevented, some not.[3] It was a frequent crime scene: petty theft, assault, a murder committed nearby by "unidentified youths" from the Baruch Houses next to the Manhattan entrance, a drop site for ransom briefcases.[4] It was peppered with graffiti and strewn with empty liquor bottles.[5] If hell is other people, as Jean-Paul Sartre wrote, the Williamsburg Bridge was heaven.

At least one person was compelled to be there every day: Ed Flood, the bridge's fifty-four-year-old inspector, who walked some six miles a day along the span, inspecting virtually every inch of the steel for cracks.[6] And one person was there every day by choice: Sonny Rollins. The Williamsburg Bridge was exactly what Sonny was looking for—a wide-open space where nobody else wanted to be. "As bridges go," wrote *Newsweek*, "it is one of New York's ugliest."[7] It was not as conventionally beautiful as the Brooklyn Bridge with its neo-Gothic stone arches, but the Williamsburg's 1.4-mile-long span of steel truss, cross-hatched fencing, and an upper rail casting geometric shadows along the footpath had a more jazz-shaped beauty. And it was rent-free. "Skyline, water, harbor—you're up above it all," Sonny said.[8] Suspended ten feet above the syncopated traffic of cars, subway trains, and tugboats—to Sonny, this was his church.

He later downplayed the Bridge sabbatical as so much jazz mythmaking. "We made a big deal out of it, but the truth is much simpler than anything that has been written," he told François Postif in 1966. "As I usually practiced at night...no one in the apartment could sleep until...I went to practice on the Bridge.... They made people believe that I was doing this for publicity or out of sheer madness, but listen: What better place than a bridge to play at night without annoying your neighbors?"[9]

"I tried the Brooklyn and Manhattan Bridges," Sonny later recalled. "Not only was the Williamsburg closest, but it also had the most favorable expanse—it was broader."[10]

Sonny's apartment was two blocks south of the commercial bustle of Jewish bakeries, haberdashers, pushcarts, pickle men, and delicatessens along Delancey Street, which led to the bridge's esplanade. Up three flights of concrete stairs, few ventured beyond where the esplanade narrowed to the footpath. Hasidim on either side used the walkway on Shabbat, and for some among the diverse working-class population on the Lower East Side and in Williamsburg, it was the morning commute.[11] But the few pedestrians traversing the bridge did not stop to listen to the lone wail of a saxophone.

Rumors about Sonny's whereabouts began to circulate.[12] In May 1960, Leonard Feather wrote that "to all intents and purposes Rollins has disappeared."[13] Nat Adderley heard he had "gone into studious isolation in New Jersey with hopes of coming up with something revolutionary,"[14] a theory that was seconded by Nat Hentoff in *Esquire* that fall.[15] Others insisted that Coltrane "drove Sonny back into the woodshed." And some, like Billy Taylor, thought it was the Gunther Schuller article that sent Sonny into exile.[16]

Sonny offered a cryptic explanation that June. "I am at present engaged in numerous pursuits, the most pressing of which are my writing and composing," he wrote in a letter published in *Down Beat*. "These endeavors are demanding of the greater portion of my time, concentration, and energies. They will best be brought to fruition by my maintaining a certain amount of seclusion and divorcing myself as much as possible from my professional career during this period."[17]

That July, Max Roach, Charles Mingus, and Randy Weston protested low pay at the Newport Jazz Festival by mounting their own counterfestival, the Newport Rebels Festival. Sonny was listed on the bill, but his protest would be silent.[18]

Sonny got rid of his phone; an operator stated that the number had been disconnected.[19] He could receive mail if the sender knew the address. Otherwise, you had to see him in person, and outside of the occasional phone-booth sighting at the Five Spot, almost no one knew where to find him.[20]

Lucille was the only person who always knew where Sonny was. At home, he was in a minimalist room with a gig bag, a photograph of himself playing, a piano, a tall stack of sheet music, some barbells, and a filing folder where he kept his handwritten commonplace book and other jottings.[21] Otherwise, he was out on the Bridge.[22]

"I found a spot by the abutments of the bridge," he later explained. "I used to stand in a place where nobody could see me. It was perfect."[23] He saw the same people walk by every day, but they couldn't see him. To them, he was the wail of a disembodied saxophone—the sound of the Bridge itself.[24]

Sonny kept odd hours. "I would go up there at night, I would go up there in the day...I would be up there fifteen, sixteen hours," he said.[25] He would often be up there at three in the morning, blowing into the dark expanse.[26] The Bridge had some drawbacks. "Yes, the bowels must not be clogged and you must not be in need of going to the toilet either," Sonny wrote in his journal. "As the latter case proved my difficulty as I could not bring air and attack thru my horn for fear of having an accidental elimination."[27] To avoid this, he took breaks. "I'd get there early, practice, go back home to refresh myself, use the bathroom, get a cognac and then return to the bridge to practice more."[28] With nothing but open air and the East River down below, there was of course a simple way to relieve a full bladder, but, Sonny said, "I would never urinate on the Bridge. . . . It was a sacred place. That would have been like pissing in church."[29]

Though his first marriage had ended acrimoniously, Sonny and Lucille led a blissful existence. "I've read several studies which prove that people who have had an unhappy first marriage are much more likely to be happy in their second one," Sonny said. "You know more and your feet are on the ground. It seems to have worked out for me."[30]

Lucille's mother had reservations about her new life in New York. Still hard at work for the IRS in Chicago, Nanette wrote Lucille that past fall, their first contact in weeks after a disagreement. "Dear L: You could sell refrigerators in Iceland. Think you would make a good salesman and since you're the only thing I have, guess I'll give in and write. Am not changing my mind, however. Will not make any comments. You've chosen your life and you are the only one who can live it."[31]

However, any tension was quickly resolved; Sonny would soon call Nanette Mom. On May 31, 1960, Lucille wrote a letter to Chase Manhattan Bank to change the name on her account to Lucille Rollins.[32] Together, they settled into a frugal domestic life on the Lower East Side.

As two ships passing in the night, they began writing daily love notes to each other. Lucille wrote hers before leaving for work, and Sonny wrote his on yellow legal paper before leaving for his. Sonny found time to take up sketching, his youthful pastime; in one sketchbook he rendered a menagerie of animals in pencil, copied from *The Golden Book of Animals*: a lion, a camel, a lynx, a cheetah, an elephant, and a series of cats.[33] While Lucille worked, Sonny ran errands; when she returned, he was on the Bridge.

As myths go, it was fairly pedestrian. They got a dog, Major, a German shepherd they loved, and several cats that lived in the back and had an apparent aversion to jazz, though one sometimes perched on the piano.[34] Sonny read the *Times*; tidied the house; took Major out for walks and gave him baths; bought buttermilk, the freshest container from the back of the cooler, of course; made sure Lucille secured the door chain; and even went to the Department of Motor Vehicles.[35] They ate well, but Sonny strove for moderation in all things but his practice routine, as he wrote her.

Whereas I am in sympathy with your overtures in the direction of self-mastery, I have purchased for you these cookies, 1 lb. Will power by itself is not sufficient to achieve the desired results which you have expressed a desire to achieve. Rather a gradual lessening of your "habit" must begin. Discretion must be now the rule of your technique....After you have consumed your meal please look in the dictionary under the letter L for Love and open the envelope which is there. I will see you soon as possible.

Sometimes, Sonny was the one lacking in "discretion."

Dear Sweetheart,

Have a nice dinner + try to nap. I ate the cookies once again in a ravenous display of indulgence even though my stomach is now suffering as I know.

Perhaps you'll realize how difficult I'm struggling to do these things like exercise and control my desires and wants in areas which I know are temporarily satisfying but ultimately demolishing.

I am very far from being the perfect meticulous human being you say I am and perhaps you'll not make that claim anymore—but instead help me by trying to overcome the same things in your own nature and thus give us a common fight—like EXERCISE!!! etc.

Well until I once again err I shall try not to. See you soon.

Love + kisses for Ever + Ever

S

Some passages were hopelessly romantic.[36]

Does not every day of our existence together underline the one-ness which completely dominates our heretofore separate free spirits. Is it not now abundantly clear that we are inseparably joined together—almost against one's will, if that can be properly construed!

With his own mother gone, Lucille provided unconditional love.

Your display of maternal concern and tenderness was noticed and was welcomed by me this morning—all in the spirit of my recent observation—MOTHERHOOD IS AN ATTITUDE...NOT A CONDITION. Remember too that life usually casts mothers in a tragic role, one in which they are rewarded by ingratitude and scorn. And yet a mother loves...How beautiful...how deep...how sweet. And how sweet and beautiful you are, my one true love.[37]

She was funny, too. In May 1960, Lucille wrote a poem for Sonny on an official Research Corporation internal memo sheet called "Rondo in W," her "first effort," sent from the department of "nuttiness."

Have you ever pondered
on the Third Avenue bus
amid the funk and dirt and chatter—

who am I[38]

It was a time of tight purse strings. One day on Norfolk Street, Sonny bent over to pick up two dimes and two pennies as people on a stoop watched him. With that, he bought an ear of corn, only to return home that morning to find the scene of a crime.

Now lest we get too complacent about luck what with my find this morning let me quickly burst the bubble—for as I came back in the house—Major had my rubbers *[galoshes]* in the middle of the floor—one of them was ruined! He had bitten out a large chunk of rubber from the top of the rubber—so such is life. No I didn't spank him—I just admonished him and he sheepishly retired to the corner, guilty as hell and realizing it.
Net result, gained 22¢
lost rubbers (price unknown)
Maybe they cost 4 or five bucks, I don't know.

Anyway dear please eat well and take a nap if possible—I will need a nap also and will be back not too late as I'll probably go on the Bridge. So be careful in the street crossing with Major and remember that I love you and can hardly wait to manifest this undying love in certain material benefits for your personal delight and pleasure. It won't be long now Lucille, and our current privation is proving to be another link in the chain of our relationship—in that I always feel closer to you during and after we have been through a lean period! That is, closer in another way for I am already as close to you in the general way as it is possible for anyone to be to anyone else.

Be careful

\+ Love

Sonny

They had a poverty of riches. The organizing principle was health: healthy body, mind, and spirit. Yet past compulsions remained. Every day, Sonny wrote, he would "face the startling and intriguing reality that there is within me a force working hard for my own destruction, even as I try to improve."[39]

For diet, Sonny took guidelines from Life Extension Examiners, an organization founded by a group of doctors and originally chaired by William Howard Taft, which promoted healthy eating and abstaining from alcohol and cigarettes.[40] The program promised weight loss of one to two pounds a week by restricting a low-carb diet to fruits, vegetables, and lean meat. Sonny and Lucille ate grapes, cherries, chicken, liver, steak, and Arnold Brick Oven wheat bread, cheating occasionally with the aforementioned cookies.[41]

Sonny committed to quitting smoking, which seemed deleterious to saxophone playing, weakening "the ability to pull power up from your lungs with the velocity and control you deem necessary."[42] Whenever he got the urge to smoke, he would concentrate on music "as a penalty."[43] He bought a wall calendar for 1960 and marked it day by day with "N.C.S.," meaning no cigarette smoking and, on the rare occasion, "box cigs."[44]

He began working out regularly and invested in barbells and exercise equipment. "I remember Monk used to come down and say, 'Oh man, what's all this stuff?'" Sonny said.[45]

He installed an incline sit-up board and, after a doorframe pull-up bar sent him crashing to the ground, bolted a stand-up apparatus to the floor.[46] He woke between eight thirty and ten after a long night on the Bridge and began an extensive workout, gradually increasing the weight: leg raises in bed, upright rows, behind-the-back presses, military press (his favorite), forward raises, bent-over rows, sit-ups (at least twenty-five per set), and thirty or more leg extensions.[47] It would all "aid in the realization of consciousness." Eventually, Sonny bought weight-lifting guru Bob Hoffman's Functional Isometric Contraction Strength Builder system.[48] "Hoffman was the guy," Sonny said. "He was one of the big proponents of bodybuilding. I used to get all his books, his magazines. I was really into it."[49] He jogged on the Bridge and did pull-ups on an overhanging beam. Sonny began to look like a bodybuilder, because he had effectively become one.[50]

To improve flexibility and mindfulness, Sonny began a hatha yoga practice.[51] In May 1960, Swami Vishnudevananda's *Complete Illustrated Book of Yoga* was published in the United States, and Sonny bought a copy.[52]

Sonny also developed his mind. He did not listen to music regularly, though Bach and Tatum were on the turntable and, as background to household chores, hillbilly music.[53] He became a self-taught student of anthropology and sociology. There was Norman Thomas, the six-time presidential candidate for the Socialist Party of America, whom Sonny saw speak in November 1960. In 1961, he attended Ashley Montagu's lecture at Cooper Union and read his antiracist *Statement on Race*, *The Cultured Man*, *The Elephant Man*, and *The Natural Superiority of Women*.[54] Sonny enrolled in an anthropology class at Cooper Union and procured the fourteen-page recommended reading list for the Columbia University Anthropology Department's PhD program, with required readings in Durkheim, Levi-Strauss, and Boas, and an extensive section on Africa.[55]

"I realized everything in music is a pattern of the life cycle itself," Sonny said of his anthropological studies. "It includes a build-up, a climax, and an anti-climax. Nothing really new happens. It's just the same thing expressed in different ways."[56]

Sonny copied notable quotes by hand, typed them out, and filed them away for future use. There was John Donne's "No Man Is an Island," as well as cleric and humorist Sydney Smith. "There is something extremely fascinating in quickness; and most men are desirous of appearing quick," Smith wrote. "The great rule for becoming so, is, by not attempting to appear quicker than you really are; by resolving to understand yourself and others, and to know what *you* mean, and what *they* mean, before you speak or answer. Every man must submit to be slow before he is quick; and insignificant before he is important."[57] He copied this passage from *The Principles of Psychology* by pragmatist philosopher William James: "We must make automatic and habitual, as early as possible, as many useful actions as we can. The more of the details of our daily life we can hand over to the effortless custody of automatism, the more our higher powers of mind will be set free for their own proper work."[58]

Then there was Sonny's spiritual life. "A great musician must be a man of great spiritual stature, ascetics + yogis or disciples of great saints," Sonny wrote in his journal. "MUSIC IS A <u>DIVINE</u> REVELATION."[59] It was Paramahansa Yogananda's best-selling 1946 book *Autobiography of a Yogi* that "convinced me that I wanted to be a yogi," Sonny said.[60] "You have to be ready to read that book," and he was.[61] Sonny kept his original copy for the rest of his life.[62] Yogananda wrote that music was a divine art, with the trinity of Brahma, Vishnu, and Shiva as the first musicians. There were "laws of sound alliance between nature and man," and a "Cosmic Song" in "personal harmony with the Oversoul."[63] Sonny found his own personal harmony on the Bridge.

Key to the journey was harmonizing with others. He and John Coltrane had deep conversations on the phone or at Sonny's apartment and swapped books on Sufism, Buddhism, and Rosicrucianism.[64] Sonny recommended *Autobiography of a Yogi*, Coltrane *The Mysticism of Sound and Music* by Hazrat Inayat Khan. They sought out "not just books about the music itself—but things that related to the larger idea of music and its uses," Sonny said. "Both John and I had ethical values we were developing at that time. So this book [by Khan] was significant, because it showed us that music and those impulses go together in a natural way. It was a wonderful realization that music, if you're trying to play honestly, and the attempt to become a better person are of one piece."[65]

Sonny joined the Rosicrucians, the Ancient Mystical Order Rosae Crucis (AMORC), a syncretic occultist movement dating back centuries that spoke of a "Primordial Tradition" that united all religions.[66] Despite his skepticism—"In the mid-fifties, I began seeing it advertised in a lot of comic books," he said[67]—Sonny began reading the literature and attending meetings. Some of his reservations were tempered by the literature: *Mystics at Prayer*[68] and *Uncommon Men*, a 1960 Rosicrucian publication that touted prominent Rosicrucians, including René Descartes, Isaac Newton, Gottfried Leibniz, Benjamin Franklin, and Goethe.[69]

The AMORC was supposedly based in science, and one night Sonny made a startling discovery during one of his own experiments as a homespun mystic. With the room lit by candlelight, he sat in front of a mirror and stared at his reflection for a prolonged period. Nothing happened, but he tried it again the next night. Still nothing. Third night: "I began looking in the mirror at myself, and my face began to change. I began to look like a sort of a caveman, a Neanderthal guy...a person that would be from ancient, ancient, ancient times.... It really unnerved me. It sort of verified what I'd always thought of reincarnation, that we were another person at one time, in another body.... After that, I realized that a lot of these things had merit."[70] That moment, as dubious as it sounds from a scientific perspective, convinced him that the sabbatical was as much in the service of his music as his spiritual self. "It's not really the occult," Sonny said. "It's really a spiritual journey that I've been engaged in ever since.... Playing my horn and gaining a 'religious' experience, they're somewhat the same thing."[71]

Music was central to Rosicrucianism. Part of the initiation entailed learning the "Rosicrucian Chant," and Sonny studied a chart of "cosmic vibrations" ranging from sound to gamma rays, correlated to the musical keyboard.[72] AMORC held a belief in the "music of the spheres" as an underlying governing force.[73] Rosicrucian mystic Max Heindel theorized that "the musician can hear certain tones in different parts of nature, such as the wind in the forest, the breaking of the surf on the beach, the roar of the ocean and the sounding of many waters. These combined tones make a whole which is the key-note of the Earth—its 'tone.'"[74]

Sonny realized he could harmonize with nature, as master musicians could supposedly "bring to us the atmosphere of our heavenly home world" and "translate them into the sounds of earth life. His is the highest mission, because as a mode of expression for soul life, music reigns supreme." So Sonny's relatively brief journey through Rosicrucianism offered a guide to hitting the very "key-note" of Earth. Soon, Sonny added a kind of Rosicrucian shrine by his home gym and began affixing a red wax AMORC seal to his letters.[75]

Then there were the out-of-body experiences. Once, on the pull-up bar in his apartment, "I was pulling myself up and holding myself in that position for as long as I could, and I called my wife, Lucille, over to watch how long I could hold that position," Sonny recalled. "While she was watching, I held my breath and really hung onto that position for a long time when suddenly I had absolutely no weight. I wasn't even holding myself up at all and I wasn't breathing, either. My brain was flooded with intense light and I was not there at all."[76] As he later recalled of the experience, "I didn't have to breathe. I was comfortable. But I said to myself, 'Oh shit! I'm not breathing!' And then I took a breath." It also happened onstage. Sometimes, he said, "I actually see myself from above."[77]

These onstage out-of-body experiences were anything but effortless. Theoretical physicist Stephon Alexander has written on the *jazz of physics*; Sonny practiced the *physics of jazz*. He would sometimes refer to his Bridge sessions as "analyzation studies."[78] He practiced breathing techniques for tone production; vibrato, tonguing, phrasing, and articulation;[79] self-designed exercises and patterns on intervals, chords, cadences, and scales;[80] the cycle of fourths (but also seconds, thirds, fifths, sixths, and so on); "evenness of embouchure";[81] modal studies (Ionian, Dorian, Phrygian, and more); whole-tone exercises; voice leading; transpositions of three-note cells into all twelve keys; saxophone fingering studies; extensive experiments in fundamental tones and the harmonic series; and "Musical Physics,"[82] which called for "hearing the first and last notes of the phrase as 'part of the first note.'" Through the bell of the horn, Sonny could seemingly resolve the paradox of quantum entanglement that Einstein referred to as "spooky action at a distance."[83]

At the top of these studies, Sonny usually wrote, in all caps, "memorize," "randomize," "chromaticize," or "mentalize."[84] Sonny didn't practice

licks, riffs, or lines: he worked out what he referred to repeatedly in elaborate diagrams as "equations," with note patterns corresponding to numbers
in their respective scales. Sometimes, he would invite a fellow experimenter
to "do some equations."[85] Despite later claims to primitivism, offstage he
was a mathematician. He never showed the work that allowed him to spontaneously let loose a cascade of notes that might sound like the Fibonacci
sequence made musical.

"Even as we learn our scales and 'run' (sound patterns) on these scales,"
Sonny wrote, "we must prepare for the time when we forget these same scales
and patterns—turning them instead into thoughts expressed, rather than a[s]
musical equasions [sic] recalled. So that when we actually go out to play and
start improvising, we may stop consciously remembering and thinking and
studying and recalling and allow the music which is as we have pointed out
already in the air just waiting for us to relax and let it come out of us and our
horns."[86]

To supplement his own self-made method book, there were classics of the
genre: Hyacinthe Klosé's clarinet text and Sigurd Raschèr's *Top-Tones for
the Saxophone* among them, and more general music books, such as *Physical Basis of Music* by Alexander Wood, *Musical Acoustics* by Charles Culver,
Sensations of Tone by Hermann von Helmholtz, and *Musical Engineering* by
Harry Olson. To become more aware of his breath, he practiced "ausculta-
tion," he wrote, the medical term for listening to the organs.[87] In his practice
log, Sonny determined that four notes could be combined into twenty-four
possible combinations of four. He then did the calculation for "twelve facto-
rial" to determine the number of combinations of twelve for all twelve notes
in the tempered scale: 479,001,600. With these limitless possibilities, there
was never an excuse to play the same chorus, much less the same measure,
more than once.

Like a weight lifter focusing on one muscle group on a particular day,
Sonny applied great discipline to these systematic studies. "Don't deviate
from one idea to another while practicing," he wrote in a journal entry. "In
other words when you hit upon something that needs doing and you are
receptive to doing this stick on that. Don't in the course of doing it get side
tracked into another area which at the time has no relation. . . . Indeed victory

is ahead—but do not forget that included in that 'ahead' is many patient slow painstaking efforts. It seems to be very far away today . . . that 'ahead.'"[88]

It seems he wasn't always certain he would ever reach that "ahead." He kept hundreds of pages of meticulous notes on his practice sessions.[89] "Now let me begin by saying that many people who have succumbed to failure in one way or another have been just that close to success so as not to see it," Sonny wrote. "And furthermore, just a small extra measure of endeavor could have resolved this unreal juxtaposition for them and in their favor. The lesson to be drawn from this is in a practical way the lesson of perseverance, for we never realize how close we are to the positive expression of our endeavors or the 'far end of our pole.'"[90]

The ultimate goal of this discipline and self-control was spiritual. Another term Sonny coined that began to appear in his practice notes was "O.T.Y.O.G."—"Oh Thank You Oh God."

"Playing my horn was more than just practicing notes," Sonny later said. "It was always something else of a spiritual nature involved."[91] His self-discipline led to greater self-awareness. "Let the inside me be me," he wrote in a journal entry. "Previously I had let the outside me designate the real me, the ME of me. Me. Now I shall let the inside me designate the real me and the outside me the OUTSIDE ME."[92]

Sonny wasn't always out on the Bridge alone. Jackie McLean, soprano saxophonist Steve Lacy, tenor saxophonist Paul Jeffrey, and saxophonist Charles Wyatt would sometimes trek out there with him.[93] He accepted visitors at his apartment; one day, pianist Bill Triglia came by and heard Sonny practicing with trumpeter Tony Fruscella.[94]

Monk had introduced Lacy to Sonny at the Five Spot in 1958, during Sonny's two weeks with Monk. On the Bridge, they would sometimes work through tunes like "Ask Me Now."[95] Lacy agreed to keep the Bridge a semi-secret. "We do rehearse on a bridge," Lacy later said. "It's not the Brooklyn Bridge, but I'd rather not say which one it is, because it's such a wonderful rehearsal spot that everyone would want to go there."[96] The Bridge tested Lacy's limits. "We were inundated with sounds," he recalled. "There was the traffic of cars, planes, sometimes a helicopter, boats, horns, and all of that very loud. So it was no easy thing, in that noisy environment, to make our own sound heard." The first time they went out, Lacy "was horrified. My sound was so small. Sonny Rollins was big, formidable and as loud as the horns from the boats."[97]

Jackie McLean had a similar experience. "Sonny could blow these low blasts that had tugboats answering him from down below in the water," he recalled. "I said, 'Jesus, Sonny, you're going to mess up the traffic in the river, man.'"[98]

He was out there, no matter the weather. Sonny and a friend "were up there one day in the winter for a few hours, and then we walked down off the Bridge to warm up," he said. "We went and got some cognac and he thought, 'Gee, we've had a nice day.' I said to him, 'Now let's go back.' He couldn't say no at the time, but he was freezing."[99]

When Sonny was not on the Bridge, he would practice elsewhere. At one point, he practiced in a room with nothing in it but a painting by abstract expressionist painter Judith Lindbloom, a friend of Steve Lacy's.[100] Mainly, he would practice at trumpeter Jake Koven's studios on Music Row, a shabby but serviceable rehearsal space in a walk-up building with wooden stairs. Sonny would walk the more than fifty blocks uptown with his tenor in one hand and a valise with a dumbbell in the other—for parity's sake.[101] "They've given me a key and I go there whenever I want," Sonny said of Koven's. "I can only play the tenor until about eleven at night, but there's a piano there and I can use that all night long."[102]

In the summer of 1960, twenty-one-year-old tenor saxophonist George Goodman was at Koven's when "the first four notes of the 1930s hit 'Three Little Words' came through the wall like shots from a nail gun," he later wrote. "The saxophonist in the other room began splintering the notes into partials, and then constructed arpeggios that swirled up from the bottom of his horn, spiraling out beyond the legitimate range of the instrument and into the stratosphere of the piccolo. He restated the notes, played them bel canto, made them waltz, turned them upside down and inside out, and ran them up-tempo in 4/4 time, taking outlandish liberties with meter and intonation. It was pure passion, power, and precision. It was pure Sonny Rollins."[103]

In that staggering display of saxophone virtuosity—isolating partials, overtone experiments, exploring the altissimo range—Sonny was working through the material from German-born classical alto saxophonist Sigurd

Raschèr's *Top-Tones for the Saxophone.*[104] That summer, Sonny wrote Raschèr "a big, bulky letter of nine pages on yellow paper in good handwriting," Raschèr recalled. Sonny identified himself as "not only an admirer of me, but also one of my students."[105] He had even extended Raschèr's technique in order to play multiphonics—two notes at once.[106] When Raschèr asked Sonny how he developed this ability, Sonny explained that he had been practicing it all summer long on the Bridge.

Soon, Sonny took on a student of his own: Alfred "Pee Wee" Ellis, the future musical director and arranger for James Brown, and co-composer of "Say It Loud—I'm Black and I'm Proud."[107] During summers, Ellis, who grew up in Rochester, used to visit his aunt who lived in Sugar Hill on 152nd Street. That summer, he had a chance encounter with Sonny. "I was walking down Broadway with my horn," Ellis recalled, "and there was a guy walking towards me with a horn, and it turned out to be Sonny Rollins. So I asked him if he'd give me a lesson, and he said yes."[108] They walked around the corner to Koven's, and so began a weekly routine that continued all summer. "Every Wednesday, I would fly into New York and meet Sonny, and spend an hour or two in that room, and I'd fly back to Rochester," he said.[109] "He didn't charge me much"—only seven dollars per lesson. "I was earning ninety dollars a week at The Pythodd Club in Rochester and the flight was $55. It was worth it. Studying with Sonny was amazing."[110]

Ellis was "like a kid in a candy store...A sponge in deep water!!" he recalled.[111] Sonny preferred to lead by example and always brought his horn with him.[112] Sometimes, Sonny would accompany Ellis on piano; other times, Ellis would accompany Sonny on piano. "We concentrated on basics," Ellis said. "Tone production, scales, intervals, and some exercises he wrote out for me." They practiced long tones, sustaining one note for a prolonged period, and harmonics, in which "you'd play a low B, for instance, and you can play four octaves, with the same fingering up and down without changing the embouchure. It kind of gives you a personal relationship with each note. . . . He helped me in a lot of ways—being true to the music and fighting the good fight."[113] It was Sonny who instilled in him a deeper sense of pride—and helped "the man who invented funk" say it *loud.*

Another student who visited Sonny during this period was René McLean,

Jackie McLean's son and Sonny's godson. He was a student at Seward Park High School, down the block from Sonny's apartment. "I would go by Sonny's house after school sometimes to get some pointers," McLean said. "He would tell me to play and learn my scales. That was my early developmental period, but just to be around Sonny and be in his presence was a lesson."[114]

Sonny also enrolled in music classes himself. He began attending an intensive orchestration class at the New School incognito, but decided to stop when a student recognized him.[115] Instead, Sonny studied with Max Hughes, a classically trained midwestern pianist who studied at the Kansas City Conservatory and taught at the University of Kansas before moving to San Francisco. When he relocated to New York, their mutual friend Kermit Scott put them in touch.[116] With Hughes, Sonny studied piano technique, composition, harmony, and orchestration.[117] Hughes worked at the Henry Street Settlement, a nonprofit social services and arts center, only a five-minute walk from Sonny's apartment.[118]

On September 7, 1960, Sonny turned thirty. The next day, he recorded his thoughts on the milestone in his journal. "Birthday now past but tendencies toward disruption still exist," he wrote. It seems he violated his strict diet and succumbed to the urge for a cigarette. "By the very documenting of these transgressions I am demonstrating my awakening strength which will come into full bloom at such time as I have suffered through the various manifestations of these problems."[119]

During his sabbatical, Sonny did maintain a modest social life. He had strictly sworn off any commercial endeavors until he was ready, but he had befriended maverick Armenian American producer George Avakian, eleven years his senior.[120] Avakian had signed Miles to Columbia and, in 1960, produced the *Billboard* number one pop album *The Button-Down Mind of Bob Newhart* and the Everly Brothers' "Cathy's Clown," a number one single for five weeks that summer. Avakian had a disarming, soft-spoken charm that belied his status as a major label bigwig—and he loved Sonny.

They first met years earlier at Basin Street when Sonny was with Brown-Roach and began talking during set breaks. With Sonny, "You could sit down and have a serious talk about almost anything, because he kept up with the news of the day and events of the world, and he had good opinions, thoughtful opinions," Avakian recalled.[121] They became friends, and in October 1960, Avakian invited Sonny to attend the World Series. Sonny gladly agreed to go to Yankee Stadium to see his team against the Pittsburgh Pirates, October 9–10.[122] During the national anthem, Sonny did not stand, in protest of social injustice.[123]

"We had very good seats," Avakian recalled. "Sonny was very knowledgeable, which was helpful, and we happened to hit some pretty good games," though the Pirates won both. Despite the Yankees' series loss, it cemented their bond, which led to a business relationship. "We just kind of drifted into it," Avakian said. "Nothing very special. It just grew out of friendship."[124]

Three months later, in January 1961, there were rumors that Sonny would be ending his sabbatical and appearing at the Birdhouse in Chicago. He never showed up, though, and Donald Byrd took his place. "The management of the club said he was still practicing and experimenting," read the report in *Down Beat*. "Rumor has it that he does his practicing in the middle of a well-known bridge in New York City."[125]

Sonny had begun to realize that the sabbatical might have to end. "I love you," he wrote Lucille in one of his daily love notes, "and we are nearing the time when our labors of the present will be our pleasures of everyday."[126]

On March 28, 1961, Sonny's restlessness and an early spring malaise was the subject of a two-page letter: "Dearest Lucille," it began. They were both experiencing some bouts of depression as the seasons changed. "As you know, hot weather incites a listlessness in me which is extremely dangerous to the progress I have made. Speaking of progress, I have reached the point to which my endeavors have been aimed and this in itself can cause me to become impatient and bored if I am not careful to guard against it." Upon his return, counterintuitively, Sonny looked forward to being able "to relax more and take more vacations." But one more summer on sabbatical remained. "However difficult this last summer might loom there is no denying that I have prepared myself and am able and ready to make the above plans materialize. Every note that I play will be played for you. The trials and hardships of these days together has invoked in me the highest feeling of devotion towards you and indeed your presence has brought about the success which I have definitely achieved."[127]

The following week, Sonny hinted at his reentry in a five-page handwritten response to a letter from Marty Burns, a college sophomore writing a paper on the contemporary state of jazz.[128] Burns, who hardly expected any response at all from the jazz scene's most enigmatic missing person, was shocked; it made for quite a term paper. Sonny had read a *New York Times* article detailing plans to create a network of jazz clubs across the Soviet Union as a bulwark against the spread of capitalism.[129] To Sonny, however, jazz was a "tremendous force for understanding and peace" that could have the power to ease Cold War tensions.[130] Sonny believed that the "National Art Form" should be used as a diplomatic tool to promote multicultural tolerance. "Contrary to some beliefs jazz music is not the sole property of any one group of people!" he wrote. "Jazz music, while no doubt utilizing the 'rhythm' of such warmer climated areas as Africa, adds to that rhythm the harmonies which have been developed and perpetuated in the colder land areas of Europe." To Sonny, "This combination of cultures has endowed jazz with a freedom which does not exist in any other music. It is therefore superfluous to speculate on the future direction of Jazz. Jazz will evolve as mankind evolves. . . . Jazz, as men, has no limits, no boundaries save those it would inflict upon itself."[131]

Sonny felt that jazz had to shift from the jazz club to the concert hall and that the "cigarette-smoking, whisky-drinking jazz great must be replaced by the clean-living, healthy, socially-aware jazz great. This transition is not so difficult as it may seem and in many respects is already in manifestation," Sonny wrote. "I hope to further the projection of this new image."[132]

Sonny got more of a push to come down from the Bridge that June, when Charles Mingus and Max Roach, who cofounded Debut Records together, came to visit him on Grand Street. Mingus was taken aback by Sonny's chiseled visage. But the change was more than skin deep. Sonny even gave Mingus a copy of H. Spencer Lewis's *Mansions of the Soul.* "Yes you have changed, Sonny, and I'm sure you realize I love that change," Mingus wrote. "It is rather quietly screaming at the top of your voice, muscles, and quiet attitude."[133] That month, Mingus went to London to film *All Night Long* (1962), where he encountered a racist atmosphere as soon as he got off the plane, and he wrote Sonny a six-page single-spaced letter on June 20 after several sleepless nights demanding his return to the scene.[134]

Mingus hadn't written anyone in years, and what came out of the typewriter was a torrent of emotion. It could be expressed only in writing, Mingus wrote, in order to keep his ego out of it and to grapple with his "<u>many</u> more than <u>two selves</u> that I have rather hesitantly learned to live with, as perhaps you have done obviously with yourself."[135]

Mingus could follow Sonny and seek salvation through the Sisyphean pursuit of study Sonny seemed to favor, he wrote, but "I'd much rather you'd save me immediately, and Max, with your saxophone. I'd like to discuss some of this on the bandstand with you. I haven't cared and have cared too much also. But since I've seen you with Max I have been born again."

Mingus's theory was that Sonny's physical transformation was motivated by more than fitness for its own sake. "I think that aside from your faith you don't want anybody messing with you," he wrote. "I know the time Jesus got the whip out on the dealers in his temple. He was a pretty strong fellow in many ways that you're not, but I don't think he could press no 215 pounds."

To Mingus, salvation could not be found in the self without being found in the community. "I'm still old-fashioned in the belief that part of finding God is finding yourself in relation to man and with man as your brother," Mingus wrote. Together they had lived through hell, and if Sonny had found a little piece of heaven, Mingus hoped they could live through that together as well.

> It is a further belief that if we seek in our music together, somewhat like the olden days when people played for beauty other than money, there we will find and give to the others and ourselves. But if we have found the sound of God itself and keep it to ourselves, there are those who must seek without you or the finder who pleases himself only with the sound of the Lord pouring from his horn. We must seek another and another so that all with ears can have the voice of God so needed. If you have this voice take it from your locked doors. Open your case. We will hear you as you hold your horn to let Him speak.
>
> Your friend,
> Chazz

Max, Mingus, and Sonny never did form that trio, but soon thereafter, Sonny came down from Sinai.

———◁○▷———

Two weeks after Mingus's letter, a journalist blew Sonny's cover.[136] It was teased on the cover of the July 1961 issue of *Metronome*: "Tenorman in Seclusion." The article, "Conversations on a Bridge," was by veteran jazz journalist Ralph Berton, the brother of drummer and Hollywood music director Vic Berton and, from 1940 to 1942, the erstwhile host of WNYC's *Metropolitan Revue*, considered the first serious jazz radio show.[137] Berton's article began with a full-page illustration of a bearded man in a broken-in blue baseball cap, freshly laundered chinos, and a sweatshirt, flanked by steel girders, eyes closed, blowing a tenor saxophone. It looked uncannily like Sonny Rollins.

"His real name is a bright one in the starmap of contemporary jazz, but out of respect for his privacy I will call him Buster Jones," the article opened. "A year or so ago, more or less at the peak of his fame, Buster Jones retired without warning from the jazz scene—vanished, in fact."[138] The mysterious "tenor man," Berton wrote, was a poll winner who recorded with Thelonious Monk, Miles Davis, Art Blakey, and Dizzy Gillespie. There was only one jazz musician in the world who fit that description.

One summer night in 1960, Berton and his wife, Phyllis, decided to watch the sunset from the Bridge on their way back home to Brooklyn when they heard something that stopped them in their tracks. "His eyes open but unseeing," Berton wrote, Sonny was "running weird changes and curves, jumping octaves with the smooth stride of an Olympic hurdle-racer," his body gyrating in constant motion, "blowing always, usually a single phrase over and over, smoothing out a sequence of triplets, superimposing a crescendo, riding the pulse of a non-existent rhythm section."

"Sonny . . . aren't you Sonny Rollins?" Berton said.

Sonny paused. "Why? Would that be important—if I were Sonny Rollins?"

"I think so," said Berton.

"Why?"

"Because, I suppose, anything Sonny Rollins does could be important."

Sonny took a deep breath and considered his options. "O.K. Yeah. I'm Sonny Rollins."[139]

Perhaps to avoid seeming sycophantic in person but dismissive on paper, Berton felt compelled to mention he had given Sonny bad reviews.

"That's one reason, maybe, why I'm out here," Sonny said. "I felt for a long time that I wasn't going anywhere, that I had ceased to speak the truth. I had to get to be myself again somehow. I had to ask myself who I was, what I was trying to do with my music."

Berton felt that by hiding his light under a bushel, Sonny was "abusing a considerable talent," that "a lot of people are worrying about you, wondering what happened."

"I'll be back. One of these days I'll be back. I just had to do this," Sonny said. "I think we're here to do good. We have to make ourselves as perfect as we can, in mind and body, in order to give the world the truth that we have inside ourselves. It can't be forced or hurried. The truth comes out in its own time."

Berton saw him several more times, and even visited him on Grand Street, intent on writing the story, but, Sonny said, there was no story unless he came off the Bridge. Berton waited a year and, when Sonny didn't come down, published it anyway.

Sonny had been found, but he didn't reemerge immediately. "I read Ralph Berton's article with a great deal of sadness," wrote one reader in a letter to the editor that September. "For a long time I have been waiting for Sonny Rollins to come out of his hiding place, to make available, again, more of that magnificent, harsh, pro-life music of his."[140] The letter came from Goleta, California. And Sonny began to realize that it wasn't just Mingus who needed him; there were countless other fans waiting, as close as the Village and as far as Japan.[141]

Atsuhiko Kawabata, a twenty-seven-year-old foreign correspondent for the short-lived Japanese edition of *Down Beat*, was one such fan. The magazine's editor, Kiyoshi Koyama, made a request: "Please find Sonny." Kawabata asked his connections on the New York scene, to no avail. Sonny didn't even have a phone. So he rented an apartment near 400 Grand Street and hoped for serendipity to strike. Yet over several months, there were no Sonny sightings. On September 18, 1961, Kawabata mustered the courage to go to Sonny's apartment. Was it even the right address? A piano being played inside suggested it could be. He rang the bell. Surprisingly, Sonny let him in, and there he was in the inner sanctum sitting across from the piano. Major was barking, Lucille reading a magazine. There was a stack of twenty books on spirituality—Rosicrucianism and other subjects and a Japanese Hakata doll. Sonny must have felt a connection, because he agreed to his first official press appearance in two years. "I didn't want to just become the bait of journalists until I knew myself what my plan would be," Sonny told Kawabata.[142] Now he knew.

On October 7, Kawabata met Sonny at 9:30 a.m., and they walked out to the middle of the Bridge, Sonny carrying his Mark VI, Kawabata a camera to document the occasion. Sonny had a spot where he always opened his case and left it, a busker for the gods. "You seem like you've mastered the sax. Do you still need to practice?" Kawabata asked as Sonny began to play. Of course, he knew the answer. Sonny was still searching for a sound, he said, practicing long tones, taking it "one note at a time."[143]

Finally, it was time to come out of his two-year self-imposed exile. At one point, Sonny began studying the meaning of exile in the work of Léopold Sédar Senghor, the Senegalese president, poet, and cocreator of the Négritude movement, which spread black consciousness throughout the African diaspora. "First, keep one's distance, refuse to take part in the headlong reckless course of a world severed from its moorings," read one passage Sonny underlined, "then recognize that the acceptance of one's exile generally satisfies the initial prescription of the coloniser." Sonny circled this passage: "The only true decolonization is that of the mind."[144] Having decolonized his mind, he was ready to bring the Bridge to the stage.[145]

"I have a family photo of me when I was one or two years old," Sonny said. "I was holding a ball and looked like the proverbial cute little boy, except for one thing: my face. It was saying, 'Damn, here I am again, having to go through this life once again.'" *Courtesy of Sonny Rollins/ Schomburg Center for Research in Black Culture, Manuscripts, Archives and Rare Books Division, The New York Public Library*

Sonny's paternal grandfather, Steadman Rollins. *Courtesy of Sonny Rollins/Schomburg Center for Research in Black Culture, Photographs and Prints Division, The New York Public Library*

Sonny's parents, Valborg and Walter Rollins. *Courtesy of Sonny Rollins*

Sonny's brother, Valdemar, born November 3, 1925. *Courtesy of Clifton Anderson and Sonny Rollins*

Sonny's Garveyite maternal grandmother, Miriam Walcott. *Courtesy of Sonny Rollins*

Sonny's sister, Gloria, born August 31, 1928. *Courtesy of Sonny Rollins/Schomburg Center for Research in Black Culture, Photographs and Prints Division, The New York Public Library*

Sonny, ready to hit Fifty-Second Street before applying his eyebrow pencil mustache. *The Collection of Faith Ringgold and Burdette Ringgold Estate.*

Sonny at approximately fourteen years old. *Courtesy of Sonny Rollins*

Sonny at approximately sixteen years old. *Courtesy of Sonny Rollins*

Sonny with one version of the Counts of Bop, without the "inner circle." Musicians unidentified. *Courtesy of Sonny Rollins*

Benjamin Franklin High School yearbook photo, class of 1947. *Courtesy of Sonny Rollins*

A jam session in Brooklyn, late 1940s. *From left*: Michael Mattos (bass), Ernie Henry (alto saxophone), Kenny Dorham (trumpet), and Sonny Rollins (tenor saxophone). Drummer unidentified. *Lillian Wright. Courtesy of Sonny Rollins/Schomburg Center for Research in Black Culture, Photographs and Prints Division, The New York Public Library*

Sonny Rollins, Art Blakey, and Curly Russell at Birdland. *Photographer unidentified. Courtesy of Sonny Rollins/ Schomburg Center for Research in Black Culture, Photographs and Prints Division, The New York Public Library*

Sonny Rollins and Roy Haynes, Club 845, 1951. *Frankie "Downbeat" Brown. Courtesy of Frank Brown, Jr./The Collection of Frankie "Downbeat" Brown*

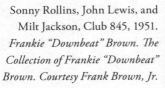

Sonny Rollins, John Lewis, and Milt Jackson, Club 845, 1951. *Frankie "Downbeat" Brown. The Collection of Frankie "Downbeat" Brown. Courtesy Frank Brown, Jr.*

Loop Lounge, Cleveland, 1956. Back row (*from left*): Lou Donaldson, Clifford Brown, unidentified woman, George Morrow, Lawrence "Jacktown" Jackson. Front row (*from left*): Max Roach, Sonny Rollins, Richie Powell. *Photographer unidentified. Courtesy of Sonny Rollins/ Schomburg Center for Research in Black Culture, Photographs and Prints Division, The New York Public Library*

The funeral of Clifford Brown, June 30, 1956, Mt. Carmel Methodist Church in Wilmington, Delaware. Top row (*from left*): Sonny
Rollins, George Morrow. Bottom row (*from left*): Max Roach's
mother, Cressie Roach, Max Roach, and his first wife, Mildred
Roach. *Courtesy of the AFRO American Newspapers Archives*

onny Rollins, Dizzy Gillespie, and Max Roach at the Music
arn, August 30, 1956. *Robert Parent. Courtesy of Dale Parent,
he Bob Parent Archive*

onny Rollins, Max Roach, Miles Davis, and (possibly) John
Coltrane at the Music Barn in Lenox, Massachusetts, August
0, 1956. *Robert Parent. Courtesy of Dale Parent, The Bob Parent
rchive*

From left: Sonny Rollins, Connie Kay, and Milt Jackson at the
Music Barn, August 30, 1956. *Robert Parent. Courtesy of Dale
Parent, The Bob Parent Archive*

Thelonious Monk, Sonny Rollins, and record store clerk and saxophonist Bob Doran at Colony Record Store on Broadway, 1957. *Jerry Lee. Courtesy of Sonny Rollins/Schomburg Center for Research in Black Culture, Photographs and Prints Division, The New York Public Library*

Sonny Rollins, Thelonious Monk, and Ahmed Abdul-Malik at the Five Spot, where Sonny joined Thelonious Monk's quartet from September 19 to October 1, 1958. *Not pictured*: Roy Haynes. This and other photos from that night were taken by photographer Marvin Scott, then a senior at NYU. *Courtesy of Marvin Scott*

Sonny Rollins on the Williamsburg Bridge, October 7, 1961. *Atsuhiko Kawabata. Courtesy of Hanako Kawabata*

Sonny Rollins at the Jazz Gallery,
soon after his return from the Bridge
sabbatical, November 21, 1961.
*Robert Parent. Courtesy of Dale
Parent, The Bob Parent Archive*

Birdland "souvenir photograph"
with (*from left*) John Coltrane,
Lucille and Sonny Rollins, Prophet
Jennings, and Arthur Taylor.
*Courtesy of Sonny Rollins/Schomburg
Center for Research in Black Culture,
Photographs and Prints Division, The
New York Public Library*

From left: Billy Higgins,
unidentified woman, Sonny
Rollins, Lucille Rollins, Max
Hughes, and Major at the Rollins
apartment on Willoughby Walk.
*Photograph by Joe Alper. Courtesy of
the Joe Alper Photo Collection LLC*

Sonny Rollins and Coleman Hawkins at the Newport Jazz Festival, 1963. *Lee Tanner. Courtesy of Lisa Tanner Photography*

Don Cherry, Henry Grimes, Billy Higgins, and Sonny Rollins at Teatro dell'Arte in Milan, January 13, 1963. *© Riccardo Schwamenthal/ CTSIMAGES*

Sonny Rollins and journalist Michel Delorme in Paris, January 1963. *Roger Kasparian. Courtesy of Studio Boissière, rogerkasparian.com*

Sonny Rollins with Don Cherry and Henry Grimes at the Stockholm Concert Hall, January 17, 1963. *Not pictured*: Billy Higgins. *Ove Alström. Courtesy of The Centre for Swedish Folk Music and Jazz Research and Inger Stjerna*

Sonny Rollins and Reiko Hoshino in Kyoto, Fall 1963. *Courtesy of Sonny Rollins/Schomburg Center for Research in Black Culture, Photographs and Prints Division, The New York Public Library*

Sonny Rollins at Masahiro Oki's Yoga Training Institute at Ikenoue in Tokyo's Setagaya Ward, Fall 1963. *Hideko Fujinori. Courtesy of Sonny Rollins/Schomburg Center for Research in Black Culture, Photographs and Prints Division, The New York Public Library*

Sonny Rollins and Don Cherry at Steve Lacy's Bleecker Street loft, circa 1963. Prophet Jennings mentioned that Sonny was playing a thousand choruses of "Ol' Man River" in the film clip. *Film still by Richard "Prophet" Jennings. Courtesy of Dominique Jennings Brandon*

Sonny Rollins and Bud Powell at Max Roach and Abbey Lincoln's Central Park West apartment, August 1964. *Film still by Richard "Prophet" Jennings. Courtesy of Dominique Jennings Brandon*

Sonny Rollins and Gertrude Abercrombie at her South Side Chicago mansion in 1964. *Photographer unidentified. Illinois State Museum, Dinah Abercrombie Livingston Archives. Courtesy of Illinois State Museum*

Sonny Rollins, Herbie Hancock, Bob Cranshaw, Ron Carter, and Roy McCurdy recording *Now's the Time* at RCA Studios, 1964. *Photography by George Avakian. Courtesy of Anahid Avakian Gregg and Maro Avakian/George Avakian and Anahid Ajemian Papers, Music Division, The New York Public Library*

Sonny Rollins and Jean-Paul Sartre at Jazzland, Paris, 1966. *Thierry Trombert. Courtesy of Thierry Trombert*

Sonny Rollins and Randi Hultin
in Oslo, 1971. *Photographer
unidentified. Courtesy of Sonny
Rollins/Schomburg Center for
Research in Black Culture,
Photographs and Prints Division,
The New York Public Library*

Sonny Rollins and Charles
Mingus at Mingus's surprise
fifty-sixth birthday party at
the Manhattan Plaza home of
Charles and Sue Mingus, April
1978. Sonny made a note at
this time: "Ask Charles: Is it
about eating and putting a roof
over your head? Is that what
life amounts to?" *Photographer
unidentified. Courtesy of Sonny
Rollins/Schomburg Center for
Research in Black Culture,
Photographs and Prints Division,
The New York Public Library*

Sonny and Lucille Rollins with Brigadier and Carrie, Germantown, 1995. *Photograph by John Abbott. Courtesy of John Abbott*

Sonny Rollins with Bob Cranshaw (bass), Kobie Watkins (drums), Clifton Anderson (trombone), and Bobby Broom (guitar), Alte Oper, Frankfurt, Germany, November 26, 2008. *Photograph by John Abbott. Courtesy of John Abbott*

Sonny Rollins with Ornette Coleman in their debut performance together at Sonny's eightieth birthday concert at the Beacon Theatre, September 10, 2010. In the background: Christian McBride. *Photograph by John Abbott. Courtesy of John Abbott*

Sonny Rollins and Bill Clinton at the 2011 Kennedy Center Honors dinner hosted by Secretary of State Hillary Rodham Clinton at the US Department of State in Washington, DC, December 3, 2011. *Photograph by Terri Hinte. Courtesy of Terri Hinte*

Sonny Rollins receives the 2010 National Medal of Arts from President Barack Obama at an East Room ceremony at the White House on March 2, 2011. *Ruth Ellis, 2011. Courtesy of Ruth Ellis*

PART 2

Chapter 24

AFTER THE BRIDGE

(1961–1962)

Before the sabbatical ended, Sonny reconnected with old friends, just as Mingus had hoped, and it happened in part through Prophet Jennings, the artist, hustler, dancer, journalist, hype man, marijuana dealer, and friend of Mingus, Monk, Miles, and Max, whom Sonny had met five years earlier in Detroit.[1]

Prophet wanted to see Sonny, but Sonny "had no telephone or nothin'," Prophet recalled.[2] If Sonny and Lucille had a phone hiding somewhere in the apartment to make outgoing calls, which remains doubtful, the number was unlisted, as Sonny's number would always be for the rest of his life.

One day, Prophet saw Sonny walking down Seventh Avenue wearing a big black hat and carrying his horn. Sonny explained that if Prophet wanted to visit him, he had to send a telegram first. Prophet sent the telegram and Sonny confirmed the time. It was one of those balmy New York summer days when rubber soles stick to the sidewalks. Sonny evidently took it as a cue to practice Bikram yoga; he had the oven on, with the fan circulating the heat. "Newk answered the door," Prophet recalled. "He was buck naked. And he had on some brogans, big old brogues on his feet. . . . Newk, he wasn't no kind of freak or nothin', it's just he'd do what he wanted in his house." In the bathroom, Sonny had written "POSTURE" on the wall in big letters. "I said, 'How ya doin', Newk?' He said, 'I—I'm fine.'"[3]

After that, Sonny spent time at Prophet's apartment, known as the Temple, a house of worship for and of "giants, royalty," many of whom became subjects of his portraiture. "Sonny Rollins said we should make this into a shrine," Prophet said.[4] In 1959, Thelonious Monk visited the Temple and saw Prophet's portrait of him on the wall,[5] and used it as the cover art for *Thelonious Monk with John Coltrane*.[6] His portrait of Eric Dolphy became the cover to *Outward Bound*; he also did the cover art for Dolphy's *Out There*. Prophet painted at least two portraits of Sonny. (There were musical portraits of Prophet, too: Freddie Hubbard's "Prophet Jennings" and Eric Dolphy's "The Prophet.")[7] Before long, Sonny would put up at least one of Prophet's paintings.[8]

The Temple was modest—bookshelves, television set, barely enough room for a party—but they were used to small bandstands. "It wasn't a big place, but it was a happy place, and there were always good happenings," Prophet said. One night, after closing at Birdland at 4:30 a.m., Monk and Nica came by. At 5, Monk put on "Jackie-ing" and started dancing. Prophet got a lot of noise complaints, which they ignored. There were quieter moments, too, many of which Prophet captured with his ubiquitous eight-millimeter camera, bequeathed to him by Dizzy Gillespie: in one, Sonny has a deep conversation with Prophet's evocative portrait of Lady Day.[9]

Before ending the sabbatical, Sonny needed a band. He would call it Sonny Rollins and Company.[10] He called bassist Bob Cranshaw and drummer Walter Perkins, his rhythm section from the 1959 Playboy Jazz Festival, who were willing to be "linemen" on the team.[11] Next, Sonny wanted a chordal instrument,[12] and soon, Jim Hall started finding notes in his mailbox.[13] The first note was matter-of-fact.

Dear Jim,
   I'd like to talk to you about music.[14]

"It was like some mystery play from then on," Hall said. "He didn't have a phone—by choice. . . . Mine was disconnected—not by my choice. So we wrote each other notes."[15] When Hall could afford it, he sent telegrams.

Eventually, they arranged a meeting at Hall's fourth-floor apartment. "He put a plastic bag down on the table," Hall recalled, "and he started talking. And he's so dignified. . . . And all of a sudden, the bag sort of jerked around and I said, 'Sonny what is that?' Typical of him, he said, 'I'll tell you about that, soon as we finish this.'" When Hall said yes, Sonny "opened the bag and there was a little lizard or chameleon or something from a pet shop that he'd brought in. And he said, 'Look at him, isn't he great?'"[16]

Hall was known for, in his words, "watching the blend,"[17] and was prepared for the "odd phrases" Sonny was known for that created an environment where "anything can happen."

"Jim had an incredible harmonic sense; he's such a sensitive player," Sonny said. "So to me, he was the perfect guy to play with."[18] Hall loved how Sonny was capable of "turning and turning a tune until eventually you show all its possible faces,"[19] and Sonny hoped he could unlock even more.

In the fall of 1961, Hall was earning a steady income as a member of the band in *An Evening with Yves Montand*, the Italian-French actor's one-man Broadway show.[20] Then "Sonny Rollins hired me," Hall said, "so I left."[21]

Some were skeptical of Sonny's hiring decision. "There was some controversy about the fact that Jim was white," Sonny said.[22] "After *Freedom Suite* some people expected me to act a certain way, and wondered why I would hire a white musician. I took some heat from that. I thought it was a healing symbol, and I didn't have any qualms about doing it. Social issues didn't have anything to do with hiring white musicians who were qualified: it was that simple." And Jim, Sonny said, "didn't have an ounce of prejudice in him."[23]

Next, Sonny needed representation. He left Joe Glaser's Associated Booking and signed with Monte Kay, another Jewish jazz impresario who cofounded Birdland and had established a career as a manager, representing the Modern Jazz Quartet, Art Blakey, Ornette Coleman, and Chris Connor.[24] He was married to Diahann Carroll; they lived across the hall from Miles Davis in Hell's Kitchen, where Sonny sometimes saw him.[25] Soon, Sonny even got a phone![26]

Finally, there was the music itself.[27] Rehearsals began at two o'clock sharp at the Five Spot after Sonny walked Major, with any changes communicated by telegram.[28] "Sonny would let me in the front door with one hand and continue playing with the other, and then disappear, still playing, into a back room and stay there maybe a half hour," recalled Hall. But it worked.

Sonny's debut was that November at the Jazz Gallery, a club recently opened by Joe and Iggy Termini and Kay Norton on Saint Marks Place, not far from the Five Spot.[29] It seated 250 and could accommodate 100 more at the oval-shaped bar.[30] The club quickly became a major venue. In May 1960, John Coltrane began his first prominent gig as a leader there.[31]

Coltrane loomed large for Sonny. The two tenor giants remained close friends, but during Sonny's sabbatical, Coltrane emerged as the dominant force. He won his first *Down Beat* critics' poll in 1961.[32] For Sonny, Coltrane's ascension had a silver lining: he no longer faced the pressure of being number one.[33]

Coltrane himself was eagerly awaiting Sonny's return. While in Europe that fall, he had Naima tape Sonny's performance at the Jazz Gallery and bring it to London.[34] "Sonny 'retired' before, and when he came back, he'd added quite a bit," Coltrane said a month after Sonny's debut. "I admire his tremendous powers of concentration. You have to do a lot of work consciously, then you can leave the rest to your subconscious later on."[35]

The Jazz Gallery had just been redesigned, and Sonny's debut would mark the grand reopening.[36] Cyma Rubin was the scenic designer, giving the club a red color palette, and Broadway luminary Abraham Feder designed a lighting system that allowed the board operator to improvise with rhythms based on the music.[37] Larry Rivers and Grace Hartigan curated works by abstract expressionist painter Ruth Mitchell and Dadaist Roy Collona.[38] For Sonny's opening, the featured artist was, naturally, Prophet Jennings.[39]

Not unlike Ornette Coleman's 1959 stand at the Five Spot, Sonny's return from the Bridge was the jazz event of 1961. A series of postponements built anticipation: Sonny had changed his mind and was never coming out of retirement after all; Jim Hall wasn't available due to other commitments; the owners just weren't ready to open.[40] It was announced for October 4, 10, and 24, and by the time November rolled around, Sonny had still not appeared.

Sonny's sabbatical officially ended on Monday, November 13, 1961.[41] It was at a Jazz Gallery benefit for trumpeter Booker Little, Sonny's Chicago practice partner, who died on October 5 from complications with uremia, leaving his wife and four children.[42] Booker Ervin, James Moody, Slide Hampton, and Duke Ellington all played.[43] Ellington "has encompassed so many aspects," Sonny said weeks later. "He's so great, and still it seems hard for us to appreciate him as much as we should while he's around."[44]

Sonny had nothing positive to say about his momentous performance that evening. "The second number I played was so poor, I couldn't be nervous about the next night," he said. "Anything I did after that would be an improvement." Self-critical as ever, Sonny was back!

Sonny's official opening at the Jazz Gallery was on November 14, when he began an indefinite run.[45] Even with heavy-traffic competition that season from Peggy Lee to Stan Getz to Roy Eldridge and Coleman Hawkins to Thelonious Monk opposite Clark Terry[46]—the new Jazz Gallery was the place to be. Sonny Rollins and Co.—Jim Hall, Walter Perkins, Bob Cranshaw—shared a double bill with the Ray Bryant Trio.[47] Tickets were $1.50 during the week, $2 on weekends. The line stretched down the block.[48] Art Blakey, Miles Davis, Bill Evans, Ted Curson, Donald Byrd, Don Ellis, Gil Evans, Jimmy Cobb, Art Farmer, Benny Golson, and Sonny's brother, Valdemar, were all there, as well as a coterie of long-haired bohemians at the bar eager to grok Sonny's new style.[49] Even Walter Winchell came, noting in his column that Woody Herman had come to "listen to the king."[50]

Sonny arrived early, dressed in a white tuxedo and black bow tie, "silhouetted against a kaleidoscopic flow of cool blues, transitory mauves or commanding reds," as John S. Wilson reported in the *New York Times*. "I want to do my bit to erase the unhealthy connotation that some people associate with jazz," Sonny told Wilson. "I want to show that you don't have to be a hophead or a juicehead to play jazz."[51] In order to resist the temptation of cigarettes and alcohol, Sonny began composing during set breaks.[52] As he weaved his way through the throngs of fans, many asked the same question. Even Miles asked him: "How does it feel to be back?" And the answer: "Not so different."[53]

Sonny was still the hardest-working artist in jazz. "I've never seen a man that determined," remarked Art Blakey when he played opposite Sonny later in the Jazz Gallery run. "He's still experimenting; he doesn't know what he wants to do yet. But he'll do it, or die trying."[54]

As ever, he mostly played standards: "East of the Sun," "Stompin' at the Savoy," "Where or When," "I'm Old Fashioned," "Polka Dots and Moonbeams," "Three Little Words," "It Could Happen to You," and "Love Letters," as well as "St. Thomas" and his own "Oleo."[55] Critics concluded that Sonny's playing was stronger all around, yet those who came expecting some tectonic shift left disappointed.[56]

Sonny was unfazed. "I don't think anybody's style can change basically," he said. "You can improve your way of saying what you want to say, but fundamentally a musician's personality can't alter once it has been formed." But Sonny himself was disappointed with the opening. In response to fans' disappointment that "I haven't come back on the scene with some brand new thing," Sonny contended, "I did come back with a brand new thing—me."[57] The audience expected some alchemical transformation, but, rather, the time spent on that suspension bridge was akin to the high-heat process of refining steel from iron ore. Sonny emerged less malleable and more secure in his own voice, having purged any recycled Charlie Parker licks from his vocabulary and expanded his timbral range; he had developed greater physical endurance that allowed him to solo as long as he wanted; and he had clarified his tone into a colossal sound that could be heard over a passing subway train.[58]

Sonny's attempt to flee the business had unwittingly created a publicity campaign beyond the dreams of any publicist, even seasoned veteran Ivan Black, who ran the Termini Brothers' PR. *Melody Maker, Cue*, the *New York Herald Tribune, New York Times, New York Post, New York Daily News*, and *Newsweek* all ran stories.[59] The *New Yorker* characterized Sonny's return as having a "millennial air." They weren't just fascinated by the music, but his whole persona, down to his fashion sense. Sonny met Whitney Balliett, the magazine's jazz critic, at a coffeehouse wearing a "gray turtleneck sweater, a blue-and-white-striped button-down shirt, open at the neck, and a handsome blue-gray V-neck sweater, above gray slacks," Balliett wrote. "This ensemble was rounded out with shined black space shoes, a black porkpie hat with a medium brim, and a gabardine overcoat." Sonny feigned indifference to the success of the opening. "I'm bringing a whole new understanding to the scene," he explained. "If no one comes to the opening, if they don't like me, if they rush out—I'm prepared for all those contingencies, and they would not influence me adversely."[60]

Yet as the facts of the Bridge became legend, everyone in the music industry wanted a piece of Sonny Rollins. Major labels were clamoring for Sonny's attention "because of the bridge and the romantic legend, and that was about it," Sonny recalled. "It was a tremendous thing for these guys in the business: 'We can really use this and use this guy. Wow, he's going to make some money for us!' "[61]

George Avakian, now one of the chief A&R men at RCA Victor, already had a positive relationship with Sonny; they had gone to the World Series together the previous year. Though primarily interested in jazz, Avakian had earned his mettle as a pop producer and convinced RCA to invest more heavily in his true passion.[62] The biggest jazz artist he wanted to sign was Sonny.[63]

Friendship or no, Avakian still had to outbid the competition. Nesuhi Ertegun, the vice president in charge of LP records at Atlantic, already had Coltrane; adding Sonny would corner the market on tenor saxophone. To that end, Ertegun arranged to professionally record Sonny at the Jazz Gallery on December 9, 10, and 16, before he was under contract with anyone.[64] When Sonny found out a few months later, he was furious, even though he was certain the tape was "a superlative effort," and he was right. Sonny would remain protective of his material for the rest of his life, superlative or not.

Ertegun captured Sonny in one of his most searing moments. A twenty-one-minute take on "Where or When" began with a rubato saxophone intro soaring into the altissimo range, with Sonny playing as though he were still on the Bridge. It seemed Sonny could manipulate time itself; a minute could feel like an hour, or an hour like a minute, with Hall bending time right there with him. Sonny could play so much, Hall could play so little; Sonny was fire, Hall ice.

What followed was a fifteen-minute rendition of "Love Letters," with Sonny taking a twelve-minute solo, never repeating himself, before segueing into an achingly beautiful "In a Sentimental Mood." Three tunes, and that's the set.[65] During another set, Sonny played a thirteen-minute solo on "Oleo" that anticipated his freer explorations on albums like *East Broadway Run Down*.[66]

Offstage, the labels jockeyed for position.[67] Then, George Avakian made an unbeatable offer: $90,000 for six albums, a whopping sum for a jazz musician at the time. Spread over two and a half years, the deal required three albums in the first year, then one every six months, and a guaranteed $10,000 minimum advance for any subsequent recordings. RCA would pay a 5 percent royalty, which would kick in whenever Sonny earned out the advance. A savvy businessman, Avakian built an initial $20,000 advance into the contract that Sonny would receive before year's end if he signed immediately, saving him money on his taxes the following year. It was the most lucrative contract RCA had ever offered a black artist.[68] Soon thereafter, Lucille quit her secretarial job.

Before signing, Sonny met with Prestige producer Esmond Edwards. "We just couldn't compete with those kinds of figures," Edwards recalled. "[RCA] could write that into some Elvis Presley profit."[69] For RCA to break even, they would need to sell more than thirty thousand copies of each album, at least as many as Coltrane's *My Favorite Things* had sold in its first year. With Sonny's top seller at Prestige selling twenty-five thousand, it was a tall order.[70]

On December 28, Sonny signed with RCA, with one unusual condition: twenty-four-hour access to the RCA Victor studios.[71] "If there was no recording going on in there, I would have access to the studio, and I had that written into my contract," Sonny said. "The watchman knew me and all that, and I'd come there and go in the studio, play as long as I wanted to, in the middle of the night, which is when I was active." Making good on the letter he got from Mingus, Sonny took him to the studio at least once for a late-night practice session with Mingus on piano.[72] However, solving the practice-space problem that had necessitated the Bridge came with strings attached. Sonny's first RCA album was due February 15, 1962, the second due May 1, so Sonny and the band had their work cut out for them.[73]

After the Jazz Gallery, Sonny Rollins and Company played the Showboat in Philadelphia from Christmas to New Year's.[74] There was rain and snow that week, so Sonny simply wore his galoshes on the bandstand.[75] Sonny came back to New York to ring in the New Year at Carnegie Hall, where the quartet played on a bill with the John Coltrane Quintet with Eric Dolphy, Thelonious Monk, and Nina Simone.[76]

With Sonny's first recording session for RCA scheduled for January 30, and a "Jazz Profiles" concert on January 25 at the Museum of Modern Art (MoMA), Sonny was concerned, as usual, about finding the right drummer. "Sonny Rollins has had more drummers recently than Heinz has varieties," reported *Down Beat*.[77] He hired Walter Perkins, Jimmy Cobb, Tootie Heath, and then Billy Higgins.

Sonny "was one of my favorites," Cobb recalled. "To young guys, he was the killer, so I used to listen to all his records." Cobb was "supposed to do a record called *The Bridge*.... I had taken off from Miles Davis for a minute, and Miles went and left town and took Philly Joe, and they went out and didn't come back for two weeks," referring to when Davis was booked in Chicago at the Birdhouse in the fall of 1961. "During that time I got hired by Sonny, but we didn't work nowhere. We just did a couple of rehearsals. By the time we was getting ready to go on a gig, I had already gone back to Miles, so I never got to actually play with him."[78]

The rehearsals were duo sessions at 400 Grand Street. When Cobb rejoined Miles, Sonny rehearsed with Tootie Heath. "He'd come to the door with no shirt on," Heath recalled. Major, the German shepherd, "would go nuts whenever I rang the bell. Then he would have to lock the dog up in the room. He said the dog had never seen anybody else in the apartment except him."[79]

Sonny told Heath to rent a tuxedo for the MoMA concert. "I rehearsed with him for a whole week, every day," Heath said. "I had told everybody, all my friends. A night before the concert, he gets Billy Higgins out of jail, and he uses Billy on the concert." Due to the last-minute cancellation, Sonny still paid Heath for the gig, but Heath never forgot Sonny's reputation as the antithesis to the stability he later experienced with the Modern Jazz Quartet. Sonny, Heath said, "would change musicians like he changed clothes."

This game of musical chairs was so rapid that Jimmy Cobb was listed as the drummer on the press release; reviews listed Tootie Heath as the replacement.[80] Over two sets, Sonny stuck mostly to standards,[81] polarizing the critics. John S. Wilson found the solos so long as to be "depressing."[82] Whitney Balliett disagreed. "Rollins isn't merely back," he wrote. "He is looming."[83]

The first RCA session was five days later. After going through so many drummers, Sonny finally hired Harry T. "Stump" Saunders, a drummer from Washington, DC, who had worked with Stuff Smith and Shirley Horn.[84]

George Avakian knew exactly what to call the album: *The Bridge*. "This is not only the bridge, the Williamsburg Bridge where Sonny worked out his comeback," Avakian thought, "but Sonny now is going to be the bridge between the Sonny Rollins of old and the Sonny Rollins of the future."[85] Sonny was also a bridge from bop to free jazz, from Coleman Hawkins, Lester Young, and Charlie Parker to Ornette Coleman and Don Cherry.

Other than the album title, and Avakian's insistence that there be an original title track, Avakian "was deferential to me in recording that album, letting me be my own producer for the most part," Sonny said.[86] Sonny wanted the conditions as loose as possible and the band to be as tight as possible. He had a technician tape the mike to the bell of the saxophone,[87] but "there were problems trying to harness Sonny and lock him down," Cranshaw recalled. "He moved all over the place while he was playing and was driving George Avakian crazy.... Sonny actually walked outside the studio into the hall while he was still playing." Instead of through-composed sheet music, Sonny "would kind of write a guide that you had to follow," Cranshaw said. "Sonny didn't want the same thing each time he played." Unlike the three-hour Prestige sessions of the fifties, they would keep going, however many takes it took.[88]

On January 30, Sonny arrived at RCA Studio B in a cashmere sweater.[89] Prophet Jennings was there, too, to "help select the tunes."[90] As RCA manager of popular artists and repertoire, Avakian was "swamped at the time," so he hired composer and vibraphonist Bob Prince as coproducer.[91] In 1961, Prince did a European tour of "Jerome Robbins' Ballets: USA," and he invited several of the musicians to sessions for *The Bridge*, including drummer Bobby Thomas and saxophonist and clarinetist Frank Perowsky.

Recording engineer Ray Hall was the first black audio engineer at RCA Victor, with credits including Vladimir Horowitz, Louis Armstrong, and the Isley Brothers' "Shout!"[92] Editing Sonny could be a challenge. "Sonny had a tendency to think in terms of relatively short phrases," Avakian said. "On the other end, when he got going, sometimes he'd spin something out so long and complicated that you couldn't edit it, not that you wanted to."[93]

On the first day, they played "God Bless the Child" over and over again for three hours.[94] But nothing was good enough to honor Billie Holiday's memory.[95] "I felt we started to go downhill because we were repeating ourselves," Cranshaw recalled. "But Sonny stayed with it, probably through ten versions."[96] Sonny changed the tempo and the arrangement until they finally recorded a satisfactory take. The final version began in concert A major, an atypical key for the tenor, and ended in C with a key change on the last chorus. Cranshaw's lush chordal intro, Jim Hall's harmonic canopy, Saunders's sensitive brushwork, and Sonny's Bridge-sized tone all made the rendition a classic.[97]

The night of the first *Bridge* session, Sonny went to see Sigurd Raschèr perform the Lars-Erik Larsson "Concerto for Alto Saxophone" at the Brooklyn Academy of Music. Afterward, he and Raschèr went to the Carnegie Deli to talk about their mutual love of the saxophone and their commitment to health.[98]

On January 31, Sonny returned to Studio B to record five takes of "Will You Still Be Mine?" None made the album, which was due in only two weeks.[99]

Starting February 2, Sonny played a weeklong revue at the Apollo Theater.[100] To stay on his game for his hometown crowd, Sonny was even lifting a barbell backstage before changing into his tux. There was at least one notable fan in the audience—James Brown. "Sonny is a weird cat," Brown said, "'cause Sonny'll be playing and everybody'll have to stop because nobody knows where he's at but him." At the Apollo, "This cat got up and started playing a tune—I don't think Beethoven would have been able to figure out those changes."[101]

In a review of the Apollo show in *Variety*, the critic wrote that the "unit could use a little more strength at the drums." Apparently, Stump Saunders was stumped by Sonny, and soon thereafter, he was fired.

The second weekend in February, Sonny inaugurated jazz programming at the Baby Grand in Bed-Stuy.[102] Around the block at the Brevoort Theatre, Aretha Franklin and Eddie "Cleanhead" Vinson were playing a weekend engagement opposite Miles Davis, Olatunji, and Redd Foxx.[103] On Sunday, Jim Hall caught an early show at the Brevoort before Sonny hit at the Baby Grand, and he was impressed with Aretha's drummer at the time, Ben Riley. He invited Riley to sit in after he finished that night with Aretha.[104] Riley grew up in Sugar Hill, but he was three years younger than Sonny, so Sonny didn't know Riley beyond facial recognition. By the end of the night, Sonny hired him for *The Bridge*.[105]

On February 12, they convened at RCA for what would be Stump Saunders's last day.[106] They recorded twelve takes of "Day In, Day Out." Sonny was not happy with the initial attack from the rhythm section: "Okay, okay, okay, okay. Stop it. Hold it, hold it, hold it. HOLD IT!" He cut them off after a few seconds. When Riley came the next day, they began with "Day In,

Day Out." Riley instantly locked in with Sonny. They then recorded "You Do Something to Me" and "Where or When." "When we halfway-finished," Riley recalled, "he said, 'Look, I'm going to California, and I would like for you to go.'"[107]

Sonny recorded three more tunes that day, "You Do Something to Me," "Where Are You," and Sonny's free-floating "John S.," meaning John and Sonny, dedicated to his relationship with John Coltrane. Cranshaw devised the bass part for "John S." in the studio.[108] The next day, they returned and recorded "Without a Song," the tune that got Cranshaw his job with Sonny in 1959, and "The Bridge," which was, according to Avakian, "virtually improvised in the studio."[109]

It was originally "like a fanfare into a solo, and it was working so well that he kept it in, and it became 'The Bridge,'" Riley recalled.[110] Over a B-flat rhythm changes progression, Sonny made 350 beats per minute sound as effortless as a breezy stroll.[111] Complicating matters further, each chorus is split into straight time and a recurring three-against-four polyrhythmic pattern in 6/8 time.[112]

Riley was learning on the job. "I tried to follow his phrasings," Riley said. "I couldn't tell what all the piano parts were that he was hearing, but I could hear his colors."[113]

At session's end, Sonny's exacting standards paid off. "The material was so good that I don't recall a single intersplice whatsoever," said Bob Prince. "The edits were so tiny as to be virtually non-existent. Every tune came out as one complete take."[114]

The Bridge married formal experimentation and improvisational openness, musical complexity and listener accessibility.[115] "I am always looking forward; if something doesn't work now, I don't worry about it because I know we'll either make it go next time, or we'll develop something else," Sonny said in the liner notes. "And if it *does* work now, I feel it will be even better in the future."[116]

The album was a commercial and critical success.[117] That April, there were already ads in magazines featuring the dignified cover photo by Chuck Stewart.[118] "At the risk of being unable to give Rollins a higher numerical rating when he surpasses this album (and I have every confidence that he will)," wrote Ira Gitler in his five-star review in *Down Beat*, "this set still has to be placed in the superlative class."[119]

After making *The Bridge*, Sonny toured California.[120] Sonny decided to travel by train, leaving Monday, February 19; he began at the Renaissance on West Hollywood on February 23. "We rehearsed going out to California in one of the sleeping quarters every day," recalled Ben Riley. "That kept it from being boring, plus it got the band much tighter together. By the time we got to California, we really had a good idea of what we wanted to do."[121]

The Renaissance[122] was next door to the Crescendo, where Billy Eckstine and Henny Youngman were appearing. Sonny's band wore a different, progressively less formal outfit for each of the three nightly sets. "We had a suit, sports outfit, and tuxedos," Riley said. "We'd open in tuxedos, and by the end of the night we'd have a sports ensemble on."

Sonny wrote Lucille in New York almost every day during the tour, on paper he borrowed from the Hollywood Travelodge where the group stayed. He missed Lucille and Major terribly.[123] "I'm glad you finally understand the difference between being home and working part-time," he wrote her. "I want you home and just my knowing this makes all the difference in the world!!"[124] Eventually, Sonny would change this regressive attitude, and he and Lucille would work together.

"Dearest Lucille," Sonny wrote after his first night at the Renaissance, "You'll never know how much I missed you last nite after I hung up the phone. In fact I started to call you back—but realized I still could not hold you or have you near by so doing so I didn't. Also couldn't find anywhere to practice so I came home with some food and looked at T.V. for a sedative and soon was asleep."[125]

That day, Sonny woke at 10 a.m., did some leg raises, and lifted some weights he got from Jim Hall. He then bought a new hundred-pound set, which he shipped back to New York at the end of the tour. He rehearsed at the club, stopped for stamps and for carrot juice at the health food store, and returned to the hotel at 5 p.m. Sonny took advantage of LA's fascination with health food, subsisting on soya bread with cheese, carrots, parsley, and quarts of spinach juice, then "honey, lemons, vegetable juice, and broth (which I make with hot tap water)." He bought a paperback copy of Carlton

Fredericks's *Eat, Live and Be Merry* and signed up for Fredericks's nutrition booklet. Like many musicians, playing on a full stomach was never his preference; he hated to eat after 4 p.m. if he was performing that night and generally took a five-hour fast before hitting the stage.

That night, he wrote Lucille a seven-page letter. He worried that Major wouldn't remember him when he got back and asked her to send sweatshirts, a black suit, mohair slacks, black slacks, olive slacks, wool neckpieces, stocking caps. He also needed a prescription filled from the drugstore by their apartment, probably for amphetamines, widely prescribed at the time to boost the metabolism and elevate the mood, which Sonny would take in order to "control my appetite," he said. "They also give me a certain necessary stamina by which I exercise, practice etc."[126] Sonny closed the letter by suggesting that they take a trip that summer, possibly with Major. "Yes, he should come along," Sonny wrote. "After all, he's part of the family."[127]

At 6 p.m., Sonny showered, shaved, and made his way over to the club by 9 before his 9:30 hit.[128] They had a great turnout for Sonny's first LA appearance since 1959, but Sonny was disappointed. The acoustics in the club were strange, and Ben Riley was jittery.[129]

By Saturday, Riley still couldn't shake the nerves. Sonny wrote Lucille that night at 3:35 a.m. to express his frustration.[130] On Monday, Sonny wrote Lucille again at 5:30 a.m. after finishing at the club late Sunday night.[131] The turnout remained high, and the standing ovations kept coming, but he was still "greatly concerned over Ben." If Ben did not improve, Sonny wrote, "I am going to drop drums from the band entirely and get a conga drum and/ or bongos—this is an idea which merits further investigation." By the following Wednesday, Riley was "still not playing as he did on the record date and it is a mystery to me," Sonny wrote. "After all, this was why I dropped the piano—because I could not find someone who contributed rather than detracted—which is now the case in the drum dept."[132]

One afternoon, the band convened at the club for their rehearsal, and Sonny decided to practice by himself in the basement while the others rehearsed upstairs. There was a cold snap, and it was frigid down there. "I didn't realize how cold it was until I felt my hands becoming numb!!" Sonny wrote. In fact, Sonny caught a cold. He picked up some vitamin C and an inhaler and went on that night. On March 1, the band was scheduled to perform on comedian Henry Morgan's late-night show; he would just have to blow through the congestion.

In LA, Sonny reconnected with Don Cherry, who was "out there going crazy" after Ornette Coleman disbanded his quartet in the summer of 1961.[133] After Cherry came to the Renaissance, "Sonny felt like playing more, so we used to drive," Cherry said, "and I would take him to different spots in California, by the sea and in the mountains, where we would practice together until the sun would come up."[134]

Before closing at the Renaissance, Ben Riley finally rose to the occasion. "If the improvement continues maybe I won't end up in an insane asylum after all," Sonny wrote Lucille. It happened just in time for the crowds to wane. "It usually works out this way. When the band sounds good the S.R.O. signs aren't up."[135]

On Monday, March 5, Sonny rented a car and drove to San Francisco, where they were booked at the Jazz Workshop from March 6 through 25.[136] There were lines down the block, even in the rain.[137] Sonny was staying up until 4 a.m. coming down from performing and struggling to maintain his exercise and practice routine, but he soon found a studio out in the country where he could practice all night after finishing at the club at 2 a.m.[138]

At the Jazz Workshop, Sonny experimented with bossa nova, which he described to Lucille as "the new rhythmic style which has swept Brazil.... It really is crazy rhythm and as you know I have an affinity towards those rhythms anyway. Everybody in Jazz is beginning to 'dig' it!"[139] It helped that Ben Riley had learned a bossa groove playing with Herbie Mann. When they played "If Ever I Would Leave You" as a bossa, some Brazilians in the audience heard it and "flipped."[140] Sonny resolved to record it on his next album.[141]

Sonny wrote Lucille that he'd enlisted the help of Art Auerbach, who owned the Jazz Workshop but made his living as a lawyer, to finalize his divorce from Dawn. "Lucille I love you and need you desperately," he wrote. "Love is an expression which I can use in respect to many people and things. So I can't use it effectively when I say goodbye to you, my WOMAN! I'm your MAN!"[142]

Ben's improvement had Sonny feeling optimistic about the band. He wrote Lucille to ask her to contact Joe Termini about getting his cabaret card formally reinstated. Termini evidently still owed Sonny money, and he wanted it resolved quickly. Meanwhile, he called Don Cherry and asked him to come to San Francisco from Los Angeles to join the group during the last week of the Jazz Workshop run.

To Cherry, who had fallen into heroin addiction in the late 1950s and was down-and-out in LA, the call came not a moment too soon.[143] "I don't think I even had a horn," Cherry recalled. It lasted only one night. "I had all these feelings in me, and just...one night I played, and I was 'out.' I played too much, or whatever," he said. "I needed the release to be free because of what I was going through. And so Sonny, that night he paid me for the whole week and said, 'Don, I don't think it's going to work out.'"[144]

To Sonny, it was nothing personal.[145] "I have just begun to break in Ben and achieve somewhat of a good rhythmic feeling," he wrote Lucille. "To add Don as we tried is analogous to starting this process all over again or to starting a new group from scratch."[146] Sonny told Cherry he would call him soon to rejoin the band. Cherry went back to Los Angeles and took a job as a busboy with United Airlines while he waited for Sonny's call.

Sonny then took a trip to the Rosicrucian Grand Lodge for the Americas in San Jose, also visiting Rosicrucian Park and the Rosicrucian Egyptian Museum. He barely got an hour's sleep the morning he went to meet Rosicrucian grand regional administrator Arthur C. Piepenbrink. Sonny's day began with an early breakfast meeting of the Knights of the Round Table, a service organization that actually met at a round table and addressed each other as "sir" or "knight." Piepenbrink asked Sonny to play a cappella for the group at 7:30 a.m. After, Sonny took a tour of the five-acre Rosicrucian Park and met imperator Ralph M. Lewis and former supreme secretary Cecil A. Poole.[147] When he got back to the Jazz Workshop, he still managed to eke out one song—"Three Little Words"—which he extended for an entire set.

Sonny did his best to avoid temptation.[148] Late in the tour, he had a brief relapse into cigarette smoking and drinking, but he caught it. To stay disciplined, after the last set he would go to the store to get yogurt and a coffee, then practice as much as he could until dawn.

The tour culminated on a high note, with Sonny's March 23 taped appearance in San Francisco as the inaugural guest on Ralph J. Gleason's televised program *Jazz Casual*, which filmed in the Bay Area and began airing on sixty-seven stations across the country that September.[149] Sonny opened with "The Bridge," taken way up.[150] Sonny spoke of the "color of the song," which he meant both figuratively and literally. Sonny had begun to investigate synesthesia, and even copied over a table from metaphysical writer Roland Hunt linking musical notes to color and scent.[151] Later on, he took down synesthetic relationships claimed by Rimsky-Korsakov, Scriabin, and Isaac Newton, as well as Don Cherry's sense of corresponding notes and colors: E was orange, red A, blue A-flat.[152] Sonny played songs in different keys, he explained, as "the same notes in a different key would produce a different color." He also discussed the idea of freedom within constraint. "We have places where we mark, I guess they could be called sort of like landmarks along the way," Sonny said of the way he structured tunes, "and of course, this discipline enables us to be free and to put things freely."[153] They closed the program with "God Bless the Child" and an eleven-minute bossa version of "If Ever I Would Leave You." Overall, the tour was a success: Sonny and the group finally jelled. He also settled his divorce: Dawn agreed to file uncontested.[154]

Sonny returned to RCA Studios on April 5, just as *The Bridge* was being released, for the first session for *What's New*. He committed to bossa nova, which had been making waves in the jazz world since 1959: João Gilberto's "Chega de Saudade," Stan Getz and Charlie Byrd's *Jazz Samba*, and Quincy Jones, Hugh Masekela, and Vince Guaraldi all covering Luiz Bonfá's "Manhã de Carnaval," the theme to the 1959 film *Black Orpheus*.[155]

Sonny's *What's New* would not be straight bossa, though, and would incorporate calypso and quelbe rhythms. The album made an aesthetic statement—all rhythms of the Afro-Latin diaspora were part of the jazz continuum.[156] Avakian hired Bob Prince to coproduce again, plus engineer Ray Hall. That first session, they concentrated on "The Night Has a Thousand Eyes," one of two bossas on the album, with Riley, Cranshaw, and Hall, adding auxiliary percussionists Denis Charles, Frank Charles, and Willie Rodriguez.

On April 10, Sonny returned to the Jazz Gallery for a two-week run opposite the James Moody Sextet and Bill Henderson.[157] Pianist and arranger Jimmy Jones was in Moody's band, and Sonny hired him to arrange two traditional calypsos for the album, "Brown Skin Girl" and "Don't Stop the Carnival."

On April 25, Sonny was back at RCA, recording a twelve-minute version of Lerner and Loewe's "If Ever I Would Leave You," the album's other bossa. They then recorded Jimmy Jones's arrangement of "Don't Stop the Carnival," the first calypso Sonny had recorded since "St. Thomas." It would eventually become a kind of theme song for Sonny, though this version would be released only on international versions of *What's New*.[158] On "Don't Stop the Carnival," Sonny didn't think of it as call-and-response, but rather Q&A, as in, "Jim + I question and answer," or "choir takes first question and Sonny answers 16 bars."[159] Rather than a call, a question demanded a direct, musically relevant answer. The choir was a vocal sextet led by Howard Roberts of the Howard Roberts Chorale, which had recently performed at Carnegie Hall.[160] Roberts starred alongside Eartha Kitt in *Shinbone Alley* and became musical director of the Alvin Ailey Dance Theater, but it was his extensive work as musical director for Harry Belafonte that made him the right choice for *What's New*.[161] The other singers had all recorded with Belafonte: Maeretha Stewart, Christine Spencer, Miriam Burton, Ned Wright, and Bill Glover.[162] On "Brown Skin Girl," Jones's arrangement is through-composed, but Sonny gave notes to the chorus with Sonny's "special lyrics."[163]

What's New was completed on May 14. The final session was a trio: Sonny, Cranshaw, and forty-one-year-old conguero Candido Camero.[164] They recorded two of Sonny's originals, "Jungoso" and "Bluesongo." As Candido recalled, it was "a conversation without telephone."[165]

Despite the popularity of the bossa nova craze, and Sonny recording some of the best work of his career, especially on "If Ever I Would Leave You," the album was not as successful as RCA had hoped.[166] *Down Beat* called it the "flop of the year in its category."[167] Nevertheless, Avakian said, "it brought Sonny into the mainstream of what was happening just then...and drew more attention than any other album he could've done at that moment."[168]

During the making of *What's New*, Sonny maintained a busy performance schedule. On April 23, he played opposite John Lewis at the 92nd Street Y. Sonny Rollins and Co. wore their tuxedoes for the concert; they were backed by the Contemporary String Quartet in Sonny's debut performance with strings.[169] On April 27, Sonny donned his tuxedo again and met the man who would later be known as Rahsaan Roland Kirk on the steps of city hall, where they played in duo alongside Mayor Robert Wagner to promote the Billie Holiday Memorial Jazz Concert at Carnegie Hall on May 7.[170] The proceeds of the concert would go to support the West Side Democratic Club's narcotics control and rehabilitation center, the first municipal narcotics center in the country.[171]

Next, Sonny gave several performances at the first International Jazz Festival in Washington, DC, from May 31 to June 3.[172] The festival was organized by President John F. Kennedy's Music Committee, part of the People-to-People Program, which began under the Eisenhower administration to promote diplomacy through cultural exchange.[173] DC native Duke Ellington served as the emcee.[174] On June 1, Sonny and the quartet performed "If Ever I Would Leave You" and "Love Letters" at the DC Armory, opposite Cannonball Adderley, Ellington, Gerry Mulligan, Dave Brubeck, Thelonious Monk, and George Russell, in addition to groups from the United Kingdom, Iceland, New Zealand, and Poland.[175] In the Coliseum, the acoustics were terrible and the heat was unbearable.[176] Having spent two years preparing for such a situation, Sonny came through loud and clear and got a standing ovation.[177]

After DC, Sonny fired Ben Riley. "I've finished with that group," Sonny told *Down Beat*'s Bill Coss. "We may have to fulfill a few engagements, but it's over. After a short time, I found we just couldn't get what I wanted. The original enthusiasm disintegrated." He hired Billy Higgins, who by coincidence shared a birthday with Art Blakey: October 11.[178] "Sonny thought I wanted to leave, and I thought he wanted to break up the group," said Jim Hall at the time. "I think we'll probably stay together a little longer."[179]

For Riley, it was a learning experience. "I was taught how to play and think," he recalled. "I tried to play my beats the way he was phrasing; I tried to keep my time between his figures."[180] Sonny taught him how to balance free playing and an internal sense of structure. "Sonny Rollins used to say,

'When you play, it's like driving on a highway you've never been on before, but there are always landmarks. You have to make those marks.'" Sonny told Riley, " 'Practicing doesn't have to mean sitting down with your instrument.' There are certain experiences in life that you incorporate into what you do on stage."[181]

From June 20 to July 1, Sonny was booked in Chicago at McKie's Disc Jockey Lounge, McKie Fitzhugh's club at the Strand Hotel, on a double bill with Gene Ammons, who borrowed Sonny's rhythm section.[182] In the audience at McKie's was eighteen-year-old tenor saxophonist Henry Threadgill.[183] "Sonny Rollins was my hero," he recalled. "[He] would walk out the club playing. He'd come back in the back door playing, and the music would constantly be changing on the bandstand. He'd just go from one piece to the other." On the last night, they played till dawn. Threadgill even began looking into Rosicrucianism. When he heard of Sonny's connection to the Gay family from Geraldine Gay's niece, who was a classmate, "I would go and sit on their front porch and wait for him....I had read in *Metronome* that Sonny used to sit and wait on Coleman Hawkins, on his doorstep. So I said, 'Well, I'll just wait on this doorstep in Chicago.' If he can wait on Coleman Hawkins, I'll wait on him," but Sonny never showed up.[184]

Threadgill was captivated by Sonny's transformation of the Great American Songbook and the pianoless trio on *Freedom Suite*; these influences led to albums like *Air Lore* by the avant-garde trio Air. "When I started Air, there was no piano," Threadgill said. "I was very much influenced by what he had done with that trio."[185]

In Chicago, Sonny also reconnected with surrealist artist Gertrude Abercrombie, of "Gertrude's Bounce" fame. Abercrombie had befriended Charlie Parker, Sarah Vaughan, Art Tatum, Dorothy Donegan, Dizzy Gillespie, Max Roach, Clifford Brown, and just about any jazz musician who passed through Chicago. Sonny visited her Victorian-style Hyde Park home, between the grounds of the 1893 World's Fair and the University of Chicago.[186] Abercrombie played the piano and would often preside over raucous jam sessions at after-hours parties at her house with Miles or Dizzy.[187] Literary figures also came: Thornton Wilder, Saul Bellow, Studs Terkel, and James Purdy among them.[188]

Sonny and Gertrude wrote letters back and forth until her death in 1977; Sonny served as a constant source of artistic encouragement.[189] They were close enough that Sonny's cowboy hat makes an appearance in Abercrombie's oil painting *The Black Hat*.[190]

Back in New York, Sonny and Lucille crossed the Bridge. The apartment at 400 Grand was homey, but small. Despite Sonny's lucrative RCA deal, they moved to Clinton Hill, Brooklyn, next to the Pratt Institute.[191] Just as Sonny Stitt suggested the apartment on Grand Street, Bob Cranshaw suggested they move to Willoughby Walk, where both he and Clifford Jordan lived. The sixteen-story, 287-unit co-op, a slab tower at 195 Willoughby Avenue, was built in 1958, so it was still relatively new at the time. Sonny and Lucille moved into unit 1712, a modest two-bedroom apartment.[192]

On Sunday, July 8, Sonny performed at the Newport Jazz Festival for the first time since 1958.[193] Even Max Roach and Charles Mingus, who organized the Newport Rebels, performed with their groups, alongside Coleman Hawkins, Roy Eldridge, Duke Ellington, Louis Armstrong, Thelonious Monk, and Aretha Franklin. Sonny was also part of a panel discussion called "Jazz and the Church" with Revs. John Gensel, Norman O'Connor, and Eugene S. Callender as well as gospel singer Clara Ward, with attorney Maxwell T. Cohen, known for his fight against the New York cabaret-card policy, moderating.[194]

Back in New York, Sonny "revamped" the band, as he wrote on July 12 to Gertrude Abercrombie.[195] He decided to dispense with any chordal instruments and amicably parted ways with Jim Hall. The new group was Cranshaw, Billy Higgins, and Don Cherry; with Higgins and Cherry part of Ornette Coleman's groundbreaking quartet, this was Sonny's foray into the New Thing. Sonny and Cherry liberated each other in different ways. The long commute to Cherry's job as a busboy with United Airlines made it impossible for him to even practice.[196]

Cherry "is a very enthusiastic young chap and he furnishes me with that word again—incentive and inspiration," Sonny wrote.[197] Two weeks later, Sonny wrote Abercrombie again. He was pleased with the new group and was progressing musically and spiritually. He had acquired a writing desk for his correspondence and composition, as well as Bob Hoffman's Functional Isometric Contraction apparatus, and was staying away from cigarettes. "My

Rosicrucian studies are progressing beautifully," he wrote, "and I am now up to the degree which reveals ways and means of 'releasing' the all-wise 'master within' (if you follow me)."[198]

From July 3 to July 30, Sonny was booked at the Village Gate, with Don Cherry replacing Jim Hall in the second week.[199] The club was a cavernous basement space in Greenwich Village. Once a commercial laundry and then a storage space, it was beneath the Mills Hotel, a flophouse with "people throwing bottles and dirt and worse than that, feces and urination," said Art D'Lugoff, "but that was the price I paid for paying a low rent."[200] The Village Gate would be the recording studio for Sonny's next RCA album, *Our Man in Jazz*. One by-product of simultaneously gaining more artistic control and more commercial pressure was that Sonny developed a growing anxiety around the recording studio that he eventually characterized as a phobia.[201] In order to ensure that Sonny met the contractual obligation to release a third album by the end of 1962, George Avakian suggested that the next album be recorded live.[202] In response, D'Lugoff had recently installed a high-end sound system to streamline the process; RCA would be the first to try it out.[203] They scheduled the recording dates for July 27–30, which would give Sonny enough time to break in the new band and the label enough time to get the right material.

The album posed challenges. As much as the idea was market tested, Sonny's long-playing explorations often exceeded the limited capacity of an LP. Furthermore, the music itself would be more radical than *The Bridge* or *What's New* and even less conducive to mainstream radio play. *The Shape of Jazz to Come* was a hit for Atlantic, though, and now Sonny had half of Ornette's band. And Sonny's band had to master "the reading of minds," recalled Billy Higgins, Sonny being "one of the most rhythmically original players...you can't take anything for granted playing with him."[204]

Sonny felt Higgins was ready for mind reading. "Billy had a grasp of the big picture," Sonny said. "It wasn't just about what was happening here in the song or there in the song. He seemed to have that understanding of where the whole thing should be, and that would be throughout the entire piece we were playing. In his mind, there was a plan."[205]

Sonny had guidelines for collective improvisation. He referred to it not as "improvised music," he wrote, but as "Logical Music." The "format of composition" was essentially a round-robin of conversations in duo, with a third and fourth voice entering to create a "dissonance" that advanced the musical discourse.[206]

1. All begin together

2. Throughout composition 2 instruments play together. e.g. Sonny + Bob play together after start. Then Sonny + Bob are joined for a dissonance by Donald which then leads to the Donald Sonny duet which incidentally should suggest a different timbre than the dissonant 'carry over' 3 part section!

3. (Billy bears a strong resemblance to Bud Powell.)

After duet of S+D., B. joins in for a TRIO which should have a HARMONIC sound rather than a dissonance sound.

Being on the same wavelength was paramount. Sonny wrote out a set of "rules." Each set began "away from the bandstand"; they entered the stage in medias res.

After finding our KEY/MOD/GROOVE/, through a series of statements we gradually involve ourselves with the rhythm and the sound and make our way to the bandstand in a rhythmic manner. Almost a DANCE! For after all do we not do everything in rhythm?[207]

The key was unity, as Sonny explained in all caps: "ALL SHOULD HAVE WATCHES SET TO THE MINUTE AT THE BEGINNING OF EVERY NIGHT. THE START OF A SET WILL BE ON SIGNAL OF AN EXACT MOMENT.—THIS WAY WE WILL ALL BE READY TO ANSWER EACH OTHER IF the situation so necessitates—which at the beginnings it will call for this conversation to find the MODE which we all hear."

Bob Prince was coproducer again, but the engineer for the album, Paul Goodman, had never worked with Sonny.[208] Complicating matters, it was not a quiet crowd. "We got quite a few complaints," said the emcee at the Village Gate. "Respect your musicians and your neighbors. Please, listen instead of talking. And now, Sonny Rollins and Company!"[209]

Our Man in Jazz sounded more like spoken dialogue than anything Sonny had ever recorded, with pregnant pauses, interruptions, and a kind of rhythmic punctuation. These improvised scenes took place over three hour-long sets a night, opposite Mose Allison's trio, and for a four-day period at the end of July, RCA recorded all of them.[210] On the first set July 27, they played a twenty-five-and-a-half-minute "Oleo,"[211] with Sonny playing in and out of metronomic time, shifting tempo from a brisk gallop to half-time, growling, playing multiphonics, then superimposing a blues onto a rhythm changes. Anything was possible as long as it was "logical."

"My heroes usually played a song without any deviation," Sonny later told saxophonist Jon Irabagon, adding: "The spirit of the way Charlie Parker played suggested freedom. And therefore, the next generation after him and so on would be leading in that direction.... It is trying to push the tradition forward and still be in the tradition."[212] In short, building a bridge.

The songs flowed into each other with no break in between—everything was a coda to a coda. The idiosyncratic repertoire spanned the Great American Songbook to the avant-garde, and Sonny had recorded much of it previously. There was the Afro-diasporic "Don's Tune" by Cherry. This was followed by a version of Sonny's "Doxy" that segued into Gershwin's "Love Walked In," with a cadenza by Sonny in the middle that quoted "Someone to Watch over Me," culminating in a bluesy take on Chopin's "Funeral March," a common reference for Sonny, who never hesitated to laugh in the face of death. Sonny twisted and turned the melody of "There Will Never Be Another You" into a half-hour improvisation that ended in "The Blacksmith Blues" à la Bing Crosby, which culminated in a far-reaching cadenza with Don Cherry until they came back to "Another You."[213] There was a twenty-four-minute workout on "Tune Up," a radical departure from the version on *Newk's Time*, that segued into "Don't Stop the Carnival," interspersed with quotes from "Bemsha Swing" that seamlessly became a blues shuffle.[214] They played Mercer and Kern's "Dearly Beloved," ending with a quote from Monk's "52nd Street Theme," and Irving Berlin's "Alexander's Ragtime Band."[215] Sonny was building a bridge from the past to the future.

This bridge could not possibly fit on one LP. Side one was taken up entirely by the July 27 "Oleo" (longer versions were taped). Side two came from the first set on July 28. "That was a tough album to work on because the best takes were very long," recalled Avakian. "We needed to be able to get something between, say, eighteen and twenty-two minutes a side. It was very hard to do."[216] They cut about forty seconds from "Doxy" to fit it on side two.[217] To round out the album, "Dearly Beloved" was edited down from eighteen minutes to eight.

The album was part of the twenty-album Our Man Series released in 1963 on RCA Victor, as though the label was a news organization with international correspondents. Ray Ellis was *Our Man on Broadway*; Henry Mancini was *Our Man in Hollywood*; Al Hirt in New Orleans; Chet Atkins in Nashville; Perez Prado in Latin America; Paul Anka was around the world. Sonny was the only man not in a geographic location and the only black man. RCA evidently had no women anywhere.[218]

Our Man in Jazz was another polarizing album; not everyone understood the logic behind Sonny's "Logical Music." Pete Welding gave it three stars in *Down Beat*, Sonny's worst review in a decade. "Much of it is just plain boring," he wrote. "It just goes on and on." Conversely, the album was listed in the *Cash Box* "Jazz Picks of the Week" as having "plenty of sales potential." The poet, jazz critic, performer, and eventual Black Arts Movement progenitor Amiri Baraka (then LeRoi Jones) wrote in the avant-garde journal *Kulchur*, "This *is* new, friends....*Assassins* is what I have been calling this group privately. *The Assassins*."[219]

Sustaining those long takes of "Oleo" and "Dearly Beloved" was difficult, as Sonny had developed serious dental problems that would plague him for the rest of his life. The expense of dental work was one reason Sonny came off the Bridge. Dental trouble could be the kiss of death for a saxophonist. Sonny's embouchure—his very sound—was dependent on his dental health.[220] He was not alone. Cannonball Adderley, John Coltrane, Jimmy Heath, and Phil Woods all had serious dental trouble, and it hung over them like a sword of Damocles.[221] For Sonny, there were still more gigs, but it was only a matter of time before he would have to take another break.[222]

On August 7, 1962, the Lower East Side Neighborhood Association organized a free outdoor concert as part of the "Evenings by the River" series at the East River Park Amphitheater, and Sonny's quartet headlined.[223] He began the concert with "The Star-Spangled Banner," with Higgins maintaining a drum roll on the snare the entire time, followed by "Oleo" and "St. Thomas." On August 11, Sonny was scheduled to perform at a benefit at the Apollo for the Southern Student Freedom Fund, an offshoot of the National Student Association. The fund supported students who were expelled from college after participating in sit-ins and other nonviolent civil rights protests, as well as put up bail money for those who were arrested. Thelonious Monk, Dave Brubeck, Tadd Dameron, Art Blakey, and Moms Mabley were also on the bill.[224]

On August 19, Sonny was booked in St. Albans, Queens, at an event at the Galaxy Supper Club, hosted by the Evolution of Jazz Club.[225] The interracial organization had 750 members and was started with the intention of bringing jazz "back to the people."[226] For Sonny's set, 200 people showed up.[227] During intermission, the club's manager asked the musicians in the audience to have an impromptu jam session. Billy Taylor, Sadik Hakim, Roland Kirk, Charles McPherson, "Big Nick" Nicholas, Attila Zoller, Roy Haynes, Joe Castro, and Kenny Dorham all "wrought heavenly havoc on Farmers Blvd," according to the ecstatic review. One account had it that Sonny walked off the stage playing and disappeared down the street into Queens, only to return an hour later, still playing.[228]

That August, Sonny won the tenor category in the *Down Beat* International Jazz Critics Poll, edging out Coltrane by one vote, fifty-one to fifty, with his hero Coleman Hawkins in third place.[229]

But at the end of August, Sonny had to cancel bookings at the Montreal and Ohio Valley Jazz Festivals, as well as a Latin American tour.[230] He needed dental surgery. One report claimed he was recovering from complications with an "improperly reset broken jaw."[231] Sonny had survived hard drugs and the criminal justice system; he never thought it would be his teeth that might do him in.

During this hiatus, Sonny connected with his fifteen-year-old godson, saxophonist René McLean, Jackie's son, who had begun seriously contemplating a career in jazz. In a letter, Sonny vividly recalled his first professional jobs, and noted, "I still feel the same thrill today." He added: "We have to be always careful in all that we do—that we do the best we possibly can in everything—that we respect and help other people.... Because René, if we stop doing good things—bad thoughts and ideas will come to 'fill the space' and as in my case, a lot of wasted energy must be used trying to get on the right track again."[232]

McLean would carry this letter with him wherever he went and turned to it as a guiding light. There was more: "He opened a bank account in my name at the Bowery Savings Bank,"[233] McLean recalled. "I still have that bank book somewhere. I think he opened it with a fifty-dollar deposit." Most significantly, McLean learned from Sonny that spirituality "is the center and the focus from where your creativity manifests," he said. Spiritual practice was as important, if not tantamount to, practicing the horn. "It's a never-ending quest to perfect oneself."[234]

On September 7, 1962, Sonny turned thirty-two years old. He wrote a brief journal entry, directly beneath a note to himself from two years prior reflecting on his thirtieth birthday and his struggle to quit smoking. Two years later, he had some of the same struggles, but a deeper sense of self-awareness: "And yet as I struggle with the exact same problems can I deny a greater awareness of them and the feeling that they will be 'conquered' more through time + understanding, gradually, than thru a pointed effort to 'break' an unnecessary habit. AND SO PATIENCE AND UNDERSTANDING IS THE WORD."[235]

On his thirty-second birthday, Sonny wrote a letter to Gertrude Abercrombie. He celebrated his birthday by enjoying the "crazy view of lower Manhattan" from his apartment and watching a televised performance of Ella Fitzgerald, Japanese pantomimist Mamako, and Dizzy Gillespie at Dodger Stadium on *The Lively Ones* hosted by Vic Damone.[236] "I am still fighting and regardless of what I ever do—I will always be striving for my self-development," Sonny wrote. "I have even gone to carrying my barbell (small one) whenever I go out so that I can keep being reminded of what I now KNOW to be 'RIGHT.'" Sonny realized some thought he was "trying to be weird," but simple actions like that kept him "like a ship on a COURSE."[237]

At the end of September, Sonny wrote Abercrombie again to note his ongoing progress in quitting smoking, though he still kept a pack in his briefcase until "I 'feel' (and thus KNOW) when to discard them," he wrote.[238] He concluded the letter with a Rollins-esque credo: "So until we see ourselves as we are, so that we may see ourselves as we should be. goodbye."[239]

In October 1962, Sonny collaborated again with Prophet Jennings. That month, at the Caravan Gallery on the Upper East Side, portraits of Monk, Sonny, Miles, and Billie Holiday adorned the walls. At the opening-night reception, Sonny performed.[240] "He asked if he could play music to my paintings," Prophet recalled. "I said sure. I'd be glad to have him do it. He said he wanted to for a long time but he was afraid to ask, because he thought he might be imposing on a friendship. I told him I wanted to ask him but held back for the same reason."[241]

This reaching out to other artistic disciplines was part of Sonny's expanding consciousness. "I definitely could get a great feeling if I go to a museum and see some of the paintings, and, boy, then I'm right in the zone, I can play forever," Sonny said. "All these different kinds of art forms have an energy that you can transfer into your music. A celestial energy."[242]

Sonny rehearsed at Prophet's Temple in advance of the show; Wilbur Ware played bass. Paul Chambers, Philly Joe Jones, and Babs Gonzales were all there for the opening.[243] The show raised Prophet's profile in the art world considerably; he even sold one piece for $6,000 cash.[244] Sonny and Prophet next worked together on *Playground After Midnight*, a choreographed dance piece. Prophet was in charge of the scenic design, Sonny did the score, and they wrote the dialogue together.[245] They planned to have a four-dancer cast—two men and two women—performing what Prophet called "life set to music in words, painting, and in dance."

It seems nothing came of *Playground After Midnight*, but through it they conceived of another production called *Jazz 'n Art*. This one was simpler—just Sonny letting Prophet's paintings be his muse. There were about a dozen pieces displayed on the stage, as Sonny, Don Cherry, Bob Cranshaw, and Billy Higgins improvised.[246] After the show at the Caravan closed, *Jazz 'n Art* was booked on November 9 at Mr. Kelly's, a club on the East Side of Detroit, Prophet's old stomping ground.[247] One review described it as a "pageant of grief and struggle," another as "one of the most excitingly unique offerings to hit this section of the country in many a moon."[248] Sonny planned to take *Jazz 'n Art* to Europe.

At Mr. Kelly's, Detroit pianist and future Supremes musical director Teddy Harris's quintet opened for *Jazz 'n Art*, and through that Sonny met Harris's tenor saxophonist, twenty-two-year-old Bennie Maupin. Maupin had first heard Sonny on "Paper Moon" with Miles Davis and considered him a hero. Harris's quintet rehearsed extensively and rose to the occasion. "As I was packing up my horn I could feel this energy next to me, and I looked and it's Billy Higgins," Maupin recalled. "And so he's standing there smiling like he always was most of the time, and he said to me, he said, 'Hey young-blood, do you know Newk?' And I said no, but I knew that Newk was Sonny Rollins's nickname, right? So he says, 'Come on, I want to introduce you to him.' He literally took me by the hand, took me back in the dressing room, and introduced me to Sonny Rollins." Meeting Sonny, "it was like I always knew him...and he just was so warm and just talked to me. He says, 'Yeah, I heard you out there playing the tenor. I can tell you love it,' and I said, 'Yeah, I do.' And so they came out and they played, and it was like being in heaven for me."[249]

To Maupin, it was a pivotal moment. "It was that night that my life really changed, really—musically," he said. "When someone uplifts you in such a way, you just know you went through something; you went through one of those life corridors."[250]

Back in New York, Sonny had more dental problems. "Sonny will be going back to work soon after a long siege of trouble with his teeth," wrote George Avakian in an RCA internal memo that November. "He is ending up with virtually a new embouchure (and almost a new jaw). He goes to Europe in early January and gets back in late February. We will probably determine what to record at that time, and do it in March. Sonny's current free-form improvisation kick will scare most people in our organization, but he is going to gain in stature with the hard core modern jazz fans who are always looking for a new thing."[251]

Sonny was booked at McKie's in Chicago for two weeks in December, but dental surgery made it impossible; Coltrane spelled him at the last minute.[252] Sonny had a European tour that was scheduled to begin in early January; he hoped to continue on to Africa, though he would not make it there.[253]

In the 1962 *Down Beat* readers' poll released that December, Sonny came in a distant third after Stan Getz and John Coltrane. Far behind Sonny in fourth place was Coleman Hawkins.[254] Sonny still revered Hawkins, and wrote him on October 13.[255]

Dear Mr. Hawkins,

Your recent performance at the 'Village Gate' was magnificent!! Quite aside from the fact that you have maintained a position of dominance and leadership in the highly competitive field of 'Jazz' for the time that you have, there remains the more significant fact that such tested and tried musical achievement denotes and is subsidiary to personal character and integrity of being.

There have been many young men of high potential and demonstrated ability who have unfortunately not been 'MEN' in their personal and offstage practices and who soon found themselves devoid of the ability to create music. Perhaps these chaps were unable to understand why their musical powers left them so suddenly. Or perhaps they knew what actions were constructive as opposed to destructive but were too weak and not <u>men</u> enough to command the course of their lives. But certain it is that character, knowledge and virtue are superior to 'Music' as such. And that 'success' is relative to the evolution of those qualities within us all. That it has been positive and lasting for you Coleman is to the honor and credit of us, your colleagues, as well as to your own credit. For you have 'lit the flame' of aspiration within so many of us and you have epitomized the superiority of 'excellence of endeavor' and you stand today as a clear living picture and example for us to learn from.

It has always been a task to explain in words those things which in nature are the most profound and meaningful. Now you have shown me why I thought so much of you for so long. Godspeed in your travels and may I be fortunate enough to hear you play the tenor saxophone again in person.

Yours truly,
Sonny Rollins[256]

Sonny would see his musical idol again soon—standing next to him on the bandstand.

Chapter 25

SONNY MEETS HAWK

(1963)

Don Cherry, Billy Higgins, and Henry Grimes referred to Sonny as "the Mae-stro,"[1] and disappointing the maestro seemed inevitable. Such was the case with Prophet Jennings. Prophet was supposed to bring *Jazz 'n Art* on Sonny's January 1963 European tour, but the national longshoremen's strike, which began that Christmas, prevented it.[2] "I was afraid to death of airplanes," Jennings, who had never flown, recalled. "Three days before sailing time, the dock strike came up in New York, so I never went." Sonny was "just so hurt that we didn't make the gig together." Prophet twisted the knife when he married a Swedish airline stewardess: "When he found out that I was flying with my wife-to-be, it upset him in a way, 'cause I turned down flying with him."[3]

On the monthlong tour, Sonny reconnected with old friends across continental Europe and made some new ones. Tour stops included Rome and Milan, Zurich, Copenhagen, Stockholm, Paris, various cities in Germany, and Amsterdam, starting January 8.[4] The tour resulted from a deal between RCA and Italian television station RAI, which brought in Odetta, Della Reese, and Sonny to tape broadcasts of *Studio Uno*, a Roman variety show.[5] Though Sonny was concerned that Don Cherry and Billy Higgins were using drugs, he kept them on cornet and drums and hired Henry Grimes in lieu of Bob Cranshaw.[6]

"The Europe group was, I think, one of Sonny's brightest groups," Cherry said. "Everybody was playing their horns…and their feelings too. When everybody's got his mind and feelings in tune, it's separate from the presence of the audience."[7]

They initially flew to Rome and stayed there a week. "Sonny had suits made for everybody—tuxedos," Cherry said.[8] Sonny's TV segment, alongside the Italian Quartetto di Lucca, was produced by Lilian Terry, the Cairo-born, Rome-based jazz vocalist, journalist, producer, and concert organizer. To prepare, Terry met Sonny at his hotel beforehand. When she arrived, she found the lobby teeming with journalists hoping to talk to Peter, Paul, and Mary, also in Rome.

"I'll be right down," Sonny said on the phone. "In fifteen minutes."

"Perfect! I'll be..."

"I'll recognize you..."

"I mean the hall is overcrowded with people and..."

"Don't worry, I'll recognize you. Fifteen minutes."

And he rang off. I laid down the receiver wondering. Had I heard him correctly? Had he said: "I'll recognize you?" Yes, twice.

Within fifteen minutes, the three singers, their manager and staff, and all the reporters had filled up the hall to confusion. Now how was I to reach Rollins when the lift was far across the crowded hall? The doors of one of the lifts opened just then and he emerged in all his presence as he stood tall and looked around. Every single head in the hall was turned towards him in fascination and his eyes searched and found mine.

He came straight to me, offering his large hand: "Ah, there you are. Let's go into the other living room, so we can talk."

From that moment I was totally mesmerized by this gentle, thoughtful artist who proceeded to ask *me* all kinds of questions even as I tried to interview him on his Roman holiday.

When I mentioned the fact of being born in Cairo, he had nodded slowly, satisfied: "Well, of course... Egypt. You know that we keep meeting every 144 years since our first encounter in ancient Egypt? Yes, you and me, and also Clifford Brown. I believe you were born in 1930, right?"

"Why, yes!" I was amazed.

"So was Brownie and so was I. Of course, you don't recall the incident, but I am sure you remember Brownie?"[9]

Sonny's insistence that they had met every 144 years was based in Rosicrucian belief. In *Mansions of the Soul*, H. Spencer Lewis asserted that the time span between rebirths was 144 years.[10] As though corroborating it, Sonny and Terry had moments of déjà vu.[11]

Terry drove Sonny through the cobblestone streets and pointed out the ancient Roman monuments. They ate their weight in spaghetti. Sonny had his photo taken at the Trevi Fountain, where Anita Ekberg and Marcello Mastroianni got soaked in Fellini's classic 1960 film *La Dolce Vita*.[12] "What fascinated me was the subject of our conversations, often esoteric," Terry wrote, "as we strolled through the streets of Rome until three in the morning. I had never walked so much in all my life, my hand clinging to his powerful arm, but somehow I was not tired as we stood on the Campidoglio and looked around and meditated on Roman and Vatican history."[13]

They passed a newsstand on Via Veneto selling the January issue of the Paris-based *Jazz* magazine, with Sonny's photo on the cover. He bought Terry a copy and inscribed it: "144 years before 1930. Do you recall the incident???"[14]

When in Rome, they jammed as the Romans did. Lele Crespi, the cousin of bassist Roberto Nicolosi, hosted a jam session where Sonny met trumpeter Nunzio Rotondo, a lifelong friend, and Don Cherry met his future collaborator, tenor saxophonist Gato Barbieri.[15] On *Studio Uno*, Sonny wore a white tuxedo; the rest of the band wore black tuxes. They performed Monk's "52nd Street Theme"[16] on a monochromatic white studio set, lit in silhouette, the spotlights making geometric shapes on the floor and walls in a rhythmic play of light and shadow.

The day before Sonny left, Lilian Terry had a backache, and Sonny claimed he could "soothe my pain with the power of his mind." When she got home, she "was aware of a 'perception,' as if my back was being soothed by a warm flow from my skull, along the cervical vertebrae and all the way down my spine." She called Sonny the next morning to tell him that it worked. "He knew it had worked and was glad he could help me. 'You take good care of your health now, and I wish you all the best in life.' "[17]

Terry paid tribute to the week when she recorded "St. Thomas" later that year with her own lyrics:

You know that I have never been to St. Thomas
Yet I have a feeling we've met in St. Thomas
Long ago, don't you know?
Hundred forty-four years before
1930![18]

On January 13, Sonny Rollins and Company performed two concerts in Milan at the 800-seat Teatro dell'Arte. John Coltrane had made the Italian debut of his classic quartet at the theater on December 2, and with the two concerts only a month apart, comparisons were inevitable.[19] Though many left Sonny's concert shaking their heads in bewilderment, the Italian critics were awestruck.[20] Arrigo Polillo felt that Sonny was more complex than Coltrane, "reconciling Pollock's formalism with Mondrian's geometry."[21] After the concert, Sonny shared some sausage with a stray cat in Piazza Duomo, as tenor saxophonist Gianni Basso and other musicians crowded around him, demanding to know how to circular breathe.[22]

On January 14, the band flew to Zurich, where they performed at the 1,200-seat Volkshaus,[23] followed by Copenhagen's Falkoner Center the next day.[24] "52nd Street Theme" was full of Sonny's sly quotations: "The Man on the Flying Trapeze," "Autumn Nocturne," and others. Over twenty minutes, Sonny took it way out, as he did with "On Green Dolphin Street" and a thrilling medley that connected "The Bridge," "You Don't Know What Love Is," and "Sly Mongoose," a calypso Sonny would have known from versions by Lord Invader, Charlie Parker, and Louis Armstrong. In the audience was twenty-six-year-old tenor saxophonist Albert Ayler, who idolized Sonny.

"Sonny Rollins is one of the smartest men in the music," Ayler later said. "Yeah, 'cause he knew how to negotiate his business."[25]

Ayler "was waiting on the sideline from the stage after the concert, and he asked me did I want to go to a session at the Montmartre," Cherry recalled, referring to the Jazzhus Montmartre, the top jazz club in Copenhagen. There, Cherry and Higgins had a jam session with Don Byas, Dexter Gordon, Niels-Henning Ørsted Pedersen, and Ayler.[26]

On January 17, they were at the 1,770-seat Stockholm Concert Hall.[27] There, Cherry met Johnny Griffin, as well as his future wife, Moki, who attended the concert.[28] On January 18, they flew to Cologne, then taxied thirty miles to Düsseldorf, making it to the theater exhausted and starving, and played the concert at the Robert-Schumann-Saal in their travel clothes—Cherry had a red sweater, while Billy Higgins and Henry Grimes wore green and gray wool shirts. Sonny traveled in style and wore a navy-blue pinstripe suit. After the concert, they returned to the hotel, ordered fried eggs from room service, and passed out.[29]

Even though the travel "was a mess," Sonny recalled, in Düsseldorf "we played the best concert on the tour. Everything was really happening. Everybody seemed to sense what everyone else was doing before they did it. And in my playing, things just came out effortlessly, I didn't have to try. It's what I strive for, where I don't have to think, because thinking impedes creativity. That's the mystery of music. That's why music is more than a science. Sure, it's an exact science, but there's something else that transcends it."[30] Naturally, it was not recorded.

On Saturday, January 19, they flew to Paris, where Sonny connected with Bud Powell before giving two concerts at the Olympia that night.[31] He walked the streets in a black hat and black custom-made Italian suit, carrying a black valise, looking like a fashion model or a double agent.[32] Ever image and health conscious, Sonny also found time to use his exercise coils, which he had carted to Europe.

At the Olympia, Sonny made the bold move of opening with a ballad, Ellington's "Solitude."[33] They played a twenty-three-minute version of "Sonnymoon,"[34] while "Everything Happens to Me" drew riotous applause, and a frisson of laughter, with references to "I Love Paris" and "Beer Barrel Polka." Sonny always quoted the "Marseillaise" when he was in France.[35] The concerts polarized Parisian fans and critics. Half the audience appreciated the group's intellectual depth, with one critic comparing the performance to James Joyce's *Ulysses*; the other half felt it barely qualified as jazz.[36] Most attendees compared Sonny to Coltrane, who played the Salle Pleyel on November 1, and critical consensus was emerging: Sonny had confirmed that "he is of the same caliber as Coltrane."[37]

Sonny was happy with his Parisian performance. "This time I really feel as if I possess all the means of communication between what I feel and the public," Sonny said after the concert. "Let the critics carp. If there is rhythm, there is jazz. Maybe people don't like the modern style, but to say it isn't jazz is just nonsense."[38] Still, he told another interviewer, he could do better.[39] And, he said in the taxi from Orly Airport to his hotel—"Coltrane prevents me from sleeping!"[40]

Before leaving Paris, Sonny arranged to return at the end of the tour for a ten-day run at the Blue Note from February 1 to 10.[41] Manager Ben Benjamin was a domineering, gay American expat who had a marriage of convenience to Etla, the club's French business manager; Bud Powell, the club's golden goose, deliberately mispronounced her name as "Hitler."[42] "The owner of this club is a son of a bitch who has a bad name among business people and musicians all over Paris," Sonny wrote Lucille. "This plus the fact that there is no Union in Paris makes it mandatory that I exert the utmost tact and business acumen before signing anything."[43]

After a January 20 concert in Munich, they were off the next day. The group hardly left their hotel room, listening to music, reading, and catching up on sleep, with the exception of Don Cherry, who visited a Klee and Kandinsky exhibit with a few Münchners. Sonny had an upset stomach, and a doctor came to the hotel. He spent the day sipping tea with lemon and reading two books he brought along for the tour in addition to his Rosicrucian texts: an encyclopedia of musical terms and a book of Van Gogh reproductions. The next morning, January 22, they went to Stuttgart: the German tour liaison, jazz critic Werner Burkhardt, convinced them to take a train instead of a plane.[44] On the platform, Sonny took out his saxophone. "Can you sing me the melody of your German national anthem?" he asked Burkhardt, who sang it, first halfheartedly, then louder for Sonny. As their train rolled in, Sonny played it back, Burkhardt recalled, "in the most uninhibited fortissimo and with variations that Father Haydn could not have thought of even in his wildest dreams."[45] Sonny planned to quote it onstage as a diplomatic gesture.

In a cramped compartment, Sonny did some band accounting and asked the group, "How long can a person live without breathing?" Billy Higgins speculated ten minutes, Burkhardt five. "Fifteen years," Sonny said. He had read of a yogi in India who had achieved the feat. "The whole thing is a question of concentration," Sonny told them. "If you only believe in it firmly enough, you can rule the body completely through the mind." In death, Sonny went on, some said the soul leaves the body and enters a realm filled with music. That led to a discussion of Germany's classical tradition. "Beethoven was above all an improviser," Sonny said,[46] also citing Bach's "The Musical Offering,"[47] Karlheinz Stockhausen's aleatoric music, and Edgard Varèse's 1931 composition "Ionisation"[48] as classical works that exemplified improvisation. Everyone went to sleep except for Sonny, who finished counting the money and putting it in envelopes; when they awoke, Sonny paid them.[49]

In Stuttgart, they looked in vain for a dentist for Don Cherry, who had a toothache. But Cherry was still able to perform that night at the Liederhalle Stuttgart; the show was recorded for a broadcast on the Südfunk station.[50] On January 23, they performed in Frankfurt, then flew to Berlin. Sonny and Cherry worked out music on the plane, while Sonny imparted survival tips for the road down to wardrobe maintenance.[51]

The tour was exhausting, especially the onslaught of reporters that ambushed him wherever he went. "As usual, I am being confronted with diplomatic type situations on every leg of the trip," he wrote to Lucille from Berlin, the stop after Stuttgart. "These occur when reporters hold their interviews as a rule. You see they always expect a stereotype and ask questions which only a diplomat would be able to be calm and intelligent about." Fortunately, "being diplomatic is a natural part of my character and demolishing those who need to be is a personal pleasure and obligation which I accept gladly."[52]

Sonny had "not been content with the deportment of Mssrs. Higgins + Cherry," he wrote. "These traits are the result of . . . the use of X and there is no doubt that certain physcological [*sic*] adjustments must be made by someone who is breaking away from a nice safe refuge, albeit made of clay and built on fantasy." To Sonny, a lack of professionalism in his group undermined his efforts to elevate the status of jazz. "I am fighting out here for dignity for them as well as myself as well as so many others, and when I think that they aren't doing what they should + can in this campaign, and for adolescent juvenile reasons I can at this writing hardly contain myself."[53]

Before leaving Berlin, Sonny was having technical difficulties with his Mark VI and decided to repair it himself—"something which I had never done," he admitted.[54] "You don't just take apart a saxophone. And then you have to do a concert that night. Anyway, I was headstrong but not head-wise, so I took apart this horn and time began going. 2 o'clock, 3 o'clock, 4 o'clock, 5 o'clock, 6. Uh-oh . . . Anyway, I put it back together. Of course, it wasn't playing any better or anything. I was fortunate . . . at that point I was grateful to just be able to play, to make the concert. It wasn't a good concert. Of course, I'm not a big fan of myself so there are very few concerts which I would find that are really acceptable."[55]

Having survived the performance, Sonny took off for Amsterdam on January 26, where they had two back-to-back concerts. The early-evening show was at the Kurhaus of Scheveningen in The Hague; the late show was at the Concertgebouw, where Norman Granz presented the group. Despite the leaky tenor, Sonny wasn't done playing. At an after-hours jam session, probably in The Hague's Jazzclub, he met Jos van Heuverzwijn, known as one of the city's leading tenor saxophonists.[56] When Sonny heard him, he asked to borrow his tenor, a Buescher Big B Aristocrat.[57]

It was one of the best saxophones Sonny had ever played.[58] "I liked American horns better than Selmer," Sonny said. "I liked those other horns— Kings and Conns and Bueschers and Martins. Somehow for me, I thought I sounded better than I did on the Selmer."[59] Jos van Heuverzwijn's Buescher produced such a good sound that when Sonny returned it, he silently hoped to one day buy it if the opportunity ever arose.[60] The group then returned to Paris to play the Blue Note from February 1 to 10 before flying home.[61]

In New York, Sonny returned to RCA Studios with Grimes, Cherry, and Higgins for *3 in Jazz*, a package LP with the Gary Burton Quartet and the Clark Terry Quintet.[62] There was more than enough "material in the can that could be used, but should not be if it can be avoided," Avakian wrote in an internal RCA memo, "as all the good things are very long and very difficult to cut without doing violence to the music."[63]

On February 20, Sonny recorded "You Are My Lucky Star," "I Could Write a Book," and "There Will Never Be Another You."[64] In an uncharacteristic show of restraint, the first two tracks were under four minutes; "Another You" was under six.[65]

On March 2, Sonny Rollins & Co. performed in Washington, DC, at Howard University's Cramton Auditorium in a concert billed as "What's New in Jazz?"[66] with Higgins, Cherry, and Bob Cranshaw.[67] Higgins showed up late for the gig, and when he walked in, Sonny put his sticks in his back pocket. Higgins took out a switchblade and started to play using that. The standoff soon ended; Higgins stopped being late.

On March 5, Sonny began a ten-day run at Detroit's Minor Key, a coffeehouse that presented contemporary jazz.[68] Bennie Maupin, who had one of his first nightly gigs as a leader, visited him at his hotel during the day.[69] "He would be in his room practicing, exercising," Maupin recalled. "He was reading some things about the Rosicrucian Order. He was studying some spiritual stuff, which was really cool. Just to see, what does a person like this do during the day, you know? I saw what he was doing. He was working on that saxophone, man."[70] Maupin moved to New York later that year; Sonny told him to look him up when he got there.

From March 15 to 23, Sonny played at Gino's in St. Louis.[71] On a set break, he sat down at the bar, where he eavesdropped on a conversation. "The only thing of his I like is *Way Out West*," a woman said to her boyfriend. "This doesn't sound like that at all."

"What could I say?" Sonny said, later recounting the moment five decades later. "I wish I could satisfy everything that everybody wants. Miles and myself, we used to talk about how the biggest thing we hated was clichés."[72]

After St. Louis, they were booked in Cleveland at the Jazz Temple, a coffeehouse in University Circle founded by Winston E. Willis.[73] One of the worshippers at the Temple was Albert Ayler, who had returned to his hometown from Copenhagen in February. According to saxophonist turned bassist Errol Henderson, Ayler kept saying "Poor Sonny" during Sonny's set. The next night, Ayler returned with his horn. "Albert could play what he knew and that was cool, but he couldn't get up there and mess with Sonny, who was playing his ass off," Henderson said.[74]

On April 19 and 20, Sonny played the Cork 'n' Bib in Westbury, Long Island.[75] It was around this time that he finally parted ways with Billy Higgins.[76] Continuing the trend of using Ornette Coleman's sidemen, Sonny replaced Higgins with Charles Moffett, a childhood friend of Coleman's who worked with Ornette after Higgins.

Sonny decided to replace Cherry as well, and caught wind that alto saxophonist Sonny Simmons and saxophonist and flautist Prince Lasha were new in town. Simmons and Lasha had recently made a splash with *The Cry!* on Contemporary.[77] Lasha already knew some New York musicians. In the 1950s, Lasha lived at 377 Edgecombe, a floor below Sonny's childhood apartment, and had once helped repair Sonny's tenor.[78] He most likely met Sonny around the time of his car accident with Richie Powell in 1956. "I took Rollins's horn up to him, as he had just got back from his first accident, and we became lifelong friends after that."[79]

In 1963, Lasha and Simmons "drove all the way across the country from

Oakland," Simmons recalled.[80] They rented an apartment on Fourth Street and Second Avenue in the East Village, not far from the new Five Spot.[81] Coltrane would come by their apartment sometimes, and Sonny "used to come around, too," Lasha said, "bringing fruit for us."[82]

"When I got here, he was the big shot of all the musicians," Simmons said of Sonny. "That included Coltrane as well."

One day, Lasha and Simmons ran into Sonny on Second Avenue on their way to Clifford Jordan's. "I looked across the street and saw this dude looking and pointing at me, and it was Sonny Rollins with his horn!" Lasha recalled. Sonny accompanied them to Jordan's studio, where they played for hours. "One person came down to where we rehearsed and said, rather than that the music was too loud, that it was too fast!"[83]

Sonny hired Simmons and Lasha for an April 22 benefit at the Village Gate for the Village Aid and Service Center, a drug rehabilitation program.[84] Sonny's set with Henry Grimes, Charles Moffett, Lasha, and Simmons was the evening's highlight.[85] "It was all kind of musicians hanging around the door waiting for the Newk, and they was begging to get in to play with him, 'cause his popularity poll was high," Simmons said.[86] "We got up on the bandstand, and I asked Newk, 'What we gon' play, man?' He didn't say shit. He just stomped his foot like a bull and charged in on it . . . not noise, but just sizzling fire."[87]

On April 25, Sonny was opening at Birdland with his quartet opposite Chris Connor and Herbie Mann.[88] Charles Moffett unexpectedly ended up on the gig after another jam session at Clifford Jordan's starting at noon and stretching into the evening. At around 7 p.m., Sonny let Moffett know that he wanted him at Birdland that night.[89]

On the stand, "Sonny asked me, 'What you want to play, Moffett?' I called a standard he played and he said, 'Naw.' At one point in the night, Don Cherry came over and told me, 'Moffett, man, go ahead and play *you*. Sonny got you for you to play like you want to play.' "[90]

At this time, Alfred Lion of Blue Note offered Sonny Simmons a contract, but he turned it down after, he claimed, "I sat down in a chair in his office, and he threw four bags of 'Dirty Harry' [heroin] on his desk."[91] Sonny offered Simmons another chance to record, along with Lasha. They convened at RCA Studios with George Avakian, yet within two takes, Avakian and Sonny got into a dispute, and the session was called off permanently.[92] That fall, Simmons returned to Oakland.[93]

It was at this time that Sonny hired twenty-six-year-old drummer Roy McCurdy, who'd played with Art Farmer and Benny Golson's Jazztet, Betty Carter, and Kenny Dorham.[94] Sonny's "rhythmic sense was unbelievable," McCurdy said. "He made me strong. I came off the Jazztet playing kind of normal, but when I came off playing with Sonny, man... it built your stamina.... You had to be strong or leave." McCurdy soon got his first sponsorship deal, from Rogers Drums: "When they found out I was with Sonny, they called me."[95]

Sonny also decided to add piano. Before closing at Birdland on May 8, he held auditions.[96] It ultimately came down to thirty-year-old Paul Bley or twenty-three-year-old Herbie Hancock.[97] Sonny held the audition on a Monday night, the night off at Birdland. That night, Miles Davis came to hold his own auditions.[98] As "the only pianist in the world who had played with Ornette,"[99] with the exception of Walter Norris, Bley wrote, he felt it might be a good fit if Sonny was still on his Ornette kick.

"These people didn't phone you, they sent word out through the grapevine," Bley wrote of the audition process. "The call had gone out for both Herbie Hancock and me to show up. When I got there, Herbie said, 'Hello Paul, which gig do you want?'"[100] Bley picked Sonny, turning down his opportunity to join the Second Great Quintet.[101] "The first time I got on a bandstand with Sonny Rollins I was amazed," Bley said. "It was so loud that not only couldn't I hear, but I couldn't see."[102]

To Bley, Sonny's "deconstruction of standards" approach was exciting. In free jazz, Bley said, "We had gone from simple standard playing to totally free playing without doing standards that had some harmonic freedom in terms of their construction. So this was an opportunity to play in a situation with masters who played standards as well as anybody on the planet and further deconstruct them, which would keep them alive for another decade or two."[103]

That first night at Birdland, Bley arrived in the middle of a set, "so I got up on the bandstand and jumped in. Sonny responded in his usual adversarial style and a marriage was born that lasted a year of touring in the U.S. and

Japan and culminated in the RCA Record, *Sonny Meets Hawk*."[104] The Sonny Rollins Quartet became Sonny, McCurdy, Grimes, and Bley.

Sonny made Bley strong, too. "Sonny is a prizefighter, 'Newk' Rollins, and Sonny always goes for the knockout," Bley wrote. "If you have to be on the stage with him you could be his target.... Sonny could play long, very long, and I couldn't play that long, so it was a question of gaining muscles."[105]

Soon, Sonny and Paul developed a friendship, where some of this macho posturing onstage translated to offstage behavior. "Sonny would come to the house sometimes and just be talking to Paul Bley," recalled iconoclastic composer and pianist Carla Bley, Paul's wife at the time. "Once he came to the house, and he brought a huge bag of fruit. And he handed it to me, and he said, 'Wash the fruit.' I said, 'Okay,' and I washed all the fruit. I didn't really take it too bad. I thought, well, it's a chance to help out." A decade later, "he apologized to me for the fruit. He says, 'Lucille now tells me that that's not the right way to treat a woman.'... So he turned out to be a very friendly guy in a way that he wasn't when he was younger."[106]

From May 21 to June 2, 1963, the quartet played at the Jazz Workshop in San Francisco.[107] "He would start a tune, play for an hour and fifteen minutes, then turn to me and say, 'You got it!'" Bley recalled. Sonny would sometimes crouch right next to McCurdy's drums to make the rhythm more visceral. McCurdy said, "Half an hour later, we'd still be playing the same tune. Up-tempo!"[108]

One afternoon, Sonny was late, and alto saxophonist Lee Konitz happened to be there.[109] "Paul Bley asked me to sit in," Konitz recalled. "I was just in the audience, and don't know how come I had my horn with me. So I played a set, and then Sonny came in, and played the most fantastic set you could imagine—nonstop outness! He just played stunningly creatively. It was *very* free, though with a groove."[110]

From June 3 to June 9, they played the It Club in Los Angeles.[111] There were turn-away crowds, but the entire band didn't always show up. As the downbeat approached for their three-hour Saturday matinee, Grimes was nowhere to be found. "Henry had been growing increasingly introverted," Bley recalled. "It was getting to the point where he would not speak unless it was absolutely necessary, and eventually he simply wouldn't speak, period."[112]

Bley continued: "Finally, we looked behind the club. . . . Henry had gone out to the backyard and climbed the tree." Eventually, "Sonny turned to me and said, 'Look, could you play a little bass for me?'" On the bandstand, "He kicked off 'This Can't Be Love' at a very bright tempo and played it for three hours. A long time to keep up a walking bass line on the piano. Fortunately, Henry Grimes made it down from the tree for the evening session, where we played a single tune for *four* hours."[113]

If Sonny felt anyone in the band was breaking the pace, he let them know in writing. Roy McCurdy soon found a letter under his door.

Roy,

I am playing my behind off. I'm playing hard. You're not playing quite hard enough. Would you please play harder?

Sincerely,
Sonny Rollins

The next night, McCurdy played harder, and found another letter.

Thank you.

Sincerely,
Sonny Rollins[114]

On the night of June 29, Sonny was in the courtyard at the New School for Social Research for the fifth and final episode of *Jazz Is Music*, a short-lived weekly TV series on WNET–Channel Thirteen hosted by composer, arranger, and New School professor Hall Overton.[115] Sonny took this opportunity to debut his new haircut: a Mohawk. "That was before the punk guys," Sonny recalled. In the late '50s, Sonny was playing at the Five Spot, and "there was a Native American guy in the crowd with some of the fans and on one of the breaks, we'd be outside, and he was talking with me, and so I got the idea, 'Well, let's give a little salute to the Native Americans, why not?'"[116] It was also economical: "I don't have to go to the barber," he said. "I do it myself, it takes a few minutes, plus I think it enhances my countenance and personality."[117]

Sonny's Mohawk bespoke an interest in indigenous music and culture as part of his syncretic approach to spirituality and music.[118] Sonny took notes on a text called "Music of the American Indian,"[119] which noted, "It is less used for entertainment and more used for and associated with Religious, Ceremonial, healing, and other of the 'higher activities,'" he wrote. His notes discussed that much Native American music was bound up with their "pantheistic creed" and that it was all part of an ongoing continuum. "In general, songs are looked upon as INSPIRATIONS not as CREATIONS," Sonny wrote. There were notes on style: "A marked mannerism of singers is attacking the note on its sharp side and then settling to its proper pitch, an excessive tremolo, and a detachment note from note by a curious contraction of the glottis. It is mostly all UNISON, with generally a PENTATONIC SCALE."[120]

Unlike future subversive cultural figures that would separate the Mohawk from its indigenous origins and repurpose it as a rebellion against conservative values, Sonny intended it as a show of solidarity for the common struggle against white supremacy, extending "The Freedom Suite" to indigenous people. "I was trying to make a statement about the Native American people," Sonny said. "They are treated the same way."[121] Sonny began sometimes performing in a cowboy hat, like in *Way Out West*, and then would take it off to reveal the Mohawk underneath. As Sonny explained, these were "the first Americans here." It was a vision of jazz as an art form capacious enough to hold the tangled dissonances of the nation's history.[122]

Sonny's five-year-old nephew, Clifton Anderson, Gloria's son, vividly recalled his first encounter with Uncle Sonny's Mohawk. "I heard the doorbell ring, and when I turned the doorknob, I saw this guy there with this Mohican haircut," he recalled. "And it scared the shit out of me! He was looming very large, plus he had this crazy haircut, so I started running screaming to my mom. She came and let Sonny in, and she says, 'Oh, this is your uncle!'"[123]

That summer, for the second consecutive year, Sonny won the tenor category in the *Down Beat* International Jazz Critics Poll.[124] He had sixty votes to Coltrane's fifty-six. Coleman Hawkins came in third with fifty-five, with Stan Getz, the perennial favorite in the '50s, getting fifty. Sonny was also named one of the three Jazzmen of the Year in a 1962 *Down Beat* retrospective, alongside Dizzy Gillespie and Stan Getz.[125]

Sonny's next major gig was at the Tenth Annual Newport Jazz Festival, which took place from July 4 to 7 in Freebody Park.[126] On Saturday night, Sonny's quartet played with special guest Coleman Hawkins in one of the most anticipated sets of the festival. George Avakian planned a series of live albums to be released under the title *At Newport '63*: Lambert-Hendricks-Bavan with Coleman Hawkins and Clark Terry; Martial Solal; Joe Williams; Joe Daley; and Sonny and Hawk.[127] The unlikely pairings bridging generations emerged from a conversation between Avakian and George Wein. According to Avakian, Wein said, " 'Dizzy Gillespie is having Milt Jackson do a few numbers with him.... Thelonious Monk has invited Pee Wee Russell to sit in. Now take the artists you're going to record up there. Sonny Rollins, for instance— is there someone special he'd like to play with?' " Avakian posed the question to Sonny. "His answer was quick," Avakian wrote: "The man to whom every saxophonist owes a debt of gratitude, Coleman Hawkins."[128]

As soon as Hawk accepted, the anxiety of influence rushed in. "To play with Coleman Hawkins was no small thing for me," Sonny wrote.[129] There was the music alone, never mind the aura, Sonny said. "It presented a challenge—how to play myself but still be natural and normal and myself while I still had this feeling of awe for him."[130]

On July 6, they had no time for rehearsal. They were a high-contrast pair. Hawk dressed dark, Sonny light; Hawk had close-cropped hair and a mustache, Sonny had a Mohawk; Sonny was a statuesque thirty-two-year-old, Hawk a stout fifty-eight.[131] Sonny began with an unaccompanied eight-bar intro to Irving Berlin's "Remember," which he, Bley, and Grimes twisted into a pretzel for fifteen minutes. Sonny played one of his kaleidoscopic cadenzas, his sound reaching out to the Newport cliffs. "Thank you very much, ladies and gentlemen," Sonny said. "Now—the great Coleman Hawkins!"

Hawk lumbered onstage. "My man!" came a shout from someone in the crowd. The rhythm section began playing "All the Things You Are," and Hawkins took the melody and the first solo. Then Bley took a solo, testing how far he could wander from the song's form without losing it entirely. Sonny played several choruses, followed by an effusive trading section, in which the two titans closed their eyes and let the spirit take them. It began to heat up with the group improvisation, but over eleven minutes, Hawk's mike was low while Sonny's was high, creating a bad balance. Beyond that, Sonny played tentatively. The same was true of "The Way You Look Tonight." It was the musical equivalent of a game of "After you"—"No, after *you*..."[132]

There would be no *Sonny and Hawk at Newport '63*. "So we did it in the studio," Avakian said.[133]

This led to more anxiety for Sonny. "I had my own feelings about being able to record with him—being on the same level, so to speak," Sonny wrote. "I didn't want to make a fool of myself, playing with the great Coleman Hawkins. So there was a little bit of trepidation, a lot of awe and respect."[134] The finances added to the tension: under Sonny's contract, he was getting $15,000, Hawk $1,200. Hawk would get an additional $750 for the studio time, coming from Sonny's RCA account.[135]

There were two days of recording scheduled, but according to Bley, Sonny didn't show up for the first: on the Monday following Newport, at 9 p.m., everyone but him reported to RCA Studios. On Monday, July 15, Sonny finally showed up in Studio B and met Avakian, sound engineer Mickey Crofford, McCurdy, Bley, and Bob Cranshaw, who was subbing for Henry Grimes.[136] "By that time, the rest of the band had been showing up every night and was put off each night by a phone call," Bley said. "When I got there, they were fed up and exhausted." Except Bley, who'd tipped the night watchman to call when Sonny arrived: "I walked in the door shaved, showered, and ready to play."[137]

Hawkins got ready to play his way. "Coleman had his little flask, and they were having fun," recalled McCurdy. "And I was having fun because just to be playing the rhythm behind these guys was a big thing....It seemed to jell almost right away."[138]

"I'm convinced to this day that Sonny had waited a whole year until it was time to unleash those phenomenal solos on *Sonny Meets Hawk*," Bley said.[139] "It was like a prizefight, and I was trying not to get hit by blows that had gone astray."[140]

Yet in a way, it was really Sonny versus himself. "When I played with Hawkins, I was trying to make a contrast between Hawkins and myself, really make a sound," Sonny said. "I didn't want to try and sound like him, because I could not sound like him anyway. It's pretty hard to sound like Coleman."[141] During the recording session, Sonny struggled with this double bind of self-assertion—seem too little like Hawkins and negate a core part of his identity, seem too much like him and be eclipsed by the great man's long shadow.[142]

In case Sonny couldn't individuate himself enough, they employed stereo sound to put Sonny in the right speaker, Hawkins and Bley in the left, leaving bass and drums in the center. They began the night with two takes of "All the Things You Are," but it only took eight bars for Hawk to see what he had gotten into. The rhythm section dispensed with the song's standard intro line in favor of a chromatic derangement. Hawk came in on the melody unfazed, and Sonny's dissonant improvised counterpoint couldn't shake him. Over three choruses, Hawk played the changes with the vigor of a man half his age. "Yeah!" screamed Sonny.

"Everybody was trying to expand perimeters," Sonny said.[143] "The idea was stretching that 'rubber band' so far that even though you were following the changes and at the same time following the 'parallel universe' of the improvised line, they were so closely related that I could skip from one to the other at any given second and do it with authority." Bley thought of what the group did as "harmonic improvising," in which "you are going from point A to point B, and it's totally up to you what you want to do in that interval, so long as you leave point A and you arrive at point B."[144] Bley went far out on his "All the Things You Are" solo. To Grimes, Bley could "bend the notes" of the piano.[145] The pianist's solo on "All the Things You Are" took Hawk's concluding statement into another dimension. Pat Metheny, who was only eight years old when *Sonny Meets Hawk* was recorded, would call Bley's solo "the shot heard 'round the world."[146]

"Of course, I didn't play the song at all," Bley said. "Not only was I 'elastically' away from the song, I never really bounced back, and when I did for a moment, it would be startling. 'Oh! He knew where he was!' I always knew where I was, that's what gives that kind of elasticity meaning."[147]

Hawk did not know where he was, though, and it was only the second take of the night. But Hawk had a plan. "Hawkins came to me after the first tune and said, 'Paul, do me a favor. For the chorus, when it's my turn to play, lead me in. Give me a nod of your head.'"

Sonny followed Bley, entering in the middle of the fourth bar with a soft tremolo. What he played was possibly even more radical—rhythmically, he was never quite on the beat; his phrases started and stopped at odd junctures; he played multiphonically, microtonally, way up in the altissimo range, and other times not at all. Then he was honking in the blues tradition. For four choruses, it was "All the Things You Aren't."

"Sonny came in just after my solo and erased everybody because he loved confrontation," Bley said. "With the fur flying between Hawk and myself, Sonny came in and said, "Oh yeah? You guys won't even know what room you are in when I get through.' "[148] Then Bley nodded to Hawkins, who came in right at the top of the chorus to take it out. To fit it on the LP, Avakian opted for a fade-out, trimming several minutes.[149]

Next, they recorded the ballad "Lover Man,"[150] with Hawk dominating through understatement as Sonny sustained a note more than an octave above the tenor range for several measures.[151] On "Yesterdays," Hawk ended his solo on a tremolo; Sonny seemed to veer into mocking territory, playing an exaggerated tremolo for the first twelve bars of his solo.

Next was "The Way You Look Tonight," with Sonny playing the head with a pronounced vibrato, further imitating the Hawkins sound. Over twelve and a half minutes, Sonny shifted back into a harsher, mostly vibrato-less sound, playing with a halting stutter before exploding into wildly inventive eighth-note runs.[152] Hawk simply played Hawk, as lyrical as ever.[153] On the trading section, Sonny dropped his imitation entirely—the contrast could not have been starker.

When the take ended, Sonny paused, then kept playing a cappella. "It's long enough," Hawk said, coughing under Sonny's noodling.

Hawk tried to get Sonny's attention; Sonny took the horn out of his mouth. "Huh?" he said.

"I can't understand how...one thing," Hawk continued. "You take all you have..." Hawkins told Sonny a quiet anecdote. "Ah, you crazy som'bitch," Hawk said.[154] He was going to drop some knowledge on his protégé.

Avakian came in. "Sonny," said Avakian. "This is fine provided one side of the LP is twenty-eight inches across."

Next up was "Three Little Words." Sonny often included it in his sets as a tribute to Pres, but Hawk had also recorded it. Sonny took it at least as far out as he did on "All the Things You Are." Then Hawk dropped all pretense and showed he could play as loudly and inventively as Sonny, without sacrificing lyricism or swing. After one line, Sonny couldn't contain himself. "Whoa!" He gradually shifted back to his stately subtone.

"We tried to get somethin' shorter," said Hawk. The take was twelve minutes long.

"Can you do it short?" shouted Avakian. "Oh yeah," said Sonny. "Five choruses." After he reiterated it, Hawk just laughed.

On the first take, McCurdy played brushes; Sonny wanted sticks. "Stop, stop!" Sonny shouted. On the third take, Sonny was frustrated: "Okay, stop! Stop! Stop. Let's get the *RHYTHM* together!" On the next take, Sonny had trouble getting into his solo. Hawk flew in with total composure, playing fortissimo. On the trading section, Sonny parroted some of Hawk's lines, seeming to invert and extend others, as he had done to Coltrane on "Tenor Madness." Yet he somehow remained deferential to Hawk, letting him establish the ideas Sonny embellished upon. And then Sonny threw in a quote from Irving Berlin's "Cheek to Cheek"—playing a tune made famous by Pres, standing bell to bell with Hawk, he truly was "in heaven."

After that quote, Hawk began playing staccato hits in the low register, seeming to cede the floor to Sonny as the tune just kept going. It was a ten-minute take, well more than the promised five choruses. "Now you see what you got to do, don't you?" Hawk called to Avakian.

"I'm glad it was a short one," said Avakian sarcastically.

"Splice all in between, that's all. Get in there, listen to it, and splice," Hawk said. And it was then that Hawk delivered his lesson to Sonny. "You got to *feel* that beat, man," said Hawk. "You gotta *feel* that shit. That's the important groove. You've got to feel somethin' in your heart. You know what I'm talkin' about?"

"But it depends on the record," said Sonny.

"You gotta feel!"

"It depends on the record."

"Not only on the record, man—anything," Hawk said. "When you play. You can feel it. You can feel somethin', whether you're in here or you're playing to some people out there! If you're not feeling that…that shit was goin' on, but I just wasn't feelin' the shit, man!"

Sonny let it sink in. "That's our music," said Sonny. "Beautiful."[155] Even out there in a parallel universe, they had to feel the beat. And Hawk was not feeling it. That summer night in 1963, Sonny saw that he didn't have to try so hard to assert his identity. Just like Hawk, he was always already himself. And there was another lesson. Logic is not enough—you've got to *feel* that shit.

It was getting late. "Let's make a good shorty—two, two, two, and one," came the voice from the booth. So over two choruses of "Three Little Words," Sonny dug down deep and played what he felt. He dropped the Hawkish vibrato and the air of self-consciousness. Hawk played his choruses with authority, followed by a trading section where Sonny seemed to really communicate with his idol.

"That's good," said Avakian. It was just over five minutes. It wouldn't end up on the final cut of the album; Sonny being Sonny, it wasn't good enough. He didn't like McCurdy's cymbal work. They laid down one more take. "Well," came the voice from the booth, "let's go home."

The band returned at 5:30 p.m. on Thursday, July 18, to finish. Henry Grimes was back, with recording engineer Paul Goodman taking over.[156] They started with "Just Friends," doing three takes, with Avakian later splicing the best material to create the finished track. In one catalytic moment, Bley locked in with Sonny with such synchronicity that when Sonny played a diminished pattern at the end and left a note out, Bley spontaneously filled it in.[157]

After a couple rehearsal takes of Ellington and Strayhorn's "Satin Doll,"[158] Sonny cut it off midtake. "No, no, no, no, no, n-no, n-no, n-no!" he shouted. They moved onto "At McKie's," a blues Sonny wrote for the session in homage to McKie Fitzhugh's Disc Jockey Lounge in Chicago. They had been going for nearly four hours, crossing into overtime after their 9 p.m. cutoff, when they decided to try George Gershwin's "Summertime."[159]

Sonny probably wasn't thinking of Gershwin so much as Mahalia Jackson, who frequently performed "Summertime" in a medley with "Sometimes I Feel Like a Motherless Child" to show the uncanny resemblance between the two. "Why should I feel or how should I feel about or upon hearing of and being made aware of the similarity of George Gershwin's 'Summertime' to 'Sometimes I Feel Like A Motherless Child?'" Sonny wrote in his journal.[160] Sonny's version reached back to the source.

Avakian didn't run the tape from the top, but he was struck by what he heard. They would record one more take before finishing that night, but, Avakian recalled, "the electricity wasn't there anymore."[161] So Avakian just went with the rehearsal take, "a marvelous, spontaneous expression which couldn't be topped."[162] On that first take, Grimes found the spiritual taproot of the music. "I was just overwhelmed," Grimes recalled. "There wasn't anything I could do but grab the ax and start playing."[163] When Sonny came back in to take it out, propelled by Grimes, all of the anxiety melted away. Sonny closed his eyes and let the spirit move him, and Hawk answered. He was feeling that beat in his heart.[164]

On July 16, Sonny began a weeklong stand at the Village Vanguard opposite pianist-vocalist Blossom Dearie's trio with bassist Jimmy Garrison and drummer Tootie Heath.[165] Miles Davis was booked there the previous week and came to see his old friend. "How happy it made life when Miles threw his arms around me smothering me literally with kisses when I walked into the Village Vanguard recently the other night," Sonny wrote Gertrude Abercrombie. "Miles is always and will always be Miles. . . . Thank the Heavens that there are still some people around whom he feels the love of. I do love him so very much."[166]

Sonny was demoralized—his dental problems were back. He pushed his ailing jaw to the breaking point, doing a gig at the Showboat in Philadelphia from August 5 to 11. Sonny and Paul Bley were "on the same wavelength,"[167] but he had to cancel his next booking, at the Grill in Pittsburgh, and postpone further recording.

Sonny wrote Avakian a letter to explain his dental predicament. Even in his correspondence, Sonny never kept to an eight-bar solo; he wrote his "dear friend" Avakian an eight-page handwritten letter, with calligraphic flourishes, distinctive punctuation, and a poetic apostrophe to "the summer-time." He wrote it on letterhead from the Palace Hotel in Gothenburg, Sweden, but sent it from "Near Jersey (AT HER BEST)." While recovering from a root canal, he hoped to devise the "means of overcoming the condition"—"DOUBLE EMBOUCHURE—UPSIDE DOWN MOUTHPIECE—NEW IDEAS sought—emergency—must carry on...I mean to produce a 'HIT RECORD,'" he wrote. "If you really want to <u>we can do it</u>."[168]

As Sonny celebrated his thirty-third birthday, he was resting and recovering for his maiden voyage to Japan—a monthlong tour that September.[169] The time off gave Sonny the opportunity to begin work on a far-ranging saxophone method book, never completed. Sonny planned to use the instrument as a guide to living well, a sort of "Zen and the Art of Saxophone Maintenance." It would variously be called "Fraternity of Saxophone," "Our Saxophone," "Saxophone Energy and Health," "Discovering the Saxophone," "Saxophone Principles," "The Almighty," and "Fantastic Saxophone."[170]

More than just a technical guide to embouchure, fingerings, and exercises, the book would present hard-earned life lessons: "An attempt to stress clean living as a <u>requisite</u> to good musicianship and an attempt to unify these ideals so as to bring about the realization of the Great American Dream, as it is so vividly exemplified in jazz, which is a derivative music—comprising many elements peoples and countries to thereby destroy the myths which separate not only jazz men of different ethnic background but indeed all men plagued by the mistrust and misunderstanding based on fear and ignorance."[171]

Sonny's holistic approach to the book was partially inspired by Paramahansa Yogananda's Self-Realization Fellowship's 1963 text *Cosmic Chants*.[172] Sonny underlined this line: "Music is a divine art, to be used not for pleasure but as a path to God-realization." He hoped to continue on this journey in Japan. Sonny bought a Buddha statue in Greenwich Village that he kept at home, and he planned to study Zen Buddhism on tour.[173]

The Japan tour was booked by Shaw Artists Corporation, Sonny's current booking agency.[174] The band was scheduled to arrive on September 18.[175] Bley, Grimes, and McCurdy had their passports in order and arrived at the airport early, but Sonny was nowhere to be found. "In the lounge we met the Shaw Artists Management rep, who was all in a sweat: 'Where's Sonny?'"

Bley recalled. Then the flight started boarding. "The Shaw Artists rep was shaking and pacing the floor," Bley said. "Here he was holding ten thousand dollars' worth of tickets. This was the last flight to Japan if we were going to make the tour, and he had no Sonny Rollins. The last call came for the flight to Tokyo. The Shaw Artists rep started shouting and frothing at the mouth. Someone persuaded them to hold the door for us—without Sonny there was no point in any of us getting on the plane—and we were given sixty seconds. Suddenly, Sonny appeared from a circular staircase. Shaved head, mohawk, carrying barbells and saxophone cases, he called out, 'Let's go.'"[176]

For his Japanese debut, Sonny was on a double bill with thirty-three-year-old vocalist Betty Carter.[177] "I think I knew her before that, but after that tour and being over in Japan together, we became pretty tight friends."[178] To Carter, the tour was a career milestone. Sonny "has the ability to swing," she said, though she couldn't get behind free improvisation. "I don't know anything about it. I must stay with what I know and try to swing."[179] Luckily, Sonny's band was equally adept at free playing and playing down the changes.

On the plane, Bley sat next to a mysterious newcomer to the group, thirty-year-old trumpeter Rashid Kamal Ali, who was born in Texas and grew up in Chicago, later serving in the army during the Korean War. Sonny had met him in Chicago, where "I heard him and liked him," he said. His nickname was Clanky.[180] Bley couldn't help but notice a briefcase chained to his wrist.

"'What's in the case?'" Bley asked. "He said, 'It's music that I've written specially for Sonny.'" Bley felt the idea was inappropriate so soon after joining the band, but Ali "didn't seem convinced."[181]

When they arrived on September 18 at Tokyo International Airport, they descended the airstair to the enthusiastic cheers of three hundred adoring fans, journalists, and a television crew from NHK. Each band member was immediately presented with a bouquet of flowers as they stood in front of a banner hung by the *Mainichi Shimbun* reading "Sonny Rollins and His Members."[182]

"I feel like an ambassador," a shocked Roy McCurdy said at the time.[183]

Even Sonny was shocked. "When I got off the plane, I just felt happy for some reason," he said. "I felt as if I was rediscovering some place that I'd been to in a previous life."[184]

And then there were the presents. The most extravagant was a gift from Sony—radios with a modified logo emblazoned on the side: *Sony Rollins*.[185]

The posh Ginza Tokyu Hotel: this was a far cry from the down-and-dirty days with Max and Brownie. It was the only four-star hotel in Tokyo when it opened in 1960, with 450 air-conditioned rooms, a rooftop with a restaurant and a driving range, a shopping arcade with a barbershop, and a cocktail lounge.[186] Sonny spent time at the Tokyu Ginza's bar and had late-night practice sessions on the hotel rooftop, gazing out at the Tokyo skyline.

During World War II, jazz was officially banned as the "music of the enemy" in Japan, but Japanese jazz musicians simply went underground.[187] Jazz surged in popularity during postwar reconstruction, when it became the Westernized sound of a youthful rebellion against conservative values and a global music of solidarity against oppression. When Sonny arrived, jazz was more popular in Japan than anywhere outside the United States, perhaps more so.[188]

Some historians date Japan's homegrown jazz scene back to 1912. Japanese jazz musicians learned the standard repertoire at the jazz *kissaten* (coffee shops),[189] where records were stacked high and managers had an encyclopedic knowledge of discographical history. There were about fifty in Tokyo alone.[190] "They had records from floor to ceiling," McCurdy recalled. "As soon as they saw you, they'd pull out all these records with you on them and start playing them."[191]

In 1961, Monte Kay booked a Japanese tour for Art Blakey and the Jazz Messengers with Bill Henderson, with the Modern Jazz Quartet following in direct succession; thirty thousand people attended eleven concerts.[192] It was, according to Japanese *Down Beat* editor Kiyoshi Koyama, "as though an invisible dam between the two countries had broken."[193] From 1961 to 1964, what became known as the *rainichi rush* (literally "come to Japan" rush) reached its peak when seventy-five American jazz acts toured Japan: Duke Ellington, Frank Sinatra, and Horace Silver among them. They were suddenly viewed as what Leonard Feather called "objets d'art in a million-dollar auction sale."[194]

Sonny's RCA albums were best sellers in the Land of the Rising Sun.[195] *Saxophone Colossus* never went gold in the United States, but it did in Japan.[196] During Sonny's first tour, he mostly played large concert halls; for repeat performances at venues, after the first time McCurdy set up his drums, "they'd set 'em up exactly the same way every time no matter what." Once, he added, "I left a broken stick on the carpet, and that broken stick was there every time!"[197]

The morning of September 19, Sonny taped a television show in Tokyo's Marunouchi Hotel, opening with a twenty-one-minute rendition of "Moritat."[198] Rashid Kamal Ali wasn't quite jelling with the band. He tried to enter several times during Sonny's solo, but Sonny blocked him. When Sonny finally gave Ali his chance, he barely played a whole chorus.[199] Then Carter came on for her set: "The Way You Look Tonight" and the tender ballad "When I Fall in Love."

Sonny then performed with a Japanese quintet: pianist Norio Maeda, trumpeter Tetsuo Fushimi, tenor saxophonist Akira Miyazawa (dubbed Japan's Sonny Rollins), bassist Tatsuro Takimoto, and drummer Takeshi "Sticks" Inomata, whose band the West Liners was one of the most successful active Japanese jazz acts. Inomata led the quintet.[200] There was no rehearsal, but the Japanese band was surprised only by Sonny's haircut. "Everyone was shocked by his Mohawk hairstyle because we had never seen anything like that before," Inomata recalled. "Japan was the place that had the most thriving jazz community in Asia at that time, and we really worshiped Mr. Rollins and his group."[201] On the broadcast, they played "Slow Boat to China" and "These Foolish Things."[202] The finale was "Oleo."[203]

"Many Japanese players have told me they were unable to understand the American artists who have already been here," wrote Charlie Mariano, who had recently moved to Tokyo with his wife, Toshiko Akiyoshi. "After hearing Rollins some of them expressed disappointment. One said, 'Do you have to understand that? If so, I'll quit music.'"[204]

That afternoon at the Tokyu Ginza, they held a press conference in the hotel's lavish ballroom with 450 eager journalists and a pair of interpreters. Sonny wore a stylish sports coat; Rashid Kamal Ali kept his sunglasses on, and a mustachioed Paul Bley smoked a pipe, which he often did throughout the tour.[205] "We're all very happy to be here," Sonny said, "and I hope that we can bring you love, understanding, and joy."

Sonny must have known that days earlier, on September 15, 1963, four Ku Klux Klansmen bombed the Sixteenth Street Baptist Church in Birmingham, Alabama, killing four girls and wounding a fifth.[206] "We taped a TV show today," he said, "and the main question that came up was the racial problem in the United States. My answer was this—I, as a musician, have my job to do. My place is to bring happiness and joy to the public with the music that I—we—play. This is what we hope to accomplish. It's obvious how I feel about the racial problem. I'll do my job—on the stand, with my instrument."[207]

On Friday, Sonny played the first concert at Tokyo's Sankei Hall.[208] Rashid Kamal Ali stood off to the side behind his sunglasses, with Sonny practically hugging the rhythm section.[209] Sonny ran through three key changes in the first three minutes of the first tune, which lasted thirty-five minutes. "We're not quite sure that we understood what he was doing," wrote *Stars and Stripes* columnist Al Ricketts. Sonny himself wasn't thrilled. "That night the group wasn't making it as a unit," he explained, obliquely referring to Ali. "I was trying to push them and apologize to the audience at the same time." Ricketts asked if he subscribed to Sonny Stitt's maxim that if you can't make it in three choruses, you can't make it at all. "That's good advice, but I don't believe it pertains to me," Sonny said. "And I don't think Sonny had me in mind when he said it. If I play long solos it's because I can *do* it. Most musicians can't." Sonny paraphrased the lesson of *Sonny Meets Hawk*: "Freedom also means discipline. When I listen to Ornette I hear New Orleans of 1923. If I couldn't hear it then I wouldn't like his playing. You must have a beat. You must have a harmonic center and conform to logic. I think Ornette does this."[210]

The next night, they opened at the twenty-four-hundred-seat Kosei Nenkin Hall in Tokyo, returning to Sankei Hall on Sunday. That night, Ali was missing. "At a jam session at a small club after the gig, there he was sitting at the bar with the briefcase still strapped to his wrist," recalled Paul Bley. "I said, 'Man, where were you tonight?' 'I'm not in the band anymore.' 'What happened?' 'I got fired.' I said, 'Gee, I sure hope you've got a round-trip ticket.'"[211] Sonny covered Ali's return ticket, as noted in his journal. Aside from this lone appearance, never released commercially, the mysterious Rashid Kamal Ali was never heard from on record again.[212]

From September 22 through 24, Sonny was at Sankei Hall; on September 25 he was at Shizuoka City Hall, and then on September 27 he was at Osaka Festival Hall. In Osaka, he met clarinetist George Lewis, the New Orleans great who was in the middle of his own extended stay in Japan, bringing Preservation Hall to the three-thousand-seat Festival Hall.[213]

On September 28, Sonny was at Kanagawa Prefectural Music Hall in Yokohama. While he was there, he asked journalist Kiyoshi Koyama to take him to Sojiji Temple, one of two head temples for the Soto school of Zen Buddhism, founded in the year 740. Koyama hired a car service to take them. "Sonny was interested, particularly with meditation," Koyama said. "He was very serious about talking to the monk in the temple and he even meditated a few minutes."[214]

In Kyoto, Reiko Hoshino, the progressive owner of the Champ Clair jazz club, gave Sonny a tour of the city. She had befriended Art Blakey, J. J. Johnson, and Miles Davis, and she began a long-standing relationship with Thelonious and Nellie Monk that past spring.[215] Champ Clair, meaning "clear field" in French, was also known as Shian Kure-ru (しあんくれーる) in Kyoto. Hoshino opened the snug two-story redbrick club in 1956 in the Kawaramachi section of Kyoto; the first floor was classical, the second floor modern jazz.[216] Hoshino introduced Sonny to shrines and sacred sites in the twelve-hundred-year-old city, as well as nearby Nara,[217] including Kiyomizu-dera Temple, a Buddhist monastery dating back to the year 778, memorable for its nail-free pagoda steeple.[218]

Before returning to New York, Sonny spent time at Masahiro Oki's Yoga Training Institute at Ikenoue in Tokyo's Setagaya Ward. Oki was the father of Oki-Do Yoga, literally "the way of Oki."[219] When a student of Oki's read about Sonny's interest in Zen Buddhism at the press conference, he offered to introduce Sonny to the forty-three-year-old yoga master, and Sonny took him up on it.[220] Sonny also met Swami Sivalingam, who worked with Oki, teaching the practice of hatha yoga and Pranayama, or breath control.[221] This practice would not only help Sonny on the saxophone but also help him delve deeper into his inner consciousness. Sonny decided to extend his trip another week to begin learning the way of Oki, laying the foundation for a lifelong commitment to yoga.[222]

Oki's asanas, or yoga poses, focused on four goals, according to his last lectures, which Sonny eventually had in his collection: "Keep your muscles flexible, keep your spine stretched, keep your breath deep, keep your blood clean." Mastering the pillars of Oki-do yoga required a combination of physical training, deep breathing, and fasting; Oki himself claimed to have once fasted for eighty-five days.[223] Rather than subscribing to one set of religious beliefs—Hinduism or Buddhism, for example—Oki's approach was syncretic, borrowing from many spiritual traditions, not unlike Sonny's own approach to spirituality. Oki's yoga practice was all geared toward developing *kokoro*, a Japanese concept that united mind, body, and heart, or "heart-mind" as Oki put it, by learning to control "desires, emotions, and intelligence" through techniques centered in the body.

"It was yoga," Sonny said, "but all the disciplines were taught together."[224]

At the institute, the day began at 6:30 a.m. and ended at 11 p.m., split between asanas, controlled breathing, and meditation.[225] Sonny practiced everything from Sukhasana, the cross-legged "easy pose," to being suspended in an aerial harness as Swami Sivalingam spotted him.[226] Sonny developed a lasting relationship with Oki, referring to him in a sketchbook as "Mr. Oki, Great Guru."[227] They had each other's phone numbers and stayed with each other when visiting.[228] Not long after meeting Oki, Sonny founded the "Sonny Rollins 'Yoga for Americans Club,'" even creating club letterhead.[229] The tour also piqued Sonny's interest in Japanese traditional music: the *shakuhachi*, Japanese modes and pentatonic scales.[230] Sonny called old Japan "what I always looked for; sought out; yearned for that when I was away from Japan."[231]

Sonny's trip to Japan confirmed that jazz could be a bridge between cultures—how everything he had begun building back on Sugar Hill could transcend language barriers—and that he was one of its ambassadors. "Music is universal," Sonny said. "Jazz music is a peaceful force, and it's received all over the world, and people in Japan are very interested in jazz music....So, when I went there, I went there as a musician, not as an American."[232]

On October 20, before coming home, Sonny wrote George Avakian a letter extolling what he had learned about traditional Japanese music—Bunraku, the work of Takemoto Gidayu, Utai or Yokyoku, the vocalizations in the Noh theater, and Nagauta, the song that accompanies kabuki.[233] Sonny wanted Avakian to find recordings of Bunraku music he could study in anticipation of incorporating it into his next record.

<o>

Sonny had recently been nominated to serve on President John F. Kennedy's Presidential Fitness Committee, a distinction he considered more significant than winning the 1963 *Down Beat* critics' poll.[234] Part of the impetus was Kennedy's recent presidential pardon of Hampton Hawes. It was meant to be "an example to other guys—staying away from drugs and all that. It was part of black jazz musicians making a change," Sonny said. "They came to see me on Grand Street. We were just in the talking stage, and it was really enticing and I was very much intrigued."[235] Then, on November 22, 1963, President Kennedy was assassinated in Dallas.

Sonny wrote to George Avakian several days later to share his grief. Having just witnessed a sense of unity in Japan, Sonny realized that in the aftermath of a tragedy, people often put their seemingly irreconcilable differences aside. Maybe Americans could form a "United Front" in the civil rights struggle in the assassination's wake. Kennedy wasn't the only leader to pass on—on August 27, 1963, Sonny's childhood neighbor W. E. B. Du Bois died in Accra, the day before the March on Washington.

"What of the colored girl crying on the white boy's shoulder at the news of what had happened?" Sonny wrote of the Kennedy assassination coverage he had seen on TV. "And this was only one of the more obvious shows of the sudden bond which made fast the assorted colors tongues and customs of our people—uniting us for the first time since maybe Pearl Harbor—as a Nation.., One Nation, Indivisible.........Yes I won't shirk from saying it...'with liberty and justice for all.' Neither George shall I ever again allow myself to be shamed into NOT standing up for the 'National Anthem'—remember—at the Series? I was weaker then and afraid of seeming naïve or insincere to you all. I guess I was naïve—by giving in; thereby endorsing cynicism. I <u>was not</u> insincere, and I swear that I shall never again be naïve."[236]

Following the Kennedy assassination, Sonny and Lucille rested during the holiday season.[237] In the annual *Down Beat* readers' poll that December, Stan Getz won the tenor category narrowly, with 2,418 votes against Coltrane's 2,377; Sonny came in third with 861, with Coleman Hawkins trailing him with 402 votes.[238] However, Sonny was still the favorite in the critics' poll earlier that year.

Polls didn't matter, though. Sonny was a global artist with an international audience that would follow him into a parallel universe. Besides, Sonny was more concerned with what he referred to as "evolutionality" than popularity. He wrote George Avakian with "holiday wishes," expressing his desire to get back in the studio soon. "Knowledge and its resultant power, success in business, material security, worldly station with its resultant fame............ ARE WORTHLESS.....if you are not ALWAYS CHEERFUL!!"[239]

Chapter 26

NOW'S THE TIME

(1964)

In January 1964, Sonny sat in with Charles Mingus at the Five Spot.[1] Mingus had a long residency in advance of a European tour that spring and wanted to keep Eric Dolphy on his toes after Booker Ervin left the group.[2] One night, Mingus invited Coleman Hawkins; another night it was Sonny. "Eric Dolphy was giving him some kind of trouble, so he brought me down to the Five Spot on Eighth Street to play with Eric," Sonny recalled. "In Mingus's mind it was something like, 'Man, I've got Sonny here, so you'd better be cool.'"[3]

Meanwhile, Sonny was getting ready for his next bout in the ring at RCA. George Avakian wanted to call Sonny's next album *The Greatest*, casting him as the jazz equivalent of Cassius Clay, whose self-declaration came after wresting the heavyweight title from Sonny Liston on February 25 in Miami Beach.[4] Rollins may not have had the soon-to-be Muhammad Ali's swagger:

he wanted to call the album *Variations on Modern Jazz Standards*, which was certainly apt. It featured compositions by Dizzy Gillespie, Thelonious Monk, John Lewis, and Benny Golson.[5] They eventually settled on *Now's the Time*.

Once again, Sonny shifted his band. Paul Bley had begun playing in a trio with Paul Motian and Gary Peacock, Henry Grimes with Albert Ayler. Sonny had scrawled phone numbers for several pianists in his notebook: Herbie H., UN-5-3972; Gillie (probably Coggins), MA-2-4538; and McCoy Tyner, who was living in Jamaica, Queens, at FL-1-2663.[6] Hancock, who had been touring with Miles Davis's Second Great Quintet, got the gig.

The first session began January 15 at 7:30 p.m. in RCA Studio B with Avakian and engineer Ray Hall, with Herbie, Thad Jones on cornet, Bob Cranshaw on bass, and Elvin Jones on drums.[7] Sonny began with Eddie "Cleanhead" Vinson's "Four," the tune made famous by Miles Davis.

Contrary to *Our Man in Jazz*, brevity was the goal, but Sonny insisted on many takes. The first two of "Four" were under three minutes; the sixth was under two. On the seventh take, Sonny quoted "Stormy Weather" to convey that it was a bad take. By the time the night was done, they had recorded thirteen takes of "Four" and some takes of John Lewis's "Django." Not one met Sonny's standard.[8] There was some kind of interfering force in the studio, whether technical, artistic, or occult.[9] Elvin Jones hit a rim shot, and according to Avakian, it sent a sudden flash of light racing across the studio. "Sonny stopped playing. He said, 'Did you see that?'" Avakian said. "I said, 'Yes, what did you see?' He said, 'I saw a flash of light, the rim shot go across the studio.' I swear I saw it, too. I'm not one to believe in anything."[10] Avakian tried to salvage the take through editing, to no avail.

On January 17, Sonny returned to RCA, this time with Paul Bley, Cranshaw, and Roy McCurdy. They recorded nine takes of "52nd Street Theme," seven takes of "Blue 'n' Boogie," and seven takes of "I Remember Clifford."[11] Not one made the album.

Back at 2 p.m. on January 20 were Sonny, Jones, Cranshaw, and McCurdy—no piano. Ten more takes of "52nd Street Theme," thirteen more of "I Remember Clifford"—with Jones taking the melody—followed by "Swanee River Rock."[12] The session closed with "Stranger on the Shore," clarinetist Acker Bilk's 1962 *Billboard* number one instrumental hit.[13] On take two, Sonny told the drummer, "Sweep for me, Roy." He wanted brushes. "Okay? Let's hear how that sounds."

It didn't sound great, and Sonny knew it. His playing was strained, halting—Sonny's sound was there, but each note was a battle. He was, if anything, overblowing. His dental problems were hurting his embouchure. As he put it in the studio: "I just got my chops fucked."[14]

After two more takes, Avakian asked, "Would you rather drop it at this point? 'Cause you've got a couple of pretty good takes on it."

"Yes," said Sonny. From that day, only Monk's "52nd Street Theme" would make it onto *Now's the Time*.

Sonny came back four days later; he'd skipped a scheduled January 23 session.[15] On January 24, he did two sessions in one day—2 to 5 p.m. and 6 to 9:30 p.m.[16] This time, he enlisted twenty-six-year-old bassist Ron Carter, Herbie Hancock's colleague in the Miles Davis Quintet; it was their first time playing together. Carter admired *Tenor Madness* and *A Night at the Village Vanguard*, and he was there to serve the music. "Everyone feels their *ones* not quite where everybody else's is," Carter said. "One of my jobs as the bass player in any group is to kind of have us all sense the same one.... Sonny is such a very strong player... you kind of go with his flow, because it feels like that's the way it must be... and my job is to make his band connect. And because he's such a positive player, it worked out five and a half out of six times."[17]

That day, they played through much of the same material, but Sonny added "St. Thomas" and "Now's the Time," playing the Bird staple in different keys and tempos. "We ended up ultimately playing it in B major," Carter said.[18] The tune was typically played in F; Sonny recorded it a tritone away. "That's always good as an improviser, to not imprison yourself in favorite keys," Sonny said.[19] One take of "Now's the Time" ran nearly sixteen minutes, culminating in Sonny taking the neck off the saxophone and blowing a chorus on a B, the note the neck plays when it's removed. He then takes the mouthpiece off and plays just the neck—connecting with that elemental sound, approaching the voice itself—before reassembling the saxophone, taking it apart again, reassembling it once more, and taking the tune out. In a journal entry from around this time, Sonny noted the similarities between the saxophone neck and the shofar, "or ram's horn, of ancient times," he wrote, "used to summon the 'HEAVENS.' Also the horn which [Joshua] toppled the walls of Jericho in the BIBLE."[20]

Sonny later reasoned, "Playing the mouthpiece would put me into a zone where I would have something else interesting to say besides playing the whole saxophone."[21]

After six and a half hours in the studio that Friday, Sonny was still dissatisfied.[22] On February 9, George Avakian wrote to RCA A&R men Steve Sholes and Ben Rosner that "Sonny Rollins is unhappy about his own performances in most of the recent recording sessions, and has offered to remake most of the selections at his own expense."[23] Sonny was willing to scrap almost everything and pay studio fees and union scale out of pocket.

The first remake session came Valentine's Day, with Hancock, Carter, and McCurdy.[24] Sonny provided written notes to Avakian with his reactions to each take for *Now's the Time*. He didn't always like his intonation on the title track, but he thought "electronical adjustment (making me sound more bright than heavy)" would help.[25] On February 18, also with Hancock, Carter, and McCurdy, Sonny did seven takes of "'Round Midnight." Sonny listened to them all and concluded only the seventh passed muster.[26]

April 14, Bob Cranshaw, Roy McCurdy, and Sonny recorded the final remake session for *Now's the Time*. They played "Blue 'n' Boogie," "I Remember Clifford," "Now's the Time," and "Four"—sixteen takes in total, all different keys. Avakian and Sonny agreed that, with the exception of "Now's the Time," all three tunes produced their best takes that day.

The title of *Now's the Time!* carried a subversive meaning.[27] "'Now's the Time' was a political statement," said René McLean, Jackie's son. "That was relative to what was going on sociopolitically with black folks."[28] The album dropped at the end of the Freedom Summer, which culminated in the Civil Rights Act being signed into law.[29]

The recording sessions for *Now's the Time* coincided with the publication of *New York: True North*, a photo book by Gilbert Millstein with images by Sam Falk, in which dozens of New Yorkers paid tribute to the city they loved. "Jazz isn't just colored people's music, but music of the country and of the world, and that is one of the messages I really want to send. It's an important one," Sonny wrote.[30] "That's been proved more in New York than anywhere else. That's why jazz moved here. The social conditions made it possible. It's become easier in New York for whites and Negroes to play together than even in Chicago. In fact, in Chicago, they still have a white local and a colored local. Not here. Here, it's [American Federation of Musicians, Local] 802, and that's it, and there's a great deal of intermingling. It's what New York should be, and is, in the finest sense—a unity of people—and jazz exemplifies that more than anything."[31]

Ben Rosner, the manager of popular artists and repertoire at RCA, was exclusively focused on the bottom line, though. "Although I have not heard the lacquers of your latest album, NOW IS THE TIME, George Avakian assures me that it's a very commercial piece of product," he wrote Sonny.[32]

To countless listeners, it was more than mere product. For guitarist John Scofield, who was twelve when *Now's the Time* was released, it was a master class in improvisation.[33] Sonny played "short phrases, long phrases, long tones, fast notes, space, melodies, intervallic structures, thematic development," Scofield said. "*Now's the Time!* is very personal for me, because not only do I love it and know it really well, but it's [what I was listening to] when I was learning how to construct modern jazz in my own playing."[34]

Sonny had continued touring while making *Now's the Time*. On February 24, he opened a weeklong engagement upstate at the Royal Arms, making his jazz-club debut in Buffalo.[35] Sonny hired McCurdy, Philadelphia bassist Spanky DeBrest, Prince Lasha, and twenty-eight-year-old guitarist Grant Green, who was between recording sessions for Lee Morgan's *Search for a New Land* and George Braith's *Extension*.[36] At the Royal Arms, Sonny reconnected with saxophonist Don Menza, who came every night after his own gig. "We heard him all night," Menza said.[37] During the day, Menza, trumpeter Sam Noto, and tenor saxophonist Larry Covelli would visit Sonny at his hotel. "He said, 'Not too early. I get up around 1 o'clock,' because they were working till 3." One day, Sonny "was looking for a way that he could hear better and he was over in the corner of the room playing right into the wall, and all of a sudden, he started playing and it sounded just like Pres! We all looked at each other, and he turned and looked at us 'cause our jaws dropped, and he said, 'Let's face it. The best of Pres is in all of us.'"[38]

On Monday, March 2, Sonny played in Montreal, following Dakota Staton into the recently opened Casa Loma Upstairs, which owner Andy Cobetto called Le Jazz Hot, on bustling St. Catherine Street.[39] Sonny's set began with Grant Green and the rhythm section laying it down before Sonny joined in. At the beginning of the run, Prince Lasha called Montreal pianist Billy Georgette, a friend of Paul Bley's, and told him to come by. Sonny wanted to meet Georgette's friend and current roommate, Stafford Eugene Harriman, a tall, one-armed mystic who bore a vague resemblance to Abraham Lincoln; his ancestors came over on the *Mayflower*.[40]

"When I brought them together, their meeting lasted four hours," wrote Georgette. Sonny "was deeply impressed with their meeting of minds and spirits, and he got very comfortable up at my pad, coming back the following day with his horn and a large Buddha."[41] Before Sonny finished his run at the Casa Loma, a snowstorm hit Montreal, dropping seven inches and delaying his flight, so he crashed with Georgette.[42] They began jamming, with Georgette on his Heinzman upright, "and what emerged was truly engaging, a combination of meditation and free jazz improvisation." Sonny taught Georgette about circular breathing. "He had the thing down...a capability to let loose a nonstop flow of notes, tones and sounds without interruption."

After the snow cleared, Sonny went to Boston on Wednesday, March 11, arriving two days late for his booking at the Jazz Workshop.[43] He performed in a black suit and black turtleneck, like "the non-communicative leader of some mysterious cult," wrote one critic, "and indeed his listeners seem to be worshippers." In Boston, Sonny replaced DeBrest with Gary Peacock, a seamless substitution. Green returned to New York, so Sonny performed without a chordal instrument. Prince Lasha, with his white plastic Grafton alto, served as a foil on long cadenzas on tunes like "Mack the Knife" and "Will You Still Be Mine," which Sonny played for at least thirty minutes each.[44]

Next was the Showboat in Philadelphia, where Philly native DeBrest was back on the gig. "Spanky had nodded out on the bandstand," recalled Ron Carter, "so Sonny called me and said, 'I'm working at a place called McKie's in Chicago.'"[45] Sonny was booked at McKie's in the last week of March and first week of April, followed by the Five Spot in New York. "'Are you available?'" Sonny asked. "I said, 'Yes, absolutely.'"[46] Carter left the Miles Davis Quintet; Gary Peacock, who had just played with Sonny, took his place.[47]

At McKie's, Sonny played in trio with Carter and McCurdy, sometimes adding Prince Lasha. Sonny wanted Grant Green back, but Green canceled at the last minute, so he called Billy Georgette in Montreal. "I told Sonny I didn't think I was ready for this, but he said 'don't worry about it, you'll have a good time and you can help me out of a jam,'" Georgette wrote. "'I'm sending you tickets, try to get here tomorrow.'"[48]

When Georgette arrived at McKie's, Sonny greeted him with his saxophone, then abruptly began the first set with "It's You or No One." He tried to keep up on a worn-out spinet, but Sonny "literally never stopped playing from the moment we'd arrived till the time we left." When sets at McKie's ended, Sonny just kept playing in the dressing room. Owner McKie Fitzhugh combed Sonny's Mohawk during one set break, but this didn't stop Sonny from playing.[49] Organist Jimmy Smith came by to say hello, but Sonny spoke only through the horn.

Sonny had begun incorporating Indian influences into his performances at this time. He wandered through the audience wearing the Bells of Sarna around his neck as a kind of talisman.[50] "I used to collect them whenever I was on the road someplace. They were all over the place at these rest stops along the highway," Sonny recalled. "I really got a charge out of wearing them when I was playing."[51] Sonny also began studying Indian classical music at around this time, learning some basic ragas and how they corresponded to different hours of the day or night.[52]

Before the end of the run, Sonny took Billy Georgette around the South Side in his rented Cadillac. "He showed me the locations of early jazz clubs and how he loved the music of a simpler time," Georgette said, "of how important it was for jazz to keep swinging, and how jazz history needed protection."[53]

Sonny then began a nine-week run at the Five Spot. The club had relocated to 2 Saint Marks Place in 1962 from its original location in Cooper Square and now had a larger capacity.[54] Sonny's trio with Roy McCurdy and Ron Carter played alternating sets opposite Roland Kirk's quartet. McCurdy and Carter would always show up a little early for the gig, but Sonny usually beat them there. "He'd come out of the cab into the club playing," McCurdy recalled, "and we'd jump out and go on the bandstand and join him." Sonny played with the Bells of Sarna around his neck, and sometimes brought sets to hand out to the audience. "He was in an abstract kind of period, and everybody was playing bells," McCurdy said.[55]

Soon, fans started bringing their own percussion instruments. The bells were "worn by the mendicants, the priests," Sonny told *Abundant Sounds'* Fred Miles and Jean French during the run. "You can see that they are very pretty. These are worn by the priests as they go around and if I am not mistaken people give them food to eat and their whole life is spent just going around and blessing people."[56]

"I remember Rollins starting his sets from behind the kitchen doors," wrote Rafi Zabor. "When he had attained the stage, the real music would begin: endless and inventive medleys in which blues faded into calypsos which were succeeded by long, fast, boppish *tours de force*. He exchanged a lot of fours with McCurdy. The music seemed to be coming out of Rollins in a single uninterrupted ribbon of sound."[57]

The theatrical, artistic, literary, and musical worlds collided at the new Five Spot.[58] Actor couple Elaine Stewart and Bill Carter, New York School and Umbra poets, and African American painter Bob Thompson turned out for the spectacle.[59] Thompson, a Five Spot regular, sketched Sonny playing with his Mohawk and black turtleneck.[60] One night during the Five Spot run, an intoxicated Thompson hopped on the bandstand and scatted alongside Sonny.[61] During daytime hours, Thompson invited Sonny to his fourth-floor studio at 6 Rivington Street to sit for a portrait.[62]

Poet Paul Blackburn "transcribed" Sonny's playing on "There Will Never Be Another You" at the club and turned it into the poem "Listening to Sonny Rollins at the Five Spot."[63] A young David S. Ware first heard Sonny there.[64] Sometimes, John Coltrane would come. "If Sonny was playing the Five Spot and Trane was around the corner, they'd be going around to see each other and check each other out," McCurdy said.[65]

Archie Shepp, who lived at 27 Cooper Square in the same building as LeRoi Jones (later Amiri Baraka), also came to hear Sonny. At the time,

Shepp was part of the New York Contemporary Five, which had Sonny's former bandmate Don Cherry on the front line.[66] "I got to sit in with [Sonny] one time," Shepp recalled. "I came in one night and asked him if I could sit in, and he allowed me to play a song with him. I think the song was 'It Could Happen to You.' It was really quite impressive, because somehow, I felt after I had performed with him that I had *learned* something. He taught me. He brought me into his space, and it's something I've never forgotten ... somehow, I felt that my musicianship had improved after I sat in with him. It was really like a musical lesson. He would play things, and then I would try to imitate what he did. I listened to Sonny a lot, but being on stage with him was really an existential experience and a learning experience."[67]

Trombonist Grachan Moncur III also stopped by. Moncur had a role in director Burgess Meredith's Broadway staging of James Baldwin's *Blues for Mister Charlie*, beginning that April. "I stopped by the Five Spot after the show one night, and Sonny asked me to sit in," Moncur told *Down Beat*. "He's always been one of my major influences, and the expectation of playing with him shook me up. However, on the bandstand, I found that I didn't have to force my groove—it was already there."[68]

Toward the end of Sonny's Five Spot run,[69] he was playing opposite Jay Cameron's pianoless quartet. On a set break, trumpeter Dusko Goykovich decided to take a cab to the Café Au Go Go on Bleecker Street to see Stan Getz.[70] Goykovich told Stan about Sonny's new sound and Mohawk haircut. "So Stan said, 'Oh, I gotta hear that,'" Goykovich recalled.[71]

They taxied back to the Five Spot. "Sonny finished the set, went to the back room, and Stan went there and started arguing with him," Goykovich said. "Stan said, 'Hey, Sonny, why did you change? Why are you playing like that?' And Sonny said, 'Hey, I play what I want to play.' Stan was really getting excited. I thought they were gonna get in a fight, because Stan was all green in the face." Soon after, "Stan left."

Getz already knew what he thought of Sonny's latest, and he didn't pull any punches. When he heard "Just Friends" from *Sonny Meets Hawk* in Leonard Feather's *Down Beat* blindfold test, he claimed he didn't recognize Hawk. "At one point one of them sounded a little like Hawk, but I wouldn't want to insult the great Hawk," he said. "It sounds like a couple of high school players. I have no rating for that record. No stars. It's not my dish of trifle."[72]

Sonny just brushed it off. "We were tight, and Stan used to come in to see me when I was working in the Village," Sonny later said. "Stan rubbed some people the wrong way; that's just the way he was. He tried to be domineering and stuff. But if you knew him, you didn't pay any attention to that."[73]

Another musician who stopped by the Five Spot to hear Sonny was Mary Lou Williams. On July 7, Sonny wrote to her.

Greetings

Please accept this rather belated acknowledgement of your presence recently at the '5 SPOT.'

It was a great privilege and deep honor to find myself playing before you. You are a 'great' and 'shining' light in our music world and indeed in all the world. You are an inspiration to so many people and you are loved by so many people—yours truly included. Let me give thanks for a moment for living in a world which includes one Mary Lou Williams.[74]

In May, Sonny's run at the Five Spot got extended.[75] During the end of the residency, Sonny was using bassists John Ore or Butch Warren, Walter Bishop Jr. on piano, and Albert "Tootie" Heath on drums. "He played basically any song in the world," recalled Heath. "He had a repertoire like I've never heard anybody else do. And he could play a segue of songs for an hour. . . . He would wave you in when he wanted to be supported, otherwise he'd be playing by himself."[76] Sonny closed at the Five Spot on June 1; the next day, Mingus, who had returned from Europe without Eric Dolphy, took his place.[77] Dolphy would tragically fall into a diabetic coma in Berlin; he died on June 29, 1964.

Meanwhile, Sonny tried to spend as much time in nature as he could. "Nature take me back I am yours," he wrote in his journal on May 17.[78] He also continued his yoga practice as diligently as possible. As he wrote Masahiro Oki earlier that year, he could "do the lotus pose fairly well," but he had "been so uneven in his daily postures and asanas!!"[79] That spring or summer,

Oki toured New York and stayed with Sonny. They attended the New York World's Fair, which began that April in Flushing Meadows and ran through the following October, visiting the Japan pavilion.[80] "A lot of them had their native instruments from their country," Sonny said.[81] At the Indian pavilion, he bought a shehnai. The fairgrounds became a favorite hangout for him while it was open.[82]

At the beginning of the Freedom Summer, Sonny turned his attention to his sixth and final album for RCA. The label was hard-pressed to break even on their famous $90,000 contract, and Sonny had his own reasons to part ways; they opted for an amicable split. Sonny told an interviewer at the Five Spot, "We now want to go with a company which is a little more oriented to the jazz idiom."[83] RCA extended the contract to July 15, enough time for Sonny to finish *The Standard Sonny Rollins*.

Sonny may have been inspired by seeing Thelonious Monk at Carnegie Hall on June 6.[84] He had also been continuing his daily study of interval relationships and leading tones. That June, he wondered if he had experienced "an evolution in hearing" when he began hearing major scales differently: "Is this a rule—an evolution of hearing which now makes the 9th and Maj. 7 trite sounding? Or is this a temporary preference of the day?"[85]

Sonny's first session for *The Standard Sonny Rollins* took place in RCA Studio B on the afternoon of June 11, with Herbie Hancock, Jim Hall, bassists David Izenson and Teddy Smith, and drummer Stu Martin, with Ray Hall engineering. In addition to "Little Girl Blue," they recorded at least seven takes of the ballad "Trav'lin' Light," with some unusual doubling—Hancock and Hall comp together, while Izenson plays arco counterpoint as Teddy Smith walks. These were long takes that Avakian decided to fade out in editing.

Sonny returned on June 23 with Jim Hall, Bob Cranshaw, and drummer Mickey Roker, who had recently recorded with Cranshaw in rhythm sections for Joe Williams, Nat Adderley, Ben Webster, and, earlier that month, Stanley Turrentine. They recorded "Look for the Silver Lining," "Nothing Ever Changes My Love for You," and "Love Look Away." Hall sat out for a Latin "I'll Be Seeing You," the only take that day that would end up on the album, edited down to under two minutes. The atmosphere in the studio was convivial; Sonny and Mickey Roker both had legendary belly laughs.

"Pretty imposing sight there, Rollins," said Avakian. "Okay, away we go. 'Nothing Ever Changes My Love for You,' take one." Sonny sang the beginning with Latin phrasing, specifying that the last tag should be "anticipated and short." On one take, Sonny extemporized on the melody before counting it off. "Nothing ever changes, everything is the same thing over again," he said. "Turn it around. How do you dig it? Do you dig it differently? Then it's changing. You see, it's the same thing, only you change it."[86] The album would capture the protean Rollins.

The next day, Sonny came back with the same group. They did "My Ship," "Three Little Words," "Night and Day," and "Deep in a Dream." All but the latter ended up on the final album—trio takes only—even though Jim Hall meshed effortlessly with Sonny.[87] For the four-hour session on June 26, Avakian kept the tape running through rehearsals in case the band unexpectedly caught fire. They ran through "Nothing Ever Changes My Love for You," "Masquerade," "Love Walked In," "Long Ago and Far Away," "Love Letters," and "Little Girl Blue." There was a lot of laughter in the studio that day. "Sonny, I understand the bonus is a free trip to Mississippi for everybody, am I right?" said Avakian. Roker responded that he would go "as far as Washington."

On July 2, Sonny replaced Jim Hall with Hancock. They recorded "Something to Remember You By," "It Could Happen to You," "My One and Only Love," "Winter Wonderland," and "When You Wish upon a Star." Still, after five sessions, Sonny was not satisfied, and he arranged for another on July 9, agreeing to pay the studio fee and union scale for the musicians out of his advance.[88] Sonny returned with just Cranshaw and Roker as well as engineer Ernie Oelrich to record "I Like the Likes of You," "When I Fall in Love," a blistering take on "Day In, Day Out," and "Autumn Nocturne," the only song that day to make it onto the album.[89] Sonny and Avakian worked on the editing together. They spliced, faded out, and selected what they felt were the best takes, aiming for an album that was "not more than 45 nor less than 35" minutes, Sonny wrote.[90]

Sonny and RCA were mutually satisfied with *The Standard Sonny Rollins*.[91] "This is in part because Sonny was seeking compactness and brevity of statement in much of the album," Avakian wrote in the liner notes. "Jazz improvisation becomes more meaningful when one can relate the source to the improvisation."[92] They even had a Christmas song in the can if they ever needed it!

Released the following spring, *The Standard Sonny Rollins* received mixed reviews. Don DeMicheal gave it two stars in *Down Beat*, describing it as "strange" and "disappointing."[93] *Variety* noted that Sonny could be a "highly uneven performer on disks," but that on this one, "he is at or near the peak of his form." *Time* wrote that "these are virtuoso saxophone interpretations."[94] The lack of consensus further cemented for Sonny that he couldn't trust critical opinion.

"The album still is my ultimate favorite in terms not of its perfection but of its portent," Sonny wrote Avakian. "Maybe you know of all of its reviews which were most peculiar in that it was 'highly praised' by some and down right (almost that is) dismissed by others who reviewed it. . . . I personally was 90% behind this album, and it was nice of you not to make it difficult for this to be."[95]

With his RCA contract fulfilled, Sonny devoted more time to practice, both spiritual and musical.[96] He continued working out with dumbbells and doing isometric jaw and lip exercises to strengthen his embouchure.[97] He even relearned how to breathe, in part inspired by his studies of yoga and Indian classical music. Sonny's method involved looking into a mirror, keeping the eyes steady, and listening and counting breaths, "feeling and hearing our own breath in our own body." Then he did it with the saxophone in his mouth. "When playing, special care must be given to the various bodily parts which are affected and 'touched' by the breath as it travels thru the body and into the instrument."[98]

He also delved deeper into interval studies and began studying the pentatonic scale used in Mongolian music, working through the modes of the scale in visual diagrams.[99] "Now that you understand how to arrive at modes—play them," Sonny wrote in his journal. "After playing them slowly and carefully"—this was followed by a drawing of a stop sign—"Stop sign . . . SLOWLY and CAREFULLY—it is important that no wrong notes are hit throughout!! Even if it takes a week before you are sure of hitting the next note correctly, wait the week so who's in a hurry—especially to make a Boo-Boo???!!"[100]

This intense technical study was geared toward leaving it all behind when he hit the stage. As Sonny wrote: "So that when we actually go out to play and start improvising, we may stop consciously remembering and thinking and studying and recalling and allow the music which is as we have pointed out already in the air just waiting for us to relax and let it come out of us and our horns."[101]

The break allowed Sonny to get more enmeshed with the jazz community. Sonny had taken down the numbers of Sun Ra (GR. 5-9802), then based at his Sun Palace at 48 East Third Street, and drummer Oliver Jackson, and made a note of performing "'Down Pat,' in honor and for Pat Patrick," the Arkestra saxophonist.[102] He also went to Nica's Cathouse in Weehawken and Prophet Jennings's Temple, where Prophet hung his portrait of Sonny with a Mohawk.[103]

On August 16, Bud Powell returned to New York with Francis Paudras, his French confidant and chaperone. A bout of tuberculosis and an ongoing struggle with alcoholism had left Powell diminished, but his return was cause for celebration.[104] One night, Max Roach came into Birdland, where Bud was playing, and invited him and Francis to dinner the following Monday, his off night. Max promised Bud a surprise.

Bud arrived at Max Roach and Abbey Lincoln's Central Park West apartment wearing a gray sport jacket and suspenders.[105] After some awkward small talk, the doorbell rang. "I think that's the surprise I told you about," said Max. There in the doorway stood Sonny, wearing a black-and-white-striped button-down and a black sport jacket, carrying two Native American drums. Prophet Jennings, also there, took eight-millimeter footage to document the big reunion.[106]

"Who's that?" Bud asked Francis. He hadn't seen Sonny since before the Mohawk.

"Why, it's Sonny, Bud," said Francis.

"Hey Sonny," said Bud. "Where'd you get the funny haircut?" Everyone cracked up as Sonny gave Bud a big hug and explained. Then Sonny gave Max the drums he had brought as a gift. Before the night was over, Sonny and Bud sat down on Max and Abbey's green sofa and looked into each other's eyes; Sonny put a comforting hand on Bud's knee. They didn't need words to convey their deep bond.[107]

Powell was scheduled at Birdland starting in late September, but on October 11, he failed to appear at the club; he was later found sleeping on the streets.[108] On October 19, his disappearance made Dorothy Kilgallen's syndicated column. "He was so homesick for his adopted country that the Birdland bosses let him out of his contract and bought him a ticket to Paris," wrote Kilgallen. "He leaves—probably never to return and Sonny Rollins will replace him."[109] A one-way ticket had been bought, but Powell decided to stay.[110]

Sonny returned to Birdland with pianist Sadik Hakim, bassist Mickey Bass, and drummer Earl "Shams" McKinney,[111] opposite the Donald Byrd Quintet featuring Jimmy Heath.[112] Rafi Zabor was at Birdland to witness what he called the strangest performance he had ever seen. "He wore a dark brown suit over a turtleneck of the same color and he was staring at the audience as if it had just gotten off a tour bus from Mars," he wrote.[113] "He walked to center stage, played two soaring, unbelievable choruses, and waved the rhythm section to a stop. He began to stare up at the lights, his head canted to one side. Every five or ten seconds he emitted a note."[114] The thought must have occurred to Sonny: he could never replace Bud Powell.[115]

On Friday, October 30, Sonny began a ten-day stand at the Plugged Nickel in Chicago after auditioning a new band. Grachan Moncur III had become available after *Blues for Mister Charlie* closed on Broadway,[116] so Sonny called him to offer him a spot pending the audition. Sonny had played with Moncur before. Moncur had composed "Sonny's Back," written after the sabbatical and recorded on the Jazztet's 1962 album *Here and Now*. Mickey Bass recommended Beaver Harris, a baseball star turned drummer whom Bass had grown up with in Pittsburgh. Sonny also tapped Detroit bassist Herman Wright.[117]

In 1963, Harris loaned his drums to a friend for travel fare and moved to New York with literally nothing but the clothes on his back. "I had this one pair of shoes that had the odor of perfume and sweat," Harris said. "I was the original funk band, I had my own original odor, man, mixed with a lot of blood, sweat, and tears...and funk."[118] He lived in the subway until he found some Pittsburgh connections to put him up and started making all the jam sessions he could. By 1964, he was living in Bed-Stuy, Brooklyn, with Mickey Bass.[119] After Bass did the gig with Sonny at Birdland, Harris saw Sonny's number on the wall and called.

Harris recalled the phone call. He was surprised by how familiar Sonny was acting: "He said, 'Oh, I know it all...all about you.'" Bass had given him the info.[120] Sonny invited him to play the following week in Chicago. It would be Harris's first major gig.[121]

"It was a good, unusual group of musicians," recalled Moncur of the group. "I had never worked with Herman before, but Herman was a very solid bass player...he gave you a lot of meat, a lot of substance in his playing...and Beaver was kind of risky. But I gave Beaver a secret...I said, 'Beaver, remember one thing. Don't play too loud.'... 'Just think in two, not four.'"[122]

At the studio, Sonny showed up wearing jeans, a tuxedo jacket, and cowboy boots painted with what Harris described as "war paint."

"Oh yeah, Mr. Harris, you've got a good snare there," Harris recalled Sonny saying. Sonny also liked his cymbal work. "You know about the time and the elements." Harris was "more or less dancing into his music."[123]

Moncur brought in his composition "The Twins" from *Some Other Stuff*, based on his younger twin brothers.[124] "When I played the tune for him, he said, 'Damn, Grachan. You're gonna have to write me a letter about that tune.'" Sonny kept telling Moncur to "tell me more" until he couldn't anymore. Leaving him with this lesson: "'Whenever you get the story together, that's when we'll play the music.'"[125]

Generally, everything clicked. "We kept a continuity of a groove going on that was very unusual. It worked, anyway. We made the gig!" Moncur said. "That's the only rehearsal we ever had for the ten days. The rest of the gigs were just impromptu. Bam, hit it! No rehearsal, no music, just hit it."[126]

When Sonny came to pick up Harris to go to Chicago, Harris was dressed in "my old mohair suit that I had from Pittsburgh cut off looking like Miles Davis," he said.[127] "I played in it so long that the sleeves were all shiny and the butt was shiny, the legs were shiny. And I walked out there like this and the arm split—rrrip." Sonny sat right next to Harris on the plane. "He said, 'Mr. Harris, when you get paid, be sure and buy you some shoes.'"[128]

Sonny played the Plugged Nickel October 30 through November 8.[129] On opening night, Sonny played from behind the drums to really feel the rhythm. "That's a helluva feeling to hear a saxophone in your back," Harris said. "Man, that was putting the sound in me, I felt it all through my body; my body just moved like a motor." By the end of the first night, Sonny said, " 'Harris, you really struggled, didn't you, but you struggled, you got it,' " Harris recalled.[130]

Sonny played recognizable tunes—he was "like a music box," Moncur said—but he rarely gave out music. On opening night, he gave Moncur a lead sheet for Monk's "52nd Street Theme" with a strict proviso at the bottom: " 'Moment' and 'MOOD' will of course always dictate any variations, and one must therefore be 'OPEN' and FLEXIBLE for such 'changes' whenever they may occur. THANK YOU."[131]

Moncur asked for more music, but Sonny demurred. "I said, 'Sonny, why don't you bring me some chords sometime or a lead sheet of some of the stuff you want to play?' He said, 'Uh, no, Grachan. I think I like the way you play when you don't know the changes.' " So Moncur just kept the mouthpiece at his lips and hung on for dear life. "For me to last ten days like that was a miracle," Moncur said, "'cause he was known to knock cats out if he didn't like how they played."[132] In musician circles, Mingus was known for this, but so was Sonny.

Yet somehow, Sonny instilled a sense of confidence in Moncur. "It was something about the way Sonny phrased and his sound that guided my sound," he said. "It seemed like I couldn't do no wrong with him. . . . It's not always about how good you can play. It's how good you can play *with* somebody."[133]

One night, Dizzy Gillespie came in; his quintet was playing at the London House two miles down the road.[134] "Dizzy got off a couple of hours before we got off during those ten days we were there, and we didn't have any piano," Moncur recalled. "And Dizzy would come in every night when he got off to sit in on piano with us. He did that the last seven days that we worked there. . . . By the time we were finished playing the last set, it wasn't like we were performing for an audience anymore. It became like it was a bebop school."[135] Dizzy would call tunes he wrote and made famous like "Woody'n

You" and "A Night in Tunisia," and he comped like Monk. "We weren't look-ing for him to solo, because his chords sounded so strong," said Moncur. For Harris, it was revelatory. "I never heard one grounded chord, he just played an endless arpeggio," said Harris.[136]

Sonny had his own lesson for the band. "The last night, the last tune, Sonny said, 'Doo boo doo boo doo boo doo'...got to the door...'doo boo doo'...closed the door of the club...'doo boo doo'...walked through the parking lot...harrrmmmmmmm...we're still standing there....We heard the car. Grachan said, 'Hey man, where's Sonny? I didn't get paid.'"[137] Back at the Sutherland Hotel, Harris found Sonny parked outside. He paid him and gave him Moncur's money. "Now don't forget, now, buy yourself some clothes," Harris recalled Sonny saying. There was a lesson: "No matter what you may feel about yourself someone that is the master of what he is doing will see something in you," Harris said. "The oddball may stand a chance of being a genius."[138]

Two weeks later, Sonny hired Harris and pianist Freddie Redd for two weeks at Basin Street West in San Francisco, followed by Shelly's Manne-Hole in Los Angeles. He planned to find a bassist in San Francisco.[139] When Sonny picked them up to go to the airport, Redd had a tenor saxophone with him.

"What do you have there, Mister Redd?" Sonny said.

"Well man, a friend gave me this tenor saxophone, man, a Selmer," said Redd, "and you know, I just thought that I'd come out and practice."

"Well, yes, you can come out and practice," said Sonny with a touch of irony. "But don't bring it on the gig."[140]

In San Francisco, Sonny hired twenty-six-year-old Philadelphia-born bassist Don Moore on the recommendation of Jon Hendricks.[141] Sonny was booked November 25 through December 8.[142] Not long before, Moore had played opposite Sonny as a member of Joe Farrell's quartet. When Wilbur Ware pawned his bass, he would borrow Moore's if he had a gig in Philadel-phia in exchange for lessons, but Moore would always attend the gig to make sure he got it back. Once in New York, Ware borrowed Moore's bass for a gig with Sonny at the Vanguard.[143] Moore came up through Philly's informal "Jazz University, they used to call it," he said, but he also had experience with

Archie Shepp and the Contemporary Five, so he was equally comfortable playing inside or outside.[144]

Sonny was one of the marquee acts at Basin Street West, an elegant club that had just opened that October on Broadway. It could accommodate 350 people, with a wall of windows overlooking the city's financial district.[145] On opening night, the band was late, so Sonny started the set solo. When the group walked in, Sonny was playing "Three Little Words" with a sense of aggravation, as if the three little words were "You are late." After the set, Sonny gave them a stern talking-to. "Listen, gentlemen, you never walk on the stand when a man's playing. These people think that we're not professionals," he said. "You're late, but the show must go on."[146] In between sets, he lifted weights.

With the club's carpet absorbing the sound, Sonny was looking for a place that would really resonate. "He went into the ladies' room, actually, during the tune 'I Found a New Baby,'" Moore said. "I remember a lady said something to the bartender: 'As long as he has his horn in his mouth, that's okay with me.'"[147]

Before the run at Basin Street West ended, Sonny took Harris up to see the Twin Peaks from the top of Telegraph Hill, where they gazed out at the social realist murals at Coit Tower.

"What do you see, Mr. Harris?" Sonny asked.

"I see a tree there, like the tree of life. I see the bananas that's like the penis and the grapes that's like the testicles and the pears are like . . ."

"You have a vivid imagination there," Sonny said. "Could I have that, please?"

On December 7, Harris asked Sonny to advance him a hundred dollars. "Oh, no problem, don't worry, Mr. Harris, anything you want, you can have anything. I really love you," Sonny said. "You really work hard."

Freddie Redd, according to Harris, overheard the exchange. "Hey Newk, lemme have a hundred dollars, man." Sonny said, "Okay, you got it."

On the last night at Basin Street West, Sonny went to pay everyone. "Ah, gentlemen, how much do I give you?" he said.

"Well, you gave me a hundred dollars last night, Newk," said Harris.

"Are you sure?" said Sonny. Harris assented. "Mr. Redd, what did I give you?"

"Oh, you gave me fifty," said Freddie.

"Okay, Mr. Redd, thank you. Okay, gentlemen, now tomorrow morning I'll pick you all up, we'll go to the airport, and we'll all go to the gig."[148] The next day, Sonny apparently left Redd at the hotel while he and Harris went to the airport.

Sonny's quartet was booked at Shelly's Manne-Hole from December 10 to 20, but he opened as a duo with Harris.[149] Sonny hired bassist Leroy Vinnegar to make it a trio. One night, twenty-four-year-old trumpeter David Hayward came in to catch his idol. "He was playing a show in Hollywood and I was there, totally loaded," Hayward recalled. "He took a break and I went up to him and asked if I could [sit] in. I would never have done that sober. It's like asking God if you can stand in for him." Sonny invited Hayward to come back to New York with him. "It was the single greatest musical experience of my life," Hayward said of his time with Sonny. "If you had asked me at the age of sixteen who I would die to work with, it would have been Sonny Rollins."[150] They became lifelong friends.

All the work Sonny had put in had finally led to a level of confidence that he could achieve some semblance of the sound he was looking for, even if he never quite found that lost chord. He was feeling positive about the future, as he wrote in a journal entry, and felt that "the great power which must be mirrored in kindness to others is magnanimous indeed."[151] He could now turn his attention more fully to cultivating a sense of magnanimity and "kindness to others," especially toward musicians in the next generation like Beaver Harris. There were many more.

Back in New York, Sonny had a couple weeks to rest before he would make his debut in London at Ronnie Scott's.[152]

Chapter 27

RONNIE SCOTT'S

(1965)

Sonny began 1965 by flying to London, where he made his British debut opposite Tubby Hayes at Ronnie Scott's for a month, from January 8 to February 7.[1] It was the original Ronnie's, a cramped basement in Soho described by critic John Fordham as a "shoebox," founded by saxophonists Scott and Pete King in 1959.[2] The club had booked Lucky Thompson, Johnny Griffin, Zoot Sims, Stan Getz, Dexter Gordon, and Ben Webster. Ronnie idolized Sonny and had been trying to book him for a long time.[3]

Sonny was excited to be on British soil, if nervous he wouldn't find sidemen up to his standard. "I like the people very, very much. And I like the atmosphere," Sonny said in an interview with British jazz journalist Les Tomkins. "Well, it's the type of place that I thought it would be, and that's why I temporarily disbanded my group to come over here and make what is an unusual...appearance as a single."[4]

So Sonny's British debut would succeed or fail based on his chemistry with Ronnie Scott's house rhythm section: pianist Stan Tracey, bassist Rick Laird, and drummer Ronnie Stephenson. Sonny's anxiety was quickly dispelled, though. Ben Webster called from Stockholm to tell Sonny "not to worry about the rhythm section—he had been so knocked out by it."[5] Yet accompanying Ben Webster, whose sets were a fairly predictable eight tunes during this period, was not the same as accompanying Sonny Rollins, whose sets were anything but predictable and sometimes might include only one tune, total.

Sonny was staying at the White House Hotel in Regent's Park, a mainstay for visiting musicians, but upon arriving, he went straight to the club. "He literally got off the plane and came with his raincoat on and his hat, and we had no idea what to be ready for, because he had a strange reputation," recalled Rick Laird. "He didn't know us, we didn't know him, and he was playing with an all-white band, which must have been a bit of a shock for him."[6] Sonny called one tune and then played it for ninety minutes straight that afternoon—"Prelude to a Kiss"—at different tempos, changing keys on a whim. They never played it again that month.[7] There were only a few hours before they would have to re-create the magic that night.

The instant connection quickly reaffirmed Sonny's belief in music as a bridge. "I didn't expect to find such a high caliber of general musicianship," Sonny said.[8] "This was especially rewarding.... The fact that we just came together and we played. The very first day, the first tune that we played together was, I think, as good as anything we will ever play...and this is what music is all about. This is its great force, the great power which it has.... The way it brings people together in communication.... I've seen this now all over the world."[9]

On opening night, the sound of Sonny emanated from the cigarette machine by the greenroom, even before Scott announced him. After he did, Sonny appeared like a bearded apparition in perpetual motion, playing an eighteen-and-a-half-minute medley with a frenetic opening cadenza including "Autumn Nocturne" and "April in Paris" before segueing to "Three Little Words" and "I'll Be Seeing You." He abruptly took the horn out of his mouth in the middle of his closing cadenza to riotous applause.

"Ladies and gentlemen, we want to say good evening to you on behalf of my staff," Sonny said, getting some laughs. "Our drummer, our bassist, our pianist!" He only paused a moment before "My One and Only Love." Sonny wandered through the packed club looking for a sweet spot.[10] At the end of the first set, Scott was dumbstruck. "Follow that, ladies and gentlemen," he said to the crowd. "What a month this is gonna be."[11]

Sonny began each performance with an exploration, not only of the physical space. "An enormous panorama begins to unfold," Scott wrote. "Beautiful sounds, awkward angular melodies, ugly noises, a series of shattering arpeggios, two or three notes played simultaneously, pauses, snatches of familiar tunes, modulations." Sonny would play continuously for his hour-long set, as these seemingly disparate threads were then stitched together, unexpectedly, into a tapestry spanning "the development of the tenor saxophone from its beginning to its possible future."[12] In one set, he only played three tunes: "Night and Day," "Tea for Two," and "This Can't Be Love." Sonny would wander off the stand, back to the greenroom, playing without pause, until the next set began, the circle unbroken.

Off the bandstand, Ronnie and Sonny became close friends; they shared a wry sense of humor. "Sonny made my father laugh when he told him the story about his daily yoga practice at the hotel," wrote Scott's daughter, Rebecca Scott. "Every day, Sonny removed the sheets from his bed, folded them and put them on the floor for his yoga exercises, completely confounding the maid who made up his bed with fresh sheets and cleaned his room. She could *not* understand why when she came back the next day the sheets were on the floor, and all she ever saw him eat was green apples!"[13]

Sonny's behavior was eccentric, but not for its own sake. The house rhythm section would sometimes encounter Sonny doing isometric jaw exercises. One night, Rick Laird found Sonny in the greenroom in his black beret, staring at himself in the mirror and practicing this announcement: "I am Pierre the Frenchman." Other times, he favored the Stetson, or a black mackintosh, atop his cleanly shaven head. On at least one night, Sonny emerged from a London taxi, bell held high, and strode across the street and down into the club playing. On another, he led the crowd out of Ronnie's and onto Gerrard Street in a spontaneous conga line.[14] Sonny soon appeared in Dorothy Kilgallen's syndicated column when he did interviews while eating a lemon rind, extolling the virtues of Barry Goldwater.[15]

The music was even more perplexing. "Bewitched, bothered and bewildered. That's been the general reaction to the enigmatic Sonny Rollins," wrote *Melody Maker*'s Bob Houston. Saxophonist and *Observer* jazz critic Benny Green described it as "a great rubbish dump sprinkled with exquisite pearls of wisdom."[16]

The fans mostly appreciated it, even if they didn't understand it; demand exceeded the snug club's 150-person capacity every night.[17] The rhythm section loved it, too, despite its being a challenge. "You'd start off on one tune and then suddenly go into bar four in a different key of another tune and maybe play that for six bars, then you'd be back playing the tune you'd started out with," recalled Stan Tracey, "and go through every number like that."[18]

Bassist Rick Laird, who would go on to join the Mahavishnu Orchestra, was on the cusp of his twenty-fourth birthday when Sonny arrived. "It was very spontaneous," Laird recalled. "You just jumped in and hopefully you knew what he was playing. He would play songs in very strange keys. Songs like 'On the Street Where You Live,' which is usually in the key of C, he'd play in E, which was fine for me, but not great for the piano player."[19]

During the run, Sonny extended this challenge to other musicians as well. He worked with Tubby Hayes's rhythm section one night—drummer Benny Goodman (no relation to the American bandleader), bassist Jeff Clyne, and pianist Terry Shannon.[20] He also met Barcelona-born drummer Ramón Farrán, who often played in the club when he came to London from Spain for work composing for television.[21]

Farrán soon got an opportunity to sit in with Sonny. "I played one day with him, and he said to me, 'Look, Ramón, I like your ting-a-ling,'" Farrán recalled. "And the ting-a-ling was when you ring the bell of the cymbal in that sort of a Cuban, Caribbean" style. Farrán was influenced by Kenny Clarke's ride cymbal, but what captivated Sonny, he said, was "the African feeling that I have inside me. I think that was what he got in my playing."[22]

When Sonny finished at Ronnie's, he would continue the music elsewhere. "We were going to play the Bull's Head, wherever, in different little bars, because he wanted to play," Farrán said. Sonny had "so many things that he wanted to do in one minute playing." If Sonny ever didn't understand something the rhythm section played, he would always ask. "He gave me this feeling of freedom playing, and you could do anything you want to do. When you have this feeling, nothing is impossible."[23]

In London, Sonny was also open to meeting fans. One day outside the White House Hotel, he met Jaap van de Klomp, a Dutch jazz impresario who, starting in 1957, ran the club Persepolis in Utrecht.[24] When Van de Klomp read the British press notices, he "went to London to look for Sonny Rollins."[25] He found him in front of the hotel. Sonny couldn't perform in Utrecht at the time, but he did have an unusual request: Could Van de Klomp arrange for him to buy Jos van Heuverzwijn's tenor? Sonny still remembered the golden sound he got on the Buescher Aristocrat he had borrowed from Van Heuverzwijn in The Hague at a jam session in 1963. As it turned out, Van Heuverzwijn suddenly passed away shortly thereafter at the age of thirty-four, and one of his last wishes was for his wife to offer the instrument to Sonny.[26]

Van de Klomp returned to the Netherlands by himself and called Van Heuverzwijn's widow, who confirmed her willingness to sell, then wrote Sonny a letter in London to find a convenient time. "He called me...early Sunday morning, and said 'I'm coming over to get the saxophone,'" said Van de Klomp. Sonny had one day off a week at Ronnie Scott's—Sundays. He flew to the Netherlands and back that day.

Back in London, Sonny immediately switched from the Mark VI tenor to the Buescher.[27] To Sonny, "it was so easy to get around on." It really sang, yet this tonal iridescence came with a drawback. "I eventually had to give it up, because I was putting too much air in the horn and it wasn't able to take that much air," he said. "It was too light...you couldn't blow into it really hard. With Selmer I could blow into it hard. It can take all of my wind and remain...everything was sort of staying where it was supposed to be. I tended after a while to overblow the Buescher."[28] Sonny was the big bad wolf of the tenor: if he blew too hard, it sounded like he might blow the keys right off the horn. Yet he loved that Buescher; soon, Sonny would even kiss it good night.[29]

At Ronnie's, Sonny noticed a man about his age there almost every night. It turned out to be Harold Pinter.[30] Pinter's wife, Vivien Merchant, had a prominent role in the upcoming film adaptation of Bill Naughton's West End hit *Alfie*. One night, producer John Gilbert, the son of the film's director, Lewis Gilbert, came out and left convinced that Sonny was the key to the film.[31]

Alfie chronicles the sexual exploits of a working-class womanizer with a cockney accent, a kind of Don Juan for the Swinging Sixties, who comes to stare into the existential abyss of his life.[32] Lewis Gilbert had optioned the film rights and got it financed as an American and British coproduction, but he did not feel he was in touch with the zeitgeist. The mod scene was entranced by modern jazz; at the same time, Herbie Hancock was hired to score Michelangelo Antonioni's *Blow-Up*. *Alfie*, on the other hand, sought to capture a less glamorous side of London life through unvarnished social realism.[33]

John Gilbert helped cast Michael Caine, a relative unknown at the time, and insisted on taking his father to see Sonny at Ronnie Scott's. "Dad, I know you've always used symphony orchestras," John told him, "but it's time for a change.... You have to listen to him, Dad. He can be jaunty. He can be mournful, everything that's Alfie." So Lewis Gilbert and his wife, Hylda, along with John all went to see Sonny at Ronnie's, accompanied by actor Tony Randall.[34]

"Sonny Rollins was as good as John said," wrote the elder Gilbert. "Hylda and I were spellbound, as was the rest of the packed house. 'You've hit it,' I said to John afterwards, and together we went backstage. Sonny was charming and, for a jazz man, surprisingly unweird. What made him happy as much as anything was talking about his wife and the rest of his family. As a musician, he was a perfectionist.... We were, in due course, to become life-long friends."[35]

As for being the sound of the film's unscrupulous protagonist, Sonny thought, "I don't know if I should have taken that as a compliment or not!" Sonny resolved that his score would serve as a counterpoint that suggested hidden depths, and, despite any reservations, he accepted. It would be his first and last film score. "I was anxious to do the film," Sonny said. "Actually, I wrote the music for the film in the club."[36]

Sonny wrote what music there was for the score overnight. "It's always hard to come down from a concert right away and just get yourself into bed," Sonny said. "So I said, 'Ronnie, after I get through playing tonight, I'd like to stay in the club, just lock me up, and I'll stay here until they come by in the morning to open up, because I want to work on the music and I'll have a nice private space to do it.'"[37] By the next morning, Sonny had finished.

There was an unintended cause for Sonny's boundless energy. "It was like eternal Christmas playing with those people," recalled Stan Tracey. "I was soon dropping drinamyl [speed] by the handful. In order to keep going at that pace, you can't do it on a sensible diet like fruit juice."[38]

Sonny was into fruit juice, and, Laird said, was "basically a very straight guy: drug-free, alcohol-free, all of that. He was clean. He was a health nut, actually." One night, Stan came in with "a big jar of pills... called black bombers," a street name for amphetamine. "They were super uppers, super-duper uppers...I had taken one before and I think I stayed up for like a day and a half in kind of hyper energy mode. So Stan's passing these around the dressing room like candy. 'Would you like some? Would you like a pill?' And I wasn't really into it, because I didn't want to stay up for the next two days. Sonny, on the other hand, decided, 'Oh, I'll have one of those.' So he took one, and the gig finished, and he was so wired that he said to the guy who was closing up the club at about four in the morning, 'I'm gonna stay here and practice.' So the club got locked up, and Sonny, as far as we know, he stayed there all day till the cleaning people came at around 2 or 3 in the afternoon and he was there playing."[39]

What Sonny came up with for *Alfie* was ingenious. Having grown up at the movies, Sonny was well versed in sweeping orchestral scores that tugged on the heartstrings. His first touchstone was the buoyant score to *An American in Paris*, the 1951 Gene Kelly–starring vehicle based on the Gershwin composition.[40] More than that, though, he was inspired by *Singin' in the Rain*, the classic 1952 musical comedy starring Kelly and Debbie Reynolds. As rain pours down on Kelly's umbrella before he sings the irrepressibly optimistic title song, an orchestral introduction begins; Kelly hums this opening motif before breaking into song. The line is based on only four notes and serves as a counterpoint to the film's iconic melody. Sonny repurposed that rhythmic motif into "Alfie's Theme."

By reframing the motif in a minor key, Michael Caine's Alfie becomes a Bizarro Gene Kelly. "Sonny took that theme," Laird said, "and he turned it into a minor blues."[41]

Though the Gilberts hired Sonny during his first residency at Ronnie Scott's, the *Alfie* score would not be recorded until the fall of 1965, with a separate album recorded that January. After the Gilberts wrapped production, with Sonny back in the United States, they flew him into London on September 12, 1965, put him up at the luxurious Dorchester Hotel, and convened to watch a rough cut of the film.[42] Lewis Gilbert had "a very good understanding of music without knowing all the technical aspects of it," Sonny said. "If the score is a success, he deserves a large share of the credit."[43] They discussed the score for the next two days, then the Gilberts flew Sonny back to New York. They recorded the score at Twickenham Studios from

Monday, October 18, to Friday, October 22, and wrapped it up the following Monday, October 25.[44]

Sonny was paid $750 upon completion of the score, with the company securing all rights to the material, giving Sonny a 10 percent sheet-music royalty, 50 percent on mechanical royalties, and 50 percent on performing, broadcasting, and rediffusion fees. In the first year after the film's release, it would earn him about $1,000 in royalties. Apparently, Sonny later felt he had been fleeced, though he attributed the acrimonious situation to the ABC lawyers representing Impulse Records.[45]

Sonny hired a British band for the score: Ronnie Scott on tenor, Keith Christie on trombone, pianist Tracey, guitarist Dave Goldberg, bassist Laird, and drummer Phil Seamen;[46] Tubby Hayes was also brought in for a few sequences.[47] As the recording approached, they didn't have any music to practice, and for many of them, this was their highest-profile gig to date. Scott and Christie went to Sonny's hotel to see if he had anything. According to Scott biographer John Fordham, "The saxophone was on a sofa with a spotlight shining on it. All three men got very stoned in the course of the discussion and eventually the two Englishmen asked to see Rollins's ideas for the score. He brought out a sheaf of manuscript paper and laid it before them. Every sheet was blank—except one."[48]

They had little more to go on when they convened in front of a big projection screen in the recording studio.[49] As Ronnie Scott told it, Sonny showed up with only one staff of prepared music, the four-bar line that became the key motif of "Alfie's Theme."[50] According to Laird, Sonny "walked in with his cowboy hat and . . . there was no score. Nothing, not one piece of music. So Ronnie was a little freaked. He said, 'Wow. No music?' So he walked up to Sonny and he said, 'So, Sonny, how do you want us to treat this?' And Sonny said in that funny voice of his, 'Very lightly, Ronnie. Very lightly.' And that was it. We made it up as we went."[51] Other than Stan Tracey's "Little Malcolm Loves His Dad," Tracey recalled, "for the rest of it there were contributions from everybody."[52]

Could it be that Sonny and the band simply improvised one of the classic major motion-picture scores? In a sense, yes. When Joe Goldberg interviewed Sonny before the score was recorded, Sonny acted as though he had not read the script, prefacing each comment with "Lucille tells me..."[53] Yet as improvised as it was, it seems there was in fact more preparation for the *Alfie* score.

The bulk of Sonny's score, or what remains, consists mostly of a single staff of music with the melody line and a corresponding single-staff bass line. However, he wrote out extensive verbal descriptions to guide the rest. "I would like to see the film 'alone' with my instrument before bringing in the group for a rehearsal," Sonny wrote. "Showing this could establish tonality of the sketches—still, the overall sound of the group would possibly change the tonality once again! Cancel then the suggestion.... Not until after seeing and hearing the band and picture at the first rehearsal showing can I really decide upon an appropriate theme."[54]

Hence, what seemed to be a lack of preparation was in fact a deliberate choice. Sonny wrote copious notes by hand, riffing off the extensive typewritten guidelines from the Gilberts, which broke each scored scene down by the second.[55] There was "Alfie's mournful theme," the "cheerful Alfie theme," the "pastoral river theme," and a "fugue type Baroque piece." The goal, Sonny wrote, was to "dramatize in music" the tension between the characters and their internal contradictions.[56]

Sonny's extensive notes were a blueprint for the score to be improvised in front of the projection screen to the click track.[57] Still, Sonny set parameters. "Guitar come in softly single line with a preview. 10 seconds enter bass, piano 18 seconds." Throughout, Sonny remained a perfectionist. "After one long morning of preparation with an unusual degree of attention to detail," wrote John Fordham, Scott drove Sonny "down to the river in his sports car for lunch. They rounded things off with a large joint. When they got back, Rollins said, 'All that stuff we did this morning, forget it.' Everybody started again."[58]

Lewis Gilbert found this highly unusual for a film score, but the results were revelatory. "The recording of *Alfie's* score was like none I had known before or was to know again," wrote Gilbert. "Those three sessions with Sonny were the most exciting of my life.... Sometimes, after a few takes, I thought we'd got it, but no. 'Please, one more, Lewis. I can do better,' Sonny would say and go on to do perhaps twenty takes. As each one was different and interesting I could see that this was not mere preciousness but an artist at work."[59]

Brilliant as the score was, Paramount wanted a vocal theme to promote the film, and Burt Bacharach and Hal David were hired to write it. George Martin produced it, with vocalist Cilla Black recording "Alfie" at Abbey Road, backed by Bacharach himself on piano and a forty-piece orchestra; later versions came from Cher and Dionne Warwick.[60] United Artists insisted on including Cher's version in the American version of the film, but Lewis Gilbert pushed back. As a compromise, it plays over the closing credits. In the finished film, though, despite the lavish orchestral production of the vocal theme, it's Sonny we hear before we see the first frame, and it's Sonny that steals every scene, even if, Sonny said, "I thought some of the best music was left out of the movie."[61] He told Bob Houston in 1967, "I didn't really get my teeth into that job."[62]

At awards season, Sonny's score was all but overlooked. The Cher version of "Alfie" won Burt Bacharach and Hal David an Oscar in 1967 for "Best Music, Original Score," snubbing Sonny.[63] At the 1967 Grammy Awards, Sonny was nominated in the "Best Original Score Written for a Motion Picture or Television Show" category, but the award went to Maurice Jarre for *Doctor Zhivago*.

——◦——

Closing at Ronnie Scott's on February 7, 1965, Sonny felt he had been treated with uncommon decency throughout the month. "When I left my engagement with Ronnie Scott's, I brought presents for some of the staff there, which I am sure was highly unusual," Sonny said. "I really made friends with the people there."[64] Without discussing it, the staff got Sonny gifts in return as well.[65]

Sonny had offers to play in Spain and France from promoter Nadine Boden.[66] Ramón Farrán recalled that Sonny made an impromptu appearance at the Indigo, a jazz club he ran in Palma, Mallorca, on the bustling street Teniente Mulet.[67] "I invited him to come to play," recalled Farrán. "And he came, and of course he came with his instrument.... It was an open house for everybody."[68]

Sonny's experience of fair treatment across the Atlantic underscored the stark contrast with the inequality and civil unrest that remained in his home country. On February 21, Malcolm X was assassinated at the Audubon Ballroom. "I can relate to Malcolm X in many ways, because I came up on the streets in the same way he did," Sonny later told Arthur Taylor. "I got into scrapes when I was younger. I think what he did was great. Like him, I tried to straighten my life out and avoid getting into a rut and getting on the wrong side of the law."[69] On March 25, Martin Luther King Jr. declared: "How long? Not long! Because the arc of the moral universe is long, but it bends toward justice."

Still, interracial marriage would not be legal nationwide until the landmark *Loving v. Virginia* decision on June 12, 1967. It was never illegal in New York, though, and Sonny and Lucille finally applied for a marriage license, issued February 25, 1965.[70] On March 7, they got married in a small ceremony. "We didn't have a big wedding," Sonny said. "We were married in my apartment when we were living in Brooklyn."[71] Sonny's sister, Gloria, and his brother-in-law, Tomlyn Anderson, served as witnesses. The officiant was William Leonard Chapman, the pastor at the Mariners' Temple Baptist Church in Lower Manhattan.[72] Sonny finally had more balance in his life, and he and Lucille even adopted a second German shepherd as a sibling for Major, named, naturally, Minor.[73]

Around this time, Sonny also reconnected with his seven-year-old nephew, Clifton Anderson, who'd gotten interested in music. Sonny bought him his first instrument: Clifton only had to decide which instrument he wanted to play, and the answer became clear when his mother took him to see *The Music Man* and he heard "Seventy-Six Trombones." "Within a couple months, I had my first trombone," Anderson recalled. "I was so little at that time that I couldn't extend the slide all the way out to seventh position.... Of course, nobody knew at that time that we'd end up playing professionally together for almost twenty-eight years."[74]

Sonny also made a strong impression on future saxophonist Eric Wyatt, the son of Sonny's close friend Charlie Wyatt. Sonny had kept in touch with Charlie since they met in the early fifties. "They used to carry the stick," Eric said. "Sonny told me my father used to help his mother with her groceries." Sonny and Charlie were both saxophone players, but had gone in different directions; Sonny was touring around the world, while Wyatt became a family man with a wife and five kids. Wyatt kept playing, though. Sonny took him on the Williamsburg Bridge. He even gave Wyatt a gold-plated Selmer Mark VI. The Wyatts lived in a two-bedroom apartment in the Brownsville section of East New York. Charlie and his wife, Phennie, slept in one bedroom, and some of the kids slept in the other; Eric and his brother slept on a pullout sofa in the living room. "It was a very bad neighborhood, so for anybody to come over there we figured you had to be family," Eric recalled. "I remember the first time that Sonny Rollins came, he brought this gigantic crate of cherries. . . . There were so many cherries in this thing, we all could take as much as we want."[75] Sonny never forgot his friends, no matter where they lived.

On April 6, Sonny signed with Impulse! Records, Coltrane's label, for a $7,500 advance per record.[76] Impulse had recently released *A Love Supreme*, and producer Bob Thiele had a good reputation. RCA had blown Thiele out of the water, but now Sonny decided to give him a chance.[77]

Thiele immediately scheduled a series of recording dates for Sonny, and Sonny began reconstituting his band.[78] At the Half Note the last weekend in April, he played opposite Toshiko Akiyoshi and Charlie Mariano, in a quartet with Herbie Hancock, Beaver Harris, and bassist Herman Wright. One set on April 30 was broadcast on Alan Grant's *Portraits in Jazz* on WABC-FM.[79] Japanese alto saxophonist Sadao Watanabe came to the Half Note; so did Bennie Maupin.[80]

"I'm standing there on the corner," recalled Maupin, "and I look in one direction, and I see Sonny—and it just happened—I look in the other direction, and I see Herbie. And they ended up right at the door at the same time. I had seen Herbie with Miles, but I didn't know him. But it was Sonny, so Sonny says, 'Herbie, this is Bennie.' That's how we met. Just like that."[81] Maupin wouldn't join Hancock's Mwandishi Band until much later, but Sonny made the initial connection.

Hancock was available to play with Sonny while Miles Davis was out recovering from hip-replacement surgery.[82] Sonny was booked at the Village Vanguard from May 5 to 23, and on opening night he used Miles's rhythm section at the time: Hancock, Tony Williams, and Richard Davis, who sometimes subbed for Ron Carter.

"Herbie had talked Sonny into hiring Tony," recalled Beaver Harris. "Sonny said, 'I'll try Mr. Williams, I've never played with him, but I think that I'll give that a try. Will you do me a favor?' And I said, 'Yeah, Newk.' He said, 'Herbie was telling me about Mr. Williams, and I've never played with him. Would you mind if I played with him this time?' I said, 'Well, no, it's okay.' He said, 'Thank you, Mr. Harris, thank you very much.' So he hired Tony. I went to the Vanguard and I was sitting on the side by the bandstand. I was pleased because Tony and I had talked about this. I used to study with Tony; he taught me some things. We had talked, he said, 'All I wanna do is play with Sonny, man, just once.'"[83]

At the Vanguard, Sonny would often start playing from the little room behind the stage. On this night, he started with "Three Little Words." Tony played the way he generally did—it was overwhelming. "He walked up to me," Harris said, "and went 'doo doo doo...please come back to work tomorrow...doo doo doo.' Tony played more shit in eight bars than I've ever heard. See, in other words, you can be the greatest drummer in the world, but if you're not playing the music, you're not playing."[84]

It was the first and last night of that rhythm section. "We weren't a passive rhythm section," Hancock recalled. "We didn't just lay back and let Sonny be free to fly on top of a steady support. We were very active. We thought that the stuff was killing! We thought that Sonny was inspiring us and he was out there and responding and sweating and playing his tail off. And we got fired! He called me later that night—and Tony and Richard, too—and said, 'I think I'll try something different tomorrow.'...We were pushing him, the way we were with Miles."[85] Sonny hired Hancock back to play solo piano during set breaks.

Sonny experimented with different rhythm sections, using Attila Zoller, Bob Cranshaw, Ron Carter, and Herman Wright in different combinations and keeping Beaver Harris as a constant.[86] "Whenever he played the Vanguard, I always made it a point to go," Maupin recalled. "When they would take a break, there used to be a little room there in the Vanguard. I don't know if it's still there or not. But he used to go in there. It was like a closet. He would just go in there and meditate. And sometimes I would go in and talk to him, ask him questions."[87]

From June 15 to 20, Sonny returned to the Vanguard in a quartet with Tommy Flanagan (the pianist from *Saxophone Colossus*), thirty-one-year-old bassist Walter Booker, and a drummer; he sometimes added trumpeter David Hayward to make it a quintet.[88] "It was thrilling to get a call by Sonny to work with him," recalled Booker's widow, Bertha Hope-Booker. Sonny gave Booker a ride home from the gig, and Booker "noticed that Sonny hadn't said anything about money. So when Sonny dropped him off, they shook hands, and said, 'Everything's good. I enjoyed playing with you.'" As Sonny pulled away, Booker realized he hadn't been paid. "Sonny called him a couple days later, and said, 'You know, you never even asked me about how much money you were going to get. So since you didn't ask me, you didn't get anything. So don't ever do that anymore. Always make sure that you understand how much money you're going to get before you do the gig.' The next time he paid him double. He paid him the money, but kind of taught him a lesson."[89]

The next night, journalist Joe Goldberg was at the Vanguard to profile Sonny for *Down Beat*. He jettisoned trumpet in order to prepare for a performance the following day at the Museum of Modern Art, which would be recorded with plans in place for it to be his debut album with Impulse.[90] As Sonny finished the set, he backed into a little closet behind the stage that Vanguard management referred to informally as the "Sonny Rollins dressing room." "The door opened again, just long enough for him to ask if I wanted to speak to him," Goldberg wrote, "and then closed."[91] The interview was done by candlelight, so as not to distract from Mose Allison's set.[92]

In the middle of the interview, a twenty-three-year-old saxophonist knocked on the door to find Sonny in front of a full-length mirror doing isometric jaw exercises. His name was Eddie Daniels, and he asked to sit in on the next set. A lot of chutzpah, but he had credentials.[93]

"What do you play?" Sonny asked.

"I play tenor," came the reply.

"You play tenor? How dare you?" Sonny said facetiously. Sonny then gave a long disquisition on the history of sitting in and how he himself had been turned down before. It would have to wait until later.[94]

"Tomorrow night?" Daniels asked.

"All right, come back tomorrow night, and we'll see," Sonny said.

The last set that night, only a handful of people were left, and Max Gordon gave Sonny the option to call it a night. His response was emphatic. "I came here to work," Sonny said. "I came prepared to play, and I can play all night." That set, a drunk walked across the stage, stumbling on his way to the men's room. But then a few familiar faces arrived and doubled the size of the crowd: Max Roach, Elvin Jones, and, limping down the Vanguard stairs with a cane from his recent surgery, Miles Davis.[95]

When Daniels finally sat in, Sonny's reaction was similar to when Charlie Parker heard Sonny and said, "That's me!" Yet Daniels did this intentionally. "I wanted Sonny to sound like the Sonny that I loved when I was hearing him as a youth," Daniels explained. "So I went there with my tenor to say 'Sonny, this is you! Play like this!' . . . I went to the Vanguard to try to say, 'I love you, Sonny. Here's the Sonny that I grew up on.' "[96]

Sonny was impressed. "He played his tail off," Sonny told Joe Goldberg a week later.[97] When the *Down Beat* article came out, it didn't identify the "phantom tenor" by name, so Daniels's wife wrote a letter to the editor under an alias identifying him. "That's how it all started, but Sonny then became a friend," Daniels said. "We got dinner at his house on occasion."[98]

For the Museum of Modern Art concert, Sonny hired Tommy Flanagan, Cranshaw, and two drummers: Higgins and Roker. Though the press release from the MoMA listed only Higgins, it was always intended as a dual drummer gig with Roker.[99] Sonny knew that Ellington had used drummers Sam Woodyard and Jimmy Johnson on "Dual Fuel," and he wanted to try it out himself.[100]

"At that time, I could have gone with either Sonny Rollins or Trane," Roker told Ethan Iverson. "I decided to go with Sonny because Bob Cranshaw was there. . . . On one chorus I play time and he would embellish, and the next chorus he would play time and I would embellish. Just color up. That's what we did on the whole record date."[101]

The concert was June 17, the first in the "Jazz in the Garden" series cosponsored by *Down Beat*, with an admission price of fifty cents after the one-dollar museum entrance fee.[102] Sonny packed the MoMA.[103] The concert took place in the museum's sculpture garden, with no rain plan. It started to drizzle as soon as the band got set up, but it didn't stop Sonny, or anyone in the audience. People who brought cushions to sit on the lawn simply used them as umbrellas. "The rain was beating on the cymbals," Roker recalled. The Colossus himself emerged from behind a tree in a green jacket and a blue beret, a kinetic statue in perpetual motion dancing with the Picasso, Matisse, and Rodin, holding the audience in rapt attention despite the rain.[104] He bobbed and weaved through the crowd, catching raindrops in the bell of his saxophone and unleashing torrents of notes.[105]

Sonny began his set with "Will You Still Be Mine?" He then played "Green Dolphin Street," "Three Little Words," and "Mademoiselle de Paris," ending that song by holding a C for a solid minute using circular breathing. He concluded with Edward MacDowell's "To a Wild Rose" and a sixteen-minute-plus rendition of "There Will Never Be Another You," with sudden key changes and an electrifying trading section.[106] Sonny was confident in his ability to relate to the common listener. "The average Joe knows just as much as I do—he knows *more* than I do," he explained to Goldberg. "*I'm* the average Joe, and I think people recognize that. That's why I play standards. Everybody knows 'Stardust.'"[107]

There that night was the Danish avant-garde saxophonist and composer John Tchicai, a leading light of the New Thing.[108] On June 28, less than two weeks after the "Jazz in the Garden" concert, he played on John Coltrane's *Ascension*. "He was playing tunes, standards, but he can still make them meaningful for me. He gets more from them than most players," Tchicai told Garth Caylor the night of the concert.[109]

Due to the rain and Sonny wandering off mike, the live recording at the MoMA was shelved until 1978, when it was issued as *There Will Never Be Another You*, much to Sonny's chagrin.[110] Plans for a studio session were immediately put in place to record on Thursday, July 8. On July 6, he began another week at the Vanguard and brought in pianist Ray Bryant, Walter Booker, Mickey Roker, and, on trumpet, David Hayward, though he would drop trumpet for the recording.[111] This would serve as a kind of rehearsal for *Sonny Rollins on Impulse.*[112] That Thursday, Sonny made his first trip to Van Gelder Studio in Englewood Cliffs, New Jersey.[113]

Designed by architect David Henken, a former apprentice of Frank Lloyd Wright and a follower in his Usonian tradition, the space, built in 1959, was a peaceful redoubt by the palisades, with thirty-nine-foot ceilings, a brick exterior, and a wooden interior. It looked more like a chapel in the woods than a typical recording studio.

Sonny pulled up to Van Gelder Studio in his Karmann Ghia coupe wearing a Yankees hat and a light sport jacket, carrying two tenor cases: the Mark VI and the Buescher. He hadn't recorded with Ray Bryant since *Work Time*. *Sonny Rollins on Impulse* "was more or less same preparation" as *Work Time*, Bryant recalled, which is to say, not much. As Roker recalled, "We rehearsed for two days to do the *Sonny Rollins on Impulse* album. Then, we got to the recording studio and did not play one thing that we had rehearsed."[114]

This sense of cultivated unpreparedness was intentional. "Although he had concepts of how he wanted to design each tune, there was no music on the date," wrote Nat Hentoff in the liner notes. "The session went swiftly because of Rollins' strong sense of structural order."[115]

Of the five tracks—"On Green Dolphin Street"; "Everything Happens to Me"; the calypso "Hold 'Em Joe," made famous by Harry Belafonte; "Blue Room"; and "Three Little Words"—the latter is the highlight. Sonny's opening cadenza on "Three Little Words," tenor saxophonist Joel Frahm later said, "is worth the price alone."[116] He's abetted wonderfully by Walter Booker's light touch, Ray Bryant's lithe concision on his solo,[117] and Mickey Roker's effervescent ride cymbal. "I just play the cymbal beat but I turn it around sometimes to keep it interesting," Roker said. "Dynamically, you got to color your music up. That's how you color your music up—by swelling, like the ocean." Gary Giddins called it "five or six minutes of perfection."[118]

Starting Monday, July 12, Sonny was booked for a week at Pep's on Broad Street in Philadelphia, but he didn't give Mickey Roker advance notice. "On Friday, Sonny calls my house: 'Mister Mickey, we have a job in Philadelphia starting Monday.' I said, 'Sonny, I have been rehearsing with Milt Jackson to play with him in Philly. I just can't…' He didn't speak to me for two years."[119] For Pep's, Sonny got Frankie Dunlop and kept Walter Booker, and after testing out pianist Mike Melillo on his last set at the Vanguard, he asked him to join the band.[120]

"It was completely free-form," said Melillo, whom Sonny had performed with earlier in May when he played as a single at the Clifton Tap Room in

New Jersey. "You never knew what he was gonna do; you never knew what he was gonna play. And I asked him one time. I said, 'Sonny, why, why did you hire me?' And he said, 'cause you know all the tunes that I know.' Because I know a lot of those standards from the '30s, '40s, and '50s, that he used to love to play."[121] Melillo's tenure with Sonny went intermittently for about a year. "He was a great cat. Everybody loved him. Even my mother loved him," Melillo said. "He used to call my mother up on the phone and ask her what she was gonna have for dinner." His parents "came to the Village Vanguard on a gig one time and met him and sat with him, and they really, really enjoyed being with him," Melillo said.

Sonny never recorded as a unit with Melillo, Booker, and Dunlop. "Some of the music that he played, I never heard again," Melillo said. "It was like a musical collage that he would do every night before a lot of the tunes, and sometimes in the middle of some of the tunes. And it would go on for like five, ten minutes. Everybody had their mouths open, because they were hearing things they never heard before...and then he would finally land on a tune. When he landed on a tune, we'd jump in and we'd play with him. We never had a rehearsal."

From July 20 to August 15, Sonny returned to the Village Vanguard playing opposite the Cecil Taylor Trio.[122] It was Taylor's first major New York booking since 1963.[123] Taylor performed with Sonny's former bassist Henry Grimes and drummer Andrew Cyrille. "Sonny lived in Brooklyn, where I lived at that time," Cyrille recalled. "So on occasion, Sonny would drive me home, and that's how we would talk to each other, and that's the closest that I've ever gotten to Sonny as far as being in his presence....Sonny never said anything to me about what we were doing. He would just talk about how... he'd want his band to jell, like if they could do the same thing every night, but that's almost impossible....He was aiming for perfection, and that's hard to get all the time."[124]

One night, Taylor later told drummer Tony Oxley, "Cecil was leaving, and as he was going up the stairs, Sonny turned to him and said, 'Cecil, don't ever let them stop you doing what you're doing!'" Oxley recalled. "Of course, it meant a lot to Cecil, to have that from Sonny Rollins."[125]

Sonny played at the Jazz Workshop in Boston's Back Bay from September

19 through 26 with pianist Milton Sealey, bassist Herbert Brown, and drummer Frankie Dunlop.[126] Sonny had the temerity to wear his Yankees hat. One set was taped for television broadcast for a series hosted by trumpeter Herb Pomeroy, in which Sonny played "There Will Never Be Another You" and "Someone to Watch over Me" and did a brief interview. "It's not the horn," Sonny told Pomeroy. "It's the man behind the horn."[127]

When Sonny returned to London to record the *Alfie* score, he brought Lucille for a subsequent European tour. That October, he was booked at Berlin Jazz Days, a three-day festival founded by Joachim-Ernst Berendt. On October 29, in Munich, he played in a trio with Danish bassist Niels-Henning Ørsted Pedersen and drummer Alan Dawson. They played the ballad "Darn That Dream" and a medley of "Three Little Words," "Over the Rainbow," "Pent-Up House," and "Valse Hot" that finally became "There Will Never Be Another You." He then played "The Song Is You" and a medley of "On Green Dolphin Street" and "Night and Day."[128]

On October 30, Sonny participated in an all-star program at the Berlin Sportpalast with Ben Webster, Don Byas, Brew Moore, Booker Ervin, and Dexter Gordon.[129] The rhythm section was Sonny's old friend Kenny Drew, Ørsted Pedersen, and Dawson. The ensuing concert was something of a fiasco, with the German producers reprimanding Ben Webster for calling out to a friend in the audience. Each of the tenor giants was asked to confine their set to three minutes, but Booker Ervin played for more than thirty. Sonny played "St. Thomas" for scarcely more than two minutes, interpolating a quote from Lauritz Melchior's "Vive la Compagnie."[130] Dexter Gordon sacrificed his set entirely. The concert was salvaged, though, by a battle royale with all six tenor giants on "Scrapple from the Apple."

Sonny had another reunion with old friends in Berlin, playing with Milt Jackson (whom he had performed with recently in Brooklyn), Kenny Drew, Percy Heath, and Art Blakey.[131] If anyone ever doubted that Sonny could still play in his fifties style whenever he wanted to, it was second nature. On October 31, Sonny appeared at Tivoli Concert Hall in Copenhagen, again with Ørsted Pedersen and Dawson, in a classic performance that was taped for television.[132] Less than three minutes into the set opener, "There Will Never Be Another You," Sonny gave the nineteen-year-old Ørsted Pedersen a solo in front of his hometown crowd. Ørsted Pedersen's upper register was crisper than just about anyone's, and he had a three-finger pizzicato technique that allowed him to play double-time lines with clear articulation. Dawson loved Sonny's rhythmic sensibility. "You don't hear much rhythmic variety from sax players," Dawson later said, "because when you've got all those pitches to deal with, you can't very well get into that much rhythmically—Sonny Rollins being the exception, of course."[133]

The tour culminated for Ørsted Pedersen on November 2 in Stockholm at the Johanneshov Ice Stadium, an eighty-three-hundred-seat arena usually reserved for hockey games.[134] Sonny played a medley: "Oleo," "Sonnymoon for Two," and "Three Little Words," which Sonny stretched out to thirty minutes.

Ørsted Pedersen was in heaven. "That tour was my first meeting with the big international mega-stars of jazz," he recalled.[135] Playing with Sonny "was the greatest experience at that point in my life....I had never experienced that kind of power." During this tour, he also accompanied Bill Evans. "It was almost too much to perform at that level on both of those gigs," he said, but he did it. Afterward, "I ended up playing everywhere in Europe...I became the man people called on the phone."[136]

On November 3 and 4, Sonny and the rest of the touring group moved on to the second Paris Jazz Festival, in the Latin Quartet at the Palais de la Mutualité. For Sonny, it was a treat to share a bill with one of his favorites, Stuff Smith.[137] On November 4, Sonny headlined a double bill with Ornette Coleman, who had recently returned from a long sabbatical himself. More than two thousand fans came, and Sonny did not disappoint. Coleman played in a trio with David Izenzon and Charles Moffett; Sonny performed with his old friend Art Taylor and bassist Gilbert Rovère. Two decades after forming the Counts of Bop, Sonny and A.T. had made it from Sugar Hill cocktail sips to Paris without losing the beat.

Sonny walked on in a sport jacket, turtleneck, and a black beret, playing "Sonnymoon for Two," and when he finished nearly an hour later, he walked off the stage playing.[138] He left almost no time for applause between songs, playing "I Can't Get Started," "Three Little Words," "St. Thomas," "There Will Never Be Another You," "When I Grow Too Old to Dream," "O Sole Mio," and "Mademoiselle de Paris."[139]

The profusion of musical quotes posed a complication for the official from SACEM, the French performing-rights association, who was tasked with noting every tune played in order to pay royalties. "The last time I saw the official," wrote a reviewer in *Crescendo*, "he was swarming up the curtains scattering the confetti of a shredded P.R. form."[140]

Back in New York, Sonny was booked for two weeks at the Village Vanguard starting November 30, replacing the Miles Davis Quintet.[141] He hired Booker, Flanagan, Frankie Dunlop, and twenty-three-year-old trumpeter Charles Tolliver.[142] He met Sonny earlier that year through Bennie Maupin, who would practice with Sonny at the latter's apartment. "Because Bennie knew him so well from doing his lesson sessions with him, I met him actually the first time at his loft," Tolliver recalled, "and then I didn't see Sonny again until I got a call from him to perform with him at the Vanguard.... I'm pretty sure he knew that I had been working for the past two years with Jackie McLean."

At the Vanguard, Sonny threw some curveballs. "He was full of all sorts of idiosyncrasies," Tolliver said. He saw him "standing on his head in between sets in that little small closet room behind the bandstand where they would usually store the drums...he was into the yoga thing at that time."[143] Sonny would play one continuous set, "going from different songs to the other," and he wouldn't announce the keys. "Of course, we grew up watching him do that, so that was one of the things that we practiced, those of us who were dead serious with the art form at that time. So that was right up my alley when I was performing with him, because it can be pretty daunting for a musician if they didn't know how or what to do when he would change the song or a key and play obscure pieces of music from the American Songbook. You really had to know the American Songbook."[144]

Playing with Sonny taught Tolliver the importance of the tradition and what it meant to build on it. It was important not to "go too astray trying to prove something that's elusive. I mean, there's only been a couple who could do that with impunity," Tolliver said. "They had a license to do that, because they had codified in so many ways how to perform this art form that they could do that. Namely John Coltrane, of course, and Sonny Rollins, too. No matter how close to the outer borders of the art form they experimented, the one thing that made them national treasures for all time is, the blues was always in their playing."[145]

Yet Sonny was ever looking for the next frontier. He finished the year with a couple of benefits that once again reunited him with old friends. On December 13, he played a benefit at the Five Spot for the late tenor saxophonist Frank Haynes, who had died on November 30. On the bill were Coltrane, Thelonious Monk, Randy Weston, Art Blakey, Walter Bishop Jr., and Billy Taylor.[146] On December 27, he played a benefit for radio station WBAI at the Village Gate, with Monk, Dorham, Betty Carter, Roland Kirk, and Charles Davis. Reconnecting with past collaborators was always meaningful, but Sonny continued to look to the future. He didn't necessarily have to go as far east as Japan or India to find inspiration; the following year, he would find it on East Broadway.[147]

Chapter 28

89 EAST BROADWAY

(1966)

On January 26, 1966, Sonny returned to Van Gelder Studio to record the soundtrack album to *Alfie* backed by a nine-piece band, with arrangements by Oliver Nelson.[1] To keep personnel costs low, they had only three hours, and no rehearsal. Nelson didn't deviate dramatically from Sonny's original score, but he gave it the distinctive Oliver Nelson treatment, "adding a little here and there and editing," Sonny said. "But this is basically the sound we got in the picture. Working with Oliver, incidentally, is enlightening. He's not only thoroughly qualified musically, but personally he is so easy to work with that he got the best out of all of us."[2]

Sonny used Walter Booker and Frankie Dunlop, part of his current working band, but Nelson brought the rest.[3] In 1965, the rest of the band had worked with Nelson on vocalist Irene Reid's *Room for One More* and Stanley

Turrentine's *Joyride*: J. J. Johnson and Jimmy Cleveland on trombone; Phil Woods on alto, Bob Ashton on tenor, and Danny Bank on baritone saxophone; Roger Kellaway on piano; and Kenny Burrell on guitar.[4] Nelson himself played second tenor if the arrangement called for it.[5]

"In those days it was just kind of a New York thing, where you would show up and you would sight-read the music but you were able to play it as if you'd been playing it for a month," recalled Roger Kellaway, twenty-six at the time.[6]

Beyond the six Nelson arrangements, much of the album, especially who would solo, was decided on the spot. "I was happy to get the call, and certainly Sonny is one of my favorite saxophonists, period," said Kenny Burrell. "I was a bit surprised when he asked me to take a solo on the first track, but I was happy to have that responsibility."[7] Burrell grabbed his Gibson and let loose on the title track. Saxophonist Dave Liebman holds up Sonny's searching solo on "Alfie's Theme" as a pinnacle. "Sonny plays everything there is to do on the saxophone," he said. "Even Trane-isms."[8]

Kellaway is featured more prominently than anyone but Sonny. He plays solos or brief solo interludes on every track.[9] On "Transition Theme for Minor Blues; or, Little Malcolm Loves His Dad," Kellaway plays two solos. "I took my solo, and in the middle of Sonny's solo, he just stopped. And just, he sunk down and sat on his haunches with the tenor between his legs and off-microphone, and my theatrical reaction was that instead of dead space, I started playing, so there were two solos on that track. We never talked about it, in fact I never talked about it with Oliver Nelson." Sonny never comes back in on the track.

To Sonny, the album was just too rushed. "I didn't have control of it, because we had to just go into the studio and make it," Sonny recalled. "It cost so much money, and there were a lot of musicians involved and you couldn't go overtime, you just had to read everything right down, which the musicians were able to do and all of that, but generally I would have preferred to have had some time to look at the arrangements myself so that I would be able to know everything and...know it beforehand."[10] Sonny, always the perfectionist, had the dissenting opinion; *Alfie* reached the number seventeen spot on the *Billboard* R&B chart.[11] Nevertheless, the rushed session under-scored that Sonny's relationship with Impulse had already begun to sour.

Then came "Titans of the Tenor!"[12] The 1966 New York City transit strike postponed the much-heralded concert, presented by Felix Gerstman and Sid Bernstein at Lincoln Center's Philharmonic Hall, from January 14 to Saturday, February 19, at 11:30 p.m.[13] The titans were Coleman Hawkins, John Coltrane, Zoot Sims, and Sonny. Coltrane's band had Albert Ayler and Pharoah Sanders; Sonny's had Yusef Lateef. If there was ever to be a papal conclave of the tenor saxophone, this was it. Tickets only cost $2.50.

The titans began with Zoot Sims, backed by Roger Kellaway, bassist Bill Crow, and drummer Dave Bailey. Sims borrowed the rhythm section from Clark Terry and Bob Brookmeyer's group, which played next. Cole-man Hawkins, dressed in a mohair suit, with a full beard, joined Terry and Brookmeyer, and played only one song—"In a Mellow Tone"—with a stately seven-chorus solo. After the intermission, Lambert, Hendricks & Ross vocal-ist Dave Lambert, the night's emcee, announced: "And now...Sonny Rol-lins!" Yet there was no Sonny. Lambert tried again, but still nothing. He went backstage to investigate, and there was Sonny, who came out with Yusef Lateef, blowing on "Sonnymoon for Two." Sonny hired pianist John Hicks, Walter Booker, and Mickey Roker. He gave Lateef the first solo and began pacing the stage, looking for a sweet spot. Instead of soloing on "Sonny-moon," he moved on to "Hold 'Em Joe," "Penthouse Serenade," and "Three Little Words," and in under fifteen minutes marched back into the wings. When the crowd demanded more, Sonny came back out and announced that he would be playing with Coltrane later in the night.

Coltrane was supposed to play with a quintet, but he brought more. *Ascension*, *Meditations*, and *Om* had all been recorded, but not yet released—*Ascension* was out that month—and most fans expected the Classic Quartet plus one. Instead, he came out with Rashied Ali and J. C. Moses on drums, Alice Coltrane on piano, Jimmy Garrison on bass, and on the front line Phar-oah Sanders, who brought a paper bag full of auxiliary percussion; Albert Ayler and his trumpeter brother, Don; and alto saxophonist Carlos Ward.

They played for forty minutes. Coltrane started "My Favorite Things," but this was just a point of departure. A man in a wheelchair drinking from a brown paper bag began a rhapsodic chant in concert with the rhythm section: "COL-trane, COL-trane, COL-trane." Coltrane began to move like a whirling dervish, then, toward the end of his set, chanted the Buddhist mantra "om mani padme hum."[14]

Critics were polarized. Dan Morgenstern called it "a chaotic, rambling, pointless 'happening,'" while a seventeen-year-old Gary Giddins left "in a state of confused elation" despite Philharmonic Hall having "the acoustic nuance of a gymnasium.[15]

Sonny never did come back out. That year Sonny scrawled in his notebook:

John Coltrane
John Coltrane
John Coltrane[16]

He also took down Coltrane's alternate saxophone fingerings.[17] Using these fingerings might be beneficial to producing that "belly sound," he wrote. That summer, while he was on tour in Tokyo, Coltrane called Sonny "a wonderful instrumentalist and musician."[18]

In March, Sonny flew back to England for the debut of *Alfie* and an engagement at Ronnie Scott's opposite Ernestine Anderson from March 14 to April 9, staying at the posh Royal Garden Hotel.[19] That past December, the club moved from its original location on Gerrard Street to the new Ronnie's at 47 Frith Street.[20] The new club could comfortably seat up to 150, had better air-conditioning, and could stay open until 3 a.m. It also honored Sonny—the swinging doors to the kitchen had half of Sonny etched on one side and half of him on the other.[21]

His sets were eclectic, with the material spanning Dvořák, Prokofiev, and "Polka Dots and Moonbeams," each often lasting more than thirty minutes. He also took inspiration from the streets. "There is a B concert blast from a foghorn, car horn or whatever heard often in the London streets," Sonny wrote. "Its equivalent for my horn is either C# on the staff or a lusty 'round toned' [high C# symbol]. If it is the latter it must not be a thin note."[22] The rotating rhythm section included pianists Stan Tracey and Gordon Beck, bassist Freddy Logan, and drummers Bill Eyden and apparently Louis Hayes, who was in London with the Oscar Peterson Trio.[23]

Sonny would play "for three and, if he felt like it, sometimes four sets a night, every night for a whole month," wrote Ronnie Scott's daughter, Rebecca Scott. "When the club closed at 3 a.m. and the punters had all gone home, Sonny would get back on the bandstand, with no rhythm section, and would play straight through until 5:30 a.m., or even later, never taking the saxophone from his mouth."[24]

On March 25, 1966, Sonny attended the gala premiere of *Alfie* at the Plaza Theatre; the American premiere wasn't until August.[25] The film was England's submission for the Cannes Film Festival, and went on to win the Special Jury Award, and the premiere was a major event, with Paul McCartney, George Harrison, Barbra Streisand (then starring in *Funny Girl* on the West End), and the *Alfie* cast all in attendance.[26] Sonny was photographed at the premiere with actress Edwina Carroll. Ronnie Scott and members of the *Alfie* band played live before the curtain as a kind of overture. A green light was supposed to cue "Alfie's Theme," and a red light would signal the end of the music. They played on cue, but due to technical difficulties with the screening, there was no red light, and they played for more than twenty minutes before the technicians could get everything in order to screen the film.[27]

Yet just as Sonny's fame reached a new peak, he decided to reconnect with the lifeblood of the music. He was never above a great hang, and they were going on every night at Kiane Zawadi's loft at 89 East Broadway, a cavernous fifth-floor walk-up. "It was a nice place to practice," Sonny recalled. "I used to practice up there late at night after I got off playing at a club." Zawadi's loft became the inspiration for the title track to Sonny's next album, *East Broadway Run Down*. "Actually it was an East Broadway walk-up."[28]

Sonny heard about the loft from Bennie Maupin.[29] "I was in touch with Sonny, and I told him that we were playing there sometimes," Maupin recalled. "I invited him over. 'You think it would be okay if, if I came by?' [Sonny said.] That humor, man. 'You think it would be okay with the guys if I came by?' I said, 'Sure, Sonny.' 'Are you sure?'"[30]

To make ends meet, Maupin took a job at Jewish Memorial Hospital taking care of research animals and played sessions at night.[31] Sonny had both his work and his home phone numbers, and they sometimes practiced together.[32] "I always managed to have an environment so that I could play," Maupin recalled, "but the loft was maybe the largest environment... and it would be so many people in there at one time."[33]

Kiane Zawadi's loft at 89 East Broadway was enormous—twenty-three by ninety-three feet—with a wooden floor and a few rugs.[34] Zawadi was born Bernard McKinney and grew up as part of the McKinney jazz dynasty in Detroit, playing trombone and then euphonium.[35] Zawadi moved to the loft in 1964 and began taking in young musicians, mostly from his native Detroit. When Maupin first moved to New York, he lived there for about eight months. The idea was "to have a little more freedom to practice and jam," Zawadi said. "There weren't too many people living down in that area, so it wasn't disturbing anybody."[36] Well, most of the time. "The only time we had problems," Maupin said, was "if it got real hot in the summertime. You can imagine the humidity on the fifth floor, it got pretty hot up there, and they would call the police, and the police basically said, 'Why don't you guys just close the window? We don't want to stop you from doing what you're doing.' They were pretty cool."[37]

For musicians at any stage of their career, the loft played a significant role. "I think it was like a perfect environment for us to do the kind of work that we needed to do," Maupin said. "To do that kind of lengthy practicing, to learn those tunes in an environment that was relatively okay. Sometimes the neighbors complained—sometimes. But it was there, and kept guys from being homeless. Some guys, they had no money, they had nowhere to stay, so you could kind of get your bearings and figure out how you're gonna do it. So I think that it served multiple purposes. Just being able to play whenever you want is a luxury, in New York especially."[38]

The loft was a raw space: some chairs, pallets, maybe a cot to sleep on, the sleep area separated by a fabric partition. And a piano. "We took a piano up there from the ground up," Maupin recalled. "We basically just moved the piano down through the streets, and when we got to the building, we carried it up the stairs. It took us a moment to get all the way up to the fifth floor." Sessions began on Friday afternoons and lasted until Monday morning. "You play as long as you want to and then find a corner, go to sleep. Get up, play some more... You just had to realize somebody was going to be practicing while you tried to sleep," Maupin said. "It may go on for a short time, it may go on all night."[39] It was Sonny's kind of place.

There was a toilet, but no shower or hot water, so they would bathe at the public showers down the block. The rent was low and the creativity was high. "The vibe of the times was good," Maupin recalled. "It was nothing in terms of what it cost. There were like five or six of us, maybe, staying in the loft. Everybody had to pay maybe fifteen, sixteen dollars. A lot of our friends—painters, and writers—we all hung out so when people came to the loft parties, that's who it was."[40]

To defray the cost of rent, Zawadi charged seventy-five cents for the semi-regular happenings that would attract an intimate crowd of up to forty spectators. Regulars got in free. "It was nothing too out," Zawadi said. "Danceable things most of the time and bebop charts.... We were in, not out." Most of the time, though, it was a musicians-only hang. "Every musician of any note who was an aspirant to be in this music at some point would come through 89 East Broadway, and just collectively take out their instruments and play whatever song was being played," recalled Charles Tolliver. "It was a great learning experience because you could sit and listen or walk around. It was a huge loft. It went from one end of East Broadway to the street behind.... This went on pretty much twenty-four/seven." As Maupin tells it, "We were more interested in playing the standard tunes that we knew, but maybe playing them a little bit differently. But there would be times when all we did was experiment. There are no recordings, because nobody had any recordings."[41]

In 1966, the Lower East Side was a bohemian heterotopia. "The whole of lower New York was just artistic—music, painting, writers," Tolliver said. He was living around the block at another loft on 18 Allen Street, where a young James Earl Jones lived across the street. "It was like what Paris was during the time of Ravel, Debussy, and all of the great French composers, and all of the great writers of the time.... New York had that artistic ebb and flow at the time."

East of the loft was a rabbinical college and the Beaux Arts headquarters of the *Jewish Daily Forward*, also the home of the Folksbiene Playhouse, a Yiddish theater company; west was Say Eng Look, one of the best Chinese restaurants in Chatham Square.[42] Artists found an affordable home and work space amid the multicultural aromas and daily commerce.[43]

The Manhattan Bridge hovered a stone's throw above the loft. The musicians who gathered there often played on the fire escape, harmonizing with the din of the passing trains. "It was loud," Maupin recalled. "But I was playing loud, so for me, it was like fun just to be out there sometimes, just working on the sound."[44] Under the Manhattan Bridge, Sonny would feel right at home.

News of the loft spread by word of mouth.[45] Once, saxophonist Wendell Harrison saw Thelonious Monk there. "Everybody that was anybody was at the loft," recalled Harrison. "Everybody was coming down to the loft and playing, and I mean major musicians and movie stars were coming down there, spending time. It was like a cultural hub."[46] David Garroway, the original host of NBC's *Today*, caught wind of it and brought a camera crew, but Zawadi put the kibosh on it. He wanted it to stay one of the best-kept secrets of the Lower East Side.

Zawadi would prepare vegetarian communal meals. "Oh man, did he cook," said Harrison. "Man, he was always cooking. Kiane was making bread, teaching people how to make bread, and teaching them how to critique and read, how to do research and what not...he was an intellectual like that. It was like college."[47]

And Sonny was a distinguished professor. "We knew all about Sonny. He was like our mentor. He was my idol," Harrison said. "We knew all of his tunes, all of his ideas. He would come around, and we were playing stuff back at him! 'Cause sometimes, he would come and just meditate. Kiane would say, 'Well, Sonny's on a speaking fast.'"[48]

The loft was also "like a referral service," said Harrison. "I got two major gigs by just me being there. They would call Kiane and say, 'What's happenin' with this tenor player?' And Kiane would say, 'Get on the phone, man! Somebody wants a tenor player.' So I got this gig with Grant Green just being there—Sun Ra—Hank Crawford...It gave us a foothold in New York and saved us a lot of money, and [gave us] a lot of camaraderie and community."

One of those phone calls to the loft would have resulted in catastrophe for saxophonist James Lockett, Harrison's stepbrother, had Sonny not been there. "He was on the roof of the loft practicing, and he had a phone call, and he left his horn on the roof and came down to answer the phone, and I guess he stayed on the phone for about five minutes, and he went up and his horn had disappeared. His horn was stolen," recalled Harrison. "And the next day Sonny heard about it and gave James a horn. He said, 'Don't worry about it!' He gave James a brand-new Selmer."[49]

Sonny embodied the spirit of 89 East Broadway. "Just Sonny being there created such an atmosphere of excitement," Maupin said. "There was one time that he came, and I think we must have played for about six or seven hours...and even when we weren't playing, he was! He was playing the hell out of the C Melody" saxophone, an early twentieth-century instrument that gradually fell out of favor; Sonny owned one. "That's what he brought with him. And Sonny's got the humor of humor, man. He was playing and he was walking around, but he was almost on his knees, just walking around with his cowboy hat and he had on some boots, and he was playing, physically sort of doing stuff. But what was coming out was seriously good. He hung with us for hours. The one time that I remember that happening, it was really great, 'cause a lot of guys did get to be on it. They happened to come by. He was just working. Sonny was *working*. In retrospect, I realized, wow, he was just working on his sound."[50]

The wide-ranging explorations that took place at 89 East Broadway—straight-ahead standards, bebop, and limitless free playing—inspired *East Broadway Run Down*.[51] On May 9, 1966, Sonny met Freddie Hubbard, Elvin Jones, and Jimmy Garrison at Van Gelder Studio to record the album. They had all played on John Coltrane's *Ascension*, which was released earlier that February.[52] But just like on *Our Man in Jazz*, in which Sonny used members of Ornette Coleman's band to take on the New Thing, *East Broadway Run Down* would still be a Sonny Rollins album through and through.

"When I got that offer, I almost passed out," recalled Hubbard. "By that time, I was very heavy into Coltrane—in fact, Sonny stopped a take, a good solo, too, my energy was up. He was right, though. He was trying to get me into his conception for the album. He already had Jimmy Garrison and Elvin Jones there, so he didn't want any trumpet coming in playing Coltrane." Similar to *A Night at the Village Vanguard*, there was "no rehearsal involved," recalled Jones. "Simply go into the studio and start playing."[53] Jones was free to expand beyond metronomic time, as Sonny, Hubbard said, had "mastered the time thing."[54]

The title track, the only tune with Hubbard, began as an eight-bar rhythmic vamp that morphed into a blues. "It seems to me," Hubbard said, "that Sonny plays different every time I hear him. He never stays in one thing. 'East Broadway Run Down' started as a blues, but soon, all three of us were moving out of the chords. It was beautiful, not having a piano, because that way we were not only freer harmonically but we were also not confined by the usual twelve-bar structure."[55] Jimmy Garrison pedals over the melody, then shifts to a walking bass line over the solo section. On his own solo, Garrison starts off playing the blues, but gradually begins to play chords, strumming the bass in the style of flamenco guitar. Jones plays a solo, building to a frenzy, then Garrison comes back in on a pedal. As Jimmy Garrison hangs on that one-note pulse, Sonny and Freddie embellish on the melody, spinning the harmony out in relation to the bass, the paragon of group cohesion in collective improvisation.

Then Sonny removes his mouthpiece, just as he had done on *Now's the Time*. The fire continues to build until it's just Jimmy Garrison strumming that elemental bass and Sonny playing wispy peals on the mouthpiece. Then they take it out. The band creates a texture, with a tactile striving for a total freedom of expression that remains necessarily just beyond reach. Over its twenty-minute run time, it seems to capture, by turns, eternity in a moment and a moment in eternity. It is the sound of Langston Hughes's dream deferred exploding.[56]

"Blessing in Disguise" repeats a two-bar riff—similar to Lionel Hampton's "Hey! Ba-Ba-Re-Bop"—over and over again. The group manages to embellish on the line and keep it dramatic for twelve minutes, but it doesn't end there—it simply fades out. "We Kiss in a Shadow" is Sonny's take on the fully orchestrated Rodgers and Hammerstein ballad from *The King and I*. In this stripped-down version, it feels totally free. Listening to the album feels like stepping inside an abstract expressionist painting, and the cover reflects it.[57]

Down Beat gave it a five-star review. It was a kind of virtuosity through restraint, and it had pathos. "Rollins' sense of dynamics, timing, phrasing, and satire would possibly stand him in better stead were he a public speaker," wrote Bill Quinn. "He probably would win public office, as did Ronald Reagan, on the basis of one speech—this LP."[58]

East Broadway Run Down would be Sonny's final LP for Impulse and his last commercial release until 1972. He had begun to feel "disillusionment with the record industry and the people around the record industry. I had a very bad experience with Impulse," he told Bert Vuijsje. "They put out records which I didn't want to be put out. In other words, I had an agreement with the company I was with before, that was RCA, that I would be involved in all the supervision and selecting of the tapes to be used and this and that...it's the only kind of situation which you should have—any artist should really have....In all fairness to Bob Thiele, I must admit that I was a little difficult to handle at that period....I might be late for a record date, or be supposed to call him and talk to him about something and wouldn't call him....But I still felt that he had the ultimate power of putting out a piece of work by me which would be out forever, and that it was up to him to cater to me to whatever degree." *Alfie*, Sonny said, he was "more or less satisfied with, although not completely." On the others, "we should have gone through more, and I wanted to do more. And he said no."[59]

Sonny told Eric Nisenson that it was mostly the legal team at ABC-Paramount, the parent organization of Impulse. "It turned out that they were a rough group of people, and they really screwed me out of stuff," Sonny said. "Not only that, the way they did it—these guys were really just thugs. Their lawyers were really tough. I never had any problems with Bob Thiele. Bob was a very accommodating fellow....I was kind of naïve and I didn't have anybody representing me at the time when I was doing contracts and working out a royalty agreement and all that kind of thing. I really got used."[60]

ABC was reluctant to get behind *East Broadway Run Down*. "They said, 'Gee, Sonny, we can't sell this record,'" Sonny told Bob Belden. "As most musicians are, I was at the mercy of these unscrupulous agents. So, I just got away from the business world for a while."[61]

The Impulse records "hurt me a lot. I mean, they really shouldn't have been put out," Sonny later told Randi Hultin. "In my history, nothing really works out as it's supposed to," appreciable irony for the improviser par excellence.[62]

As Sonny's disillusionment grew, he just went deeper into the woodshed. "I used to drive and play," Sonny later recalled. "I'd be driving with one hand and holding my neck and my mouthpiece with the other, mainly holding out extended tones, which is good for your embouchure....Like a guy once said, 'I never want to *not* be practicing. I want to be there when the angel comes and gives me the message.'"[63]

When possible, his woodshed was in the woods. This one was in Alpine, New Jersey, on the side of the Palisades Parkway in a wooded area overlooking the Hudson River and the New York skyline—an area called the Alpine Lookout only a five-minute drive from Van Gelder. There, the only sounds were the birds and insects, the far-off thrum of passing traffic on the parkway, and the occasional plane overhead. Sonny usually drove there early in the morning, before dawn, when there were almost no human noises.

"I went there to practice," Sonny recalled. "See, that's the constant in my life—practicing. It's always about that in one way or another. Driving up the Palisades Parkway, there's an overlook...where you can park your car and walk down along the palisades there....One time, I said, 'Hey man, let's see.' I parked my car...and then I'd walk there. There's a spot I found there that was great, and then I'd go there and practice."[64]

Occasionally, police would check to see who was out in the woods with a saxophone, sometimes in the middle of the night. "I don't think there was an ordinance against it," Sonny said, "so they never bothered me, but they might have waited for me till I came up." In 1967, when filmmaker Dick Fontaine was directing his documentary "Who Is Sonny Rollins?," his camera captured footage of Sonny playing there. Fontaine also interviewed one of the officers who heard the unusual sound on his typically quiet beat. "One morning, about, oh, 5:30 in the morning," the officer said, "I was pulling into this area here, the Alpine Lookout, and saw the car parked and got out, started to walk, and all of a sudden I heard this music in the distance. The only thing you have out here is Mother Nature at that time. Nobody else. Something to see at 5:30 up here."[65]

After Sonny found this sylvan practice space, he began taking musicians out there with him, everyone from his good friend saxophonist Charlie Wyatt to a group of teenagers he met while they were practicing on the Brooklyn Bridge.[66] Once, he and Eddie Daniels played "Airegin" in a duo with the trees.[67] He would take Grachan Moncur to the Palisades, "like one step from falling two thousand feet below," Moncur recalled. "We wouldn't practice tunes. We'd be matching our sounds—just sound. Sounds!"[68]

Bennie Maupin went a number of times. "Sometimes he would call me and come and pick me up, and we would go and practice over in New Jersey," Maupin recalled. "He would want to practice at night.... Then he would take me back home, 'cause I had to go to work in the morning."[69]

One night, Sonny pulled up in front of Sonny Simmons's East Village apartment at 4 a.m.[70] "He blew his horn and got out of the car... 'Simmons!!!' You could hear him all the way to Brooklyn." Simmons got dressed, grabbed his alto, and ambled downstairs. "He took me all the way across the George Washington Bridge into the New Jersey forest. I was wondering what we were doing out here in the woods, and I reflected upon the days when he used to practice on the Bridge." At noon, they were still blowing. " 'Newk, when we gonna eat, man?' " Simmons asked. No response. He asked again later, but Sonny just kept on playing, "from 5 a.m. in the morning to 5 p.m. that night in the Englewood Cliffs forest, looking out at the Hudson." When Sonny drove him back to the East Village, "he gave me a hundred-dollar bill. I couldn't believe it, but boy did I need it."[71]

Soon thereafter, Rollins paid Simmons another 4 a.m. visit. This time, they went to Sonny's Brooklyn apartment on Willoughby Walk, where, laid across the bed, there were five "brand-new saxophones companies had given him." The phone kept ringing, but Sonny didn't answer. He made an exception for Coltrane—they talked for hours while Simmons practiced in Sonny and Lucille's bedroom. Freddie Hubbard and Larry Ridley knocked on the door, but Sonny just kept on blowing.[72] "My wife kept calling. He would let me talk to her, but nobody else.... After the third day, I said, 'This cat done kidnapped me!' " Finally, Simmons's wife showed up at the door. Sonny let her in, put some vegetables in the blender, and the three of them drank. Before Simmons and his wife left, "He gave me one of them brand-new saxophones."

In mid-May, after the *East Broadway Run Down* recording session, Sonny brought bassist Larry Ridley and drummer Freddie Waits to Baltimore to play at the Jazz Society for Performing Artists' Monday-night concert series at Forest Manor.[73] Due to a scheduling mix-up, Sonny was booked the previous week but didn't show for the packed house, and when the right date finally came, an overflow crowd arrived. One medley lasted forty-eight minutes—the *Down Beat* reviewer timed it—and after the first set, he received a standing ovation.[74]

"Sonny said to me, 'Larry, you remember when we played Baltimore, man?'" Ridley recalled. "'We could have been like the Pied Piper and led the people into the streets and they would have followed us, man!' I said, 'All right, Newk, you've got that right,' 'cause when he gets that calypsonian rhythm thing that he does, man, his use of syncopation and that West Indian kind of lope that he would do, where he would be building solos, man, people would be screaming."[75]

From June 7 to 26, Sonny returned to the Vanguard, playing opposite the Thelonious Monk Quartet. Sonny hired Freddie Waits, Walter Booker, and Mike Melillo for the three-week run.[76] It was probably then that Sonny met teenage saxophonist David S. Ware, taking him home after finishing at the Vanguard to teach him how to circular breathe.[77] "I was sixteen years old, man, you know, that was a big deal for me," Ware said.[78]

That July, Sonny mourned two painful deaths. On July 11, Sonny's friend Ahmad Basheer, a former roommate of Charlie Parker and Ted Joans who came from St. Louis, suffered a cerebral hemorrhage and died on his thirty-eighth birthday.[79] Sonny and Yusef Lateef both attended the funeral.[80] Lucille described Basheer in a note as exemplifying the defiant path Sonny had come to symbolize: "a big, dark, bear of a man who passed thru. He was a kind man in an unkind world, a gentle man in a violent world, a peaceful man in a warring world, a soft-spoken man in a hard-sell world, a trusting man in a deceitful world, and a loving man in a hating world." He was there when Sonny needed him, a rare friend he could confide in. "The world, who didn't know him, or wouldn't have appreciated him—is only the worse for his loss." To Sonny, "Everybody loved Basheer . . . He was almost like a saint."[81]

Then on July 31, 1966, Bud Powell died.[82]

Sonny had another reminder of his mortality when his dental problems began to flare up again. In the first week of August, he was booked at Lennie's in Boston, but he had to cancel.[83] Sonny had started going to Dr. Stanley Earl Nelson, a prominent fifty-year-old reconstructive dentistry expert who specialized in dental prosthetics and was one of the first black dentists to open a practice in midtown Manhattan—probably the first.[84] His office at 30 Central Park South overlooked the Plaza Hotel. Dr. Nelson was a civil rights activist who sought to integrate the profession.[85] He was also a serious jazz fan whose patients included Charles Mingus, Ben Webster, Cannonball Adderley, and Joe Williams. "Stanley was very accomplished," Sonny said. "Unfortunately, having to play a wind instrument and having a lot of dental problems was a bad choice that I made. I didn't know that originally. I might have taken better care of my teeth."[86] Incidentally, Sonny's general practitioner, Earl Shaw, was an African American doctor and amateur guitarist who had an office in the same building.[87]

Dr. Nelson found some new shadows in his dental X-rays, news that could send any saxophonist into a state of despair.[88] Sonny continued doing isometric exercises to improve his jaw strength, but this problem required surgery.[89] Bennie Maupin bore witness to Sonny's ongoing dental troubles. "He had a difficult period with his teeth, and during that time I saw him quite a bit," Maupin said. "He wasn't really able to do what he wanted to do. . . . [B]ack then, dental surgery was a real crapshoot. They were just starting to develop implants. . . . He's so diligent about working on the sound. He was always very concerned about what the sound was like. But the thing with the teeth is that you can't feel anything. You can't feel."[90]

That August, Sonny was voted second in the tenor category in the *Down Beat* International Jazz Critics Poll, with John Coltrane in first and Stan Getz in third place. Sonny was sidelined until he recovered from dental surgery. From October 9 through 20, he was booked at the Vanguard with his quartet, opposite Bill Evans.[91] On October 25, he was back at the Vanguard, opposite Pete La Roca's quartet, and to take some pressure off his teeth, Sonny brought Eddie Daniels and Bennie Maupin, who were also friends with each other.[92]

"We played one night," recalled Maupin. "Sonny just put us through our paces, played a bunch of tunes, a bunch of tempos, and it was just one of those incredible times, but because he was having problems with the teeth, we played that one night, and then the next night he didn't come. So Max Gordon, the owner, was going crazy. But Sonny was telling him, 'Max, I just really don't feel well,' 'cause he talked to him on the phone. He said, 'I'm going through this thing with my teeth.' So Eddie and I played the second night, and by then, people were trying to figure out who are these guys? Max is refunding money, and it got real deep. So he fired us."[93]

Another reason Sonny couldn't make the Vanguard was that he was called to deputize for John Coltrane on a European tour, and he had to rest his chops.[94] Coltrane had canceled his appearance at the 1966 Berlin Jazz Days due to his own health problems. No one knew, but Coltrane was suffering from liver cancer.[95] Alice Coltrane was also pregnant with their son Oran, who would be born on March 19, 1967, and it's likely she may not have been able to fly under doctor's orders. After Coltrane returned from his Japan tour that summer, he only took gigs within driving distance.[96] Alice herself canceled her appearance due to "impending motherhood."[97] So the Max Roach Quintet was booked as a replacement, with Sonny enlisted to make up for the absence of Coltrane.

The Roach Quintet—Freddie Hubbard on trumpet, James Spaulding on alto saxophone and flute, Ronnie Mathews on piano, and Jymie Merritt on bass, all of whom played on Roach's recently released *Drums Unlimited*—was already scheduled to play George Wein's Newport Jazz Festival in Europe, so it was an easy substitution. The quintet would play part of the set, and Sonny would play the last twenty minutes in a trio with Roach and Merritt.[98] Sonny's reunion with Max—their first major appearance together in nearly a decade—would be one of the main attractions.

Sonny and Lucille first flew to Paris. He sat next to James Spaulding on the plane. "I was nervous in a way, because he had so much under his spiritual cap, he was so skillful with his rhythms, and he drew from so many things going all the way back," Spaulding recalled. "He had the history of the music inside his playing." They barely spoke, but Spaulding, seven years younger, picked up a lot by osmosis. "He said everything he wanted to say through the horn," Spaulding said. "He spoke through his instrument—very clearly."[99]

At the end of October, Sonny met journalist François Postif in his hotel room with Lucille for a laid-back interview, with Sonny lying on the bed eating an apple. Postif began by asking whether Sonny perceived any significant shift in his critical reception since the "Angry Young Tenor" days. To Sonny, the audience's perspective was beyond him. "People don't judge my music the same as I do," he said. "Some evenings, I am aware of having played well and the audience is wooden while other evenings, for me, I am frankly bad, and the audience gives a standing ovation. For this reason, I do not know at all where I am with the public, their reactions being sometimes diametrically opposed to mine."[100]

As for his records, he felt similarly disconnected. "These are just moments in my life and, in general, unsatisfying moments," he said. The only record he liked, he said, was *The Standard Sonny Rollins*. This surprised Postif—that Sonny would prefer himself playing standards over his own compositions—but to Sonny, that posed more of a challenge. "It's not the composition that's important in jazz, it's the treatment you give it," he explained. Given enough time to develop his treatment of standards, "they become mine; it is exactly as if I had composed them."[101] Was Sonny a perfectionist? "If this word means someone with a constant search for perfection, then I am a perfectionist," Sonny said. "But I would like to add that everything I do...is far from perfect!" Yoga tempered the worst aspects of his perfectionist tendencies. It allowed him to acknowledge that he was "generally doing my best....I think you have put your finger on one of the main characteristics of my personality: this thirst to do better. But...you cannot spend your life constantly regretting what you have just done. Life is meant to move forward, not to always be looking backwards."[102]

It had been seven years since Postif last interviewed Sonny—not long before his Bridge sabbatical—and he wanted to know if Sonny felt he had made any progress toward his goals. "Honestly, I got older and, in a man's life, seven years is huge," Sonny said. "During these seven years, I have reflected a lot and experimented with a lot of new things; in short, I learned a lot. What matters is experience, and, you see, I think my music is a lot more mature than it was seven years ago. The word 'maturity' perfectly expresses the parallel that exists between my music and my experience. Don't get me wrong, just because I'm seven years older doesn't mean my music is better, or more advanced. But I believe that, quite naturally and without my being able to do anything about it, my experience has carried over in one way or another into my music."[103]

Was Sonny lonely? "Yes, on reflection, I feel alone, very alone even," he said. "But I don't make it complex; loneliness is the lot of all of us, and who has not felt alone at least once in their life?"[104] The tour would show just how mature Sonny had become.

There were moments of levity to temper the strain of successive one-nighters, mostly in a different country every night, but there was tension on the tour from the start. Stan Getz and Astrud Gilberto agreed to the tour despite a conflict between Getz's second wife, Monica Silfverskiöld, who was also his manager, and Gilberto, who had an affair with Getz after making *Getz/Gilberto*. Separately, Freddie Hubbard was his combustible self.[105] On November 5, they played the four-day Berlin Jazz Days.[106] They performed at the Berlin Sportpalast, and the audience was ecstatic, boosted by four hundred British jazz fans who flew over on chartered planes as part of what they called the "Jazz Trip of the Year."

After the Roach Quintet played, the crowd could barely contain themselves. When Sonny entered, they erupted, hooting and hollering. Sonny was in good spirits following a fifteen-minute workout on "There Will Never Be Another You." It sounded like Max had four hands. "Beautiful, Max, beautiful—thanks," Sonny said from the stage.[107]

On November 6, the Roach Quintet and Sonny performed at Reading University in Reading, England, as part of the *Jazz Goes to College* television series hosted by trumpeter Humphrey Lyttelton: Roach's British debut. They played for nearly thirty continuous minutes. Tubby Hayes, Ronnie Scott, Keith Christie, and others took the train out from London for the event.[108] On November 8, they played in Rotterdam at the twenty-two-hundred-seat De Doelen concert hall on a bill with the Albert Ayler Quintet.[109] They then played in Oslo and, on November 10, at the Konserthuset in Stockholm. The Roach Quintet played "For B.P.," Hubbard's composition for the recently departed Bud Powell, and "Nommo," Jymie Merritt's composition in 7/4 time.[110] For twenty minutes, Sonny, Roach, and Merritt ripped through "There Will Never Be Another You."[111]

On November 12, they flew from Copenhagen to Vienna, where they would be bused to Graz. "I met them on a November morning in fog-bound Copenhagen airport awaiting a delayed flight to Vienna and it went downhill from there," wrote tour manager Joe Boyd, then twenty-four. "Everyone else was on their way to Paris for a concert or a day off. The young guys in Max's group—Freddie Hubbard, James Spaulding, and Ronnie [Mathews]—were disgruntled: everyone had a girl in Paris or knew where to find one. Their day off that week had been in Oslo." To raise their spirits, they passed around a bottle of duty-free Scotch while they waited; Max and Sonny stayed sober. "The three of them were drunk by noon in the airport and snoring on the plane to Vienna," wrote Boyd.[112]

In Vienna, they boarded a bus that would take them two hours south to Graz. The Austrian promoter left a case of beer on the bus, which, Boyd wrote, "they eagerly attacked. Nondrinkers Sonny and Max sat up front ignoring the storm brewing in the rear. First it was the Beatles, who had 'ripped off black culture and made a fortune,' then George Wein, 'the Jew who was sending us off to play for a bunch of Nazis' (Freddie had read that Hitler came from Graz)." As Spaulding tells it, "Freddie became paranoid on the bus from the airport to the concert hall. We fell asleep, we woke up, had to get dressed, 'cause we were late getting to the concert hall. We had to dress, we had to change clothes. Max, you know, he liked to perform in tuxedos and bow ties. . . . The only thing we had was drinking some Scotch we had going down there. I don't remember having any stimuli. We just had some Johnny Walker Red. We were just sipping on that. We didn't get drunk or nothing."[113]

The concert was at the Stefaniesaal, a twenty-four-hundred-seat concert hall in Graz built in 1885. "When we arrived at the beautiful opera house," wrote Boyd, "the crowd was calmly seated, dressed very formally and glancing at their watches: the three musicians were raving and out of control." As Spaulding recalled, Hubbard was fulminating against the audience before he even took the stage. "It wasn't the crowd," Spaulding said. "In fact, they were quite attentive. They wanted to hear what Freddie had to say, and they weren't very nice things that he spoke of."

"Damn, I don't see no soul whatsoever!" Hubbard said. "There's one, there's one." Jymie Merritt played the bass line to "Nommo," his composition named for the Dogon teacher figures.[114] On Hubbard's cadenza, he began to play higher and higher, staggering across the stage.[115] Finally, laughter rang out from the crowd, and some boos. "Jive motherfuckers," said Hubbard, softly at first. He continued his cadenza, blasting a note into the rear of the auditorium. The crowd began to hoot and holler. "Fuck you white mother-fuckers. Fuck you white motherfuckers!" Some people in the crowd laughed.

"Go home!" called someone from the audience.

"Well, okay, I'll go home. If you don't like me, kiss my ass!"

The audience chortled, like some kind of dystopian laugh track. "Go away!" said someone from the crowd.

"That's right. 'Cause you jive. You jive! You jive! You white motherfuckers! You the ones who started this shit! Let me tell you. You the one. . . . Fuck you! Fuck you! You jive white motherfuckers! If you don't like me, kiss my black ass! You motherfuckers! Fuck it! I don't care!"[116]

Merritt, who was still sober, resumed the bass line to take it out. Mean-while, there was drama brewing backstage. "I had to talk fast to convince the promoter not to stop the concert, refund the tickets and have the three of them arrested by the fierce-looking police who had suddenly appeared," recalled Boyd. "Having negotiated a five-minute reprieve, I signaled Max to play a stage-clearing drum solo."

Roach unleashed a fusillade on the snare drum, and the crowd applauded. Five minutes later, Sonny took the stage, flanked by Roach and Merritt.[117] The concert proceeded as though nothing had happened. Sonny played "Love Walked In," "Lover," and "Poinciana." Though Hubbard's outburst meant they would forfeit half the fee, it also extended Sonny's set, and Sonny was on that night.

As the concert continued without incident, wrote Boyd, "one of the ine-briated trio started throwing furniture out of the window of the locked dress-ing room."[118]

Spaulding hoped to hear Sonny from the wings, but, he said, "before I could get out to see Sonny play, they had already arrested Freddie and put him in handcuffs, and then I was in the dressing room still, and I was trying to open the door, and I kicked the door and the door flew open and it was one of the German security, and they came in and smacked me across the face and knocked me to the floor, put handcuffs on me, and twisted handcuffs on my wrist, so I thought that my wrist was gonna break. They snatched me out of there with Freddie, put us in a Graz paddy wagon, took us to the jailhouse, and put us in some jail cells. It was a nightmare for us."[119] The trauma would stay with Spaulding forever. "Every time I think about...it's implanted in my brain," he said. "I can still see it. I can still look at it."

That night, Boyd wrote, "Max, Sonny and I cruised Graz in a taxi until 2 a.m. trying to find out where they were being held. I would go into police stations and say 'Schwarzers?' and get a shake of the head until we finally found them in the medieval castle that overlooks the city. Early the next morning, I sprang them with a three hundred dollar fine for violating an Austrian statute against 'insulting the public' and we headed for the airport and Paris. They were exhausted and Freddie's wrist was swollen from the cuffs. Someone asked him whether it had been worth it. 'No, man,' he said. 'But almost.'"[120]

After the incident, they continued with the tour, but Spaulding and Hubbard, who had come up together in Indianapolis, were not on good terms. "We didn't speak to each other until we got back to New York," Spaulding said.[121]

———◄○►———

After the tour ended in Paris, Sonny met the great existentialist philosopher Jean-Paul Sartre. Sonny was booked that December for a week at the basement club Jazzland, where he reunited with his childhood friend Art Taylor and bassist Gilbert Rovère, the trio he used the previous year.[122] Sonny had hoped to use a pianist, and he called René Urtreger, whom he had met at the Club Saint-Germain in 1959. Yet since Sonny had last seen him, Urtreger had become a heroin addict. Urtreger told Sonny he could do it, and he was advertised on the bill, but he didn't show up for the rehearsal or at the gig.[123]

Sonny called again and insisted that Urtreger come to his hotel room.

Much to his surprise, Sonny gave him some cash, and said, "'Take care of yourself, go see doctors. I mean, get out of that shit,'" Urtreger recalled. "He told me that he had already gone through exactly the same thing that I did." Urtreger never forgot the kindness Sonny showed him in this rock-bottom moment. It took a long time, but in 1977, Urtreger finally got completely sober. "He changed my life, really."[124]

At Jazzland, critic and filmmaker Michel Contat brought Jean-Paul Sartre and his wife, Arlette Elkaïm, to hear Sonny at Jazzland. "Jazz is like bananas—it must be consumed on the spot," Sartre wrote in 1947 of a night out at the stalwart jazz club Nick's in Greenwich Village.[125] It had apparently been years since Sartre, who was then sixty-one, had set foot in a jazz club.

"We were seated comfortably, but far from the exit," wrote Contat. "Sartre had to make a call, but he couldn't cross the small room while Rollins was playing, that would have been disrespectful. [Sartre] was getting a little impatient; Rollins couldn't find what he was looking for."[126] After the show, photographer Thierry Trombert shot a photo of the two giants. It made the cover of the January 1967 issue of *Jazz Hot*.[127]

As for what Sonny and Sartre discussed, it was not easy to surpass the language barrier. "I'm sorry we didn't get into any deep philosophical conversations," Sonny later said. "I think he liked the music."[128]

Chapter 29

WHO IS SONNY ROLLINS?

(1967)

In 1967, many were predicting the end of jazz. What was killing jazz—this time—was a profusion of rock that brought Jimi Hendrix's "Purple Haze," the Monkees' "I'm a Believer," Aretha Franklin's "Respect," Jefferson Airplane's "Somebody to Love," and James Brown's "Cold Sweat" onto the airwaves all at once. Janis Joplin headlined the Monterey Jazz Festival in the worst financial year in the festival's history, while the George Wein–produced Pittsburgh Jazz Festival was canceled altogether. "But the times, they have changed," lamented Nat Hentoff in "Will Rock 'n' Roll Take over from Jazz?"—a 1967 *New York Times* feature. "*Down Beat* now covers the pop scene. *Jazz* magazine has become *Jazz & Pop*."[1] Drummer Shelly Manne was irate when he heard that the annual *Playboy* jazz poll was becoming a jazz and pop poll. "If the public is confused into thinking commercial pop and pure jazz are all one and the same," Manne said, "then the great creativity of the jazz artist will be smothered, because people are letting dollar signs obscure their vision."[2]

Sonny commiserated with the notion that a smaller pie could mean more competition than solidarity. "That period might have been one of jazz being not accepted or popular," Sonny recalled. "Maybe that was true to some extent…there was no direction, there was no camaraderie, among the musicians."[3] In 1967, he would find that sense of camaraderie in unlikely places.

To many in the jazz world, the issue was less one of market share than definability. "After 50 years of false alarms," wrote Leonard Feather, "it seems that in a sense the Cassandra call may at last have some basis of truth." Even Cannonball Adderley claimed that "the jazz we knew and loved in the 1930s, '40s, '50s—yes even in the early '60s—is gone. The audience for it is gradually fading away." Considering Louis Armstrong's oft-repeated remark that "If you have to ask what jazz is, you'll never know," even those who had never felt the need before were suddenly asking—"Okay, but is it jazz?"

Jazz, to the arbiters of tradition, was having a genre problem. Richard Goldstein, who famously panned *Sgt. Pepper's Lonely Hearts Club Band* that summer, gleefully imagined the newly released "Light My Fire" as modern-day scat singing and a future cover of "Hello, Dolly!" "slashed and siphoned through the cool keyboard of a Moog synthesizer." Even within its own ranks, jazz seemed irredeemably divided to some that year, with fault lines drawn between the avant-garde and the traditionalists. The Art Ensemble of Chicago was coalescing, and AACM cofounder Muhal Richard Abrams released *Levels and Degrees of Light*, his first album as a leader; Miles Davis was moving in a more experimental direction with *Sorcerer*; on the more traditional side were Louis Armstrong's "What a Wonderful World" and Ella Fitzgerald's second Christmas album. Frank Sinatra defected alto-gether with "Somethin' Stupid," a *Billboard* number one hit that year. "Jazz has been hag-ridden for years with silly ideological splits," wrote Ralph J. Gleason that January. "Semantic hassles about 'Chicago style' and 'New Orleans style,' 'West Coast jazz' and 'East Coast jazz,' 'funk and soul' and 'bebop' and 'mainstream' and 'Third Stream' and all the rest."[4] Gleason's solution: shoring up the genre with what he referred to as "bargain basement packages" highlighting jazz classics advertised on late-night radio.

In response to this capitalist agenda, Archie Shepp wrote in "Black Power and Black Jazz" that the spirit of protest that galvanized Sonny's *Freedom Suite* was all that mattered. To Shepp, those pointing a finger at the revolutionary avant-garde as the purveyors of "angry" music, albeit justifiably angry, and thereby ruining the commercial viability of jazz, needed to listen beyond the cash register. "It does not proscribe on the basis of color," wrote Shepp of the music made by Bird, Sonny Rollins, Miles Davis, Cecil Taylor, and Ornette Coleman. "Its only prerequisites are honesty and an open mind. The breadth of this statement is as vast as America, its theme the din of the streets, its motive freedom." Yet commercial-minded jazz impresarios also had a similar thought—the answer to resuscitating jazz lay outside American borders. "For American jazz fans, 1967 is the Year of the Pessimist," wrote Bruce Cook. "Jazz—which many call America's sole indigenous contribution to western culture—is getting to be a scarce commodity in the land where it was born."[5]

Sonny was becoming increasingly jaded and was unsigned to any record label, having left Impulse after *East Broadway Run Down*, finding the whole process "pretty mercenary."[6] "I was disillusioned with the record business and I was very disturbed by all the social turmoil of that time," Sonny recalled. "The injustice of it all bothered me then, and still bothers me now. Every-thing is still the same—really, we haven't gone anywhere. We have the same type of people leading the country, and the same type of shit that was going on then is going on now. As a musician and an artist it bothered me. Every time someone looked at me like I was an animal instead of a human because I was black. It could be then, it could be now. The same thing happens. That was the climate of this country, and it still is."[7]

In Japan, jazz was still big business, and they treated African Americans with a sense of dignity—if they could get in. That January, Sonny had a twenty-six-date tour across Japan planned alongside Art Blakey and the Jazz Messengers.[8] That past November, on a "Drum Battle" tour of the country produced by George Wein with Elvin Jones, Tony Williams, and Art Blakey, Williams and Jones were arrested on narcotics charges. In response, Japanese immigration officials held visa applications up to higher scrutiny, and a process that ordinarily took about a week suddenly took two months. On December 29, all tour visas for Sonny's band were denied due to the mere possibility of narcotics use, and the tour was summarily canceled.[9] The New Japan Booking Corp., which was coproducing the tour with Wein, sustained a $30,000 loss.[10]

Sonny's first reported gig that year was on March 27, when he followed Eddie "Lockjaw" Davis into Ronnie Scott's in London for four weeks. When he swung into Swinging London, Sonny had grown out his sideburns well below the ear. Touring as a single, Sonny's rhythm section was the stalwart pianist Stan Tracey, bassist Dave Green, and drummer Tony Oxley, with Ronnie Scott himself sometimes sitting in.[11] Sonny was staying at the Strand Palace Hotel, not far from Ronnie's on Frith Street. After he finished in the middle of the night, he would walk home, spread some newspapers on the floor of his room, and have his daily yoga session. Sonny was always practicing, whether the saxophone or yoga. These early-morning asanas would "usually go on long enough for him to catch the dawn," wrote Bob Houston, who interviewed Sonny for *Melody Maker* during his run at Ronnie's, "and he loves the grey, indeterminate dawns we have in London."[12]

Sonny knew Tracey well, but he had never played with Dave Green or Tony Oxley. Green had just turned twenty-five; he was a childhood friend of drummer Charlie Watts, and cut his teeth with trumpeter Humphrey Lyttelton, Buck Clayton, and Big Joe Turner. Oxley was twenty-eight and had a distinctly more avant-garde approach; he came up with bassist Gavin Bryars and guitarist Derek Bailey in the trio Joseph Holbrooke and would go on to work with Cecil Taylor for decades.[13]

Green first encountered Sonny as a fan at Ronnie Scott's. "I was sitting in the front row on the side, and he was playing, and I don't know how he did it, but he arched his back way over and he's kind of playing the horn virtually into my face, but upside down," Green recalled of Sonny's yogic performing stance. "It was the most amazing experience."[14]

When Ronnie Scott called Green and offered him a month with Sonny, Green was elated, but intimidated.[15] "I was overawed, really," said Green. "I got on great with Roland [Kirk], I had a ball with him and Ben [Webster], but Sonny—Sonny is another level." Green would come to think of it as "forever one of the high spots of my life."

Oxley had played with Johnny Griffin and Charlie Mariano, but having seen Sonny at Ronnie's before, he seconded Green's sentiments.[16] On the set breaks, Sonny kept playing continuously; fans followed him down the stairs past the basement bar to the greenroom, where they stood outside and listened. At the end of the break, he walked back up the stairs playing and marched onto the bandstand. "He never stopped playing—all the time—five hours, which I thought was tremendous!" Oxley recalled. "I thought, now there's the lesson for me to learn about how you're supposed to approach the tunes—the freedom. . . . He never hardly spoke, he didn't really say much at all, but you could learn by listening to him."

Stan was used to Sonny's unpredictability at this point, but the gig would be a challenge for Green and Oxley. Sonny would play a half hour without interruption, then play a cadenza, then play a half hour more. On opening night, Sonny was spurred on by the presence of Eddie "Lockjaw" Davis and Ben Webster, though it seems they did not sit in.[17] "We knew the language, but we were quite used to playing a tune from beginning to end," Oxley said. "I haven't got the harmony to worry about, but he'd be playing two bars of one tune, free for a little while, and one bar of another, three bars of another, and freedom in between. With bass and piano, they were trying to deal with the harmony. . . . It was right up my street, because my playing is called 'free,' which is not free . . . it's very demanding. . . . You don't do this as a formula, you do this as a way of life."[18]

Standards were a springboard into the unconscious—"Love Walked In," "Bye Bye Blackbird" with Ronnie Scott, "It Could Happen to You," "My Reverie," "The Night Has a Thousand Eyes," or the lesser-known "True Love."[19] "When I change songs during a set, I'm not doing it for effect," Sonny said. "I'm doing it to maintain interest. If we play a song and it's not getting over or the guys begin to lose interest, rather than bore the audience I'll try another song to keep the mood going." The band's willingness to play straight-ahead or out complemented Sonny's approach of planting one foot firmly in each. "It's a very fine line which separates playing changes and not playing changes," Sonny said. "I have been brought up to play chords, but I can deviate from them, but it's not haphazard."[20]

Sonny took the trepidation of his rhythm section at Ronnie's and worked with it. "Although I felt kind of in a way inadequate for the gig," Green said, "he never made me feel that way." If Sonny sensed that someone in the band was feeling it that night, he let them take it. "Yeah, go ahead, man!" he said to Ronnie on the stand. And he got to know them and their families off the bandstand. "I was still living at home with my mom," Green said, "and I went to do some shopping for my mom at the local shops, and when I came back, my mom said, 'Oh, Mr. Rollins rang for you.' And I went, 'What? What did he say???' She said, 'Oh, he was very nice.... We spoke for an hour.'"

A call from Sonny could be as long as his solos. "He did ring me up one night after the club, which used to finish at half past 3," recalled Oxley. "I got home to my flat, and the phone went, and it's about half past 4 in the morning. And he wanted to talk. I felt, 'Bloody hell. We only finished playing five hours.' And we talked and talked, and we talked about concepts, time, all sorts of things like that. Very inspiring."

Yet Sonny was contemplating another break, not only from recording, but also from performing. "I don't know how classical artists are treated, but I do feel that in jazz the attitude is simply that an artist goes into a club and does business or he doesn't do business," Sonny told Bob Houston. "And if you don't do business, everybody in the club starts giving you funny looks.... I've had arguments about this, but for me, you don't have to starve to be a great jazzman."[21]

A few days later at Liverpool University, Sonny "was in one of his strange moods," recalled Ronnie Scott, "and he just never played anything. He'd start a snatch of something, and the guys would catch on and start to play; as soon as they did, he'd drift into something else—fragments. And really after half an hour it just got boring—very weird. People slow handclapped, walked out, all sorts of things. Eventually he said, 'Play with me,' so the two of us had to kind of play something more or less understandable, because there were two of us."[22]

The next night at the Club 43 in Manchester, Sonny was feeling it. Fans were queuing up before sunset. At 9:50, Sonny took the stage, with a standing-room-only crowd. It was nearly ninety degrees and humid in the club, but no one left until the last note was wrung out at 2:30 that morning. "It was *incredible*, absolutely incredible," said Ronnie Scott. "About the best music I've ever heard."[23] The British tour culminated at the Nottingham Playhouse on Sunday, April 30, when Sonny played a concert billed as "The Giants" on a double bill with Ben Webster. Sonny played with Tracey, Green, and Oxley; Webster played with the Johnny Patrick Trio with Jackie Dougan and Kenny Baldock.[24]

"I remember, we were in the band room, and Sonny was saying, 'Oh, Dave, this is a special gig, man. We're playing opposite Ben,'" Green recalled. "He was really kind of, I wouldn't say nervous, but he was really conscientiously saying, 'It's a really big night, man.' He was honored to be playing opposite Ben Webster. And that's the thing about Sonny. He's such a humble human being. He has that heritage. His respect for those guys knows no bounds. That comes out in his whole attitude about music—it's a complete line which you can hear in Sonny's playing, directly from Hawkins, Ben, and those guys. That love is there. And that came out that night at the Playhouse. He was really determined to make that a special one, and it was a very special evening."[25]

Green learned a lot on that brief tour. "He did give me something quite specific, which I really valued," Green said. "I must have asked him, in my youthful way, if everything was okay. And he said to me, 'When you're playing four—four in the bar—emphasize two and four.' . . . That's what he did. And of course, that's so important." But the greatest lesson was how to listen closely. "There was one occasion at Ronnie's where we went on the stand and he was searching, playing little flurries and little phrases and little bits of tunes, starting, stopping, and pausing and starting again with something different," Green said. "But all of that is part of the adventure, isn't it? He's so in the moment, Sonny. There's nothing preordained. . . . He's a total giant of an improviser. And that's what I learned. If I can learn anything, if I can learn that in my own playing, it's to try and think in the moment, purely about the music."[26]

Jaap van de Klomp, the Dutch jazz impresario who helped Sonny buy Jos van Heuverzwijn's Buescher in 1965, wrote Sonny again, intent on finally booking a Dutch Rollins tour. With his schedule clear, Sonny agreed to do several dates.

Sonny arrived in Holland right as what became known as, depending on where you were, the "Long Hot Summer of 1967" or the "Summer of Love" was heating up in the United States. Hippies flooded San Francisco's Haight-Ashbury neighborhood in search of a cultural utopia, while in urban ghettos across the country, what Martin Luther King Jr. decried that April as the "giant triplets of racism, materialism, and militarism" had led to a rise in police brutality, economic insecurity, and white flight. That summer, 159 riots broke out in cities across the country, culminating in the Detroit riot memorialized by John Lee Hooker's "The Motor City Is Burning." Sonny experienced a strikingly different atmosphere abroad.

"I have to say that jazz was making a terrific impression in Europe at the time," Sonny recalled. "And it was such a wonderful hands-across-the-ocean thing, if you will, and a wonderful time. I love Holland and the people in Holland. I met so many musicians in Holland; and not just musicians, people...in this crazy world where it's so hard for people to become friendly, and all of the racial problems people had in the States and a lot of Americans not really understanding or appreciating jazz. But we went to Europe and wow!...I really enjoyed not just the music; the music exemplified the whole way that we were. 'We,' I mean black American jazz musicians. We were appreciated over there."27

Still touring as a single, Sonny would play with a rhythm section not so different in its orientation from the group in England: twenty-five-year-old drummer Han Bennink and twenty-nine-year-old bassist Rudolf "Ruud" Jacobs. Not unlike Tony Oxley, Bennink, who would also go on to play with Cecil Taylor, was becoming synonymous with the emergent Dutch avant-garde; Jacobs was the paragon of straight-ahead playing. Though already formidable, some would say they were not ready for Sonny, especially without a piano, but they were the best available and would either exceed expectations or be left behind. "I always found looking back at it, you know, that when he played our club, that should never have happened," recalled

Van de Klomp, who ran the Persepolis, in Utrecht. "It was a low point in the history of jazz somehow, you know...that he did those gigs. That there was nothing else better and bigger available for him."[28]

Despite the belief that the market for jazz was more robust beyond American borders, even in the Netherlands, times were tough.[29] A small but loyal audience for jazz and new music remained, but by 1967, most Dutch youth had fallen for rock.

In the Netherlands, Sonny had his chance to demonstrate the vitality of jazz, but it would not be easy. Together, Jacobs and Bennink backed Johnny Griffin, Ben Webster, Wes Montgomery, and Clark Terry, but they had grown apart musically, and by 1967, they had little in common except for their mutual admiration of Sonny's *A Night at the Village Vanguard*.[30] Jacobs was still in the mold of Oscar Pettiford and Ray Brown; Bennink had branched out from the ride-cymbal pulse of Kenny Clarke and Max Roach and played on Eric Dolphy's *Last Date*. Jacobs rarely strayed from the changes; when the mood called for it, Bennink played on a curious add-on to his drum set: a flowerpot with a pig's bladder in it that he procured from a local butcher. "I knew that I could be the glue that could bring them both together, so that it wouldn't sound like, hey, this guy is in Nova Scotia and this guy is in, you know, Los Angeles or something."[31] But Bennink and Jacobs weren't so sure.[32]

After Sonny flew to Amsterdam, he made his way to Hilversum, a twenty-five-mile drive from the Dutch capital. There, he stayed at the Gooiland Hotel across from the neo-Gothic Sint-Vituskerk, the tallest neo-Gothic church in the Netherlands. He later moved to a summer home along the Otter Marina in Oud-Loosdrecht. Sonny, Han, and Ruud went to the Dunne Dirk Café, and Sonny even met Han's newborn daughter, Suki, on his houseboat in Loenen aan de Vecht, but there was no time for rehearsal.[33] What happened when they hit would be a surprise to everyone, both in the audience and onstage.

On Wednesday, May 3, Sonny opened the tour at the Academie voor Beeldende Kunst in Arnhem, where a makeshift bandstand was set up by pushing some stage blocks together.[34] Underscoring the trio's stylistic differences, Sonny and Ruud wore plain button-down suits; Han wore a striped button-down with rolled-up sleeves and an Aztec-print beanie. If there wasn't enough trepidation, it was also Ruud's twenty-ninth birthday.

Before the concert, Sonny tried out the different mouthpieces he brought with him—Otto Links and Berg Larsens—searching for the right pairing with the Buescher for that night. Then he went through his isometric jaw exercises. "He was doing very strange things with his mouth," recalled Han. "I said to myself, 'Hello! What shit is going on here?' " Then, Ruud observed, "He looked at us with a bit of a frown: What should I do with these young whippersnappers?"[35]

Sonny played an opening salvo. "Let's go," he said. Then, something miraculous happened. "From the first note," Ruud recalled, "everything fell off my shoulders, and I said, 'What is going on?'... He was just smiling at us and enjoying.... I could do anything I want without any nerves and I felt very good all of a sudden, without any dope or any drinks. It was something spiritual."[36] The feeling was pure freedom, a weightless sensation that neither Jacobs nor Bennink had experienced before or since. "Sonny had such a strong timing, he made you feel like you were in an elevator," said Bennink. "You didn't have to catch or carry him—he carried you."[37]

That night, Sonny maintained a "take no prisoners" approach, as he thought of it, for two hours and fifteen minutes.[38] On "Four," he drew from a stream-of-consciousness musical expanse: a calypso vamp, a shuffle, the Great American Songbook, Indian ragas, Nat Adderley's "Work Song," and Gershwin's "An American in Paris."[39] After twenty-two minutes, Sonny still had more to say, but they moved on to the next tune. "It was just getting good," Sonny said to the rhythm section. Next, Sonny blended "On Green Dolphin Street" and "There Will Never Be Another You," followed by "They Can't Take That Away from Me" and "Sonnymoon for Two," interspersing a quote from Wilson Pickett's "Land of a Thousand Dances," a hit in 1966. The concert reached a zenith with a twenty-two-minute-plus rendition of "Three Little Words." Sonny quoted "I Can't Get Started," "St. Thomas," "Autumn Nocturne," "Pent-Up House," and, perhaps with some irony, "The Stars and Stripes Forever," all while Ruud and Han vamped with increasing intensity. It culminated with a hard-swinging shout chorus that ended in "If I Were a Bell."

The polarity between Han and Ruud created a productive tension. Han pulled him out, and Ruud pulled him back in. He was in a flow state as he wandered across the makeshift platform, widening the gap between the blocks. It looked like he was about to fall, but that night, nothing could topple him. By the end of the set, Bennink was floating. "I'm close to tears that we are playing this great with that cat," he told Dutch jazz critic and presenter Michiel de Ruyter.[40] "It was my birthday," Jacobs recalled, "and it was a present."[41] When de Ruyter asked Sonny about his reaction to Bennink, Sonny's reply was unexpected: "I can learn from him."[42]

"I certainly didn't feel that there was nothing I could learn from them," Sonny recalled. "I learned playing with everybody!"[43]

The Dutch critical response was overwhelming. One critic wrote that the Arnhem performance was "a force that would have made the siege of Jericho a joke at the time."[44] The crowd was so energized that one gobsmacked concert organizer lost all control and cut off his necktie in delirious excitement.[45]

On Thursday, May 4, Sonny, Han, and Ruud performed at the Go-Go Club, the Loosdrecht lounge where Pim Jacobs, Ruud's pianist brother, hosted a regular thirty-minute NCRV television show called *Jazz met Jacobs*; this was a dry run for the next night's taping.[46] On Friday morning, the trio convened at 10:30 a.m. at VARA Studio 5 in Hilversum for a radio recording for the Dutch NCRV station, which was also arranged by Pim Jacobs.[47] They recorded "Blue Room," "Four," "Love Walked In," and "Tune Up."[48]

"He's a verbal improviser, rather than Coltrane," said Bennink. "Coltrane is like structures. Sonny also, but he's like, he's telling stories." It was a breezy session; Sonny left plenty of space for the rhythm section. "Sometimes he stopped playing and was just listening to my bass," Jacobs recalled. "And smiling," said Bennink.[49]

That night, they taped *Jazz met Jacobs* at the Go-Go Club.[50] The scene at the Go-Go Club was more buttoned-up than it was in Arnhem, and Sonny felt the shift in tone. Yet the rigid atmosphere of a nationally televised broadcast hardly changed his freewheeling approach. "He will play a number of pieces and even I don't know which ones," a tuxedoed Pim Jacobs announced to the TV audience with nervous anticipation.[51] Sonny began with "Sonnymoon for Two." At one point, an audience member remarked loudly to his wife that this was not like the Lionel Hampton record they had at home.[52] Others began whistling "St. Thomas" at random moments. Some called for Bennink to stop playing altogether. The trio played right through the harangues, digging deeper into the blues. Sonny then segued into "Love Walked In."[53] When Pim Jacobs's wife and cohost, vocalist Rita Reys, came on to cut him off, Sonny just kept on playing.[54]

Sonny had one more engagement on the tour, at the Persepolis that Saturday night, May 6. It would be at the smallest venue, but perhaps had the biggest heart. "Rollins belongs in the Concertgebouw, but we couldn't book it so soon," said Jaap van de Klomp.[55] The Persepolis was a cavernous jazz cellar, sixty-five feet long and twenty feet wide, with a jury-rigged hominess. To improve the acoustics, Van de Klomp affixed egg crates to the ceiling.[56] They would cram more than two hundred people in for a big show, and with no windows, it was a Dutch oven. "Condensed water dripped from the ceiling," recalled Van de Klomp, "and there was not enough oxygen for the candles to burn."[57] This gritty atmosphere was where Sonny finished his Dutch tour, but even there, he felt the love.[58]

"As far as I know, Rollins himself has never played better in the Netherlands," wrote critic Rudy Koopmans of the Persepolis gig. Pianist Misha Mengelberg, Bennink's ICP cofounder, sat in, as did Belgian alto saxophonist Jacques Pelzer and bassist Wim Essed, and Sonny just went along with the free-for-all. The highlight was "Sonnymoon for Two," with Bennink and Jacobs jamming out for thirty minutes. Jazz critic Arne Zuidhoek described the performance as a *hartewensconcert*, referring to a Dutch concert series at the time.[59] There is no direct translation for this—it literally means a "heart's desire concert." In this case, it was a *hartewensconcert* not only for the Dutch audience at the Persepolis, but also for Sonny.[60] His appearance at the Persepolis was the final guest appearance ever at the club, which went out with a bang.[61]

Han and Ruud learned a lot that week. "Sonny's timing and his character, and his presence on the stage, his spiritual power, what he had inside," recalled Jacobs, "it influenced me in a very good, positive way." Sonny was "standing in life and living by concepts that we have to think about the world. That's what I learned from him," said Bennink.[62]

Of all the musical references Sonny made during the Dutch tour, the most common was Chopin's "Funeral March."[63] It captured what Ralph Ellison called "blues-toned laughter," a gallows humor in the face of death, but also a memento mori. And an insistent rebuke to the jazz prophets of doom.

It wasn't until June 16 that Sonny began another publicized gig—two weeks at the Both/And in San Francisco.[64] He played with Prince Lasha (who had moved back to California), drummer Beaver Harris, and Los Angeles–based bassist Herbie Lewis.[65] Lewis got a DUI, though, and had to be replaced at the end of the run by bassist John Heard, the Pittsburgh native who had recently moved to San Francisco. Sonny also replaced Harris with drummer Richie Goldberg.[66] After closing at the Both/And, Sonny was booked at the Penthouse in Seattle through July 8, but he canceled at the last minute.[67] Sonny was also booked at the Newport Jazz Festival that year, but canceled that as well.[68]

Around this time, Sonny and Lucille separated. Lucille's mother, Nanette, had retired from the IRS in 1965, and Lucille returned to Chicago to live with her in an apartment on Addison Street on the North Side.[69] Lucille took a job at the University of Chicago as a secretary to Robert W. Thompson, a professor of high-energy physics.[70] Thompson had worked at Los Alamos during World War II and headed a twelve-member research group funded by the National Science Foundation that worked at the university and at a high-altitude laboratory in Sunspot, New Mexico. Lucille had standard secretarial duties, but also helped manage the group's annual $200,000 budget. After spending 1961 to 1966, according to her résumé, as a " 'Housewife' only," resuming her career must have been invigorating. She took the dogs, Major and Minor.[71]

Then, on July 17, 1967, John Coltrane passed away at forty after a battle with liver cancer. Not many were aware of Coltrane's worsening condition, and it seems he never disclosed it to his closest confidants, Sonny included. The disease may have stopped Coltrane from performing, but it didn't stop him creatively. As late as June 1967, it was reported that Coltrane turned down an engagement at the Vanguard because he was "practicing, working on something new, and he didn't feel ready to play in public yet."[72] Though Coltrane told no one about his failing health, Sonny could sense that something was not quite right with his musical brother. Right before Coltrane "made his transition," Sonny recalled, "I remember one of the last times I talked to John, his voice sounded ... I could hear the fundamental tone and the overtones in his voice ... I could hear the bottom tones and I could hear the higher partials." These conversations undoubtedly influenced Sonny, just as Sonny must have influenced Coltrane's explorations on *Interstellar Space* and *Expression*, both recorded in February and March 1967.[73]

Coltrane was instantly canonized, another jazz immortal joining the ancestors all too early.[74] "I was not at his funeral," Sonny recalled. "I must have been out of town. I'm not too big on funerals."[75] Sonny preferred to grieve more privately for his brother and friendly rival. "There is a certain element of competition in music, but between people that respected each other, it mitigates that," Sonny later recalled. "People want that competition or that element. But Trane liked me and I loved him. We had great admiration and respect for each other, which was great because we remained close friends. He used to come to my house and we shared music, but we did a lot of other things as friends. We remained close until his passing."[76] And to Sonny, Trane was not gone. "I still feel John's spirit with me," Sonny later said. "All the time."[77]

Sonny played no more gigs for the rest of the year. He was voted best tenor saxophonist in the fifteenth annual *Down Beat* International Jazz Critics Poll in August 1967, with Coltrane coming in second—not that it mattered to Sonny or Coltrane at that point.[78] Sonny was never one to rest on his laurels. He knew that he had to continue working on his inner self, not only for his own musical and spiritual development, but for everything Coltrane would never be able to do.

As New York got colder, Sonny was contacted by British filmmaker Dick Fontaine about being profiled by *Creative Persons*, a television documentary series that would air internationally.[79] Fontaine had previously directed *Sound??* in 1966, a documentary short with John Cage and Rahsaan Roland Kirk, and the same year a documentary on Ornette Coleman's group with David Izenson and Charles Moffett. Sonny was paid $3,500 for his participation. The episode title posed a simple question with a complex answer: "Who Is Sonny Rollins?"

The film was shot between November 18 and November 24, during a period when Sonny had seemingly decided to retreat from the world.[80] Fontaine followed Sonny back onto the Williamsburg Bridge, where he harmonized with the foghorns. He captured a lively exchange between Sonny and tenor saxophonist Paul Jeffrey, a close friend, in a saxophone duo on the Bridge, as well as in candid conversation.[81] The events of 1967—personally and politically—had plunged Sonny into a funk.

"I didn't hate anybody for a long time. I wouldn't say that I hate now, but in order to avoid becoming a hateful person, I have to remove myself from this society," Sonny said. "I was really sold on the whole American idea, you know, until I began to realize that I was being really foolish and naïve, although I wasn't really, because I'm not going to let people—hateful people—destroy my basic spirituality, because they've taught me how to dislike someone else, just from, you know, their dislike. Things have gotten out of hand like that to me. Enough times that I realize that the most important thing to me is my sanity."

Did this mean retirement? "I don't want to cop out. Really, I couldn't. I don't think I could," Sonny told Jeffrey. "You can blow your horn and if you get great at it, you'll live a good life, so to speak...and the public don't really give a damn. As long as you sound good, they don't care what you do. You can use drugs, you can do anything you want as long as you sound good when you get up on the stand. Well, I don't know if it's worth that."

Jeffrey was supportive of Sonny taking another break from public performance.[82] "Well, eventually, of course, I want to communicate," Sonny said, "but it might take being alone to communicate." Sonny had spiritual business to attend to: "One gets to the point where you want to have these conditions of complete harmony. It gets back down to a spiritual thing. I've just spent my life trying to find me, and there's just enough light there for me to see at the end of the cave."

But it was not time for the next sabbatical yet. Fontaine took Sonny to Brownstone Music Hall, where Charles Moffett was the band director in a multiyear after-school program.[83] Sonny sat in with the band as Moffett conducted, blowing a blues and giving pointers to a young saxophonist. Sonny had one main piece of advice, a credo for saxophone playing and life in general: "Just keep putting as much air into it as you can."[84]

Chapter 30

SANDEEPANY SADHANALAYA

(1968)

In January 1968, Sonny returned to Japan on a monthlong tour produced by George Wein. "Before I left I was going through a difficult period," Sonny recalled. "I had a weight problem and was using a lot of pills—amphetamines. I was very paranoid. I wasn't getting much done. I was doing things, but I wasn't going anywhere."[1] He hoped a trip to the Far East might renew his sense of purpose.

The tour was scheduled to begin on January 3, but visa issues with the Japanese immigration authorities delayed Sonny's arrival. Sonny hired three midwesterners: his erstwhile bassist Larry Ridley; drummer George Brown, who had worked with Wes Montgomery, Gene Ammons, and Yusef Lateef; and pianist Hugh Lawson, who had also worked with Lateef.[2] When they flew to Hawaii en route to Japan, though, Lawson's visa was denied due to tightened restrictions that began before Sonny's scuttled 1967 Japan tour.[3]

Throughout the tour, Japanese road manager Hideko Ataka recalled, "we were followed by police.... Two middle-aged men were always watching us at the station and venue. They weren't particularly suspicious of the Rollins group at a time when the Japanese government was showing a strong attitude toward the repeated scandals caused by jazz musicians, but Sonny wasn't pleased at all and everyone was frustrated."[4]

As for Lawson's visa denial, Sonny simply played some of the concerts with a pianoless trio. For others, Sonny picked up twenty-eight-year-old pianist Masabumi Kikuchi, who had performed with Lionel Hampton. On Sonny's previous tour, Kikuchi came every night Sonny performed at the Marunou-chi Hotel.[5]

When they arrived in Tokyo, Sonny walked down the airstair with a compact suitcase, slacks, a tan overcoat, and, much to the surprise of the Japanese press and fans, a full head of hair and a beard.[6] Seeing Sonny without a Mohawk, numerous fans insisted to promoters that this "wasn't the real Sonny Rollins, but an impostor." The complaints grew to the point that before a concert later in the tour, Sonny gave in and restored the Mohawk. On tour, Sonny also paid tribute to local traditions, donning a broad-shouldered *kataginu* vest.[7]

Sonny performed on Japanese national TV on *Young Jamboree* opposite Japanese pop groups including the Tempters, the Spiders, and the Blue Comets,[8] but otherwise, the tour consisted mostly of one-nighters. They were scheduled to start on January 3 and 4 at Tokyo Sankei Hall and play on January 5 at Tokyo's Koseinenkin Hall, then move up to Muroran Cultural Center in the north. They were able to cover large distances on the Shinkansen, known in the United States as the bullet train, which arrived in 1964.[9]

For Sonny, the tour was the beginning of a spiritual pilgrimage. In Mishima, near Mount Fuji, Sonny reconnected with Masahiro Oki in the yoga studio he established there in 1967.[10] Sonny played Kyoto, Kobe, and Fukuoka, followed by Hiroshima.[11] Through Oki, Sonny recalled, "I remember going to the Hiroshima site where the bomb fell. . . . I played my soprano there for a little commemoration."[12]

They continued on to Osaka, Utsunomiya, Ueda, Nagano, Kanazawa, Aichi Prefecture, and back through Tokyo.[13] Sonny stayed past the scheduled end of the tour to perform a concert on February 3 at Tokyo Video Hall with alto saxophonist Sadao Watanabe.[14] On January 27, in the city of Hitachi on the Pacific Coast, Sonny "stood still against the waves crashing into the lead-colored winter landscape of the sky and the sea," wrote Ataka, then asked, "'Why don't you take us to Sojiji Temple in Tsurumi?'" After returning to Tokyo, Kiyoshi Koyama and Ataka went with Sonny to the temple. "It was sunny but cold," she recalled. "We arrived at the vast precincts of Sojiji Soin Temple of the Sojiji sect in front of Tsurumi Station in Yokohama City. Doves flew out all at once from the mirror-colored roof of the temple. Birds were singing in the distance. It smelled like a bonfire. Quietness. Cold." They went into the dimly lit, high-ceilinged Zazen training dojo and meditated on tatami mats. "I'm not sure how much this short visit gave him, but there was the illusion that the air was somehow calm and light on the way back." About a week after the tour ended, George Wein called Japan looking for Sonny. "Where is Rollins? I can't get in touch," he said. A few weeks later, Ataka heard from Sonny that he had arrived at the next leg of his spiritual journey.[15]

From Japan, that February, Sonny went to India looking for answers. "I had begun to realize that it was impossible to get, on a day-to-day level, any kind of satisfaction out of this world," Sonny recalled. "I decided to go to India because I believed that it was the place where I would be able to get deeper into the spiritual element of life and be able to find a way to deal with that kind of reality. At this time, Lucille and I were separated. I went there by myself. . . . I just took my horn and a bag and got on the plane to India."[16] Jazz had a presence in India as early as 1935, when jazz violinist Leon Abbey toured with his band. The US State Department began sending jazz ambassadors to India in 1958, when Dave Brubeck came; Duke Ellington was dispatched in 1963, inspiring the *Far East Suite*. But generally speaking, American jazz musicians came to India to play, not to study Vedanta.

In 1968, a great malaise was sweeping across the culture—it was the year of the Prague Spring and its crushing defeat by Soviet forces, the Tet Offensive in Vietnam, worldwide student protests, and, in the span of two months, the assassinations of Martin Luther King Jr. and Robert F. Kennedy. That year, Sonny was not the only music icon, or even the only jazz musician, who felt India calling. That February, the Beatles, their romantic partners, and a coterie of fellow seekers—Mia Farrow (sans Sinatra), Donovan, the Beach Boys' Mike Love, jazz flautist Paul Horn, and others—all flew to India looking for nirvana. They went to Rishikesh in the foothills of the Himalayas by the Ganges, where the controversial Maharishi Mahesh Yogi had established an ashram in 1963 before exporting Transcendental Meditation across the globe. Transcendental Meditation was gaining traction in the West, and the Beatles would serve as gateway.[17] They would write most of the White Album during the weeks they were there, but curtailed their three-month trip after only a month, leaving on acrimonious terms.[18]

It was by chance that Sonny did not meet the Beatles in India. Maharishi Mahesh Yogi had become an icon in the West, not only because he counted the Rolling Stones, the Beatles, and the Doors among his followers. "Meditation Movement Is Invading Hollywood," read one headline that past

October—and the Maharishi was the star.[19] The *New York Times* referred to him as "Chief Guru of the Western World." Transcendental Meditation centers began sprouting up across Europe and the United States. On January 21, 1968, the Maharishi filled the four-thousand-seat Felt Forum at Madison Square Garden for a public lecture on the benefits of Transcendental Meditation, signing autographs and receiving floral offerings on the dais from teenage girls in miniskirts.[20] "If Jesus Christ came with his message today," the Maharishi boasted in advance of the talk at a press event at the Plaza Hotel, where he was staying, "he would be speaking at a press conference like this." What Jesus was lacking, he added, was PR. His two-month self-realization course promised the results he claimed religion had failed to deliver—for a price.[21] If the Beatles were "more popular than Jesus," it seemed the Maharishi fashioned himself his Second Coming.[22] Through his Spiritual Regeneration Movement, His Holiness promised "200 percent" value of life—100 percent material and 100 percent spiritual—as well as an end to racism and lasting world peace.[23]

Transcendental Meditation worked for many in the West, yet some were skeptical of the Maharishi's panacea. Many saw what seemed like a cultural moment ripe for a genuine revival of Hinduism both in India and abroad being compromised by the Maharishi's break from classical tradition.[24] Sonny expressly intended to find an ashram in the Himalayas. He would have heard of the Maharishi, and could likely have studied with him alongside the Beatles, but the story would not have been as interesting.

"On the last leg of the flight, I was talking to some Indian people and one fella knew something about ashrams," Sonny recalled.[25] "He suggested this particular place to me just outside of Bombay and this swami, Chinmayananda." " 'You are going all the way to the Himalayas,' " the Air India passenger said. Chinmaya Mission was much closer. " 'If I were you, it's only fifteen minutes from the airport. You can go and meet him and come.' "[26] A thousand miles south of Rishikesh, on the outskirts of Bombay in Powai, there would be none of the drama that ended the Beatles' brush with the Maharishi. Where Sonny was going, the course in self-realization lasted much longer than two months.

Sonny stayed at Sandeepany Sadhanalaya, an ashram run by Chinmaya Mission, the organization founded by Swami Chinmayananda Saraswati in

1953 to teach Vedanta through the serious study of the Bhagavad Gita and the Upanishads. Swami Saraswati was only fifty-one years old when Sonny arrived and found his spiritual path as an adult. He was born into a secular life as an upper-class Brahmin, completing a master's in English literature at the University of Lucknow and working as a journalist in Delhi.[27] His reporting on the ascetics of Rishikesh introduced him to the teachings of Swami Sivananda, and in 1949 he became a disciple. Soon, Chinmayananda had disciples himself. His approach was controversial to orthodox clerics, but Chinmayananda's classes were taught in English in order to reach the middle class and secular society in Bombay. "A new type of swami is emerging in this country who will serve as missionaries to their own people," wrote Chinmayananda. "At this crucial time in our history, we do not need those who live in a cave and meditate."[28]

When Sonny arrived at the ashram, he encountered not Chinmayananda, but rather Swami Parthasarathy, the Pradhan, or ashram manager, one of Chinmayananda's disciples. Chinmayananda went on intermittent lecture tours; at around this time, he was doing large-scale events in New Delhi, nearly nine hundred miles away.[29] Like Chinmayananda, Swami Parthasarathy had given up a successful career in shipping and a Rolls-Royce to pursue a life of Vedanta.[30] Parthasarathy was forty years old at the time, only three years older than Sonny. "Sonny appeared, and he came to my room," Parthasarathy recalled. "I was editing the commentary on the Gita, Upanishads. That's all I'd been doing."[31]

Parthasarathy got up from his work. "He was standing in my room. He said, 'Do you teach yoga?' I said, 'I don't know what you mean by *yoga*. Yoga is derived from the Sanskrit root *Yuj*, to join, so yoga means joining with the infinite. You are the infinite. You are now living in the realm of the body, mind, intellect—you have lost the infinite. So to get back, to join back, to unite with the ultimate is called yoga. So it could be done through study, education like this. Not by standing on your head. It'll improve your muscles, that's about all. So you can't reach the self, the Atman, through yoga.' . . . So he was listening to me for next to one hour, standing. I didn't know what the guy wanted. And he said, 'I have a ticket to go to the Himalayas.' In front of me he tore it to bits. He tore it, and then he said, 'Can you teach me this?'

I said, 'I can't teach you in one day or two days. You have to stay here for a while.' He said, 'I'm prepared to stay if you allow me to stay here.' Then that's how he stayed... and then he learned."[32]

Parthasarathy lived at the ashram with his wife and daughter, and Sonny was given a separate room. "I went strictly as a neophyte," Sonny said. "I was just trying to find some real, deeper understanding of life. Nobody knew who I was, and I was unknown to them as far as who I was in the jazz world. There were a few Americans at the ashram, and one guy knew who I was. The focus was never on me. I only rarely practiced because I was in an ashram and I did not want any undue focus directed on me."[33]

Sonny grew his beard out and adhered to the ashram dress code, a loose-fitting white kurta and lungi, worn so that "the purity of white provides a peaceful aura and serves as a reminder to live a life of austerity in thought, word, and deed."[34] The uniform was light, as temperatures generally rose to the nineties and rarely fell below seventy at night.[35] The beautiful campus was situated on a hill not far from Powai Lake. A day at the ashram began at 4 a.m., followed by Vedic chanting and a series of classes on Vedanta; communal meals of rice, chapatti, and dal; and, to conclude the day, the ritual chanting of Jagadeeshwara Arati and a *satsang* gathering with the swami.[36]

Swami Chinmayananda taught that the unenlightened life was akin to eating a plantain without taking off the peel; his course would help students peel away the layers of illusion. Parthasarathy taught additional classes in South Bombay, about fifteen miles from the ashram, and he invited Sonny.[37] The class met every Friday from 6 to 7:30 p.m. and was attended primarily by a group that called themselves the "Teenagers Club," but anyone could join; attendance averaged about forty students. Parthasarathy would assign a reading in Vedic philosophy for the week—Adi Shankaracharya, Chinmayananda, the Upanishads or Bhagavad Gita—and ran the class as a seminar.

Haresh Jagtiani, who was studying law at St. Xavier's College in Bombay, applied a legal skepticism to the teachings, but Parthasarathy welcomed his doubt.[38] "Halfway through, Parthasarathy said, 'You know, there is a musician who comes from America,' and he didn't know what he played, so he said 'he plays the trumpet.' So he said, 'Would you like to meet him?' Music was somewhat of a passion for me, so I said, 'I'd love to meet him.'"

In class, Sonny was deeply inquisitive. "I think that for him Indian philosophy was in one sense so different from Western philosophy...which is more empirical and relies on scientific proof, whereas with Indian philosophy there is a bit of intuition and the whole approach is different," Jagtiani said. "He was very, very curious, and we had a lot of exchanges while sitting next to each other or asking questions of the teacher."[39]

Jagtiani knew his name, but "had no idea how famous Sonny Rollins was." Then, "I had a discussion with my friend. I told him, 'Well, I think that Stan Getz is the best tenor sax ever.' This friend of mine was a little more initiated into music. He said, 'Well, for me, Sonny Rollins is number one.' So I said, 'What Sonny Rollins are you talking about?' And I described him. And he said, 'Yes. What about it?' So I said, 'Well, I know him!' When I met him the next time, I said, 'Are you *the* Sonny Rollins?' And he said, 'Yesss...'" Sonny visited Jagtiani's home and spent some time with him before the course with Parthasarathy ended. "I found him superbly intellectual, very curious, wanting to know much more about the Indian way of life and the Indian philosophy," Jagtiani said. "He was just really trying to understand it and see how it could give him a code of living and how it really could translate into a way of life.... [H]e obviously had a great appetite for philosophy."

Parthasarathy taught that "the fundamental requirement in spiritual training" was differentiating between *swadharma*, or "one's own nature," and *paradharma*, or "alien nature." "If your tendency is for music or art, then you must choose your vocation based on music or art.... [T]he same rule holds good for religion as well." Desire clouded that natural path. "Your desires cause the gulf between you and Atman," he wrote. He distilled the elimination of desire to three principles: *Karma yoga*, or a course of action "without selfish interest"; *Bhakti yoga*, the course of devotion, which calls for thoughts and desires to "rise from the secular to the sublime"; and *Gnana yoga*, a course of knowledge and awareness of "Brahman as the substratum of your experiences," actively changing "the direction of your thoughts from the world to that which supports the world."[40]

"He told me, 'Sonny, your karma yoga is to play music,'" Sonny recalled. "I would be bringing joy to people. That was a proper way to live."[41]

As Chinmayananda's student, Parthasarathy wrote that there are two types of sound, articulate and inarticulate.[42] Articulate sound comes from the alphabet and deals with "knowledge of the head," while inarticulate sound "deals with the heart," transcending language barriers. Om is a combination of the two—"the most potent, most natural" sound, a sound that "represents the entire phenomenon of sound." In Indian classical music, there was always a drone note in the background played on a *shruti box* or *tanpura*.[43] The musician is "constantly aware of that note in and through his variable manipulation of songs, tunes and beats," and there was a corollary to the search for self-realization. Sonny could work to translate the sound of the Om, of the Atman, to the saxophone.[44]

Sonny heard this in action on March 24, 1968, when Parthasarathy took him to see the Indian shehnai player Bismillah Khan opposite vocalist Latafat Hussain Khan at the Swami Haridas Music Festival in Bombay's Birla Hall.[45] Khan would become an influence on Sonny's artistic development.[46]

Sonny did compose two tunes there—"Ashram" and "Powai." The latter was based on an Indian chant Sonny heard at night; he later recorded it on *Sonny Rollins in Japan*.[47] He sat in at an Indian dance, and another night, Parthasarathy "asked him to get his saxophone," the swami recalled. "It was a real sensation."[48] It was a duo with the *nadaswaram*, a South Indian oboe-like instrument similar to the North Indian shehnai.[49]

There were at least three jazz fans in Bombay who would have done anything to be there. Jehangir Dalal, Niranjan Jhaveri, and Coover Gazdar were St. Xavier's College graduates who cofounded the short-lived *Blue Rhythm* magazine, publishing it from 1952 to 1953.[50] "There was a growing number of people who were very devoted to jazz and very dedicated to it, and they searched," Dalal recalled. In this case, the search was more literal. Jhaveri "found out somehow or other that there was an American jazz musician staying with a swami up in an ashram in Powai," Dalal said. "There are many of these ashrams, and he drove around to several until he found Sonny. And then the next time he took me down, and another friend also, and we went down to see him there. Later on, he came to my house and we had a meal. We talked, he listened, and that was it. . . . We spent as much time as we could with him."[51] Having gone to India to escape the jazz scene, Sonny wasn't thrilled to be found, and he was even less thrilled when he arrived at Jhaveri's house to find a full rhythm section set up and a tenor saxophone, though he obliged.[52] But he must have been gratified to see that the gospel had spread to Bombay.

It was one of Sonny's few meetings with Chinmayananda himself that helped him realize that spiritual practice and musical practice were not mutually exclusive. "I told the swami, 'Well, you know, it's hard for me to sit down and meditate,'" Sonny said. "So the swami said... 'Sonny, you know, when you play your horn, that's a form of meditation.'...After that, I was ready to come back to the States."[53]

Dalal and Jhaveri helped Sonny get home. "We went to the Air India office to arrange for his ticket," Dalal said. "We documented a picture of him standing outside Air India, and that was it."[54]

Sonny left India with more questions than answers. "I knew what I was looking for, but I didn't really find it. I expected supermen who'd provide the key to understanding," Sonny said, "but there weren't any supermen....Of course, that was something valuable to learn."[55]

At around this time, Sonny read Dane Rudhyar's 1928 treatise *The Rebirth of Hindu Music*.[56] "When knowledge decays, when dharma is no longer perceived, civilization becomes rapidly distorted, then disintegrates," Rudhyar writes, "and music, which is the clearest mirror of civilization, loses its true intonations, its inner strength of tone, and becomes a mere repetition of formulas and modes which have lost their <u>vital</u> meaning and no longer rouse in Nature and in man powers and visions, but only please the senses or thrill the intellect." Sonny underlined the word "vital." He double underlined the idea of the musician as an "arouser of spiritual forces." To Rudhyar, "Tone-alchemy is soul-alchemy, for tone and soul are one."[57] Sonny copied this last passage—"TONE & SOUL are ONE"—in a journal. He distilled it to this schematic:[58]

WE HEAR   MUSIC   WITH OUR EARS
WE READ   WITH OUR EYES
WE EXPERIENCE   WITH OUR HEART

So Sonny would focus less on the intellect, as he had when he was younger, and more on the spirit. Sonny had learned that the deepest path to the listener's soul was not through the mind, but through the heart.

Back in New York, Sonny hoped to find the kind of spiritual exaltation he experienced at the ashram not only in his tone but also in his home.[59] Yet the environment posed a perennial challenge. "When I came back from India, where I was living in a place of great spirituality, both in its culture and its religion, I felt as if I was actually elevated," Sonny said. "I felt like I was walking three feet over the ground. This lasted for maybe three or four weeks. Gradually I felt I was dragged back down to the reality of this way of life here...dragged back down to earth, so to speak."[60]

The spiritual quest continued on the bandstand. On the weekend of June 28 and 29, Sonny played at the Village Vanguard opposite the Bobby Hutcherson–Harold Land Quintet. He would continue at the Vanguard through most of July on double bills with Coleman Hawkins, then McCoy Tyner, and finally Freddie Hubbard.[61] Sonny hired a quartet: a changing rhythm section with pianist Pat Rebillot as the only constant.[62]

Rebillot had recorded with tenor saxophonist Frank Foster and with Chico O'Farrill and was music directing *Jacques Brel Is Alive and Well and Living in Paris* at the Village Gate Theater when he got the call. Rebillot was friends with the Colomby brothers, and Jules Colomby, who had just taken over as Thelonious Monk's manager from his brother Harry, recommended Rebillot to Sonny.[63] The only problem was that he would have almost no time to make it from the Village Gate to the Vanguard. "I would play at the Village Gate and then literally run over to the Vanguard to work with Sonny," Rebillot recalled. "I was in shape to run it, so I did. It was a nice warm-up for the gig."[64]

The rest of the band shifted night to night. Sonny tried bassist Miroslav Vitous and drummer Joe Chambers. That night at the Vanguard, "it's not happening, we're not making it," Chambers recalled. "It's not jelling, so I remember Sonny, in the middle of a song, he came and kneels down next to me and says, 'Well, you know, Joe, what's going on? What seems to be the problem? I'm trying my best.'...We started the next set and he walks up out the door. I mean, he leaves the stage." After the gig, one of the Colombys paid them, and that was that.[65]

Next, Sonny tried bassist Stanley Clarke, then Larry Ridley, and, finally, Reggie Johnson. Then, Sonny hired drummer Rashied Ali, channeling Coltrane's spirit.[66] "I think he hired Rashied to try to find some of that current flowing through that style," Rebillot said, "and it was kind of discombobulating, 'cause Rashied never played 'ding-ding-a-ding.' He would hint at it for one second and then leave it. So you never really knew where things were at, where he was thinking of the time." Sonny was playing mostly standards—"Old Devil Moon," "In a Sentimental Mood," "Three Little Words," and his own "Doxy" and "St. Thomas"—and it didn't jibe with Ali's interstellar rhythms.[67]

"It was wildly experimental," Rebillot said, and Rashied "was a real sweetheart of a guy...but Sonny often would just keep playing the melody over and over, trying to find a groove, and he would never really get to improvising and it would be over, and the audience would applaud and Sonny would say 'No, no, no, no!' Like he was in pain. He originally told me that he likes to stroll," meaning that the piano would lay out, "and I knew that, but he was just reminding me, so I would drop out at the appropriate chorus, but shortly after that, he changed his mind, and I think it was because of Rashied and the different bass players."[68]

Soon, Sonny brought in drummer Leroy Williams on a recommendation from Wilbur Ware, with Reggie Johnson and Rebillot.[69] "That was one of the highlights of my musical career," Williams recalled. Williams had listened to Sonny from an early age; he was in the audience in Chicago in 1956 when it was announced that Clifford Brown and Richie Powell wouldn't be coming because of the car accident.[70] Sonny used Rebillot on one final gig on August 3 at the Jazz Runs at Laurel festival in Laurel, Maryland, playing a virtuosic midnight set.[71]

That summer, Dick Fontaine's "Who Is Sonny Rollins?" began airing around the world.[72] In August, he once again topped the *Down Beat* International Jazz Critics Poll in the tenor category, with eighty-one votes to Stan Getz's forty-seven.[73] But the wide recognition did little to temper his growing disillusionment with the business.

Sonny then flew to Copenhagen, where he was booked for three weeks at the Jazzhus Montmartre through September 22, along with a recording for Dutch radio and television.[74] He played with the house rhythm section: bassist Niels-Henning Ørsted Pedersen, drummer Albert "Tootie" Heath, and pianist Kenny Drew.[75] At the Montmartre, Sonny played his Mark VI with an Otto Link mouthpiece; his sound had a stoic elegance.[76] One of the performances was filmed for broadcast, with Sonny wearing a black beret.[77] Sonny was a flawless technician, but his performance lacks the emotional resonance he so often reached. It seemed he was just going through the motions; the sound of the struggle, of the search that brought the creative act to life, was missing.[78]

One surprise at the Montmartre was seeing Jehangir Dalal, Sonny's friend from India.[79] In the audience at Sonny's last performance was Norwegian jazz presenter and journalist Randi Hultin. She was in Copenhagen to see psychedelic rock band the Savage Rose, and decided to see Sonny. Hultin was an old friend of Kenny Drew's, and she asked him to introduce her. "Talk to him yourself," Drew said curtly.[80] After Sonny's first set, she went up to his dressing room. "Sonny Rollins, could I have a word with you?" Hultin asked.

"Okay, come on," he said. She asked if she could take a few photos of him, and he said okay. Sonny relaxed when he found out that Hultin had also been a friend of Bud Powell's. According to Hultin, Sonny returned for the second set invigorated. "That's because you were listening. I could feel that that's what inspired me," Sonny later told her. Sonny went past his allotted time that night, or early that morning, and he asked Hultin to wait for him. They took a long walk through Copenhagen in the wee hours. "I love trees," he told her. Back in the hotel lobby, Hultin asked if Sonny would ever consider coming to Norway. Sonny asked, "What are the people like in Norway? Are they like you?" Sonny gave Hultin Lucille's address in Chicago where she could write him, then flew home.[81]

Sonny had no more gigs for the rest of the year. Meanwhile, "Who Is Sonny Rollins?" continued to air. "Negro jazz tenor saxophonist Sonny is shown struggling with himself," read TV listings across the United States, "trying to decide whether he can stay in a country which he no longer understands."[82] Sonny did understand—all too well. Martin Luther King Jr. had been assassinated, and every night brought a new episode of an unjust war in its deadliest year.

Sonny wrote about his disillusionment in his journal:

I feel like giving up. All of the business part is devoid of moral underpinning. This enables me to function but lessens my moral fiber:

commitment, purpose—In other words the only commitment I have now is to getting food for my next meal. Of course when I perform I endeavor to do what [seems] to have to be done and try to get into a trance-like state as seems to be what allows me to do this thing for which I am being paid and for which the bread for tomorrow's meal comes.

The point about the Gita's view of work is that if I deteriorate or am not up to snuff I should not expect success and should gracefully exit. But I cannot participate with a priori view of negativism. I have to keep practicing and hope that I can improve a little musically but basically by practicing derive the moral underpinning to keep it happening and to keep trying to make it happen.

...Things are never constant. Disaster is coming. Disasters are coming.[83]

Sonny, it seemed, was depressed about a moral universe with such a long arc that any bends toward justice were all but imperceptible. To stave off pessimism, all he could do was practice—yoga and his instrument. Spirituality and music were one and the same. "Projection of Spiritual Devotion into the music," he wrote in a journal. "Concentrate on the messages which the music will bring to the hearers."[84]

Chapter 31

MUSART

(1969–1970)

Sonny's way out of his disillusionment with the music industry was through other people. Usually from the next generation—a subtle, often unheralded mentorship he developed and never spoke about as such. "I'm all for anybody who is coming along new with whatever they are doing and then they have to add their mark to the book," Sonny later said. "The book has already been written, and then these young people have to come on and see if they can put their names into it."[1] They thought of him as a musical father figure; to Sonny, they were just practicing together.[2]

In 1969, Sonny saw a familiar face at Eighth Street and Sixth Avenue: twenty-year-old David S. Ware. "We saw him at a fruit stand. He loves fruit. I said to him, 'I'd like to play for you. I'd like you to listen to my playing.' He looked me straight in the eye to see my sincerity and said, 'All right.' We went back to his apartment and started practicing together. We practiced together from '69 until the early '80s."[3] Ware was with drummer Marc Edwards, two-thirds of the trio that would become Apogee with Gene Ashton, later known as Cooper-Moore. Ware had recently moved home to New Jersey after three semesters at Berklee. He was ready to transfer to "Rollins College."[4]

"There were times when we practiced together I heard things coming about that I hadn't heard him record," Ware recalled. "There are certain things he wanted to perform in public, and this is something I never quite understood. But Sonny is Sonny."[5]

Ware learned by osmosis, from the rudiments of saxophone technique to yoga. "He was always able to take a piece of material and make it his own, because he made it his business to know what the past possibilities of the tune were, and then found a way to somehow expand on those possibilities through complete mastery," Ware said. "It's what true improvisation is about. Dealing with a melody on that level takes time—it takes time to know how to discard the bar lines and move through the forms in a new rhythm, and then again to use those rhythms you're playing in to bring out new tonalities of the individual notes."[6]

Their sessions focused equally on spirituality and music. "I heard this in both Coltrane and Rollins, but here Sonny presented me with an actual method to obtain this on a personal level," Ware said.[7] "Sonny would talk about some of his spiritual experiences, to the effect that there is an experience you can have where you more or less are witness to what you are doing, what you are playing... from deep within yourself, outside of your everyday self."[8]

"I have never ever thought just music, just jazz," Ware later told Sonny.

"No, for me the two have always been together. I must have both. And that's what I heard in your music. So much, you know…using that saxophone as a pathway to God."[9]

Sonny continued his search at Musart, a basement-level jazz loft at 149 Spring Street in SoHo. Musart Spiral Foods was mostly a musicians' hang, but it served organic food that was "natural as hell."[10] The loft was a neighborhood place with New Age decor that *New York* magazine described as "vegetative imagery, mushrooms and planets and astral spirals running over waterfalls."[11] Multireedist George Braith founded Musart in 1966; in 1967, he released an album of the same name on Prestige.[12] Inspired by Rahsaan Roland Kirk, Braith had the ability to play two horns at once, including the C melody saxophone and stritch; he later invented a hybrid instrument dubbed the Braithophone.[13] According to Sonny, there was "always music going on there…and you could get high down there and it was cool…it was always somebody smoking pot or using LSD."[14]

Braith opened Musart in order to have a space where he could play with Coltrane, whom he met in the mid-'60s, but Coltrane never set foot in the place. "Right after Trane died, Alice told me that John had come to her in a dream and said that he'd visit me every day at 3 p.m.," Braith recalled. "So I told all the musicians I knew never to come to Musart at that time. Everybody knew not to bother me at three o'clock, because that was the time I would be with Trane. And I did feel his spirit. This went on for a while, until one day I hear a knock at the door. I didn't answer, but then I heard someone on the other side of the door say, 'Hey George, open up.' It was Sonny Rollins. So I let him in."[15] According to Braith, Coltrane's spirit never returned after Sonny's arrival, but Sonny did.[16] Braith recorded much of the goings-on, and at one of these sessions, Sonny played only the pads of his saxophone in rhythm.[17]

He also sought out spiritual connections with nonmusicians. He began a relationship with Jackie Lewis, the owner of Grand Hotel, a high-end boutique on St. Marks Place in the East Village. "She was a respected black businesswoman," Sonny recalled. "I met her in the Village at one of her stores there."[18] Lewis grew up in Salt Lake City and moved to New York to chase her dream of owning her own clothing store. She opened Pourquoi in 1964, and by the following year she was selling custom-made seamless bell-bottoms and other designer clothes to artists, movie stars, and musicians. At Grand Hotel, she sold "the best from California and on and off Seventh Avenue designers," it was reported in the *New York Times*, but "also buys from and encourages undiscovered talent, particularly Negro."[19] Like Sonny, she viewed life through the prism of a "spiritual and metaphysical perspective," and would eventually leave high fashion to move to Negril, Jamaica, and open up her own spa, Jackie's on the Reef, "designed to allow your temple to reconnect to your special purpose." They were kindred spirits, and she and Sonny would remain friends for life, but the relationship began and ended while Sonny and Lucille were separated.

During this period of spiritual rejuvenation, Sonny would perform in public only when he was ready. On February 18, while the Modern Jazz Quartet performed at the Metropolitan Museum of Art, Sonny was at the Whitney to take part in the Composers' Showcase series "New Directions in Jazz."[20] Nearly one thousand people packed the Whitney's third floor, sitting on the ground, for premieres by Cecil Taylor, Ornette Coleman (in absentia), Jimmy Giuffre, and Sonny. One of them was Orrin Keepnews, the erstwhile Riverside producer who in 1966 had cofounded Milestone Records.

"The small venue was sold out and somehow my promised press-list ticket wasn't there," Keepnews recalled. "Frustrated, I decided to wait and at least say hello to Sonny, whom I had not seen in years and had not worked with since the *Freedom Suite* sessions for Riverside. That turned out to be a very far-reaching decision. I told him my sad story, he smuggled me into the concert with him, and I ended the evening in possession of a rare prize: the always-unlisted Rollins telephone number."[21] After playing roadie and carrying Sonny's saxophone into the museum, Keepnews expressed interest in signing him, but Sonny brushed off the overture.

For the performance, each grantee composed their premiere in advance—Coleman and Giuffre each wrote string quartets—but Sonny's new composition, "Tone Poem for Saxophone," would be composed spontaneously that night. "I had been working on a piece for strings," Sonny recalled, "but I just did not have my string quartet chops up, so I did the next best thing—a solo improvisation."[22]

Sonny finally felt ready to realize a goal he articulated in 1958: solo saxophone. It was a stream-of-consciousness performance, akin to one of his cadenzas, only much longer. The spectators were riveted, and demanded an encore, so Sonny played "St. Thomas" solo.[23] Surrounded by art, Sonny must have been thinking of Coleman Hawkins's landmark 1948 solo saxophone recording "Picasso."[24]

On March 15, Sonny gave a similarly experimental performance in front of an audience of twelve hundred at Town Hall. This time, he was backed by seven bassists, with his "powerful upper torso encased in a dashiki," wrote Ira Gitler.[25] Sonny and the New York Bass Violin Choir headlined opposite the Jaki Byard Quartet and Artie Simmons and the Jazz Samaritans. Led by bassist Bill Lee, the father of Spike, the bass choir also included Lisle Atkinson, Richard Davis, Milt Hinton, Michael Fleming, Ron Carter, and Buster Williams, with a piano and drums; Williams anchored the rhythm section.[26] They played arrangements of "Valse Hot," a bossa nova, and a blues, with Sonny bestriding the stage.

"We took him someplace," Atkinson recalled. "A different style. It was like an orchestra, but not a customary orchestra. Six in the front line and Buster played in the rhythm section. In the beginning of the concert, I had the feeling that we unrelaxed him for a minute. However, it was gorgeous."[27]

They only had twenty-five minutes of material prepared, leaving the crowd wanting more, calling out their requests, so Sonny played solo for a few minutes.[28] "I could have played longer," Sonny said. "I tried to show them that I was thinking of them. I didn't intend it to be that way. It's nice to let people know what's going on on the other side of the footlights—a rapport. I usually don't play that short a time. I work very hard. I wear out suits playing. I hope they forgive me."[29]

The next week, Sonny played at the Village Vanguard with a rotating rhythm section opposite vocalist Novella Nelson.[30] He began the week with pianist Albert Dailey, bassist Wilbur Ware, and drummer Tootie Heath, playing standards: "Three Little Words," "Dancing in the Dark," "Yesterdays," "Sonnymoon for Two," "St. Thomas," and the Beatles' "Eleanor Rigby."[31] At the end of the week, he retained Dailey but hired Walter Booker on bass and Gerald "Sonny" Brown on drums.

Sonny was working so sporadically that it was difficult to keep a consistent rhythm section "until I get a steady itinerary and offer steady work," Sonny said. One of the reasons for his frequent absences was his unwillingness to negotiate his fee. "If you play for one price in one case, they expect you to play for that all the time," Sonny said. "If they want Sonny Rollins, then they have to pay my price. If I don't get it now, when am I going to get it?"[32]

Sonny began negotiations to sign with a record label, and considered joining the jazz faculty at Queens College, but neither prospect came to fruition.[33] Sonny was not worried about the future, though. "There are so many possibilities in music. It's an open sky," he said. And he was not worried for the future of the art form either: "I've been out here long enough to know that things go in cycles. Jazz will always survive."[34]

That April, Sonny was back at the Vanguard opposite the Tony Williams Trio—later, Tony Williams Lifetime. He hired twenty-six-year-old drummer Al Foster, a native New Yorker who had worked with Blue Mitchell, Walter Davis Jr., and Monty Alexander. "I had met Sonny the day before at the rehearsal," Foster recalled. "He asked me if I could play the calypso. So I played the calypso. And Sonny said: 'Okay, see you tomorrow!' Wilbur Ware was on bass. He was one of my heroes. Albert Dailey was on the piano. I was so nervous because Tony Williams was there with his band and I had to play on his drums."[35]

Next, Sonny was at the Aqua Lounge in Philadelphia with Albert Dailey on piano, Walter Booker on bass, and Louis Hayes on drums before giving a concert at the Famous Ballroom in Baltimore for the Left Bank Society.[36] At the concert, Sonny quoted from "Valse Hot," "St. Thomas," "I'm an Old Cowhand," "Oleo," "Paul's Pal," and "Bewitched, Bothered, and Bewildered." The energy was electric in the room, and Sonny was at his madcap best; he received a five-minute standing ovation.[37]

On Sonny's next gig, he played solo again. It was at the 1969 student-run UC Jazz Festival at the University of California, Berkeley's outdoor eighty-five-hundred-seat Greek Theatre.[38] It was a celebration of black culture in the backyard of the Black Panther Party, headquartered in Oakland.[39] Two months before the Harlem Cultural Festival, known as Black Woodstock and immortalized by the *Summer of Soul* documentary, the 1969 UC

Jazz Festival was a precursor to the first Pan-African Cultural Festival that July in Algiers. The Berkeley festival presented some of the same artists that would soon bring the Panthers' revolutionary spirit and global solidarity to Algeria, including UC festival artist-in-residence Archie Shepp, and Nina Simone, who performed "Four Women" and the yet-to-be-recorded Lorraine Hansberry tribute "To Be Young, Gifted and Black."[40] The Reverend Charles Belcher introduced the festival by asking the artists in the program "to do their thing in memory of those who have died or suffered for freedom... in the names of Jesus, Malcolm, and Martin."

Sonny performed on Friday, April 25, at 8 p.m. on an unseasonably cool opening night of the three-night festival.[41] With NASA preparing for the moon landing that summer, Sonny attempted his own moon shot.[42] He strode onto the 125-foot stage with his Mohawk haircut and horseshoe mustache, wearing a chocolate-colored double-breasted blazer, an ivory turtleneck, and black-and-white plaid bell-bottoms, playing unaccompanied tenor under the full moon: "Full Moon and Empty Arms."[43] Sonny unspooled a sweeping Americana suite, from "Camptown Races" to "Dearly Beloved" and "I Thought About You" to "I'm an Old Cowhand" and "St. Thomas," from minstrel songs to spirituals to the Great American Songbook.[44] Time seemed to stand still. Critics differed as to the length—some said it was twenty-five minutes, others twice that.[45] At the end of "St. Thomas," he let out a triad, then approached the microphone and chanted to the melody, "I thank you, I thank you, I thank you, I thank you, thank you."[46] Sonny quietly left the stage to a standing ovation, then came back out for an encore, continuing "St. Thomas" until he spun on the balls of his feet and skipped off the stage.[47]

Blues guitarist Albert King came on after Sonny, but Sonny "stole the show that night," wrote Ralph J. Gleason. "The next day, even after the searing intensity of Nina Simone's 'Four Women' and the purely religious joy of her 'I Shall Be Released,' musicians were still talking about Rollins.... It is no comment on Mozart to suggest Sonny Rollins, in a 45-minute spontaneous composition, stream-of-consciousness style, with strung-together quotations and references to hundreds of popular songs, folk songs and familiar musical phrases, is just as good. It is only to say they are different."[48]

In the audience was fourteen-year-old Oakland alto saxophonist David

Murray, who would go on to cofound the World Saxophone Quartet and win a Grammy and a Guggenheim. "He was walking around just blowing, man, making all this kind of shit on and off the mike. He was out," Murray recalled. "The next day, I told my dad I needed to get a tenor."[49] Just as Coleman Hawkins caused Sonny to switch from alto to tenor, Sonny led David Murray to take up the bigger horn. "People, they try to make like Coltrane is god, but no! God is still alive. Sonny's god. He won by just being there. I mean, Sonny is Fidel. Trane was Che Guevara."[50]

Murray saw Sonny as a bridge between the traditionalists and the avant-garde. "He never looked down on that kind of music," Murray said of free improvisation, "but he had to learn everything about his horn, everything about bebop...then he came back to the avant-garde. A lot of people can't do that." And "Sonny could do the most corny-ass shit and make it hip. See, a lot of people can't do *that*." Murray would spend the ensuing decades "trying to not be like Sonny in order to be like me, but you've got to go through somebody to get to who you might want to be."

That summer, the person Sonny had gone through to get to who he wanted to be rejoined the ancestors.[51] On May 19, 1969, Coleman Hawkins died of liver disease at Wickersham Hospital in Manhattan. He was sixty-four years old.[52] Sonny handwrote his remembrance in a musicians' tribute in the French *Jazz* magazine that summer.

> this about my Master and Idol
> I should like to be sad now at his passing. But alas!, this thing is impossible, for instead I find myself happy—forever happy and greatful [sic], that He came.
>
> Sonny Rollins[53]

For the first two weeks in July, he played at the Village Gate in a quintet with trumpeter Bill Hardman opposite the Dizzy Gillespie Quintet with James Moody.[54] Sonny's band was billed as the Sonny Rollins Celebration, and on the weekend of July 11, the Charles Mingus Quintet made it a triple bill.[55] Sonny's band shifted, but at one point it was pianist Albert Dailey, drummer Doug Hammond, and on bass George Braith, sometimes minus Dailey. Sonny then brought in bassist Jimmy Garrison, allowing Braith to stay on playing reeds.[56] Sonny then played another weekend in Philadelphia at the Aqua Lounge with Tootie Heath on drums before taking most of August off.[57]

That August, Sonny was again voted top tenor in the *Down Beat* International Jazz Critics Poll.[58] He was getting ready for a West Coast tour in August and September, and he hired a new band, starting with drummer Tootie Heath and bassist Buster Williams, on hiatus from Herbie Hancock's sextet, but he needed a pianist. He auditioned twenty-four-year-old pianist George Cables on the recommendation of Freddie Hubbard.[59]

"I picked up the phone, and I said, 'This is George Cables.' And he said, 'This is Sonny Rollins.' And all I could say was 'Who?' That was just beyond anything my imagination could gather," Cables recalled. The audition was at Musart. "When I went and knocked on the door, I heard this saxophone. He kept on playing it, and I heard it coming closer to the door. This imposing figure opens the door, who was very gracious, but still, I'm basically a kid, and it was just an impressive situation. . . . This audition was just him and me. I can remember just about every moment. Once I got in and sat at the piano, he asked me if I knew 'Love Letters,' which I didn't, and right away he pulled out the sheet music, so we went through it, and I think it was in C. And then, he said 'Okay, after that, let's do it in D-flat.' So we went through it and I got through it, and then after that, he said ' "Night and Day" in E-flat.' I said, 'Okay, cool. I know this. This is cool.' But then he said, 'Okay, let's do it in E.' And I got through that." Sonny turned to Braith. " 'Oh, this guy is really good,' " Sonny said. "I was trying to be cool, but I felt like I had a grin from ear to ear." Sonny wanted to test Cables's ability to change keys spontaneously, as Sonny was wont to do. Changing keys "gives you another perspective on the piece," Cables said, "because each key has its own personality and its own timbre."[60]

The tour was Cables's first trip to California.[61] They played from August 19 to 31 at Shelly's Manne-Hole in Los Angeles and from September 2 to 14 at the Jazz Workshop in San Francisco.[62] The rhythm section stayed in a suite in one hotel; Sonny stayed in a different hotel. They would meet at the club. The Manne-Hole was always packed. On the first night, George Cables showed up early to find Walter Bishop Jr. already there. "He was waiting in the doorway just in case," Cables recalled. "He said, 'I heard that Buster was coming, I heard that Tootie was coming, but I didn't hear anything about the piano player!' I said, 'Well gee, you ready to take my gig already before I even play the first note!' But we got to be really good friends and hang out quite a bit in LA."[63]

Another musician who came out to see Sonny was percussionist James Mtume, Tootie Heath's nephew and Jimmy Heath's son.[64] Mtume was a member of the US Organization, part of the movement for black cultural nationalism, and Sonny took an interest. "Sonny would come and listen to the lectures, and my uncle Tootie was very much involved," Mtume said.[65]

Sonny was in high spirits when he did an interview with Los Angeles radio host Jim Gosa on the KCBA program "Jazz Dialog."[66] "Between 1960 at least and 1969 I feel I've matured somewhat on my instrument and music," Sonny said, "although I must add that as far as my own playing is concerned, I feel that I've really not got my message across yet, you know. I mean, I haven't really come into full power yet....I know that there's a lot more music that I have inside of me which I haven't really played yet." There were off nights, but some nights Sonny was on fire. "There's nothing as great as really having a good performance and reaching the people," Sonny said, "and the interplay that goes between you and the people. It's really a wonderful thing. So like one of these nights is almost enough to keep you going for a few weeks, you know, at least. If you have one good night at times it's enough to last you for a while."

Moving on to the Jazz Workshop, "the setup was like that old piano trio setup," Cables recalled, "where the drums and the bass are behind the piano, and Sonny was playing, so I couldn't see Sonny, he was behind me, and his sound was so big that I'm saying, 'Wow, I wish he wouldn't play in my ear like that.' And I turned around, and he was all the way on the other side of the stage!"

One of Cables's key lessons was to listen with open ears. "At that time, I'd been really enamored with guys like Herbie Hancock and McCoy Tyner, and I'd been playing with Art Blakey and Woody Shaw, so I was interested in alternate harmonies and playing against the chord, so sometimes I did that accompanying Sonny," Cables said. "It was my first lesson: Stay home sometimes. But he just said to me very nicely, 'Could you play closer to the changes for me?' When you play in a band, it's not like you're just doing your own thing. You're playing for the whole and for the bandleader and for the music in general. I would kind of go where he went when he was playing outside of the chord. I needed to stay home, because at least the contrast would be there."[67] Sonny "really plays the song. Each song, he tells a story and plays what the song is rather than playing technical stuff. So I learned to try and just play the song you're playing, to get the joy out of it."

Yet Sonny was not getting much joy out of it himself. "I finished my job in California and I had had it," Sonny recalled in 1971. "I didn't want to play, I didn't want to hear music and I didn't want to know about music or anything. I was very, very upset because that was the first time I had gotten to the point where actually I didn't even want to know about music."[68] He would not make another public appearance for nearly two years.[69]

Sonny canceled his remaining bookings for the year.[70] He was fed up with the atmosphere of liquor and drugs he felt still prevailed in the clubs and of not being paid a reasonable rate for someone of his stature. "I think what I was really trying to do was find a philosophical, spiritual basis for playing so that I could be out among those things and still be pointed in one direction," he later explained. "To just be concerned with playing."[71]

That October, Sonny took a much-needed vacation to Jamaica, his first trip to the Caribbean to explore his West Indian heritage.[72] He called the trip a "real homecoming," according to the Jamaican Tourist Board. "I was just there as a tourist," Sonny recalled. "A friend of mine that I met in Jamaica took me around to see different people living in Jamaica—this fellow Dermot Hussey."[73]

Through Hussey, a Kingston radio deejay on RJR,[74] Sonny met guitarist and composer Ernest Ranglin, RJR deejay Fred Wilmot, and Karl Parboosingh. Known to friends as Parboo, the Jamaican artist was inspired by jazz musicians, having met Max Roach, Kenny Clarke, Lester Young, and Charlie Parker while he was studying in New York at the Art Students League under George Grosz.[75] Sonny also met American expatriate novelist William Melvin Kelley. In 1968, Kelley had moved to Kingston from Paris and was living with his wife, Aiki, and daughters, Jesi and Cira.[76] A major novelist,

Kelley was a Harvard graduate and author of *A Different Drummer*, *Dancers on the Shore*, *A Drop of Patience*, and *dem*, and then at work on *Dunfords Travels Everywheres*.[77] According to his wife, the protagonist of *A Drop of Patience*, Ludlow Washington, was in part inspired by Sonny, with hints of Clifford Brown, Charlie Parker, and Louis Armstrong, "with a side of Bud Powell.... He was so influenced by Sonny, *East Broadway Run Down* on constant rotation. He loved the image of Sonny on the Williamsburg Bridge, practicing, exploring, expanding.... All Kelley's work is jazz."[78]

Kelley was playing *East Broadway Run Down* when Sonny and Dermot Hussey arrived at the Kelley residence at 38 Montgomery Avenue in Kingston. "My father was a HUGE jazz fan," recalled Jesi Kelley, who was four at the time. "I remember the day he brought Sonny to the house; my father was beside himself. Poppy had his 'office' where he wrote in a tiny room in the back of the house; what would have been the maid's room. I remember Poppy calling me from out the backyard where I was playing to come meet Sonny Rollins, and I knew EXACTLY who he was; we had all his albums. We stood in the yard outside Poppy's office and I remember looking up at Sonny; he was so tall, taller than Poppy. And he had a quiet kindness about him."[79] Sonny and Kelley may have partaken of some sacramental ganja, she recalled.

Six months later, Kelley typed Sonny a letter written in Jamaican patois, asking Sonny to spend his sabbatical in a warmer climate. *Chief Sonny: kneekneenee-deep in Water, n Eye on dHorizon in dSea: See it? N dWaves calling, calmly, come back, Chief Sonny.*[80]

However, Sonny would mostly be in Brooklyn for the next two years, never appearing publicly. It was another sabbatical. Some would report that he stopped playing entirely, but this was not the case. He continued to see David S. Ware and other friends and collaborators.[81] "I always was playing. I was not *working*," Sonny said. "I always had my horn with me when I was not appearing publicly. I didn't get away from music...I just got away from performing."[82]

During this sabbatical, Sonny "became the ultimate recluse," he recalled. "I didn't go out at all; well, maybe just to buy groceries or something. I think I had something called agoraphobia—a phobia about going out and being among people." It was not depression, Sonny said, though "maybe I was depressed over the condition of human existence." It was a solitary time of yoga and music. "I was still practicing yoga. I was able to get into these states where I could leave my body; they call it floating. I used to do these practices to find out what was possible in life. Life is not what we see around us. It's something else. This is a screen. Behind the screen there is something else."[83]

So Sonny withdrew, searching for the atman. "For a time I considered becoming a yoga teacher," he recalled, "which was the only other thing I was qualified to do."[84] He described his mental state in a journal entry.

> My problem is motivation, in that I had decided to get completely uninvolved—and do not want to listen to music—which is necessary to keep into the music thing. I don't want to hear music, I don't want to know what somebody is doing. This is what I have to drive myself to do. Because I have to listen in order to be involved in music. I have to hear what they are doing so that I can do it if I have to, and formulate my ideas around what's happening out there. In other words, I am declining from LIFE as it is happening.[85]

Chapter 32

SATCHMO LOVE-MO

(1971)

In June 1971, Gordon Kopulos wrote a story for *Down Beat* with the headline "Needed Now: Sonny Rollins."[1] The reason was that "Jazz, whether or not we like to admit it, is in a serious crisis." Eric Dolphy, John Coltrane, and Coleman Hawkins were gone, and on November 25, Albert Ayler was found floating in the East River. Sonny was presumed to be alive, and rumors were rife as to where he had retreated. "The darkest one has it that this time he's put down his horn for good and is living on bread, water and agony, the most likely that he is in the Far East, meditating," Kopulos wrote. The reality was far more mundane: Sonny was in Brooklyn dealing with more dental problems and still fed up with the industry.

In 1971, it wasn't so much that jazz had changed, but it had bifurcated into two warring factions: rock-jazz fusion and the avant-garde. "About 10 years ago, you couldn't get jazz and rock in the same room," Nathan Cobb wrote in the *Boston Globe* in early 1970, at the beginning of Sonny's sabbatical. "But today, the term 'jazz-rock fusion' is being bandied about by critics and musicians alike, and the musical marriage is being hailed as the sound of the '70s."[2] Meanwhile, downtown New York City lofts had sprung up: Sam and Beatrice Rivers's Studio Rivbea, which opened in 1970, and, over the next few years, Joe Lee Wilson's Ladies' Fort and Rashied Ali's Ali's Alley. Where did that leave Sonny at the beginning of the '70s?

He was there through the '40s, and what he thought of as "the aspiring '50s," "the inspiring '60s," and now the "cynical '70s."[3] He was already considered an elder statesman at forty. Sonny even told one friend at the time that he was an "old-timer."[4] As battle lines were gradually drawn in the '70s jazz wars, Sonny was still a bridge, exemplifying what the Art Ensemble of Chicago called "Great Black Music: Ancient to the Future."

David Murray certainly felt this way as someone coming up on the scene caught between fusion and the avant-garde. "The one thing I think everybody could agree on, they all liked Sonny Rollins," Murray said. "Sonny Rollins was never a point of discussion as far as 'Do we like Sonny?' It was more about what period of Sonny do we like."[5] To some, Sonny was already part of the history books, but to Sonny himself, he was just getting into a new period. Yet few knew where he was.

In May 1971, Sonny considered ending his sabbatical just as he and Lucille were considering ending their years-long separation. "I thought I had really reached a very bad point in my life, but then recently I began to want to play again," Sonny told Nigerian journalist and photographer Tam Fiofori that year. "So I'm trying to get another go at it...this time, I hope I don't get caught up in the same things."[6] There was some financial exigency as well; in the first half of 1971, he received no royalties from ABC Records, the parent company of Impulse, his most recent label; though *Alfie, Sonny Rollins on Impulse*, and *East Broadway Run Down* were selling, five years after recording his final album for the label, Sonny had not yet earned out his advance.[7]

Sonny's return was galvanized by Norwegian journalist and jazz presenter Randi Hultin, with whom he had maintained a platonic friendship.[8] In 1971, Hultin gave Lucille's Chicago address to the organizers of the Kongsberg Jazz Festival, the annual international festival inaugurated in 1964. The organizers sent a letter into the void in the vain hope that it would reach Sonny. Against all odds, he said yes, on the condition that he play with a Norwegian rhythm section. "I thought that a Norwegian group would probably enjoy playing with me and would be really enthusiastic to play with me," Sonny told Hultin.[9]

In part as a result of Norway, on May 20, Lucille sent Sonny a letter from Chicago addressed to Mr. S. T. Rollins. She was worried about his health and bored in her job working for Professor Robert Thompson in the Physics Department at the University of Chicago. Lucille had resolved to quit and to start fresh in either Chicago or New York. Her letters tempered the gravitas of the decision at stake with what she called "idle chatter." She was buying organic bread from a new bakery, sent a *Mad* magazine cartoon of General Patton (then depicted on movie screens across the United States),[10] discussed her progress in weekly koto lessons and, casually, the possibility of starting over.[11]

A week later, she wrote again to say that Major and Minor, their German shepherds, were doing well and that she would be leaving her job at the end of June, unsure of where she would be on July 1, which she called "my moment of truth."[12] By mid-June, they decided to give it another shot. She resigned from her job and booked a one-way ticket to New York in mid-July. "I hate the 4th of July in New York (it always gets me uptight, and it would be a bad way to start off nervous)," she wrote. Mid-July "would give you a week possibly to be back after being in Europe to rest and 'prepare' for my great (??????) homecoming (I hope!!—I mean I hope you think it's great, that is)." This amid a discussion of a recent dinner (shrimp tempura and plum wine) and logistical matters, like procuring a parking space in Brooklyn.

So enough of this idle chatter. Will write my note of quitting now and throw it on his desk.

Take care, and hope all goes well, and hope now to see you very soon.

Love, always,

L.[13]

"We had a contentious relationship," Sonny said. "I was a civil rights guy, and we had our political differences, but we always got back together."[14] So in the summer of 1971, Sonny was poised to resume his career and his marriage all at once. He was happy to be in Norway for the first time, where he knew his father had visited during his naval career.[15] The seventh annual Kongsberg International Jazz Festival took place June 24–27, with Dizzy Gillespie backed by a Norwegian big band, George Russell, Don Cherry, Mal Waldron, Johnny Griffin, and others, but the return of Sonny was the festival's marquee event. His rhythm section was twenty-five-year-old bassist Arild Andersen, twenty-eight-year-old drummer Jon Christensen, both Norwegian, as well as twenty-six-year-old Swedish pianist Bobo Stenson.[16]

In 1964, when they were twenty-three and eighteen, respectively, Per Ottersen and Kjell Gunnar Hoff founded the Kongsberg Jazz Festival in their hometown, and it was their dream to book Sonny. When they picked him up at the airport in Fornebu, Sonny was carrying a copy of the latest issue of *Down Beat*, with his photo on the cover. "WANTED: SONNY ROLLINS!!!" it proclaimed in all caps.

"When I got home, I sent a telegram to *Down Beat*," recalled Hoff. "Sonny Rollins is in Kongsberg!"[17]

The festival hotel was the Grand, though Dizzy Gillespie had to vacate after he showered and accidentally went out the wrong door, wandering the hallway naked.[18] Sonny arrived at the festival four days early, but didn't spend that much time in the hotel; he took trips up to Knutehytta, a lodge overlooking the Gruveasen mountain, where he could practice outdoors.[19] The Nordic air convinced him to go on a fast, "just eating fruits since I've been here.... It's light most of the time, and it just changes your body chemistry, I guess, but that's one of the things I like about Norway."[20] Sonny fasted periodically to counteract a tendency to overeat.[21]

On June 25, Sonny arrived for his concert at the Kongsberg cinema in style—he had grown out his hair and had a full beard with sideburns that would rival Elvis's, with an untucked, flowing button-down with pleated sleeves over a white turtleneck and white slacks.[22] He performed for a packed audience—the festival directors had to sit on the floor. "Before people came into the concert, and we were just running over a few things, it was very light and relaxed and everything was fine, but as soon as the concert started, I noticed it was different," Sonny said. The band "had gotten more tense, but it came out fine anyway. Maybe they were a little bit nervous. They didn't have to be nervous around me, because I like the way they played."[23]

The band *was* nervous. "He came into the rehearsal and he said, 'Can you guys play some calypso?'" recalled Arild Andersen.[24] The concert started with a seventeen-minute version of "Sonnymoon for Two."[25] More than thirty minutes of the forty-five-minute set were recorded for TV broadcast on the state-run NRK station. Sonny played eleven choruses on "Sonnymoon," but then stepped aside and let the band really stretch out. He gave a masterful rendering of "In a Sentimental Mood," heavy on vibrato à la Ben Webster, before passing it off to Stenson after the melody. Stenson takes a full chorus, unusual for a slow ballad, followed by Andersen, who dug deep as Sonny stood back, swaying behind the drums. At the end of the first full chorus, Andersen expected Sonny to come back in, but he didn't. Andersen played an entire second chorus; the bass solo ran a full four minutes. Then, Sonny signaled to Stenson to play an entire additional chorus. Only then does Sonny come back in for the head out, playing an inspired cadenza.

It turned out Sonny was nervous, too, and his teeth were bothering him. "This is my first concert in some time, and I'm not really up to one hundred percent like I should be, 'cause I've been away for a while," Sonny told Hultin a few days later. "But it was great to start again playing here in Norway. It was great to begin again and it gives me a nice boost and a nice inspiration to get back into playing again on a full-time basis."[26]

Sonny and Hultin attended much of the programming during the festival.

On June 26, they went to the baroque Kongsberg Church to see the live recording of George Russell's *Listen to the Silence*.[27] They also went to the Odd Fellow club in Kongsberg to see Johnny Griffin and Sonny's old friend drummer Arthur Taylor. Taylor had begun working on *Notes and Tones*, a collection of interviews he conducted with jazz musicians that would be published in 1977, and Sonny agreed to sit down for one.

"Do you play for yourself, for the musicians or for the audience?" Taylor asked.

"I would say I'm playing for the sake of music," Sonny said. "This is my first appearance since 1969. One of the reasons I stopped then was because things had got to the point where I found that playing was getting to be a real job and a chore, which I didn't dig."[28]

Before the Kongsberg festival ended, Hultin invited Sonny to come back to Oslo with her and stay at her house, the legendary residence at Gartnerveien 6. Starting in 1953, Count Basie, Ben Webster, Sonny Clark, Kenny Dorham, Stuff Smith, Hampton Hawes, Freddie Green, Zoot Sims, and just about any jazz musician who passed through Norway passed through Gartnerveien. Sonny agreed to come for a few days. He didn't practice—dental problems prevented him—but he enjoyed his time in the pastoral environment. As part of his yoga routine, Sonny did a headstand for at least ten minutes every night. "Sonny liked to spend time in the yard," Hultin wrote, "and for some reason took to mowing grass, even though he maintained this was the first time he had ever pushed a mower in his life."[29]

They spent the days listening to music, with Sonny singing the lyrics; Sonny also met Hultin's daughter Christina. The night before he left, they sat down for a recorded interview. In New York, he said, he had been leading a solitary life, watching television sometimes, painting watercolors, and not listening to much music. He had given away most of his own recordings to friends. "I kind of keep myself so closed off and secluded from people. A lot of times, people don't even know how to contact me," he said. "I still have my students, they always keep in contact with me, but I haven't been actually doing steady teaching recently." Lucille was still in Chicago, but was "supposed to be coming back to New York...so I don't know how that's going to work out."[30]

Hultin kept a guest book signed by her illustrious guests, and Sonny added his own message:

Randi
    Now its' my turn to say how wonderful you are.
    May the Lord bless and keep you through this life and may we meet again in the next. = I KNOW WE WILL
                                                                    Sonny Rollins[31]

When Sonny left on July 4, he flew to Reykjavik and decided to stay in Iceland for a day.[32] He celebrated the holiday digging the Armed Forces Network broadcast of Ramsey Lewis's "Oh Happy Day" from *Them Changes*. Then it was back to New York.

Back in Brooklyn, Lucille returned the next week. Sonny was reunited with Major and Minor, and a cat—it was suddenly a full house. Lucille started a new position as an executive assistant at New York University (NYU). Sonny wasn't back on the scene yet himself, though. "I must admit that my physical plant has been breaking and that I am in not the best health currently," Sonny wrote Hultin that July. "Also not to mention my teeth (or lack of) which produce pain when I blow my horn—now that I have just decided to really blow my horn again!! I must get the above mentioned things resolved, before I can get into full swing. On top of all of this I am currently attempting to normalize a domestic situation which is taking a lot of attention. It is all a matter of giving—I don't think it is too bad to give but I must shore up my own condition so that I will be able to give (vis a vis personal health)."[33] Max Roach recommended a new dentist, and Sonny began $3,000 of treatment.[34] As it altered his embouchure, it would inevitably alter his sound, making it throatier, but still undeniably Sonny.

Sonny and Lucille successfully restarted their marriage, and that December, her mother, Nanette, would move into the apartment on Willoughby Walk to join them.[35]

Right then, Louis Armstrong and Charlie Shavers died two days apart. On July 6, Armstrong died of heart failure,[36] and on July 8, Shavers died of throat cancer. Then Sonny and Lucille's dog Major also passed. Wynton Kelly transitioned earlier in April. Sonny and Randi Hultin had just watched Armstrong on television earlier in the month. "[Armstrong] found the Rosetta stone," Sonny said. "He could translate everything. He could find the good in the worst material."[37]

On July 27, Sonny wrote Hultin a stream-of-consciousness meditation on mortality in all caps:

> RANDI HULTIN:
>
> SO MUCH OF LIFE HAS PASSED SINCE LAST WE SPOKE. LIFE DEATH, ...POPS' PASSING OF COURSE AND THEN MY DOG OF ELEVEN YEARS AND CHARLIE SHAVERS, (WHICH WAS A REAL DRAG COMING AS IT DID SO CLOSE TO LOUIS...AND NUMEROUS OTHER THINGS AS MY FINDING A NEW DENTIST AND CURRENTLY PLANNING TO PLAY MORE OF MY INDIAN OBOE IN THE FUTURE, AND MY WIFE AND PEOPLE AND TREES AND BOOKS AND LOVE AND RESOLVE AND FAITH AND BELIEF AND STRUGGLE...TO ATTAIN ANYTHING WORTHWHILE...AND NEIGHBORS AND FEAR OF NOT TAKING CARE OF SOMETHING WHICH YOU KNOW YOU SHOULD AND IS IMPORTANT. AND RESOLVING TO TAKE CARE OF SUCH THINGS WITH DISPATCH... AND FRIENDS AND PEOPLE WHO LOVE AND PEACE AND HAPPINESS AND MOMENTS OF GRATEFULNESS AND REAL JOY AND PUTTING ALL OF THESE THINGS INTO A HORN AND HEARING IT COME OUT AND BRINGING IT OUT AND THIS IS LIFE AND I WONDER HOW STUPID I LOOK IN THOSE HOME MOVIES WHICH RANDI TOOK AND ICELAND WAS OUT OF SIGHT
>
> ...THE PEOPLE OF THE UNITED STATES WILL NEVER LET JAZZ DIE AND LOUIE IS SO LARGE THAT HE WILL NEVER DIE.[38]

Sonny had a handwritten lead sheet in his archives for a tune called "Satch," apparently never recorded.[39] It has a complex chord progression, often with a change per beat, full of sharp nines, flatted fifths, and half-diminished chords, but the melody and the message were simple:

Some folks called him Lou-ie
While Others knew him as plain ole Satchmo
But if you'll re mem-ber
His one creed was Love-mo

There was one more line in the bridge: *Nev-er die, and that is why*

In late July, galvanized by Pops' death and with his latest bout of dental work behind him, Sonny's thoughts returned to music in full force.[40] By August 4, Sonny was "proceeding along alright as I have been adjusting to my teeth and I am rehearsing with some bright young musicians some of whom I may use in future things," he wrote Hultin. "For instance I may soon make a recording for a 'friend' of mine who has been after me to do so. He formerly headed Riverside Records."[41] The friend was Orrin Keepnews.

As Sonny continued adjusting to his new embouchure, he had no documented gigs for the rest of the year. Despite his long absence, he was still voted second in the *Down Beat* International Jazz Critics Poll, with Dexter Gordon winning.[42] Sonny still hated the industry. "We all sit around and smile on album covers and to hell with the life blood of music which is slowly being drained away," Sonny wrote Hultin.[43] "My own playing? It is still exciting to me and my desire to create is alive once again after being stifled for over a year. I must admit that this pleases me."[44]

On October 26, he was still getting ready for his return to performing in the United States. "Today the sun is now coming up and there is a beautiful patch of blue sky through the clouds," he wrote Hultin. "My windows face east and so I see the big red ball of sun coming up in the morning. I am looking forward to today because I am going to play at a private studio in the Bronx. Since I am unable to practice my horn in my Brooklyn apartment in the unencumbered uninhibited manner I prefer, my problem has been one of finding somewhere to practice alone—since I really enjoy this type of solitudinal working." He was "on the verge" of being where he wanted to be, and thinking about returning to teaching, but it still wasn't time yet.[45]

Two days later, he wrote Hultin again, this time discussing spiritual matters. "You must live on a constant plane of BEAUTY PEACE LOVE AND TRANQUILITY, BASKING IN THE SUN OF THE LOVE SHARED FOR YOU. THIS IS THE PLANE WHERE I AM EXISTING, CAN YOU IMAGINE IT????" he wrote. And then there was the more earthly plane. "Oh—oh—my cat has just gone to her (its) box and I'll be right back. Excuse me."[46]

That December, Swami Chinmayananda came to the United States on a lecture tour, and Sonny was "helping arrange things for him," he wrote. "It has gotten me to be very busy."[47]

Sonny had come to deeply respect Hultin, who became a close confidante. "I do feel that you are more completely qualified to write on jazz than anyone in Scandinavia or Europe," he wrote her. "Maybe they discriminate against you because you are a woman. They are probably jealous of your intimate understanding of the music and the musicians. I think your articles can be 'hard-hitting' as much as you want—no one can censor you, as you are obviously more knowledgeable than they." Later on, when Hultin was having marital troubles, Sonny wrote, "Unfortunately we live in a world where women are second class people—(like Blacks.) Many men feel that they should have as many women as they want. This is unfair and maybe one day this will all change. In my opinion the social set-up of our world is way out of line and has to fall—so don't despair—1 out of 3 marriages fail in the U.S. and in Los Angeles 1 out of 1. The social set up is all wrong. It is not your fault!!"[48]

Sonny's youthful idealism had hardened into a middle-aged cynicism born of experience.[49] The sabbatical had awoken feelings of exile. Being in Europe, he told Arthur Taylor, "I feel I'm in another man's country. In the States it's difficult, and I'm the type of person who can withdraw into myself, so a lot of times I choose to withdraw and not to go out and get involved with hostility from white people," Sonny said.[50] "Of course, I know you have to get out in it; you can't just withdraw and try to forget that it exists. I'll say this—about ten years ago I used to be very much in favor of trying to bridge all the people in the world together and trying to bridge the gap between white and black. I used to read a lot of philosophy and look for ways of bringing everybody together. I would go out of my way to try and make friends. But now I know that this is redundant on my part as a black man, because it's not up to me to do it; it's up to the white man to be friendly with me....I can't do it. I had to give up that idea because it really doesn't work."[51]

Even if Sonny had concluded that music would not end racism, he still felt that music was "a beautiful way of bringing people together, a little bit of an oasis in this messed-up world."[52]

With this shift in perspective came a renewed focus on the individual.

"Now that I've been away for a while I want to get back into playing a little more, and I also want to try to fulfill myself," Sonny told Taylor. "I'm beginning to just want to be in a natural state all the time and not have anything to do with alcohol or any kind of stimulant. I'm also reaching a stage where I can really dig life as it is. I've always heard people ask, 'Why can't you dig life the way it is? Why do you need to get high?' I couldn't relate to that at the time. I felt I wanted to get high before playing. I'm beginning to find that I can make it without stimulants—not only that I can but that I want to, and that I can enjoy life the way it is without using whiskey or anything. This is the first time that this has ever happened to me."[53]

Sonny had nearly killed himself in the past, but it was time for a middle path. This was Sonny Rollins in his forties.

Chapter 33

NEXT ALBUM

(1972–1973)

In 1972, listeners across the world were holding out hope that Sonny would return to regular performing. In the Netherlands, jazz publicist Fred "Cigar" Canté launched the "ROLLINS COME BACK" campaign, with stickers signed "some concerned jazz fans."[1] Sonny had returned to live performing in the United States and signed a new recording contract. The recordings and the live shows would tell two very different stories of who Sonny was as a musician. To say he disliked recording was too mild—he hated it.

"I hate it because I'm a perfectionist, and I'm a person that considers myself constantly evolving as a musician and a performer," Sonny later said, "so I hate to put anything down that's going to be there forever. And this is what recording is all about."[2]

Unlike being onstage, a studio recording, it seemed, could be perfected, take after take, until he got it right, a painstaking process that sometimes led to revelations from behind the glass, but often proved antithetical to an art form where perfection was tied up with spontaneity. Live, audiences would swear Sonny was the sun, moon, and stars on a good night, but if he wasn't, he was Icarus flying too close to that sun. Sonny's perfectionism in the studio and the unpredictability of an off night live obscured the fact that he was still the greatest living tenor saxophonist. When he was on, he was playing as brilliantly as ever, maybe better.

Others wondered why Sonny had departed from his 1950s style. But he wasn't hearing that sound.[3] Some would be disappointed at his turn to electric instruments and an R&B influence, considering it a betrayal of his hard-bop roots. To Sonny, though, it was as much a departure as a return to the music of his childhood idol Louis Jordan.

He shared this propensity for artistic evolution with Miles Davis. Miles "got a lot of flak from people who said 'Miles, why aren't you playing the way we want you to play, like back in the forties?'" Sonny later said. "I think Miles is also a person that doesn't want to be a relic, and I share that with him. . . . I want to keep contemporary and I have a great love of music myself and we want to keep active. . . . Some people can just be what they are and live their whole career like that. Beautiful. I'm not that kind of musician and I don't think Miles is."[4] Furthermore, Sonny claimed, despite the ample evidence onstage that he could still play however he wanted, that he had no choice but to change: "I'm always completely improvising. I keep fresh because I'm never the same. I'm always trying to reach a point in my music and I'm always reaching for it."[5]

Completely improvising required preparation, and Sonny continued his daily practice: daily hatha yoga and woodshedding, methodically working through his asanas, the saxophone rudiments, and his own written-out saxophone exercises or "dailies," a routine he maintained for the rest of his career. The ephemerality of the stage lent itself better to the notion of complete improvisation. "I became very self-conscious about recording around the seventies," Sonny recalled. "I wanted to make sure that what came out was the best representation of Sonny Rollins, and I thought I knew what that is. Now, I might not be perfect in that."[6]

Recording was a necessary evil. The industry dictated that a steady touring schedule required physical product to promote. "Whereas recordings are good, and I'm very happy to have made successful ones that helped people find out about me," Sonny said, "the actual playing experience [in the studio] is nothing like being with real people, and creating music for real people, and getting the feedback from real people."[7] For a supposed recluse, Sonny was desperate to reconnect with his audience, and he could only do it on the stage. Since the fifties, recording technology had progressed, but to Sonny this was in some ways more of a hindrance than a help. His early recordings had "no overdubbing, no going back and forth. In effect, it was live, but no audience except for the engineer and producer," he said. "Now, of course, I employ overdubbing and other modern techniques myself for my recordings, but I prefer f-to-f. I think there's something that happens in actual live performance. It can't really be captured; even a live recording is not like being there live.... So there's no way to capture what's happening right at the moment, which is what jazz is all about anyway—that creative spontaneous thing."[8]

For a neurotic perfectionist perpetually moving forward, going back and listening to the studio masters was painful. "The guys that I played with are like redwood trees. I have a high standard to keep up with the people that I've been associated with," Sonny later said. "So I hear my shortcomings when I listen back to myself. Hopefully, too many other people don't hear them! But I hear them."[9]

That January, Sonny was feeling optimistic. "I have just taken some engagements and will be doing some more performing than recently," he wrote Gertrude Abercrombie. "So wish us well Gertrude, and send us your love and thoughts then I'll send back my vibrations and we'll build a bridge to infinity of steps along the ladder. THE POWER OF GOOD VIBES you dig? Of course you do! Don't you?"[10]

Orrin Keepnews had tried signing Sonny to Milestone since 1969, but Sonny never picked up the phone. "For what turned out to be nearly three years of intermittent attempts, I never succeeded in reaching him," Keepnews wrote, "until the day I returned from a trip to find the message that Mr. Rollins had phoned—leaving a quite different call-back number. In quick sequence, I called, he informed me that he was thinking of recording again and wanted to know if I was still interested, we met briefly and agreed in principle, and a details meeting was set up with his attorney, [S. Edward Katz], a longtime guardian of Sonny's best interests. Most points were easily dealt with: royalty, advance, my never-in-question commitment that Rollins would have total artistic control over his work, and also that it would initially be a one-year, two-album contract, with two successive one-year options."[11] The contractual terms were fairly standard, and Milestone agreed to a $7,500 advance per record.[12] It was half of what Sonny got from RCA a decade earlier, and a smaller label, but it was worth it to Sonny to have total control over his artistic output.

"The only thing I have is my autonomy, as much as my bankroll will allow," Sonny wrote Randi Hultin, "and I will not prostitute myself unless I want to play and the people involved are groovy. I'll starve or whatever until such conditions are met to my satisfaction."[13]

Sonny's contract with Milestone was executed on March 1, 1972.[14] By the end of the year, Milestone was acquired by Fantasy Records, which transferred over the contract. The deal was mutually beneficial, especially given his experience at Impulse: Sonny got control and Milestone got Sonny. "Milestone seemed to be a label which was very laid back," Sonny recalled. "Nobody told me what to do, what to record, when to record, and I missed that, which was precisely what I wanted."[15] Sonny's lawyer ensured that the label had to issue the two albums, and the label ensured that they would have a three-month production period after completion to release each album, freezing the contract year if there was a delay in recording. Keepnews knew about "Sonny's aversion to the record-making process," and anticipated that the six albums they agreed to would take about six years, twice as long as the contract dictated—and he was right.

It's a byzantine story: In 1964, Riverside filed for bankruptcy.[16] In 1966, Keepnews left Colpix Records to become A&R producer for the newly formed Milestone label, which he cofounded with pianist Dick Katz.[17] In 1967, producer Robert Bialek bought Milestone and kept Keepnews on as general manager. In 1969, Sol Rabinowitz at CBS negotiated foreign distribution for Milestone; in 1970, the label became a subsidiary of Herman Gimbel's Audio Fidelity. In 1967, Gimbel made an unsuccessful bid to buy

Fantasy Records, the Berkeley, California–based label run by the Weiss brothers, plastics manufacturers turned jazz record producers.[18] In 1967, they sold Fantasy to their associate Saul Zaentz—well before Zaentz produced *One Flew over the Cuckoo's Nest* or *Amadeus*. In 1968, Zaentz took a chance on a young mailroom worker with a band called the Golliwogs. The worker was John Fogerty, and the band was renamed Creedence Clearwater Revival.

"All of a sudden, Fantasy had this pop hit on its hands," recalled Keepnews. "I guess it was at that point that they felt they had the money to indulge their desire to scoop up this Riverside stuff."[19] In 1971, Zaentz brought on Ralph Kaffel to run the label.[20] In 1971, Fantasy bolstered its jazz catalog by acquiring Prestige, home of Sonny's early work, then, in November 1972, the Riverside catalog.[21] Fantasy eventually bought Stax, Pablo, Contemporary, and others. With these jazz catalogs all part of Fantasy, Kaffel launched the "twofers" program, reissuing two albums in one package and, later, the Original Jazz Classics reissue series.[22] Suddenly a jazz conglomerate with a glut of classic material, Fantasy needed help managing it all, and given Keepnews's relationship to the source, Zaentz and Kaffel hired him as director of jazz A&R. Keepnews left Milestone.

"To be told eight years after I'd bombed out [with Riverside] that I really was a success and that my material had lasting value—that was important," Keepnews said.[23] However, taking the job at Fantasy meant leaving behind the Milestone artists Keepnews had signed: McCoy Tyner, Joe Henderson, Lee Konitz, and Sonny. Then, within weeks of Keepnews's departure, Zaentz acquired Milestone from Herman Gimbel.[24] With the Milestone, Riverside, and Prestige catalogs in addition to their own existing roster, Fantasy had in short order become the largest indie jazz label in the country, and all of Sonny's classic Prestige and Riverside albums would be brought under one roof, with new work on Milestone in the pipeline.[25] "I don't think anything normal ever happens in the jazz record business," Keepnews said.[26]

Practically before the ink had dried on his contract, Sonny's new label was issuing his old material. "My wife hates any kind of reissue; she thinks it's the worst thing that could happen to someone," Sonny said. "I don't really dig the reissue scene, although in my case I had stopped playing for so long that the company probably felt the need to get something of mine back into the shops."[27]

Eventually, when Lucille took over as Sonny's manager, his Milestone contract was renewed on an album-by-album basis. To avoid repeating the exploitative fate of his earlier work, Sonny would retain all publishing for his own music under the banner of Son Rol Music Co. This was his "doing business as" entity, or DBA, allowing him to collect the writer's and publisher's share of royalties to his own material. "I don't know of any such arrangement in the industry," recalled Kaffel.[28] "It really was a unique arrangement. We'd do an album and Lucille would say, 'You want to do another one?' And I would say, 'Yeah,' and so we'd do a one-page letter and we'd be set for the next album. That went on for his duration with Milestone." What this amounted to was that Sonny "had total freedom," Kaffel said, with Fantasy showing "respect for the music and a lot of respect for Sonny. It was really a very wonderful relationship."[29]

There was some concern that after so much time away, Sonny had lost his edge. "Maybe my skills atrophy," Sonny said. "I think that's normal. But, maybe there's things more important.... I'm always hoping there's a certain correlation between a person and his art. I'm hoping I'm going to be gaining something through the experience of life that's going to compensate for skills."[30]

Sonny was committed to reaching the widest-possible audience. "I feel there's a virtue in playing simple, so I would like to do things that are simple," he said. "This is nothing profound, but people sometimes might think of jazz as being something involved.... I want a basic recognizable song, melody, something people will be able to relate to.... [T]here's no sense in playing music if there's no communication."[31] Yet Sonny's journals and practice notes reveal that he approached simplicity through complexity. He dissected harmonic progressions, intervals, and upper extensions with exhaustive detail. Simplicity, it turned out, was a challenge for him.[32]

From March 14 to 19, Sonny was booked at the Village Vanguard for his first New York gig in two years.[33] "I remember one year I couldn't find him," wrote owner Max Gordon. "I had his phone number on Willoughby Street in Brooklyn, where he lived, but every time I tried it, I got his wife or mother-in-law." He finally reached Sonny at 3 a.m.: " 'How're you doin'?' he asked matter-of-factly, as if he talked to me every day. 'What's happenin'?' "[34]

Sonny had been across the river in Brooklyn all along, but it was a homecoming nonetheless. Sonny hired pianist Albert Dailey, bassist Larry Ridley, and New Orleans–born drummer David Lee, who was equally adept at playing timpani, funk, R&B, boogaloo, and straight-ahead jazz.[35] "Dizzy Gillespie recommended me to Sonny, 'cause I had played with Dizzy about a year," Lee recalled. "I was playing with Roy Ayers and then Sonny called me, so I went with Sonny."[36] Dailey was a piano prodigy from Baltimore who had worked with Sonny before, but this would be his longest stint in the band. He was, according to Max Gordon, "the only piano player Sonny never fired."[37]

Ankle-deep slush and heavy rains did not bode well for Sonny's opening, but the weather did not stop fans and fellow musicians from lining up around the block on Seventh Avenue. According to Whitney Balliett, it was the busiest week ever in the Vanguard's history. On opening night, the Sonny Rollins Celebration opened with a nineteen-minute "Sonnymoon for Two," followed by "Moritat" with "There Will Never Be Another You" and "St. Thomas" interspersed. Quoting "The Man on the Flying Trapeze," Sonny's high-wire act featured dozens of choruses on Monk's "Straight, No Chaser" and a soulful "In a Sentimental Mood." As Balliett wrote in the *New Yorker*, Sonny had "surfaced like a whale."[38] Not every set was equally thrilling, but Victor Stein wrote in the *Village Voice*, "I would gladly sit through what I heard Sunday ten times to catch one set like the two I heard Thursday night."[39] On the final night at the Vanguard, Sonny played only three songs per set, but each tune lasted fifty minutes.

"There'll be no more hiatuses for me from now until the end, which isn't that far away when I consider the time I have left," Sonny said.[40] Sonny was happy to have a well-received homecoming, as he wrote Gertrude Abercrombie shortly thereafter, sending some positive press notices. "To me they are of course not <u>really</u> meaning anything," Sonny wrote, adding, "but here they are just in case they mean anything to you."[41]

At the Vanguard, Sonny met nineteen-year-old alto saxophonist Bob Mover.[42] He was teaching in Boston, working with pianist Jaki Byard, and considering moving to New York, but he wanted a second opinion—from Sonny.[43] Mover had written Sonny a letter asking if he could study with him, but decided to approach him in person instead. At the Vanguard over two nights, Mover sat right in front of the bandstand and was so blown away that decades later he remembered in exquisite detail, from Sonny's red jumpsuit to the standards he played. "He looked like Santa Claus," Mover recalled.

On a set break, Sonny sat at the head of a receiving line. "So I didn't stand in line," Mover said. "I sat next to him. And he kind of looked at me, and I looked at him and smiled, and he smiled back." When the line thinned out, Sonny turned to Mover. " 'So what brings you here?' " Mover told him how much Sonny had influenced him; Sonny asked if he knew Chu Berry's playing. " 'It must be wonderful to just feel all this love and adulation and all these people want you back,' " Mover said. " 'I can't imagine that feeling.' And Sonny said . . . 'I just try to find the middle ground, because audiences are a very fickle thing. They can love you one day and not dig you at all the next, so if you depend on them, you'll be very unhappy.' "

The next night, Mover returned and sat next to Sonny on a set break. Sonny offered to share a Scotch. " 'From the way you talk about music, you must play good horn. Do you?' " Sonny asked. "It took me a minute, and I thought, compared to what? Compared to what I had just heard? No! This profound silence for ten or fifteen seconds. I said, 'Well, Sonny, yeah, I can play.' And he gives this huge grin like the sun coming out, and he says, 'Isn't it nice when you know you're good?' " Mover then asked if Sonny would take him on as a student. "He said, 'I'm not quite sure how I do what I do even though I have some knowledge, and I think explaining it might make it more elusive, and make me have to think about how I do what I do which I don't want to do, so that's why I don't teach. But . . . we can practice together.' "

Mover called every day, but Sonny couldn't make it. "While he's canceling, we're on the phone for an hour," Mover said. "We just had a good flow, we'd tell each other jokes." A week passed, but Sonny came.[44] Mover pulled out a bottle of Cutty Sark, and they started playing the standard "Invitation." Sonny worked through some interval exercises, and Mover played it back.

Then Sonny asked Mover to call a tune, and he called "There Is No Greater Love."

"He said, 'Sure. What key?' I said, 'Well you play it in E-flat. I noticed that.' I don't have perfect pitch, but I could tell from watching his fingers sitting so close. So Sonny says, 'Oh, do I?' Then he starts playing it in G." After the better part of an hour, Sonny asked if they could switch horns. "Sonny played my alto, and he played only Bird on my alto, but he overblew the horn. I almost had a hallucination of the keys just flying off. And he had me play his tenor...and I sounded just like Sonny Rollins," he said jokingly. It was the only time they would ever practice together, but the philosophical conversations continued.

Mover recalled that Sonny began studying the Schillinger System of composition at around this time. "I asked him what he got from it, and he said that the only chapter that he really found useful to him was the part about expansion and contraction of melody," Mover said. Perhaps the greatest lesson was this: "'Within me, there is a pianist, a drummer, and a bass player, and they're all there within my tenor,'" he said. "'You have to be an orchestra within yourself.'"[45]

That spring, Sonny was awarded a Guggenheim Fellowship to work on a concerto; other recipients that year included George Russell, Mary Lou Williams, Keith Jarrett, and Carla Bley.[46] Sonny wouldn't realize his concerto for another fifteen years.

It was time for Sonny to end his recording hiatus.[47] On July 14, he went to Mercury Sound Studios at 110 West Fifty-Seventh Street to begin recording Sonny Rollins's *Next Album*, a tongue-in-cheek title.[48] The band consisted of George Cables on electric and acoustic piano, Bob Cranshaw on electric and upright bass, drummers David Lee and Jack DeJohnette alternating, and Arthur Jenkins on congas. So Sonny could explore the studio space, recording engineer Elvin Campbell constructed a microphone that could be clipped onto his bell; he ended up sitting for most of the session.[49] "Everybody was out on the floor. We weren't in booths," recalled David Lee.[50]

It was DeJohnette's first time recording with Sonny.[51] He'd conceived of his role in Sonny's band as "providing intensity but also sort of a base where

Sonny could go and come back and play against the music," he said. "He plays with and against the music. That's why sometimes he likes to have the rhythm section provide a base so that when he goes out and comes back, there's a cushion to support him when he lands. But he takes off."[52]

That first day, Orrin Keepnews invited journalists Gary Giddins and Kiyoshi Koyama to the studio. "I remember we used something like twenty reels of tape, culled down to one in those days," Lucille later wrote.[53]

"The first rehearsal, we played 'Skylark' in E-flat," recalled George Cables. "The second rehearsal he called it in B-flat. And when we got to the date, he said B-flat, but when he put the horn in his mouth, it came out in G!"[54]

"It might sound different in a different key," Sonny said. "I was probably searching for a key that would bring out the better aspects of the tune."[55] "Skylark" turned out to be the session highlight, opening and closing with Sonny's signature cadenzas.

The album led off with "Playin' in the Yard," a simple funk tune with Cables and Cranshaw playing electric instruments, officially marking Sonny's entrance into the seventies on record. When they recorded Sonny's new calypso, "The Everywhere Calypso," George Cables looked up in the studio to see Monty Alexander, who was from Jamaica, standing in the booth. On the standard "Poinciana," Sonny recorded on soprano for the first time.[56] "Since Coltrane had reintroduced the soprano, everybody had started playing soprano," Sonny said. "So I guess playing soprano was sort of the thing to do after Coltrane."[57] Coltrane's influence also emanates from "Keep Hold of Yourself," a C-minor blues that evokes "Mr. P.C." and, at times, "Cousin Mary."[58] Sonny dropped a beat in the ninth chorus—it turned out he was only human.

The album got mixed reviews. "This album is a hard disappointment, primarily because Rollins serves up such uninspired performances," wrote Hollie West. Conversely, Gary Giddins wrote in his five-star *Down Beat* review, "If there is a Platonic perfection to which all tenorists aspire that resides in our collective unconscious, then Sonny must be the cat with the goods."[59]

That August, Sonny reclaimed the top spot in the *Down Beat* International Jazz Critics Poll and toured Europe as a single. Lucille came with him; she had begun taking a more active role in managing his career.[60]

In September, Sonny returned to California for three engagements—at the Los Angeles County Museum of Art,[61] and his first appearance at the Monterey Jazz Festival since its 1958 inauguration. He brought George Cables and David Lee. Cables recommended bassist Henry Franklin, a Los Angeles native who had just returned from a European tour with Hampton Hawes.[62] When Sonny "called me about 10, 11, 12 at night," Franklin recalled, "I thought somebody was putting me on. . . . And then finally, after a couple minutes, I said, 'Wow. Maybe this really is him, man.' And it was. So I had to apologize."[63]

On September 11, 1972, Sonny played at the LACMA sculpture plaza.[64] "That's the first time I had ever seen a standing ovation before [someone] even played," said Franklin. "People were standing for the whole concert. He didn't call tunes. He just started playing. Whether you know it or not, Sonny's gonna play it. That was our rehearsal." To George Cables, it was one of the best gigs he ever played. "I could swear I saw a rainbow over the audience," he said.[65]

In San Francisco, Sonny was scheduled to appear at Black Expo '72, also known as Black Quake, billed as "America's first international exposition devoted exclusively to black culture," which took place from September 7 to 10 at the Civic Center. The festival celebrated black culture across the arts, presenting, among others, Ray Charles, Bobby Womack, the Delfonics, Ornette Coleman, Bobby Hutcherson, and Herbie Hancock; New Federal Theatre founder Woodie King Jr.; poets Haki Madhubuti, David Henderson, and Sonia Sanchez; artists Joe Overstreet, Elizabeth Catlett, and Charles White; photographer and director Gordon Parks; and director Melvin Van Peebles.[66]

Next, Sonny taped a thirty-minute episode of the arts anthology series *One of a Kind* for KCET, which would air nationally on PBS.[67] They played "In a Sentimental Mood," "Keep Hold of Yourself," and "There Is No Greater Love."[68] On September 16, Sonny performed at the Monterey Jazz Festival opposite Herbie Hancock's Mwandishi band, Joe Williams, Mary Lou Williams, and a group billed as the Giants of Jazz: Clark Terry, Roy Eldridge, Kai Winding, Sonny Stitt, Thelonious Monk, Al McKibbon, and Art Blakey.[69] Sonny performed in a royal-blue African robe and decided to play a medley for his set, jumping from "There Is No Greater Love" to "I'm an Old Cow-hand" to "St. Thomas," followed by "Three Little Words."[70]

At the beginning of November, Sonny was booked at the Berlin Jazz Festival, but he didn't perform—his teeth were bothering him again.[71] Following dental work, Sonny was off for the rest of 1972.[72]

On December 5, Sonny's good friend Kenny Dorham died of kidney failure at the age of forty-eight; Sonny would help support his family.[73] Sonny also won the *Down Beat* readers' poll—he was hailed as the "comeback man of the year."[74]

⎯⎯◦⎯⎯

In 1973, Lucille began transitioning into work as Sonny's full-time manager, and her new role freed Sonny up to focus solely on the music. On February 5, Sonny and Lucille attended Norman Mailer's gala birthday party at the Four Seasons, paying a fifty-dollar admission fee to be donated to the Fifth Estate, an organization Mailer was launching with a to-be-determined agenda. At the black-tie affair, Sonny mingled with Charles and Sue Mingus, Jimmy Breslin, Eugene McCarthy, and George Plimpton; Andy Warhol shot photos.[75] At this time, novelist James Purdy sent Sonny an inscribed copy of his new novella, *I Am Elijah Thrush*, a comic tale of unrequited love told by a black narrator.[76] Sonny knew Purdy through Gertrude Abercrombie, and Sonny wrote Abercrombie for his phone number so he could thank him.[77]

Sonny had an opportunity to see Abercrombie when he performed in Chicago from February 28 to March 4 at Joe Segal's Jazz Showcase, downstairs at the Happy Medium.[78] Sonny hired David Lee, pianist Walter Davis Jr., and bassist Cecil McBee. Davis was a forty-year-old former sideman to Charlie Parker, Max Roach, and Art Blakey, who following a stint in the sixties as a tailor had returned to music.[79] McBee was thirty-seven at the time and had just worked with Charles Lloyd.[80]

At the Jazz Showcase, it was standing room only.[81] Sonny was on fire that week, playing "Strode Rode," "Pent-Up House," "In a Sentimental Mood," "Poinciana," "The Folks Who Live on the Hill," and "Paper Moon." Musicians flocked to the Showcase to hear Sonny—Bunky Green, Willie Pickens, Eddie Harris, Jack DeJohnette, Stan Getz, Wilbur Campbell, Herbie

Hancock, Bennie Maupin, AACM cofounder Muhal Richard Abrams, and all the members of Air.[82]

On March 11, Sonny played in Washington, DC, as part of the Smithsonian's Jazz Heritage Series at the Natural History Auditorium. Beforehand, Sonny gave a public master class at Howard University to three student saxophonists selected by Donald Byrd: Allan Barnes and Stephen Johnson of the Blackbyrds as well as Larry Thompkins.[83] That night, 650 fans, among them Representative John Conyers, flooded the 550-seat auditorium. Sonny wore a velvet suit.[84]

"The power of the sound of his horn, of whatever he intended to express, was absolutely beyond anything that I could imagine," McBee recalled. Two weeks after they got back, Sonny asked if McBee would go on tour to Japan with his band later in the year, but McBee had a prior commitment. "Sonny never got back to me again," he said.[85]

On April 2, Sonny began a two-week engagement at the Half Note in New York with a new band.[86] He retained Walter Davis Jr. and David Lee and brought on bassists Bob Cranshaw and James Leary, who sometimes played simultaneously, and twenty-six-year-old guitarist Yoshiaki Masuo, who went by the monomym Masuo.[87] Masuo got his start with Sadao Watanabe and, after moving to New York in 1971, working with Elvin Jones and then Lee Konitz. That March, Sonny invited Masuo to audition at a rehearsal studio on Nineteenth Street between Fifth and Sixth Avenues. Just the previous week, based on his performance on Elvin Jones's *Merry-Go-Round* session, Masuo auditioned for Chick Corea's Return to Forever in advance of Corea's *Hymn of the Seventh Galaxy*. At the studio with Sonny, Masuo met bassist James Leary, Bob Cranshaw, and Walter Davis Jr.; they played "God Bless the Child." Sonny and Chick Corea both offered him a spot, but "the feel was so good playing with Sonny" that he joined his band.[88]

At the Half Note, Sonny played opposite the Newport All-Stars, with George Wein on piano,[89] and he "reached such a level of excellence, it scared you," said Wein.[90] Masuo was in heaven. "It's not easy, but to play his music, to me it felt so good," he said. "His music sounds happy, but in that happiness there are lots of other things. It's deep." When they were really on, Bob Cranshaw would exclaim, "All right!"[91]

After the run at the Half Note, Sonny returned to Mercury Sound Studios to begin recording *Horn Culture*. "They want me to record again, although I'm not sure I'm ready," Sonny remarked that February. "I've made some good albums and some bad albums, so this'll be nothing new."[92] Sonny hired Walter Davis Jr., Cranshaw, David Lee, Masuo, and twenty-seven-year-old percussionist James Mtume, the son of Jimmy Heath. Mtume met Sonny when he was a teenager.[93] While attending Pasadena City College on a swimming scholarship, he joined the black nationalist US Organization. There, Ron Karenga gave him the name Mtume; he was one of the first to celebrate Kwanzaa. In 1971, he joined Miles Davis's band.[94]

"Sonny was playing so long, I thought by getting another player in the band that was playing rhythm, it would be easier to play," recalled David Lee. "David was an extremely talented drummer who never got his just due as many artists are," Mtume said. Truthfully, Sonny "had the drums in his head," Mtume said. "Forget the technique—and he was an absolute monster on the instrument—it was his sense of timing that always gassed me. Being a percussionist, timing is everything."[95]

Mtume added: "Sonny also helped me understand simplicity of melody. It's not about how many fuckin' notes you *play*, it's really about how many notes you *don't* play.... What is your signature?"

Yet much of Sonny's relationship with Mtume moved beyond the music. "We discussed politics a lot, because I came out of the Black Power movement in the sixties, and we would have discussions about that period—Malcolm X or Elijah Muhammad and Farrakhan," Mtume said. "The politics and the music have always kind of been locked, but the politics was kind of downplayed. Art is always adjacent to politics."[96]

On *Horn Culture*, Sonny experimented with fusion. It was an inherently risky process and not always successful. *Horn Culture* would mix one-chord funk vamps like "Pictures in the Reflection of a Golden Horn," on which Sonny trades with himself on an overdubbed track, and a new version of "God Bless the Child."[97] Sonny recorded one of Mtume's tunes, "Sais," named for the Egyptian city that was the last pharaonic capital before the Persian conquest, and asked Mtume to play piano on it.[98]

At the first session, Masuo had a raging cold. They recorded again on

June 13 and again on July 23 at Fantasy Studios in Berkeley.[99] Gary Giddins was at the studio with Orrin Keepnews and his son Peter on one of the New York–based sessions. "Apparently there's a thing that musicians know about Orrin: He hates the tune 'Stella by Starlight,'" Giddins recalled. "No matter what the tune was, Sonny constantly quoted that song over and over again. Orrin remarked, 'This is Sonny's way of telling me that he doesn't want us to use any of this stuff. But that's OK. We needed a rehearsal session. We'll continue tomorrow and then we'll get the record.' Well, the record came out, *Horn Culture*—and much of it consisted of what we heard on that 'rehearsal' day."[100]

Sonny knew it was not his best work.[101] "As soon as I appeared in public people wanted a record," Sonny said later that year. "It's a business thing also. And it's probably good to have a record out, even though it might not be one that I necessarily feel is the best thing that I've ever done. . . . But I also realize that this can go on forever and ever and ever, and I would never make a record. So I listen to other people on that. I listen to my wife on that, and she advises me on what she thinks is acceptable."[102]

Lucille's notes on the *Horn Culture* sessions were largely positive. She thought "Sais" was "Beautiful!!!" "God Bless the Child" was "lovely," though she found another take, likely left off the album, "terrible," "overall as a group effort nowhere. All in all NO STARS."[103]

Gary Giddins would refer to *Horn Culture* as the nadir in Sonny's recorded output—"a confused jumble that should never have been released."[104] In Neil Tesser's two-and-a-half-star *Down Beat* review, he wrote, "To be blunt, the music is largely uninspired."[105] Yet the fuller picture is that *Horn Culture* was a record of a band still getting comfortable with itself; much of Sonny's post-sixties material came to life on the stage.

"Love Letters," which was jettisoned from the album, had coalesced by June, when Sonny embarked on a brief West Coast tour with George Wein's Newport Jazz Festival West.[106] "We call him 'the walker,'" recalled Wein, "because when he's onstage we have to put microphones all around, because he starts walking all over."[107] They flew back to New York, where they played the Vanguard followed by the Newport Festival in New York at Philharmonic Hall.[108]

Around this time, Sonny and Lucille, who was not yet Sonny's full-time manager, decided it was time for a change of scene.[109] Clinton Hill, the neighborhood where they lived by the Pratt Institute, "began to change, to go down," Sonny recalled. "Lucille was working and I had to go and meet her at the subway when she came back from work every day. We began to feel that we had to leave, which we hated to do because we had a nice big apartment."[110] In 1973, there were 1,680 murders recorded in New York City, the second highest in its history up to that point; the highest murder rate occurred in 1972, the previous year. As Sonny wrote in his journal, it was time to "get the hell out of New York."[111]

Lucille and Sonny began driving upstate to house hunt, as far north as Washington County. "We used to do that every day, and finally we found a house. It was not perfect and it was a kind of compromise, but you have to compromise when you buy your first house," Sonny said.[112]

They wanted seclusion, while still along a main road. "An interracial couple can't be too isolated," Sonny later said. "It's better to be in the middle of things. You know, even up here the KKK is still around."[113] It was a modest four-bedroom, two-bath farmhouse with a fireplace, built in the 1880s, overlooking the Catskill Mountains in provincial Germantown on about ten acres of land along a quiet state highway—Route 9G. There were four outbuildings, most of which were eventually painted a teal blue: a two-story barn, a garden shed, a small studio, and a chicken shed, which they converted into a recording studio and practice space. With the Guggenheim money, Sonny had a rehearsal studio and practice space custom built.[114] Sonny and Lucille slept on the second floor, her mother, Nanette, downstairs.[115] They grew apples, tomatoes, and string beans.[116]

In rural Columbia County, Sonny could practice as much as he wanted without disturbing anyone and could practice meditation and yoga without being disturbed. "It was a two-hour drive, and we loved the quiet and privacy. We weren't really social people who hung out and went to parties and everything," Sonny recalled. "I had plenty of open sky and could see the stars at night."[117] Most in town knew him as Theodore, Sonny and Lucille as the Rollinses. Soon, Germantown residents shopping at Otto's Market might bump into the Colossus in the produce aisle; a local hotel clerk once referred to him without irony as Teddy.[118] Minor the dog had a lot more space. For the first time, Sonny's woodshed was an actual woodshed.[119]

That August, Sonny went on a European tour for the summer festival circuit with Masuo, Davis, Cranshaw, and Lee. On August 17, they played Jazz Middelheim in Antwerp, and Sonny welcomed an old Belgian friend onstage. "We did our last tune. I unplugged my guitar, and I'm heading for the exit, but this guy came up to me and he grabbed my guitar, and he really looked crazy," Masuo recalled. "I said, 'What's going on?' I look at this guy and I kind of recognize his face... the guitarist René Thomas. He was heavily into drugs, but he wanted to play. So I gave him my guitar. Sonny of course knew that was him, so they played one more tune."[120] Sonny had worked with Thomas on *Sonny Rollins and the Big Brass*; he would pass away at forty-seven on January 6, 1975.

On August 21, they played at Chateauvallon in the South of France and Laren in the Netherlands on August 24.[121] It would be the first time many had seen Sonny playing with an electric bassist. Bob Cranshaw made the switch to the Fender after injuring his back in a car accident that year, and Sonny liked the sound, despite the objection of some traditionalists. "He made the electric bass sound very much like an acoustic bass," Sonny said.[122]

Yet to some fans, Sonny going electric was as controversial as Dylan doing so.[123] At Laren, Bert Vuijsje suggested in an interview that Sonny's heyday was from 1956 to 1959, but Lucille strongly objected. "I have to say this," she interjected. "Because I mean, and I don't think I'm being prejudiced, but never in his whole life, I don't think there's any question about it, now, this is it! I mean as far as the image part and as far as being wanted and as far as being the number one person, I don't think there's any question about it."

"You think my most impressive period is right now?" Sonny said.

"I think there's no doubt about it," said Lucille.

"I think that would be more for other people to say," said Sonny.

Sonny hoped his heyday was yet to come. "I haven't really reached what I've been trying to reach ultimately in my playing," he said. "So I can't put myself in a period of saying, 'Well, I've done it.'"[124]

That September, Sonny went on a ten-city tour of Japan. Sonny and Lucille stopped in Fairbanks, Alaska, for a brief vacation en route to Tokyo.

Lucille's mother, Nanette, who lived with them, had to spend some time at the hospital, and every day, Sonny wrote her a postcard with a photo of Alaskan wildlife or an iconic image from Japan.[125]

In Japan, Sonny's appearance was greeted with the enthusiasm of a Vladimir Horowitz concert, maybe greater: "Both events are as infrequent and as awesome to behold as total solar eclipses," read a story in the *Mainichi Daily News*.[126]

Sonny and Lucille flew to Tokyo on September 14.[127] Mtume was available, so he came on the tour as well. Between September 7 and October 2, they played Fukuoka, Hiroshima, Yokohama, Tokyo Festival Hall, Kosei Nenkin Hall, Yamagata, Kanazawa, Niigata, Nagoya, Kyoto, Nishinomiya, Tokyo again, and Sapporo.[128] The September 30 performance at the Nakano Sun Plaza Hall in Tokyo was recorded for release on the Japan Victor Company (JVC) label.

Sonny Rollins in Japan was the explosive album everyone expected of *Horn Culture*; it was released only in Japan. "Powai," a nineteen-minute modal exploration that Sonny wrote at the ashram in India, was based on a ritual chant he heard on the outskirts of Bombay.[129] Sonny never recorded the song again. They played "St. Thomas," "Alfie's Theme," "Moritat," a twenty-nine-minute version of "Sais," "God Bless the Child," and "Hold 'Em Joe."

Back in the United States, Sonny played from October 22 to 28 at the Jazz Workshop in Boston, where bassist Roland Wilson filled in one night for Cranshaw.[130] He was back at the Half Note from November 19 to December 1—two weeks at $3,000 per week—and getting regular standing ovations.[131] Sonny had revised his earlier thinking about clubs versus concerts. "I generally prefer concerts to club dates, although both have their advantages," he said.[132] "In a concert you usually have an attentive audience. You don't get the expense-account businessmen who don't seem to have much interest in music; you're not competing with banging trays, rattling bottles and ringing cash registers. On the other hand, a concert is a one-shot deal; you don't get another chance. With a club date, if one set doesn't work out, you can make up for it on the next one. You can play all night in a club, begin to relax and stretch out musically. You don't really have the time to do that in a concert."[133]

Sonny was feeling closer to content. "I can't say I'm happier with my playing now, but I am beginning to accept myself a bit more," he said during the Jazz Workshop run. "I'm not happier because I haven't reached the point which I should be at." His teeth remained his Achilles' heel. "I've had a lot of dental problems, which have really been the bane of my existence. . . . I eventually wind up back at the dentist." Sonny was convinced that he was running out of time, probably because so many of his peers had already passed on. "Time is running out," he said. "Now I definitely want to play as much as I can."[134]

As Sonny was looking to the future, the past remained fresh in his mind. "I still get a lot from John [Coltrane]. I feel that at one point, he got a lot from me, and now I'm catching up with him," Sonny said. In Germantown, Sonny continued studying what he referred to as the "literature of the instrument." He was still in touch with Roach, Monk, and Miles. He had seen Max on the European tour with his group M'Boom and just recently been at Miles's concert; Monk, though, was in poor health. And Sonny was moving forward, with the help of Lucille. "She's a real straight arrow," Sonny said. "She keeps me in line. Left to my own devices, I can get pretty wild."[135]

From December 14 to 15, Sonny played at the East, an African cultural center at 10 Claver Place in Bed-Stuy, founded by Jitu Weusi in 1969.[136] The East operated independently and had to fund itself through community organizing and cultural events, first and foremost a popular concert series. Alcohol was prohibited, but home-cooked meals were always served.[137] Mtume recorded an album there in 1971, *Alkebu-Lan: Land of the Blacks*; and Pharoah Sanders, Freddie Hubbard, Nina Simone, and Sun Ra all performed there.[138]

Sonny's appearances at the East were a highlight of the concert series. "Rollins was on fire that night," recalled one concertgoer. "It seemed like he was spitting sparks out of his horn on his tune 'The Cutting Edge.' The audience was on its feet screaming, like they were at an old fashioned, country church revival meeting."[139]

Sonny finished the year with a concert at the Brooklyn Academy of Music on December 30 opposite the Vermeer Quartet.[140] That month, he was voted into the *Down Beat* Hall of Fame; that August, he had won in the critics' poll.[141]

"There is a jazz renaissance in New York," wrote Bob Porter in *Down Beat*. "In a bit less than two years, the number of clubs actively featuring jazz has tripled."[142] More jazz records were being produced; there was increased media attention. It seemed to many that one of the driving forces in the jazz resurgence was Sonny's return. These accolades cemented Sonny's status as an elder statesman at forty-three years of age, but he still wouldn't rest on his laurels.

Chapter 34

THE CUTTING EDGE

(1974–1975)

By the beginning of 1974, Sonny and Lucille were living a life of relative solitude, intermittent touring, and recording, a rhythm they would maintain for the next thirty years. Sonny woke up at 6 a.m. and spent hours practicing in his custom-built studio in Germantown, while Lucille managed his business affairs. "I'm as good technically as I'm going to get, so the thing to do is work on myself, so I can play ME," Sonny said later that year.[1] Lucille made sure Sonny could do that. She left her administrative position at NYU and, that June, informed *Down Beat* that she was to be listed as Sonny's booking agent and personal manager.[2]

"At first, I felt like such an amateur dealing with club-owners and record producers that I used the pseudonym Janice Jesta for a while," Lucille said. "Jesta was one of our cats. But I became more self-confident once I realized how much I love this business."[3]

"Lucille loves it, she's good at it, and I don't have to face the real world of people who are just there to make money," Sonny said. "If I did I don't know how long I would be in the business, because music is a tough, cutthroat business."[4]

In addition to managing bookings, arranging tour itineraries, and serving as road manager, Lucille looked after Sonny's health, reputation, and their finances with a perspicacious eye for detail—nothing slipped past her. She also made sure Sonny wasn't overbooked. If Sonny's sabbaticals were truly behind him, they had to find a middle ground. This meant saying no more often than not. "I've heard that some music-industry people call me Mrs. No," she said.[5]

Lucille had a midwestern civility that complemented her shrewd business sense; she was as polite as she was direct. In her personalized letters, she could say no with grace and made sure that Sonny was given a fair deal and accorded the respect he deserved. She had no compunction about dressing down anyone who deserved it with a professional courtesy that could be withering in its restraint. And no matter what, she always responded.[6]

In 1977, Sonny received a Christmas card addressed only to him from a French concert organizer and record producer who had impugned Sonny's current style while offering to book him at a festival. Lucille let him have it.

> Although you choose to ignore the fact that I do Sonny's booking and am also his wife (I have never heard of the rudeness of a family sending a card to just the husband—if we had sent you a Christmas card it would certainly have been addressed to both of you out of courtesy) I just have to write this letter.
>
> First of all, you profess to respect Sonny—if you did, you could never have written your letter about a year ago (which he showed) which carried the assumption (completely erroneous) that Sonny was doing anything musically in order to capitalize on any crazes, fads or anything. Sonny is a great artist who does what he wants, plays with whom he wants, and neither you, I, any writer, anyone can or should tell him what to do. He has always however (unlike you) been open and finds exciting things in what is happening today, some of which (and some of the songs) he likes, finds compatible, and he enjoys playing with versatile musicians. He could make a very comfortable living simply reliving the 50's and never changing—fortunately he is not so closed up and is always changing, always going forward, never looking backward. Perhaps you didn't realize how insulting it is—if you don't like what

he's doing—fine—that is certainly your privilege—but please don't <u>assume</u>, especially if you think you know him and respect him, that he has ever had any motives other than making the best album at the time he is doing it—sometimes it works, sometimes it doesn't. He also (yes, even Sonny) has an off night—although being slightly prejudiced I would say that even one of Sonny's "off" nights will top anybody else's "on" nights.[7]

Their relationship was a ménage à trois. "Strange as it may seem," Lucille wrote, "Sonny's main interest is in music (I hope I come second) and my main interest is in keeping Sonny healthy, happy, and to do whatever I can to see that he gets the proper respect and is kept free from the things that are distracting and distasteful to him so that he can concentrate on the great gift he has. This is not easy in this life."[8]

Many fans, critics, and peers hoped that Sonny would continue "reliving the '50s"—even Cecil Taylor. "Sonny Rollins was burnin' in fifty-one man, but he told me in seventy-four that he wanted to do...well, let's say this: He feels now he wants to make money," Taylor said. "I think that Sonny could do anything he wants and still make money. But those chumps he's playing with ain't making him think about anything. He's one of the cats I learned a lot from so it hurts me when I, you know, hear him playing this simple shit."[9]

Sonny vehemently denied this accusation—to him, he was just responding to the contemporary scene and expanding his musical vocabulary. The backlash was largely a response to Sonny's perceived embrace of fusion and his use of electric instruments in his bands. In 1974, Sonny himself had begun contemplating using an electronic instrument himself. "I'm not against it.... It's not so much the attachments. It's still the player," Sonny told a radio host that year. Sonny recognized that there would be some "subtleties" lost, but potentially something gained.[10] "I feel it's important for a person to get out what's inside of him, you know, whichever way he can do it. If he can do it on an electric instrument, okay, good. An acoustic instrument is more personal. I don't think there's any doubt about that. But I think it's the time now to try to blend the two forms.... It's hard to project now whether we'll have to let go of everything and go into a complete new thing or whether the two can coexist. I'm trying to touch all bases, so to speak, and keep my ears open for whatever's happening without putting down what's been done before. It's another one of those fine lines—one of those cutting edges." "The Cutting Edge" was a new Sonny original, a modal tune that would have the master of playing changes suddenly playing virtually none.[11]

Sonny was booked at the Etcetera Club in Washington, DC, from February 11 to 16 at a rate of $3,300 for the week, which was standard for him for club work at the time.[12] He had his regular band—Walter Davis Jr., Masuo, and David Lee, with bassist Roland Wilson subbing for Bob Cranshaw. Sonny reconnected with twenty-year-old saxophonist and DC-area native Ron Holloway, whom he had met the previous year and came to the show with his father.[13] Sonny asked if he wanted to sit in, but he didn't have his horn and vowed he'd bring it the next time.[14]

From March 4 to 9, Sonny played at Just Jazz in Philadelphia with Masuo, Walter Davis Jr., and David Lee. Masuo recommended his friend Chin Suzuki on bass, and Mtume and Robert Kenyatta joined on percussion.[15] On March 17, Sonny played a benefit for drummer Ed Blackwell, who was suffering from kidney disease. The benefit took place at Mackenzie's Corner House in Toronto alongside Salome Bey, Sadik Hakim, Karl Berger, and others.[16] From April 1 to 7, Sonny played in Boston at the Jazz Workshop and adjacent Paul's Mall, which were under the same management.[17] Sonny used Masabumi Kikuchi on piano, Don Pate on bass, Dave Earle Johnson on drums, and Ray Mantilla on congas. It was at this time that he invited twenty-year-old saxophonist Ricky Ford and thirty-year-old trombonist Ray Riperton, the brother of Minnie Riperton, to sit in.[18]

"I was probably one of the only people who was studying Sonny Rollins on a level that you could really see that he listened to Sonny Rollins," Ford recalled. "I made scientific observations of things he was doing, his finger position. They say you can learn more from a musician by observing them than by actually studying with them."[19] For example, Ford noticed that Sonny would never use the high F-sharp key. "Sonny Rollins is more like Benny Carter. He never really succumbed to peer pressure. His style pretty much is very consistent throughout his whole career, even though the people are going to say, 'No, he became more commercial.'... Fundamentally, he was always playing the way he played in the sixties. Maybe you're not gonna hear it on the record but you could hear it when you go to hear him live."[20]

Ford had been practicing twelve hours a day and, leading up to Sonny's arrival in Boston, had learned all the material on *Horn Culture*.[21] "Each night he told me to come back. I played with him for the whole week, me and Ray." After the gig, Sonny invited Ford to New York to rehearse, paying his airfare and hotel.[22] Sonny suggested that he might bring Ford on tour with him to Europe. When he didn't hear from Sonny, "I went to the telephone booth to call," Ford said. "He said, 'Well Ricky, if you were in the band, I would have to work too hard.'"[23]

Instead, Sonny hired someone who sounded nothing like him: twenty-eight-year-old Philadelphia-born saxophonist and bagpiper Rufus Harley.[24] Sonny and Harley met years earlier. Friends once called Harley "Little Sonny," and it was Sonny who convinced him to switch from saxophone to bagpipes. When Harley first approached Sonny for advice as a young saxophonist, Sonny told him to play long tones to develop his sound. "He told me to play whole notes, way before I came to the bagpipes, and he told me to sustain them. The whole essence of music is about that—the Om is the whole note . . . it is the sustaining force."[25]

"After Coltrane and Sonny Rollins broke big, the rest of us were in a funny place," Harley said in 1969. "After they put it through the horn, there wasn't much any of us could do but get another instrument." When he saw the Black Watch, a Scottish pipe-and-drum regiment then on tour, perform at the funeral of John F. Kennedy, Harley was inspired to seek out a set of bagpipes.[26] Harley traced the origin of the bagpipes back to ancient Egypt, claiming it as part of the African diaspora.[27] The bagpipes could only play a nine-note scale, but beyond the limitation in repertoire, he found that the possibilities for jazz were limitless.[28] Soon, Harley was signed to Atlantic Records. Coltrane and Roland Kirk both asked Harley to show them how to play the pipes, and so did Sonny.[29]

Sonny had bought a set of bagpipes on his first trip to England. "I got enamored with the pipes, and I wanted to play," Sonny recalled. "I was learning to do the circular breathing, so it was all part of a concept I had which on the saxophone was mimicking in a sense the bagpipes, the way the bagpipes produce their sounds. And I heard the bagpipes in myself besides just listening, and I loved Rufus, but as an instrument I had ideas about, one—playing them myself, and two—incorporating their sound in some way into my saxophone playing."[30] He even bought a practice chanter.[31]

Harley was a strict vegetarian who delivered his nine children himself.[32] He dubbed himself an "international ambassador of freedom" and eventually began bequeathing hundreds of miniature replicas of the Liberty Bell to people he met around the world. He performed either in a kilt or in a flowing bishop's robe with a cross emblazoned on it. To Harley, the bagpipes allowed him to represent "just what an American is."[33] Rufus had what he described as the "life-force energy," and Sonny felt it.[34]

"I just thought, what an interesting, courageous move," recalled Mtume of Sonny's decision to hire Harley.[35] "I mean, it's Sonny Rollins and a bagpipe! That's how he heard. He just was so open, man. Who else would do that of his stature? He caught a lot of flak from those square cats. They couldn't hear that. Sonny didn't look at Rufus as a novelty. He looked at him as a component. I'm sure Rufus played with some horn players, but he's standing up there with Sonny Rollins, man. That's a statement."[36]

Sonny planned for Harley's debut performance with the band to be on May 3 at Carnegie Hall, slated as Sonny's only US concert appearance that year. Leading up to the show, though, he made an unheralded appearance, at least as significant: at the Bronx Men's House of Detention, for an audience of prisoners, who were allowed to wear civilian clothes. The concert, staged in a prison auditorium, was presented by Hospital Audiences, Inc., an arts nonprofit founded in 1969 by Michael Jon Spencer with the simple premise—"Art heals!!!"[37] Sonny performed with Cranshaw, Lee, Masuo, and a pianist recommended by Mtume—Stanley Cowell.[38] Two songs sent a message of perseverance to the men: "God Bless the Child" and "Don't Stop the Carnival."

For the May 3 concert at Carnegie Hall, Sonny added Mtume and Harley to the band. It was presented by New Audiences, the concert production company founded by Julius "Julie" Lokin and Art Weiner in 1971 in New York.[39] Sonny and Lucille did not want an opening act, and in lieu of that, New Audiences convinced them to have Sonny perform with a special guest:

Freddie Hubbard.[40] Orrin Keepnews hoped to record the concert for Sonny's next Milestone album, but Hubbard, recently signed to Columbia, agreed on the condition that there be no recording due to the potential conflict.[41] Lucille wanted Sonny's photos and biography kept very current. "You'll note that nothing much goes back further than 1972," she wrote Lokin, "and if possible that's the way we'd like it to be for, say, the program—no looks or 'wallowing' in the past."[42]

The afternoon of the concert, Freddie Hubbard abruptly canceled. Hubbard "was not very reliable," Lokin recalled.[43] "Even in booking, the guy who was representing him said, 'I'm not guaranteeing he's gonna be there. You want to take the chance, go ahead and do it.' So my partner and I went after Mingus, and Mingus got Dizzy."[44]

It was too late to change the program. "They made an announcement that Freddie Hubbard was not gonna be there and people were pissed off," recalled Clifton Anderson, who attended the concert with his family. "A lot of people went to the box office and got a refund. Sonny comes out, he plays a couple tunes. He said, 'Freddie Hubbard can't be here tonight, so I called a couple of my friends to come in. Ladies and gentlemen, Mr. Dizzy Gillespie and Mr. Charles Mingus!' That was the best concert I'd ever been to. The blissful energy backstage, there was so much love. And that made up my mind at that point that I was going to become a musician."[45]

"In the '70s, Sonny Rollins dominates the realm of the tenor saxophone the way Ellington dominates the big band, the way Armstrong once held sway over all trumpet players," wrote Gary Giddins in the *Village Voice*. "He may frequently play as well as he did last week in Carnegie Hall but I doubt if he has ever played better. For that matter I doubt if I have ever attended a more extraordinary concert."[46] And like the Titans of the Tenor concert, it was not recorded by anyone.[47]

From June 18 to 23, Sonny played the Village Vanguard.[48] On June 28, Sonny, Masuo, Harley, Lee, and Cranshaw flew to Europe for a monthlong tour. They began on June 30 in Norway at the Kongsberg Jazz Festival.[49] On July 6, Sonny appeared at the Montreux Jazz Festival, adding Mtume and Stanley Cowell, in a performance that was taped for Sonny's next Milestone release, *The Cutting Edge*.[50] Sonny stuck to the set they had developed throughout the tour—his original "The Cutting Edge," his arrangement of Edward MacDowell's "To a Wild Rose," another original called "First Moves," Burt Bacharach and Hal David's "A House Is Not a Home," and "Swing Low, Sweet Chariot" (pronounced "Chario," with a long *o*), which was part of Rufus Harley's bagpipe repertoire.[51]

"Sonny is such a powerful figure on the saxophone," Cowell said, "and the energy level that he plays with after he plays for thirty minutes—and then it's the piano solo. Gee, what are you gonna do? You've been comping... trying to. It's quite a challenge." After Montreux, Cowell joined the Heath Brothers. "You could relax a little more, breathe a little more. I just felt that Sonny's stuff was so powerful that I didn't want to continue in that vein."[52]

Reviews were mixed, but in France, *The Cutting Edge* won the Grand Prix du Disque in the jazz division of the Charles Cros Academy Awards, the French equivalent of the Grammys.[53]

From July 8 to July 20, Sonny performed at Ronnie Scott's, his first London appearance since 1967.[54] Every set was standing room only; *Melody Maker* called it "Britain's jazz event of the year."[55] Sonny played, among others, "Poinciana," "There Is No Greater Love," "A Nightingale Sang in Berkeley Square," "Alfie," and "East Broadway Run Down."[56] On "Swing Low, Sweet Chariot," Sonny used circular breathing to play in unison with Harley's drone. To those who had read the tepid reviews of his recent releases and worried that Sonny had lost his edge, the Ronnie's run confirmed that he was still the world's greatest improviser. "All the Rollins elements are still there," wrote Ken Hyder. "The tone—as big, wide and fiery as a blast furnace; the dramatic cliff-hanging sense of timing; and the almost sardonic—but never sentimental—treatment of ballads, which would surely be doomed to corny failure under other singers."[57]

Sonny focused on the concept of a "sustaining" sound, "rather than a lot of notes. I think there's more expression in getting the true meaning of the sound... and this gets back to the drone on the pipes. It's all related." To Sonny, his '50s compatriots were still with him. "Sometimes I just have to think about these guys and I can get their spirit," he said. "Sometimes I can just think about Clifford Brown and I will start to play better myself."[58]

On July 26, Sonny concluded the summer European tour at the Antibes

Jazz Festival.[59] The annual festival was held in La Pinède, the pine grove in Juan-les-Pins overlooking the beach. Sonny wore a bright-red shirt and a matching red beret. According to Leonard Feather, Sonny "shook the Pinède to its foundations." In a week that included solo performances by Keith Jarrett, Randy Weston, and Martial Solal, as well as Lee Konitz, Muddy Waters, Freddie King, and the Dave Holland Quintet, Sonny's concert was "the scene stealer and, artistically, the week-stealer."[60]

That August, Sonny won the tenor category in the *Down Beat* International Jazz Critics Poll again.[61] Earlier in the year, he was named Jazz Man of the Year by the Japanese *Swing Journal* for the second consecutive year.[62] He took August off. On September 10, he was booked for one night only at the Jazz Showcase in Chicago, then from September 16 to 28 at the Half Note opposite Attila Zoller. On October 4, Sonny played at the University of Pittsburgh Jazz Seminar's culminating concert. In the band were Thad Jones, Jim Hall, Jaki Byard, Ron Carter, Alan Dawson, and on tenor and soprano saxophone Pitt's own Nathan Davis, who originally met Sonny in Paris.[63]

From October 27 to November 15, Sonny went on a fall European tour for George Wein's Festival Productions, with Lucille as road manager. Sonny brought Masuo, David Lee, Rufus Harley, and bassist Gene Perla. Perla had met Masuo in Japan in 1970 and stayed in touch; it was through this connection and his several years working with Elvin Jones that he got the gig.[64] They played in Stockholm on October 27, Copenhagen on October 30, at the Berlin Jazztage on November 1, at Newport in Paris on November 6, a date in Belgium, at the Belgrade Jazz Festival on November 12, and at the Mednarodni Jazz Festival in Ljubljana, Slovenia, on November 15.[65]

"I would say logistically, it was probably the best tour I ever did in my life," Perla recalled. "We went to Europe for three weeks; we had seven concerts. So we'd have two or three days in each city and play one concert. It was wonderful."[66]

Perla and Sonny did all their talking on the stand. "In those nine months, maybe there were twenty or thirty words spoken between us," Perla said. "He kind of kept to himself—quiet, never had a conversation about anything, maybe just like, 'The bus leaves at 4.' He wouldn't hang out. I don't have any issue with that. It makes absolute sense to me, because I think that he handled his fame extremely well...because he's a god! Who else is there? Coltrane, him, Stan Getz? You know, a few guys who rise to the top like that that have such a heavy influence on the scene? And so everybody's on you. Put the glass wall up."[67]

Sonny continued focusing on that sustaining tone. In Stockholm, he would sustain a note on "My Reverie" or Jerome Kern's "Look for the Silver Lining," then suddenly let loose a stream of eighth and sixteenth notes.[68]

Sonny took the rest of the year off from performing.[69] That year, he won the tenor category for the third year in a row in the *Down Beat* readers' poll. Sonny himself was looking for the silver lining. Around Christmas, he wrote Randi Hultin that he was composing new material, "(which is the only salvation for me at this time) and trying to not 'over-eat' and 'under-anything' else, and in general keep myself in good busy habits as these days go by, one by one, by one, by one, by one, by one etc. Actually I am working on a new album on which I will be using some new elements and this is giving things a big beautiful energy and great anticipation and Great Expectations."

And here is how he signed off for 1974:

Well—time to get to work

LATER[70]

————◁○▷————

At the beginning of 1975, Sonny continued focusing on communicating more immediately with the audience. "I like to play and let the crowd settle and then pull a little then wake them up with something outrageous," he wrote in his journal. "Just when they begin to lose interest I shock them back to reality."[71]

He was thinking of adding a keyboard, possibly a synthesizer, to his band, to be played by himself. "I used to be a talented piano player," he said. "I'll have a keyboard of some sort on stage and comp a little when it feels good and solo a little and gradually work it in." In the meantime, "my life, besides music, is very happy."[72]

Sonny and Lucille finally left the apartment on Willoughby Walk in Brooklyn and rented a studio pied-à-terre at Independence Plaza in Tribeca by the Hudson for when they needed to be in the city.[73] On January 15, 1975, Sonny and Lucille moved into 310 Greenwich Street, apartment 39A, though they would still be in Germantown, Lucille wrote George Wein, "95% of the time."[74]

That year, Sonny gave a series of master classes at universities. On January 28 and 29, he led two three-hour master classes for a capacity crowd at the three-hundred-seat Ira Aldridge Theater at Howard University.[75] On the first day, Sonny was backed by guitarist Bill Harris, pianist Lawrence Wheatley, bassist Duane Alston, and drummer Maurice Lyles, his old friend from Lexington. Alto saxophonist Earl Anderza, a former San Quentin inmate and a current resident at the Regional Addiction Prevention center (or RAP, Inc.), took the stage and started playing an unaccompanied duet with Sonny. The crowd began to shout. "Burn! Cook!" Others leaped to the stage with their instruments as the rhythm section joined in. They all played "Take the 'A' Train" in honor of Duke Ellington, a native son of Washington, DC, who had passed away on May 24, 1974.[76]

The next day, Sonny talked about the relationship between music and politics, diet, and jazz pedagogy.[77] WHUR deejay Dyana Williams asked Sonny if he felt that black women should be limited to certain instruments in jazz. Sonny responded, "Black women cannot be prevented from doing anything, especially in the creative and spiritual."[78]

For the musical portion, Sonny was backed by bassist Steve Novosel and invited several people onstage, among them tenor saxophonist Ron Holloway.[79] Sonny mostly played his own material, but when someone asked about "Giant Steps," Sonny played it unaccompanied. "His approach to the tune was more melodic lines, so it was a very different approach," said Holloway. After the performance, Holloway's mother suggested that he invite Sonny to dinner with his family, and Sonny said yes. "We kept in touch from that performance on," Holloway said.[80]

Holloway had studied Sonny's "sense of construction, timing, humor, personality, choice of notes, note displacement, drama wit . . . All this and more!"[81] Note displacement meant that "everybody has their pet phrases and their licks, so to speak, and Sonny is no exception, but the thing that he would do in order not to become too repetitive or monotonous, he would take some of his phrases, and put a rest in a very unexpected place and change the phrase...almost like he was trying to trip himself up." Perhaps most significantly to Holloway and to Sonny, Sonny was a guiding light in keeping Holloway off drugs. "One of the reasons I avoided getting into drugs was because of Sonny Rollins. So for me, Sonny had the reverse effect that Charlie Parker had on his generation. His tribute to Charlie Parker is to tell younger musicians, 'Don't even go down that road. It's not worth it.'"[82]

From February 4 to 9, Sonny played at the Village Vanguard with Masuo, Stanley Cowell, Bob Cranshaw, David Lee, and, on congas, Robert Kenyatta, who was on hiatus from touring with the Beach Boys. One night, Woody Shaw sat in on "Dearly Beloved."[83] From February 18 to 23, Sonny played at In Concert in Montreal, with Gene Perla on bass.[84] University appearances followed: on March 7, a concert at SUNY-Binghamton and, from March 12 to 14, a master class at the Rutgers Livingston College campus in New Jersey organized by Music Department chair Larry Ridley.[85] On April 4 and 5, Sonny was a clinician and gave a performance at the Pacific Coast Collegiate Jazz Festival at the University of California, Berkeley alongside Ed Shaughnessy, Jamey Aebersold, Tom Hart, and Freddie Hubbard. From April 10 to 12, he was a judge at Notre Dame's Collegiate Jazz Festival, alongside Willis Conover, Dan Morgenstern, bassist Chuck Rainey, Jack DeJohnette, and Cecil and Dee Dee Bridgewater.[86]

Sonny sometimes invited Dee Dee Bridgewater to sing with him. "He called me on several occasions to perform with him for the New York Jazz Society. Then he had me sit in with him one time at Montreux for the Montreux Jazz Festival in Switzerland," she recalled. "I was in my early twenties and I was just starting out, and he was one of the first people that called me to work with him.... He was always very kind with me, and we would work out the keys of songs. We would do standards.... What I remember more is his calling me on the phone because of his voice... He just always made me feel good and like I was just part of the band."[87]

From May 7 to 11, Sonny played at Paul's Mall in Boston.[88] Gene Perla, who had been with the band on and off since the fall 1974 European tour, voiced his growing disenchantment that Sonny had deviated from the sixties mold. "I'm frustrated musically.... I'm there about nine months now. I

had been bitching about, 'Ah shit, I wish we could play some swing, man,'"
Perla recalled. "I'm playing the electric bass, which I can swing out on, and
so Sonny plays a swing tune. Masuo lays out, Sonny does his thing, walks
out in the audience, and David [Lee] and I, we jumped on that shit, man. . . .
And I was drinking. I had a little buzz going. We took a break...so I went
to Sonny. I said, 'Can we talk briefly? In the back.' And I'll never forget the
way I opened the conversation. These are my exact words: 'Let's stop fuckin'
around. It was great what we just played.' And Sonny said, 'Okay, okay.' A
couple of weeks later I got the phone call. I had a sense it was coming." Lee
left the band at around this time as well, apparently of his own accord.[89]

From May 19 to 24, Sonny played at El Mocambo in Toronto.[90] That
June, he took a weeklong West Coast tour with a new band: Masuo, Robert
Kenyatta on congas, and, replacing David Lee and Gene Perla, bassist James
"Fish" Benjamin and drummer Eddie Moore.[91] Moore had worked with
Dewey Redman and as part of the house rhythm section at the Jazzhus
Montmartre in Copenhagen, backing Stan Getz and Dexter Gordon. Ben-
jamin, who was recommended by Bob Cranshaw, worked with Harry Bela-
fonte from 1970 to 1975, as well as with Jackie McLean. Benjamin had
family from St. Croix and St. Thomas, so between that and his work with
Belafonte, he was ready to play calypso, and he specialized on electric bass, so
he could play in the fusion bag when the mood called for it.[92]

"We were thrown together from recommendations from different people,
but we jelled pretty good," Benjamin recalled. "We accepted the challenge
that we could play his music and just support him."[93] From June 17 to 19,
they played at Concerts by the Sea in Redondo Beach, from June 20 to 21 at
the Great American Music Hall in San Francisco, and on June 22 at Pioneer
Banque in Seattle.[94] Sonny appeared at the 1975 Newport Jazz Festival in
New York at Avery Fisher Hall on July 4 at 11:30 p.m.[95] The rider to Sonny's
contract made only three stipulations: that Sonny receive top billing, that
flautist Bobbi Humphrey be the opening act, and that Sonny be allowed to
choose whether she played before him or after him.[96] At Avery Fisher, Wein
had three microphones set up so Sonny could freely wander the space without going off mike. He strode onto the stage to a standing ovation, wearing yellow pants, a multicolored velvet hat, and a navy body shirt, playing

"My Reverie," his take on the Larry Clinton version of the Debussy song.[97] He had two guitarists, Masuo and Nathen Page, as well as James Benjamin, Robert Kenyatta, and Eddie Moore. Page was known as the "Wayne Shorter of the guitar," a self-taught guitarist from West Virginia who had worked with Jimmy Smith, Roberta Flack, Herbie Mann, and Jackie McLean.[98]

From September 2 to 5, Sonny recorded *Nucleus* at Milestone Studios in Berkeley. He ventured further into crossover territory, exploring funk rhythms with five originals of his own ("Lucille," "Gwaligo," "Are You Ready," "Cosmet," and the thirty-six-bar form of "Azalea"); Mtume's "Newkleus," with the double entendre; and "My Reverie," which he had previously recorded on *Tenor Madness*. In a sense, this was Sonny's answer to Herbie Hancock's *Head Hunters*, the first platinum-selling jazz album and the best-selling jazz album up to that point. He even hired his old friend and protégé Bennie Maupin, who was in the Head Hunters band. "That was one of those special gifts," Maupin said of *Nucleus*. "He was moving somewhere."[99] Sonny hired George Duke on keyboards, synthesizer, and piano; Bob Cranshaw and Chuck Rainey alternating on electric bass; David Amaro and DeWayne "Blackbyrd" McKnight on guitar; Eddie Moore and Roy McCurdy on drums; Mtume on percussion; Raul de Souza on trombone; and Maupin on tenor saxophone, Lyricon, bass clarinet, and saxello.

Maupin described Sonny's demeanor in the studio as "very relaxed, and very critical of his own work. We sure had some great moments in the studio that day. The stuff that didn't get released—it's there somewhere."[100] Sonny and Lucille returned to Berkeley from October 6 to 8 to mix the record, though Sonny never set foot in the mixing booth; it was released by the end of the year.[101] As a "crossover" album, it had an edge. Sonny growled as viscerally as any funk saxophonist ever did, but his kaleidoscopic solos on "Azalea" and "Cosmet" defied genre convention.

Reviews were polarized. The *San Francisco Examiner* called it "strictly 'jazz'-funk 'crossover' material that is a total disaster on both levels."[102] The *Village Voice*'s Robert Christgau gave the album a rare A rating, writing, "This is as rich an R&B saxophone record as I know, combining repetition and invention, melodies recalled and melodies unimaginable, in proportions that define the difference between selling out and reaching out."[103] In its first month, *Nucleus* sold 8,350 copies. On a royalty statement not long thereafter, Lucille marked the $45,936.38 negative balance forward—against past advances, not an outstanding debt—with the comment that "you 'owe' Milestone!" Sonny made most of his money from live performance.[104]

On September 27, Sonny played a benefit concert for the intellectually disabled at Yale University's Sprague Hall with Nathen Page, James Benjamin, Robert Kenyatta, and Eddie Moore.[105] The surprise of the night came when Sonny pulled out a Moog synthesizer and proceeded to play, making good on his promise earlier that year.[106] In the middle of the month, he played a week in Montreal at In Concert.[107] On October 24, Sonny was scheduled to play at the Nassau Coliseum on Long Island for the First Planetary Celebration, a benefit to promote the United Nations in its thirtieth anniversary year.[108]

Sonny won the tenor category in the *Down Beat* readers' poll for the third consecutive year, and this time there was a nationally televised awards show in which the winners all played.[109] Taped in Chicago in the last week of October, the hour-long *Down Beat* Awards was hosted by Quincy Jones and Chick Corea, with appearances by Sonny, McCoy Tyner, Rahsaan Roland Kirk, Hubert Laws, Bill Watrous, Freddie Hubbard, George Benson, Stanley Clarke, Lenny White, Airto Moreira—all playing together—and Weather Report.[110] Sonny wore a brown newsboy cap and a blue-and-white polka-dot button-down. The program began with Nat Adderley's "Work Song," a tribute to Cannonball Adderley, who died on August 8 that year after suffering a stroke. Sonny took the first solo, then traded briefly with Kirk.

Before Sonny's feature, Corea gave his introduction. "This is a really special introduction for me. The cliché is I can't find the adjectives to describe this man whose contribution to the American music scene is hard to calculate," he said. "He's been a great inspiration to me and to every musician I know that's heard him." Sonny played a heartfelt duet with McCoy Tyner on Ellington's "In a Sentimental Mood," their tribute to the late Duke.[111] The program ended with a group tribute to Ellington. "There's only one way to end it," announced Quincy Jones, "and that's to pay homage to a man that I'm sure is a part of every one of us up here tonight, and he's a guy that epitomizes the process of going from the roots to the fruits. We're talking about Duke Ellington! Get down! C'mon, McCoy!" On "Take the 'A' Train," Sonny took the first solo.

On November 2, Sonny and Lucille flew to Japan for a nationwide tour starting November 4. Sonny brought James Benjamin, Robert Kenyatta, Eddie Moore, and Nathen Page.[112] The tour ended on November 22 with a five-hour all-night concert starting at 1 a.m. at the Royal Akasaka Club, on a bill with saxophonists Sadao Watanabe, Kosuke Mine, pianist Takehiro Honda, and vocalist Yasuda Minami. "After the gig," recalled Benjamin, "there were some people backstage who wanted to meet Sonny. And then a young guy came up to me and said, 'James Benjamin, you're Fish Benjamin, you worked with Jackie...' Holy cannoli! The guy knew my whole résumé. It just shows how the Japanese were so into the music, whoever came over there, they knew their whole history."[113]

Sonny and Lucille flew back to New York on November 25.[114] He would give no more performances for the rest of the year, taking some time to relax and practice. That December, he wrote Gertrude Abercrombie. He wanted to know how Chicago pianist Eddie Baker and his wife were doing and whether Gertrude had "taken the plunge and started working again"—he always supported her art. It would be the last letter she saved from him. She had pancreatitis and severe arthritis, and succumbed to her ailments on July 3, 1977, at sixty-eight.

Things here are fine in that I am playing and working and feeling strong and stronger! I am currently up here in the country trying to complete some composing for some upcoming concerts but I have been having trouble with my heat system in my studio and this has just temporarily stymied me until it is fixed. I guess you know how difficult it is to get people to fix things these days! Anyway everything else is fine and God is still in his heaven, you dig?![115]

Chapter 35

THE WAY I FEEL

(1976–1977)

In June 1976, the *Real Paper* in Boston asked Sonny to name his five favorite albums. He listed, in no particular order, "Lester's Savoy Jump" by Lester Young, *A Love Supreme* by John Coltrane, "I Surrender Dear" by Ben Webster, "Body and Soul" by Coleman Hawkins, and *Head Hunters* by Herbie Hancock.[1] The list conveyed Sonny's desire to combine these influences: Pres's linear storytelling, Trane's spirituality, Ben Webster's emotional depth, Hawk's harmonic genius, and *Head Hunters'* deep funk.

Sonny noted the shift toward funk in his journal. "Concentrate upon jump up funk rhythms.... Occasional selected ballad material can fill out repertoire." He wanted "Funk with Feeling... and more funk rather than jazz now."[2] Despite the traditionalists' harangues, Sonny was intent on adapting to the changing times instead of rehashing the past. "There are more and more young white kids listening to jazz—turning away from rock," Sonny said that past fall.[3] "So many college students know there is more meat there, that there's more to jazz than rock. It's actually a good thing in terms of economics. We need the interracial people listening. We need the support."[4]

Lucille was pleasantly surprised that, at the age of forty-five, Sonny had managed to reach a new generation of fans.[5] "His audiences are almost exclusively young now (I can't explain this fully, but it is there) so that aside from the simple facts of money, availability of dates, etc. we have become careful and very selective of the type of thing we do." Booking Sonny at a festival highlighting the music that he had once typified, she wrote, would have him "completely out of place at this point, both from the festival's and our viewpoint."[6] It was as though she was claiming that if Shakespeare were alive today, he would be out of place at a Shakespeare festival. And maybe he would be.

From Sonny's perspective, though, he would not be out of place anywhere.

"As far as I'm concerned, all music is unified and there's branches and differences of course," he said that year. "I don't just do one thing. So I'm always about the unity of the whole musical experience. . . . I think I try to locate the unifying principles in a lot of things."[7]

One college student who was inspired by Sonny was soprano saxophonist Jane Ira Bloom, then a student at Yale. She met Sonny around this time through audio-equipment designer Mark Levinson in advance of his January concert at Carnegie Hall. Sonny had long had a penchant for strolling, quite literally. Festival organizers wanted to capture every note on their sound system, but Sonny never wanted to be tied to a stationary mike.[8] There were sonic sweet spots in every club and concert hall waiting to be discovered, but only if Sonny was free to roam the stage. Levinson had developed a high-fidelity clip-on microphone Sonny could attach to his bell, so Sonny could, as he put it, "move around, and wave the horn up and down."[9] Sonny came to test it out in Stamford, Connecticut; Levinson invited Bloom, who was "just over the moon about the chance to meet Sonny Rollins."[10]

"*Saxophone Colossus* was like a bible," said Bloom. "He's a man who reinvented himself. It's no small thing. Every time you listen to him, he was following his own vision, his own ideas, and that's something I really related to. . . . He came from a time where he pulled it out of the air. The same thing as Ornette Coleman. These people didn't go to school. They immersed themselves in the religion of music making and they invented a sound that had never been heard before and a way of thinking and playing that had never been heard before. And Sonny was the champion."[11]

In advance of the Carnegie Hall concert, Gary Giddins went up to Germantown to interview Sonny for the *New York Times*. "I hope they're not disappointed, because you have to be a Sonny Rollins believer; if you're a Sonny Rollins believer, I won't let you down," Sonny said. Believing, to Sonny, did not mean dwelling on his past. "Remember what Satchel Paige said: 'Don't look back—something may be gaining on you.'" He asked Giddins to throw a softball with him in the yard. "Don't ever shrink from the belief that you have to prove yourself every minute, because you do," he said.[12] To Sonny, he was only as good as his last inning.[13]

The sold-out January 10 show was presented by New Audiences.[14] Sonny played with special guest Tony Williams on drums and flautist Hubert Laws, whom Sonny had invited during the *Down Beat* Awards. The rest of the band included Hal Galper on keyboards, Masuo on guitar, Cranshaw on electric bass, and Kenyatta on congas. Sonny paced the stage, newly unrestricted by technology.[15] Other than mobility, the new microphone allowed him to "get the sound I need with all those electric instruments backing me up."[16] In an acoustic setting, not even a subway train could overpower Sonny Rollins, but with his *Nucleus* band, he was contending with amplification. After an uninspired first set, Sonny came back and was so energized that he played three encores. "His final note was a long, low, sardonic honk," wrote Giddins. "It seemed to say, 'Okay? Are there still any disbelievers?'"[17]

It was Sonny's first meeting with Tony Williams since the ill-fated 1965 Village Vanguard date that resulted in his abrupt firing of the legendary drummer, but it seemed it was water under the bridge. "I have a strong sense of rhythm, so his playing complemented me perfectly," Sonny said. "It was so rhythmic."[18]

Laws, nine years younger than Sonny, discovered *Jazz in 3/4 Time* during high school. "That record impressed me so much, so when I finally got the opportunity to play with him, I was just so overjoyed by that," Laws said. Laws immediately connected with Sonny's spirituality. Laws's conception of the spirit went back to "a Hebrew word, 'ruach,' and it talks about being breathed," Laws said. "It's a thing that's intangible or you cannot see it, but it still moves you to do what you do."[19]

Yet to *New York Times* critic John S. Wilson, who panned the show, no amount of spirituality could cut through the amplifiers and backbeat.[20] This was a minority opinion, held by scarcely more than two people who heard the show. "Despite the unduly negative attitude of people like John Wilson and Sonny Rollins, we have not found anyone, including the most critical listeners who did not find Sonny's concert absolutely great," New Audiences cofounder Art Weiner wrote Lucille. She wrote back, "Sonny is still rather 'down' and doesn't think he is playing well—I've been listening to him for 20 years now and have never heard him play better. But I guess his musical imagination takes him places he still is seeking to reach and so he is never satisfied."[21]

To continue expanding the college audience, much of Sonny's US performances for the rest of the year were either at universities or in clubs with a mixed booking policy—"heavier on rock than jazz," Lucille wrote an executive at Fantasy Records at the beginning of 1977. Lucille bristled at the suggestion from Fantasy that Sonny might not have sufficient draw to play the legendary Roxy in Los Angeles. "What I am saying is that I believe that a record company should be aware of where the artist's career is going and where his audience is," she wrote. "If there is a lack of understanding of this and what type of audience the artist is drawing (in Sonny's case almost exclusively 18–25 weaned-from-rock-to-some extent audience) it becomes very difficult to deal with." It was not Fantasy pushing Sonny toward fusion, but his own vision in tandem with Lucille.[22]

For a brief California tour in February, Sonny enlisted much of the *Nucleus* band: bassist Chuck Rainey, electric guitarist David Amaro, and drummer Eddie Moore, picking up keyboardist Larry Nash.[23] Then Sonny and Lucille took a rare three-day vacation to Mexico.[24] On February 25, he played at the Longhorn in Minneapolis with Masuo, James Benjamin, Eddie Moore, and Robert Kenyatta. Minneapolis critic Jim Fuller was surprised by what he heard. "It may be that he felt the folks out here in the hinterland weren't ready for his latest persona, or perhaps he was just in a good mood Wednesday. Whatever the reason, he was the full-toned, unamplified, marvelous creative Sonny of the 1950s and '60s through both sets of his one-night stand."[25]

From March 17 to 21, Sonny followed Bill Withers into Paul's Mall in Boston.[26] On March 27, he played at Swarthmore College and from April 2 to 4 played at Amazingrace, a bohemian club in Evanston, Illinois, not far from Northwestern that served no liquor and could accommodate up to four hundred seated on the carpeted floor.[27] From April 8 to 10, he played at Michigan State University.[28] On April 11, Sonny made his first Detroit appearance in more than a decade at the Showcase Theater, in a booking preceded by Albert King and followed by Ravi Shankar and Tom Waits.[29] On May 9, Sonny performed at SUNY–New Paltz for their annual spring celebration, playing on a bill with Hot Tuna and Ry Cooder.[30] From May 18 to 23, Sonny was booked at the Village Vanguard for one of his only New York jazz club appearances that year.

That summer, Sonny took a break in anticipation of recording his next album. "Everything's fine here," Lucille wrote to Fantasy Records that June.

"We're enjoying country life, fresh air, and just planted our vegetable garden today—a quiet summer, to prepare for the fall."[31]

When Sonny began recording *The Way I Feel* that August, George Benson's *Breezin'* was not only the *Billboard* number one R&B album; it was the number one *Billboard* album period. *The Way I Feel* was aiming for similar crossover success. "Now if the new record can get on the charts," Lucille wrote Fantasy publicity director Gretchen Horton, "I'm going to consume singlehandedly a bottle of champagne."[32]

Arrangements were done by Wade Marcus, Stevie Wonder's former music director who had recently done the arrangements for Stanley Turrentine's crossover album on Fantasy, *Everybody Come on Out*.[33] The band was up to the task: pianist Patrice Rushen; guitarist Lee Ritenour;[34] drummer Billy Cobham, who had just worked on Stanley Clarke's *School Days*; bassists Alex Blake and Charles Meeks; and percussionist Bill Summers. Fantasy brought in a large horn section: trumpeters Oscar Brashear, Gene Coe, and Chuck Findley; trombonists George Bohanon and Lew McCreary; French-horn players Alan and Marilyn Robinson; tuba player Don Waldrop; and multireedist Bill Green. The songs were all new: George Duke and Flora Purim's "Love Reborn," Duke's "The Way I Feel About You" (which was dedicated to Sonny),[35] and Patrice Rushen's "Shout It Out," alongside four originals by Sonny—"Island Lady," "Asfrantation Woogie,"[36] "Happy Feel," and "Charm Baby."

Rushen was a twenty-one-year-old pianist and singer from Los Angeles then signed to Prestige.[37] She was preparing her third album for the label, *Shout It Out*, but she first recorded the title track with Sonny. "We were labelmates, and back at that time, it was a very common practice for the record companies to take somebody who was a newcomer and pair them with someone who was more established," Rushen recalled.[38] "Sonny was always really nice to me, and probing about what I wanted to do. I think maybe he heard something in my playing or in my writing to get that I was very serious about the music and appreciative of the pathway that I knew that he had laid."[39]

To Rushen, Sonny opened the door to subverting genre conventions.[40] "Sonny was one of the architects that gave us permission to just be about the music," she said. "No one puts their hands on the piano or puts their horn up to their mouth and decides which notes are jazz notes, and which notes are pop notes, and which notes are classical notes. They play and address the music first, and the nuances of whatever idiom that you're playing, the essence of whatever dialect you're using."

Bill Summers, who was a member of the Head Hunters and lived in the Bay Area, was also enlisted by Orrin Keepnews. Sonny "had zero ego and it was just great to be with him," Summers recalled. "No one played like Sonny, and he didn't play like anybody else. He was open, too. He wasn't afraid to try some popular concepts and put it into his music."[41]

Despite its lavish production, *The Way I Feel* was mainly indicative of how Sonny felt in the studio.[42] There are a few rapturous moments that hint at a complexity beyond the hummable themes—Rushen's polyrhythmic solo on "Love Reborn" or Sonny's pushing of the boundaries at the end of his solo on "Happy Feel"—but otherwise, the album fell short of the solo flights that characterized Sonny's live shows. It got mixed reviews; those who were open to Sonny incorporating contemporary styles mostly liked it, while purists did not. *Record World* wrote that "the transformation of tenor titan Sonny Rollins into Mr. Funk is complete." According to *Down Beat*, Sonny had done what many of the artists on the CTI label were already doing, only with more sophistication: "performing a brand of jazz-funk-fusion better than just about every other saxophonist around."[43]

And how did Sonny feel? He had resigned himself to the fact that he couldn't make everyone happy, that pleasing the critics and pleasing the general public were sometimes mutually exclusive. "Some people don't like what I'm doing," he told Hollie West shortly after the album was released. To Sonny, though, he was in a kind of catch-22. "There's a certain energy that's important in music, especially the music I play," he explained. "Now, to play standards and older songs you need a group of people to interpret them. It requires a certain energy and familiarity. Many young musicians today are not familiar with the standards. But many guys of my own age don't have the energy to play these things in a fresh way."[44]

In October, Sonny played the Great American Music Hall in San Francisco followed by his Vancouver debut at Oil Can Harry's.[45] Sonny hired a new, young touring band: twelve-string-guitar specialist Aurell Ray, drummer Eddie Moore, pianist Michael Wolff, and electric bassist Don Pate.

Pate was the son of the legendary Chicago bassist and arranger Johnny Pate, who mentored Bob Cranshaw and Richard Davis before they moved to New York. Cranshaw, who played in the *Saturday Night Live* band for the show's second season, recommended Don to Sonny.[46] Aurell Ray joined the band after Sonny fired Masuo; Masuo had a prior engagement with Sadao Watanabe and wasn't available for Sonny, and Sonny didn't ask him back.[47] Ray loved *East Broadway Run Down*, but his experience with Melba Moore and Charles Earland prepared him to bring the funk.[48]

Wolff grew up in Berkeley, California, having been blown away by Sonny's solo concert at the Greek Theatre in 1969.[49] He had played with Cannonball Adderley until he passed, then joined Jean-Luc Ponty's band before Eddie Moore recommended him to Sonny. At the audition, Sonny gave Wolff the music and he played it down; Sonny invited him back the next day. "I show up the next day, and there's no music. I go, 'Hey, Sonny, can you give me the music?' He goes, 'You're a good musician. I don't think you need the music.' I go, 'Come on, man. I'll memorize it.' And he wouldn't give me the music, so I just walked out. Then he came after me—'Come on back.' He was kind of testing me, man. And then I got the gig." Generally, Sonny was "super respectful," Wolff said. "One time we were playing, and...he started soloing while I was soloing, and he came over to me and apologized." Wolff could also get funky, but before the gig he often practiced Ravel.

Moore grew up in San Francisco and was a bear of a man with a big heart. "He was a beautiful, beautiful person, a beautiful soul," recalled Ray. According to Pate, "We used to call him the black Orson Welles." Sonny hired him three weeks after he left Stanley Turrentine, so Moore also had his crossover bona fides. Sonny "made me go for myself," Moore said. "Sonny plays the saxophone like Elvin Jones plays the drums. You really have to know where the one is to work with Sonny."[50]

On October 28, Sonny, Lucille, and the band flew to London to begin the European tour with George Wein's Newport in Europe. Sonny had grown his hair out, let his sideburns widen, and grew a pointed beard, complemented by a pair of bug-eye sunglasses. On October 30, he was on a bill with Muddy Waters and McCoy Tyner at the New Victoria Theatre,[51] on October 31 at the Dortmund International Jazz Festival opposite Tyner and Anthony Braxton,[52] on November 4 at the Barcelona International Jazz Festival,[53] and on November 5 at the de Doelen in Rotterdam.[54] The touring package caused a bit of a riot in Paris in the first week of November, when, according to Lucille, "there were two thousand people outside, two thousand with tickets, crashing by young people—George Wein fled in panic—and lots of controversy"[55] over "electrique vs. acoustique" in Sonny's playing. On November 12, they played at the Bologna International Jazz Festival in Torino in a televised broadcast;[56] and on November 13 they played at the Cascais Jazz Festival on the Portuguese Riviera.[57]

"We didn't have a roadie," recalled Wolff. "Lucille told me, 'You can't have rock and roll expenses making jazz money.'" Still, everything was comfortable. "We always had excellent travel and accommodations," said Aurell Ray. "When we'd go to Europe, there were only four or five of us in the band, and we had a whole bus."[58]

No two concerts were alike. Some entire sets were shorter than another set's first tune; some sets, "Don't Stop the Carnival" wouldn't stop for an hour; some consisted entirely of funk; on others, Sonny waxed poetic on Billie Holiday's version of "Easy Living."[59] At one show, said Wolff, "they were playing music during the changeover and it was a Freddie Hubbard tune, and Sonny came out and started playing along with it. We had to learn that tune immediately, and we came back in and they turned off the tape and we just kept playing that song. That was fantastic ear training." Sonny wanted the energy to keep building, even if a song lasted an hour. "It felt like he didn't even really need the band. Like here's the band, and there's Sonny. He was just on another plane of energy." According to Don Pate, that energy remained before and after the concert; he practiced in his dressing room and sometimes later in the hotel. "At one point," Pate said, "he was in his hotel room practicing to Barry White."[60]

Sonny ran a clean tour. "That band wasn't a drug band," Wolff said. They did smoke marijuana on occasion, for spiritual purposes. "When I get high," Sonny wrote in a journal at around this time, "I get high to get closer to God."[61] The focus was always on the music. "He pretty much had the spirit every night," Wolff said. "He was a guy that was hard on himself, which made him get better, but truthfully, he didn't need to get better. He just needed to play. He was already Sonny Rollins."[62]

Back in the United States, Sonny played the *Boston Globe* Jazz Festival on November 25 on a bill with Herbie Hancock and Gato Barbieri. Hancock even sat in on acoustic piano on "There Is No Greater Love."[63] From November 26 to 28, they were at the Village Gate.[64] On November 29, Sonny and Lucille flew out to Berkeley to finish mixing *The Way I Feel*.[65] Gigwise, that was it for the year.

In December, Sonny won the tenor category of the *Down Beat* readers' poll for the fourth consecutive year.[66] Though Lucille monitored such developments, it was about the furthest thing from Sonny's mind. While not touring, they were enjoying a quiet life upstate. Lucille made sure the rent in New York and the mortgage in Germantown were paid on time, and she managed Sonny's thriving career from far out in the country;[67] Sonny maintained his daily practice routine and took care of the dogs, Minor and Kendo the Akita, and focused on nutrition, "eating fruit and broiled chicken for my diet while I'm up here in the country," as he wrote in a journal entry. "So far one big meal a day. For instance, I had today 2 mangoes, 1/2 half broiled chicken, 2 small cantaloupes, plus my juice which I drink throughout the day. Grape, pineapple, papaya, etc."[68]

And then there was the way he felt, which as he wrote Randi Hultin, had nothing to do with chart performance or the music business.[69] On December 16, his father, Walter Rollins Sr., passed away at the age of sixty-five.[70] There was no obituary.

Randi, there is also a type of Indian religious art, one of which shows the world's peoples, the birth DEATH, BLOOD—ALL SHOWN ON A POSTER. This is how I feel now. I am caught up in the world. On the wheel. Jerking and lunging. Like this planet spinning through space.[71]

————◦————

On August 8, 1977, Herbie Hancock and V.S.O.P. made the cover of *Newsweek*, bathed in pink neon light, with the headline "Jazz Comes Back!"[72] "The signs of rebirth are everywhere," wrote Hubert Saal. Jazz, of course, had never left, but fusion was driving the renaissance as far as the market was concerned.[73] According to Saal, artists like McCoy Tyner were selling one hundred thousand copies an album, with Anthony Braxton selling more than twenty thousand. Even Dexter Gordon, living in Europe for the previous fourteen years, was back. Fusion remained divisive among critics, but it created a burgeoning jazz fan base that had Sonny playing standing-room-only shows at university coffeehouses and auditoriums.[74]

"Sometimes we don't see reviews," Lucille wrote Fantasy publicity director Gretchen Horton on December 27, 1976, "and sometimes that... is lucky in the case of bad ones—this is a strange time of course for Sonny, as he gets flack for not being 'pure' from a few people but fortunately some critics and almost unanimously audiences are happy—what counts after all."[75]

Critics and some fans continued wearing out the grooves in Sonny's early work while railing against his electric turn with Jacobinic zeal. "Sonny Rollins has become the most potent contemporary symbol of the devastation wrought by the Big Dollar on a jazz artist's creative development," wrote Thomas Albright, "but that is only because he is the most conspicuous of established jazz giants to 'cross over' to the puerile, numbing world of sound-alike disco-funk formula music."[76]

As far as Sonny was concerned, he was still experimenting. "There are more esoteric sides to my playing and they need to be fed right now with a new background/up," he wrote in his journal. "Where I can experiment more with phrasing and fashioning my own thing."[77]

Some continued to project a narrative onto Sonny: tunes like "Wagon Wheels" or "Surrey with the Fringe on Top" were signifying on corny pieces of Americana; Stevie Wonder's "Isn't She Lovely" or his own R&B tunes signified selling out. To Sonny, they were all part of the same continuum of American music. "I'm not a good enough musician to play something that I don't like," Sonny said that year. "I can't do it. Whatever I play, most of it is me. But you have to think about whether or not it will reach audiences and whether it will sell."[78]

The gigs in 1977 began in February. The band remained Moore, Wolff, Pate, and Ray. From February 10 to 13, Sonny played the Showboat Lounge in Silver Spring, Maryland.[79] According to Hollie West's review, Sonny was "stirring up controversy by performing an amalgam of raucous rock and jazz." Overheard at the club: "How can he play that garbage?"[80]

"I'm writing this review with a good deal of sadness," wrote saxophonist and *Down Beat* critic Bill Kirchner of the Showboat gig.[81] There was a bias that funk and calypso tunes were intellectually lightweight—not *real* jazz. Sonny didn't hear it that way, and neither did a lot of young listeners who connected to it, as well as some devoted fans, who saw it as just another facet of Sonny's expansive musical personality. Sonny invited Ron Holloway to practice with him in the Showboat Lounge for three hours one afternoon, and he sat in for a set that night. They played fusion, but also "Strode Rode" and "My One and Only Love." For Sonny, it was all jazz.

Ironically, Sonny returned to his least commercial act ever—the Bridge sabbatical—through his starring role in a commercial for Pioneer Electronics stereo equipment. Produced by advertising agency Scali, McCabe, Sloves, the national sixty-second spot was shot by legendary commercial director Steve Horn. *Clash of the Titans* star Burgess Meredith provided the voice-over, convincingly proclaiming that after the Bridge, Sonny was "at last good enough," a sentiment that assuredly did not resonate with Sonny.[82]

Filmed on February 17, Sonny wore a trench coat, sweater, and hat. "We went up on the bridge and shot it just the way I did it then. The one I actually used the most was the Williamsburg Bridge, but we used the Brooklyn Bridge in the commercial because it was more scenic. It's kind of a pretty bridge, it's got the archways like a church, and it's really very nice. And, as a matter of fact, I did go up on the Brooklyn Bridge sometimes, so it wasn't really an inaccuracy as far as that was concerned.... We did it on one of the coldest nights of the year, and, of course, we had to do retakes on it, and my fingers were just frozen! I had to keep stopping and trying to warm up my fingers."[83]

Much of Sonny's other work that year was on college campuses. That February, he made his Miami debut at the Miami-Dade Community College jazz festival and performed at SUNY–Stony Brook.[84] In March, he returned to Paul's Mall in Boston,[85] where he played "Easy Living," which had become a mainstay of his set, alongside Stevie Wonder's "Isn't She Lovely." "How many of you remember Billie Holiday?" Sonny said from the stand. "I fell in love with her the first time I met her, she was so beautiful. Here's a tune she made famous."[86]

Appearances at colleges and clubs continued: Champaign, Illinois; Amazingrace in Evanston; Memorial Hall in Dayton, Ohio, on a bill with McCoy Tyner; then a benefit near his home at a high school in Red Hook, New York, to oppose a proposed nuclear power plant. On April 11, he played a concert at Cornell College in Mount Vernon, Iowa, taking time to offer guidance to the student musicians and graciously fielding off-color questions about drugs and the jazz life at a punch-bowl reception. On April 13, he played a sold-out concert at the University of Tennessee, followed by the New Orleans Jazz and Heritage Festival aboard the SS *President* opposite the Crusaders.[87]

At the end of April, he had a short West Coast tour, beginning with the Trojan Horse in Seattle. One night, in walked Milt Jackson and Percy Heath, in town with the Modern Jazz Quartet. "Play me some blues!" Jackson shouted. Then Heath started dancing in the aisle. Sonny was on that night, playing an incandescent two-hour set. "Do you realize that you've been playing for two hours?" Lucille asked when he got off the bandstand. "No, really?" Sonny said incredulously.[88]

It was around this time that Sonny added a new percussionist to his band: twenty-eight-year-old conguero Sammy Figueroa,[89] who had played with Herbie Mann, the Average White Band, and the Brecker Brothers. "He taught me how to be real groomed onstage, how to be really clean and look good onstage," Figueroa said of Sonny. "And the other thing he taught me was that people pay you according to how much you think you're worth. If you think you're worth ten dollars, then you're a ten-dollar musician.... You have to believe in who you are. You don't go too over or too low. You stay within a happy medium.... Then you might lose one gig, but you're gonna gain twenty. You have to be fearless."[90]

Fearless or not, Sonny was rarely satisfied. "There will only be one night out of a week, or, at the least, one night out of five that I will like, that I will feel I've accomplished something in," he said at the time. "I've learned to live with it. I used to have a lot of anguish over it. I mean, I really used to *suffer* bad if things didn't go right. I'd really get down. But now I take it a little better, more like, 'Well, there will be another night.'"[91]

Sonny sometimes applied the same standard to his band. At one concert, Figueroa recalled, "In the middle of the show, he goes, 'You're all fired!' So after the show, he's walking out like this. 'Meet me in my dressing room!' And everybody was there standing like West Point, but no one said anything. So he points at the first musician. 'Why did you play that? I told you not to play that. You played it!' 'I don't know.' 'And you! What do you think you're...' And man, I started laughing so hard I couldn't hold it. And he screwed his whole face up. 'Are you laughing at me?' 'Sonny, you're a funny motherfucker, man.' He said, 'Get out of my dressing room!' And I just went back. I left those guys hanging. And just like I thought, he called me up the next day, we were off, and he said, 'Hey Sammy, what did you just eat?' I said, 'I had some eggs.' He said, 'Oh, I had the same thing.' He didn't even talk about what happened! And I didn't even ask him."[92]

From June 13 to July 3, he toured Japan, where he was still treated like royalty.[93] "He would play thirty bars of Sonny Rollins solo, and then he expected you to do the same thing as strong as he did," recalled Figueroa of those early gigs. "If he saw any weakness, he'd go, 'This motherfucker, he's not making any effort.' Then he would go onto the next one. That's how he tested me. I had to be on my toes all the time. He'd give me these long-ass solos. In Japan one time, he said, 'Go up onstage and start by yourself.' And I went on and started playing a solo for twenty minutes, and I started singing and doing some Cuban stuff and the people went nuts. And right in the middle of all that, he walks in playing. Every night was a whole different adventure."

This kind of unpredictability changed Figueroa's approach to improvisation, in music and in life. "When you're playing and you're improvising, you sometimes lose your train of thought, and then you start repeating another scale that you did before. What Sonny told me was 'Think of something beautiful that happened to you and don't think about the audience.'...Otherwise, he said, 'If you don't have any ideas, don't play shit at all.'"[94]

From August 3 to 6, Sonny was in Berkeley recording *Easy Living* at Fantasy Studios. Sonny's new contract with Milestone raised his advance to $10,000.[95] The idea was to record an album more representative of Sonny's eclectic live shows, with a blend of originals, ballads, and a pop cover: "Isn't

She Lovely." He hired George Duke on keyboards, Tony Williams, Paul Jackson on electric bass (with Byron Miller playing bass on "Isn't She Lovely"), Charles "Icarus" Johnson on guitar, and Bill Summers on congas. Lucille convinced Sonny to record "My One and Only Love" on his new curved silver Selmer soprano, though he wasn't confident in his soprano playing.[96] Sonny bought a copy of the piano sheet music for "Easy Living," something he did for much of his repertoire, so he really knew the tune, which was the album highlight.[97]

Reviews were mixed. *Down Beat* gave it three and a half stars;[98] others felt it was his best album of the decade.[99] "I listen to the way he plays 'Easy Living,' and not that other stuff," Cecil Taylor remarked. After the album came out, Lucille tracked its position on the *Billboard* jazz charts, where it peaked at number thirteen.[100] Broadening commercial appeal partially motivated the decision to have George Duke and Tony Williams guest on the album in lieu of Mike Wolff and Eddie Moore, Sonny's regular band members. For Wolff, that was a signal it was time to go. "I just said, 'Sonny, I can't stay with you if you do that.' He said, 'Well, but you're great, and the company wants me to do it.' I said, 'I don't care. Cannonball [Adderley] didn't use [George Duke]. I think Cannonball and you are an equal level.' He wouldn't do it, so I said, 'I'm out.' On good terms, though."[101]

Wolff stayed for one last European tour, August 13 to 21.[102] Sonny played at the Laren International Jazz Festival on August 13; at Jazz Middelheim in Antwerp, where an audience of about thirty-five hundred broke the festival's attendance record;[103] and from August 16 to 18 in Copenhagen at the Club Montmartre.[104] Lucille forwarded the mostly favorable reviews to Fantasy's publicity team, omitting the bad ones, as she wrote: "I refuse to acknowledge bad reviews."[105]

With Mike Wolff out, Sonny held open auditions for a guitarist or pianist to replace him. Armen Donelian, a twenty-six-year-old pianist who had graduated from Columbia University and played with Mongo Santamaria's Afro-Cuban octet, got the gig.[106] Sonny's involvement in yoga and Eastern thought resonated with him. "There was one time when I had to go to Sonny's hotel room to get some music from him. So I knocked and Sonny answered the door, and he was dressed only in his briefs. I was like, 'Sonny, I can come back another time.' He said, 'No, no, come in,' and he gave me the music, and he had laid out newspapers on the floor. He was doing yoga on the floor of the hotel room."[107]

In late September, Sonny and Lucille returned to Berkeley to mix *Easy Living* and begin another sold-out college tour: the University of Michigan at Ann Arbor, Indiana University Bloomington, and the University of Minnesota.[108] From October 21 and 22, Sonny played a gig at the Foxhole in Philadelphia, in the basement of the parish hall of St. Mary's Church; Hank Mobley sat in one night.[109] "This was after one of [Mobley's] lungs collapsed, so he only had one lung, so his sound wasn't as big as it might have been," recalled Donelian. "He looked rather ill, but he and Sonny seemed to have a mutual admiration for each other."[110]

Shows followed in Richmond, Silver Spring, Miami, Atlanta, and Dayton, Ohio.[111] In December, after a period of touring that would rival his fifties schedule, he was off for the rest of the year.

"I am very happy," he said during an interview in Dayton. "I could be working 365 days a year, if I wanted. But I don't. I've always been ambivalent about performing. I like to be on stage. But I like my privacy, too. I like the freedom of playing two weeks and having three weeks off. I wouldn't advise it for everyone, but it's worked for me. And I'll tell you why. Playing is hard on me. You see that?" he said, pointing to a glass of brandy on the ice maker. "When I'm at home I never touch that stuff. When I'm out in the club milieu, it gets to me. I have to watch myself. I want to be working twenty years from now, not at home sick in bed."[112]

Touring had taken a toll, and in Minnesota that October, Sonny Rollins had a cold. His throat felt like sandpaper, but he still made time for a University of Minnesota jazz critic to do an interview at his motel.[113] Sonny ambled out of bed in his bathrobe and slippers, towel wrapped around his inflamed throat, and let the eager student in. He had cough syrup and a vaporizer and was burning incense. Part of the interview was done with Sonny in bed, part in front of the Vikings game. Yet onstage that night, Sonny would come alive.

His young interlocutor wanted to know how Sonny felt about the purists' disdain for his contemporary backbeat. "I think a lot of rock people like it for the—now I may be wrong, you can explain this to me better—they like it for the dance," he responded. "They're able to dance to it, to boogie and everything like this. That could be a reason. This is an element of accessibility which I think is good.... Well, my wife, she's my manager, she's very down on purists, you know. I'm sort of in the middle, cuz I kinda know where they're coming from, and there's a lot of things that I'd like to preserve. I mean, I'm basically a sentimental person. I know a lot of old songs and melodies from the past.... I'm not really down on the purists, you know—although they've been knocking me a lot recently."

"Are you pretty thick-skinned about that?" the interviewer asked.

"Well, more so than I was at one time. Yeah, I am, a lot more, mainly because I don't read everything that's written about me, that's one thing. Secondly, I've been around long enough to know that, especially in my case, I mean I'm always able to come back and do something. They might put me down, but I'll always come back and get to 'em later."

Chapter 36

DON'T STOP THE CARNIVAL

(1978–1979)

Sonny began 1978 at Carnegie Hall on Friday the thirteenth. It was his first New York appearance since November 1976, and he wasn't taking any chances. "People forget," he told John S. Wilson in advance of the show.[1] There would be no accidents as he had with Monk that fateful Friday the thirteenth; he rehearsed for two weeks.[2] As a Virgo, he said, he was predisposed to be a "perfectionist" who "wants everything to come out just so."[3]

Before Carnegie Hall, Sonny held auditions for a second guitarist. Aurell Ray recommended sixteen-year-old guitarist Bobby Broom. Ray was impressed when he saw Broom perform alongside Marcus Miller in Weldon Irvine's *Young, Gifted, and Broke*.[4] Sonny "brought me in the room and we played for about an hour, and he asked me to go wait in the waiting room. He came out a few minutes later, and asked me to go on tour: 'I've got some college dates that I want you to do.' I said, 'Well I can't, 'cause I've got to go to college next year, so I'm trying to graduate high school.' He said, 'Oh yeah, yeah, yeah, that's right. I'm sorry. I forgot.' I must have looked all of twelve at the time."[5]

A couple weeks later, the phone rang. "I'm sitting at my desk doing homework, and my mom knocks on the door and I'm waving her off," Broom recalled, "and she says, 'Well, I think you should get it. It's Sonny Rollins.'" Five days shy of his seventeenth birthday, he made it to Carnegie Hall.[6]

In addition to Ray and Broom, Sonny used Bob Cranshaw, Mike Wolff, Sammy Figueroa, Eddie Moore, and special guest Donald Byrd. "It's really nice to play with old friends," said Byrd. "It was the first time we'd played together in twenty years.... To me, he's the greatest sax player alive."[7] To the audience, it was worth trekking through a winter slush storm to watch Sonny take control of the elements with his tenor and curved soprano.[8]

On January 28, Sonny played to a packed house at Washington University in St. Louis, followed by a concert at the Detroit Institute of Arts auditorium on February 1.[9] Then he went to India.

The first international Jazz Yatra Festival was in Bombay from February 12 to 18, organized by Sonny's friends from the nonprofit Jazz India, Niranjan Jhaveri and Jehangir Dalal.[10] *Yatra* means a religious pilgrimage in Hindi; participating artists were not paid by the festival. Instead, their consulates supported them, and Air India flew everyone in gratis. The festival took place at the open-air Rang Bhavan auditorium.[11] Billed as "A festival of Indo-Afro-American music," it was truly international—Clark Terry, Stan Tracey, Albert Mangelsdorff, Karin Krog, and Sadao Watanabe all performed. Sonny performed on Saturday, February 18, the last night of the festival, with Aurell Ray, Eddie Moore, and bassist Leon Gaer, whom he borrowed from the Don Ellis Quartet.[12] The festival was an overwhelming success—twenty-two thousand people in total.[13]

Sonny was happy to be back in India spreading his brand of jazz diplomacy, even if "the tremendous amount of poverty was a little difficult for Lucille to handle," he wrote Randi Hultin. The symbolism of the festival was not lost on him. "I am proud to be associated with Jazz Yatra," Sonny wrote in a program note the following year, "because it shows so beautifully how music can be used to lead the world's people toward harmony and understanding."[14]

From March 1 to 5, Sonny played Paul's Mall in Boston. One night, there was a leak at the restaurant upstairs, and water damaged the soundboard below. "The house was packed and everybody's sitting there listening to Sonny Rollins and we were like twenty minutes into the first set and all of a sudden all the power went out in the sound system," recalled Armen Donelian. "No mikes, no electric piano, no electric guitar, nothing...the only people that could play were Sonny and the drummer. So Sonny turned around and said, 'Eddie, drop out.' So Eddie dropped out and Sonny played by himself for twenty minutes until they got the power back on. He was phenomenal. He just kept playing and playing."[15]

It was on this gig that Sonny hired twenty-four-year-old Brooklyn native Jerome Harris on bass. Harris was self-taught on bass and guitar and graduated from Harvard with a degree in social relations. After graduating, Harris decided to pursue a second undergraduate program at the New England Conservatory, starting as a freshman the next fall.[16] After graduating in 1977, he stayed in Boston and soon got the call from Sonny, who needed a sub for bassist David Jackson.[17] Luckily, Harris had honed his skills in a variety of genres. "The genre components of his repertoire were the same, it was just that he was on this level of intensity and focus that was so much higher, but at least I knew how to play a calypso, which some jazz players didn't," Harris said.[18]

To Harris, much of the criticism of Sonny's recent work stemmed from a perceived hierarchy that placed duple- or straight-time feels beneath a triplet or swing feel.[19] "Because the duple feels were so significant in pop, be it rock and roll or rock, R&B, funk, whatever, certain people in the jazz world associated duple feels with being 'commercial,' selling out. But there's all kinds of duple-feel music that's very developed, that swings in its way, where the rhythms are elastically approached, and there's improvising," Harris said. "I think as time went on, there were younger audiences who maybe didn't grow up being all about the swing feel, but they could relate to the calypso feel, so he was able to kind of bridge that and bring those people in."[20]

On March 17, Sonny, Donald Byrd, and the Blackbyrds appeared at the Atlanta Civic Center in a tribute concert for Atlanta native Duke Pearson.[21] Sonny and Byrd received keys to the city from Mayor Maynard Jackson.[22] Sonny's image was soon emblazoned across a brick "wall of respect" on Auburn Avenue, painted by local artists, next to Martin Luther King Jr., Frederick Douglass, Malcolm X, W. E. B. Du Bois, and John Coltrane.

From March 20 to 24, Sonny and Lucille took a much-needed vacation to Petit St. Vincent in the Grenadines before continuing Sonny's rigorous performance schedule.[23] For two weekends in late March and early April, Sonny was at the Village Gate, where Al Foster replaced Eddie Moore on drums.[24] This marked the end of Moore's tenure with the band, as well as Armen Donelian's.

The following week, Sonny was going to San Francisco to record a live album at the Great American Music Hall, and Tony Williams was hired instead of Moore. "It hurt Eddie that Sonny didn't use him on that thing," Ray recalled.[25] Adding insult to injury, San Francisco was Moore's hometown. According to Ray, it was Orrin Keepnews who made the difficult decision to exclude Moore from the album. "I think they were trying to put some name artists, featured people on there for recording purposes," Ray said.[26] After putting in so much time in the band, though, Moore understandably wanted the album credit and decided to quit.

Don't Stop the Carnival was recorded live at the Great American Music Hall from April 13 to 15, with opening night, April 12, as a kind of dress rehearsal.[27] Williams and Byrd both guested, with Harris on bass, Aurell Ray on guitar, and pianist Mark Soskin, who lived in San Francisco at the time. "Orrin said 'Sonny wants to audition you for a live recording,' and at the time, he was going through a lot of piano players, quickly," Soskin recalled.[28] At the late-night audition, it was just the two of them plus Orrin Keepnews. "We played for hours, and after we played he said, 'Okay, you got it.' And then like a day or two later, we recorded the album."[29]

"My role in the band was—I soloed quite a bit—but it was really to be supportive of him and to not interfere," Soskin said. "It was the most spontaneous gig I'd ever done and probably ever will do."[30]

Soskin had firsthand proof of Sonny's legendary woodshedding routine.

"He would practice right up until the performance," Soskin recalled. "Many times, I'd hear him warm up with Coleman Hawkins's 'Body and Soul' note for note.... Basically, what we did was go to the gig real early for the sound check, but it really wasn't a sound check. We just played. We'd play for hours, take a short break, then play the performance." As Bobby Broom later experienced, "Those sound checks were sometimes better than the gig."[31]

There was some backstage drama with Tony Williams. Orrin Keepnews organized an afternoon rehearsal before the run began. "We get there, the drums are there, Tony's not there," recalled Jerome Harris. "He arrived late and left early. We're playing and at some point, he just got up and said, 'See ya,' and split!"[32] Williams's curtness stood in stark contrast to Donald Byrd. "He was totally warm and cracking jokes and trying to put others at ease," Harris said.[33]

Williams showed up for the concerts, though. He was an overwhelming force on the title track. Sonny contributed two originals, "Silver City," a high point of the album, opening with an extended duo with Williams, and the funk tune "Camel," with the drummer in full Lifetime mode. Williams could still swing harder than almost anyone, as he demonstrated on the standard "Nobody Else but Me." "Non-Cents" was a funk tune by Kevin Toney of the Blackbyrds; Byrd also brought in his own tunes "A Child's Prayer" and "President Hayes."[34] The album ends with the crowd clapping along to Mtume's "Sais." The standout moment is the visceral cadenza on "Autumn Nocturne." The audience seemed to hold its breath as Sonny played what Soskin thought of as an "encyclopedia of jazz" before the rhythm section came in and the crowd let out a cathartic cheer.[35]

That magic didn't quite happen on every track, but the scattered moments when it does capture the raw power, inventiveness, virtuosity, and stylistic range that to some were absent from much of Sonny's studio output that decade. In his review of *Don't Stop the Carnival*, Stanley Crouch wrote of "a guy who loved Sonny Rollins so much that he prayed to him like a patron saint and, once when he was getting his ass kicked, cried out, 'Sonny, please save me!' ... If he has been bothered by the consistently mediocre recordings Sonny Rollins has made over the last few years, the tenor saxophonist's new recording...may not only renew his faith but provide him with revelations as well."[36] In a *Down Beat* blindfold test that year, Stanley Turrentine gave "Autumn Nocturne" five stars. "I have all the respect in the world for that man," he said. "That solo. Just beautiful, man."[37]

At this time, Sonny reconnected with Charles Mingus, who was battling ALS (amyotrophic lateral sclerosis), confined to a wheelchair, and unable to play. "When he had Lou Gehrig's disease, my wife and I used to go by his place," Sonny recalled. "I'd spend time with him when he couldn't move. He was just in that position, which was really tragic."[38] Armen Donelian was living at Manhattan Plaza in midtown on the West Side, and Mingus was his neighbor.[39] Mingus's wife, Sue, who was also friends with Lucille, organized a surprise party for Mingus's fifty-sixth birthday on April 22, and Donelian and Paul Jeffrey were the decoys. "I didn't even know Sonny was coming," recalled Donelian. "Sonny and Charles were very close. Sonny came in and everyone else came and we started playing 'Happy Birthday,' and Charles was very moved. He didn't say anything. He was speechless. And Sonny came over and he just sat down and the two stared at each other, right into each other's eyes without looking sideways. It must have been for about eight minutes like that." It was just like how it used to be with Monk. To Donelian, their connection was beyond words—"just a silent transmission."[40]

Next, Sonny auditioned new drummers and pianists for an upcoming two-week domestic tour.[41] Sonny hired drummer Akira Tana, a friend and former roommate of Jerome Harris, and pianist Delmar Brown. Tana was a twenty-six-year-old student at the New England Conservatory who, like Harris, did two undergraduate degrees, the first at Harvard.[42] Growing up in the Bay Area, Tana was also at Sonny's solo concert at the Berkeley Jazz Festival in 1969. Tana took an overnight train from Boston and, when he arrived at Blue Rock Studio, began playing duo with Sonny. "That's kind of a daunting situation to be in a room by yourself with Sonny Rollins, just playing duets with him," Tana recalled. At the end of the day, Sonny offered him the gig.

It was on such short notice that Tana had to miss playing Stravinsky's *Petrushka* at the New England Conservatory. With his grade hanging in the balance, Tana appealed to the president of the conservatory. "He said the choice is up to me. So I made the choice—and I got an F for orchestra."

The tour ran from April 28 through May 6—Scottsdale, Arizona; the

Quiet Knight in Chicago; the Vogue in Indianapolis; and the Bank Nite-club in Akron, Ohio.[43] The concerts demanded all Tana had: sets lasted up to two and a half hours. "He would play forever," Tana recalled. "Once he started going, he wouldn't stop. I had never experienced that kind of intensity before.... I just remember being totally drenched and just exhausted after playing with him." Things were more laid-back offstage. "The whole band would be in this big old car and he'd be driving about fifteen miles an hour on these wide streets in Indianapolis. And I asked him—'I'm going to the store tonight. Can I get you anything?' And he said, 'Can you get me some cream cheese?' "[44]

On June 18, Sonny played at the inaugural White House Jazz Festival with Ron Carter, McCoy Tyner, and Max Roach. President Jimmy Carter hosted; it was recorded by Radio Free Europe for broadcast in the Soviet Union and Eastern Europe.[45] The festival was organized by George Wein in partnership with White House social secretary Gretchen Poston as part of the twenty-fifth anniversary of the Newport Jazz Festival. They brought forty all-star artists to the White House South Lawn spanning most of jazz history: Eubie Blake, Mary Lou Williams, Cecil Taylor, Herbie Hancock, Chick Corea, Benny Carter, Illinois Jacquet, Stan Getz, Dexter Gordon, Ornette Coleman, Roy Eldridge, Doc Cheatham, and Clark Terry were all there.[46] The peanut farmer was a jazz fan.

Though Carter wasn't the first president to bring jazz to the White House, his words at the festival brought a sense of validation to everything artists like Sonny and Max had fought for. "This is an honor for me, to walk through this crowd and to meet famous jazz musicians and the families of those who are no longer with us but whose work and whose spirit, whose beautiful music will live forever in our country," Carter said. "If there ever was an indigenous art form, one that is special and peculiar to the United States and represents what we are as a country, I would say that it's jazz.... I believe that this particular form of music, of art, has done as much as anything to break down those barriers and to let us live and work and play and make beautiful music together."[47]

To stick to a strict two-hour time limit, solo performances were confined to five minutes; larger ensembles got eight. Sonny's set with Tyner, Carter, and Roach was introduced by Sam Rivers. They played a blistering "Sonny-moon for Two" through the ninety-degree heat.[48]

"We all got a souvenir picture of shaking hands with the president," Sonny later recalled. "Eubie Blake was there; the bass player we used to call the Judge, Milt Hinton, he was there. There was a gang of people there. It was really quite remarkable....I remember talking to Ornette. My wife was there with me. It was a really hot day, a typical Washington, D.C. day.... [Carter] made everyone there feel quite at home, he and his wife Rosalynn." A buffet with jambalaya, salad, wine, beer, and pecan pie was served to the four hundred attendees: "Lots of pecan pie," Sonny emphasized.[49]

As 8 p.m. approached, George Wein approached the president. "Sir, I was told to end the concert in exactly two hours. Unless those orders are countermanded, that's precisely when the show will end."

"Consider the orders countermanded," Carter said, cracking a smile. "Anybody who wants to is free to go, but I'm going to stay and listen to some more music."[50] After Pearl Bailey, Gerry Mulligan, and Illinois Jacquet's "Flying Home," it was Carter's turn to swing.[51] "Now, the president, his Highness, has asked us to play a tune that we played at the White House when we were here before," said Dizzy Gillespie. "We're gonna play this tune...the name of it is 'Salt Peanuts.'" The crowd erupted. "Now, wait a minute, but there are some diplomatic strings attached. To wit: that the president himself, his majesty, sing the lyrics to 'Salt Peanuts.'" It turned out that Carter's knowledge of the subject went beyond agriculture. "Wait a minute. I've just got one question," Dizzy said after the brief performance. "Would you like to go on the road with us?"

Carter, without missing a beat: "I might have to after tonight!"[52]

The most moving moment of the day came earlier when George Wein acknowledged Charles Mingus, sitting in his wheelchair in the front row. President Carter approached him to honor his contribution to the music; Mingus was moved to tears. Mingus died on January 5, 1979, only six months later. At the memorial service, Joni Mitchell and Sonny both performed.[53]

On June 25, Sonny played at Carnegie Hall for Newport in New York, with Mark Soskin, Jerome Harris, Al Foster, and Sammy Figueroa. "Moon over Miami" was a highlight, with an epic cadenza that got more than a minute of applause. "After Sonny Rollins's Newport Jazz Festival performance at Carnegie Hall Sunday night, I was asked to recant all suggestions I had ever made, in print or in conversation, that any living tenor saxophonist is Rollins's equal," wrote *New York Times* critic Robert Palmer. "I did so gladly and with hardly a second thought."[54]

From July 8 to 9, Sonny played Milwaukee Summerfest with Soskin, Harris, Ray, Sammy Figueroa, and drummer Adam Nussbaum.[55] "I was pretty freaked out to say the least, but Sonny was a gentleman," Nussbaum said. "He's a very kind person, but I felt so in awe of being in his presence."[56]

On August 10, he performed at the Chicago Fest.[57] In Chicago, Sonny was a special guest on an episode of the *Soundstage* television series profiling singer-songwriter Garland Jeffreys. Jeffreys chose Sonny and Carmen McRae, a distant relative, for cameos. Sonny and Jeffreys performed the Jeffreys original "Nothing Big in Sight," which was not recorded elsewhere. "I'd like to dedicate this to Miles, Monk, Mingus, Chet, Bird, Trane, Dizzy, the Duke, the Count, and Mr. Sonny Rollins," Jeffreys said, introducing the song. Sonny gave a master class on performing with a singer, playing tasteful obbligato during the vocal, then letting it rip on his solo.[58] "It was fantastic, the way he played," Jeffreys recalled. "He steps out just a little bit, and plays his solo, and steps back and supports me again, just comps like he's supposed to do in a jazz band. He doesn't step out, take over, move me out of the way. He doesn't have to. I really learned something from that show."[59]

That fall, Sonny reunited with his group from the White House Jazz Festival for the Milestone Jazzstars tour: McCoy Tyner and Ron Carter, who were labelmates at Milestone, and, in lieu of Max Roach, Al Foster, Sonny's current drummer.[60] The gamble was to see if it was possible to produce a jazz tour with a rock tour's box office. Montreux Jazz Festival founder Claude Nobs realized that Sonny, McCoy, and Ron were all on Milestone and tried to book them for the festival together. It didn't materialize, but out of that kernel came the Jazzstars tour.[61] It was conceived by Fantasy "creative liaison" Bill Belmont, a self-professed "music business bureaucrat" who did not fit the stereotype—he was more counterculture than the typical suit, but more business savvy than the hippies.[62] Belmont had experience road-managing Country Joe and the Fish, the Rolling Stones, the Doors, and the Grateful

Dead, but he also knew jazz and loved Sonny. He came to Fantasy in 1975, managing the international side of the business, and got to know Sonny and Lucille when they came to Berkeley to record and mix albums.[63] Belmont had a sardonic wit—Lucille dubbed him "Gloom Disco"—but he also had a shrewd business sense, and in 1978, he saw an opportunity to try something bigger than the concert halls Sonny was already filling.

Norman Granz "brought American jazz musicians to Europe in a way that elevated not only their social status, but their musical status," Belmont said. "He presented people in classical music halls, kind of the same way the Milestone Jazzstars played halls that rock and roll bands played. And many of those promoters continued to present jazz after that."[64]

Orrin Keepnews thought of the Milestone Jazzstars as a "spiritual child of last year's V.S.O.P. tour,"[65] referring to the supergroup with Herbie Hancock, Wayne Shorter, Tony Williams, Ron Carter—Miles Davis's Second Great Quintet—and Freddie Hubbard, who stood in for Miles. Like V.S.O.P., the Jazzstars would perform an entirely acoustic set. It was the return to tradition that many of Sonny's die-hard fans were waiting for.

"We've been complaining for years that the record companies only put their promotion behind the million-selling pop or fusion stars," said Carter. "All we needed was someone to recognize that a substantial demand exists for the best acoustic jazz, and to back it with their money and enthusiasm."[66]

Fantasy spared no expense, taking out ads in *Rolling Stone* and major newspapers, prerecording a radio interview with each band member, setting up television appearances, making T-shirts and a souvenir program, planning autograph sessions. Concerts were recorded in Madison, New Haven, and San Francisco, leading to a well-received double album.[67] Unlike the typical model of touring on the back of a studio album, the release came on the back of the tour. It ran September 16 to October 29, nineteen shows through the West Coast, Midwest, and Northeast, at halls ranging from twenty-five hundred to four thousand seats:[68] San Francisco's Masonic Auditorium, New York's Beacon Theatre, the Kennedy Center, and the Philadelphia Academy of Music among them. In Seattle, Pat Metheny opened.

"I talked Bill Graham into promoting it," Belmont recalled. "The one thing that Bill Graham was concerned about was, 'Well, what kind of audience am I gonna get here? What are you expecting? Am I gonna have any trouble?' I told him no. And then after the show, he said, 'I wouldn't have believed it if I hadn't seen it.'" Belmont was shocked by Graham's racial bias. "That's the attitude that people had as recently as 1978 about jazz in America at someplace other than the Keystone Korner," Belmont said. "And I think a lot of that attitude really in many ways never left Sonny's mind. In other words, 'Am I an interloper here?'"

Graham was surprised not only by the sellout crowds but also by the predominantly white audience. "The only audience that had a large African American presence was Philadelphia," Belmont said. "And somewhat Washington, DC."

This underscored the lack of diversity in the concert business; virtually everyone presenting black music was white. "There are relatively few black concert entrepreneur types," Sonny said at the time. "This is mainly due to the fact that you have to have a lot of money in order to get started as a concert promoter. It's a highly competitive field, and it's difficult to get started. The only black major promoter-entrepreneur that I know of is Don King, the boxing promoter." On tour, "Sonny used to stay at airport hotels," Belmont recalled. "I once asked him why, and he said, 'Well, you never know if you have to get out of town quick.'"[69] Well into the eighties, Sonny would carry some press clippings on tour in case he had any problems on the road with white people who didn't recognize him.[70]

They rehearsed for a total of four hours. It was a leaderless group, so everything had to be decided collectively. One of the primary concerns was the dynamic between Sonny and McCoy. Sonny famously found piano restrictive; McCoy was known for sweeping harmonies on the sustain pedal. Sonny saw no problem with the idea of "trying to be more accessible," while McCoy staunchly opposed fusion. "In acoustic music," Tyner said, "the player's sensitivity supersedes his instrument, not vice versa. But I have a lot of respect for Sonny, and our musical rapport is genuine. It's obvious that this is no one's group in particular, so there's no reason we can't be a little accommodating and make beautiful music together."

To avoid stepping on anyone's toes, each show had multiple configurations: three or four full-quartet performances; a duet with Sonny and McCoy, usually on "In a Sentimental Mood," which they had played earlier at the televised *Down Beat* Awards; a trio with just the rhythm section; a duo with McCoy and Ron; a pianoless trio; and a solo piece from each of the three Jazzstars.[71] Everyone contributed compositions: Tyner's "Nubia," Sonny's "The Cutting Edge," and Carter's "N.O. Blues." The encore could be Monk's "I Mean You" or Coltrane's "Impressions."

The tour was a huge success. Most performances got standing ovations.[72] In the *Billboard* box-office charts for auditoriums under six thousand, the tour outsold Tom Petty and came in just short of Bonnie Raitt, Thin Lizzy, and Cheap Trick.[73]

Each of the three Jazzstars had records out: Sonny's *Don't Stop the Carnival*, Tyner's *The Greeting*, and Carter's *A Song for You*. "The tour was a tremendous promotional thing because McCoy, Ron, and I are all with the same label, so the company was able to give all our records a boost by having us play together," Sonny said. "This was one of the considerations that persuaded me to do it, but I wouldn't want to play in that context all the time."[74]

Carter hoped it would continue. "We had a great tour, man," Carter later recalled. "I was disappointed that the tour didn't continue for the next year."[75]

However, Sonny was through. "It's the first time that this has happened and maybe the last time, because everyone has their own groups, and they really want to pursue their own careers," Sonny said. "So this is a momentous thing."[76] He was ready to go back to his own band: "I can't play in what they would call now an all-star context all the time."[77]

Belmont compared the success of the Jazzstars tour to the Grateful Dead's 1987 single "Touch of Grey," their only song to make the *Billboard* top ten. "When that single happened, they all of a sudden had a multigenerational audience," Belmont said. "That single did for the Dead what the Milestone Jazzstars tour did for Sonny. Sonny just went kaboom into some other stratosphere." Suddenly, promoters in Sonny's native country realized what they had known for a long time in Europe and Japan: Sonny drew big crowds. "Miles never played dates like Sonny," Belmont said. "He played some big shows, but never for such an extended period of time as Sonny did."[78]

It was a level of success that was finally sufficient to dismiss Sonny's self-doubt, to a point. "I've started to realize that since people have appreciated my music, I should do it completely," Sonny said during the tour. "It's a way of being prayerful and praying to your god, and being thankful for having it. It's a religious thing."[79]

———◄○►———

Sonny became a household name not during his heyday in the fifties, but much later.[80] It was twenty years since he began the Bridge sabbatical. "It's taken me a long time to get [to] a place like this, where there is such a productive environment," Sonny said in 1979. "Today I have everything I really want out of life."[81] He and Lucille weren't living extravagantly; the only luxury they had was a Mercedes.[82] What Sonny wanted came from the music.

Sonny viewed critical and popular acclaim as the "kiss of death," he said that summer in a major profile in *Rolling Stone*. Sonny was the rare jazz musician to get that kind of coverage in the magazine; the cover read "Jazz '79: Sonny Rollins." "I always feel a new something happening; that's why I'm still around," he explained. "Maybe history will limit me to a style or period, but I refuse to limit myself. I never want to get to a point where I won't take a chance. . . . I like to think of myself as relating to all these things, not just as some guy who made great records in the fifties."[83]

Sonny had a loyal team assembled that would for the most part remain with him for the rest of his career, with Lucille as the nucleus: his label, Milestone; sound engineer Richard Corsello; publicist Terri Hinte; booking agent Ted Kurland; lawyer S. Edward Katz; and his saxophone technician, Emilio Lyons, the legendary Italian "Sax Doctor," who would give his tenor a tune-up every April and September while Sonny ate home-cooked spaghetti at his Boston home.[84] "I never see a man like Sonny Rollins, who loves the saxophone and treats the saxophone like a human being, like a life," Lyons recalled. "Sometimes he'd come with a limousine here and when he got out with the saxophone, he wouldn't give it to me. 'Don't you understand? That's not dead. That's *alive.*'"[85]

"There was a time when jazz musicians didn't play a lot of major concerts," Kurland said. "There were festivals, but in the seventies and eighties, it was a good time for heritage music . . . blues and jazz. . . . Colleges and universities started to embrace it, and performing arts centers that maybe up to then were predominantly classical concerts, they started to book jazz musicians."[86] Kurland did not book Sonny into any clubs and, at festivals, always tried to ensure that Sonny would be the final performance of the program out of respect for him and all other artists; for anyone, following Sonny Rollins was "a ludicrous undertaking."

To Kurland, Sonny was the type of icon that transcended any labels. "He was the only musician that did what he did," Kurland said. "It was so dramatic and profound and captivating, but he also onstage had a charisma and an energy. The way he moved around the stage, it was almost hypnotic, and he would pull people into a transcendental realm."[87]

Kurland never overbooked him. This approach stemmed from Lucille, whom Kurland described as "probably one of the best managers of any manager I ever worked with. Her judgment was usually impeccable. She was a very, very wise, smart person with certain business lessons I learned—in terms of not compromising and knowing when to say no." Bookings incorporated a travel day, a rest day, and a performance day. "There is a very overused phrase about performers leaving it all on the stage. He personified that," Kurland said. "I would get exhausted at his concerts."[88]

His life was in balance at this point. "Too much road time makes it a job instead of enjoyment," Sonny told Leonard Feather that year, "and happily, enjoyment's what it is right now."[89]

On May 14, 1979, Sonny, Lucille, and the band flew out to Berkeley to record *Don't Ask* at Fantasy Studios.[90] Sessions took place from May 15 to 18, with Soskin, Harris, Foster, Bill Summers on auxiliary percussion, and guitarist Larry Coryell. At Lucille's suggestion, Sonny simply called Coryell on the phone. "I listened to him for a number of years, and I always thought that his playing and mine would be compatible," Sonny said not long after making the record.[91]

For Coryell, it was a career highlight. "Sonny was all everyone said he was and more; his sense of what he wanted was impeccable," Coryell wrote.[92] Sonny played two tracks in duo on the album—Coryell's "The File" and the standard ballad "My Ideal," done rubato, ending with Sonny quoting "Oh, Susanna."

Fantasy decided to market "Harlem Boys" as a single. It referred to Sonny and Al Foster, the "Harlem Boys" in the band.[93] Orrin Keepnews cut it down from the seven-minute album version to a four-minute radio edit, and it got airplay on major R&B stations as an instrumental single.[94] Sonny's "Tai Chi" was a novelty that Sonny had been playing during his live set on Lyricon, the electronic wind instrument developed earlier in the decade. The most interesting tune on the album was Sonny's "Disco Monk." Despite its kitschy title, there was substance there—it combined an infectious disco beat with shifting tempos, an overdubbed tenor line also by Sonny, some inspired improvisation from Sonny and Coryell, and Mark Soskin on Clavinet and synthesizer. Sonny even plays piano, paying his own Monkish tribute to his guru.[95]

It was Sonny attempting to do for disco what he had done with westerns on *Way Out West*, even if it would never be as iconic. "During that period of time, this sort of fusion was the big thing," Sonny recalled. "So for some reason, the people that I grew up with—Monk, Miles, et al.—they weren't being heard as much. Some people call that 'con-fusion,' but I didn't go to that level. I respected it.... There was so much disco-type music going on at that time, which is okay, I have no problem with any kind of music. But the sentiment was that I wanted people to remember Monk."[96]

Sonny was aiming for a synthesis of the past and present. "I like to walk a tightrope," he said that year. "I appreciate the Art Ensemble; I appreciate Ornette; I appreciate Grover Washington and Stanley Turrentine and all those more melodic players. Through listening to all of them, I am able to make a statement of my own, without having to align myself with one school or the other."[97]

As part of that evolutionary process, in 1979, Sonny went disco. "When I came up, you played for dancers and it was a mark of your ability if you could play for people to dance," he said. "I think you can use disco to make people more aware of music."[98]

Initially, there were audio problems with *Don't Ask*, and Fantasy brought in Richard Corsello to fix them. "There really wasn't anybody there who knew which end of the microphone was the pickup, which end the cable gets plugged into, so with my repairing the *Don't Ask* record and making it sound as good as it did, it really opened everybody's eyes up," Corsello recalled. "Sonny and Lucille and I bonded, and we worked together for the next forty-plus years."[99]

In the short term, *Don't Ask* became Sonny's best-selling record ever.[100] One critic called it "one of the happiest albums the master has ever made."[101] He brought that energy on a national and European tour that spring and summer: the Berkeley Jazz Festival; the Catamaran in San Diego; Tulagi in Boulder, Colorado; and the Newport Jazz Festival in New York.[102] In Europe from June 26 to July 14, he played Wembley Conference Centre in London, Kongsberg in Norway, Pori Jazz in Finland, and the Velden Jazz Festival in Austria.[103] Late that summer, Sonny played two gigs in upstate New York, at the Joyous Lake in Woodstock and the Lewiston Artpark.[104]

On September 24, Sonny appeared on *The Tonight Show*. It aired at 12:45 a.m., an hour Sonny hadn't gone on in quite some time, but it was beamed out to an audience of fifteen million, his largest ever. Sonny was invited by guest host Bill Cosby, once an aspiring jazz drummer, who had recently seen Sonny on *Soundstage* with Garland Jeffreys. Cosby's first paid stand-up gig was apparently at Pep's in Philadelphia, opening for Sonny.[105] Decades before Cosby's career ended in disgrace, in 1979 he was riding high.[106]

In the morning walk-through at NBC Studios in Burbank, the producers explained that Sonny had eight minutes, thinking he would spend part of his airtime on the couch, but Sonny had no plans for late-night banter.[107] That night, Cosby held up *Don't Ask* and introduced Sonny as "one of the greatest musicians in the world. . . . I feel that you all, after you hear him, will feel that I did a good thing when I asked him to be with me tonight." It was Cosby's idea that Sonny play solo.

Sonny strode through the blue velvet curtains with a matching blue hat, dark slacks, a black T-shirt tucked in, a white blazer, and black Chuck Taylors.[108] Out of the saxophone came a flood of old-school jokes, comic non sequiturs in the spirit of Sonny's old favorites Bob and Ray, moments of pathos, stories, and songs: "Playin' in the Yard," "Dizzy Atmosphere," Grieg's *Peer Gynt*, "St. Thomas," "March of the Toys" from *Babes in Toyland*, "Brahms' Lullaby," Bird's "Ornithology," and, finally, "Shave and a Haircut." He sustained a high G on the tenor as the camera panned to Doc Severinsen's band, which, dumbstruck by Sonny's tour de force, could do nothing but applaud.[109] As the applause continued, Sonny didn't remove the mouthpiece. "All right!" Cosby said. "Get the last note out, Sonny! Get the closing note!" Sonny picked it back up with a quote from Percy Grainger's "Country Gardens," the staid folk melody and frequent bebop reference.[110] In referencing Grainger, Sonny was both skewering any bourgeois viewers of *The Tonight Show* and making a sly reference to Bird. Two weeks after his forty-ninth birthday, Sonny's tight five was one of the most remarkable late-night TV debuts.[111]

That image—Sonny standing tall on *The Tonight Show* stage after being introduced by a black host who grew up in the Philadelphia projects—Sonny bobbing and weaving with his tenor like Muhammad Ali,[112] Sonny stepping inside the time and smashing categories—underscored his outlook not only on the music but on the music business, which had not changed substantially since "The Freedom Suite." "Explain to Lu how we are fighting THE SYSTEM," he wrote in a journal around this time.[113]

> It's all about that people want to control you/present you/picture you as they want you to be/fit you into their category. This constitutes what life out here is all about; the battle lines as it were. This is where the system tries to crush us as it did me one time. Watch yourself. They try to BLACKBALL you in the business, to bring you in line. I'm working on this album and we gonna tell em F em.

Four days after *The Tonight Show* appearance, on September 28, Lucille's mother, Nanette Pearson, died at seventy-eight. She was buried in Germantown, where she lived with Sonny; Lucille; their Akita, Kendo; and their cats. Sonny and Lucille were devastated.[114] But the show went on.

That fall, Sonny, Foster, Soskin, and Harris played at the University of Kentucky, Sonny's first time back since his stay at Lexington. He followed this with Berkeley's Zellerbach Hall and Western Washington University in Bellingham. Then he played rock clubs: Stars in Philadelphia and the Bottom Line in Greenwich Village.[115] Sonny wanted to make sure that his band was as committed as he was. "Jerry: Don't forget to always play more up on the beat than below the beat," he wrote in a note to Jerome Harris. "There should be no change in intensity downwards once the blowing section begins."[116]

Sonny closed out the seventies in the late thirties, back where it all began. The band was on a short Texas tour, playing the Houston Jazz Festival and Armadillo World Headquarters in Austin.[117] "This was among the great performances," recalled Harris of the Austin show. "The building was kind of a Quonset hut, and had an elevated stage and an area between the stage and where the seats started, and I remember we were playing a ballad, I'm pretty sure it was 'The Very Thought of You.' We were getting towards the end of the tune, when all of a sudden, a bunch of couples got up out of the audience and started dancing in that open area between the seats and the stage, so Sonny motioned—'Keep the tune going.' And he started playing all this Coleman Hawkins stuff. It was as if someone had flipped a switch and we were back in 1939 or '40. I have never heard anything like it, and these couples are on the floor. It was like 'Oh . . . my . . . god.' We knew that Hawk was one of his guys, but I had never heard him go so deeply into pulling that influence out and manifesting it. I was nearly in tears."[118]

Sonny was always unstuck in time. The past was there in the rhythm, not preserved in amber but more like quicksilver. "To me," he said, "it's all just one thing anyway."[119]

Chapter 37

THE STONES

(1980)

At the outset of what Sonny called "The Bombastic Eighties," he continued pursuing as much artistic freedom as possible.[1] Financial success and artistic integrity were often at odds in the music business. The money was there—even Rick James, that quintessential eighties artist, was a Sonny Rollins fan—but it came at a price.[2] By the end of the year, Sonny would be put to the test. He had the opportunity to make more money than he ever had in his life when he was approached by a band he genuinely didn't know: the Rolling Stones.[3]

The year 1980 culminated with the Stones, but it began at Dooley's in Tempe, Arizona, where Sonny played on January 29 with Mark Soskin, Jerome Harris, and Al Foster.[4] Sonny played in California in February—two nights at the Roxy in Los Angeles, one night at the Great American Music Hall in San Francisco, and a series of college dates.[5] He cut a striking figure and wore many different hats, literally—black, blue, red, purple, all velvet, and his Chuck Taylor Converse sneakers. He also doubled on the Lyricon as part of his set, playing "In a Sentimental Mood." On March 8, he played at the Boston Globe Jazz Festival opposite Freddie Hubbard.[6]

After Sonny and Lucille took a weeklong vacation in March in Petit St. Vincent, Sonny continued touring domestically.[7] On March 23, he was scheduled at Merlyn's in Madison, Wisconsin, a punk club that also booked jazz acts;[8] then on April 10 in Philadelphia at Stars, another club with a similar booking policy.[9] On April 12, Sonny played in Nashville at Vanderbilt University's Rites of Spring Festival,[10] and then he was in the Midwest: on April 16, in Indianapolis at the Vogue; from April 18 to 19 at George's, a newly opened club in Chicago; and on April 21 in Minneapolis at the Walker Art Center. He then went to the South: on April 25 at the New Orleans Jazz and Heritage Festival aboard the SS *President*, Sonny received a standing ovation after every tune. In Austin, he returned to Armadillo World Headquarters on April 26; he played Rockefeller's in Houston on April 27.[11]

That May, Sonny went to Berkeley to record *Love at First Sight* at Fantasy Studios with George Duke, Stanley Clarke, Al Foster, and Bill Summers.[12] Sonny and Lucille signed a one-album contract for a $12,000 advance. They were given the option to serve as dual coproducers with Orrin Keepnews for no additional compensation—Lucille was effectively already serving in that capacity and had considered taking a more substantial role in production. The idea was to operate as their own production company, tentatively called Snillor Productions (Sonny's name backward), inspired by Ron Carter's Retrac.[13] Neither Sonny nor Lucille ultimately took a producer's credit on the record, but the seed was planted for the future.[14]

Fantasy Studios was a state-of-the-art facility. In 1980, Saul Zaentz invested in the new Studio D, a massive thirty-by-fifty-foot space outfitted with top-of-the-line equipment, funded in part from the success of *One Flew over the Cuckoo's Nest*, which was coproduced by Zaentz and Michael Douglas. In addition to Fantasy's own artists, the facility became the studio of choice for pop and rock bands and postproduction on major studio films, among them Journey's "Don't Stop Believin'" and *Apocalypse Now*. "It was just an amazing facility, with moving walls, moving ceilings, all kinds of different surfaces and environments to be able to work in, the best equipment," recalled engineer Richard Corsello, who after mixing Sonny's *Don't Ask* was working with him in the studio for the first time.[15] Fantasy had twin twenty-four-track tape recorders, which allowed Sonny to play as long as he wanted uninterrupted. "We'd have both of them armed and ready to go," Corsello said, "so when we got toward the end of a reel we would start the second machine up so that if it was a good take we could edit them together."[16]

Recording Sonny posed unique challenges that demanded creative improvisation. "We would get it all set up and he'd be standing in front of a microphone, and then I would go in the control room and say, 'Okay, all right, let's hit it, man. We're rolling.' And he would turn and walk away from the microphone and start walking around the room," Corsello recalled. Corsello began using a clip-on Sony ECM-50 lavalier mike. "I clipped it to the bell of his horn, and I gave him fifty feet of cable so he could wander around the studio."[17] The only problem was that the clip-on microphone's sound was not up to Corsello's standard. "What I would do afterwards is I would take his horn and send it out to the studio and play it back through a speaker and record the room and add that in to give his horn some depth. I had to be very creative on how to figure out how to record him. What was I gonna do? Have somebody go out there and hold a microphone and follow him around while he's playing?"[18]

The one place Sonny would never wander is the control room. "While Lucille and I would be in the control room mixing records, Sonny would be out in the studio practicing his horn," Corsello said. "Sonny was never involved in any of that.... He just really disliked hearing himself, period."

On *Love at First Sight*, Sonny recorded his up-tempo calypso "Little Lu," named for Lucille; Stanley Clarke's lilting "The Dream That We Fell Out Of," with Sonny doubling on Lyricon; "Strode Rode"; "The Very Thought of You"; George Duke's "Caress"; and "Double Feature," a loping saxophone-bass blues duo that Clarke and Sonny shared composer credit on. Compared to the *Saxophone Colossus* version, "Strode Rode" was recorded a sixth up from the original key, the blue note in the ninth bar was raised a half step, and Sonny tongues the melody more crisply. Duke plays an electric keyboard and Clarke an electric bass, giving the piece an overall cleaner, more sterile feel than the insouciant swagger and grit of the iconic original.[19]

Love at First Sight was recorded from May 9 to 12 in Fantasy Studio C, about two songs a day. Sessions were long, at Sonny's insistence: the first went from 2 p.m. to 7:30 p.m.; the second from 3:30 p.m. to 10 p.m. "Little Lu" had thirteen takes. Lucille and Sonny had wanted Bill Summers to lay down some overdubs. In particular, they felt "Little Lu" was missing a key element—cowbell, preferably on every beat.[20]

Sonny pulled no punches. He may not have entered the control room during recording or participated in mixing, but he did listen to the album to offer postproduction notes. Lucille had a range of responses to the different takes. "<u>Deadly</u> take BORING," she wrote of the second take of "Caress," while the third was "beginning to get feeling." On "The Very Thought of You," Sonny was "beautiful (magnificent)," George Duke "lovely." Some takes were rejected outright with a big "NO," while others got a resounding "YES."

Sonny, on the other hand, remained his own worst critic. In his written notes, he reserved most of the opprobrium not for the band but for himself, from intonation problems to "fumbled" notes to what he perceived as a hollow-sounding high D missing a partial of the overtone. No errant note escaped his critical ear—from a missed change to "heavy-handed" playing on some takes.[21] At best, Sonny was self-damning with faint praise.[22] Of the four takes of "Double Feature," the duet with Clarke, Sonny liked only the first. The second had "bad sax opening—an embarrassment"; the third, "a trifle better opening—an embarrassment." Throughout, the best takes were all "usable," the worst an "embarrassment." One take was "probably best but it's just not enough music. The whole album musically is cliché ridden and what else can I tell you." In a mock mock-up of the album cover, Sonny gave an alternate title for the record: "SHOOT ME IN THE HEAD! I'm Sorry I Was Born."[23]

That doesn't mean he hoped the critics would see *Love at First Sight* the same way. Most didn't fall in love, but the album got lukewarm to positive reviews, even managing to crack the Top 200 album charts.[24] Despite Sonny's own private assertion, one critic called the album "non-cliched"; another concluded that "this album is more proof that Sonny Rollins is indeed the greatest living tenor sax player."[25]

On the summer festival circuit, Sonny played Milwaukee Summerfest, Chicago Fest, the Jazz City festival in Edmonton, and an appearance in Vancouver.[26] On September 7, he turned fifty years old, but Sonny was hardly slowing down. That month, he played the Great American Music Hall and the Long Beach festival in California, then returned to the Walker Art Center in Minneapolis.[27]

That October, Sonny embarked on a European tour with Soskin, Harris, and Al Foster organized by Alexander Zivkovic, a London-based Serbian journalist turned jazz promoter.[28] On October 18, they played a sold-out concert at London's Royal Festival Hall, on October 22 at Groningen Cultural Center in the Netherlands, on October 23 in Warsaw at Sala Kongresowa, on October 25 in Sweden at Umea Dragon Skol, on October 27 in Lyon, on October 29 in Munich at Circus Krone, on October 31 at the Théâtre de la Ville in Paris, on November 1 at the Zurich Folkhaus, and on November 2 in Belgrade at the Dom Sindikata.[29]

In Warsaw, it was Jerome Harris's first time behind the Iron Curtain, and the symbolism of Sonny's freewheeling music hung heavy in the air. He played "Little Lu" for nearly forty minutes. There were only four radio stations in Poland, and records were smuggled in as contraband, then recorded from vinyl onto reel-to-reel tape and distributed through an underground network of deejays and record enthusiasts. Listening to jazz, in a live concert setting, was a political act of defiance.[30]

"It was during the Solidarity movement period," Harris said of the anticommunist Polish trade union that was founded earlier that summer. "Before the trip, I had bought a new pair of shoes, these Bass jazz oxfords, and as we're walking on the streets of Warsaw, I see people looking at us, and people would come up and whisper, 'Change money,' trying to get dollars for zlotys. Hard currency was hard to come by, but I also noticed that people were looking at us, and person after person was staring at my shoes and going up. We passed a place that looked like a department store and I said, 'Mark, I'd like to go in here and look at the shoe department,' and what was offered were these clodhopper, anti-style shoes. Now I saw why people were staring at my shoes."[31]

Sonny was a hit at Warsaw's Jazz Jamboree, presented by the Polish Jazz Association, and after the show, the band was invited to a jam session. "The atmosphere at the gig was really kind of intense," Harris said. "It was a jam session after-hours club, and you really had the feeling of the patrons there being like, 'Okay, we are into this music and we don't know if Russia's gonna send tanks in tomorrow.'"[32]

At the Paris International Jazz Festival, Sonny's concert at the 1,750-seat Théâtre de la Ville almost caused a riot. It sold out two months in advance and frustrated French jazz fans showed up to find they couldn't get in.[33] The show went on, though, and Sonny played an electrifying four-hour set.[34] He then conducted a master class at the Salle Wagram, with saxophonists Charles Schneider and Marc Thomas, bassist Yves Torchinsky, and drummer Stéphane Grémaud. The class was filmed and released as *La Leçon de Musique*. Sonny taught the young musicians how to play "Little Lu," but the lesson cut much deeper than running down changes. "So what we're basically proving here is that jazz is something which is, it's not so much what's written down there, it's what you bring to it. It's what we do with it," Sonny explained. He taught them how to circular breathe, to imbue each song with the emotion the song projects, and how to listen to each other as a collective—"When we all are playing together, all separately, yet all the same."[35]

The last tour date was in Belgrade on Alexander Zivkovic's home turf. "He played during communist era. Tito was still alive when Sonny Rollins played," Zivkovic said.[36] "The Communist Party was in power and in charge of everything—culture, music—and they actually considered jazz and rock as sort of a bad influence on Yugoslav youth," he said. With the economy in a near-perpetual state of crisis, payment was complicated. "During the communist regime, there was always a problem with hard currency, so I had to accept dinars instead of dollars—local currency—for Sonny Rollins's gig," Zivkovic said. "That was of course illegal."[37] Nevertheless, they played the gig and made it home fine.

Sonny finished the year with one more domestic tour in November and a brief tour of the Caribbean, performing in Martinique and Guadeloupe.[38] It was during this string of dates that one of the most unlikely collaborations of the eighties was sparked.

At Sonny's shows at the Bottom Line from November 7 to 8, his nephew Clifton Anderson brought his girlfriend and had a close encounter with an unexpected Sonny Rollins fan. "We go backstage, and we're hanging with Sonny in the dressing room," Anderson recalled. "Chick Corea's back there, and the chief engineer at Fantasy, Jim Stern. These two other people come in and sneak in the door. And I'm looking at the guy, and I'm saying, this guy looks kind of weird. He's got this funny beard, and funky looking. And the woman that he's with is fine as shit. What a weird-ass couple. So after the show is over, we went back to the dressing room, and Sonny's driver said, 'How'd you like that funny disguise that Mick Jagger had on?' It was Mick Jagger and Jerry Hall!"[39] Apparently, filmmaker Dick Fontaine, who had made the 1968 documentary "Who Is Sonny Rollins?," took Jagger to the Bottom Line and served as a point of connection.[40]

Soon thereafter, "Sonny called me up and said, 'Hey Clifton, you ever hear of this rock band called the Rolling Stones?' I said, 'Yeah, Sonny!' He said, 'How is their music?' I said, 'You know, they're pretty hip. From what I understand, their stuff comes out of the blues, so you're gonna like it.' 'This guy keeps following the band. He wants me to play, and he keeps—it's like he's stalking me or something.' So I said, 'That's Mick Jagger, man. Sonny, you should do it. I think you'd probably like it. I think you'll like their music. They're cool.' So he said, 'Well, I'm not gonna do anything yet.'"[41]

The idea of Sonny making a record with the Rolling Stones originated with drummer Charlie Watts. Before he was a Stone, he was a jazz fan, and also a jazz drummer in his own right. Growing up, he lived across the street from bassist Dave Green, who played with Sonny in the sixties.[42] "My love for Sonny goes back a long way," Watts recalled. "I would have been fifteen or sixteen when I first played his records, first with Max Roach and Clifford Brown, then his stuff with Miles, and then of course on his own. . . . I first saw him in 1964 in the original Birdland club on 52nd Street, playing with a trio. To sit there and watch Sonny Rollins, my God!"[43]

When Mick Jagger asked Watts to recommend a saxophonist for *Tattoo You*, Watts instantly thought of Sonny.[44] "I had a lot of trepidation about working with Sonny Rollins," Jagger said. "This guy's a giant of the saxophone. Charlie said, 'He's never going to want to play on a Rolling Stones record!' I said, 'Yes he is going to want to.'"[45]

Tattoo You was culled from discarded material the Stones had already recorded for *Emotional Rescue* and other albums. "The thing with *Tattoo You* wasn't that we'd stopped writing new stuff, it was a question of time," said Keith Richards. "We'd agreed we were going to go out on the road and we wanted to tour behind a record. There was no time to make a whole new album and make the start of the tour."[46] In order to finish the tracks, they had to bring in additional personnel for overdubs. This meant that Charlie Watts would never have the direct experience of recording with one of his idols. "Probably just as well," said Watts. "My goodness, I'd sit there and think, 'Bloody hell, what am I going to do here?' I'd feel like an impostor, because that's the highest company you can keep."[47]

Ahmet Ertegun made the initial approach. "Ahmet Ertegun, the president of Atlantic Records, whom I've known for a long time, called and said Mick wanted to talk to me," Sonny recalled. "So I spoke to Mick and he said, 'Well, look, man, I'd like to use you on the date.' I said, 'Are you sure?' and he says, 'Yeah,' so I told him to send me some cassettes of what he had in mind and I'd see if I could get into it."[48]

It took some coaxing from Lucille. "She was familiar with the Rolling Stones," Sonny later said. "I mean, I heard the name Rolling Stones but Rolling Stones didn't mean anything to me . . . so I didn't want to do it, so Lucille said, 'No Sonny, please do this.' So I said, 'Okay, well, I'll do it.' And the rationale that I'll have for doing it is that I'll see how my playing as a jazz musician can somehow meld with these guys, you know, British rockers or whatever they were called."[49] On multiple occasions, Sonny doubled down on his resistance to the idea. "I'd considered them—and it's faulty—not on the level of jazz," Sonny said. "But my wife said, 'No, no, you must do it.' So I said, 'OK, let me see if I can relate to what they are doing; let me see if I can make it sound as good as possible.' "[50]

When Sonny played the tape Jagger sent him, he just didn't relate to it. "It might be wrong for me to feel that way because I do like a lot of white artists," Sonny said. "I like the Beatles. Paul McCartney is a good tunesmith. But the Rolling Stones, I didn't relate to them because I thought they were just derivative of black blues."[51]

That December, Sonny met Mick Jagger at Atlantic Studios at 1841 Broadway in Columbus Circle to lay down his overdubs, but as punctual as he usually was, Sonny was late.[52] "I had a hard time finding the studio," Sonny said. "I hate being late to anything, and usually I am not. But this time I was late, although not purposely. Mick seemed to feel that I was dissing him...but it was completely inadvertent.... I just could not find the studio."[53]

It was just Sonny and Mick Jagger in the studio that winter day; it's not clear if anyone other than Mick was in the booth. "Sadly I was not on the session," said Chris Kimsey, who was engineer and associate producer and even played electric piano on *Tattoo You*. "I think it may have been Bob Clearmountain.... Wish I had been there!" Yet Clearmountain wasn't there either. "Although I did mix 'Waiting on a Friend' that he played on, I never met the man," Clearmountain said. "Mr. Rollins had recorded his beautiful solo before I was involved with the project." Neither was Barry Sage, who worked with Kimsey on much of the rest of the album.[54]

"I said, 'Would you like me to stay out there in the studio?' " Jagger recalled. "He said, 'Yeah, you tell me where you want me to play and DANCE the part out.' So I did that. And that's very important: communication in hand, dance, whatever. You don't have to do a whole ballet, but sometimes that movement of the shoulder tells the guy to kick in on the beat."[55]

Sonny played on three tracks: "Neighbours," "Slave," and "Waiting on a Friend."[56] Despite Sonny's misgivings, he still approached the album as a perfectionist. "I really wasn't sure that they'd use the takes I'd made. But Mick liked them, and put them out," Sonny said. "But it *was* work, it wasn't something I just fluffed off. It took a lot of time. Of course, anything I do takes a lot of time. I always tell people I'm not a good enough musician to be able to do things half-heartedly. Anything I do to get the results I get, I'm really working my ass off."[57]

"He came in and asked to hear the tunes," Jagger said, "and came up with these amazing solos the first time out. He thought he was just warming up; we thought what he had played couldn't possibly be improved on. But in a couple of cases, he did improve on it."[58]

"Neighbours" was apropos for Sonny. Ostensibly about the aggravation of noisy neighbors—"Screamin' young babies, no peace and no quiet, I got TVs, saxophone playin'" (that is, one of the concerns that drove Sonny onto the Bridge), the song turns out to be about the Golden Rule ("Do unto strangers what you do to yourself"). "Waiting on a Friend" was the stand-out track, released as the album's second single after "Start Me Up." Sonny may have known it was partly recorded in Kingston, Jamaica; it ends with Sonny adding a frisson of calypso. Yet there is something more subversive here. Sonny steps inside the time, never quite on the beat, hanging on a note, making us wait, bending it down a whole step like a wild palm in the wind, then back up again, before drifting off into the horizon—a fugitive, far-off sound, totally free. Sonny was adding the element he felt was not quite present in the mix. "With the Stones the free spirit is more implied if not there," Sonny wrote in a journal entry from this period.[59]

Clearmountain, who mixed "Waiting on a Friend," was one of the first to hear Sonny's solo, but he didn't know it was Sonny. "At the time, I didn't even know who played the sax solo as Mick never mentioned it and the track sheet only said something to the effect of 'sax solo,' with no mention of the player's name," Clearmountain recalled. "What a great solo! But anyone on Planet Earth hearing that song would likely say the same thing."[60]

Sonny wasn't just omitted from the recording log; he went uncredited altogether on the album. This was a mutually agreed-upon omission and, if anything, more insisted on by Sonny. "I didn't want to be credited on the record or *anything*," Sonny later said. "Because to me, that was sort of a lower step down . . . and I was already Sonny Rollins. I was one of the top names in jazz. I represented jazz. Jazz is higher than rock and roll, okay? Simple as that. I didn't want to be, 'Oh man, Sonny Rollins is playing on a rock and roll record?' You know, that's a disgrace."[61]

In fact, no one was credited on *Tattoo You*, not even the Stones themselves. "I just got fed up with writing all those credit lists out," Jagger said, "and everyone wants one above the other one, and then I couldn't remember who is playing, so I thought, 'Oh, everyone got paid anyway. So it's much easier to leave the whole thing."[62] There were complete credits on their previous album *Emotional Rescue*, as well as on their next two, *Still Life* and *Undercover*. For one thing, Nicky Hopkins, Pete Townshend, Sugar Blue, and a handful of others contributed to *Tattoo You*, and with Sonny's refusal to be credited, it would be hard to explain the conspicuous absence of Sonny Rollins on the personnel list.[63]

"Sonny didn't want to be on anybody else's record as a sideman, so he had a clause in his contract that he could not appear as a sideman," recalled Clifton Anderson, "but anybody who ever listened to Sonny knows exactly who it is."[64]

"In retrospect, it was a little naïve of me to think I could do something with them and let it be sort of under the table," Sonny said.[65] In reviews, the Stones bore the brunt of Sonny's uncredited appearance. How could they publicly say that Sonny simply refused to be credited on a Rolling Stones record? *Tattoo You* was at the top of the *Billboard* 200 for nine weeks in 1981; Michael Lindsay-Hogg's music video for "Waiting on a Friend" was in heavy rotation on the fledgling MTV channel.[66] Critically, it was hailed as one of the best albums of the eighties by *Rolling Stone*. As critics noted, it was in good part due to Sonny's presence.[67]

Sonny worried that appearing with the Stones on top of the charts could undermine his artistic integrity. And the concern was justified. His old friend Betty Carter issued a harsh rebuke of those who dipped their feet into the pop world, the latest example being Sonny. "We've got George Benson, Donald Byrd, Herbie Hancock, and, before that, Tony Williams. And now, even Sonny Rollins recording with the Rolling Stones," Carter said. "Now what would he want the Rolling Stones for if they're not the source? It would seem to me that a black man would go to the source—which would be Chuck Berry—record an album with him and you've got history in the making. But he wants to make some money and make it fast."[68]

Sonny was aware of the backlash, but at the time, he "didn't really comprehend why," largely due to his lack of familiarity with the Stones. Later on, Sonny read Martha Bayles's critique of the Stones in *Hole in Our Soul: The Loss of Beauty and Meaning in American Popular Music*.[69] As for *Tattoo You*, Sonny said, "in some ways, I do regret it."[70]

It had nothing to do with the money. "I got my little five figure check," Sonny recalled of the recording session.[71] But then the Stones came back with a serious proposition.[72] In 1981, as they were gearing up for their three-month American tour of 1981, starting at the end of September, they had high hopes that Sonny would accompany them. "We're just at the point of seeing if we can do any and if so how many," Lucille said at the time. "So much of it is Sonny's schedule. We're going to Europe in a few weeks." Sonny and Lucille adhered to the musician's code that you never renege on a commitment, but Lucille was optimistic that they could work it out. There was a strong incentive, recalled drummer Tommy Campbell, who was in Sonny's band at the time. "When that record came out, they asked Sonny to play on tour," Campbell said. "He said nope... I know it was in the millions—one or two or three million dollars—back then."[73]

Sonny Rollins could not be bought. "I said, 'No way, no way,'" Sonny said. "Regret not going? Just the opposite... I couldn't have lived with myself if I'd played with the Rolling Stones. No, no, no, no." Had they wanted Sonny to open for them, maybe it could have happened. "I would have been playing with the group. See, the Rolling Stones had concerts where they had Stevie Wonder not playing with them. They had him opening for them, something like that. That's fine, that's different. They didn't approach me that way; I was supposed to re-create that record that we made together. So I had to be part of that group... there's no way that I would do that."[74]

The Stones hired saxophonist Lee Allen for the first three shows, followed by Tonight Show Band member Ernie Watts, who was recommended by Quincy Jones and played the rest of the tour.[75] They played for crowds up to ninety-five thousand, with $52 million in ticket sales. It was the highest-grossing tour of the year; the December 5 show at the Superdome in New Orleans set an indoor attendance record that held for thirty-three years. It also yielded *Let's Spend the Night Together*, the 1983 concert film directed by Hal Ashby, which grossed an additional $50 million. "It was a historical event, like the King Tut exhibit on the road," said Watts.[76] But Sonny would not be part of the museum.

Later on, the Stones tried to get Sonny again, this time to re-create his "Waiting on a Friend" solo on the Bridges to Babylon tour in 1997. "The Stones were doing this tour and they wanted Sonny to fly into St. Louis and play that solo onstage," recalled Bill Belmont. "Sonny and I talked about it, and all he had to do was fly from New York to St. Louis, be treated like a hero, star, general, celebrity, important icon of the universe, play the date and leave.... They offered him the moon. It was probably a lot of money. I've heard various figures. Private plane, the whole deal. Anything to get him to do it." Sonny and Lucille turned them down again. They got Joshua Redman instead. "I wasn't tempted by that," Sonny said.[77]

Later, Belmont asked the Stones about procuring a quadruple-platinum album for Sonny for his work on *Tattoo You*. "Charlie said 'Absolutely, at any time. Right away, we'll do it,'" Belmont said, "and so they generated an album which they sent to me, and I sent it off to Sonny. I don't think he mentioned it, but they did get him the record. He probably has it in the closet." As Sonny tells it, "They sent me a copy of the record and a lovely letter, but I never listen to my old recordings." It's unclear if Sonny was referring to the vinyl or the platinum record; either way, he didn't care.[78]

Sonny would remain friendly with Charlie Watts, but he never performed with the Rolling Stones. What was ultimately a one-day collaboration dogged him in interviews for the rest of his career. "Playing second fiddle to a British rock group didn't make sense to me," Sonny later said. "I made the record for [Lucille] and that was it. I'm not a fan of theirs and I do not know their work."[79]

As reclusive as he could be, Sonny couldn't entirely escape the Rolling Stones, though.[80] "I was in the supermarket up in Hudson, New York, and they were playing Top 40 records," Sonny recalled. "I heard this song and thought, Who's that guy? His playing struck a chord in me. Then I said, 'Wait a minute, that's me!' It was my playing on one of those Rolling Stones records."[81]

Chapter 38

PASSING THE TORCH

(1981–1983)

"I like to think there is a direct link between early jazz and jazz of any time," Sonny said. "I like to think that jazz can be played in a way that you can hear the old as well as the new. . . . I listen to Louis Armstrong and hear something that I want to be able to hear in anything that's called 'jazz.'"[1] In the early eighties, Sonny was that bridge, linking the legacy of Armstrong to the next generation. He began what might be thought of informally as the eclectic Sonny Rollins Invitational Series he hosted regularly for the rest of his career. Between 1981 and 1983, he passed the torch to Grover Washington Jr., Pat Metheny, and Wynton Marsalis while continuing his own robust touring schedule.

After a January 1981 tour of Japan, and a gig at Rockefeller's in Houston, in March, Sonny turned to his health: intermittent fasting, some days drinking only tea, stretching, and yoga practice.[2] He conserved his energy leading up to his highest-profile US show of the year, on April 25 at Town Hall with Grover Washington Jr.[3]

Washington had become synonymous with smooth jazz.[4] In the week leading up to the concert with Sonny, Washington was enjoying the greatest commercial success of his career when "Just the Two of Us," his collaboration with Bill Withers, reached the *Billboard* top five.[5] Yet no amount of commercial success could curb his excitement to share a stage with Sonny. "Sonny called and asked me to do this, and it didn't take very long for me to say yes," Washington said. He hoped that appearing with Sonny could shore up his artistic integrity, and Lucille hoped that some of Washington's commercial appeal would rub off on Sonny. "Lucille loved the idea, because she was always trying to make Sonny more contemporary, not just a bebop player," recalled Julie Lokin of New Audiences, which presented the concert.[6]

"Grover really has that common touch which people can relate to. I mean, he's got it. He's a great player as well as being a beautiful human being which means to me a great deal also," Sonny said. "But one thing about Grover, he always wanted to play more jazz."[7] Playing only soprano that night, Washington would have his chance to prove his jazz bona fides—Sonny didn't bring a piano player; he just had Al Foster and Bob Cranshaw. There would be no safety net.

Sonny opened the night with a long free-form cadenza, preemptively winning whatever saxophone battle anyone expected. They each played a couple tunes by themselves with the rhythm section, but for most of the night they played in tandem, "God Bless the Child" and "You Do Something to Me" among them. They finished the second set with the audience clamoring for more and came back out for an encore. Sonny counted off "Oleo" at a brisk tempo, and Washington played through the changes on his best solo of the night. Then Sonny played some choruses in double time. At fifty, Sonny still had it.[8]

The concert grossed $35,000, with Sonny receiving $9,000 of that.[9] Julie Lokin wrote Lucille to report the success, calling it "the best presentation we've done."[10]

After the concert, Sonny hired twenty-seven-year-old pianist Bill O'Connell, having him mostly play a Rhodes. A graduate of the Oberlin Conservatory of Music, O'Connell established himself in New York with Mongo Santamaria. Sonny's repertoire remained obscure, including the Friedrich Hollaender song "Illusions" from *A Foreign Affair* with Marlene Dietrich or "Cabin in the Sky" from the eponymous film, and Sonny generally didn't supply lead sheets. "He would just teach me the tune and I'd find the chords, which was really different from just about every rehearsal I had been to," O'Connell recalled. "When that rehearsal was over, you knew the tune. I had it memorized."[11]

In July, Sonny returned to Japan as part of Live Under the Sky, a jazz festival that began in 1977.[12] He appeared with the group from *Love at First Sight*—George Duke, Stanley Clarke, and Al Foster.[13] Sonny radiated joy from the stage as he broke into a full sweat on "St. Thomas," "Moritat," and "Isn't She Lovely"—with Duke and Clarke both playing acoustic and electric; Sonny also played soprano.[14]

In August, Sonny played Jazz City in Edmonton, the Stratford Shakespeare Festival, the Great American Music Hall, and the Park Central Jazz Festival in Dallas.[15] He kept Bill O'Connell, hiring bassist Tom Barney and drummer Steve Jordan.[16] Barney, Bob Cranshaw's son, knew not to follow Sonny into the stratosphere. "No matter where Sonny goes, stay put," he said. "Because if you try to follow him, that's a rabbit hole. I think my dad is probably the only person who could follow Sonny when Sonny would veer off because they had such a history together and their depth of tunes was so deep. Anybody else, you need to just stay put. He'll come back around and find you."[17]

Journeyman drummer Steve Jordan was only twenty-four, but he had already established himself as a first-call session player across genre: Don Cherry, Don Pullen, and Ben Sidran as well as the Blues Brothers Band, Spyro Gyra, Herbie Mann, and Aretha Franklin. Jordan got the gig through Bob Cranshaw, his bandmate in the *Saturday Night Live* band; he had also gone to the High School of Music and Art with Clifton Anderson. "I'm not interested in being flashy if it's cutting into the person that we want to hear play," Jordan said. "I'm providing a bed for him to soar. He would always stay in the pocket, so that was number one. When you're playing with Sonny, particularly at that time, your focus is beyond . . . a heightened focus—every sixty-fourth note. High intensity, almost like meditation."[18]

The band all responded to Sonny's sense of comic timing. "Some of the most amazing stuff was just sitting at the piano when he took a cadenza, and he would go off and play all this ridiculous stuff on the saxophone, but then he'd go [sings "Pop Goes the Weasel"] and the crowd would go crazy," recalled O'Connell. "It taught me something. How many people can really express humor in this music? Most don't. Everybody tries to be so serious and profound, but humor's profound, too."[19]

That fall, Sonny did a ten-city European tour from October 10 to 25 through Stockholm, Rotterdam, Rome, Torino, Perugia, Angers, Angouleme, Grenoble, London, Chichester, and Cork.[20] He brought O'Connell, bassist Thomas Palmer, Yoshiaki Masuo, and twenty-four-year-old drummer Tommy Campbell.[21]

Campbell was the nephew of organist Jimmy Smith, and joined Sonny from Dizzy Gillespie's band, but the first lesson was that playing with Sonny was an endurance sport.[22] For one, Sonny's suitcase was the single heaviest piece of equipment on tour. "I picked up his suitcase. 'Holy smokes, man! What's in it?' They were his weights," Campbell said. He and the band would watch in disbelief as Sonny would "grab his briefcase and his horn and hit the stairs. And when we got up he wasn't even breathing hard." Yet Sonny demanded that his much younger band keep up, always an estimable task. Campbell played basketball, but playing with Sonny was like four straight quarters without a break. "He loved to get the most out of his band. Don't get caught napping," Campbell said. "If you're playing like the song is gonna end soon, you are badly mistaken. He'll sense that, and play sixty more choruses.... I'm not a heavy sweater, but I've never been so drenched."[23]

Campbell looked to Sonny for any feedback, positive or negative—any sense of connection or mentorship at all, really—but never got it, not verbally at least. Offstage Sonny was "somewhat untouchable."[24] Then one night, something clicked. Sonny had been communicating all along—his own history, his thoughts on Campbell's playing, and much more—through the music. "I was going, 'Man, he's not telling me shit! I don't know what!' And as soon as I said 'what,' he came back and started playing song after song that I just happened to know every song and the lyrics. He told me a story that you would not believe, but we were onstage, so I couldn't get it all and file it all, but he was telling me, 'Yeah, you're fine, you're doing great. How you like playing with me so far?' All in his horn!... It was just like him sitting down and talking for the first time."[25]

From December 9 to 15, Sonny recorded his next album for Milestone, *No Problem*.[26] He hired vibraphonist Bobby Hutcherson and drummer Tony Williams (both local to the Bay Area), Bob Cranshaw, and guitarist Bobby Broom. It had been a few years since Sonny had last worked with Broom, and Broom had learned a lot in the interim. Sonny called him up for the record after seeing an ad in the paper that year for *Clean Sweep*, Broom's debut as a leader on Arista; he liked what he heard when he checked it out.[27]

No Problem would be the first record that Sonny and Lucille coproduced without Orrin Keepnews's involvement. "I have been thinking about producing for a long time," Sonny said that November. "I was listening to Roberta

Flack talking one night, and what she described was similar to me. She was actually producing her own albums anyway; she was selecting the material, picking the people. What I haven't been doing is talking to people on the date about money and various arrangements. The rest is something I think I should be doing—it just means more control over what you do."[28]

This was "financially disturbing" news to Orrin Keepnews. Earlier that year, he resigned as vice president of jazz A&R at Fantasy. "I've wanted for quite some time to get rid of the executive-administrative paperwork load and to concentrate on what has always been my first priority, producing records," Keepnews said.[29] Yet the decision relied on maintaining a relationship with Fantasy and continuing to produce artists under their umbrella, especially Sonny.

So that there was no bad blood, Sonny agreed to have Keepnews's producer's fee included as part of the recording budget, even though he would not be involved. Keepnews wrote Sonny a letter in late August to explain that he had for years shielded Sonny from the myriad logistical details that allow the creativity to flow in the studio. "I only hope I haven't done _too_ good a job of shielding you from such problems and details, thereby possibly providing the inaccurate impression that such matters are small and easy to deal with... Thus I really do not understand why you feel it necessary to plunge into total responsibility without taking advantage of my offer to make the next album a transitional and instructional process in such areas." Ultimately, the split was amicable. "It wasn't anything against Orrin, because we're still friends," Lucille said, "but it was just we wanted to do it all our own way."[30]

Keepnews would never produce a new Sonny Rollins album again—the rest would be self-produced by either Sonny, Lucille, or both. "Producing was a mountain that was there to be climbed," Sonny said later that year, "so I did it."[31]

No Problem consisted of three originals by Sonny ("No Problem," "Coconut Bread," and "Joyous Lake"), Bobby Hutcherson's "Jo Jo," Bobby Broom's "Penny Saved," Friedrich Hollaender's "Illusions," and the 1977 Dolly Parton hit "Here You Come Again." Of the latter, Sonny said, "That one I always just liked a lot, from the minute I heard it on the radio."[32] Richard Corsello had other work during the day, so sessions were held from around 7 p.m.

until 2 a.m. at the latest. On the first night, they recorded seventeen takes of "Joyous Lake" until 1:30 a.m., returning the next night to record an eighteenth; the album version was edited from multiple takes.[33] Throughout the album, Sonny ascends high into the altissimo register. He wrote an ironic note in a journal about playing beyond the natural range of the horn, which he seemed to take seriously: "Generate certain frequencies which can bring animals under your sway. As a wind player you have the possibility of all frequencies such as dog range and all animal ranges."[34] It was even more impressive that Sonny could maintain this level of control of the horn considering his ongoing dental problems, which had flared up again during the European tour.[35]

No Problem was among Sonny's more pop-friendly albums. Broom recognized that the album was aiming for the widest-possible audience. "You want to reach people, then certainly don't play only to a musician audience," Broom said. "If you do, you'll starve for sure."[36]

On February 17, 1982, Thelonious Monk died.[37] Sonny paid no public tribute and grieved privately.[38] Monk was "a complete conceptualist," Sonny recalled at this time, but one of the key lessons he took from Monk was his total commitment to the art form. "He had a great dedication in his work. He was completely absorbed and serious about his music. All else came secondary to us getting that sound. This kind of integrity was important to me."[39]

To Sonny, Monk was not gone. "After Thelonious Monk died," Sonny recalled, "I remember telling someone that in many ways Monk was really my guru, my teacher figure. But I had to reach a certain point of knowledge myself before I could really appreciate this."[40]

Following a benefit concert in San Francisco, the *Boston Globe* Jazz Festival, and a week's vacation with Lucille in Petit St. Vincent, Sonny did a series of shows with twenty-seven-year-old Pat Metheny.[41] The guitarist had turned down dozens of sideman offers, not having accepted one since touring with Joni Mitchell in 1980, but the chance to play with Sonny was worth "a million Grammys."[42] "You can imagine what a thrill it would be for any young guy to get on the bandstand with somebody like that—as well as playing with him night after night," Metheny said. "He's always been an influence. I remember sitting down with his records at thirteen or fourteen when I first got to thinking about improvising and trying to figure things out."[43] Later, Metheny got tapes of some of their performances together and for a period listened to them every day. Growing up in Kansas City, listening to Sonny inspired him to begin experimenting with different amps to get a fuller tone. He was such a jazz head that he missed Hendrix; that midwestern Metheny sound came more from the impetus to translate saxophone to guitar.[44]

On April 9, Sonny gave two concerts with Metheny at the Academy of Music in Northampton, Massachusetts, with Bob Cranshaw and Al Foster.[45] This was followed by shows at the Smithsonian in DC, at Purdue University in Indiana, and at Kent State in Ohio.[46] The pairing was tenuous at first, but by the end of the run, Sonny and Metheny began to jell.[47]

For the last three gigs, Foster was replaced by twenty-two-year-old drummer Ronnie Burrage.[48] He was a child prodigy himself from St. Louis; he played with Duke Ellington when he was nine years old and was most recently touring with McCoy Tyner. "What I took away most from Sonny was his incredible stamina and power," recalled Burrage. "When I played with him we played a lot of duets together. In the middle of shows, he would just go into it. A couple of times he would squat next to the drums, and he would start playing a rhythmic figure, and I'd start playing it. The thing that got me was that he would be squatting for probably ten minutes. When he was squatting he was like a steady barge pushing through, but when he stood up, it was like a freight train."[49]

Starting in July, Sonny played the summer circuit with Jack DeJohnette, Bob Cranshaw, Masuo, and Bobby Broom.[50] Sonny played ecstatically, but he was feeling down. "July of 82—Mental Depression—Physical Draining," he wrote in a journal.[51] Perhaps it was in response to the death of Thelonious Monk that February and then, on July 22, Sonny Stitt, of cancer.[52] The depression may have also had something to do with Sonny's recent discovery that in 1981 the French subsidiary of RCA had commercially released a bootleg album without his permission.

That July, Sonny sued the label when he found out about the album, a two-LP set of alternate takes from the RCA years titled *The Alternative Rollins*.[53] The masters were intended to sit in the RCA vaults in Indianapolis and Fogelsville, Pennsylvania, never to be touched without Sonny's consent. Sonny's lawyer, Ed Katz, secured an injunction against the label prohibiting any further distribution of the album, and Sonny eventually won the ensuing lawsuit.[54] *Sonny Rollins v. RCA Records* dragged on in New York Supreme Court until RCA settled in 1986. The settlement agreement required RCA to pay Sonny a retroactive $20,000 advance for the unauthorized release, against future royalties, and a $10,000 flat fee, in addition to his legal expenses. Most important, it ensured that any future Rollins releases from the RCA vaults would require the approval of Sonny or his estate.[55]

What is perhaps most revealing in the pages and pages of depositions, old contracts, and other legal proceedings is Sonny's neurotic perfectionist tendencies coming out in the paperwork. None of the material on the unauthorized album met Sonny's standard.[56] The thing was, the unauthorized material was fantastic, but of the eleven tracks on *The Alternative Rollins*, Sonny deemed only three satisfactory; the other eight were "imperfect."[57]

"I believe that the release of such imperfect renditions credited to me does adversely affect my reputation as an artist," Sonny said. "The release of such renditions caused me great embarrassment with respect to my public and peer professionals. While every rendition of a musical composition by an artist is not necessarily perfect, certainly, where the artist and/or his producer has control over the situation—such as in a recording situation—there is no reason whatsoever for any recording short of perfection or at least of artistically satisfactory quality to be released for sale to the public. The very essence of artistry and the appreciation by the public of artistry is the degree of artistic purity and perfection representative of and by the artist. To allow the public to realize less taints the artist and hurts his career. And I believe the defendant has hurt my career in releasing these admittedly imperfect renditions."[58]

To add insult to injury, the album erroneously gave him composer credit for "Winter in [sic] Wonderland" and "When You Wish upon a Star." "These grossly negligent acts of the defendant has caused me even greater embarrassment, stress and mental anguish," Sonny said.[59]

Sonny perpetuated his perfectionist streak when he went back to Fantasy

Studios from August 17 to 22 to record *Reel Life*. He used the band he toured with all summer: DeJohnette, Masuo, Broom, and Cranshaw. Two guitarists "gives it a sort of a surreal sound at times," Sonny said.[60] The album title may have partially been inspired by the fact that it was originally supposed to have three film songs: "Cabin in the Sky," "I'm Old Fashioned," and "Look for the Silver Lining."[61] They were all left on the cutting-room floor for *Reel Life*, but remained in Sonny's rotating set list for subsequent tours.[62]

The title referred more to tape reels. The cover depicts Sonny in the lotus position sitting atop a giant tape reel in the sky—the serenity of yoga and trauma of studio time being the yin and yang of Sonny's anxiety cycle. During the *Reel Life* session, he filled at least twenty reels. To Bobby Broom, some of the best material was cut. "There are some outtakes, there's some stuff that I remember of his playing being 'Oh my gosh.' And I remember saying, I hope they choose that take because it was out of this world. And of course, they chose something else."[63] A rehearsal take of Masuo's tune "Sonny Side Up" wound up on the album.[64] Some tunes, like "Reel Life," really took flight in a live setting. Sonny's rendition of "My Little Brown Book" was inspired by the version on *Duke Ellington and John Coltrane* and Herb Jeffries's version.[65] "McGhee," based on a line Sonny heard Howard McGhee play back in the day, harked back to 1949, when Sonny was touring with him in Utica and running the hot water all night to keep warm. The tune, the album's highlight, captured some of the energy Sonny brought to live shows; Gary Giddins called it his best recorded solo since "Autumn Nocturne" on *Don't Stop the Carnival*.[66]

That fall, Sonny went on a European tour and needed to hire a new bassist, as Bob Cranshaw couldn't make it.[67] After auditions, the gig went to Lincoln Goines, who specialized in fretless electric bass, and joined Campbell, Masuo, and Broom. "He was really into connecting with the audience as a band," Goines recalled. "He thought that was really the primary mission, for him to go out and just radiate this big, wide, warm energy that he had and that's what he did most of the time."[68]

At the beginning of 1983, Sonny became an NEA Jazz Master.[69] Donald Byrd, a member of the Music Panel for the National Endowment for the Arts and chairman of the NEA Jazz Music Committee, played an instrumental role in beginning the Jazz Masters program in 1982. The award was initially given every year to three living jazz artists who, according to Byrd, "significantly altered the language of the music" and carried a $20,000 cash prize.[70] In the inaugural year of the program, it went to Roy Eldridge, Dizzy Gillespie, and Sun Ra, with a posthumous induction for Thelonious Monk; in the sophomore year of the program, it was Kenny Clarke, Count Basie, and Sonny, who was cited for his contribution to the language of improvisation.[71]

Refusing to rest on his laurels, Sonny continued practicing as much as possible. He had found a rock in a remote area near his home in Germantown. "I have the privacy and serenity to play as loud and as long as I like without disturbing people who might not like what I'm rehearsing," he said early that year.[72]

"I'm trying to play the complete experience of my whole career, and my endless quest for the lost chord. I'm not sure if it was partly a joke, or had some meaning to it," he said. It was in part a joke popularized by Jimmy Durante in the song "I'm the Guy Who Found the Lost Chord," a comic tale of a pianist who could play Mozart in his right hand, Bizet's *Carmen* in his left, whistle a sextet—"food became secondary"—when he stumbles upon the fabled lost chord. Sonny took this quest—and struggle—seriously. "The idea is that there is music in the universe that is that sound, that perfect harmony, and we're trying to get to it. I'm trying to find my lost chord, trying to hook on to that thing which I've been on the road for all these years. The quest for musical perfection, if you will, or salvation."[73] Yet with all that time on the road, at fifty-two, albeit a virile fifty-two, Sonny was coming down with a case of what became known in the industry as Road Fever.[74]

From January 4 to 23, Sonny did a thirteen-city tour of Japan with Masuo, Bobby Broom, Tommy Campbell, and a new electric bassist, twenty-one-year-old Russel Blake.[75] Blake was the Brooklyn-born younger brother of bassist Alex Blake, who worked with Sonny on *The Way I Feel*. The younger Blake had already toured with Hugh Masekela and most recently, with drummer T. S. Monk, the son of Thelonious, when he got the call in December 1982. Sonny's nephew Clifton Anderson, who was also on the Monk tour and had worked with Blake since 1979, recommended him. "I was of course playing my role as safely as possible, you know, and let Sonny be the quarterback, and this was the new team that I was trying out for," Blake recalled. After a two-and-a-half-hour audition at SIR Studios, Sonny had Blake leave the room, conferred with the band, and offered him the gig. "Sonny shook my hand and said, 'Welcome to the team.'" On New Year's Day 1983, they took off for Tokyo. In Japan, Blake was stunned by the reverence for jazz and for Sonny, unheard of in the United States—an overwhelming media presence and police escort service—as soon as they touched down. "I felt like I was part of the Rolling Stones or something," he said.[76]

Back in the United States, Sonny mostly kept a clear performing calendar for the rest of the winter.[77] In March, he and Lucille took a vacation to Virgin Gorda, spending some time in St. Thomas on either side of the trip, taking his horn with him, of course.[78] Mostly, though, Sonny was preparing for an upcoming New York concert at Town Hall presented by New Audiences with special guest Wynton Marsalis.

The brash twenty-one-year-old trumpet prodigy from New Orleans burst onto the scene with a ferocity few had equaled since Sonny himself arrived in the bebop era. He could play the dozens on just about anyone in a trumpet battle, a debate, or even on the basketball court.[79] He turned down scholarship offers from Harvard, Yale, and the Massachusetts Institute of Technology to go to Juilliard, but, like Miles Davis before him, dropped out when he realized it was stifling his jazz education; he would later return as director of the jazz program. He enrolled in the university of Art Blakey and the Jazz Messengers and eventually toured alongside Herbie Hancock, Tony Williams, and Ron Carter with V.S.O.P. in 1981. In 1982, his self-titled Columbia Records debut sold a hundred thousand copies. He swept the 1982 *Down Beat* readers' poll, winning Jazz Musician of the Year, Jazz Album of the Year, and best trumpeter, with 823 votes to Miles Davis's 330. In 1983, his album *Think of One* and his recording of the Haydn, Hummel, and Leopold Mozart trumpet concertos made him the first artist to win classical and jazz Grammy Awards in the same year. Critics and public figures from Stanley Crouch to Ed Bradley hailed Wynton as the savior of jazz. Yet some felt that all of this acclaim had gone to his head.

Marsalis was the unofficial leader of a group of neoclassicists that would come to be known as the Young Lions, intending to restore the hard-won respect they felt jazz had lost when it opened its doors to funk.[80] In what many would refer to as the "jazz wars," the Young Lions were pitted against the avant-garde.

Wynton boldly answered a question that Leonard Feather had posed rhetorically for decades but never dared to answer: What is jazz? To Marsalis, jazz was Louis Armstrong, Duke Ellington, Charlie Parker, and Thelonious Monk, and everything that embodied the formal principles they codified. The aesthetic openness characteristic of the avant-garde was not jazz—first and foremost, it had to swing.[81]

To Wynton, bebop's old guard were revolutionaries who in trading the ride cymbal for a backbeat had betrayed their own revolution. Plenty of that old guard disagreed.[82] Miles Davis, one of Wynton's formative influences, became an outspoken critic: "I knew he could play the hell out of classical music and had great technical skills on the trumpet, technique and all of that, but you need more than that to play great jazz music, you need feelings and an understanding of life that you can only get from living, from experience."[83] Sonny was one of the few willing to give him the experience.

During a *JazzTimes* interview with Hollie West that year at the Washington, DC, Four Seasons, Wynton and Branford pulled up in a rented Rolls-Royce. Wynton explained that he wanted to learn, but "there's nowhere to apprentice." This was in part due to the fact that he lashed out at many of the masters in the press, and Sonny was not immune. "The thing that's really painful to me about jazz is that some of the greatest musicians have sold out at a point in their careers when it wasn't necessary for them to sell out, and what that has done is fucked up the music," he said. "Ornette Coleman, Sonny Rollins, a whole bunch of cats. I don't even have to name them. They know who they are. When you see a cat walk out on the stand with a skirt on, robes and shit, you know who they are. We know what's happening.... Some cats portray me as a punk asshole who went to Juilliard. They say I'm arrogant. That pisses me off because I'm a sincere cat who's just trying to learn how to play. I respect them. But I resent them fucking with me."[84] This comment would not see print until July, after the showdown with Sonny.

So it seems that Wynton saw the meeting with Sonny as both an opportunity to grow and a title bout. Contrary to what many thought,

Wynton was more open to learning and more self-aware than his arrogant twenty-one-year-old posture might have suggested. "I can play the trumpet well. My ability to play the instrument is good. So far as being a jazz musician, I have a lot to learn," he said in early 1982, listing Sonny as one of his influences. "My playing isn't spontaneous enough. I play too many eighth notes. It's not open enough. I have a lot to learn...we all have a lot to learn. Even Trane was looking for stuff until the day he died. I'm doing what I want to do: I'm playing jazz, period. And if I get squashed—there's always that possibility—I just get squashed."[85]

Sonny thought of the meeting more as an olive branch than a gauntlet thrown. "Jazz is a *living art*," Sonny said. "I don't put down Wynton and those guys that are doing repertory. They are doing an especially important job by educating young people about this music." And Wynton was about to get a lesson in the art of living.

Sonny "did that for a reason," recalled Clifton Anderson of the invitation to Wynton and other up-and-comers. "Those particular guys were getting a lot of play as being the next guys to come along and carry the music, and Sonny believed in the old-school way, the actual way the music has always been passed along. You have to play with the elders. There has to be some kind of definite interaction at some point for you to get something that you're gonna need to have if you're supposed to be one of the next cats."[86]

Wynton grew up with Sonny. *Clifford Brown and Max Roach at Basin Street*, Sonny's first album with the quintet, was one of Wynton's favorite albums; pianist Ellis Marsalis, the family patriarch, named Wynton for Wynton Kelly. The younger Wynton also loved *Newk's Time*, which Sonny recorded with Wynton's late namesake a quarter century earlier.[87] So like Hawk met Sonny in 1963, in 1983, Sonny met Skain.[88] The tension here was different: instead of the older man showing he was still hip to the present, it was the younger man showing he was hip to the past.

The critics would inevitably view the concert as a cutting contest, and Sonny didn't want a decision victory declared in the next morning's paper.[89] So leading up to Town Hall, he practiced even more than usual.[90] "I try to rehearse as much as possible," Sonny said in anticipation of the concert. "It's not always possible to rehearse twenty-four hours a day, but sometimes it's a good idea to rehearse a whole lot."[91] Sonny was getting up before dawn to practice. This routine was more complicated in the Tribeca apartment, where Sonny's neighbors spent all day rehearsing covers of Van Halen and Led Zeppelin.[92]

Wynton himself approached the music as a pugilist—each sixteenth note a jab, side-slipping landing like a right hook, arpeggios like so much fancy footwork. "Music is like boxing. It's like any sport," Wynton said. "Before a game, there's all the hype and bullshit. But the game has got to be played. Somebody's going to win."[93]

On April 23, 1983, the day of the concert, Sonny was so focused on the music that he forgot to eat.[94] He came onstage dressed in all black. He looked out, and there was Yoko Ono in the audience. All seemed copacetic at first, but quickly, the guitarists noticed that something was not quite right.[95] "The first tune, Sonny gave me a solo, which was kind of rare," said Bobby Broom. "He usually played the first tune by himself." According to Masuo, "I knew when he was not feeling good. I felt it."[96] Then Wynton came out in his starched business suit and tie.

On the third tune of the night, Sonny called "Big Foot," a Charlie Parker blues Bird recorded with Miles Davis. Sonny pulled no punches, playing like a man possessed. "Sonny must have took eighty choruses, man," said Tommy Campbell. "I know Wynton didn't want to play. I *know* that." But then, "Sonny stepped back right next to me, and passed out, and he was right beside my floor toms, and his eyes were in the back of his head. You never know when cats are faking like that, especially Sonny. I didn't hear him hit the ground hard, but he fell and it did seem he got dizzy. But then, of course, we tried to finish the song."[97]

"I went to see what was going on, but Sonny was unconscious already," said Masuo.

"I'm looking around, and I don't see Sonny," said Broom. "And I'm starting to lean and look at the wings and I don't see him, and my eyes go down, and I see his head sticking up from behind something. And I just gasped and unplugged and I walked off to the side. And it was bedlam."

"We all ran over to him out of concern that god forbid he busted his head open or there was a concussion, and he was still blinking his eyes and he didn't move. The amazing thing was that he did not let go of the saxophone. He was still holding firmly onto his instrument."

" 'Is there a doctor in the house?' " someone called. Luckily, there were several, including Sonny's older brother, Valdemar.[98]

"He went straight back like a tree, when a tree just falls," recalled Clifton, who was in the audience. "Someone yelled out, 'Somebody shot Sonny Rollins!' Anyway, they closed the curtains, and when I got back there, he was lying on his back, his eyes were rolled back, and his horn was laying on his chest. He was basically unconscious, but he knew where that horn was!"

Wynton was shocked. "Strange," he thought. "He just fell down. He fell backwards but he held his horn up. It looked, actually, like he had tripped over one of those boxes the guitar players use to get all those different sounds. I kept waiting for him to get up, but he didn't get up." It was as though Ali had KO'd Liston without a phantom punch—Sonny knocked himself out.

"We cut the tune off and he finally got up, fifteen minutes later, and asked where his horn was," Wynton recalled.[99] He was assured that, thankfully, his tenor was fine—he bore the brunt of the fall. Then he was rushed to Bellevue for oxidation.[100] The doctors wanted to keep him overnight to make sure he was stable and determine what caused the fall, but Sonny checked himself out against medical advice. He got the diagnosis from his personal doctor— hypertension exacerbated by nervous exhaustion.[101]

"Sonny was just overworked," Lucille explained to the *Daily News*. "I had worked myself into a frazzle," Sonny added.[102] There was an unreported reason for the collapse: "I was smoking some bad weed before the show," Sonny recalled. "They took me down to Bellevue, but they let me out. I wasn't crazy or anything, just . . . this was some messed-up pot."[103]

The irony would not have been lost on Wynton if Sonny was in fact felled by the very electric equipment the Young Lions were crusading against, but someone in the Marsalis camp suggested another cause for his spiking blood pressure. According to Clifton Anderson, "Somebody said, 'Wynton played so much shit he made Sonny collapse.' And it got back to Sonny."[104]

The concert was rescheduled for June 3 at the Beacon Theatre, and in the meantime, Sonny took a month's respite in Germantown.[105] He kept a strict natural diet—no salt, seasoning, or sugar—eating "things that come in God's wrapper." He spent quality time with Lucille as well as their dogs, Flory and Kendo, and their three cats. He did yoga. He practiced with a greater sense of moderation. In one typical day, Sonny woke up at 4 a.m. to feed the dogs, installed some insulation, rode his stationary bike for forty-five minutes, and took out the horn for the rest of the day. He was in bed by around 9.

The rest did him good, and on May 20, he played his first concert since the collapse at the University of Illinois at Chicago Jazz Festival—hailed as a triumphant return to form.[106] But this was just an exhibition match. Back in New York, Sonny was concerned that the people who saw him collapse at Town Hall would opt for a refund instead of the rematch. "After what happened last time, will people come back?" Sonny asked Robert Palmer of the *New York Times*. "Everything I've done is still very much a part of me. But to be able to play across different styles the way I can play across bar-lines—*that* is the reason I practice every day."[107] And Sonny intended to step inside his opponent's sense of time onstage.

Before the June 3 concert, Lucille reminded Sonny to eat. He swapped the all-black suit for more color and a purple satin hat. He replaced Tommy Campbell with Jack DeJohnette, opening with a twenty-five-minute calypso. Wynton looked on in awe as everyone felt a silent amen—the heavyweight champion was back in fighting form.[108] Then Sonny invited Wynton out. The young Marsalis played with a maturity that belied his youth, showing flashes of Lee Morgan's rhythmic attack and Clifford Brown's harmonic sophistication, creating a sense of dynamic range in the electric Rollins rhythm section, but he was no match for Sonny. "He was afire from the very first notes," wrote Gary Giddins. "Marsalis, though he played extremely well, was lucky to remain perpendicular in the relentless gusts of Rollins's genius."[109]

"I knew at the downbeat," recalled Anderson. "I said, 'Oh shit, I hope Wynton's ready for an ass-whooping tonight,' because that downbeat was like take no prisoners, and by the time they got through the first tune, Wynton was already kind of demoralized." Then they came back to where they left off at Town Hall: "Big Foot." "Sonny says, 'Okay, my friend Wynton Marsalis wants to play an old tune—Charlie Parker played it. A blues, so we're gonna do this one for you called 'Big Foot,'" Anderson said. "Oh no! Sonny said something about 'Wynton wants to trade with me on a blues.' I said to myself, 'Why would Wynton want to trade with Sonny on a blues? What the fuck is the matter with him?'"

Wynton got what he asked for. "Sonny Rollins gave me a lesson in the second concert," he said later that year. "He pulled the blackboard out: 'Check this out, son.'"[110] On "Big Foot" redux, wrote Giddins, "Rollins burst in like life itself, paraphrasing the theme in staccato notes, interpolating 'St. Thomas,' and piling cross rhythms on cross rhythms."[111] Sonny dazzled on cadenzas on "My Ideal" and "I Got It Bad," with allusions to "Nobody Knows the Trouble I've Seen," "Rhythm-a-ning," "How Are Things in Glocca Morra," "To a Wild Rose," "Country Gardens," and a Scottish jig, before putting his own spin on Marsalis's "Hesitation" and Sonny's own "Hear What I'm Saying." It was quite a quilt: there were Bird, Miles, Bean, Duke, Paul Robeson, Monk, Mary Lou Williams, Bing Crosby, Edward MacDowell, and Jimmie Rodgers, woven together by Sonny's endless musical imagination. Did Wynton hear what he was saying?[112]

"I saw him stand people up on their chairs by smoking through some rhythm changes," Wynton recalled. "I knew then that when somebody who can play that much horn unleashes the highest level of knowledge and fire and swing, that the purity of the music will touch listeners with the deep love and respect that it takes to become a master of that stature."[113]

As far as who "won" that night, "it was pretty unanimous," said Broom.[114] According to Lucille, it was the best Sonny Rollins concert she had ever heard. Even Sonny conceded that it was "okay." It wasn't recorded, of course, but had Sonny known a tape was rolling, he said, "it might not have been okay."[115]

After the concert, Clifton Anderson went backstage at the Beacon to congratulate his uncle on a great performance. "At the end of the show, I'm starting up the stairs, 'cause I figured Sonny was back there on the first floor. But he wasn't," he recalled. "Wynton was sitting there. The door was partway open. He had his trumpet in his lap. So I knocked on the door. I said, 'Hey, man, you did okay.' He looked up and he said, 'Sonny Rollins, man. Sonny Rollins.' I said, 'Don't worry about it, man. You did all right.' He just said, 'Sonny Rollins, man.' That's all he could say."[116] Between the two concerts, Sonny had learned he was not invincible—and so had Wynton.

When the *JazzTimes* story with Wynton's lacerating remarks came out that July, the magazine was deluged with letters from incensed readers. Chastened, Wynton explained in a subsequent issue that the article "would give the impression that I lack any real degree of respect for my predecessors—which is far from the case. Sonny Rollins is the greatest living saxophonist and Ornette Coleman made an invaluable contribution to the music."[117] Of his experience onstage with Sonny and other masters, he called it "the biggest honor I ever had."[118]

On Sonny's next album, recorded six months after the Beacon concert, he recorded a tribute called "Wynton," "written for both Wyntons," Sonny said, "because Wynton Marsalis is named after pianist Wynton Kelly."[119] Wynton's homage came in the form of a poem, a rondeau à la Sonny. "Rollins rarely rests," the alliterative poem states. "Sonny reinvigorates rituals."[120]

In part inspired by Wynton, in part to lighten the load, and in part because he was hearing polyphony, Sonny decided it was time to add another horn to the band, and he hired Clifton Anderson, keeping it in the family.[121] After all, Sonny had begun his recording career with J. J. Johnson.[122]

Clifton had come a long way. He graduated from the Manhattan School of Music in 1978, cutting his teeth with Carlos Garnett, Slide Hampton's World of Trombones, T. S. Monk, Stevie Wonder's *Secret Life of Plants* tour, and others, and at twenty-five, Sonny felt Clifton was ready to join the family business. So it was "out of the frying pan, into the fire," Anderson recalled. Initially, Sonny began inviting him to rehearsals and let him sit in on a few tunes, but that July, he wanted him on the front line. "I said, 'Where are my parts?'" Anderson recalled. "He said, 'Learn the songs off the record.' So I learned the songs off the record, and then when we got on the job, he didn't call anything that was on the record. He played a bunch of old songs. I think I might have known maybe one or two of them. So it was a real wake-up call."[123] Over the nearly three decades Sonny and Clifton would work together, Sonny never gave him music, and he learned quickly to have the tunes down in all twelve keys, lest he be caught off guard.

In anticipation of his debut with the band, Clifton asked Bob Cranshaw for advice. "He said, 'Just find some good notes to play under Sonny. Play against him sometimes. The first thing to do is to figure out what key he's gonna be in,' 'cause he changes keys all the time.'" To learn Sonny's obscure repertoire, Cranshaw recommended finding a recording of Ella Fitzgerald or Fred Astaire singing it. "He said the two of them sing the exact melodies as the composers wrote them. If you want to learn, those are the two to listen to.'"

Clifton's first concert with Sonny was on July 9 in Toronto at the Ontario Place Jazz Festival.[124] The outdoor festival took place on a man-made island on the Toronto waterfront, with seating for twenty-five hundred and room for eight thousand on the lawn. The amphitheater was positioned in the center, with a seventy-foot revolving stage that rotated constantly so spectators could see the band from any vantage point: Russel Blake, Bobby Broom, Ronnie Burrage, and Clifton.[125]

"When I was in rehearsals with Sonny, he'd just let me play, and when he wanted me to stop playing, he would just come in and start blowing so I knew that was the end of the solo," Anderson said. "So I thought that was gonna happen. But I started my solo, and this is a hot summer day, man. So I played one chorus, and I played another chorus, and I played another chorus. And I'm playing into the mike, and I'm waiting for Sonny—okay, like I don't have nothing really much left to play and so I'm waiting and looking out the corner of my eye, and Sonny's just standing up there, not coming in. And the stage is going around; I see the same people come back around. I was playing so long, and then Bobby Broom drops out. And I'm just playing with Russel and Ronnie. And then Russel drops out, and it's just me and Ronnie. And at this point, I definitely don't have anything left to play. I'm sweating so hard, my mouthpiece is sliding all over my face and shit, and so I didn't have any more chops. I just hit a note and it was like a blurt. The people must have thought that was what I wanted to do, but I just didn't have any chops left. And I put the horn down. Everybody's like, 'Yeah, yeah, yeah!' and then they came back in with the rhythm section.

"So it's the end of the gig. I'm totally pissed. I go back in the dressing room. 'You motherfuckers. What the fuck! You left me hanging out there, man. You dropped out on me.' And they're laughing. They say, 'Yeah, man, that was your initiation.' . . . So then there's a knock on the door. It's Lucille, Sonny's wife. And she says, 'Clifton, Sonny wants to see you in his dressing room.'

I'm like, 'Oh shit!' I go in his dressing room and I said, 'Hi, Sonny.' 'Yeah, Clifton, okay, it's gonna be all right. Yeah, I think it'll be okay. But one thing you have to do, you have to watch how long you play.'" Clifton and the band learned that day that Sonny would not be going easy on his nephew.[126]

To Clifton, who grew up listening to Sonny starting in the sixties, Sonny had just begun to reach a creative peak. "A lot of people look to the fifties into the early sixties as the height of his career, but the shit that he was playing that I witnessed was way beyond that," Clifton said. "At a certain point, I said, 'saxophone players need to start getting with this shit, man,' because I don't know what the fuck he's playing. It dawned on me that maybe what he's playing is so advanced that they don't want to try to fuck with it."

On July 27, Sonny and Lucille flew to Japan for the outdoor Live Under the Sky Festival, which took place from July 29 to August 5. Sonny played in a specially formed quartet, with Pat Metheny, bassist Alphonso Johnson (known for his work with Weather Report, Billy Cobham, Bob Weir, and Phil Collins), and Jack DeJohnette. They played opposite Weather Report, the Crusaders, and Trio Music with Chick Corea, Miroslav Vitous, and Roy Haynes.[127] Sonny always loved his time in Japan, and the energy level of the Japanese fans fueled his own.[128]

At the Chicago Kool Jazz Festival on August 31,[129] Sonny was welcomed back to his second home by twenty-five thousand fans in Grant Park.[130] In what felt like the final tune of the night, Sonny counted off "Cabin in the Sky," punctuated by a lengthy closing cadenza. But then he began a calypso. Festival organizers scrambled to figure out what to do to avoid breaking their hard cutoff. At least one critic had to leave to meet a review deadline, but the carnival could not be stopped. "The audience was practically hysterical," wrote one critic. "People were standing on their chairs, screaming and waving their arms."[131] Suddenly, the stage lights came on. Then the lights went out. But the band played on. Finally, the audio system was unplugged. So the night ended in darkness, with the sounds of the islands in carnival. For Sonny, the carnival stopped when he stopped.

From September 1 to 8, Sonny, Lucille, and the band went to Europe for three concerts, in Saalfelden, Austria; Alassio, Italy; and Helsinki, Finland.[132] It was then that Russel Blake realized how spiritually connected Sonny was.

"I learned more from him offstage than I did onstage," Blake recalled. In Europe, Blake called home before the September 7 Helsinki show to find that his mother was very ill. It happened to be Sonny's birthday. That night, Blake's brand-new bass amp kept shorting out. "That day at the sound check, it was working perfectly, but every time Sonny gave me a solo and I walked to the front of the stage, the amp would go out," he said. "We just couldn't explain it, and it happened about eight times during a two-hour concert."[133] When Blake arrived at his family home back in New York, the house was filled with people. His mother had died thirty minutes after he called her from Finland on Sonny's fifty-third birthday.

Distraught, Blake called Sonny to break the news. "We were going to be leaving in two days to go to Montana and a couple other gigs, and I had to inform Sonny that I would not be able to make it," Blake said. "My mom had passed, and Sonny was so impacted by this. One of the reasons he was impacted was because he had a deep and close and intimate relationship with his mother similar to the one I had with my mom. And when his mother died, I believe he was around the same age I was and he could empathize with what I was going through." Sonny was also the same age his mother was when she died—fifty-three. "So of course, he said, 'Don't worry about the gig, I've got your back. Do what you have to do. Take care of the family.' So the next thing I know, about an hour later, a truck showed up with about four thousand dollars' worth of flowers. Huge—just flowers everywhere. It was from Sonny and Lucille. It was a very challenging time for me to try to absorb and understand the transition, and Sonny was right there taking the lead sort of like an uncle as well as a big brother."[134]

Sonny and Lucille kept the schedule sparse for the rest of 1983. He continued working with Blake, Anderson, Broom, and Campbell, then switched from guitar to piano, rehiring Mark Soskin that fall.[135]

"God was very good to give us this warning," Lucille wrote Randi Hultin of the incident at Town Hall, "so that whatever changes needed to be made could be." Yet Sonny kept pushing to keep searching for that lost chord. "Sometimes guys who've been around awhile don't have anything to prove, in terms of making a name for themselves, so they may not work as hard," Sonny said earlier that year. "I'm still trying to prove something."[136]

Chapter 39

WHO BY FIRE

(1984–1989)

Sonny began 1984 in one of his least favorite places: the studio. From January 23 to January 27, he recorded *Sunny Days, Starry Nights* with Clifton Anderson, Mark Soskin, Tommy Campbell, and Russel Blake at Fantasy Studios in Berkeley.[1] It was Lucille's first album with sole producer's credit, and she earned it—her preparations generated more than a hundred pages of paperwork in order to create the ideal conditions for the band to sound as natural as possible.

To dispel performance anxiety, they turned on the red light and didn't turn it off. "We tried the method of letting the tape roll, and that changed everything," Sonny said. "We could loosen up and go back to what was good."[2] Perhaps for Sonny, the perfect was the enemy of the good.

Sunny Days, Starry Nights conjured the euphoric energy of Sonny's live shows. The band came in with an already established rapport, allowing them to keep the intensity and intimacy nearly as high as a live-performance setting. "Even though we were still in the studio, he still wanted to bring that live festival energy, in spite of the fact that there were not fifteen thousand people out there in front of us," recalled Russel Blake. "So given the fact that we were still well-oiled from the tour, and given Sonny's ability to take it into the second and third dimension with his solos, it was very easy to go with him and just forget that there were four walls around us and a ceiling."[3]

Unlike some earlier albums, Sonny road-tested the material before going into the studio. They recorded Sonny's calypsos "Mava Mava," "Tell Me You Love Me," and "Kilauea," and his ballad "Wynton," for Wynton Marsalis, with Mark Soskin on celeste; two standards, "I'll See You Again" by Noël Coward and Jerome Kern's "I'm Old Fashioned," a tour de force that had been a longtime staple of Sonny's live set list.[4] Lucille played cowbell on

"Mava Mava" and "Kilauea." On "I'll See You Again," Sonny overdubbed his own part, letting listeners hear what a Rollins-Rollins duo might sound like.[5]

"You're supposed to be happy and joyful, at least in your music," Sonny said that spring. "They say something about that in the Bible—make a *joyful noise* or something—and it's true, it's right."[6] The calypso Sonny initially titled "Won't Give Up Just Yet (on Life)" became "Kilauea," the Hawaiian volcano that seemed to resonate with the broad rhythms of Sonny's life. It was dormant in the 1930s, erupted intermittently starting in 1952, and after a series of sabbaticals began erupting more or less continuously in 1983. "Kilauea," which closes the album, does not end; it merely fades out.[7]

That year, Sonny's domestic touring schedule focused on appearances on college campuses. "One of the reasons we play universities is that the money is always there," Sonny said. "Musicians are always worried about money. The other reason is that I pick up young listeners there. They really appreciate my music."[8]

In February, Sonny was booked at the University of Georgia and the University of Florida.[9] On February 17, he played the Bottom Line, where the material from *Sunny Days* really set sail. After an explosive five-minute cadenza on "I'm Old Fashioned" that had the crowd screaming, Sonny launched into "Reel Life." Suddenly, a trumpeter joined the band. "Who is that?" came calls from the audience. Some recognized him: Don Cherry. The rhythm section went into stop time as Cherry developed a groove. They "did a musical dance together," recalled Russel Blake, as the crowd started to clap in unison, with the band and the audience both "in a place of awe as well as support."[10]

It was around that summer that Sonny fired Clifton Anderson. "He called me at like seven o'clock in the morning. I thought I was dreaming 'cause I was fast asleep and I picked up the phone," Anderson recalled. "He said, 'Hey Clifton, it's not happening. We're gonna have to let it go. Just keep working on your thing and we'll try it again.' So I said, 'Oh, okay.' Later I woke back up and realized, 'Oh shit. Sonny just fired me!' And the funny thing about it was when he fired me, I was just starting to have a feeling that I could figure out where I was supposed to go in the band."

At the same time, Sonny rehired Jerome Harris on bass.[11] Harris had been soaking in Caribbean rhythms with Oliver Lake's reggae band Jump Up since he had last worked with Sonny, and was ready for the even more calypso-heavy sets Sonny favored at the time.[12]

On August 2, Sonny played what he referred to as "one of my best nights ever"[13] at Wolfgang's in San Francisco.[14] "It was one of those nights when I could do anything that came into my head. I was able to connect with that music from the stratosphere and make it materialize for everybody. Then it's like I'm not really there, and the music is taking over. It's coming through you so fast and so strong that you are inconsequential. It's thrilling beyond words. Those are nights you never forget. And since it doesn't happen every night, the times it does give me inspiration to keep going in hopes it will happen again."[15] Was it recorded? No.

Sonny gave relatively few performances for the rest of the year, touring nationally.[16] Late that October, Lucille wrote to Randi Hultin. They were doing well, but Sonny had to undergo dental surgery and would be off recovering until the beginning of 1985. Not that anyone would notice; Sonny played through the pain. It didn't stop him from sustaining a ten-minute cadenza in Pittsburgh that November that ended in a standing ovation. They enjoyed a quiet fall and winter in Germantown.[17]

———◄○►———

In 1985, Sonny continued searching for that lost chord. "I want to play for my younger fans, my new fans, as well as my older ones," Sonny said that year. "It is hard to make everybody happy. I like to believe it can be done. My job is to make them hear me; my obligation is to reach people, period."[18] His older fans continued to hold out hope for the Sonny of the fifties to return, and sometimes he did. "I know more than I knew then, as a musician. It is just a matter of whether it always comes out," he said. "There are some physical limitations as I get older, but aside from that I am ready anytime to take a crack at the old Sonny Rollins. I will take him on in a session anytime and we will see."[19]

Sonny had not renounced the past, as some had thought. "In many ways I consider myself as preserving the era that I came up with," he said.

"Everything I came from, not just me, is on the line. I feel I have to present it in the best light."[20]

The year began with a Japanese tour from January 6 to 21 with Mark Soskin, Jerome Harris, Tommy Campbell, Clifton Anderson (whom Sonny had rehired), and special guest Bobby Hutcherson on vibes.[21] Concerts generally ended with an effervescent "Don't Stop the Carnival."[22] "Sonny put me in the middle of the stage, with Sonny on my right and Bobby Hutcherson on my left," Anderson said. "I was getting so much fucking music every night. That tour was one of the highlights of my musical life."

In February and March, Sonny mostly recovered from dental surgery. That March, he and Lucille grieved the death of Kendo, the beloved Akita that they got in Japan in 1973. "He used to be with me every day when I practiced and I miss him a lot," Sonny said.[23]

In April, Sonny appeared outside Cleveland at Lakeland Community College, Oberlin College, and at the Mary Lou Williams Jazz Festival at Duke in North Carolina.[24] Williams died in 1981, and Sonny paid tribute to her legacy and impact on his own career at the festival. These university performances often exerted a strong influence on the students in the audience as well as the other musicians on the bill. Also performing at Duke was Terri Lyne Carrington, a nineteen-year-old drum prodigy from the Boston area. Sonny had met her in Boston some years earlier through her father, a saxophonist who was president of the Boston Jazz Society. "He's always been very friendly to me, I'm sure because of my dad but also because he knew I was serious about the music," Carrington said. "He displays an incredible sense of rhythm by not playing simple subdivisions of the quarter note.... He plays very free. It's as if he were talking and since music is a form of communication, it makes sense that he strives to do that, but no one does it quite like him."[25]

Sonny played some domestic dates that spring,[26] and then in May, he went on a European tour with Mark Soskin, Bobby Broom, Tommy Campbell, and bassist Victor Bailey, who was off from touring with Weather Report.[27] In Rome, Sonny commemorated the thirtieth anniversary of the death of Charlie Parker, playing an electrifying set, but as a result of pushing it to the limit, the following night in Palermo his teeth were not cooperating.[28]

On a good night, Sonny would play for two hours; an off night the set could be oddly truncated. "I never wear watches on or off the stand," Sonny said during the tour. "Anyway, it's kinda ridiculous for a guy to be looking at his watch on the stand! The time frame I have to work in is something like an hour on each set. Sometimes I have someone on the side to tell me, but I have no idea at all. Sometimes I play too short and go off, and promoters don't like it . . . but I don't really think about it."[29]

Sonny rested in June, doing daily yoga, meditation, saxophone practice, and painting as well as taking long walks around his neighborhood in the Financial District when he was in the city. "I do yoga all the time," he said that year. "When I'm in the city, I walk. Down here, around lower Broadway and the Battery, it's a really nice part of the city, the last part they're building up. There's a new building blocking my view, taking away a chunk of my northerly view of New Jersey, and I'm mad as hell about it."[30]

On July 19, Sonny recorded *The Solo Album* at the Museum of Modern Art's free "Summergarden" series in the outdoor Abby Aldrich Rockefeller Sculpture Garden. Dan Morgenstern, who produced Sonny's rain-soaked 1965 concert, was "certain that tonight's event will surpass it," he wrote in the press release, "if only because Sonny Rollins at 55 is an even greater artist than he was at 35, though he was already peerless then."[31] On the suggestion of Summergarden organizer Andrew Caploe, Sonny decided to perform his concert alone, al fresco, in what he conceived as his final solo performance.[32] Milestone agreed to have it professionally recorded by engineer Tim Geelan. It is as close as we'll come in a commercial release to hearing what Sonny might have sounded like on the Bridge. Two hours before the concert, the line wrapped around the block; twenty-five hundred came out, and about half that made it in, though nothing could stop the overflow crowd from listening on Fifty-Fourth Street.[33]

It was a balmy summer day in New York, the type where your shirt clings to your body and a fetid urban stew steams up from the concrete, but that night, the temperature dropped to the midseventies for some much-needed relief.[34] At ten past eight, Sonny strode alone into the sculpture garden between the reflecting pool and Henry Moore's "Family Group" wearing a Breton fisherman's tee, white linen pants, and white sneakers, and began playing.

"It makes you get closer to the elements, to the sky, and it inspires me to play more celestial music. It makes me feel free and very creative when I play out in the open," Sonny told a CBS crew reporting on the concert. "I hope my music is still here. I can sort of hear it still in my mind, and music never leaves the atmosphere. It always comes back again, so my horn sounds are someplace out in space going on forever."[35]

Sonny thought he would sit down like Andrés Segovia, a touchstone of solo performance for Sonny, but when he felt the kinetic energy that night he had to move.[36] Gazing out at the crowd and into the reflecting pool, Sonny played an a cappella stream-of-consciousness solo for seventy-five minutes under a spotlight. As was the case for his other solo performances—at Berkeley, the Whitney, at the ashram in India, or on *The Tonight Show*—there was no repeating form to navigate. However, this dive into the breach was more ambitious than those shorter performances.

This jukebox of the unconscious was a deeply personal expression, a kind of musical autobiography; Sonny was communing with the audience and also his past. This performance represented an attempt to synthesize it all, representing "the complete experience of my whole career"—transcending genre to be "inclusive of the best of everything."[37] It was visceral: "Me. My horn. Out to the people."[38]

Playing an improvised autobiography that was also a unified field theory of music was a tall order, but it was exhilarating to hear Sonny try the impossible and fail. His spontaneous self-portrait came drifting out to Fifth Avenue, a declamatory sound collage that bubbled up from the recesses of his consciousness, conjuring bright spots from Sonny's childhood and four-decade career. There was Edward MacDowell's "To a Wild Rose," "When I Grow Too Old to Dream," "Pop Goes the Weasel," "Alfie's Theme,"[39] the diminished patterns and interval studies he had "mentalized" on the Bridge, "Mairzy Doats," "A Tisket, a Tasket" ("It's Raining, It's Pouring"), Grieg's *Peer Gynt*, "Rock-a-Bye Baby," Coltrane's "Mr. P.C.," "Autumn Nocturne,"[40] "St. Thomas," "Someday I'll Find You" (the Noël Coward theme song to a childhood-favorite radio show, *Mr. Keen, Tracer of Lost Persons*), and the obligatory "I Can't Get Started" quote to convey his own disapproval as well as a nod to Bird—it was all there. Sonny harmonized with the sound of the city; at several points, a car horn honks and Sonny honks back.[41]

His intermittent pausing to say "Goodbye now" or "Gotta go" to the audience conveyed by turns a resignation and an ironic wit. "What can I do now that I didn't do before?" he bellowed out to the crowd. Finally, delving deep into the past, the album ends in a blues-drenched conjuring of Coleman Hawkins's rhythm changes "Stuffy."[42] Finally grasping hold of the beat, elusive or nonexistent for the rest of the concert, the audience began clapping on two and four. Anyone could "feel that shit," as Hawkins had once told him;[43] Hawk would have been proud. Sonny rocked with a religious intensity, like a ring shout, and suddenly they were in Mother Horn's church. "Keep goin', man!" "Beautiful!" shouted the crowd. Sonny was sweating profusely, and his jaw was killing him, but he kept it going through the final low-register foghorn blast of the night, marching back into the museum still playing as the crowd erupted.

Yet Sonny was dissatisfied. "I had been going to my dentist, and something he was doing with my teeth made my embouchure not as comfortable, but I had no time to see him before the show, and so it wasn't my best," Sonny recalled, adding: "Well, I can say that about any performance I do: It wasn't quite what I would have wanted it to be."[44]

Sonny dedicated the album to his dog Kendo. It was edited down to two tracks, "Soloscope Parts 1 and 2." The portmanteau implies not only a looking into the self, but the instrument that allows it; to Sonny, the saxophone was a kind of "soloscope."[45] It was almost too much of himself in one continuous musical expression. "The amazing thing about Rollins is that even when he's off he's on," wrote Gary Giddins of the performance. "He kept starting up again, as though he'd find what he was looking for this time for sure. And had he continued searching until dawn, I suspect a good part of the audience would have remained no less vigilant."[46]

Leonard Feather hated *The Solo Album*. He wanted a coherent form and a clearly delineated beat—terra firma, not the musical equivalent of what Freud called the "oceanic feeling." "It is alarming that a genuine colossus of jazz, a man rightly hailed twenty-five years ago as an emperor, can remove his raiments and be seen by responsible critics as fully clothed," he wrote.[47] Perhaps what Feather missed in Sonny's racking his consciousness for the ultimate sound was the touch of mortality hanging over this defiant dance with death—how naked it all was—and the overwhelming sense that we will all stand alone one day and play our own halting song.[48]

It would be Sonny's last solo concert. If nothing else, the juxtaposition between *The Solo Album* and his ensemble work proved that part of the magic of the shambolic excursions of a cadenza was the moment when it resolved into the order of a recognizable song and the band came in to catch him. That night, the audience was the band.

Sonny's next tour passed through Baltimore, Rio de Janeiro, Philadelphia, Buffalo, Detroit, the Russian River Festival in Sonoma, Troy in Montana, Kansas City, Webster University (in Missouri), Lincoln, and Poughkeepsie.[49] The most meaningful of those was at the historic Folly Theater in Kansas City. It was Sonny's debut in the birthplace of Charlie Parker, made all the more poignant by the fact that Philly Joe Jones, who was on the *Collectors' Items* session in 1953, had joined the ancestors on August 30, the day after what would have been Bird's sixty-fifth birthday.[50]

Sonny was presented the keys to the city. "As you know, my idol, the great Charlie Parker, was from here. Do you remember Charlie Parker...I hope?" he said to the audience.[51] That night, Sonny was on fire, propelled by Bird's memory. He played an eight-minute solo improvisation, quoting Monk's "Straight, No Chaser," "Greensleeves," and an operatic "Figaro! Figaro! Figaro!" Yes, Monk was right up there with those European folks. Then Sonny went baroque and finished with Chopin's "Funeral March." When Sonny heard a tape of this tour de force decades later, he insisted: "I can do better than that."[52]

In 1985, Sonny won the *Down Beat* and *Swing Journal* polls in the tenor category again, but what he was striving for transcended any mortal sounds.[53] "The glory isn't in grasping the ring," he said in an interview that year. "It's in reaching for it."[54]

———◄○►———

Sonny was developing more and more of a reputation as an endurance artist. In the winter of 1986, he had a bad cold and ear infection, but he went on anyway. Another incident that year would cement his reputation for death-defying acts. While recovering from dental surgery, much of his attention was focused on his *Concerto for Tenor Saxophone and Orchestra*, which would have its world premiere that spring in Japan.[55] Ironically, though, it would be a much smaller concert several months later that would be better remembered.

For the first half of the year, Sonny performed in colleges and clubs in the United States, refusing to let a lingering cold detract from the intensity of his performances.[56] That May, he played an eleven-concert tour of Japan, his twelfth time visiting. Sonny had developed a strong affinity for the country and its people; he found parallels between Japan and the islands of the Caribbean.[57] He was primarily in Japan for the world premiere of his concerto, which would be filmed by documentary filmmaker Robert Mugge as the centerpiece of *Saxophone Colossus*. The concerto was the realization of work reaching back to his Guggenheim Fellowship in 1972. He had been doing sustained work on the piece since 1983 and had a committed collaborator in Finnish pianist Heikki Sarmanto. Sonny met Sarmanto in 1972 when they played together at the Helsinki Jazz Festival and reconnected with him in the early eighties.[58]

The *Yomiuri Shimbun*, which sponsored Sonny's Japan tours, gave Sonny the opportunity to premiere a large-scale orchestral work for the one-hundred-piece Yomiuri Nippon Symphony Orchestra. Sonny wrote the themes for each movement, but as he considered himself more of a "spontaneous orchestrator," with no experience as a symphonic orchestrator, Sarmanto would orchestrate and conduct the symphony.[59] Sarmanto came to Germantown to fine-tune each movement, with Sonny sometimes sitting at the piano, other times playing saxophone while Sarmanto played the different themes from the seven movements. "Those little thematic patterns, they were so incredibly strong, melodic, very meaningful melodies," Sarmanto said. "They were the seed for this whole piece."[60]

Aside from the preparation, everything about the piece was relatively spontaneous, an experiment in subverting the binary between jazz improvisation and classical fixity. "The whole point of it is to be unclassifiable," Sonny explained.[61] "I tried to make a blend of the so-called 'classical' idiom with my own music and thinking."[62] There was no rhythm section; it would be less like *Clifford Brown with Strings*, in which a traditional rhythm section was supplemented by an orchestral backdrop, than like the Glazunov saxophone concerto, only with a strong element of improvisation, not unlike Gunther Schuller's Third Stream.[63]

There was only time for two rehearsals with the orchestra and concertmaster Kiyomitsu Obana before the world premiere on May 18, 1986, in Tokyo at Koseinenkin Kaikan; an encore performance took place the next night. Sonny played with a faster vibrato and a tighter embouchure, typical of classical saxophone technique. His improvisations over the sentimental themes, reminiscent of Aaron Copland or classical Hollywood cinema, largely took the form of filigreed double-time lines, devoid of the familiar references he was known for.[64] It exemplified the internationalism Sonny had come to embody: a collaboration between a Finnish composer with a jazz background, a Japanese orchestra, and an African American soloist of Caribbean descent, blending improvisation, the European classical tradition, and calypso. Though it was performed in 1987 in Ravenna and Parma, Italy, no US premiere was planned.[65] Sonny considered the possibility of recording it, but the concerto was immortalized solely by Mugge's film.[66]

"The concerto was difficult, because I wanted to do something that was free and me—yet with the full flavor of playing with an orchestra," Sonny said. "It was certainly restricting for me, because in that medium, everyone has to play a certain way."[67] The rest of the concert cast Sonny in a more natural setting. Special guest Hubert Laws played a set with the Yomiuri Nippon Symphony Orchestra.[68] The night concluded with Laws on piccolo, Sonny, and the orchestra playing a medley Clifton Anderson arranged of "Moritat," "Falling in Love with Love," and "St. Thomas." Laws and Sonny then played a four-minute unaccompanied tenor-piccolo duet on "Airegin," each taking a solo.[69]

It was a less heralded gig documented in Mugge's *Saxophone Colossus* that would steal the concerto's thunder. On August 16, Mugge and his film crew were in Saugerties, New York, at Opus 40 for Sonny's open-air performance with Clifton Anderson, Bob Cranshaw, drummer Marvin "Smitty" Smith, and Mark Soskin. Sonny paced across the bluestone stage at the former quarry site turned sculpture park in white slacks and sneakers, sweating through a red V-neck sweater. He was playing his heart out—the Saxophone Colossus playing to the gods at what some call the Stonehenge of North America—but otherwise, it was an unremarkable gig compared to the concerto premiere.

"Before a concert, I try to meditate on what I have to do. I try to block out any extraneous thoughts. I try to think about what it's going to be like," Sonny says at the outset of Mugge's film. "I try to will the band to sound good. I try to act in a positive way, and I try to create a picture of what I hope is going to happen on the stage, so it's sort of a meditation in a way, prior to performing."

What happened at Opus 40 that evening was neither what Sonny had hoped for nor what he could have predicted. His horn had recently been relacquered, restoring its gleam but altering the tone. No one else could hear the difference, but to Sonny, it was painfully obvious: "You can think you're going to play a vowel, and out comes a consonant," he later explained. For the rest of the concert, he struggled in vain to buy a vowel. He burned through the modal "G-Man" and "Kim," two of his own tunes, before playing a smoldering "Don't Stop the Carnival" and "Tenor Madness." Then he played a cadenza, as though wrestling with the instrument like Jacob, trying to bend the unyielding metal into the shape he wanted. It began with Verdi's "Anvil Chorus," Chopin's "Funeral March," Louis Armstrong's "A Kiss to Build a Dream On," "It's Raining, It's Pouring," and "Over the Rainbow" into "The Man on the Flying Trapeze," Grieg's *Peer Gynt*, and "How Are Things in Glocca Morra?" Apparently, not good. "Huh!" he grunted. Then, like the man on the flying trapeze he embodied, Sonny leaped from the six-foot stone stage, breaking his right heel and landing on his back. Clifton Anderson put down his trombone, thinking Sonny had ventured into the audience, not realizing what had actually happened. But then there was a silence.

The camera crew had heart palpitations as they lost sight of their star. "We were really concerned that he seriously injured himself," recalled Robert Mugge. "I ran to the other side to find out if he was okay."[70] Unable to get up, Sonny started playing "Autumn Nocturne," crossing his right leg over his left. The audience gasped as though what seemed like mere theatrics was part of the act. Bob Cranshaw let out a laugh, then locked in with Sonny, and the rest of the band came in as Sonny played the pickup to "Autumn Nocturne." The band was so dumbfounded that they missed a few of the changes. Little did anyone realize how much pain Sonny was in. He finished "Autumn Nocturne" flat on his back. Yet that was not the end of the concert. He played "Tenor Madness" (which ends *G-Man*), "My One and Only Love," "Kim," and "I'll Be Seeing You."[71]

Tad Richards, the stepson of sculptor Harvey Fite, the sculptor and visionary behind Opus 40, had only recently begun booking concerts with his wife, Pat; this would become their most iconic show. "After a few minutes, Sonny is still playing, still out of sight and Lucille says—'I'm a little worried, can you go and check on him?'" Richards recalled. "So I did and I found Sonny lying on his back, playing with the cameraman standing over him. We waited until he finished his solo and then helped him to his feet....Sonny asked how long we wanted him to play and I said I would stop the concert right then, if he needed medical attention. 'No man,' he growled, 'I'm going to finish the gig,' which he did standing, propped up on one foot. Afterwards, two of our volunteers who were EMTs took him over to Northern Dutchess Hospital where they confirmed he had broken his heel."[72]

To Sonny, it was all in a day's work. "Well, I jumped off the stage, because I didn't realize how deep it was," he said. "During that time, I used to leave the bandstand and walk around the club and then return to the bandstand....Now I didn't realize how high up we were...so that's why I jumped off. It wasn't that I thought I was Superman or something like that. I thought that I would just land on the ground and keep playing. Well, I did land on the ground and keep playing, but I didn't realize it would be under duress. I broke my heel, and see, I kept playing because, you know, the show must go on....I was in excruciating pain. If you ever break your heel, you'll know what I mean. Try to avoid it."[73]

This indelible moment immediately became part of jazz lore. "It's a magical moment that was legendary in the jazz community before the film was released," recalled Mugge.[74] If Sonny Rollins falls off the stage and there's someone there to hear it, he still makes a sound.

Despite Sonny's frustration with the performance, Lucille felt that the Opus 40 version of "G-Man" was a masterpiece and that it would be "criminal" not to put it out.[75] Critic Robert Christgau gave *G-Man* a rare A+ rating; when Chip Stern heard it, he thought, "Gee, this is historic, this is a breakthrough, I want to go out in the street and yell hooray and walk through ground glass and hot coals in my bare feet." This was not how Sonny felt, though. "I'm glad that people liked it, but I didn't do what I wanted to do; plus I got a horn that I'd just gotten fixed, which meant that it was different than usual—it takes a while to break a horn in," he said. "So I was very frustrated on that; it was not what I wanted to do at all."[76] At the *Saxophone Colossus* premiere, Sonny couldn't watch himself on-screen and had to walk out.[77]

For most artists, breaking a heel might be enough to sideline a tour, but the next week, the usually kinesthetic tenor titan was on the Hudson River Dayliner Musicruise, giving a performance from a leather armchair and ottoman, his foot wrapped in a cast as the ship motored around a rainy Manhattan. This was initially planned as the setting for the *Saxophone Colossus* shoot, though the sweeping vistas along the Hudson turned out to be less of a spectacle than Sonny's giant leap.[78] For three hours, Sonny kept the crowd on their feet as he sailed through dozens of choruses on "Tenor Madness," extending the blues for a full half hour, then a similarly expansive "Don't Stop the Carnival."[79] The ship passed the Statue of Liberty, then celebrating its centennial year, and the crowd erupted. At the end of the night, Sonny welcomed his old friend Tommy Flanagan to the stage to play "In a Sentimental Mood." Stanley Crouch's review was ecstatic: "What he can't do with the horn we haven't heard, what he doesn't know no one knows, and what he provides in saxophone *force* has no rivals."[80]

To Lucille, Sonny was playing better than ever. "I'm not talking just technically. But I think because he's changed as a person over the years," she told Robert Mugge. "There's now more warmth, and more feeling, and more depth than ever in his playing."[81]

It was the height of the Reagan era, and Sonny had long abandoned the youthful dream of bringing an end to injustice through music. Yet Sonny knew that if he could not reach all of society, he could still reach individuals— that perhaps more holistically than ever, he exemplified the humanities in his very existence. "There was a time in my career when I thought that my soloing and my playing would be able to turn the world around. I'd be able to change politics and influence things for the better," Sonny says at the end of Mugge's *Saxophone Colossus*. "I don't have these illusions anymore. Now all I want to do is to maybe bring enjoyment to myself and enjoyment to those people that appreciate a little bit of my art and what I'm doing. And I think that just being able to do that is plenty."[82]

———◄○►———

By the fall of 1986, Sonny's heel had healed, and he was able to pace the stage again on a four-week European tour with Mark Soskin, Jerome Harris, Clifton Anderson, and Tommy Campbell.[83] He had to keep giving it everything he had, in part as a tribute to his predecessors, like Eddie "Lockjaw" Davis, a childhood mentor who died of cancer at sixty-five on November 6.[84]

In his quest for spiritual communion, Sonny was always honoring the giants whose shoulders he stood on. "Go back to Louis Armstrong and listen to his solos—there's something really moving, something deep about it. The music itself is a spiritual music," he said early in 1987. "Being a musician is not an easy life in this country, *especially* in this country. A jazz musician is looked down on with derision by a lot of people, you can't get a credit card, and so on. You're on the outside of society in many ways, yet you know you're doing something worthwhile. So you need things to hold onto and give you strength."[85]

Sonny did not only find the spiritual in the secular through the genius of Pops, whose "A Kiss to Build a Dream On" was making regular appearances in Rollins cadenzas. Sonny practiced a religious syncretism that borrowed the best of everything.[86] Next to his bed in his thirty-ninth-floor pied-à-terre, he stacked books on religion: the Bhagavad Gita, *Autobiography of a Yogi*, and texts on Shintoism, Islam, Hinduism, yoga, Christianity, and Judaism, even *Dianetics*; books by Toni Morrison, Kafka, James Joyce, and Noam Chomsky lived in the house upstate.[87] He had begun building a video collection: *The Maltese Falcon, The Blue Angel, The Bank Dick, The Sky's the Limit, Casablanca*.[88] Above his bed loomed a portrait of an African drummer painted by Prophet Jennings. Near the upright piano was another stack of books, this one on politics, and, nearby, a koto and a tamboura. Sonny still had his Buddha statue, but just as important was his Louis Armstrong bobblehead.[89]

All of this came together in a new original composition, "O.T.Y.O.G." It stood for "Oh thank you oh God," and this simple mantra and statement of humble gratitude was a part of his daily practice. Years earlier, Sonny had begun to make daily numbered to-do lists, and "O.T.Y.O.G." was usually close to the top. One Friday's activities began with "O.T.Y.O.G." before making calls to Bobby Broom and Ronnie Scott, and making sure to "wrench every note out."[90]

"I have a spiritual place that I feel everything emanates from," Sonny said. "You can call it the big picture, we can call it universal reality, universal spirit, all of these things, but anyway, playing my horn was always a way of my going right to that place. . . . Playing my horn was more than just practicing notes. It was always something else of a spiritual nature involved. And O.T.Y.O.G. was just a way of putting things in order that I could refer to right quick, because of course the world we live in is just the opposite from those types of thoughts."[91]

It was a prayer that went back to Sonny's childhood. "When I was a kid, being brought up in a religious family, we had to say our prayers before going in bed. We would say, 'Oh thank you, oh God.' I always kept that in mind . . . but I didn't want to write the words in black and white. I thought that sounded too pretentious, and besides, I didn't want to display religious aspects too conspicuously. Besides, all of this is very personal. This piece is a little prayer that I address to my God."[92]

The song itself mirrors this eternal quest. Sonny subscribed to a position of agnostic theism, and preferred to think of God as an "It"—no gendered pronouns. "I don't know what God is, except that I know it's there," he said. In "O.T.Y.O.G." an eight-bar ascending line over a harmonic pedal leads to a descending line over a walking bass line that resolves to the tonic. In other words, it's eight bars of climbing over one unchanging chord followed by eight bars of returning home as the chords shift rapidly. Once stating the melody line several times, Sonny would climb as high as he could, improvising during the pedal section as though striving for that goal of ecstatic spiritual enlightenment, and in the next section, he tended to restate the melody in a kind of genuflection as the chords shifted beneath him. Yet to Sonny, in music and in spirituality, unlike for many jazz players, "the melody never stops."[93]

"In 'O.T.Y.O.G.,' there's moments there that could be Ornette, could be Frank Wright, but in the frame of this really hearable, hummable, feelable structure," said Jerome Harris. "It includes popular taste while not pandering. There's a way in which it harkens back to New Orleans–style polyphony where the melody doesn't have to always be stated up front. People can harmonize and prod it a little bit and have a flexible relationship to it, but it's there somewhere in the band enough that the audience can always hear it or feel it."[94]

To Sonny, part of the key to life and music was finding the complexity in simplicity and the simple in the complex. "A piece of music, it's sometimes very simple lines, and then as we play on it and play on it and play on it, it becomes more complex and more involved. This is what I try to do—to become more involved as we go, but the simplicity is basically the beginning and the end," Sonny said. "Just like life, it's very simple but it's very complex at the same time. It's very abstract, but it's still, basically, it's the simple things we relate to in life."[95]

Sonny recorded "O.T.Y.O.G." on *Dancing in the Dark*, his next studio album, but like so many of his tunes, it was designed as a vehicle for live performance, more conducive to exhaustive improvisation over twenty minutes as the spirit moved him. It was in live performance that Sonny would really testify.[96]

At fifty-six, Sonny knew exactly who he was and the uplifting spiritual message he was trying to communicate: hope and love, what he thought of as "the verities." Jazz was demanding, Sonny recognized, but it was his challenge to make it accessible even to people who claimed they did not like jazz without pandering, and sophisticated enough for the cognoscenti without alienating the masses.[97] Sonny would never deny that "jazz is protest music"[98] by its very nature and history, but he ultimately came to the position that "everything I try to do when I get on the stage is anti-politics."[99] This quest for spiritual unity was in itself a political act.[100]

After playing all over the country for the first half of 1987, on June 6, Sonny was invited by Dizzy Gillespie to play at his seventieth birthday concert at the Wolf Trap National Park for the Performing Arts in Virginia.[101] The performance took place four months prior to Gillespie's actual birthday: it was later shown on television. Carmen McRae, Freddie Hubbard, Wynton Marsalis, Oscar Peterson, Mongo Santamaria, and others were on the bill.[102] "When they asked me to name someone that I wanted to come to this, I immediately thought of Sonny Rollins, and he said yes!" said Gillespie.

"We jammed together in different places, but we never, you know, worked together, and he's always been one of my favorite musicians."[103]

When Sonny came out onstage, he bowed before Dizzy as a sign of respect. Dizzy's seventieth was not the only milestone they were marking; it was also the thirtieth anniversary of Sonny and Dizzy's only two meetings in the studio, for *Sonny Side Up* and *Duets*, both recorded within two weeks. They decided to play "Wheatleigh Hall," the B-flat blues from *Duets*. They took it only a few clicks slower than the original blistering tempo, with pianist Hank Jones, bassist Rufus Reid, and drummer Mickey Roker holding down the rhythm section. The performance deviated from the original recording in two ways. Sonny played the first three choruses of his solo a cappella—not even in stop time, as he did on "I Know That You Know" from the *Sonny Side Up* session. At nearly fifty-seven, he possessed close to the stamina of his twenty-seven-year-old self. His articulation was clear, even at fast tempos, and he remained a master of pecking. Only now he had the confidence of an elder statesman; he jettisoned some of that frenetic speed for a more lyrical call-and-response statement that harked back to the elegance of Pres.

"I see myself paring down things," Sonny said not long after the concert. "I remember hearing Coleman Hawkins, one of my heroes, one night when he was sick. He was playing much less than he normally did but the notes he was playing were so pure. That's what I'm looking for."[104]

Then Dizzy and Sonny traded a cappella. It was a bold move to invite comparisons to their playing in the prime of youth, but they still had it. Sonny let it rip, but when Dizzy didn't up the ante, opting instead for more concise rhythmic hits, Sonny held back. The goal was to communicate with Dizzy and with the audience—and they did.

After a European tour and several concerts in the United States and Canada, on August 22, 1987, Sonny performed on the Musicruise in New York.[105] Aboard the Hudson Dayliner, Sonny was able to walk this time and played an inspired show with Clifton Anderson, Bob Cranshaw, Marvin "Smitty" Smith, and pianist Monty Alexander. "It was something to remember, because it was one of those boat cruises up the Hudson, and as we liked to say, we rocked the boat," recalled Alexander. "The people were dancing and grooving, and Sonny was in his element."[106] Betty Carter was in the audience, and when Sonny invited her up, they did "Pent-Up House" together.

From September 15 to 25, Sonny and Lucille were at Fantasy Studios in Berkeley recording *Dancing in the Dark* during a series of eight-hour sessions.[107] Sonny used Clifton Anderson, Jerome Harris, Mark Soskin, and Marvin "Smitty" Smith. They recorded "O.T.Y.O.G.," the calypso "Duke of Iron" (dedicated to the eponymous calypsonian Sonny had seen in New York when he was young), the ballad "Promise," the straight-ahead "Allison," and the 1981 Quincy Jones hit "Just Once." The title track opens with a cadenza so tightly captured on the Shure condenser microphone that the friction of the saxophone pads on the keys is audible; the other standard, "I'll String Along with You," was updated with a reggae beat.[108]

Sonny heard Jerome Harris and Marvin "Smitty" Smith experimenting with a reggae version of "I'll String" between takes and decided he liked it. Later, Sonny had Harris overdub some skanking rhythm guitar.[109] During rehearsals, Anderson recalled, "Just the two of us worked through the piece for an hour or so, finding the harmonies and arrangements that seemed to work best. I remember leaving the rehearsal/music lesson very excited, thinking this was going to record great! When we got in the studio, and Sonny called the tune, the first thing he did was change the key (while the tape was rolling). Then he completely changed the arrangement we had worked on."

Dancing in the Dark got generally positive to rave reviews when it came out in 1988, and spent weeks on the jazz charts. Yet rather than approximating a live concert, the album served as more of a template for the volcanic performances to come. "Being a thematic player, I always want to embellish things ad infinitum," Sonny explained. "Playing in a recording situation, you have to be much more circumspect. You've got to condense all your ideas."[110]

Sonny finished the year by attesting to the power of jazz to promote freedom across the world. He was one of the speakers at the Jazz Freedom Concert on December 7, a fundraiser at the Duke Ellington School of the Arts in Washington, DC, organized by the International Jazz Coalition on behalf of the dissident Czech Jazz Section. The five-thousand-member Jazz Section was founded in 1971 as an offshoot of the Czech Musicians' Union. Its bulletin primarily published jazz-related content, but also poetry, polemic, and serial novels.[111] The government slashed the tires of the Jazz Section's lawyer and confiscated the mailing list, but members just picked up the bulletin in person. In 1985, the government ordered the union to disband the Jazz Section; when they refused, the government disbanded the union and imprisoned the leaders of the Jazz Section for alleged tax evasion. The Jazz Freedom Concert was organized to protest this Kafkaesque injustice; proceeds also went to offset production costs for the continued publication of the bulletin. Recent dental surgery prevented Sonny from performing, but he was able to speak in support of his positive experiences onstage in Eastern Europe promoting jazz as a language of freedom.[112] To Sonny, the radical spirit of protest never died.

———◄◦►———

"Soon, I'm going to be a senior citizen," Sonny said at the beginning of 1988. "I'll be able to ride half-fare on the subway."[113] Yet he was far from the twilight years of his career; the search for the ultimate sound continued.

So much had to go right for it to be a good night.[114] Vibrating reeds— "Sometimes I'll get maybe two good reeds out of three boxes," he said. His horn not acting up. The band had to be on. His own health—he and Lucille caught bad lingering colds that year. The theater's sound system. A responsive audience. And even if the precise alchemy was in place, Sonny never knew when *Sonny Rollins* would show up.[115]

Sonny's near misses at what he called a "direct pipeline to the heavens" could be exhilarating.[116] It happened in Tokyo that March. There was the New Audiences show at Town Hall that April where Gary Giddins wrote that "Rollins played with a vivacity and amplitude so far beyond the ken of most musicians that it might shame many into another line of work."[117] A few days later, Sonny sat down for an interview in his apartment for a major feature in *Down Beat*. He didn't mention Town Hall once.

"He would be so consistently on fire," recalled Jerome Harris. "He was damn consistent."[118] But Sonny could feel the difference, and audiences came to recognize when he was merely great and when he took it beyond. "When I'm soloing, I'm striving for a state of blankness," Sonny said. "I don't want to have to think. I want it so my horn just responds to what I'm feeling. I practice a lot, of course, so all the tools are in place. But it's only when the subsconscious part takes over that I'm really doing what I set out to do."[119] No amount of preparation could prevent the trepidation Sonny felt going into a performance. "Even though I might play certain songs," Sonny said, "they're *recomposed* each time."[120]

One of the challenges of "playing to reach myself," as he put it, was the isolation of being a bop survivor, of speaking with ghosts who loomed large and could answer back only in a dream. Early that year, Sonny had one of his first Coltrane visitations in years. "It wasn't just a vision, it was very realistic," Sonny recalled. "We were hanging out together, like back in the old days. We were talking, and he was telling me some of his stories with his wry sense of humor. It was very upbeat; everything was harmony and love, you know, and when I woke up I was happy—smiling. I'm sure glad he came back."[121]

Sonny continued giving it everything he had, touring through Miami, California, Japan, New York Town Hall, then throughout Europe and the United States.[122] After a show in Waterford, Connecticut, a fan asked Sonny why he was using piano; why wouldn't he play trio again? "The man was holding me to a standard from thirty years ago," Sonny said, "but his comments still disquieted me....I worry about falling into patterns I should avoid. I'm always concerned with getting the most out of myself. The mere suggestion I might not be unnerves me."[123]

Sonny finished the year by recording a brief part for a radio commercial for Listerine Antiseptic.[124] He occasionally did this kind of work; in 1986, he recorded the theme music for the BBC true crime series *Indelible Evidence*.[125] For someone with near-lifelong dental problems, Sonny was perhaps not an apt choice for Listerine, but of course J. Walter Thompson's copywriters had not tapped Sonny for his teeth. "That's why it never gets old and new people discover it every day—just like the music of Sonny Rollins," said the announcer as Sonny wailed.[126]

———◄o►———

Who will die after a long life and who before his time
Who by water and who by fire[127]

Leonard Cohen adapted the "Unetanneh Tokef," a central prayer of the

High Holy Days in which it is determined who will be inscribed in the Book of Life and who in the Book of Death, as the song "Who by Fire." Sonny ostensibly had no ties to the Canadian poet and songwriter or to the song itself. "I heard the title, but I didn't know the genesis of it," Sonny said, but he would forge a strong connection that winter.[128] Sonny played with a deep *ruach*, the Hebrew word for breath, wind, and spirit. Sonny was familiar with this trinity of the breath. "When God spoke about the breath of life going into the human being and it became a soul, this is the wind, the breath," Sonny said at the beginning of that year.[129]

It was producer Hal Willner who conceived of the idea of pairing Sonny and Leonard Cohen. At first blush, "Hallelujah" and "Don't Stop the Carnival" did not mesh well, but Willner specialized in orchestrating unusual collaborations. In a series of tribute albums representing his omnivorous taste, he cast classic songs in a whole new light: Muhal Richard Abrams and Henry Threadgill doing music from *La Dolce Vita*, Dr. John doing "Blue Monk," Lou Reed singing Kurt Weill's "September Song," Betty Carter covering "I'm Wishing" from *Snow White*. Starting in 1980, Willner began selecting the music used in *Saturday Night Live* sketches, so it was natural when he came on as music coordinator for *Night Music*, an hour-long Sunday-night program also produced by Lorne Michaels's Broadway Video. Its midnight Sunday time slot—1 a.m. in some markets—allowed it to take greater risks on network TV while drawing in night owls nationwide.

Jools Holland, the keyboardist in British rock band Squeeze, and David Sanborn, the alto saxophonist whose dulcet tones enlivened James Taylor's cover of "How Sweet It Is," were the cohosts. Both played in the house band. They had a jazz background—Sanborn idolized Sonny—and *Night Music* aired footage of Billie Holiday, Charlie Parker, and Coltrane as interstitials between segments. "The idea was to break down some of the artificial barriers that just seem to sprout up like weeds that separate musicians," Sanborn said. "I thought it would be great to try to find that common thread that connects the music...to cross over the boundaries and transcend those stereotypes."[130]

Despite the ethos of radical openness, orchestrating the meeting of Leonard Cohen and Sonny Rollins as Willner's first act on *Night Music* seemed risky.[131] Willner's mantra was "Stay away from being boring at all costs."[132]

This meeting would not be boring, but would it be good? "It was almost as if someone was sitting around with a Sears chemistry set and said, 'What would happen if we put this with that? Maybe it will blow up, maybe it won't,'" mused Branford Marsalis, the future leader of the Tonight Show Band.[133]

Sonny and Leonard Cohen had not met until the rehearsal. "Leonard said he wanted to do 'Tower of Song,' but I had a fantasy in my head of doing 'Who by Fire,'" Willner said.[134] "Usually when people jam they go with up-tempo things; that song had a spiritual aspect, but I knew that people would relate." Willner suggested it to Cohen, "then there was this silence. Then he said—tentatively—'Will he do that?'" Willner had a feeling Sonny would. "It was something that Rollins could relate to: the prayer aspect of it."[135] Sonny related, especially to the frank meditation on mortality; he was a survivor and that meant saying a lot of goodbyes.

At the rehearsal, there were some nerves. Sonny stood back and observed Cohen, just as he had with Mick Jagger. Cohen sang the opening bars, and when they came to Sonny's solo, Sonny, Willner recalled, "who was sitting there staring at Leonard the whole time, picked up his horn and started wailing in a different kind of understanding of the song." When they finished the rehearsal, Sonny approached backup singer Julie Christensen with an earnest look. "Do you think Mr. Cohen likes what I'm doing?"[136] Mr. Cohen more than liked it.

They saved the meeting for last. Sonny played "Kim," his song from *G-Man*; Cohen sang "Tower of Song." At the end, Sonny came back out in sunglasses, a vision in black with his Chuck Taylors, and started his cadenza. He played some pentatonics, then some harmonic minor flourishes as those klezmer intervals crept in. When Leonard Cohen came in on the melody backed by George Duke, a chorus including Perla Batalla, and members of the band Was (Not Was), it was clear that something special was happening. Cohen stood still, delivering the lyrics in his lugubrious basso profundo. "Who shall I say is calling?"[137]

Sonny was calling. Cohen turned his back to the audience to watch Sonny channel a religious fervor. Sonny played one of the bluesiest solos of his career and still managed to squeeze in a tongue-in-cheek reference to "Pop Goes the Weasel." He had internalized the laughing-to-keep-from-crying impulse common to both klezmer and the blues.[138] When Sonny finished his chorus, the notoriously stoic Cohen turned back around, struggling to suppress a smile as he intoned the solemn lyrics.

Cohen let Sonny take it out. And as he did, Sonny began to rock. When some devout Jews pray, they sway back and forth in a hypnotic rhythm, a *shuckling* motion; Sonny was *davening* as though his life depended on it. He ended with a final peroration as the rhythm section dropped out, circular breathing to repeat an insistent motif without taking in the breath of life. He descended into the depths chromatically, then tilted the bell of his saxophone into his knee to mute it, but the breath continued. He let out one final *tekiah* like a shofar blast. "For me, it was old hat. It was playing with Uncle Sonny," recalled bassist Tom Barney, who was in the *Night Music* band. "You can see his cheerfulness, his playfulness with music and he makes fun of things, sounds, the moment. There's always a lot of humor in his playing, but there was a serious side of it, too, so you had to catch both worlds. It was an extraordinary moment."[139] Everyone applauded, including Cohen, as Sonny cracked a smile himself.

The polarity between the two—that antagonistic cooperation—led to an unexpectedly beautiful catharsis. Sonny's transcendent performance was more about the endless struggle to survive than the meditation on mortality the lyrics suggested. "There was definitely something of a higher nature going on that night," Sonny said. "This was the message there—we have to go on even though we don't always reach any kind of satisfaction. That's the struggle in life, you know?"[140]

Hal Willner later called it "probably the best collaboration I ever did."[141]

Sonny and Lucille were financially comfortable enough that they could turn down half their offers.[142] More time off meant Sonny could stay fresh enough to increase the chance of having a good night. "I realize that I am not going to reach the point I once thought I would be able to, where every performance is a sort of nirvana," he said. "This is life, after all."[143] Sometimes, he did get there, though, and May 19, 1989, was a high point. Sonny played Carnegie Hall in a show presented by New Audiences with Clifton

Anderson, Bob Cranshaw, Mark Soskin, Jerome Harris on guitar, Al Foster, and special guest Branford Marsalis.[144] Wynton's older brother was thirty years younger than Sonny, but he didn't think for a moment that his relative youth would help him keep up.[145] "People say, 'Well, how do you play like Sonny Rollins?' " Branford said. "I said, 'Well, I think the first thing you have to do is you have to learn about ten thousand songs."[146]

Marsalis told the *New York Times* that he expected it to be like going toe to toe with Tyson; that would make him Spinks. Yet Sonny didn't envision it as the battle royale the public expected. "I don't approach it as, 'We'll have a cutting contest,' " Sonny said. "I've gotten into some competitive things with Sonny Stitt, Dexter Gordon, John Coltrane, and Ben Webster, situations which had more of a competitive focus. Even there, when you play with them you learn, especially if you really respect the guy you're playing with. I have the highest respect for Branford—I wanted to choose someone compatible."[147]

At the rehearsal, Branford played Sonny's solo on "Toot, Toot, Tootsie." It wouldn't cut it; he would have to play himself. "Just to stand there on a stage with him is an honor. And I figure, what's wrong with getting slaughtered by Sonny Rollins?" Marsalis said. "There's going to be an incredible amount of knowledge passed on in that whipping. I'll pick myself up off the floor, and maybe I'll cry, because I do that sometimes after a tough gig. But then I'll internalize the stuff he played and be a better person for it."[148]

"I knew he wasn't going to do to Branford what he did to Wynton," recalled Clifton Anderson, "but Branford came backstage before the concert, and said, 'Man, why did I take this gig?' I said, 'It's gonna be fun, man, don't worry. It's gonna be fun.' "[149]

At Carnegie Hall, Sonny danced circles around Marsalis through "East of the Sun," "The Tennessee Waltz," and "Three Little Words" in the first set. Sonny made sure he and Branford didn't solo back-to-back, but Sonny's vertiginous arias were enough to throw anyone off-balance. At one point, Anderson said, Branford "played two or three choruses, and he ended his solo in the middle of the third chorus. He was completely fucked up, as was everybody else."[150] On "Three Little Words," Sonny played what seemed like everything he knew and then found more. It was a breathless display of brilliance that had the crowd erupting several times during the solo. Then he and Branford traded briefly, the young protégé swept up in the deluge.

Drummer Jeff "Tain" Watts witnessed it firsthand. "He gave Branford his six choruses or something like that, and then he just wrote a whole encyclopedia on it," Watts said. "It just came and it just kept coming. The first three choruses were beautiful and perfect and then he just had volumes to say about it. And he probably could have played even longer."[151]

"I was standing directly behind him, behind the drum set, just looking," recalled Anderson. "Every chorus, you thought you heard everything, and the next chorus, the shit just kept going." Finally, Sonny arched his back in a yogic position, holding the horn high above his head. "I looked at the people in the audience, and everybody was on the edge of their seat. This is at Carnegie Hall as far as you could see. You could see a good fifteen rows or so, and their mouths were open, and I wish to this day that I had a camera, because this was an iconic shot."[152]

When the lights went up, stunned silence pervaded the room as Jeff "Tain" Watts locked eyes with Delfeayo Marsalis, Vernon Reid, Stanley Crouch, and the other jazz professionals in the audience. "Every musician was looking across the room at each other, like what just happened here?" Watts recalled. "It was like somebody threw a bomb in there."

After intermission, Sonny came back out as though it was just business as usual. "Thank you, ladies and gentlemen, for staying for the second half," he began. Branford continued to hold his own, but according to Watts, "he'd get out of the way and just stand on the side of the stage and shake his head, because it was that deep.... Coltrane in his prime, it would have been a very good one. It would have been apples and oranges, but no one could defeat him that day. It was one of the most amazing things I've ever seen." Sonny spared Branford the potential humiliation of trading fours on the final tune of the night: "Tenor Madness."[153]

They came back out for the encore, and Branford reported on the Knicks playoff game; Michael Jordan and the Bulls won that night. Sonny called "Strode Rode," and he somehow still found more to say. Everyone in the band and audience left Carnegie Hall in awe. "I can't say how many shows

I played with Sonny. It's hundreds, but of those hundreds and hundreds of shows, there are shows that stand out, that I can call up from my memory," said Anderson, "and that's one of them."[154]

"The only time I ever spent with Sonny was the day he kicked my ass at Carnegie Hall," Branford recalled nearly twenty years later. "It was as though he was using everything in the room as a source for improvisation. He is easily—with the exception of Louis Armstrong—the greatest improviser in the history of jazz."[155]

Two weeks later, Sonny invited Branford to play on his next studio album, *Falling in Love with Jazz*. "He's a great player, and if anyone thinks I blew him offstage, Branford can redeem himself on the record, because he sounds real good," Sonny said, adding a touch of irony. "But you know how it is with these young guys.... They've got all their physical powers, so that we older guys have to really keep on our toes and try to keep up with them. They're strong; they can play, and they know everything."[156]

The album was recorded that summer over three days: June 3, August 5, and September 9. On the June date, Jerome Harris was the only regular member of Sonny's band; the other players were Branford, Watts, and Tommy Flanagan. For the August and September dates, Sonny used Clifton Anderson, Mark Soskin, Bob Cranshaw, Jerome Harris, and Jack DeJohnette. To Watts, just being in the presence of "one of the most obviously full-of-love artists ever" was a learning experience. "A lot of it is from being in the room with them," Watts said. "There's so much information and so much emotional sonic impact."[157]

Sonny and Lucille opted for a different approach to *Falling in Love with Jazz*, geared toward loosening up the studio session even more. First, they decided to record it entirely in New York at Clinton Studios—in Hell's Kitchen, also known as Clinton—to avoid the stress and expense of travel and accommodations. Second, each of the three sessions was only three or four hours in the afternoon. They recorded two to six takes of each tune, instead of the typical seventeen or more, and put them all on the album except for the "Merry Widow Waltz." "This turned out to be a great way to do this as no one had a chance to get tired and we were able to use different

660 | Saxophone Colossus

people," Lucille wrote Fantasy president Ralph Kaffel. "Even Sonny was pleased I think—and the whole atmosphere was more like not really recording but just some friends getting together to play."[158]

The band with Branford and Flanagan recorded two standards, "For All We Know" and "I Should Care." Nothing could hold a candle to the Carnegie Hall show, but Tommy Flanagan added another dimension with his sensitive ballad playing and comping. With the other band, Sonny recorded the standards "Little Girl Blue" and "Falling in Love with Love"; two originals, "Sister" and "Amanda," the latter named for journalist Hugh Wyatt's daughter; and "Tennessee Waltz," the lovelorn country hit, which Sonny added to the band's repertoire that spring.[159]

"It was a little bit outside the repertoire and what we could do at the time," Sonny said of the country turn. "I wanted to have a real country sound, although it was me playing, but I wanted to bend the genres there and still be a piece of itself."[160]

Sonny's connection to country music stretched back to childhood. "I listened to a lot of country when I was growing up. We used to listen to the Grand Ole Opry when it came on," Sonny recalled. "Roy Acuff and all those people. Cousin Minnie Pearl. I think the Grand Ole Opry used to be on every week.... They used to have Amateur Night in Harlem coming from the Apollo Theater. We wouldn't miss that. *And* the Opry."[161]

The song became a guitar feature for Jerome Harris, who had recently switched from the bass chair in Sonny's band.[162] Harris played a solid-body Stratocaster clone, but he channeled the spirit of a pedal steel to bring out some country twang. As a musical omnivore who listened to Doc Watson, Dolly Parton, and Bill Monroe, Harris knew the tune well. The arresting sight and sound of two African American men from New York City standing onstage belting out the "Tennessee Waltz" with more force and feeling than just about anyone ever had affirmed the unkept promise of a truly inclusive American ideal. Sonny knew that the roots of country music were as tangled as the roots of the American Dream.[163]

Sonny continued touring through the summer and fall.[164] At fifty-nine, as he contemplated the end of his fifties, Sonny had no plans for another sabbatical. He had recently reconnected with classical saxophone lodestar Sigurd Raschèr, who lived about ninety miles north of Germantown in Shushan, New York; they wrote frequent letters. Sonny was surprised that on the verge of eighty-two, Raschèr had stopped touring. "It is unfortunate that people won't be able to see you perform," Sonny wrote in disbelief. "Why did you stop?"[165]

That year, Raschèr arranged for Sonny to become an honorary member of the North American Saxophone Alliance, a group founded by saxophonist Frederick Hemke.[166] Sonny was grateful for the acknowledgment, but he hoped the organization would dedicate itself to using the saxophone to promote loftier ideals beyond the instrument itself. Sonny was reading Rudolf Steiner and Bill McKibben's recently published book, *The End of Nature*, on the incipient global warming crisis.[167] To Sonny, it was incumbent on such organizations to confront these social and political issues.

"What did you think of the idea of raising the consciousness of saxophone players so that they can become an ethical and moral force at this particular time in our civilization?" Sonny wrote.

> I assume you agree that it would be a positive thing, but do you believe it can be done? You didn't really discuss this in your note. Again, these various saxophone organizations and societies are meaningless and irrelevant at this point in time unless they face up to the "larger picture," and confront the challenge of "EARTH 1990." What a wonderful opportunity to put our instrument upon the face of history.[168]

This was Sonny Rollins. Never "Can it be done?" Rather, "Do you *believe* it can be done?" It was the belief that belied impossibility.

Chapter 40

HERE'S TO THE PEOPLE

(1990–1996)

In the nineties, Sonny dedicated himself to preserving the tradition as he slowly watched the giants who walked alongside him rejoin the ancestors one by one. By the end of the decade, Sarah Vaughan, Dexter Gordon, Art Blakey, Stan Getz, Miles Davis, Dizzy Gillespie, Don Cherry, Ella Fitzgerald, Carmen McRae, and others would all pass on. During this changing of the guard, the battle between the neoclassicist Young Lions and the avant-garde divided the jazz scene. In New York alone, the divide was most pronounced between Jazz at Lincoln Center, which became an official branch of the city's preeminent cultural institution in 1991, and the iconoclastic Knitting Factory—uptown versus downtown.[1]

"I come down in the middle," Sonny said in late 1989. "I agree that the music of the old masters is important. How can you forget about guys like Art Tatum? And I agree that some guys should try to create new things. But, really, I think a musician should play what he feels. I don't think you should necessarily try to do something for the sake of doing something. But, if you have command of your instrument and an understanding of the tradition, then there's nothing wrong with experimenting."[2]

As the gulf between factions widened, Sonny felt that he could remain a bridge. And he was still playing some of the best music of his life.

Sonny later spoke of the "expansive ancestry of jazz,"[3] going back to New Orleans and African roots. "If 'jazz,' in quotes, was supposed to have been spawned in New Orleans as the legend goes, and it happened in Congo Square—which was the one place where all these players could play their drums and their music—my feeling is that music from all the different areas, which would include African and Caribbean components, was included in New Orleans," Sonny said. "Now here I am, a guy with Caribbean roots, but who was brought up in New York and exposed to the blues and classical traditions. Then as a jazz player—just as Dizzy was able to bring jazz and the Afro-Cuban traditions together—I had the opportunity to introduce these Caribbean beats into jazz, which I feel were present at the very creation of jazz. In fact, a good friend of mine in Jamaica—Dermot Hussey—related to me how Duke Ellington told him that he felt that jazz came up through the Caribbean." To Sonny, that expansive ancestry expanded into the past and the future. "People shouldn't feel, 'This is jazz. The door is closed on its possibilities and it's got to be very close to a certain tradition,'" he said. "The whole tradition of jazz is very open-ended."[4]

To Sonny, even hip-hop fell "under the jazz umbrella," and he had begun resonating with zydeco.[5] "I think jazz is big enough to contain and use all these elements. But I also think there should always be something definable as jazz," he said in 1993. "I wouldn't want it to get submerged into some big eclectic stew. There's got to be some improvisational element, and the blues feeling—which is very defining—and some kind of rhythmic thrust."[6]

Sonny still felt the obligation to push the music forward while respecting tradition, a dictum so ingrained in jazz discourse that it had almost become cliché, but as a living link to the past, he felt this obligation more keenly than others. "It's very important jazz doesn't become a museum piece," he said.[7]

What was once kept out of the schools eventually gets taught at universities. The New York Schools of Music, where Sonny took his first lessons in the 1930s, actively abhorred jazz; in 1990, three of his first gigs were at the University of Pennsylvania Jazz Festival; a middle school in Bethlehem, Pennsylvania; and Finney Chapel at the Oberlin Conservatory of Music. That spring, he played Princeton.[8]

Sonny was concerned that improvisation could not survive a college curriculum. "Now, with jazz being taught in schools, which is a good thing, and more and more of it written down, we're in danger of losing what's most important about jazz," he said that year. "Who knows? Jazz may not have a future.... In my neighborhood there was a cultural milieu for jazz, but I don't know where a place on Earth like Harlem in the Renaissance exists anymore. I don't know. Maybe jazz is going to be a kind of chamber music in the future. It's something like that in Europe and Japan, where they have a tradition of taking music more seriously. Jazz is a music of the head, as well as the heart. . . . We don't want to make jazz too written, or even too acceptable, because that is what can kill it."[9]

Keeping jazz alive meant "keeping fresh," Sonny said,[10] and also keeping himself alive, so he continued adhering to a regimen of daily yoga, healthy diet—"none of that fried stuff"[11]—twenty-five minutes on the stationary bike four times a week, and constant practice.[12] "Do I dye yet?" Sonny quipped to a reporter. "Remember Ronald Reagan never answered that question."[13] As Sonny approached his sixtieth birthday, he was beginning to go gray, but he was not about to settle into a gilded retirement.

The Germantown house was kept free of the awards and accolades. It was decorated tastefully but with a minimalist aesthetic, with a basic stereo system, an old TV, and baby gates to block off different rooms for the dogs. They had two cars, a Volvo and a Mercedes, and a swimming pool, but otherwise led a modest, undisturbed life in upstate New York. Every day after breakfast, Sonny went out to the barn to practice, where there were few mementos of his past. Concert posters adorned the walls, but there was little else to distract him, other than Carrie, the daughter of their dogs Flory and Brigadier, who often accompanied him to the studio.[14] His old Buddha bust looked down on his electric keyboard and a gigantic Swiss alphorn he picked up in Switzerland.[15] Sonny rarely used the stereo or the Sylvania record player, he explained with his characteristically wry wit. "It would be like asking a guy who drove a cab for a living to take a vacation and drive across country."[16]

Sonny had more aches and pains, but this only increased his resolve, even though he had decreased his practice routine from a Bridge sabbatical high of fifteen hours a day to a meager three to six hours. He practiced what he referred to as "Sonny's Rudiments," everything from scales to sight-reading to alternate fingerings, the overtone series from Sigurd Raschèr's *Top-Tones*, and the patterns he began obsessively documenting on manuscript paper in the fifties. He generally called these "Dollies," "Dailies," or "Dallies" in his workbook; he did them slowly but methodically.[17] He had begun going through arias from Wagner's *Tristan und Isolde* to open his mind and exercises in his friend Yusef Lateef's *Repository of Scales and Melodic Patterns*.[18] Finally, he would arrive at free blowing. Sonny wrote Raschèr that he was actually making progress in the clarity of his upper register and the overtones in the altissimo range. "I am beginning to get some hints that the facility is coming," he wrote. "It comes in ways I never envisioned but that is why Sigurd says practice diligently and you will be rewarded." Still, he wondered, was there such a thing as "undertones," notes below the horn on the lower frequencies?[19]

In his studio, Sonny was painting with sound and was still broadening the palette. "I hope that I haven't found my sound yet because I'm still searching for some other things which I hope will develop," Sonny said that year. What were they? "Colors, you know. Different colors."[20] There was always more to learn.[21]

He and Lucille still turned down half of their offers and reduced Sonny's performance schedule to an average of five nights a month. Sonny was slowing down, but not diminishing in focus. He would usually sweat through at least two shirts over the course of a performance. "Two hours of my playing is equivalent to ten hours of a lot of others' playing," he said.[22]

Before the encore at the Bottom Line in April 1990, he had flu-like symptoms, but the crowd never suspected. "Jazz is always happening," he told the audience. "Different every time, so come see us later."[23]

That April, Sonny toured Japan with Bobby Hutcherson, Clifton Anderson, Jerome Harris, Bob Cranshaw, and Al Foster.[24] Earlier in February, Sonny flew to Japan to shoot a television commercial for Amada, the metal processing company, which was arranged by his Japanese road manager, Hideko Ataka.[25] In addition to Amada making a donation to a drug treatment organization, Sonny was paid about $75,000 for the spot. Making a bridge from Sonny to industrial metal processing would be a challenge, but the spot featured him playing on a steel "suspension bridge of hearts," the theme that Amada and Sonny both never stopped searching for perfection.[26]

Sonny was still at the top of his game during a national tour in 1990.[27] At Blues Alley, Cecil Taylor, who was in the audience, got up and started dancing.[28]

For Sonny's sixtieth birthday, he returned home to Germantown for a few weeks hoping to have some rest and relaxation, only to find himself reflecting on "the usual unexpected problems which life brings with it," as he wrote Sigurd Raschèr. This took the form of emergency plumbing work—walls broken down to repair old pipes—and having the house repainted. Sonny applied this idea more broadly to world events, especially the growing conflict as the Soviet Union moved toward its official dissolution. "This is the way the world has always been, has it not? Constant challenges to man's courage, faith and intellect!! There just seems to be less courageous faithful people around these days to confront the issues!"[29] As he began his seventh decade, Sonny also wanted a small birthday present—a signed portrait of Raschèr himself to add to the collection he started when he had Coleman Hawkins sign his headshot five decades earlier.

As a keeper of the flame, Sonny continued passing the torch to the next generation of musicians. In 1991, the guest of honor was twenty-one-year-old trumpeter Roy Hargrove. Hargrove grew up in Dallas, attending Booker T. Washington High School for the Performing and Visual Arts, where he soon caught the ear of Wynton Marsalis, who invited him to sit in at concerts while Hargrove was still in high school. He attended Berklee and then the New School in New York, where Hargrove began recording with Bobby Watson, Superblue, Ricky Ford, and Frank Morgan.

Sonny had only recently become aware of his explosive arrival on the scene. "The first time I came in contact with Roy was at a George Wein show that was done on the East River pier," Sonny recalled decades later. "Roy was quite a musician and quite a musical personality, and he just was sort of a mystical, beatific character, you know, and . . . he was here and he left. A great guy and a superb musician."[30]

Despite his precocious talent, Hargrove had butterflies. "During rehearsal I was overwhelmed that I was just standing next to him," Hargrove said. "He's history in person, the whole history of the music."[31]

The Carnegie Hall concert promised another exciting meeting—the reunion of Sonny, Jim Hall, and Bob Cranshaw, three out of four members of the band from *The Bridge*, with Al Foster on drums. At the beginning of the night, Sonny walked onstage in a bright-red shirt, a black ascot, and a black jacket with white trim and played so many dizzying choruses on "Long Ago and Far Away" that it seemed he had blown a hole through the wall. He played a calypso, then welcomed Hargrove, "that fine young musician we've all been hearing so much about." Hargrove came out in a suit and tie, young enough to be Sonny's grandson.

In the same way that Miles Davis never tried to compete with Bird's speed, Hargrove followed Sonny with a ballad, playing Michael Edwards's "Once in a While," which Hargrove had recently recorded on his sophomore album, *Public Eye*. He was the quintessence of hip. Hargrove took it into double time on his solo, but that was not what immediately distinguished him. As hard as Sonny could swing at a fast tempo, Hargrove could swing just as hard on a ballad. It was clear to everyone in the audience at Carnegie Hall that Hargrove had it—they applauded that ballad for a full minute. But then came the real test.

"When we got on stage, I felt this tremendous amount of energy coming from him," Hargrove said. "You don't sleep when you play with him. He's really unpredictable. When he throws it at you, you have to catch it—or you're in trouble."[32]

Sonny called "Big Foot," the Charlie Parker blues he had played in 1983 with Wynton Marsalis. Sonny took the first solo. But Hargrove stood his ground, starting slow and building to a climax. When they traded—fours, twos, ones, free-for-all—Hargrove could pick up Sonny's lines and complete them and vice versa, a native speaker of the language of bebop.

Then it was time for *The Bridge*. Hall had only gotten deeper since the time Sonny slipped messages in his mailbox in the early sixties. When they played "Without a Song," "The Bridge," and "Where Are You," they conjured that bygone era three decades earlier as though not a day had passed. Cranshaw even played upright bass and soloed brilliantly on "Without a Song," the tune that landed him his lifelong gig with Sonny. Yet thrilling as it was, the night belonged to "Young Roy," immortalized by a new composition Sonny had written for Hargrove they premiered that night. Sonny brought him back out, "if he's still here," for a medley of "Don't Stop the Carnival" and "St. Thomas," and Hargrove could hang on calypso, too. When the audience demanded an encore, they played "Tenor Madness." Sonny closed with a cadenza that resolved into "This Is Always," the ballad made memorable by Charlie Parker and Earl Coleman. To Sonny, there was a direct line from those days to the present. And Roy Hargrove had *arrived*.[33]

That August, Sonny invited Hargrove to record with him on *Here's to the People*. Sonny obviously loved Hargrove's ballad playing; he recorded on two,

"I Wish I Knew" and Sonny's "Young Roy." Sonny and Lucille decided to break up the record into four three-hour sessions between August 10 and 24 with at least a few days in between each, all recorded at Clinton Studios in New York to avoid travel. They had also done this on *Falling in Love with Jazz*.[34] The rest of the band included Clifton Anderson, Mark Soskin, Jerome Harris, and Bob Cranshaw, with the drum chair alternating between Jack DeJohnette, Steve Jordan, and Al Foster.

Sonny wrote the beginning of a set of lyrics to the title track, an original thirty-six-bar composition. "Here's to the people that live in the country..." "I am not a lyricist, but I still get the first words on the first bars of the song," he explained. The populist "Here's to the People," with its four-bar "semi-military style drum break," according to Sonny's lead sheet, was meant as a "sort of salute," Sonny said, to hardworking people like his parents.[35]

Sonny dedicated "Doc Phil" to Dr. Phil Terman, his longtime dentist and friend who kept him playing for so many years. Terman was a jazz clarinetist and saxophonist who developed an expertise helping musicians with the full gamut of dental problems. He treated most of the Duke Ellington Orchestra, Dizzy Gillespie, Stan Getz, Jimmy Heath, Perry Robinson, and Phil Woods, who recommended him to Sonny in the early eighties.[36]

Despite Sonny's chronic dental troubles, Dr. Terman allowed him to maintain his embouchure. Sonny sent him a signed picture, inscribed "To Phil Terman—My Savior."[37]

Although it lacked the fire of the recent Carnegie concert, between Sonny's originals and the collection of standards he chose, *Here's to the People* garnered positive reviews. Gary Giddins wrote that "the latest tour de force by the greatest living tenor saxophonist almost qualifies as the Sonny Rollins Record We've Been Waiting For."[38]

That October, Sonny went on a twelve-concert, three-week tour of Japan.[39] Right before the Japan tour, Miles Davis died on September 28, 1991, at the age of sixty-five. Sonny had visited him in the hospital previously, and when he was "getting ready to transition, his sister was there with him," Sonny recalled. "She talked about different people, and she brought my name up, and he squeezed her hand hard."[40]

Miles's death underscored Sonny's growing sense of responsibility as one of the last of his generation. "Miles and I were very close, and I never thought of him as not being around," Sonny reflected in the months after Davis's passing. "Although during his last few years I didn't communicate that much with him, we were just close from years gone by. It feels funny. It really is strange. I never thought I would survive all this time. I think I'm actually overdue. All the saxophonists, most of the guys didn't really stay around that long—Coltrane was in his forties, Bird in his thirties, even Lester Young was [forty-nine] when he passed. It's a hard, hard life from every standpoint. You've got to take care of yourself. The environment is so hostile, both the music environment and the social environment. It's getting better I know, but when I was coming up, musicians were kind of outcasts. I could see why most of the guys don't stay around till past fifty."[41]

At around this time, Sonny hired two new band members: percussionist Victor See Yuen and drummer Yoron Israel.[42] See Yuen auditioned for Sonny in the eighties, but didn't get the call until 1991, when Sonny was playing at the Charles Hotel Ballroom in Cambridge, Massachusetts, that May.[43] Two months later, Sonny asked him to come on a European tour as the sole percussionist in the band—no drummer. See Yuen was of Chinese, African, Spanish, and French ancestry, but it was probably his native country of Trinidad and Tobago that forged the most powerful connection to Sonny. Growing up surrounded by calypso and soca, even the cadence of his speech patterns were more rhythmic, Yuen said, so it wasn't so much Sonny's polyrhythms that threw him at first but the endurance test. Playing at the ancient Roman theater in Vienne, France, on one of his first gigs, See Yuen quickly learned that he had to be in gladiatorial shape. After two and a half hours, Sonny announced they would take a fifteen-minute intermission.[44] Then he came back and played for two and a half more.[45] "It was an awakening for me to realize that I had to condition myself to be with the band," See Yuen recalled, "to step up my game to be on the same level as Sonny. Physically, I had to do push-ups, sit-ups, stretching, I had to do training—running and practicing in my room with mallets—just to condition myself to go the distance in case there was another five-hour concert."[46]

Native Chicagoan Yoron Israel was working with Art Farmer when he got the call to play with Sonny in early 1992 on Bob Cranshaw's recommendation.[47] Israel had grown up on Sonny with the Brown-Roach Quintet and was initially surprised by the electric sound of Sonny's band, but soon realized that "He didn't change what he played . . . it was just a different sound palette, playing just as energetic, just as much vocabulary."[48]

Compared to the concerts, rehearsals could not have been more leisurely. At SIR Studios in midtown Manhattan, Sonny did not stick to the common practice of running through everything they might play in concerts. "They would be booked for four to six hours, but in that one day, we may have gone through maybe three songs," Israel recalled. Mostly Sonny listened intently, making sparse but specific suggestions, exploring the harmony, and playing through different sections of the song, sometimes the entire thing. "That concept and foundation that was set in those rehearsals set a framework. . . . Leave enough space where the music can take on its own life."[49]

On May 6, 1992, in Munich's Philharmonic Hall, Israel learned the reason Sonny built a travel day and a rest day into the tours. "All the great players have this in common. Once they hit the bandstand, that's all that matters. I mean, they give their heart, mind, and soul to that hour or, in Sonny's case, that two hours," Israel said. "There's no taking prisoners. It's like, if I leave this planet after this concert is over, I've left it all there."

Sonny came out in a flowing red shirt and a black ascot and proceeded to give everyone in the band a workout, even on the ballads. Israel had learned from Abbey Lincoln that sometimes a ballad required even more focus than an up-tempo tune, which was the case as Sonny closed his eyes on "Tennessee Waltz" in one of his most lyrical performances of the song.[50] An hour into the concert, Sonny decided to trade with Israel for more than fifteen minutes on "Long Ago and Far Away." Then Israel really started to sweat.

"I'd never run out of things to play," Israel recalled. "If I listened to him and focused on building and communicating, he never seemed to run out of ideas and it just put me in a mode where there was just such a wealth of information going back and forth that it was just . . . man!" The key to speaking the language was to listen. Sonny came back after the intermission in a yellow shirt and a new ascot, but Israel had the same white button-down, still soaked through. So that was another lesson—always bring a change of clothes.

At the end of 1992, Sonny hired drummer Greg "Vibrations" Williams, Betty Carter's cousin, who came from his home in Detroit to make the gig at the Ann Arbor Blues and Jazz Festival. "I said, 'What you want me to do, man? How you want me to play?' He said, 'Well, just listen, contribute to the music, help me create the music, and push me.' I never played with Sonny. He didn't tell nobody what to play. He just started playing. You had to do that shit by yourself," Williams said. He played with him for more than a year. "It was two and a half, three-hour concerts and shit. Lucille had to stop me playing one night—'Sonny has to quit this shit now.' He'd put his horn up in the air like he was playing to god, and we'd go. Wasn't no catching him."[51]

Sonny kept touring in moderation, and not just because he felt an obligation as an ambassador of a bygone era. He also had to make a living. "I've been recording for many years and get certain royalties from my compositions and record sales," Sonny said in 1992, "but I couldn't live on that sum. Most of my income comes from live performances. If I break my arm or can't play, I'm out of luck. That's how close to the edge a jazz musician lives."[52]

For Sonny and Lucille, though, it was never about making as much money as possible.[53] Sonny received constant offers, and Lucille always responded promptly, generally with a no, with an air of professional courtesy, if a touch of frost from rejection fatigue. Regarding, for example, the prospect of releasing the extended Village Gate recordings from the *Our Man in Jazz* dates in 1962, it was an emphatic no. "In this age of CD's, it is tempting for people to put out everything they have, but we'd just rather not. In fact, absolutely would not," Lucille explained. "I am telling you definitely, as we feel it is better to say no and mean it or yes, but not maybe. And in this case, we really mean a no."[54] The rejection letters—and Lucille kept piles and piles of them in her records, marked "NO" in black ink—were couched as diplomatically as possible. He "had absolutely no time,"[55] was "project-overloaded,"[56] or was "severely over-projected."[57]

This heightened discretion concerned not only the density of his calendar but also the travel required. During the nineties, Sonny turned down two concerts in Montana for $14,000; $17,500 to play Newport in 1995; $15,000 for a concert in Saskatoon; $14,000 for one concert in Jacksonville, which "especially doesn't sound too appealing," Lucille wrote Kurland Associates; and a whopping $120,000 in 1997 for two shows at the Sardinia International Jazz Festival.[58] Sardinia was a no largely because Sonny had begun promising exclusive European appearances, in this case at the Antibes festival that summer. This was in part because Sonny "hates the festival scene, hates being around a lot of musicians and other people and is not a recluse but really doesn't enjoy being around these scenes," Lucille wrote. "So what might be normal for others can be torture for him."[59] They maintained a long-standing policy of no small clubs, regardless of the fee. In 1996, the Blue Note in New York offered Sonny $10,000 a night for as many nights as he wanted. It was a hard pass. But the previous summer, Sonny played Lincoln Center Out of Doors in Damrosch Park for only $7,500.[60]

It's not that Sonny was accepting more lucrative offers. "I don't want to be rich, strange as it may seem to most people," Sonny said in 1998. "I want to live lightly on the planet; I don't want to be a part of what they used to call the rat race."[61]

Sonny was not above playing regional venues a long car ride or plane flight away like North Carolina State University; the Music Hall in Portsmouth, New Hampshire; Gretna Music in Mount Gretna, Pennsylvania; or the Caravan of Dreams in Fort Worth.[62] Once they decided his schedule was full, though, it was full.

Sonny also appreciated awards if they seemed to elevate the status of jazz. In May 1992, he was given an honorary doctorate at Bard, his first. "The commencement was a kick for me," he wrote the novelist Marcelle Clements. "It represented a recognition of American jazz by the mainstream establishment and in accepting it, I (in my mind) did so for all of my compatriots who were never so honored during their lifetimes—Lester Young, John Coltrane, Coleman Hawkins, et al."[63]

While Sonny and his generation were increasingly accepted by the cultural establishment, they were also gaining acceptance in hip-hop. Jazz-rap progenitors Gang Starr included a verse about Sonny in "Jazz Thing," which played in the closing credits to Spike Lee's 1990 film *Mo' Better Blues*.[64]

Dizzy Gillespie's death on January 6, 1993, and then Billy Eckstine's on

March 8 underscored the heavy responsibility Sonny carried.[65] Sonny and Dizzy crossed paths one last time earlier in the summer of 1992 in Rotterdam when Gillespie was on his Diamond Jubilee tour for his seventy-fifth birthday year. "He came in my dressing room and was talking to me and my wife, Lucille, for a while," Sonny recalled. "Well, when I was on stage, I played 'Happy Birthday.' Then he came out to the stand, it was a surprise. He just came out and we played."[66]

This sense of responsibility was in his mind when he made plans to record *Old Flames*, his next album on Milestone, which was recorded at Clinton Studios on July 16 and August 24, 1993.[67] Sonny asked his old friend Jimmy Heath, with whom he had "been tight for a hundred years,"[68] to write arrangements for brass choir, which Heath also conducted. The album consisted almost entirely of ballads, with only one original, "Times Slimes." Sonny hired Clifton Anderson, Bob Cranshaw, Jack DeJohnette, and Tommy Flanagan as the core group, with the brass choir composed of Anderson on trombone, Jon Faddis and Byron Stripling on flugelhorn, Alex Brofsky on French horn, and Bob Stewart on tuba. Heath's lush arrangements of "Darn That Dream" and "Prelude to a Kiss" brought out Sonny's gentle side; *Old Flames* showed off Sonny's exquisite ballad playing.[69] "People haven't heard these songs for millions of years," Sonny said. "That's something of a challenge in itself. But I think the more simple you can get, the greater it is, really. For me, this is the essence of the whole thing. I like to hear Louis Armstrong play a simple melody. I can hear the whole thing in that. That doesn't mean you can't approach it in different ways and make it more complicated. But I'm afraid that getting older, I'm just beginning to search for that real simplicity, and trying to honor it, I guess."[70]

Amid all this beautiful simplicity, "Times Slimes" stood out, not least for its jarring title. Sonny explained the meaning at great length in interviews—a story in the *New York Times* about a white man "who had lived in the Bronx for maybe three generations.... It showed a picture of him barricaded in his house. He was in a state of siege and wouldn't move. His house looked like a concentration camp. It was covered by barbed wire to keep the burglars out. The story was, no matter what, he wasn't moving. This story, this picture on the front page of the Sunday *Times* incensed me. What got me mad was this—why didn't they have a member of a minority group from the Bronx going through the same thing, with his house boarded up, fighting the same thing? It was the perfect opportunity for a paper like the *Times* in a peaceful way to make a statement. Instead, the *Times* is putting out the same old crap. The face of crime is crime. It's not black or hispanic. Minority people are also victims. They're living behind barbed wire, too."[71]

Yet Sonny had other, more personal, issues with the Gray Lady. In June 1991, *New York Times* critic Peter Watrous wrote a feature on Ornette Coleman in advance of a major concert at Carnegie Hall, Coleman's first show in the United States in four years.[72] The story focused on the act of self-creation that made the free-jazz iconoclast a legend and the backlash he faced from critics, presenters, and his peers. According to Coleman, Sonny was one of those dismissive artists. " 'When I went to California to play with the master be-boppers, they all—Clifford Brown, Max Roach, Sonny Rollins—one night let me sit in, and they walked off the bandstand,' Mr. Coleman said. 'I was playing 'Donna Lee' faster than they could play it, but they walked off and left me playing there and said I was crazy, that I didn't know what I was doing. Oh, man, I was so hurt. I said, 'Well, I'm not going to play music.' "[73]

This humiliating incident did in fact happen, but Rollins was not there to witness it—it was apparently Sonny Stitt. It took place in April 1954 at the California Club in Los Angeles, during an early gig of the Clifford Brown–Max Roach Quintet, then Brown, Roach, bassist George Bledsoe, pianist Carl Perkins, and briefly on tenor, Stitt.[74] Ornette attended a Monday-night jam session during the quintet's extended run,[75] waiting until 1:45 a.m. to get his chance. Brown and Roach had already left, and after just a few notes, the rhythm section "walked off."[76] In 1957, Ornette had a starkly different encounter with the Brown-Roach Quintet—because it was then that he met Sonny Rollins, who immediately recognized his genius.[77] Much later on, Sonny realized that Ornette "misremembered that I was always in his corner musically," he said. "A lot of guys were not. So that's what happened. He knew that."[78]

Apparently, Watrous called Sonny to confirm Ornette's story and Sonny denied it, but the error was printed nonetheless and never corrected. Sonny was so hurt by what he considered an old friend's deliberate betrayal—in truth an innocent misrecollection—that tension lingered between him and

Ornette for years. He felt that he was one of Ornette's early champions, not part of the chorus of naysayers. Sonny and Watrous would never speak on the record again. Ergo "Times Slimes."[79]

After the perceived slight from Coleman, whom Sonny continued to respect, he just kept moving forward. After recording *Old Flames*, he brought it to a sold-out concert at Carnegie Hall on November 4, 1993, with Jimmy Heath's brass choir and special guests Terence Blanchard and Tommy Flanagan.[80] Blanchard came up in New Orleans and replaced Wynton Marsalis in Art Blakey's Jazz Messengers when he was only twenty, later forming a quintet with Donald Harrison that was signed by Columbia. He began collaborating with Spike Lee, composing the score to such films as *Mo' Better Blues* and *Malcolm X*, and thought of Sonny's score for *Alfie* as one of the key contributions that "laid the pavement and the framework for us to be able to be successful, because of what they did."[81]

Blanchard idolized Sonny and had opened up for him at the 1980 New Orleans Jazz and Heritage Festival when Blanchard was playing in the New Orleans Center for the Creative Arts high school big band.[82] "I remember watching Sonny Rollins walk to the stage, and you could see why they called him Newk. He looked like a professional athlete, man, like a boxer heading to the ring," Blanchard recalled. Leading up to the 1993 Carnegie Hall show, "I called Branford [Marsalis]. I said, 'Man, Sonny called me to do a gig with him at Carnegie Hall.' Branford said, 'Go ahead and get your ass kicked like all the rest of us. This is your time.'"

The show was revelatory. "It was one of those things where I learned an immense amount just being on the bandstand," Blanchard said. "And you learn those things you can't learn just by talking to a teacher. You learn the things about how he interacts in the moment, how the energy starts to just build and rise and rise throughout the show, how it goes from what you rehearsed to actually what you play live on the stage."[83]

From the stage at Carnegie, Sonny welcomed that "young man that's following right in the wonderful trumpet tradition," naming Clifford Brown, Fats Navarro, Miles Davis, Dizzy Gillespie, and Wynton Marsalis. "We all love him and we are behind him 100 percent. I hope you feel the same way about him."[84]

In the first five seconds of Sonny's opening cadenza on "Keep Hold of Yourself," Sonny fired off so many notes that when he abruptly paused, many in the crowd couldn't help but laugh; it was like a gushing spigot he could control at will. The song lasted twenty-five minutes in what trumpet players might refer to as a "chops buster," building and building until Blanchard and Sonny upped the ante in a ten-minute trading section, eliciting the first of two standing ovations that night.[85]

"I remember when I started trading with him, man, it just went on and on and on, and his ideas were just flowing and flowing and flowing, and I just felt like I played everything I knew three times over," Blanchard said. "It was one of those things where you start to really understand what technique was about. Technique was about not being able to play what you know, but being able to reach for some of those things you haven't played yet."[86]

Lou Reed was there, skipping most of the release party for *Live MCMX-CIII*, the Velvet Underground's long-awaited reunion album, and stayed until the bitter end.[87] The response was ecstatic, but there was one carping critic who left Carnegie Hall dissatisfied. "The concert could have been better," Sonny said a few weeks later. "There's no doubt about it."[88]

———◄o►———

At the beginning of 1994, Sonny hired Billy Drummond as his new drummer, another gifted onstage conversationalist. "He's like a drummer on the saxophone… 'turn and stop on a dime'–type phrasing that defied the laws of gravity," he said, "so when you're trading with him, he's coming at you with as much rhythmic variation as you could even imagine. For a drummer, that's going to the mountaintop."[89]

Sonny's legendary work ethic persisted. At concerts, Drummond said, "He gave it up every night. You'd just go, 'Man, this is impossible for somebody to be this giving of himself. It's a good lesson. All those guys were like that."[90] At one concert that year, Sonny accidentally chipped off a piece of his mouthpiece the size of a postage stamp during the first song. No one in the audience suspected a thing.[91]

Sonny worked with still more drummers, as well as pianists Mike LeDonne and Carlos McKinney and bassists Konrad Adderley and John Lee, and as long as they had the right stuff, he didn't care if they had won the Thelonious Monk International Jazz Competition or came off the street. "I used to play on the street and Bob Cranshaw used to see us on his way to Sesame Street," recalled drummer Bruce Cox of his street band with alto saxophonist Vincent Herring and others. One day Cranshaw invited Cox to audition for Sonny. "I had heard that was the hot seat," he said of the drum chair, "and it worked out. I think that was one of the best gigs I got from playing on the street."[92] Cox played intermittently with Sonny at first and eventually became a regular in 1997. "It was like working with a king, but he's laid-back, as far as not a lot of glamour," Cox recalled of touring with Sonny in Japan and elsewhere. "Even though he's one of the world's best, he was still humble."[93]

Harold Summey won the 1992 Thelonious Monk competition and joined Sonny in 1994. "When you get to meet a guy and you spend time in their orbit for a minute and you figure out that it's all true, that somebody could be that good, it's an overwhelming experience," Summey said. "He could control the whole band from his saxophone. A lot of times I felt like I couldn't catch up to him; he was always just a little bit out in front of me. And I've never felt that way since.... Everything I do as a musician, it's like pre-Sonny, post-Sonny."[94]

Summey learned how to lock into the elusive time feel established by Sonny and Bob Cranshaw. "Sonny used to say, 'The hard thing about jazz is figuring out how to keep the forward momentum going without rushing,'" Summey recalled.[95] "I think he probably figured out the same thing that Louis Armstrong figured out. You can be really strong and present without being overbearing or nervous. Armstrong was an unassuming sort of person but his playing was completely compelling. He sucked you in, and it's the same thing with Sonny. He's just playing really powerful music that stays on the forward edge of that beat. Charlie Parker could do that, too. John Coltrane... What it really boils down to is that's what swing is. It's not just about the first and third partial of the triplet... it goes beyond that."[96]

In 1995, Sonny hired pianist Kevin Hays and sent him a tape of old vocal tracks to prepare him for the gig. "That was really a revelation for me. It was all of these songs that we were going to play, at least the standards, and it was all singers, like Ethel Waters singing 'Cabin in the Sky,' Sarah Vaughan,

Billie Holiday," Hays recalled. "He was like, 'I want you to hear how these songs really go.' You knew what was important to him—the melody is paramount. He's definitely a melody man. As far out as he could take it, I think in a way that's why it was so effective when he would stretch, because he was so rooted in the melody he could reach his metaphorical branches out so far."[97]

On August 30 and October 7, 1995, Sonny recorded much of this material on *Sonny Rollins +3* over two four-hour sessions from 1 to 5 p.m. at Clinton Studios in New York.[98] For the August session, Sonny hired Bob Cranshaw, pianist Stephen Scott, and Jack DeJohnette; the October session had Cranshaw, Al Foster, and Tommy Flanagan. Flanagan was ideal for the session, given his long relationship with Ella Fitzgerald; Stephen Scott had a maturity that belied his youth and had worked with Ron Carter, Joe Henderson, and, most important for this vocal-centric album, Betty Carter.[99]

There were two originals—"H.S.," a sixteen-bar blues dedicated to Horace Silver, and "Biji," which referred to "back in the days when guys had nicknames like Rahsaan and Famoudou," Sonny said. "I adopted Brung Biji as mine. It was sort of African style."[100] The core of the album was influenced by classic jazz vocals. Sonny knew the lyrics to this material, allowing him to delve into the emotional complexity of the songs. "I match up with the melody first since I'm an instrumentalist, but the words are part of what I take in," Sonny said.[101]

"What a Difference a Day Makes" was made famous by Dinah Washington in 1959. Irving Berlin's "They Say It's Wonderful" was probably the 1958 Sarah Vaughan version on the tape Sonny gave to Hays. "Mona Lisa" was recorded by Nat King Cole with Nelson Riddle's orchestration in 1950. "Cabin in the Sky" was sung by Ethel Waters and Eddie "Rochester" Anderson in the 1943 film of the same name and emerged as a highlight on +3, with a lyrical cadenza. "I've Never Been in Love Before" was recorded by Bing Crosby in 1950, though there were many other versions.

Though the album garnered some of Sonny's most positive reviews in years, he was dissatisfied with it. "I'm still trying to make the perfect record for me," he said. "My performance could be more dynamic. I'm a perfectionist. Hopefully my standards will always be more stringent than the standards of my listeners."[102]

The music coalesced on tour. Persistence was a key lesson; Sonny was "leaning into the music with full commitment," Hays explained. "You're not wasting any sound, you're not wasting any notes or breath on something unless you're connected to it on a kind of feeling level." During one memorable evening concert at an outdoor venue in Istanbul, Sonny kept playing through a power outage, inspired by the call to prayer, which he harmonized with at dawn while practicing in the city. "Everything went dark and Sonny kept playing. He started doing these particular 'call to prayer' sounds that you would hear at regular intervals in Istanbul, just kind of beautiful microtonal music going on, and he started doing that. And then the lights came back on and everybody started playing and the crowd went crazy. It was almost like Sonny had adopted their language."[103]

Monday, November 13, 1995, was proclaimed Sonny Rollins Day in New York. "I made a few jokes about using the proclamation they gave me to get on the subway for half price," Sonny said.[104]

That Saturday, November 18, 1995, was a little different. Sonny organized the first-ever Sugar Hill reunion at the Beacon Theatre in New York. Jackie McLean, Walter Bishop Jr., Gilly Coggins, Connie Henry, and Percy Heath all came. Trumpeter Wallace Roney was invited to fill the shoes of Miles Davis, who loomed large at this family gathering.[105]

"We did two rehearsals," Roney recalled. "In the first, I went in and we rehearsed for maybe five minutes. Sonny was playing light and my chops were so strong because I had just gotten off the road. I went home and told my brother that we played for five minutes and Sonny wasn't sounding too strong. I joked that I was going to tell Sonny he's got to play more than that. So, the day of the gig, I got to the soundcheck a bit late and Sonny was already playing. And he was burning. *Burning.* I was so caught up in being late that I didn't notice the intensity he was playing with. He was looking right at me, and with his body he's saying, 'C'mon, man. Play!' He was so much stronger than I remembered, and he was really going for it. I took my horn and started going for it, too. We were doing it right there at the soundcheck, and everyone was hollering. When we got to the concert, he played his butt off. But I think some of his best playing was at that rehearsal. The tunes were 'St. Thomas' and 'Tenor Madness.'"[106]

Leading up to the sold-out concert, Jackie McLean went to Boston to give his horn a checkup with legendary saxophone technician Emilio Lyons. "He said, 'Emilio, check my instrument, 'cause I got to go in the ring with Sonny Rollins,'" Lyons recalled.[107]

Sonny himself was concerned that at sixty-five, his age had finally begun to show. They don't generally mount career retrospectives and name days on the calendar after artists still in the prime of life. "I accept that I don't have the same energy or the amount of teeth that I had then," Sonny said at this time. "But that's okay. Age...on one hand you learn some things; you compensate by developing a whole lot more mental finesse. It's like a big league pitcher who can't bring it quite like he used to; he's lost a yard off of his fastball. So he compensates with guile, starts throwing a lot of junk and off-speed pitches. So maybe he can't blow it by the hitters anymore, but, hey, he can still outwit them."[108]

Yet onstage together at the Beacon somehow they turned back time. Of the Counts of Bop, Kenny Drew had passed on in 1993 and Art Taylor on February 6, 1995. In 1994, Sonny's musician friend John Reid from Stitt Junior High School, whom he had kept in touch with since 1943, also passed.[109] Sonny dedicated the concert to Taylor, with whom he had joined Local 802 nearly fifty years earlier. However, much of the original Sugar Hill Gang was still standing on that stage. They had come a long way since Goof Square.

Sonny served as emcee. Early on, he welcomed Roney to the stage for a duet with Percy Heath. "This is a beautiful number written by another friend of mine, Thelonious Monk. We used to hang out right around here by the Beacon not so long ago... it seems like yesterday," Sonny said.

"'Straight, No Chaser!'" yelled one enthusiastic fan.

"'Straight, No Chaser,' right," Sonny replied. "That's what we used to get in those days—straight, no chaser. But this is now."

Bishop thought of Sonny as "The Colossus of the Collage," a quilter of melody who brought people together. "When it actually happened, Sonny was the one that had the clout to pull it off," Bishop recalled, "at the Beacon Theatre, with young audiences, and man, it was like a rock concert. When he called me onstage, you would have thought I was Bruce Springsteen. I couldn't believe it."[110]

At the end of the first set, Sonny went toe to toe with J-Mac. In the opening cadenza, McLean began taking it out, an old-fashioned throwdown just like the old days. Both men had a speech-like quality to their playing, and Sonny responded, attempting to bring it back to the minor pentatonic scale to lead into "Keep Hold of Yourself," punctuated with a growl. McLean was not having it, though, taking it back out, then back to the bebop language they had learned to speak together. They echoed each other, picking up on the other's phraseology, chewing it up and spitting it back out, as Sonny kept returning to "Keep Hold of Yourself" and McLean kept taking it further out. This went on for a full seven minutes as the audience began egging them on as the old sparring partners duked it out onstage in a pitched battle of brinksmanship. McLean began ascending to the top of the alto's range as Sonny played a descending pattern simultaneously. Now they were really speaking. The rhythm section finally came in and they played the head, but nothing could top the prelude. Gene Seymour called it "one of the most epochal dialogues between two master improvisers ever conducted on stage."[111] The Counts of Bop had become the Kings of Bop.

With the concert's climax coming unexpectedly at the halfway point, the night ended with an anticlimactic free-for-all on "St. Thomas" and then "Tenor Madness" that apparently did not live up to the rehearsal. But that interplay with Sonny and Jackie McLean was a moment to savor.[112]

Sonny was "The Last Jazz Immortal." This appeared, writ large on the front page of the January 1996 issue of the *Village Voice*, superimposed on a photo of Sonny playing hard, a bandanna on his head.[113] One fact in this major career retrospective surprised Sonny himself: he had been with Milestone for twenty-five years. To mark the relationship milestone, Sonny and Fantasy president Ralph Kaffel planned a compilation album: *Silver City: A Celebration of 25 Years on Milestone.*[114] The track list came straight from Gary Giddins's overview. "How's this for a critic's wet dream?" wrote Giddins in his introduction to the album. "Impatient with the flippant, glib, and ignorant dismissal of a quarter century of Sonny Rollins's finest work, you write an article suggesting his label compile a selection of milestone (to coin a phrase) performances, listing what you believe those performances to be."[115] And then it came to fruition.

The argument behind *Silver City* was explicit: Sonny's postsixties work deserved a major critical reappraisal. The prevailing notion among the purists was that the Milestone albums represented a twenty-five-year slump. Some had made a similar case, unfairly, against Louis Armstrong's later work after the genius of the Hot Fives and Sevens, but there was a subtlety and luminescence to be gleaned from late Louis and likewise from the later Sonny. Many of the albums were uneven, with one or two gems; in part, they never measured up to what Sonny could do on a stage. Fans who appreciated only the early work did not realize that on a good night, Sonny was playing as well as he ever had if not better. Yet the evidence was there for all to hear in the double CD's curated selections. Despite its attempt at bottled transcendence, though, *Silver City* could not make the case convincingly enough; freedom, as it turned out, could not be easily captured on record. "There's no way to capture what's happening right at the moment, which is what jazz is all about anyway—that creative spontaneous thing," Sonny said when the album came out.[116] Sonny would still have to prove himself night after night, forever chasing a fugitive sound.

Chapter 41

OLD FLAMES

(1997–2012)

In the late 1990s, Sonny became increasingly outspoken about politics, specifically consumerism, racism, and environmental destruction. He feared that if things did not change, the world was coming to an end.[1] He maintained a steady reading diet, mostly nonfiction: Ross Gelbspan's *The Heat Is On: The High Stakes Battle over Earth's Threatened Climate*, Sandra Steingraber's *Living Downstream: An Ecologist's Personal Investigation of Cancer and the Environment*, Bill McKibben's *Hope, Human and Wild: True Stories of Living Lightly on the Earth*, Benjamin DeMott's *The Trouble with Friendship:*

Why Americans Can't Think Straight About Race, Michael Parenti, Howard Zinn, a lot of Noam Chomsky.[2]

In interviews, Sonny spoke with a lacerating wit. What about Mayor Rudy Giuliani? "I think Giuliani's just another cheap politician," Sonny said. "He thinks that if he cracks down on minorities, it'll get him further up in the Republican Party. He also drives one of these gas-guzzling sport-utility vehicles, so you know that he has no environmental sense, and it's a tip-off that he has no sense about anything. I give him some credit for the drop in the crime rate, but that doesn't mean that I want to be harassed on the street because I'm black." The environment? "Right now, it's like we're on the Titanic, but everybody's just watching *Titanic*."[3]

He realized that the problem was endemic to capitalism. A model of infinite growth with finite resources was unsustainable. "Economic growth at 3%, a conventional standard, means that the economy doubles every quarter century," he wrote in a journal entry, "typically doubling society's use of raw materials expenditure of energy + generation of waste. Obviously this is a system existing as it were on borrowed time."[4] The circularity of his music flew in the face of the prevailing system.

Yet as erudite as Sonny was with the pen, he wanted to find a way to express his politics through the horn, as he wrote to Sigurd Raschèr in 1997.

> Every time I do interviews these days I try to bring up subjects such as the environment and the faith in consumerism which I see as the end of the world coming soon.... Very often music people are not sympathetic to the discussion of anything outside of their very narrow concerns but it is sheer folly to be living in the 1990's and not see what is going on around us! Pesticide ridden food, chemicalized air, toxic water—these are the result of greed and our reliability on technological answers to life's problems.[5]

Sonny acknowledged that aesthetics and politics were to a certain extent inseparable. Political beliefs, yoga, his reading material, a mostly vegetarian diet—it all went into his expression. "It's all music," he said, "because all these things are what comprise Sonny Rollins."[6]

In 1998, he was concerned enough about society's inaction on climate change, which he had already been studying for a decade, that he decided to release his first political concept album since *Freedom Suite*, forty years earlier. He thought of *Global Warming* as "my *Freedom Suite* of '98."[7] Sonny hoped his music would exemplify our collective interdependence. "We're destroying the planet. We are sawing the limb that we're sitting on."[8]

The album was recorded in two four-hour sessions on January 7 and February 8, 1998, at Clinton Studios.[9] The January session had stalwart bassist Bob Cranshaw, pianist Stephen Scott (who plays kalimba on the title track), and drummer Idris Muhammad, with whom Sonny had never played. For the February session Sonny added Clifton Anderson, used percussionist Victor See Yuen, and subbed drummer Perry Wilson for Muhammad. "Island Lady" was an old tune of Sonny's from *The Way I Feel*; Irving Berlin's "Change Partners" takes on a socially conscious double meaning. Four originals channeled his environmentalist credo—"Global Warming," "Mother Nature's Blues," "Clear-Cut Boogie," and "Echo-Side Blue." The title track retitled Sonny's "Kilauea." With its buoyant calypso feel and kalimba intro, it was meant to harmonize with nature. The doleful "Mother Nature's Blues" conveyed the message that the earth would keep on going around the sun with or without us in its own twelve-bar cycle. The ballad "Echo-Side Blue" was initially called "Ecocide Blue," "but I thought that might be a little bit too stark."[10] The album closes on "Clear-Cut Boogie" with a fade-out on an unresolved chord. The clear-cut situation called for an immediate response, but the title also suggested clear-cutting forests, and a grim pronouncement in Sonny's oaky voice: "And then there were no more."[11]

At the February session, something cosmic happened. "The first record I did with Sonny, man, was actually the most spiritual recording I had ever been a part of because I had an out-of-body experience," recalled Perry Wilson. "There was a point in the session where I literally could see myself. I was looking down on the room, and I'm looking at everybody, and the feeling that I had was that I better hurry up and get back in my body, otherwise I wouldn't be able to. At the time, when I went home after the session, my girlfriend told me I went to sleep for two days."[12]

Wilson was a recent addition to Sonny's working band. He had played with Stanley Clarke, the Crusaders, the Temptations, and Patrice Rushen and moved to New York from Los Angeles, where he began working with Cassandra Wilson. Sonny saw Perry's jitters on his first gig with the band and said, "Just go with me." He went with him for four and a half years. Sonny jelled with Wilson because he not only grew up in the musical melting pot of Chicago but was also not afraid to "just swing." And Wilson loved Sonny and Lucille; every Christmas, they bought him round-trip tickets to go back to Chicago to see his children. Likewise, Sonny looked out for his saxophone fraternity. Clifford Brown's nephew Rayford Griffin might come backstage or Coltrane's cousin Mary. "Michael Brecker was a bad motherfucker, but he knew," said Wilson. "One time, I remember him coming to the dressing room and sitting with Sonny for a while. Joe Lovano, occasionally we'd see him. What I loved about playing with Sonny was that all of the cats that played saxophone *knew* and they understood and they paid homage and they respected him and they would come see him and support him. What I really liked about the jazz community was that it was a mutual admiration society."[13]

To Wilson, Sonny's ability to communicate was a result of the "endless vocabulary" that allowed him to connect with audiences and musicians of all generations without ever resorting to gimmicks. Of course, there was also the legendary work ethic. "It was not uncommon for Sonny to play until his gums bled," Wilson said. "He played till his mouth was bleeding and then kept going, and then played the next night."

To Wilson, the experience of playing with Sonny represented the most radical freedom of his life. "Brothers from my generation, we cannot fathom what Jim Crow was like," he said. "Guys like Sonny and Bob [Cranshaw], for them to have lived through that, man, and still be as optimistic about life and still always feel compelled to educate a guy from my generation and bring us along and make us understand some responsibilities that we have with this music, and all that it had done to bring our people, black people in particular, out of, not necessarily poverty, but to bring them a sense of hope, is really the perfect expression," he said, "because on the bandstand is actually the freest place a black man in America can be."

As the turn of the century approached, Sonny grew increasingly wary of technological advances, none of which in his view led to greater freedom. He was a bit of a Luddite; Lucille handled email correspondence.[14] Sonny may have sent the rare fax and listened to the radio obsessively, but otherwise avoided television and the Internet. He was more concerned with the lack of progress in achieving much older ideals, which he wrote about in his ever-present legal pad. "We will soon be entering the year 2000, the new century! The old century has produced for us many scientific and technological tools. But are we living together any better? Our world is still full of hatred, fear, + suffering. What good is science if it is used to kill people and animals and to pollute our planet?"[15]

On May 8–9 and July 29, 2000, Sonny recorded *This Is What I Do* at Clinton Studios. He hired Cranshaw, Clifton Anderson, Stephen Scott, and, alternating on drums, Jack DeJohnette and Perry Wilson. Photographer John Abbott, with whom Sonny would have a twenty-five-year professional relationship, shot the cover image. "I have never taken a bad photograph of Sonny—and I credit Sonny—he has an outer beauty as well as an inner beauty," Abbott wrote.[16] Sonny recorded three songs from the classical Hollywood cinema he loved: "Sweet Leilani" from the 1937 film *Waikiki Wedding* and "Moon of Manakoora," sung by Dorothy Lamour in the 1937 film *The Hurricane*. "A Nightingale Sang in Berkeley Square" was recorded by Bing Crosby in 1940. In fact, Crosby had recorded all three.[17] Complementing this youthful nostalgia were three originals, "Charles M.," for Mingus, featuring a rare bass solo from Bob Cranshaw; the samba-laced calypso "Salvador"; and "Did You See Harold Vick?" Of his funky tribute to the late unsung tenor saxophonist, Sonny said, "I wrote this song actually thinking of a friend of mine who many years ago was coming out of Minton's, where Harold had been playing. So this guy was standing outside the club and he said, 'Did you hear *Harold Vick*?!' I tried to get the cadence of his speech into the song."[18]

For *This Is What I Do*, in 2001, Sonny won a long-overdue Grammy for Best Jazz Instrumental Album, his first win in any category.

With Sonny now seventy, Sonny and Lucille reduced his performance calendar to only forty concerts a year, and his legendary practice routine had shrunk to two to three hours a day, but he continued searching for that lost chord. "I know I'll never be satisfied," he said in March 2001. "I just want to get a little closer to some of the things I'm practicing, you know, some of the things that jazz will allow you to do if you can get a little more mastery of it."[19]

Between 2000 and 2001, so many of Sonny's friends, collaborators, and contemporaries passed on it would be difficult to name them all: Tommy Flanagan, Sigurd Raschèr, Randi Hultin, Buddy Tate, Joe Henderson, Stanley Turrentine, John Lewis, among others. It was getting lonelier out there, but Sonny could still find communion on the bandstand. To properly honor their legacy, Sonny would never retire—"I don't play golf."[20]

Yet 2001 would make perseverance difficult. On Tuesday, September 11, Sonny was six blocks from the World Trade Center in his thirty-ninth-floor apartment at 310 Greenwich Street, getting ready for a day of practice and running errands. Most people saw the image; for Sonny, it started as a sound—American Airlines Flight 11 passing overhead. "Then I heard a big 'POW!' "[21] he recalled. He looked out on the Hudson to see if a plane had crash-landed, but there was no sign of disturbance. Then he switched on his black-and-white television as Flight 175 crashed into the South Tower.

In a state of shock, Sonny went downstairs to survey the scene around Ground Zero. "The streets were bedlam, women running around screaming. When the South Tower came down, we started to run because we thought it would take everybody if it fell over. Since it imploded on itself, that didn't happen, but a tremendous amount of toxic dust filled the air."

He immediately returned to his apartment, called Lucille in Germantown, and did the only thing he could think of—he started practicing. Quickly, the power was shut off, but Sonny never needed electricity to keep the music going.

By 2:30 p.m. that day, Lucille had already lost contact with Sonny. "I'm out of touch with S. today—keep getting circuits busy recordings—which in a way is not too surprising. Hopefully we'll get him out of the city tomorrow," she wrote a friend by email.[22]

Sonny was stuck in the apartment until the next night, when the National Guard came to evacuate him and three other stranded residents. Without power, Sonny had to walk down thirty-nine flights of stairs. He grabbed a flashlight and his tenor.

As Sonny boarded an evacuation bus, he was caught on camera by CNN's Jason Bellini. One neighbor had left her cancer medication behind. "Most of her neighbors took the first things that came to mind," said Bellini.[23]

"Wherever I go, this goes with me," said Sonny, clutching his saxophone.

"Wherever you go, this goes with you?"[24]

"That's Sonny Rollins," said another neighbor, "one of the top jazz saxophonists in the world!"

The evacuation bus took them to the makeshift shelter at Washington Irving High School by Union Square. "It was like a scene from a World War II movie about the London Blitzkrieg, where the place has been bombed, everybody's out, and the sirens are going off," Sonny recalled. "There were so many ambulances, firefighters going into [Washington Irving High School] for oxygen and new guys coming out. Everybody had to put on masks because the air was acrid with toxicity."[25]

From the shelter, Sonny had a car service pick him up and take him to Germantown.

After being reunited with Lucille, she wrote an email to a friend on September 13:

> HE IS HOME—AS OF ABOUT 2 A.M.—HALLELUJAH. WE'LL BE DRIVING TO BOSTON TOMORROW—HOPE YOU GUYS ARE O.K. TOO—IT WAS QUITE AN EXPERIENCE (POWER AND PHONE HAD BEEN OUT FOR 24 HOURS AND THEY HAD TO WALK DOWN 39 FLTS. AND THE NATIONAL GUARD TAKE THEM OUT OF THE AREA, ETC. BUT THINGS LOOK BETTER TO ME TODAY.[26]

They were going to Boston for a concert on September 15, and as a "reluctant troubadour,"[27] Sonny decided that the show must go on. It was not clear initially if the show would be canceled. "Within days, I'm saying forty-eight hours, everything that he had booked for the next year was canceled. Not postponed—it was canceled," recalled Perry Wilson. "Lucille said, 'I don't want you to panic. We've got deposits for over 50 percent of the gigs, so we'll pretty much be okay for some of it, but just bear with us.' He had a gig that

Saturday in Boston and we didn't think we were gonna do it." Flights 11 and 175 originated at Logan Airport in Boston, making it seem even riskier.

Sonny credited Lucille for realizing the symbolic significance of the concert. "Lucille was right, because there's no point in my just stewing in my own juice, so to speak, during that time, and be all messed up in thinking about this thing that just happened," Sonny said. "It *was* the best thing to do it, and besides that, it was beneficial to some people to hear us playing right after that incident. It was inspirational. My wife opened my eyes. I said, 'Okay, she's right,' and if I was thinking clearly, I would have realized that it was my opportunity to do something right, which was the concert, instead of thinking about myself—what a bad situation I was in and how I was put upon and all this stuff. Instead of thinking like that, I should do something for other people."[28]

Despite misgivings, the decision to perform was unanimous.[29] "We all felt like the best thing to do was to play. We needed to play for our spirits," Wilson said. "I'm glad we did that gig, because we needed that. We *all* needed that. And man, he played his ass off. He played his *ass* off."[30]

Fenton Hollander booked the concert at the 1,215-seat Berklee Performance Center in Boston. "I said, 'My take on it is we cancel, they win,'" Hollander recalled, holding back tears. "Announcing it, I was like this, because I was so impressed that he had done it. I was better than this—I covered it—but my wife knew. She said, 'You almost lost it there, didn't you?'" Only one person called to cancel. "People came, and they were buoyed by the fact that it went on."[31]

That Saturday night, Sonny walked onstage with a slight limp. He had just turned seventy-one the previous week. "My legs were wobbly and I was mentally disjointed," he said.[32] Onstage, he started speaking about the first song: "Without a Song." "It's very appropriate at this time. Of course, it's appropriate in my life every day, but I think everybody feels this way," he said.

I only know there ain't no love at all
Without a song

When he started playing the first bars, the years fell off him; it was 1959 again, and Bob Cranshaw still caught the key change. Sonny gave one of the most inspired performances of his career; he knew he had to.

Sonny's spirits were lifted by the audience and also his band, Scott, Anderson, Cranshaw, Wilson, and Afro-diasporic percussionist Kimati Dinizulu, whom he hired earlier that year.[33] That night, at the end of the first set, Dinizulu, Wilson, and Sonny played off each other for the last fifteen minutes of a twenty-one-minute "Global Warming" with an indomitable sense of rhythm.

"Yes, ladies and gentlemen, we're here tonight, and we must remember that music is one of the beautiful things of life, so we have to try to keep the music alive some kind of way," Sonny said at the end of the first set. "Maybe music can help. I don't know. But we have to try something these days, right?" At the end of the concert, Sonny played a moving five-minute cadenza spanning his career from "St. Thomas" to "To a Wild Rose," and it was more of an effort than anyone quite realized. He had breathed all of that toxic debris into his lungs, but playing this concert was part of his karma yoga. Such a momentous rebuke of terrorism and affirmation of survival could end only one way—with "Don't Stop the Carnival."[34]

A recording of the performance would eventually be edited and released as *Without a Song: The 9/11 Concert*. "That record is not indicative of the concert itself, 'cause we did two sets," said Perry Wilson. "At the time I played with Sonny, he was only contracted to play seventy minutes of music per night, but we never played seventy minutes of music." That night in Boston, each set was nearly eighty minutes; with a brief intermission, the whole concert was three hours long. Sonny would play until he had left it all on the stage.

It was recorded surreptitiously by Carl Smith, a lifelong jazz fan and Harvard graduate who had written a book on Bud Powell but had only in his early sixties become a Sonny convert. "I was never a particular Sonny Rollins fan until I heard him play live in 2000 for the first time," Smith recalled.[35] What he had heard on Sonny's recent records could not compare to what he heard that night. "Five minutes into the concert I was absolutely transfixed," Smith said. "I turned to the guy next to me and said, 'We are in the presence of greatness.' And I meant not past greatness. What I was hearing then, in the year 2000, was beyond what I had ever heard before. It was truly a life-changing experience. I went home from that concert as if I had stumbled upon a continent nobody knew about."[36]

Smith hoped to persuade Sonny's harshest skeptics, convinced of a decades-long slump, that Sonny was still at the peak of his powers. Most musicians, Smith explained, "only go for doubles. Sonny wants to hit a grand slam every single time. So he strikes out. He didn't care if his concert was a flop because he was always seeking to find that spectacular moment when he could just hit it out of the park." To document those moments, Smith began collecting every concert recording he could find through a global network of enthusiasts, eventually amassing more than 450 tapes dating back to the 1950 jam session at Seymour's in Chicago, with Sonny on alto.[37]

However, Smith's main ambition was to secretly record Sonny in the present. "People who tried to record a concert were thrown out. I saw it happen," Smith said. He had never made a professional recording before, but as the co-owner of Maine-based high-end audio company Transparent Audio, he was in the right business. "I spent six months developing a secret recording system with tiny state-of-the-art micro-microphones sewn into my shirt in the shoulders and a small DAT recorder," Smith said. He bought second-row tickets to create some cover and had his friends sit on either side of him, instructing them not to applaud. It turned out the second row was still slightly in front of the speakers, "so my microphones captured the live sound of the instruments rather than the amplified sound."[38] That night, Sonny hit it out of the park.

Ironically, the biggest hurdle to Smith's quest to redeem Sonny's late-career legacy turned out to be Sonny and Lucille themselves. When Lucille discovered Smith's handiwork, she was irate and told him that she would have concert security staff on high alert if he ever tried it again. She didn't even want Sonny recording his own concerts and assumed that Smith was just another exploiter in a long line of unscrupulous characters.[39] After Stanley Crouch caught wind of Smith's staggering performance archive, Smith asked if Crouch could somehow prevail upon Sonny and Lucille to at least listen to the tape. Crouch had no such luck. "The idea of someone like you doing this for any reason other than profit for yourself," Crouch told Smith, "is the same as my telling them that I have a martian in my office that I want them to talk to."[40] Lucille put a stop to Smith's project; there was simply "no such thing as a good 'bootlegger.'"[41]

In the wake of the tragedy of 9/11, Sonny was dealt another blow several months later when Lucille suffered a stroke in February 2002.[42] Sonny took care of her while she recovered. They were devoted to each other and continued writing love letters and sending cards on birthdays and holidays. To Sonny, "Love=Lucille=Love." He was just "that guy that you married."[43] They never saw eye to eye on politics, but even when they were at a gas-station rest stop on tour, they would get off the tour bus holding hands.[44]

Lucille didn't want Sonny to retire, and definitely not on her account. Her unwavering support for his artistry and career was foundational to their relationship, as Lucille explained in an earlier undated letter to Sonny written while recovering from another physical ailment. She was inspired after watching televangelist Tammy Faye Messner.

> Playing like you do (or like any genius, of whom there are few) is not completely technical—your aforementioned strength comes through in your playing—without the trials you have had you would not have that kind of strength—it doesn't come with getting everything with no obstacles. Maybe it isn't fair—but it's the way it is—and you must have faith that God meant it to be that way.
>
> I sound like Tammy or Rev Ev. (I'm even weeping like Tammy as I type this).
>
> The reason I'm telling you about how I'm feeling (I've had 3 constant days of barely being able to walk, not going past Germantown, trying to be very peaceful and get a lot of rest—but the pain involved prevents the rest) is not so you'll say, oh, poor Lucille. It's to say I believe I'm being given this to let me appreciate—for a long time I've felt that things have just been too good, I have you, whom I love, adore, worship—and not so incidentally separately have respect, admiration, awe for your talent. So in trials, why didn't He give you this—because (I believe) in His wisdom He knows that you must use your fingers, your arms, your legs—if I did what you do that wouldn't be possible right now—and so consequently maybe He's letting me take over this to "teach" and "advise" us both. Also, He knows, since he gave it to you, that your talent is such a unique and special gift that he won't take away your ability to play. That is why I think He has time after time

given you the warnings, the pain, the everything with your teeth—but somehow has managed to leave you enough to do what you must do.[45]

So Sonny continued touring, albeit in a limited capacity. With Lucille unable to maintain her previous duties as road manager, Sonny had help from veteran audio engineer and trumpeter Peter Downey, Sonny's tour manager starting in 1999.[46] Downey specialized in audio equipment and live mixing, but he managed the kitchen sink: hotels, flights, merchandise, and procuring Sonny his first wireless mike. "He became like a grandfather-type figure, so I wanted to look out for him," Downey said.[47] Yet Sonny looked out for Downey just as much—they talked about everything from Eastern religion to the importance of sobriety to Sonny's beloved Mets (he abandoned the Yankees when they became too "mercenary").[48] "There are so many things that I learned. I would go back to the hotel with him at the end of the night, and the rest of the guys would go to their rooms, and the crew would clean up their gear, and I would sit in his hotel room, and it was like 'Alright, I'm leaving, see you later...' Three hours later, sitting there listening to him go off on these intelligent tangents of the meaning of life and everything else. It was amazing."[49]

Sometimes they would talk about music, and Sonny's fabled search for the lost chord. "He always said that he could never get there.... He couldn't figure out what it was that was holding him back," Downey said. "And I'm like, 'What you played last night was genius! You can't get there? Where the hell is here?' That went on for years, and then one day, he said, 'I think I know where I'm going.' "[50]

In the early 2000s, Sonny began working again with drummer Steve Jordan, who immediately noticed that Sonny lived entirely in the present. "He's not a nostalgic person. It was a twenty-five-year span of playing with him before he played 'Tenor Madness,'" Jordan recalled. "He's never gonna lay back on his laurels. He's always moving forward—trying to get better, trying to get over the plateau, and that's really the biggest lesson I can think of."[51] Sonny would not rest, not even after winning a Lifetime Achievement Award at the 2004 Grammy Awards.[52]

That year, despite debilitating back pain, Lucille was resilient enough to produce Sonny's next album, just as Milestone was in the process of being acquired by Concord. Sonny hired his current working band: Cranshaw, Anderson, Jordan, and Dinizulu. The recording took place at Clinton Studios in New York over two six-hour sessions at the end of September 2004, with plans for Lucille to spend two days mixing in October. Sonny and Lucille stayed at the Four Seasons during recording; they had given up their apartment that year, after spending increasingly less time in the city in the wake of 9/11 and Lucille's stroke.[53]

Lucille and engineer Troy Halderson spent two six-hour days mixing as planned, and by early October the album was "in finished order ready to manufacture and should not be tampered with," Lucille wrote. "Think we are pleased with the results and hope everyone will feel the same." She then went back once more in late October to mix "I'll Look Around," a song Billie Holiday recorded in 1946. Sonny dedicated the CD to their dog Miko.[54] Yet the project would never materialize.

On November 27, 2004, only a month after finishing work on the record, Lucille passed away at their home in Germantown at the age of seventy-six.[55]

Sonny was devastated. Lucille was his rock. Every night, she turned on the porch light to light his way from the studio. "I came out here a few times," Sonny said, "and then I looked, and there was no light on the porch. It just kind of highlighted that, well, there's nobody there now."[56] He gradually stopped using the studio; he practiced in the house with Miko.

"I grieved for a long time," Sonny said the following year. "I'm still grieving because it hasn't been that long. After she left me here, I couldn't play for a long time, man. I took my horn out and tried to play a little bit, a few minutes at a time. Gradually, as I began to accept engagements again, I got back to practicing a little more.... We lived together a long time. I'm laying on the bed my wife died in, and she was right next to me, and I was trying to do things for her, and I'm still here."[57]

Sonny and Lucille had carved out what Sonny thought of as "a perfect existence," with Lucille managing their business affairs, leaving Sonny to focus entirely on music and ideas.[58] Sonny had to step into the role his wife had occupied for nearly thirty-five years. Sonny didn't own a cell phone or use email. Not many people ever pictured the Saxophone Colossus looming over a fax machine while he waited for the spin cycle to finish.[59] To manage his ongoing career, Sonny enlisted help from trusted longtime colleagues. Clifton Anderson became his right-hand man; Peter Downey was tour manager; Terri Hinte, for years the director of publicity at Fantasy, managed PR; Bret Primack launched Sonny's personal website; and Ted Kurland continued national and international bookings. Sonny would collaborate on all aspects; he even entered the dreaded mixing booth.

When Lucille passed, Sonny owed Milestone one more album to satisfy his contract, but, still grieving, he decided to shelve the unfinished 2004 studio project.[60] It was then that Richard Corsello contacted Carl Smith. In August 2004, Gary Giddins had written a column in *JazzTimes* on Smith, arguing that his collection served as a corrective, preserving "the revelatory power of a matchless artist at his peak."[61] Lucille was furious, but in the wake of her passing, Giddins and Stanley Crouch helped convince Sonny that Smith had no interest in taking advantage of him.[62] "Lucille was adamant about shutting that door and keeping it shut," said Terri Hinte, "and Sonny was not."[63]

Nearly four years after the fact, Sonny finally agreed to listen to Smith's tape from the Berklee Performance Center. He described the experience of listening to the concert as "like Abu Ghraib," but he hoped the public would have a different reaction.[64] When *Without a Song: The 9/11 Concert* was released in 2005, it won a Grammy Award for Best Jazz Instrumental Solo for "Why Was I Born?"

With his Milestone contract fulfilled and the label brought under the umbrella of Concord, Sonny did not renew. Instead, he launched his own label, Doxy Records, and his own merchandising and concert production company, Oleo Productions.[65] Under the Doxy banner, Sonny would release a series of albums, new and archival, in addition to *Sonny Rollins in Vienne*, a DVD of his summer 2006 performance for an audience of more than seven thousand, and also produce several large-scale concerts. Though Doxy would eventually be distributed by Universal Music Group and Sony, Sonny's label operated independently, and initially they did not make a distribution deal, selling CDs only at concerts and on Sonny's website. It was the logical next step in a career marked by artistic self-determination. "The record business is sort of going in that direction now," Sonny explained. "I've been out here a long time. People know me. The jazz fans that know me, that buy my stuff—they're probably going to buy it anyway. So I just figured, why don't I have my own company and try to bring some of that money for myself?"[66]

At the end of 2005, following a Japanese tour, Sonny began recording *Sonny, Please*, his first album under the Doxy label. At seventy-five, Sonny recalled, "Towards the end of the tour, the group really began to come together. I began to be able to play much more fluently and my mind was getting clear and my focus was getting clear and the band was beginning to jell. The whole thing was beginning to happen."[67]

The album was recorded over five sessions between December 2005 and February 2006 at Carriage House Studios in Stamford, Connecticut.[68] Sonny used his touring band from Japan: Cranshaw, Anderson, Broom, Dinizulu, and Jordan, with drummer Joe Corsello, Richard's brother, who played on "Serenade" by Riccardo Drigo. "Serenade" reached back to Sonny's childhood and the halcyon days of radio; it was the theme song to *When a Girl Marries*. Noël Coward's "Someday I'll Find You," which Sonny also recorded on *Freedom Suite*, was the theme song to *Mr. Keen, Tracer of Lost Persons*. Sonny's calypso "Park Palace Parade" conjured the Park Palace Ballroom, where he attended calypso dances as a child with his mother. "Remembering Tommy" was a tribute to the late Tommy Flanagan, and "Nishi" was a blues dedicated to Osaka-based bassist, jazz promoter, and educator Mitsuru Nishiyama. The title track, "Sonny, Please," was dedicated to Lucille, whose spirit infused the album. "He used to come off and get upset about the audience," recalled Peter Downey. " 'Oh, they had to pay to listen to that?' Lucille would always say, 'Sonny, please!' So that became the name of the record."[69]

Drummer Joe Corsello never expected to get an opportunity to join Sonny's band, but the opportunity presented itself in January 2006 when Richard Corsello told him that Steve Jordan was going on tour with Eric Clapton and Sonny was auditioning drummers.[70] "Talking to him, I just felt like I knew him my whole life, and he just kind of took me under his wing, like a member of the family," Corsello said.[71]

Sonny worked with other drummers, among them Victor Lewis, Jerome Jennings, and Willie Jones III. "Sometimes you can be oversold when you hear stories about certain legendary musicians," Jones said. "Maybe they don't play quite the same. But in 2007, he was still playing. The stamina, the vocabulary, everything. So I was on my toes."[72]

In the fall of 2006, Sonny began working with Chicago-born drummer Kobie Watkins, who was recommended to him by Bobby Broom. "He wanted African feel, which is based in a deep groove," Watkins recalled. "He was trying to take it away from...'You take a solo, then you take a solo. Now you take a solo.' How about everybody soloing together? Music is a conversation."[73]

As Sonny remained fiercely in the present, accolades honoring his past followed. In June 2006, he was inducted into the Academy of Achievement.[74] On May 21, 2007, Sonny traveled to Stockholm, where he was awarded the Polar Music Prize, a Swedish international award given out annually to one contemporary and one classical musician; Sonny won alongside Steve Reich. Eagle-Eye Cherry, the Swedish son of Don and Moki Cherry, announced the award, which was bestowed by King Carl XVI Gustaf of Sweden. By the end of his career, Sonny received ten honorary doctorates, the Austrian Cross of Honour for Science and Art, an Edward MacDowell Medal, and a National Medal of Arts; was inducted into the American Academy of Arts and Sciences; and received numerous other accolades. As honored as he was, though, Sonny was adamant that what he later referred to as "this victory-lap, lifetime-achievement crap" did not make him a relic. "No, man. I haven't been out here all these years for them to stick me in a museum. They can take me out and shoot me before I'll allow myself to be some oldies act."[75]

On September 18, 2007, to celebrate the fiftieth anniversary of his Carnegie Hall debut, Sonny organized a concert at Carnegie Hall that would replicate the program from his 1957 show.[76] It was a rare return to the piano-less trio format he defined five decades earlier. Sonny arranged a reunion with drummer Roy Haynes, rounding out the trio with thirty-five-year-old bassist Christian McBride. The program consisted of "Sonnymoon for Two," "Some Enchanted Evening," and "Moritat."

McBride had never formally met Sonny until he got the call.[77] Two days before the concert, Sonny called a rehearsal at SIR Studios in Manhattan for just the two of them so they could work out material and Sonny could hear McBride's "beat center." The rehearsal was scheduled for 1 to 3 p.m., so McBride showed up forty-five minutes early to be safe. He found Sonny already there, hunched over some manuscript paper. "I said, 'Mr. Rollins, I'm so sorry I'm late. I thought I was supposed to be here at 1.' He said, 'You were, don't worry. You're early.' "[78]

McBride looked at the patterns and rudiments scratched out on Sonny's paper. "I said, 'Well, what are you doing here?' He said, 'Well, I just wanted to come here and practice.' I thought, 'Wow, that's intense, man.' And he had all of this manuscript paper laid out and I said, 'What are you practicing?' He said, 'I've just got some scales I'm checking out and some modes, just some different kinds of things to keep me sharp.' And at that point, I remember thinking—'None of us—none of us have any excuse for the rest of our careers not to practice that intensely.' I know all of us have different demands in life, but you've got to make some time for that. If the world's greatest living jazz improviser can decide 'I need to take an hour or four to get these scales together,' then what's everybody else's excuse?"[79]

The next day, the trio convened for a rehearsal at Avatar Studios. McBride was overwhelmed by the weight of history; Sonny had just turned seventy-seven; Haynes was eighty-two. "Damn. The mob!" McBride exclaimed.[80]

"Sugar Hill, man," Haynes said, waxing nostalgic. "Me and Sonny Rollins, from Sugar Hill. Shit."

"The Hill!" said Sonny. "You dig?"

McBride was about to become an honorary member of the Sugar Hill Gang. Haynes called it "Sonnymoon for Three."

Sonny and Roy Haynes had not played together since the Five Spot with Monk's quartet in 1958, but their relationship was as tight as it was then. When Haynes looked at Sonny, he saw the same young kid who knocked on his door in 1947 and later recorded with him on Bud Powell's "Dance of the Infidels" and Miles Davis's "Morpheus." Sonny heard that same vertiginous snap-crackle on the drums.[81]

Sonny was deeply moved by the experience. "I've played with Roy from the beginning of my career," he said. "We speak the same language. We understand each other."[82]

"Mmm...That is really something," Haynes replied. "We're talking, man, and even when it's silent, there is some shit going on."

At the concert, the emcee was Sonny's childhood friend Gil Noble, who had gone on to host the weekly television talk show *Like It Is*. When Sonny came out, he got a standing ovation.

"Thank you for coming out to celebrate the fiftieth anniversary of one day in the life of one man that you know," Sonny said from the stage.[83] Sonny displaced the time in a way he had not done fifty years earlier; the group interplay was more intense and speechlike, particularly on a restrained "Some Enchanted Evening," on which Sonny spoke through the silences. It wasn't better than 1957, but different; there were fifty years of constant change there.

"I've always felt that many jazz improvisers are much too legato," said McBride. "There's no emphasis on the long, short, and medium-length notes. And Sonny always addresses all three every time he plays a phrase. When you have that sort of rhythmic sharpness, I really think it separates the good improvisers from the great improvisers."[84]

Sonny and his team recorded the concert and planned to release it on Doxy alongside the 1957 recording with Wendell Marshall and Kenny Dennis—jazz as artistic evolution. Blue Note had considerable success with the 2005 release of *Thelonious Monk Quartet with John Coltrane at Carnegie Hall*, recorded at the same 1957 concert. However, after hearing the tape from the 2007 concert, Sonny abandoned the idea. The recording did not meet his standard.[85]

For McBride, that one night imparted a lifetime of lessons from his elders. "I do know that he confirmed what I already believe, in that you are a lifelong student," he said.[86]

At this time, Sonny began working on a new archival release culled from Carl Smith's collection. First, though, Smith had to earn Sonny's trust. As Sonny explained to him, "he still couldn't count on being able to hail a cab in NYC." Smith established his integrity, and soon he was "sitting alone with Sonny in his studio behind his modest Germantown home for a couple of hours while Sonny took notes on a yellow legal pad."[87]

The collaboration yielded the first of four volumes in the *Road Shows* series—compilation albums of previously unreleased live tapes, all released on Doxy, in 2008, 2011, 2014, and 2016, with material drawn from the Carl

Smith Collection dating from 1979 to new recordings from Sonny's ongoing tours. To keep the series current, Sonny brought audio engineer Richard Corsello on tour. "That's the best way to work with Sonny, is to not lock him up in a room and tell him to go ahead and play," Corsello said. "It's just being able to go back and listen to a month or three months' worth of performances and pick out the best one."[88]

Yet what Sonny described as the "torture" of locking himself in a room and listening to his own less-than-perfect performances was often tantamount to being locked in the studio. "When you're hoping you're really going to sound great and you listen and you get sort of dashed, it can get discouraging," Sonny said. "Hopefully I'll be able to do something better than that in the future."[89]

In the spring of 2010, Sonny told his new guitarist Russell Malone that he needed a hip replacement, but he refused the surgery because "he didn't want to deal with the recuperative process," Malone recalled. "But you know what, man? He'd get up on that bandstand and wear everybody out. Bob Cranshaw had been listening to Sonny forever, but there would be some nights, man, Bob would have that look on his face like, 'What the heck did I just hear?' He'd be smiling." Once, Malone asked Sonny if there was anything he could do to improve as a musician. "Sonny's not one of those kinds of guys who would give you a technical answer. The old-timers don't do that. But what he told me, he said, 'Keep your karma clean. Don't steal from anybody, treat people right.' I never forgot that."[90]

It was in this spirit that Sonny planned his eightieth birthday concert at the Beacon Theatre on Friday, September 10, 2010.[91] Sonny had not played at the Beacon since 1995, when he hosted the historic Sugar Hill reunion. They had all since passed on. His older sister, Gloria Anderson, Clifton's mother, had passed away in June 2008. The concert was as much a celebration of their lives and legacies as it was a celebration of Sonny's.[92]

At the Beacon, Sonny split emcee duties with Stanley Crouch, who in 2005 had written a *New Yorker* profile of Sonny.[93] Sonny hobbled onstage with his shock of white hair, shades, flowing white beard and white shirt, black pocket square, ascot, and slacks. One critic described him earlier that year as "Methuselah in sunglasses."[94] But when the mouthpiece touched his lips, Sonny was God.

Backed by his working band—Cranshaw, Russell Malone, Kobie Watkins, and Sammy Figueroa—Sonny began the night with "Patanjali," a modal tune inspired by the father of modern yoga. Next came "Global Warming."

"In the world of jazz, people are not doing it by themselves," Sonny told the crowd. "There's a higher force that takes people and picks people and says, 'You are the one.'" Out came Hargrove, who joined Sonny for "I Can't Get Started," which Sonny had played on *A Night at the Village Vanguard*, and "Rain Check," from *Work Time*. Then Jim Hall joined them for "In a Sentimental Mood," from *Sonny Rollins with the Modern Jazz Quartet*, and "If Ever I Would Leave You," from *What's New*. Then Sonny brought out Christian McBride and Roy Haynes for a reunion of their 2007 trio. They started with "Solitude" from *Way Out West*, then "Sonnymoon for Two."

It was then that the big surprise of the night came. Sonny played a series of sparse, Monkish blues choruses, as though he was waiting for the muse to visit. And he was.

"Ladies and gentlemen, somebody told me that there's somebody in the house that is going to say happy birthday to me...and he's someplace backstage, and he's got a horn. And I wish he'd come out now. He's here. He's here!" No one there, not even Sonny, knew if anyone was truly going to come out. The song had been going for eight minutes. But then, Ornette Coleman walked onstage. Sonny had not played with Ornette since 1957 when he made *Way Out West*. Sonny was eighty, Ornette had turned eighty-five months earlier, but they had *never* played together onstage.

"I was standing backstage," recalled Russell Malone. "Ornette was scared to go out there. You heard how great Sonny was playing that night. Ornette's son Denardo and maybe another person, they were trying to get Ornette to go out there, and he was literally frightened. Imagine you've got a dog who's scared to go into the pool. It was like they were trying to push this dog into the pool, and the dog was resisting."[95]

Ornette came out in his fedora and suit, cracking a half smile as Sonny kept playing. He bowed and shook Sonny's hand, and Sonny could hardly contain his jubilation. There was a tinge of that big Texas blues sound in Ornette, but he then took the blues out into something else, and McBride and Haynes followed him.

"Yeah, baby!" Sonny exclaimed at the end of Ornette's solo. And then Sonny ventured out along the path Ornette had paved that had led to *Our Man in Jazz*. Suddenly, they were back in Malibu in '57. Over a twenty-one-minute version of "Sonnymoon," these two saxophone giants played until they had resolved whatever tension remained between them from the hurtful remark Ornette had made in the *New York Times* nearly two decades earlier. Some conversations are best had through music.[96]

At the end, Sonny turned to Ornette. "I love you, man," he said. "I love you, man."

The concert ended in an encore with everyone playing "St. Thomas." It had been fifty-four years since Sonny recorded *Saxophone Colossus* in Rudy Van Gelder's living room, but it seemed like just yesterday.

After the concert, Sonny truly felt they had buried the hatchet. "I'm glad that we could make up," Sonny said. "After we played, we were there in the dressing room . . . and we were talking about life. It was great."[97]

Sonny was awarded the National Medal of Arts, presented by President Barack Obama on March 2, 2011. During the ceremony, Obama said that he still had "these old records where they were still vinyl, Sonny—before they went digital—that helped inspire me or get me through a tough day or take risks that I might not otherwise have taken. . . . The fact is that works of art, literature, works of history, they speak to our condition and they affirm our desire for something more and something better."[98]

"I'm very happy that jazz, the greatest American music, is being recognized through this honor, and I'm grateful to accept this award on behalf of the gods of our music," Sonny said.[99] To have the first black president stand in the East Room of the White House and explain that Sonny's music inspired his own fight for freedom fulfilled the dream of "The Freedom Suite."

That year, Sonny was named a recipient of the Kennedy Center Honors alongside Barbara Cook, Neil Diamond, Meryl Streep, and Yo-Yo Ma. On December 3, 2011, Hillary Clinton hosted the Kennedy Center Honors State Dinner. Bill Clinton made a toast to his childhood idol:

I discovered Sonny Rollins when I was about fifteen or sixteen—about fifty years ago. I loved jazz, and I fancied that someday I might be good enough to do it. And I bought my first Sonny Rollins LP. I listened and listened—I listened the grooves off of it. I subscribed to *Down Beat* magazine and I kept thinking: if I read every edition, sooner or later I will find one article that will explain to me what in the hell I just heard.

...At eighty-one, he told me tonight, he said "I still practice every day." Every day. I said, "I love that eightieth birthday gig at the Beacon." He said, "I wasn't very good."[100]

Sonny used this official recognition to continue advocating for social justice. Two months later, he wrote to former president Clinton, announcing his plans for the Sonny Rollins Foundation and asking him to sit on the board of directors.[101] Sonny's foundation did not come to fruition immediately, though. In 2017, he endowed the Oberlin Conservatory of Music Sonny Rollins Jazz Ensemble Fund.[102] Oberlin, Ohio, was an important stop on the Underground Railroad, and the school became one of the first integrated colleges; Will Marion Cook studied violin there in the 1880s. The audition-only "Sonny Ensemble" was conceived to perpetuate Sonny's legacy of altruism. Each ensemble member would be entered into the "Sonny Scholar Ledger," with Sonny's signature first. The ledger cover displays a Rollins maxim: "Trust that later on in life, there's something bigger for you when you serve others."[103] In 2022, he began work on the Sonny Rollins Freedom Suite, a nonprofit organization dedicated to the principle that leading an ethical life according to the Golden Rule is central to playing *real* music. "You have to be *real*, and music is real, and ethical behavior is real," Sonny said.[104]

Following the Kennedy Center Honors, Sonny also wrote Michelle Obama a heartfelt letter in defense of the NEA Jazz Masters program, which was planned to be eliminated after 2012.[105] Sonny, who became an NEA Jazz Master in the second year of the thirty-year program, wrote a draft of the letter in longhand, as he did with most of his correspondence.

The strength, beauty and moral spirituality of this music has meant so much for generations of striving black Americans. That it has kindled the spirit of freedom in every corner of the globe says so much about its universality and what America really stands for and represents for human beings everywhere.

I know this is cost-cutting time, but the Jazz Masters program gives back so much more than it costs.[106]

The Obama administration reversed course and extended support for the NEA Jazz Masters program.

In 2011, Sonny continued searching for that lost chord. "You have to go a hundred percent the entire gig," recalled Jerome Jennings, who first toured with Sonny in 2007 and was playing with him again in 2011. "It's an intensity thing and if I go ninety-five, he can feel that. I've never played with anybody like that." Sometimes Sonny would call Jennings on the phone while practicing. "I would pick up the phone, he would be playing into the phone for like five minutes. I didn't even say hello after a while. 'You should always be working on something.' "[107]

Sonny told Jennings, who was thirty at the time, of the importance of health and sobriety. On tour, Jennings said, Sonny drank green tea religiously, and he was relieved when Jennings told him he was not on drugs. " 'It catches up to everybody,' " Sonny said, " 'so I want to make sure you're not doing these things.' " Yet mostly, Sonny taught him about music. "It's not licks, man!" Jennings said of Sonny's style. "I call it *information overload*."[108]

Guitarist Peter Bernstein joined the band in 2010 and played intermittently with Sonny through the summer of 2012. More than any one concert, what stood out for him the most happened during an audition. Different drummers came in for a half hour each, and one was struggling with the calypso feel. There was some back-and-forth with Sonny until it began to coalesce. "The guy was so reverent and wanting to do a good job. He said, 'So Sonny, in this calypso, like, what's the traditional way? Would the snare drum be open or closed? Do you want the snare to have that snare sound or it's more of a high tom-tom sound?' Sonny was quiet. It seemed like a long time. It probably was twenty seconds, which is a long silence. So then he said, 'You're here to make decisions. And as long as the music feels good, you can do what you want. And if you think about it, you couldn't be in a more privileged position.' Those were his exact words."[109]

It was a realization. "I never quite thought of it in those exact terms. Improvising, being able to make decisions about how to interpret, from the dynamics to the voicings to rhythms to everything, it's all your choice. That's a privilege."[110]

In 2012, Sonny continued touring, but on the cusp of eighty-two, his health began to falter. Guitarist Saul Rubin, who joined the band in the summer of 2012, recalled that the only cure for Sonny's ailments was onstage. "He couldn't really stand up straight. His back was all messed up, but then he started playing and he's standing up straight and dancing around, it was like, 'Whoa, what happened?'" Rubin recalled. "I think he transcended the pain."[111]

Earlier that summer, Sonny finally found the lost chord, not onstage, but in a hotel room in the South of France. On July 29, 2012, he was playing at the Jazz in Marciac festival in pastoral Gascony. "There's a big festival out there, but it's in the middle of nowhere," Sonny recalled.[112] It was the end of the tour, and Sonny was driven out to his hotel in the French countryside on a rainy night. He went through his usual routine—he picked out his clothes for the concert, laid out his shirts to get pressed, left his dental partial in the bathroom (or so he thought), and went to bed.

The next morning, the maid came in to clean the room, and Sonny heard what sounded like something clatter to the floor of the bathroom. As the concert got closer, Sonny discovered that his partial was not in his briefcase where he usually kept it.

Sonny scoured the room frantically, but it was nowhere to be found. He called the front desk and managed to explain the dire situation in broken French and English. The hotel staff began searching through the garbage.[113]

There he was, not bestriding the narrow world like a colossus, but on the floor of a hotel room looking for his teeth. "I really began panicking," Sonny said. "I was in a depressed mood, man. I looked up and I saw the sky and I saw a cloud....And suddenly, the cloud, it was like a window...it just cracked a little bit; and what can I say, man? I saw it. What was beyond there was—there's no words to describe it. I was sitting there and went back and looked over in one of the bags I had been opening, looking through. In the bag, my briefcase was in there and it was opened, like something fell, and there on the floor was my partial."

"That's sort of like some playful spirit or something playing a joke on me to say, 'Well, see, everything is okay.' But... once I had that thing that I saw, everything *was* okay. I didn't care what happened, whether I found it or not. Didn't matter." It turned out that finding the lost chord meant being willing to give it all up.

And soon, he would have to. That fall, Sonny was diagnosed with pulmonary fibrosis. According to the Centers for Disease Control, the degenerative condition is "a chronic and progressive lung disease without a known cause" with "limited treatment options" and an average survival time of three to five years. One of the only treatment options is a lung transplant, which carries enormous risk.[114] A 2019 study has shown a significant correlation between exposure to the toxic dust and debris at Ground Zero and the incidence of pulmonary fibrosis, though whether Sonny developed the disease as a result remains unproven.[115]

Sonny mostly shrugged off the grim prognosis. He continued to practice, although he had to cancel some tour dates on medical advice. He even found time to play himself on an episode of *The Simpsons*.[116] Sonny jokingly suggested donating his lungs to medical science: "Sonny Rollins' lungs, the most blown lungs in jazz." With whatever time he had left, he was going to get to the next level. "I'm going toward this breakthrough, this piece of music that is going to explain it all to me," he said. "It will matter."[117]

"You mean," said the interviewer, "like you're going to play this music and the rivers are suddenly going to run backward?" What more could he play that he hadn't already played in the past sixty-five years? Sonny laughed his deepest belly laugh. "Don't you see, that's exactly the point. Those notes you mention, those notes have already been blown. People say, 'Sonny, take it easy, lean back. Your place is secure. You're the great Sonny Rollins; you've got it made.' I hear that and I think, 'Well, screw Sonny Rollins. Where I want to go is beyond Sonny Rollins. Way beyond.'"[118]

A few weeks later, despite his diagnosis, Sonny began a monthlong European tour. At the Barbican in London, he blew a few notes midway through his first set, and stopped. "Sonny, Sonny, Sonny, get yourself together!" he bellowed.[119] The crowd laughed, but to Sonny it was no laughing matter.

Four days later, on Tuesday, November 20, 2012, Sonny played at the Voll-Damm Jazz Festival in Barcelona. His performance coincided with 20-N, the anniversary of Generalissimo Franco's death, when far-right white supremacist groups demonstrate for a return to fascism in Spain.[120] Sonny's concert would be a de facto counterprotest. He performed at the twenty-two-hundred-seat Palau de la Música for an ecstatic audience, playing "St. Thomas," "My One and Only Love," and ending the night with an endless "Don't Stop the Carnival." Sonny played every concert like it would be his last. This time, it would.

Chapter 42

THE BIG PICTURE AND THE LITTLE PICTURE

(2012–)

So Sonny began his final sabbatical. Not long after his diagnosis, in December 2012, he moved to Woodstock. "Last year the farmhouse became physically uncomfortable for a guy my age," he said. "The staircase leading to the second floor was steep and dangerous—I fell there one time. The house also was drafty in the winter and spring. My feet get cold easily now and I needed to be warm, so it was time to move." Central heating was not the only reason to move on; Sonny had lived alone in Germantown since Lucille's death in 2004, and it was time. "A house has a soul," Sonny said. "Its personality is shaped by its history. The personality of this house and my personality—we had to join and realize, well, we're going to be together for a while."[1]

As drummer Jerome Jennings recalled, Lucille's voice had remained on Sonny's answering machine. "I know that was a humongous cavity in his heart when he lost her," Jennings recalled.[2] As Sonny continued on his spiritual journey, his instrument was his "second wife," he said. "I don't sleep with it in bed. But I don't let it out of my sight."[3]

Realtor Sara Cohen helped Sonny move to Woodstock and began assisting him regularly with household obligations from that point on.[4] In the new house, Sonny soundproofed a bedroom to convert it into a practice room, but his practice sessions were getting fewer and further between. Soon, he was practicing in the living room; it had a resonant frequency of E. Sonny put his alphorn on top of the bookcases, but over time he began turning to books and yoga for spiritual communion as his condition worsened. He grew increasingly prone to dizzy spells and fatigue. It slowly sunk in that he would no longer be able to play. For a man with such a Herculean work ethic, retirement was a hard pill for Sonny to swallow. Yet as he had learned from Monk, it was important to learn to play the silences. For Sonny, the silence was deafening at first, then he gradually found a sense of inner peace.

When people came to visit, Sonny tried to put on a good face, but it was hard to conceal his despondency. Ed Sanders, the writer, activist, and founding member of the Fugs, lived nearby and became a friend. Sonny inspired "The Sad Sax," a piece in Sanders's series of glyphs, his drawings "charged with literary, emotional, historical or mythic and poetic intensity."[5]

Sonny Rollins'
Sad Sax
which he kept
out in the open
in his Living room
when his Lungs
  no longer allowed
  him to play[6]

In 2014, he stopped playing entirely. "I went through a period of depression; I was really low," Sonny recalled. "I'd been on this life quest to try and fulfill my potential with music, and not being able to play anymore meant

I wasn't going to get a chance to do that. But I eventually came out of my depression when I realized that rather than being depressed I should be grateful. I had an opportunity to live a life as a musician, which I always wanted to do. I was even able to achieve some prominence—that was a wonderful, wonderful gift. I didn't want to be like a spoiled child, 'Gee, I didn't get everything I wanted to get under the Christmas tree.' It would be selfish of me to think like that. I decided I didn't want to be that person. Once all of those feelings jelled in my mind, I was able to come out of my depression and accept my circumstances and be grateful for what I'd had."[7]

The hardest part was knowing for certain that he would never improve on his past performances. Even if he realized that the perfection he sought would always just elude his grasp, he never stopped trying. "I can't make it better," Sonny said. "I can't do anything. That's it. It's there, and that's it. I can't *redeem* myself."[8]

Sonny ultimately found redemption through spirituality. He had a deep and abiding belief in reincarnation and accepted that even if he couldn't play that perfect sound in this life, he would do it in the next. In spite of Sonny's unwavering belief that he was coming back, it never gave him any excuse to let up in his quest in this life to find that lost chord.

"Life is not forever," he said. "We have a short period to learn and do something correct. . . . Life is not about cake and ice cream and enjoyment. Life is short, and it's important to do something."[9]

As for companionship, Sonny stayed in close contact with his extensive circle of friends, collaborators, and fans, but led an increasingly solitary life. He would periodically change his phone number, and people he was once close to might lose contact for years, until out of the blue, the phone rang with an unidentified caller on the other end. There was that familiar woody New York accent, maybe a bit fainter, but otherwise it was as though not a day had passed. There was one friend who perhaps wanted something more, but Sonny had decided he would live out the rest of his days alone. "We both said to each other that we were O.K. with living our lives out by ourselves. I am," Sonny wrote. "Seeing a 'spiritual path' opening up for me as I negotiate my octogenarian days. I don't think I am insulting you by observing that this might not be your actual preference—and again you are younger than I—and I totally can accept that. I love and respect you completely. I always have and always will."[10]

There is perhaps something melancholy about the Saxophone Colossus rebuffing one last chance at love and living out his last days in this life alone in pursuit of spiritual solemnity. Yet it is also unsurprising. Sonny had indeed proved that he could make it alone on the bandstand, in this world—could be, in a word, a colossus. Larger-than-life as they are, colossi remain lone figures. The Colossus of Rhodes, or that "New Colossus," Lady Liberty, was not shown in scenes of love or hedonistic pleasure, but pointing the way to greatness, to freedom. This, Sonny believed, was his destiny.

"I like being alone, actually," he said. "I have my yoga books. I have my Buddha books. I have a lot of spiritual material that I need to get with. At my age, all my friends are gone. At one time I began to lament that and then I said, 'No, this is good that I have nobody to call and waste time talking.'"[11]

It may seem sad that this is where the story ends, with Sonny alone, his bags packed for the next life—the great gig in the sky. But it makes perfect sense. Of course Sonny Rollins believes in reincarnation. It has been said that in order to write his plays, Shakespeare had to become his characters and in so doing lived many lives. In the same sense, Sonny had lived thousands of lives onstage. Can a song have a life? For Sonny, it could. The concept of Samsara, so central to Buddhism, Hinduism, and Jainism, is the cycle of birth, death, rebirth, and redeath, and it finds a musical parallel in the interpretation of the American songbook Sonny had come to typify. Every chorus has the same essential structure, but as Sonny proved, there are infinite ways to play "Three Little Words." He made the most out of every phrase, through sudden bursts of brilliance and unexpected silences, each note a part of him and the story he was telling, a timeless tale made new every night. And with each improvised life, Sonny would return the next night and the next, hoping again to reach musical nirvana. Maybe he did, but he certainly didn't think so. Is not jazz a kind of Samsara? To Sonny, this was the challenge of jazz, and also of life. It was his karma yoga.

In advance of his 2010 birthday tour of Japan, Sonny defined jazz for a Japanese magazine:

Jazz is life as shown through music. Jazz is life in musical form. Jazz is the musical expression of life. As we all know life changes every second. Each snowflake that falls is different. Every sunset is different. Every surprise is different. The clouds in the sky are never the same—always changing. Jazz mimics life.

Real jazz music is changing from note to note. When I play a song, I can never play it the same way twice! Even if I'm playing the same song, it's different each time I play it! That's why they call jazz the 'music of surprise,' the greatest and most challenging music in the world.[12]

And there were other lives that had passed through his. On September 23, 2014, Sonny got a call from Cornel West. Dr. West was at John Coltrane's grave site in Pinelawn Memorial Park. "This was in the evening, almost at nighttime," Sonny said. "I'm in concert with him going there and having that reverence for our prophet, John Coltrane, and I was there with him in spirit. And we talked a little bit about it."[13]

"Sonny, he's full of so much wisdom, and he's from the same tradition," West said. "And the whole world knows we must learn how to live in the blues idiom. The blues is about compassion in the face of catastrophe. We black folk, we've been on intimate terms with catastrophe ever since we've been here. But you keep track of Howlin' Wolf, you keep track of Bessie Smith, and you're going to see some compassion, some creativity, in the face of catastrophe. And despair won't have the last word."[14]

In 2015, the Jazz Foundation of America presented Sonny with a lifetime achievement award at the Apollo Theater. At eighty-five years old, his life had come full circle. "The Apollo Theater was my school," Sonny said. "I used to be here every week when a new band would open up here. Sometimes we'd come two or three times a week. This is my university right here." Sonny began a roll call of those who were there that night carrying on the tradition: James Carter, Kenny Garrett, Billy Harper, Gary Bartz, Jimmy Heath. And then he summoned the ancestors whose legacies lived through them. "Jimmie Lunceford. How about Lester Young? How about Coleman Hawkins? How about Ben Webster? How about Johnny Hodges? How about

John Coltrane? How about Charlie Parker? How about Miles Davis? How about Thelonious Monk? How about Bud Powell? How about Dizzy Gillespie? How about Roy Eldridge? How about Fletcher Henderson? See, these are the people that set our world in motion with the music....I'm one of the soldiers in the spiritual battle of jazz. I heard all those here tonight, in the past. We're all here together."[15]

There were not many giants left, and Sonny found himself saying goodbye to the last of his generation. When Ornette Coleman died on June 11, 2015, Sonny was the first to enter Riverside Church behind Ornette's casket.[16] When Bob Cranshaw died on November 2, 2016, Sonny sent a message to be read at his memorial at St. Peter's Church in New York. It was a brief message, not for those celebrating Cranshaw's life but for his departed musical colleague himself: "Can't be there tonight, but I'll see you on the next gig."[17] In 2018, Sonny's older brother, Valdemar, passed. Jimmy Heath was one of Sonny's best friends, and he had to say goodbye to him too when he passed on January 19, 2020. "When you get to be my age," Sonny said that year, "your friends drop off one by one."[18] Yet to Sonny, they were not gone.

"I believe in reincarnation, which means that a person playing music has got a lot of things in his mind that he's heard already," Sonny said in a 2020 essay for the *New York Times*. "He puts them together and that comes out in his style. So you might recognize Louis Armstrong's style, but it's still derivative of every kind of music that exists. Any experiences that he's had, or things that he's played, he takes and folds into himself, and they become something new. Charlie Parker, Dizzy Gillespie, John Coltrane—their styles are ultimately made up of many lives, spanning back to that first sound. And that material is there for all musicians and artists to access. It's an accumulation of wisdom, the context art gives us that puts life into perspective. When I go to the museum and I look at a piece of art, I'm transported. I don't know how, or where, but I know that it's not a part of the material world. It's beyond modern culture's political, technological soul. We're not here to live forever. Humans and materialism die. But there's no dying in art."[19]

With Sonny's career behind him, he left a timeless legacy. There is the music he gave us, much of which is preserved on record. There is his archive, a material repository of his life at the Schomburg Center for Research in Black

Culture in Harlem, only two blocks from where he was born. In that sense, Sonny came home to Harlem.

Then there is the legacy of what Sonny Rollins means to American culture and to the global jazz tradition. Sonny was famously known as the architect of thematic improvisation, a concept he did not consciously create but that was thrust upon him. Yet his life was quite deliberately a thematic improvisation. Sonny was a freedom fighter for everyone, but also for himself. He was a "second Paul Robeson," a calypsonian who could dance around raindrops, a saxophone-toting cowboy chasing the new frontier, a lone figure wailing on the Bridge, a Mohawked warrior honoring the past, a yogi in Japan and India, the Saxophone Colossus holding the stage, and, finally, a jazz prophet preaching the Golden Rule. It was all a thematic improvisation defined by an enduring quest to find out what it truly meant to be free. He sought freedom from injustice, from addiction, from the predations of unscrupulous businessmen, from invisibility, from hypervisibility, from the technical constraints on his instrument, from what the Buddha calls impure thoughts, from desire and the material world, and, finally, from his earthly body. He did it with a sense of humor, by working harder than anyone, and with a profound recognition that democracy does not always mean equality, that freedom rarely comes freely, on the bandstand or in life.

"The law? That's a joke, man's law.... You can see that doesn't work," Sonny said. This to Sonny was where karma came in—to balance the scales of justice. "You don't get away with anything. You reap what you sow.... You're going to have to pay for it.... That's real justice," he said. "Call it the universal justice system, call it God, call it Jehovah, or Buddha. Call it anything. But there's something there that is real and just, whether we can understand it or not.... I'm still learning that. You might say, 'When I die, will I figure it out?' You will, but not in this life. Not as Sonny Rollins. That's learning. You do the best you can do." Yet to Sonny, playing music brought people just a little bit closer than the rest. "Music is one of the bridges," he said. "People who are playing music have a special dispensation. They have an edge on other people just by the fact that they are involved in music."

This applied especially to those involved in jazz. "Jazz is a music of freedom," Sonny said, "because we had to create. We had to fight. We had to struggle. We had to break down barriers. . . . That entailed freedom, to even attempt to do what the jazz people were doing."[20]

It was a frustrated quest, but not without meaning. "The world will never change," he said. "Individually, we have to change. That's what life is about. It's a testing ground for us to go through individually and change."[21]

Making these changes was the improviser's greatest test, and Sonny was the art form's greatest improviser. Through his singularly virtuosic improvisation—the rhythm, the lyricism, the sheer sound—Sonny compelled us to hear what so many could not see: that within a world beset by racism, capitalist greed, and environmental destruction, that maybe another world was possible. Sonny was in this world, but not of it.

While he was in this world, though, he learned "not to take life too seriously," he said. He made tentative plans for gallows humor on his tombstone: "Thanks to Andy Capp, Bob and Ray, and *Mad* Magazine." He kept his Bob and Ray comedy tapes for life, was a lifetime subscriber to *Mad*, cut out Andy Capp comics and carried them around for a rainy day. "These characters have enriched my life and hit the right note. . . . It's one of the things that has made my life bearable. It's very important to me, my sense of humor." When he was not here anymore, he knew his music, and that sense of humor, still would be.

Sonny knew that the music would find new life across the generations. "Jazz is a spirit," he said. "It is freedom. It is reality put into musical form. It will never leave until this planet leaves."[22] He understood that it is our responsibility to harmonize with nature, not nature's responsibility to harmonize with us.

When the COVID-19 pandemic hit in the spring of 2020, Sonny's life did not change dramatically. "I have been more or less quarantined for a couple of years," he said. "I have pulmonary fibrosis, I have a walker, and I don't really go out much. I just go out when my friend takes me to the doctor or the bank. So having to stay in the house is not an entirely new situation for me. Actually, I'm quite happy as far as that is concerned."[23]

To Sonny, it all came down to the Golden Rule. "All of the ancient disciplines and religions that we know of in our world, every one of them—Christianity, Islam, Judaism, Taoism, Buddhism, Confucianism,

Zoroastrianism—all of these disciplines preach the Golden Rule," Sonny said. "Do unto others as you would have done unto you."[24]

The Golden Rule was always a radical idea—something so simple yet nearly impossible to truly live by. To Sonny, Jesus would not have been a capitalist. However, he said, "Most of the world is in that sphere: 'Let me get mine.' If Jesus came back, would he be wearing a Rolex? No! These people would like to have the blessing of being like Jesus, but then they're not doing it. You have to live like that! You've got to do it...you have to do it individually. It's too much to try to think about everybody acting in concert. It doesn't happen. We all have to face so-called death individually, so let's face life. We're here with all this ignorance and hatred. Well, that's why we're here—to make a contrast to that."

To Sonny, making that contrast was a lifelong challenge and then some, but finally, the legendary perfectionist, always his own worst critic, had made his peace with coming up short. "It's all good. That's what I've come out of this life with.... If something happened that I thought was horrendous... it's here for us to learn. That's how you learn. You really have to experience it. What station I'm on, I don't know, but I know I'm on the right track."[25]

To Sonny, a life lived according to the principles of jazz meant going onstage night after night, without any sheet music, until we get it right, rolling the tape take after take until, as Coleman Hawkins told him, you could "feel somethin' in your heart."

"There is no ending," Sonny insisted.[26] Even when it seems the story's all told.

And here's why: "You can't look at life like this is separate from the universe," he said. "I call it the Big Picture and the Little Picture. Here on earth, this is the Little Picture. The 'universe' is not even a good word, because what I'm talking about is much bigger than the universe. We have to connect ourselves with that! Our body turns to dust like everything else on the planet. If I'm in the funeral parlor, my soul is long gone. See? But you're going to have to keep coming back, coming back, coming back, coming back—until we begin to learn."[27]

ACKNOWLEDGMENTS

This book has been a seven-year journey that proved more colossal than I ever could have imagined. It began in the summer of 2015, when I took a short pilgrimage downtown to 400 Grand Street on the Lower East Side, where Sonny lived in 1959 during his legendary sabbatical. He was twenty-nine and lauded as the greatest tenor saxophonist of his generation; I had just turned twenty-nine myself, and Sonny was the reason I practiced the saxophone in the first place. When I first interviewed Sonny in 2012, I told him that as a young saxophone player I struggled to play "Airegin." "Making it through the changes was like a rite of passage," I said. "For me, too, by the way," Sonny replied. Of course, he had written it.

Developers were razing the tenement building for a luxury high-rise, and I wanted to experience Sonny's daily commute to the Bridge before this brick-and-mortar piece of jazz history was gone forever. After finding the five-story walk-up on its tree-lined block, I took a left on Clinton, then a right on Delancey, and walked a few more blocks to the foot of the Bridge lugging my baritone case over my shoulder. It is not exactly a short walk to get to the middle. As the train rumbled beneath my feet, I stood suspended in the air, nothing but a slatted fence and crisscrossing cable separating me from the water down below. There was something sublime about the Bridge itself—its sprawling history, everyone who had passed over it. I assembled my horn and blew into the expanse, poised between two worlds—Manhattan and Brooklyn, but also the fleeting present and the irretrievable past. Graffiti dotted the pavement, and as I walked, just about where Sonny must have held his epic Bridge sessions hidden behind an abutment, I noticed one word scrawled in purple chalk over and over again: HEAVEN. How to get back to that place, sealed off to the past, before the rain washed it all away? One thing was certain: I could not get there alone.

The journey of this book echoed Sonny's sabbatical in a sense, with so many people stepping onto that metaphorical Bridge with me along the way. This book would be nothing without the contributions of a global jazz community of musicians, scholars, industry veterans, and friends. Far and away, I want to thank Sonny himself for his generosity, brilliance, humor, and trust, for the many bridges he crossed and for living the many lives he has lived in this one life alone. Terri Hinte has been immensely supportive throughout the process, and I cannot thank her enough for everything she has done for the music. Clifton Anderson has been another source of support, as has Eric Wyatt.

If this book is a kind of cantilever bridge into the past, having the musicians and others who lived this history tell the stories in their own words is the superstructure. Many of them have passed on since we spoke, and their legacy lives on through their words, music, and the continuing impact their voices have had on this living art form. I had more conversations than I can list here. Thanks to John Abbott, Konrad Adderley, Monty Alexander, Stephon Alexander, J.D. Allen, David Amram, Arild Andersen, Lisle Atkinson, George Avakian, Clarence Banks, Tom Barney, Mickey Bass, Bill Belmont, James "Fish" Benjamin, Han Bennink, Peter Bernstein, Alex Blake, Russel Blake, Terence Blanchard, Jane Ira Bloom, Leroy Brannigan, Dee Dee Bridgewater, Bobby Broom, Ras Moshe Burnett, Ronnie Burrage, Kenny Burrell, George Cables, Candido Camero, Tommy Campbell, Terri Lyne Carrington, Shirley Carter, James Carter, Ron Carter, Joe Chambers, Bob Clearmountain, Jimmy Cobb, Bill Coggins, Joe Corsello, Richard Corsello, Stanley Cowell, Bruce Cox, Bill Crow, Michael Cuscuna, Andrew Cyrille, Jehangir Dalal, Eddie Daniels, Richard Davis, Frances Davis, Jack DeJohnette, Kenny Dennis, Iris, Ivy, Derrick, and Denzil Bailey, Bob Dogan, Lou Donaldson, Armen Donelian, Bob Dorough, Peter Downey, Basile Drossos, Cécile Drossos, Alexis Drossos, Billy Drummond, Laura Dunlop, Roy Eaton, Pee Wee Ellis, Ramón Farrán, Sammy Figueroa, Dawn Finney, Ricky Ford, Henry Franklin, George Freeman, Donald Gay, Terry Gibbs, Lincoln Goines, James Goldwasser, Jeff Gordon, Dusko Goykovich,

Dave Green, G. Earl Grice, Henry and Margaret Grimes, Steve Grossman, Troy Halderson, Ralph Hamperian, John Handy, Billy Harper, Joe Harris, Jerome Harris, Barry Harris, Louis Hayes, Kevin Hays, John Heard, Jimmy Heath, Tootie Heath, Frederick Hemke, Olaf Hendricks, George Hicswa, Fenton Hollander, Ron Holloway, Bertha Hope-Booker, Will "Zeke" Hubel, Grachan Moncur III, Willie Jones III, Takeshi Inomata, Yoron Israel, Javon Jackson, Ruud Jacobs, Haresh Jagtiani, Jerome Jennings, Sheila Jordan, Steve Jordan, Ralph Kaffel, Roger Kellaway, Aiki and Jesi Kelley, Chris Kimsey, Jaap van de Klomp, John Koenig, Kiyoshi Koyama, Sam Kulok, Ted Kurland, Pat LaBarbera, Rick Laird, Hubert Laws, David Lee Jr., James Brandon Lewis, Dave Liebman, Kirk Lightsey, Julie Lokin, Emilio Lyons, Harold Mabern, Russell Malone, Doris Mason, Yoshiaki Masuo, Bennie Maupin, Cecil McBee, Christian McBride, Roy McCurdy, Rene McLean, Mike Melillo, Don Menza, Bob Mintzer, Roscoe Mitchell, Don Moore, Dan Morgenstern, Tommy Morimoto, John Morrow, Bob Mover, James Mtume, Wulf Müller, David Murray, Adam Nussbaum, Bill O'Connell, Tony Oxley, Ron Parry, Swami Parthasarathy and his assistant, Abha Hule, Don Pate, Allan Pepper, Gene Perla, Frank Perowsky, Bob Porter, Bret Primack, Aurell Ray, Pat Rebillot, Freddie Redd, Ishmael Reed, Robert Richer, Larry Ridley, Joe Rigby, Roberto Romeo, Fabrizio Rotondo and Nunzio Rotondo Jr., Saul Rubin, Patrice Rushen, Barry Sage, Ed Sanders, Heikki Sarmanto, Bill Saxton, Steve Schapiro, Don Schlitten, Archie Shepp, Norman Simmons, Sonny Simmons, Whitney Slaten, Mark Soskin, James Spaulding, Janis Sproles, Bob Stewart, Ira Sullivan, Bill Summers, Harold Summey, Yoshio "Chin" Suzuki, Lew Tabackin, Akira Tana, Philip Terman, Lilian Terry, Theresa Thomas, Henry Threadgill, Charles Tolliver, Mark Turner, René Urtreger, Bert Vuijsje, Sadao Watanabe, Kobie Watkins, Jeff "Tain" Watts, Joan Weinstock, Jerry Weldon, Randy Weston, Leroy Williams, Greg "Vibrations" Williams, Perry Wilson, Carl Woideck, Michael Wolff, Ken Yagoda, Victor See Yuen, Kiane Zawadi, and Aleksandar Živković.

The archive forms the other pillars of this book. The Schomburg Center for Research in Black Culture, which houses the Sonny Rollins archive and Quincy Troupe Papers, became a second home for months. Thank you to Cheryl Beredo, Lauren Stark, Barrye Brown, Serena Torres, and the rest of the staff in the Manuscripts, Archives, and Rare Books Division; Mary Yearwood; Matt Snyder, who processed the Rollins Papers; Shola Lynch and the staff of the Moving Image and Recorded Sound Division (MIRS); and Michael Mery and the staff of the Schomburg's Photographs and Prints Division. Thank you as well to Easy Corner Restaurant around the corner.

For research on the New York City criminal justice system, Rossy Mendez at the NYC Municipal Archives helped locate thousands of pages of minutes of the Parole Commission. During a monthlong mandatory stint on a Special Narcotics Grand Jury at Manhattan Criminal Court in 2018, I was able to access Sonny's criminal case file through the help of grand jury warden Christopher Stottmann. A reference assistant in the city clerk's office dislodged the indictment docket book and was able to unearth the 1951 records. Thank you as well to the staff of the New York County Clerk's Record Room.

Thank you to the staff at the Library of Congress Music Division, Recorded Sound Research Center, and Performing Arts Reading Room. In particular, thank you to Larry Appelbaum and Christopher Hartten for their assistance and insights into the Max Roach Papers. Thank you to the staff of the Music Division at The New York Public Library for the Performing Arts, Dorothy and Lewis B. Cullman Center, especially Jessica Wood, for help with the George Avakian and Anahid Ajemian Papers, the Ivan Black Papers, and other materials. Thank you to the following archives and librarians: Darcie Riedner, Courtney Berge, and the staff of the University of Idaho Library Special Collections and Archives for help with the Leonard Feather Papers; Kimberly Taylor of Archives and Special Collections at SUNY Fredonia for help with the Sigurd Raschèr Collection; Marc Brodsky at the Newman Library at Virginia Tech; Penny White in Special Collections at the University of Virginia; and Cindy McGuirl of the Paul Motian Archive. Thank you to the staff of the Tamiment Library/Robert F. Wagner Labor Archives at the Elmer Holmes Bobst Library at NYU, which holds research material in the American Federation of Musicians, Local 802 Records and Robert Steck Papers, where I was able to learn more about Sonny's union membership and the background of Camp Unity. Thanks to Alexandra Bainbridge at the Eberly Family Special Collections Library at Penn State for her assistance with the Harry J. Anslinger Papers; to the staff of the Smithsonian

Institution's Archives of American Art for their help with the Gertrude Abercrombie Papers; and the staff of the Smithsonian's Archives Center and National Museum of American History, where I was able to access essential oral histories.

My visit to the Jazzinstitut Darmstadt was extremely fruitful; thanks to Wolfram Knauer, Arndt Weidler, and Doris Schröder for their research assistance. In Oslo, I did research in the Randi Hultin Collection at the National Library of Norway. Thank you to Wivi-Ann Wells, to archivist Finn Kramer-Johansen for research assistance, and to Per Husby, who discussed the collection and Sonny's time in Norway while I was at the library. The Institute of Jazz Studies houses oral histories with Wilbur B. Ware, Kenny Clarke, Walter "Foots" Thomas, and others that were important to my research. Thanks to the IJS staff and in particular, Tad Hershorn for his assistance and insights, and help with the Mary Lou Williams Collection. Thanks to Hope Ketcham-Geeting and the staff of the David M. Rubenstein Rare Book and Manuscript Library at Duke University for their help accessing the tapes in the W. Eugene Smith Collection; to the staff of the Rare Book and Manuscript Library at Columbia University; to Anne Rhodes at the Oral History of American Music program at the Yale University Library; to Nathan Coy at the Archive of Recorded Sound at Stanford University; to Debra Madera at the Pitts Theology Library at Emory University; to Brenda Nelson-Strauss at the Archives of African American Music and Culture at Indiana University; to the Felix E. Grant Jazz Archives; and to the HistoryMakers.

Thank you to Resonance Records for the opportunity to share the story of Sonny's 1967 tour in Holland with Han Bennink and Ruud Jacobs for the *Rollins in Holland* package. Thanks to Annemiek Ebbink, Liselore Gerritsen, Frank Jochemsen, and Jurjen Donkers for their help and company, and to George Klabin, Zev Feldman, John Koenig, Zak Shelby-Szyszko, and David Weiss. Thanks to David as well for sharing his oral history with Freddie Hubbard, which I was able to transfer from MiniDisc.

At the Columbia University Libraries, thanks to Nick Patterson, Adrian Thomas, and the staff of the Microforms Reading Room. Thank you to Bob Scott at the Digital Humanities Center, who helped me while I spent several months reading through and digitizing about forty years of *Down Beat* magazine from the microfilm. Following the completion of this project, the RIPM Jazz Periodicals database, another indispensable resource, became available. I would also like to thank Walter Hellebrand, George Tyson, Ricki Marshall, and Hazel Brookes for assistance with genealogy research on St. Eustatius, St. Thomas, and St. Croix, and to Modianne Cathalina of the National Archives of Curaçao.

Thanks to the government records agencies that were able to provide documents, among them, the National Personnel Records Center and the City of New York Office of the City Clerk Marriage License Bureau, and various other departments.

Dominique Jennings Brandon shared archival material from her father, Prophet Jennings. Thank you for your insights and generosity.

Thank you to the scholars who helped me throughout this project: Ammiel Alcalay, Genji Amino, Matthew Clayton, Kwami Coleman, Brent Hayes Edwards, Krin Gabbard, Ben Givan, Farah Jasmine Griffin, Robin D.G. Kelley, Yulanda McKenzie, the late Douglas Mitchell, Robert G. O'Meally, Montana Ray, Alyn Shipton, John Szwed, as well as the Jazz Study Group and African American Studies Colloquium at Columbia University. It was a pleasure to talk about the book at the Popular Music Books in Process Series with Yuval Taylor and Rob Kenner, and thanks to Kimberly Mack, Eric Weisbard, and Carl Wilson for organizing. Thanks as well to Chris Budnick, Nancy Campbell, JP Olsen, Marjorie Senechal, and Gary Falk for insights into Lexington. I had more conversation with and support from Frank Alkyer, Bob Blumenthal, Aaron Cohen, Stanley Crouch, Phil Freeman, Ben Givan, Ashley Kahn, John Litweiler, Howard Mandel, Matt Merewitz, Lee Mergner, Bill Milkowski, Dan Morgenstern, Ted Panken, Emilie Pons, Mac Randall, Giovanni Russonello, Neil Tesser, Natalie Weiner, and David Yaffe. Thanks to the journalists, musicians, and scholars cited throughout this volume whose research and writing on Sonny Rollins amounted to tens of thousands of articles. Thanks as well to Richard Seidel, Hank O'Neal, Allen Lowe, Don and Maureen Sickler of Second Floor Music, George Schuller, Will Glass and the Jazz Foundation of America, and Loren Schoenberg of the National Jazz Museum in Harlem. Thank you to Dimitri Vassilakis, who organized the Jazz Democracy event at the United Nations, where I spoke on behalf of the Jazz Journalists Association (JJA) on Sonny's *Freedom Suite* in 2018. Thank you to Shiho Kataoka for help with translation. Thanks to Jeff Caltabiano for his support and for launching the Sonny Rollins Bridge Project. Thank you to the members of the Stan Rubin Orchestra, many of whom discussed this book with me between set breaks, among them, Bob Curtis, Jeff Newell, Nate Sutton, and the late Tom Olin.

Thanks as well to those who provided photos: John Abbott, Clifton Anderson, Bertrand Alary, Anahid, Maro, and Greg Avakian and the Ava-kian family, Roger Bergner, Dominique Jennings Brandon, Frank Brown Jr., Edward Elbers, Ruth Ellis, Terri Hinte, the Illinois State Museum, Mac-cha Kasparian, Linda Noel-Kawabata and Hanako Kawabata, Dale Parent, Michele Wallace and Faith Ringgold, Marvin Scott, Cynthia Sesso, Inger Stjerna, Lisa Tanner, Thierry Trombert, and Savannah Wood.

I began this book on a fellowship at the Leon Levy Center for Biography at the Graduate Center, CUNY. The center was then under the direction of Gary Giddins, whose work I have long admired. Gary's insights into the music of Sonny Rollins were vital to my research, and I thank him for his support and encouragement at every stage of the project. Kai Bird became the director of the center in the middle of my fellowship year and was a key advisor on the craft of biography. David Nasaw read an early chapter draft and offered incisive feedback. Thank you to Michael Gately and Thad Ziolkowski for their help and guidance during that generative year. Other readers of early drafts include Melina Moore and Madison Priest. Cynthia Carr, Heather Clark, Justin Gifford, Matthew McKnight, Abigail Santa-maria, Eric K. Washington, Lindsay Whalen, and Adam Plunkett were all there for me, offering feedback and camaraderie throughout what can be very solitary work. Thank you to Adam, Berit Erickson, and Mari for having me at their home after we left New York for Pennsylvania. I also benefited from meetings of the NYU Biography Seminar and other informal interac-tions, some with biographer heroes of mine including David Levering Lewis, Brenda Wineapple, as well as the late Les Payne and James Atlas. Thank you to Shelby White for her support through the center.

Special thanks go to Carl and Mary Smith, who invited me to their home in Portland, Maine, for a weekend of listening and discussion that I will never forget. Carl loaned me a copy of his entire Rollins collection—more than 450 live tapes of Sonny Rollins—for the duration of the project. Thanks as well to Carl's associates, Tom Ferrara and John Scherrer. For the Sonny Rollins discography, Tom Lord's *The Jazz Discography* and the Jazz Discography Project (https://www.jazzdisco.org/sonny-rollins/discography/) are excellent resources.

Special thanks also go to Lewis Porter, who has been a true mentor, provided immeasurable help with research, and read the entire manuscript at an early stage. Thank you to Lewis and Odella for having me in their home.

I believe Sonny deserves the thick spine he has in this book, but containing the story between two covers presents a biographical challenge alluded to in one of the epigraphs. "The greatest work of the painter is not a colossus, but a *historia*," wrote Leon Battista Alberti in his Renaissance treatise *On Painting*. By *historia*, Alberti was referring to narrative painting, and by colossus, any of the colossi of Rome, such as the Colossus of Rhodes, one of the Seven Wonders of the World. Sonny is the "Saxophone Colossus," but his music also epitomizes jazz as *historia*. Telling the story of a colossus like Sonny required balancing perspective and scale: get too close and miss the big picture, but stand too far away and lose the definition. The first draft of this manuscript was colossal: 586,482 words. (Just shy of *War and Peace*, one friend told me.) I was able to cut nearly 250,000 words. Michaelangelo Matos, a singularly perspicacious editor, cut 70,000 more. Though some of the cut material survives in the notes, I am certain that the book is better for it. Thanks to Ben Schafer, my editor, first at Da Capo and then Hachette, for patiently sticking with me for so many years. Thanks to production editor Fred Francis, Annette Wenda for her thorough copy editing, publicity manager Michael Giarratano, senior marketing manager Quinn Fariel, associate editor Carrie Napolitano, attorney John Pelosi for legal vetting, and the staff at Hachette Books. Thank you to my indefatigable agent, Russell Galen at Scovil Galen Ghosh, for his unwavering belief in this project from the moment I mentioned it.

Finally, thanks to my family: to my parents, Pattie and Harlan, and my sister, the brilliant vocalist Allegra Levy. My daughter Diana developed her sense of rhythm as an infant listening to "St. Thomas" on the playmat, drumming along with Max, and as a toddler, grooving along with her toy saxophone. Thanks to Debbie Sylvester, Diana's caretaker in New York, and the faculty and staff of New School Montessori in Lancaster. This book is also dedicated to my second daughter, Isabel, who heard *Way Out West* in the womb. The last thank you goes to Kaitlin Mondello, the love of my life and closest confidante, who has offered insights and constructive criticism, helped select photos, and listened to me read aloud from and talk about this book, sometimes incessantly, for what turned out to be the better part of the first decade of our relationship. You deserve a medal. Sonny's ballads remind me of you, or the way he strolls on "Oleo" with Miles, or how he plays a calypso. Our cats, Wuftie and Jody, were with us when I began this book but have since passed on. We now live with Sunny, an orange tabby, who, as if by divine providence, came into our lives from the rescue already bearing that name. Sonny always asks about him.

NOTES

Reference notes for this book can be found online at the following location:

https://hach.co/saxcolossus

INDEX

Note: Performer's musical recordings can be found by the name of the specific title. Credits in parentheses may refer to performer, composer, or other relevant contributor.